Why Do You Need This New Edition?

If you are wondering why you should buy this new edition of *College Reading and Study Skills*, here are six great reasons!

1. Would you like to read and study from your textbooks more efficiently and effectively? **New *Using College Textbooks* sections** guide you in integrating and applying the skills you learn throughout this book to all of your other courses.

2. Do you need to master the skills necessary for today's classroom? New *Success Workshops* on how to **"Read and Think Visually," "Manage Your Electronic Life,"** and **"Communicate and Network with Other Students"** provide you with the tips you need to succeed in today's visual, electronic, and social environment.

3. Do you want to read about topics that are interesting and contemporary? **New thematic readings** and a **new sample textbook chapter** focus on issues that are important in today's culture like the ethics and science behind genetically modified food and human cloning, as well as the implications of Web 2.0 and social networking.

4. Do you want your textbook to be visually engaging? Not only is material throughout the text presented visually, but **new *Visual Thinking* activities** challenge you to think critically about visuals and how they are used.

5. Would you like to know what is important before you read? **New Learning Goals** begin each chapter to help you focus on the key skills you need to learn to understand and apply in order to become a skilled reader.

6. Do you want extra practice? **New *MyReadingLab* icons** provide directions for accessing activities for additional practice on Pearson's MyReadingLab program.

College Reading and Study Skills

Twelfth Edition

KATHLEEN T. McWHORTER
NIAGARA COUNTY COMMUNITY COLLEGE

BRETTE McWHORTER SEMBER

PEARSON

Boston Columbus Indianapolis New York San Francisco Upper Saddle River
Amsterdam Cape Town Dubai London Madrid Milan Munich Paris Montreal Toronto
Delhi Mexico City Sao Paulo Sydney Hong Kong Seoul Singapore Taipei Tokyo

Editor in Chief: Eric Stano
Senior Acquisitions Editor: Nancy Blaine
Development Editor: Erin Reilly
Marketing Manager: Kurt Massey
Senior Supplements Editor: Donna Campion
Executive Digital Producer: Stefanie A. Snajder
Digital Project Manager: Janell Lantana
Digital Editor: Rob St. Laurent
Production Manager: Ellen MacElree
Project Coordination, Text Design, and Electronic Page Makeup: PreMediaGlobal
Cover Design Manager: John Callahan
Cover Designer: Kay Petronio
Cover Image: Erik Degraaf/Veer
Senior Manufacturing Buyer: Dennis J. Para
Printer and Binder: RR Donnelley
Cover Printer: Lehigh-Phoenix Color/Hagerstown

This title is restricted to sales and distribution in North America only.

For permission to use copyrighted material, grateful acknowledgment is made to the copyright holders on pp. 504–507, which are hereby made part of this copyright page.

Lexile® is a trademark of MetaMetrics, Inc., and is registered in the United States and abroad. The trademarks and names of other companies and products mentioned herein are the property of their respective owners. Copyright © 2011 MetaMetrics, Inc. All rights reserved.

Library of Congress Cataloging-in-Publication Data

McWhorter, Kathleen T.
  College reading and study skills / Kathleen T. McWhorter, Brette McWhorter Sember. — 12th ed.
    p. cm.
  ISBN-13: 978-0-205-21302-3
  ISBN-10: 0-205-21302-2
 1. Reading (Higher education)   2. Study skills.   I. Sember, Brette McWhorter, 1968-   II. Title.
  LB2395.3.M386 2011
  428.4071'2—dc23

                                                              2011045838

10 9 8 7 6 5 4 3 2—V003—15 14 13

Student ISBN-13: 978-0-205-21302-3
Student ISBN-10:   0-205-21302-2

AIE ISBN-13: 978-0-205-21731-1
AIE ISBN-10:   0-205-21731-1

CONTENTS

Across eleven editions, *College Reading and Study Skills* has demonstrated that reading and study skills are inseparable. A student must develop skills in each area in order to handle college work successfully. With this goal in mind, I have tried to provide complete coverage of both reading and study skills throughout and to show their relationship and interdependency. In doing so, my emphasis has been on direct instruction. My central aim is to teach reading and study through a how-to approach.

NEW TO THE TWELFTH EDITION

The primary thrust of the revision is to build a text that recognizes and accommodates visual learners and thinkers, emphasizes new forms of classroom communication, and recognizes that students need guidance in learning from textbooks and other academic sources effectively. Specific changes include the following:

NEW USING COLLEGE TEXTBOOKS SECTIONS. Using textbook excerpts from a wide range of disciplines, this section guides students in integrating and applying the skills taught in each chapter to their other courses.

NEW VISUAL THINKING ACTIVITIES. These new activities prompt students to think analytically about visuals. In chapters devoted to study skills, *Visual Thinking: Applying Skills* photos ask students to consider the skill they are learning in that chapter in light of the visual. In reading skills chapters, *Visual Thinking: Analyzing Images* photos prompt students to explore an image and the purpose it serves in relation to a reading passage.

NEW THEMATIC READINGS. Part Five of the book contains 9 readings, grouped according to three themes. Theme A on body adornment returns to this edition. A new Theme B raises controversial issues having to do with genetics. Finally, Theme C on the Internet and technology addresses the implications of Web 2.0 and social networking.

NEW SUCCESS WORKSHOPS. The college classroom is changing, and students need new skills to meet the challenges of increasingly visual, electronic, and collaborative school and work environments. To meet this need, new Success Workshops titled "Read and Think Visually," "Manage Your Electronic Life," and "Communicate and Network with Other Students" have been added.

NEW FULL-LENGTH TEXTBOOK CHAPTER. The twelfth edition features a full-length sample chapter titled "Emotion and Motivation" from an introductory psychology text, allowing students an opportunity to apply skills taught throughout the text to actual textbook material.

NEW LEARNING GOALS. Listed at the beginning of each chapter, new objectives appear as a numbered list and correspond to the major headings in the chapter. At the end of each chapter, revised "Self-Test Summaries" provide students with an opportunity to test themselves on their mastery of these learning goals.

UPDATED TEXTBOOK SELECTIONS FOR EXERCISES. All selections have been checked for reading level; many have been replaced with excerpts from the most up-to-date editions of textbooks.

NEW ANNOTATED INSTRUCTOR'S EDITION.   For instructors, the Annotated Instructor's Edition is an exact replica of the student text with answers provided on the page.

NEW LEXILE MEASURES.   A Lexile® measure is the most widely used reading metric in U.S. schools. Lexile measures indicate the reading levels of the longer selections in the Annotated Instructor's Editions of all Pearson's reading books and the reading level of content in MyReadingLab. See the Annotated Instructor's Edition of (text) and the Instructor's Manual for more details.

CONTENT OVERVIEW

College Reading and Study Skills, Twelfth Edition, presents the basic strategies for college success, including time management, analysis of learning style, active reading, and note taking. The text offers strategies for strengthening literal and critical comprehension, improving vocabulary skills, and developing reading flexibility. Students also discover methods for reading and learning from textbook assignments, including outlining and summarizing, and for taking exams. The reading and study skills I have chosen to present are those most vital to students' success in college. Each unit teaches skills that are immediately usable—all have clear and direct application to students' course work.

Because I believe that critical thinking and reading skills are essential to college success, these skills are emphasized in the text. I introduce students to critical thinking skills by explaining Bloom's hierarchy of cognitive skills early and then showing their academic application throughout the text. *College Reading and Study Skills* offers direct skill instruction in critical reading and includes key topics such as making inferences, asking critical questions, analyzing arguments, and evaluating Internet sources.

The units of the text are interchangeable, which enables the instructor to adapt the material to a variety of instructional sequences.

SUCCESS WORKSHOPS.   Appearing at the beginning of each part, the Success Workshops use a fun, lively, and accessible format to provide students with skills that will directly and immediately contribute to their college success. Topics include acclimation to the college environment, academic image, concentration, stress management, and reading and thinking visually.

PART ONE: BUILDING A FOUNDATION FOR ACADEMIC SUCCESS.   This section provides an introduction to the college experience and presents skills, habits, and attitudes that contribute to academic success. Chapter 3 in this section establishes the theoretical framework of the text by discussing the learning and memory processes and the principles on which many of the skills presented throughout the text are based.

PART TWO: READING AND THINKING CRITICALLY.   This section focuses on the development of reading skills for both textbooks and other common academic reading assignments. Critical thinking and reading skills are emphasized. Students are shown methods of learning specialized vocabulary and discover systems for vocabulary learning. Techniques for reading graphics are presented. Critical thinking topics in Chapter 9 include making inferences, distinguishing between fact and opinion, recognizing tone, and analyzing arguments. Chapter 10 focuses on evaluating an author's techniques. Reading and evaluating electronic sources, including how to adapt reading strategies for online and other sources and how to avoid cyberplagiarism, are discussed in depth in Chapters 13 and 14.

PART THREE: READING TEXTBOOK CHAPTERS AND ASSIGNMENTS.   These chapters teach skills that enable students to learn College Textbook assignments. Chapter 15 focuses on how to highlight and mark a textbook. Chapter 16 teaches students to organize information using outlining, summarizing, and mapping.

PART FOUR: STRATEGIES FOR ACADEMIC ACHIEVEMENT.   The purpose of this section is to help students prepare for and take exams. Organizing for study and review, identifying what to study, and methods for review are emphasized. Methods of learning through writing—paraphrasing, self-testing, and keeping a learning journal—are described. Students learn specific strategies for taking objective tests, standardized tests, and essay exams, as well as for controlling test anxiety. In Chapter 20, students learn to adjust their reading rate to suit their purpose, the desired level of comprehension, and the nature of the material they are reading.

PART FIVE AND SIX: THEMATIC READINGS AND SAMPLE TEXTBOOK CHAPTER. This section contains 9 readings, grouped according to three themes: body adornment (sociology/cultural anthropology), controversies in science (biology/genetics), and technology and the Internet (media studies/business). These readings, which represent the kind of texts that may be assigned in academic courses, provide students with an opportunity to apply skills taught throughout the text. Finally, a sample textbook chapter taken from an introduction to psychology college text, titled "Emotion and Motivation," allows students to work with actual textbook material to apply skills taught throughout the text. The chapter is representative of college textbooks and of the learning aids they contain. An "Understanding Your Textbook" quiz following the chapter tests students' familiarity with the learning aids contained in the chapter.

SPECIAL FEATURES

The following features enhance the text's effectiveness and directly contribute to students' success:

- **Learning Style.** The text emphasizes individual student learning styles and encourages students to adapt their reading and study techniques to suit their learning characteristics, as well as the characteristics of the learning task.
- **Reading as a Process.** This text emphasizes reading as a cognitive process. Applying the findings from the research areas of metacognition and prose structure analysis, students are encouraged to approach reading as an active mental process of selecting, processing, and organizing information to be learned.
- **Metacognition.** Students are encouraged to establish their concentration, activate prior knowledge, define their purposes, and select appropriate reading strategies prior to reading. They are also shown how to strengthen their comprehension, monitor that comprehension, select what to learn, and organize information. They learn to assess the effectiveness of their learning, revise and modify their learning strategies as needed, and apply and integrate course content.
- **Skill Application.** Students learn to problem-solve and explore applications through case studies of academic situations included at the end of each chapter. The exercises are labeled "Applying Your Skills." "Discussing the Chapter" questions ask students to reflect on how the advice in the chapter will work in their assignments. "Analyzing a Study Situation" questions present students with mini-cases and ask them how to best approach an academic challenge. Finally, "Working on Collaborative Projects" exercises provide opportunities for group work.
- **Learning Experiments/Learning Principles.** Each chapter begins with an interactive learning experiment designed to engage students immediately in an activity that demonstrates a principle of learning that will help students learn the chapter content. The student begins the chapter by doing, not simply by beginning to read.
- **Visual Literacy.** A new Success Workshop titled "Read and Think Visually" introduces students to the basics of visual literacy, while "Visual Thinking" activities in each chapter encourage students to think critically about visuals.
- **Chapter Learning Goals and Additional Practice on MyReadingLab.** Each chapter opens with chapter learning objectives that correspond to the major headings in the chapter. Suggested click paths through MyReadingLab lead to activities related to major headings.
- **Chapter Focus and Purpose Questions.** The first section of each chapter opens with a question that models the question students commonly ask before beginning an assigned chapter: Why should I learn this? Following each question are several answers that establish the importance and relevance of the skills taught in the chapter.
- **Interactive Assignments.** The Success Workshops and the learning experiments at the beginning of each chapter engage students and function as interactive learning opportunities.
- **Writing to Learn.** The text emphasizes writing as a means of learning. Writing-to-learn strategies include paraphrasing, self-testing, outlining, summarizing, mapping, and keeping a learning journal.

- **Realistic Reading Assignments.** Exercises often include excerpts from college texts across a wide range of disciplines, providing realistic examples of college textbook reading. Furthermore, new "Using College Textbooks" sections guide students in making the most of their textbooks.
- **Thematic Readings.** Nine readings, grouped according to three themes, are contained in Part Five. These readings provide realistic materials on which to apply skills taught in the text. They also provide students with an essential link between in-chapter practice exercises and independent application of new techniques in their own textbooks, and valuable practice in synthesizing and evaluating ideas.
- **Self-Test Chapter Summaries.** Linked to the chapter's learning goals, the chapter summaries use an interactive question–answer format that encourages students to become more active learners.
- **Quick Quizzes.** A multiple-choice quick quiz is included at the end of each chapter. Each quiz assesses mastery of chapter content, provides students with feedback on their learning, and prepares students for further evaluation conducted by their instructor.
- **Visual Appeal.** The text recognizes that many students are visual learners and presents material visually, using maps, charts, tables, and diagrams.
- **Using Technology.** The text offers students advice for using technology to make their study habits more effective. See "Tech Support" boxes throughout the text.

THE TEACHING AND LEARNING PACKAGE
Book-Specific Ancillary Materials

- **Instructor's Manual/Test Bank.** This supplement contains teaching suggestions for each chapter along with numerous tests formatted for easy distribution and scoring. It includes a complete answer key, strategies for approaching individual chapters, a set of overhead projection materials, and suggestions for integrating the many Pearson ancillaries. The Test Bank portion of the supplement includes content-based chapter quizzes and mastery tests to enable students to apply skills taught in every chapter. ISBN: 0-205-21732-X.
- **Annotated Instructor's Edition.** This supplement is an exact replica of the student text with answers provided. ISBN: 0-205-21731-1.
- **PowerPoint Presentations.** A presentation for each chapter, which is structured around the chapter learning objectives, can be downloaded at Pearson's Instructor Resource Center. You can use these presentations as is or edit them to suit your lecturing style. ISBN: 0-205-21721-4.
- **MyReadingLab.** This Web site is specifically created for developmental students and provides diagnostics, practice tests, and reporting on student reading skills and reading levels.
- **Expanding Your Vocabulary.** Instructors may choose to shrink-wrap *College Reading and Study Skills* with a copy of *Expanding Your Vocabulary*. This book, written by Kathleen McWhorter, works well as a supplemental text providing additional instruction and practice in vocabulary.

ACKNOWLEDGMENTS

In preparing this edition, I appreciate the excellent ideas, suggestions, and advice provided by reviewers: Kathy Barker, Grays Harbor College; Shawn Bixler, Summit College; Joan Lippens, Washtenaw Community College; Janet Michalak, Niagara County Community College; Betty J. Perkinson, Tidewater Community College; Mary Lee Sandusky, Kent State University at Trumbull; Ann Thomas, Dekalb Tech; Hollie Van Horne, Kent State University/Salem Campus; and Carla Young, CCAC–Allegheny Campus.

The editorial staff at Pearson deserve special recognition and thanks for the guidance, support, and direction they have provided. In particular I wish to thank Erin Reilly, my development editor, for her valuable advice and assistance and Nancy Blaine, acquisitions editor, for her enthusiastic support of the revision.

KATHLEEN T. MCWHORTER
www.pearsonhighered.com

SUCCESS WORKSHOP

1 Learn Everything You Can in the First Week

Your first week of classes and your first week on campus are some of the most important days you will ever spend.

Discovering . . .
What Your Courses Require

When you accept a new job, your manager spends time explaining your job and its responsibilities. These first few days are important because you learn what is expected and what you must do to earn your paycheck. The first few days of a college course are equally important. You learn what your instructor expects and what you must do to earn a grade and receive credit for the course. Often, much of this information is contained in a course syllabus—a handout distributed on the first day or in the first week of class. Look and listen for the answers to the following questions.

Course objectives: What are you expected to learn in the course? (Pay particular attention to these; exams measure your ability to achieve these objectives.)

Course organization: How is the course structured? What portions will be lecture, conferences, discussion, small group work, and so forth?

Exams, quizzes, and assignments: When are exams scheduled, and what assignments are due? (Record dates for each in a pocket calendar.) What are the penalties for late assignments? Are make-up exams offered?

Grading system: How will your grade be determined? How much does each test or assignment count?

Class participation and attendance: What are your instructor's policies regarding attendance? Is class participation part of your grade?

Office hours: Where is your instructor's office, and what hours is he or she available?

If any of this information is not provided during the first week of class, be sure to ask your instructor.

Analyzing . . .
Your Course Syllabi

Examine the syllabus for each of your courses. Identify the course objectives and course organization. Highlight or underline the schedule for assignments, quizzes, and exams. Then immediately transfer these dates into your calendar. After your first week of classes, go through your calendar, noting the due dates for the next month. Begin now to plan how you will schedule your time to meet your due dates.

Examining . . .
A Sample Syllabus

Course Syllabus

Course Number: BIO 201

Course Name: Human Anatomy and Physiology I

Instructor: Dr. Jack Eberhardt

Prerequisite: BIO 102 with a grade of C or higher

Office Location: 322 Olympic Towers

Office Hours: MWF 1–3

E-mail: joberhardt@mcc.edu

Course Objectives:

1. To identify the major parts of a cell and know their functions.

2. To understand the structure and function of the human organ systems.

3. To learn the types of human body tissues and understand their functions.

4. To perform laboratory activities for collection and analysis of experimental data.

....

Course Grade: Grades will be based on three multiple-choice exams and weekly laboratory reports. Exam questions are based on lecture notes, textbook assignments, and the lab manual. The exams will test factual knowledge as well as critical thinking skills.

....

Attendance: Regular attendance is required for both lecture and laboratory. If you miss a class, you should get the missed material from a classmate. The instructor will not distribute or post lecture or lab notes. Make-up labs will not be allowed. If you miss an exam, you must provide written documentation to explain your absence. If you fail to do so, a grade of zero will be entered.

....

Tentative Lecture Schedule:

DATE	TOPIC	CHAPTER
Sept. 16	Course Introduction, The Scientific Method,	1
Sept. 21	Atoms, molecules, water, Chemical bonding	1, 2

....

>>

2 Learn About and Use Campus Resources

Rating . . .
Your Knowledge of Your College

Answer each of the following questions about your college.

1. What are the hours of your college library?
2. How would you find out the last date by which you can withdraw from a course without academic penalty?
3. Where do you go or whom do you see to change from one major (or curriculum) to another?
4. What services does the student health office provide?
5. Who is your advisor and where is his or her office located on campus?
6. What assistance is available in locating part-time jobs on or off campus?
7. How would you find a tutor for a course in which you are having difficulty?
8. Where can you get help with writing a paper?
9. Where are the computer labs and what services do they offer?
10. Where would you go to find help with personal problems?

Each of the questions above points you to an important college resource or service. In addition to learning about the services referred to above, be sure to study your college catalog.

Studying . . .
Your College Catalog

The college catalog is your primary source of information for staying in and graduating from college. Be sure to obtain a current edition or access it online. It is your responsibility to know and work within the college's regulations, policies, and requirements to obtain a degree. Although faculty advisors are available to provide guidance, you must be certain that you are registering for the right courses in the right sequence to fulfill requirements to obtain your degree. Furthermore, be sure to obtain a complete catalog, not a preadmissions publicity brochure. Keep the catalog that is in effect during your freshman year. It is considered the catalog of record and will be used to audit your graduation requirements. A complete catalog usually provides several types of information:

Academic rules and regulations	Course registration policies, grading system, class attendance policies, academic dismissal policies
Degree programs and requirements	Degrees offered and outlines of degree requirements for each major
Course descriptions	A brief description of each course, the number of credits, and course prerequisites (Note: Not all courses listed are offered each semester.)
Student activities and special services	Student organizations, clubs and sports, student governance system, and special services

Examining . . .
Your College's Web Site

Many colleges have a Web site on the Internet that contains useful general information about the college, as well as information about degrees, programs, and services. These Web sites frequently include such valuable information as campus maps, an academic calendar, course and program information, and employment opportunities.

TEST YOUR ABILITY TO FIND INFORMATION

Use your college catalog or Web site to answer the following questions.

1. Does the college allow you to take courses on a Pass/Fail or Satisfactory/Unsatisfactory basis? If so, what restrictions or limitations apply?
2. What is the last date on which you can withdraw from a course without academic penalty?
3. On what basis are students academically dismissed from the college? What criteria apply to readmission?
4. What is the institution's policy on transfer credit?
5. What rules and regulations apply to motor vehicles on campus?
6. List five extracurricular programs or activities the college sponsors.
7. Describe the health services the college provides.
8. What foreign languages are offered?
9. What systems/media does the college use to notify you of on-campus emergencies or other essential information?
10. What courses are required in your major or curriculum? Are any general education courses required?

3 Use College Textbooks Effectively

Have you ever wondered?

Question: How do textbooks differ from other information sources, such as dictionaries, reference books, and most nonfiction books?

Answer: Textbooks contain numerous features to help you learn. Most are not just page after page of print. They contain charts, tables, diagrams, and photographs, each of which is designed to help you learn.

Question: Who writes college textbooks?

Answer: Textbooks are almost always written by college teachers. (Check the title page of your textbooks; you will see the author's name and the name of his or her college or university.) College teachers know what you are likely to need help understanding. They know when you need, for example, a diagram to help you visualize a concept. Consequently, when they write textbooks, they build helpful features into each chapter.

Analyzing . . .
The Features of Your Textbook

Get acquainted with *College Reading and Study Skills* and its features. Place a check mark in front of each item you find as you flip through this book. (Note that the book does not include all the features listed below.) Describe how you can use each feature to learn.

Feature	Value
❏ Chapter objectives	_____
❏ Chapter opening visual/graphic(s)	_____
❏ Informational boxes	_____
❏ Charts, graphics, and/ or photographs	_____
❏ Marginal vocabulary definitions	_____
❏ Examples	_____
❏ Exercises	_____
❏ Tables	_____
❏ Chapter summary	_____
❏ Writing activities	_____
❏ Internet exercises	_____
❏ Index	_____

Getting an Overview . . .
The Preface

The preface is the introduction to the book; it describes its organization and use.

- Read the preface or "To the Student" in one of your other textbooks.
- Write a list of information you learned about your textbook from reading the preface or "To the Student." Look for the answers to these questions:

    How is the book organized?
    What topics does the book cover?
    What makes the book unique?
    What learning features are included?

- Of all the information in the preface or "To the Student," what strikes you as most interesting? Why?

Examining . . .
The Table of Contents

The preface usually gives a summary of the book's organization and content. The table of contents provides you with a more detailed outline of the book's topics. The chapter titles are the main divisions of the book, and the subtitles within each chapter indicate the smaller subdivisions of the topics.

- Look at the table of contents of one of your textbooks for another course. Choose one chapter that you will have to read soon.
- Examine the title and subtitles for that one chapter. What is the main topic of the chapter? What are the major divisions of that main topic?
- Think about what you already know about this topic from talking to other people, watching the news, reading, or listening to the radio.

- What do you expect to learn from reading this chapter?

Learning More . . .

Each chapter in this book has a section titled "Using College Textbooks." In it you will learn how to apply the skills you learned in the chapter to reading and studying college textbooks. For example, in Chapter 7, "Understanding Paragraphs," you will discover the features within a textbook chapter that help you find main ideas (p. 158), and in Chapter 15, "Textbook Highlighting and Marking," you will learn how textbook authors help you decide what is important to mark and highlight (p. 324). Be sure to use each of these valuable sections to make textbooks easier to read and study.

Setting Goals and Managing Your Time

LEARNING GOALS

In this chapter you will learn to

1 Establish goals and priorities

2 Analyze your time commitments

3 Build a term plan

4 Build a weekly schedule

5 Use time efficiently

6 Avoid procrastination

LEARNING EXPERIMENT

Form two groups, Group 1 and Group 2. Each group should follow the directions given below for their group.

DIRECTIONS FOR GROUP 1

Study the photograph on the right for one minute at the beginning of class and one minute at the end of class. Focus on the details of the photograph.

DIRECTIONS FOR GROUP 2

Study the following photograph for two consecutive minutes at the beginning of class.

DIRECTIONS FOR BOTH GROUPS

The members of each group should meet, right after studying the photograph, separate from the other group. The group should write down as many

details from the photograph as they can remember. Group members may want to do this partly in the form of a diagram or sketch of the photograph, so they can indicate the placement of the various details.

Each group should then appoint someone to speak for them. The speaker from each group will tell the whole class what his or her group remembered about the photograph. Then the class will compare each group's details with the actual photograph to find out how much they remembered.

THE RESULTS

Which group remembered more details, more accurately? Why? Most classes find that the group that studied two separate minutes (Group 1) recalled more items than the group that studied for one two-minute block of time. Group 1 also had a goal in mind as they studied, whereas Group 2 did not.

LEARNING PRINCIPLE: WHAT THIS MEANS TO YOU

Several short periods of study are more effective than one long period of study. Having a goal (purpose) for studying also improves recall. This chapter will show you how to set goals and how to plan and manage your time. As you create a semester or weekly study plan, be sure to spread out your study; include three or four short periods of study and review for each of your courses.

WHY SET GOALS AND MANAGE YOUR TIME?

It is important to learn to set goals and manage time because:

- Setting goals can keep you on track, motivate you to work, and help you measure your progress.
- Managing your time allows you to finish your course work and still have time for family, work, and social activities.
- Managing your time allows you to make steady progress on long-term projects instead of being surprised at the last minute by rapidly approaching due dates.

ESTABLISHING YOUR GOALS AND PRIORITIES

Goal

Establish goals and priorities

One of the first steps in getting organized and succeeding in college is to set your priorities—to decide what is and what is not important to you. For most college students, finding enough time to do everything they *should* do and everything they *want* to do is nearly impossible. They face a series of conflicts over the use of their time and are forced to choose among a variety of activities. Here are a few examples:

Want to do:		Should do:
• Take family to park	*vs.*	Finish psychology reading assignment
• Go to hockey game	*vs.*	Work on term paper
• Go out with friends	*vs.*	Get good night's sleep

These day-to-day choices can be frustrating and can use up valuable time as you weigh the alternatives and make decisions. Often, these choices can be narrowed down to wanting to take part in an enjoyable activity even though you know you should be studying, reading, or writing a paper. At other times, there may be a conflict between two things you need to do, one for your studies and another for something else important in your life.

One of the best ways to handle these frequent conflicts is to identify your goals. Ask yourself, "What is most important to me? What activities can I afford to give up? What is least important to me when I am pressured for time?" For some students, studying is their first priority. For students with family or work responsibilities, caring for a child or being available for their shift might be their first priority, and attending college is next in importance.

How to Discover Your Priorities

1. **Make a list of the ten most joyous moments in your life.** A phrase or single sentence of description is all that is needed.
2. **Ask yourself, "What do most or all of these moments have in common?"**
3. **Try to write answers to the question above by describing why the moments were important to you—what you got out of them.** (Sample answers: helping others, competing or winning, creating something worthwhile, proving your self-worth, connecting with nature, and so forth.)
4. **Your answers should provide a starting point for defining life goals.**

Defining Goals Based on Your Priorities

In defining your goals, be specific and detailed. Use the following suggestions:

- **Your goals should be positive (what you want) rather than negative (what you want to avoid).** Don't say "I won't ever have to worry about credit card balances and bill collectors." Instead, say "I will have enough money to live comfortably."
- **Your goals should be realistic.** Unless you have strong evidence to believe you can do so, don't say you want to win an Olympic gold medal in swimming. Instead, say you want to become a strong, competitive swimmer.
- **Your goals should be achievable.** Don't say you want to earn a million dollars a year; most people don't earn that much. Set more achievable, specific goals, such as "I want to buy my own house by the time I am 30."
- **Your goals should be worth what it takes to achieve them.** Becoming an astronaut or a brain surgeon takes years of training. Are you willing to spend that amount of time?
- **Your goals should include a time frame.** The goal "to earn a bachelor's degree in accounting" should include a date, for example.
- **Expect your goals to change as your life changes.** The birth of a child or the loss of a loved one may cause you to refocus your life.

Tip *Time frame* means the length of time from the beginning to the end of an activity.

You will find that clearly establishing and pursuing your goals eliminates much worry and guilt. You'll know what is important and feel that you are on target, working steadily toward the goals you have established.

Exercise 1

DIRECTIONS   Write a list of five to ten goals.

_____

_____

_____

_____

_____

How a College Education Contributes to Your Goals

College can help you achieve many of your life goals. College can provide you with the self-awareness, self-confidence, knowledge, skills, practice facilities, degrees, friendships, business contacts, and so forth that can help you achieve your life goals.

Try to make the connection between college and life goals clear and explicit. College demands hard work and a stick-with-it attitude. You will be more motivated to work hard if you can see directly how that hard work will pay off in helping you fulfill your life goals.

DIRECTIONS   For each of your life goals listed in Exercise 1, explain how attending college will help you achieve that goal.

Exercise 2

_____

_____

_____

_____

_____

ANALYZING YOUR TIME COMMITMENTS

Your time commitments should reflect your priorities. For example, if a work or family obligation has high priority, then you must reserve time for it. You can reserve enough time to study for an exam in psychology, do library research, and read biology assignments. To do this, though, you must determine how much time is available and then decide how you will use it.

Let's begin by making some rough estimates. That way, you'll see where your time goes each week. Fill in the chart shown in Figure 1-1, making reasonable estimates. After you've completed the chart, total your hours per week and write the answer in the space marked "Total committed time per week." Next, fill in that total below and complete the subtraction.

Goal 2

Analyze your time commitments

myreadinglab

To practice analyzing your time commitments, go to

> Time Management, Memorization, and Concentration

    168   hours in one week

  _____   total committed time

  _____   hours available

Are you surprised to see how many hours per week you have left? Now answer this question: Do you have enough time available for reading and studying? As a rule of thumb, most instructors expect you to spend two hours studying for every hour spent in class. Complete the following multiplication:

_____ hours spent in class × 2 = _____ study hours needed

Do you have this much time available each week? If your answer to the question is no, then you are overcommitted. If you are overcommitted, ask yourself the following question: Can I drop any activity or do it in less time? Can I reduce the number of hours I work, or can another family member split some time-consuming responsibilities with me? If you are unable to reduce your committed time, talk with your advisor about taking fewer courses.

**Figure 1-1
Weekly Time
Commitments**

	HOURS PER DAY	HOURS PER WEEK
Sleep		
Breakfast		
Lunch		
Dinner		
Part- or full-time job		
Time spent in class		
Transportation time		
Personal care (dressing, shaving, etc.)		
Household/family responsibilities (cooking dinner, driving sister to work, etc.)		
Sports		
Other priorities		
Total committed time per week		

If you are overcommitted or feel you want to use your time more efficiently, now is the time to develop a weekly schedule that will help you use your available time more effectively. You are probably concerned at this point, however, that your time analysis did not take into account social and leisure activities. That omission was deliberate up to this point.

Although leisure time is essential to everyone's well-being, it should not take precedence over college work. Most students who develop and follow a time schedule for accomplishing their course work are able to handle family and community obligations and still have time left for reasonable leisure and social activities. They also find time to become involved with campus groups and activities—an important aspect of college life.

Goal **3**

Build a term plan

BUILDING A TERM PLAN

A term plan lists all your unchanging commitments. These may include class hours, transportation to and from school and work, family commitments, religious obligations, job hours (if they are the same each week), sleep, meals, and sports. A form for a term plan is shown in Figure 1-2. You'll use your term plan to build weekly time schedules. Adjust your schedule each week and make a new copy.

Exercise 3

DIRECTIONS   Use the form shown in Figure 1-2 or a computer software program to build your own term plan. ●

Goal **4**

Build a weekly schedule

BUILDING YOUR WEEKLY SCHEDULE

A weekly schedule is a plan of when and what you will study. It includes specific times for studying particular subjects as well as specific times for writing papers, conducting library research, and completing homework assignments for each course.

At the beginning of each week, decide what you need to accomplish that week, given your unchanging commitments. Consider upcoming quizzes, exams, and papers. A schedule will eliminate the need to make frustrating last-minute choices between "should" and "want to" activities. The sample weekly time schedule in

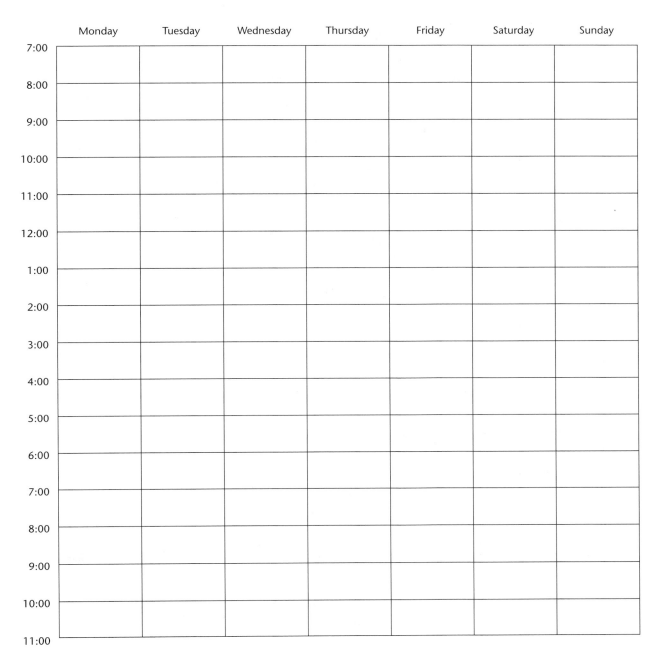

Figure 1-2
Term Plan

Figure 1-3 was developed by a first-year student. Her unchanging commitments are shown in *yellow*. Her weekly study adjustments are shown in *brown*. Read it carefully, noticing how the student reserved times for studying for each of her courses.

Tips for Creating a Weekly Schedule

Now that you have seen a sample weekly schedule, you can begin to build your own, using the following guidelines:

1. **Before the week begins, assess the upcoming week's workload.** Reserve a specific time for this activity. Sunday evening works well for many students. Check your course management system or your class Web site for updates

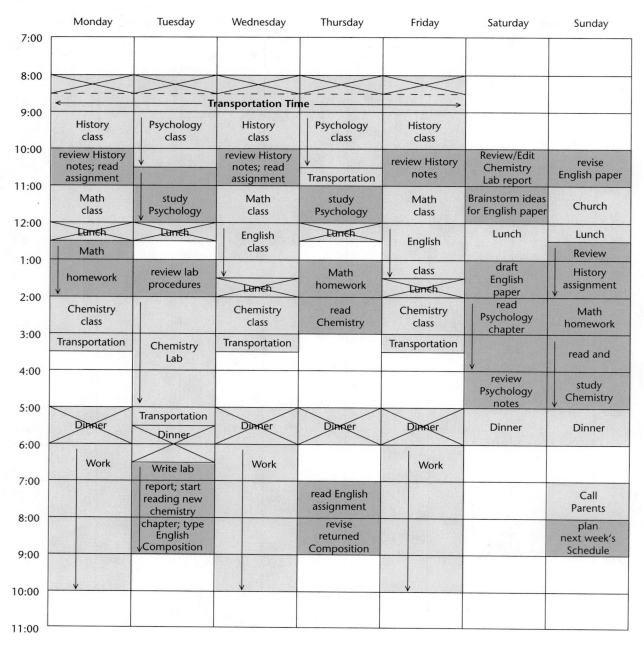

Figure 1-3
Sample Weekly Time Schedule

and new assignments. Review your assignment notebook or calendar for upcoming quizzes, exams, papers, and assignments.

2. **Write in any appointments, such as with the doctor or dentist or for a haircut.** Add in new commitments such as babysitting your niece on Saturday afternoon or helping a friend repair his car.

3. **Estimate the amount of time you will need for each course.** Add extra time if you have an important exam or if the amount of reading is particularly heavy. Block in study times for each course using the suggestions in the box on page 15.

4. **Plan ahead.** If there's a paper due next week that requires library research, allow time this week to begin your research. If you share computer access, make sure you reserve access in advance.

5. **Block out reasonable amounts of time, especially on weekends, for having fun and relaxing.** For example, mark off the time when your favorite television show is on, or allocate time for going for a run.

6. **Build into your schedule a short break before you begin studying each new subject.** Your mind needs time to refocus—to switch from one set of facts, problems, and issues to another.

7. **Include short breaks when you are working on just one assignment for a long period of time.** A 10-minute break after 50 to 60 minutes of study is reasonable.

8. **Set aside a specific time each week for developing next week's plan.** Be sure to review your prior week's performance, as well.

When to Study Which Subjects

The order in which you study various subjects and complete various tasks does matter. Use the following suggestions to use your study time effectively.

GETTING THE MOST OUT OF YOUR STUDY TIME

1. **Study difficult subjects first.** It's tempting to get easy tasks and short assignments out of the way first, but don't give in to this approach. When you start studying, your mind is fresh and alert and you are at your peak of concentration. This is when you are best equipped to handle difficult subjects. Thinking through complicated problems or studying complex ideas requires maximum brain power, and you have the most at the beginning of a study session.

2. **Leave the routine and more mechanical tasks for later in the evening.** Activities such as printing out papers or alphabetizing a bibliography for a research paper do not require a high degree of concentration and can be left until you are tired.

3. **Schedule study for a particular course close to the time when you attend class.** Plan to study the evening before the class meets or soon after the class meeting. If a class meets on Tuesday morning, plan to study Monday evening or Tuesday afternoon or evening.

4. **When reading or studying a particular subject, try to schedule two or three short, separate blocks of time for that course.** One long, continuous block can be fatiguing.

5. **Schedule study sessions at times when you know you are usually alert and feel like studying.** Do not schedule a study time early on Saturday morning if you do not really wake up until noon on weekends, and try not to schedule study time late in the evening if you are usually tired by that time.

Visual Thinking
APPLYING SKILLS

How could this student study more efficiently?

6. **Plan to study at times when your physical surroundings are quiet.** If the dinner hour is a rushed and confusing time, don't attempt to study then if there are alternative times available. Turn off your cell phone. If you are studying online, disable instant messaging.

Using your weekly schedule will be a challenge because it will mean saying no in a number of different situations. When friends call or stop by and ask you to join them at a time when you planned to study, you will have to refuse, but you could let them know when you will be free and offer to join them then. When a friend or family member asks you to do a favor—such as running an errand—you will have to refuse, but you can suggest some alternative times when you will be free. You will find that your friends and family will accept your constraints and may even respect you for being conscientious. Don't you respect someone who gets a great deal done and is successful in whatever he or she attempts?

TECH SUPPORT

Using Electronic Calendars

Many Internet services, such as Google and Yahoo, offer Web-based electronic calendars. These calendars provide daily, weekly, or monthly scheduling options in which you can enter your academic, work, and social activities. You can share your calendars and coordinate activities via e-mail with your friends and classmates; set repeating obligations (such as classes that meet on a regular basis) by typing them in only once; have meeting or appointment reminders sent to you via e-mail or cell phone; and even link activities to other Web sites or online documents. Because these calendars are Web-based, you can access them from just about any computer or most cell phones. The main advantages to online calendars are that they don't get lost, they are password-protected (you need to log in to your private, free account to access your calendar), and they can be updated easily. And you can always print out a hard copy to carry with you, if you prefer.

Exercise 4

DIRECTIONS   Using the term plan you wrote in Exercise 3, create a plan for next week. ●

Goal 5
Use time efficiently

USING TIME-SAVING TIPS TO MANAGE A BUSY SCHEDULE

Here are a few suggestions that will help you to make the best use of your time. If you are one of the many students who balances family responsibilities, work obligations, and college work, you will find these suggestions particularly valuable.

1. **Use your computer to save time.** For example, check the library's Web site to see the hours it is open; send an e-mail to confirm an appointment.

2. **Set priorities.** There may be days or weeks when you cannot complete every assignment. Many students work until they are exhausted and leave remaining assignments unfinished. A better approach is to decide what is most important to complete immediately and which assignments could, if necessary, be completed later.

3. **Use spare moments.** Think of all the time you spend waiting. You wait for a class to begin, for a ride, for a friend to call, for a pizza to arrive. Instead of wasting this time, you could use it to review a set of lecture notes, work on review questions at the end of a chapter, or review a chemistry lab setup. Always carry with you something you can work on in spare moments.

Tip *Spare moments* means "small amounts of extra time."

4. **Learn to combine activities.** Most people think it's impossible to do two things at once, but busy students soon learn that it's possible to combine some daily chores with routine class assignments. Some students, for example, are able to do laundry and, between loads outline a history chapter or work on routine assignments. Others review formulas for math or science courses or review vocabulary cards for language courses while riding a bus.

5. **Use lists to keep yourself organized and to save time.** A daily "to do" list is helpful in keeping track of what daily living/household tasks and errands, as well as course assignments, need to be done. As you think of tasks to be done, jot them down. Then look over the list each morning and try to find the best way to get everything done. You may find, for instance, that you can stop at the post office on the way to the bookstore, thus saving yourself an extra trip.

6. **Don't be afraid to admit you're trying to do too much.** If you find your schedule is becoming too hectic or unmanageable, or if you are facing pressures you can't handle, consider dropping a course. Don't be too concerned that this will put you behind schedule for graduation. More than half of all college students take longer than the traditional time expected to earn their degrees. Besides, you may be able to pick up the course later during a summer session or carry a heavier load during another semester.

CONTROLLING THE TENDENCY TO PROCRASTINATE

Goal 6
Avoid procrastination

Have you ever felt that you should work on an assignment, and even wanted to get it out of the way, but could not get started? If so, you may have been a victim of procrastination—putting off tasks that need to be done. Although you know you should review your biology notes this evening, for instance, you procrastinate and do something else instead. Tedious, difficult, or uninteresting tasks are often those that we put off doing. It is often these very tasks, however, that are essential to success in college courses. The following suggestions can put you on track for success by helping you overcome or control a tendency to procrastinate.

Regardless of What You Do, Start!

If you are having difficulty getting started, do something other than sit and stare, regardless of how trivial it may seem. The tips on page 18 will help you get started.

HOW TO FIGHT PROCRASTINATION

Do you . . .	Try this:
Get distracted?	• Turn off the television. • Set your cell phone to silent. • Disable instant messaging and new e-mail alerts. • Clear your desk; get rid of clutter; move other unfinished projects out of sight. • Avoid stimulus overload—don't listen to music while sitting in a busy and loud student lounge, for example.
Feel overwhelmed by the task?	• Break the task into manageable parts; this will make the task seem doable. Work on one piece at a time.
Try to avoid the task?	• Don't fall into the trap of overdoing routine tasks such as cleaning or balancing your checkbook. • Sit and stay at your desk. You will be unable to run errands, pick up takeout food, etc.

JUMP START!

- Start with a small task that takes very little time, such as rereading your instructor's assignment.
- Start with easy-to-do tasks, such as making a list of what needs to be done.
- Give yourself five minutes to get started. Once you are involved with the task, it will be easier to continue.

Recognize When You Need More Information

Sometimes procrastination is a signal that you lack skills or information. You may be avoiding a task because you're not sure how to do it. You may not really understand why a certain procedure is used to solve a particular type of math problem, for example, so you feel reluctant to do math homework. Similarly, selecting a topic for a term paper may be difficult if you aren't certain of the paper's purpose or expected length. Overcome such stumbling blocks by discussing them with classmates or with your professor.

Think Positively

As you begin a task, it is easy to get discouraged by negative thoughts. A positive attitude will make the task more enjoyable so it moves along more quickly. Use the following tips to help you avoid negative thoughts.

HOW TO STAY POSITIVE

If you think . . .	Try telling yourself . . .
This is boring.	I'll be able to stick with this (and give yourself a reward when you finish).
I can't wait to finish.	It will feel great to have this job done.
I'll never be able to remember all of this.	I'll highlight what is important for later review.
This is not useful to learn anyway.	My instructor would not assign this if it weren't important.
If I didn't have to do this, I could be _____.	When this task is finished, I'll find time to _____.

DIRECTIONS Read each situation described, and then answer the questions that follow. Discuss your responses with another student, or write your answers in the spaces provided.

Exercise 5

1. In analyzing his amount of committed time, Zabir filled in a weekly chart, in hours, as follows:

Sleep	56
Breakfast, lunch, dinner (total)	14
Job	35
Time in classes	23
Transportation	10
Personal care	15
Household/family	20
Study time	30
Total	203

Zabir is overcommitted; his total commitments add up to more hours than there are in a week (168). He has to have at least a part-time job in order to pay for school. He is enrolled in science lab technology, so he must spend a lot of class hours in lab. He estimates that he needs 30 hours of study time per week to maintain a high B average this semester. It is also important to have a small amount of time for leisure and recreation. Look at his chart again. What could he do? What are his choices? Try to find as many alternatives as you can.

_____

_____

_____

_____

_____

2. Tiffany is a serious student but is having difficulty with her accounting course. She has decided to spend all day Sunday studying accounting. She plans to

lock herself in her room and not come out until she has reviewed four chapters. What is wrong with her approach? What study plan would be more effective?

_____

_____

_____

_____

3. Mark realizes that he has three assignments that must be completed in one evening. The assignments are to revise an English composition, to read and highlight ten pages in his anatomy and physiology text, and to recopy a homework assignment for sociology. He decides to get the sociology assignment out of the way first, to do the English composition next (because English is one of his favorite subjects), and then to read the anatomy and physiology text. Evaluate Mark's plan of study.

_____

_____

_____

_____

4. You are taking a course in music appreciation, and your instructor often asks you to listen to a certain part of a concert on FM radio or to watch a particular program online. You cannot predict when these assignments will be given or at what time you will need to complete them. What could you do to include them in your weekly study schedule?

_____

_____

5. Carlos is registered for the following courses, which meet at the times indicated:

Business Management 109	T-Th 12–1.30 P.M
English 101	M-W-F 11 A.M.–12 Noon
Math 201	T-Th 9–10:30 A.M.
Biology 131	Class M-W-F 2–3 P.M.; Lab W 3–5 P.M.
Psychology 101	M-W-F 9–10 A.M.

The workload for each course is as follows:

Business Management	Two chapters assigned each week; midterm and final exams; one term paper due at the end of the semester
English	One 250-word essay per week
Math	A homework assignment for each class, which takes approximately one hour to complete; a quiz each Thursday

Biology	Preparation for weekly lab; one chapter to read per week; a one-hour exam every three weeks
Psychology	One chapter to read per week; one library reading assignment per week; four major exams throughout the semester

Because Carlos has a part-time job, he has the following times available for study:

Between his classes
Evenings: Tuesday, Wednesday
Afternoons: Monday, Thursday, and Friday
Weekends: Saturday morning, all day and evening Sunday

What study schedule would you recommend for Carlos? Indicate the times he should study each subject and what tasks he should work on. Use a blank term plan (Figure 1-2) to plan a schedule for Carlos.

_____

_____

_____

USING COLLEGE TEXTBOOKS:
Keeping Up with Reading Assignments

An important part of time management is keeping up with textbook reading assignments. It is easy to let assignments slide, especially since your instructor is not checking to be sure you have completed them.

Use the following suggestions to keep up with assigned reading.

USE AND MARK YOUR SYLLABUS

A syllabus (see pages 2–3) often contains a list of assigned chapters along with the week they are due. Use the margins of the syllabus to mark when you plan to complete each assignment and check it off when complete. Subdivide long chapters into sections to be completed on different days. Here is an excerpt from a syllabus for an art course.

Week 1	Chapter 1 The Nature of Art		9/15
Week 2	Chapter 3 Visual Elements of Art	✓ pp. 112–130	9/19
		✓ pp. 131–148	9/21
Week 3	Chapter 4 Principles of Art	pp. 149–160	9/26
		pp. 161–175	9/28

Annotate the Text's Table of Contents

Keep track of when assignments are due and when you have completed them using the book's table of contents, as shown below. Feel free to add notes to yourself indicating sections that need further review or those that you had difficulty with.

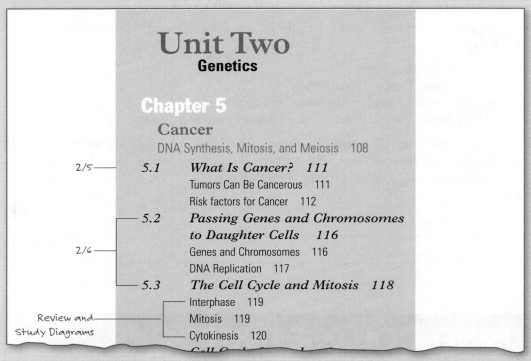

Experiment with both of the above methods of keeping track of reading assignments. Decide which one works better and use it for several weeks.

FURTHER PRACTICE WITH TEXTBOOK READING

Part A: Sample Textbook Chapter

Below is a section of a syllabus that assigns the sample textbook chapter (p. 489) to be studied over a one-week period.

> **Feb 13: Lecture on Emotion.** Read "Theories of Emotion," "Emotion and the Body," "Nonverbal Emotional Expression," and "Experienced Emotion" sections of Chapter 13.
>
> **Feb 15: Lecture on Motivation.** Read the remainder of Chapter 13 and complete the "Test Your Understanding" section.
>
> **Feb 17: Quiz on Chapter 13:** Emotion and Motivation

Using the guidelines above, annotate the table of contents provided on p. 23 according to the syllabus.

Part B: Your College Textbook

Choose a textbook that you are using in one of your other courses. Using the syllabus for that course, annotate your textbook's table of contents according to the guidelines above.

13

EMOTION AND MOTIVATION
What Drives Us to Do the Things We Do? 192

SELF-TEST
SUMMARY

Goal ① Why should you set goals?	Establishing your goals will eliminate the need to make many day-to-day choices, eliminate conflicts, and keep you focused. Begin by establishing your priorities and following them to achieve your academic goals. Next, compare the time you have allotted to various commitments with the priorities you have assigned to those activities. Finally, build a term plan that you will adjust weekly.
Goal ② How can you analyze your time commitments?	Analyze how you spend your time each week on non-academic tasks to determine if you have enough time for classes, studying, and homework.
Goal ③ What is a term plan?	A term plan is a time schedule that lists all your fixed time commitments, including your classes, transportation time, job hours, sleep, meals, sports, and family commitments. This is your basic time schedule for the semester. From it you can build your weekly schedules easily.

Goal 4 What is the value of a weekly time schedule?	A weekly time schedule helps you to plan your study time in advance and avoid last-minute choices of how to use your time best. It is your commitment on paper to how you intend to do what is necessary to accomplish your goals for the week.
Goal 5 What can you do to save time when you have a busy schedule?	Many students who have heavy family and work responsibilities need to find ways to make the most of their time. They can do this by setting their priorities, organizing their time with lists, using the computer as a time-saving tool, learning to combine activities, and using their spare moments for study tasks.
Goal 6 How can you overcome the urge to procrastinate?	Procrastination can knock even the best students off the success track. To help yourself deal with difficult, tedious, and uninteresting tasks, clear your work area of anything that will distract you, break the task up into manageable parts, get into the task immediately, avoid thinking negatively about it, avoid typical escape routes such as television, and be aware of when you need more information and get it.

APPLYING YOUR SKILLS

DISCUSSING THE CHAPTER

1. What are the advantages of working on assignments in several short sessions over a period of time rather than in one longer session all at once?
2. What are some of the ways that you use spare moments and combine activities to help you save time?
3. Why is it more important to overcome procrastination in college than in high school?
4. How can establishing goals and developing plans help you in a job you might hold after finishing college?

ANALYZING A STUDY SITUATION

DIRECTIONS   Working in pairs, analyze this situation and discuss answers to the questions that follow.

Sarah decided she didn't need a time schedule because every day is the same for her. She gets up, makes breakfast, gets her children ready for school, and puts them on the bus. Then she goes to two classes, has lunch, goes to another class, and comes home to study for an hour until her children return. She spends the rest of the afternoon and evening with her husband and children. Recently, Sarah's grades have begun to fall. One of her instructors told her he feels she should spend more time preparing for class.

1. How could making a time schedule help Sarah? What might she learn?
2. Make some suggestions about how Sarah can get more study time.
3. What kinds of changes would she need to make?
4. What important decisions does Sarah need to make?

WORKING ON COLLABORATIVE PROJECTS

DIRECTIONS   Working with another student in your class, exchange and critique the term plans and weekly schedules you wrote in this chapter. Answer the following questions:

1. Where do you see potential problems in the schedule presented?
2. Is enough study time included?
3. Are study times scheduled appropriately? (See the suggestions on p. 15.)
4. Are there "empty hours" that could be used more efficiently?

For support in meeting this chapter's goals, go to **MyReadingLab** and select **Time Management, Memorization and Concentration**.

Quick QUIZ

DIRECTIONS Write the letter of the choice that best completes each statement in the space provided.

CHECKING YOUR RECALL

_____ 1. If you are taking 12 hours of classes, you should expect to study each week for at least
 a. 6 hours.
 b. 12 hours.
 c. 24 hours.
 d. 30 hours.

_____ 2. An example of a well-defined goal is
 a. "I never want to go bankrupt."
 b. "I want to earn a B.A. degree."
 c. "I want to be a millionaire someday."
 d. "I want to earn a degree in art by the time I am 27."

_____ 3. A term plan is intended to
 a. list all of your unchanging commitments in a semester.
 b. indicate specific study times for each course.
 c. serve as a record of class assignments.
 d. be constantly revised as your weekly schedule changes.

_____ 4. An example of an effective time-saving technique is
 a. waiting as long as possible to complete an assignment.
 b. reviewing class notes while riding on the bus.
 c. eliminating optional assignments from your weekly plan.
 d. studying with a friend.

_____ 5. It is usually best to study for a difficult course
 a. in two or three short blocks of time rather than one long block.
 b. only when you really feel like it.
 c. after a warm-up session.
 d. after you have studied for your easier courses.

APPLYING YOUR KNOWLEDGE

_____ 6. Maurice is a first-year college student who just started playing on an intramural water polo team. Maurice was an A/B student in high school and is working a part-time job to help pay for college. Which of the following goals is the most appropriate for Maurice?
 a. I will never get a grade below an A.
 b. I will make the U.S. Olympic Water Polo Team next year.
 c. I will study for 40 hours each week.
 d. I will graduate from college with at least a 3.0 grade point average within five years.

_____ 7. If you have a biology class on Tuesday mornings, you should plan to study for it on
 a. Monday evenings.
 b. Thursday afternoons.
 c. Friday evenings.
 d. the weekend.

_____ 8. Of the following tasks associated with a math course, the best one to work on early in the evening is
 a. recopying a friend's notes from a class you missed.
 b. learning a difficult method for computing statistics.
 c. copying math formulas from the textbook onto index cards.
 d. checking to make sure you have the assignment written down correctly.

_____ 9. Sarah has an economics examination tomorrow. She has been cramming for four hours straight and is starting to panic. Which of the following suggestions would _not_ have helped Sarah to study more effectively?
 a. studying her easier topics first
 b. studying in short blocks of time, rather than one long block
 c. taking a ten-minute break for each hour that she studies
 d. scheduling her study session at a time when she is alert and feels like studying

_____ 10. Tonight, Justine needs to prepare for a math midterm examination that she'll take tomorrow, make vocabulary flash cards for tomorrow's Russian class, and read three chapters in a novel for her English class in two days. In what order should she attack these assignments?
 a. math, Russian, English
 b. math, English, Russian
 c. Russian, math, English
 d. English, Russian, math

Learning Style and Learning Strategies

LEARNING GOALS

In this chapter you will learn to

1 Analyze your learning style

2 Develop an action plan

3 Understand instructors' teaching styles

4 Understand instructors' expectations

5 Use active learning skills

6 Explain and illustrate critical thinking

LEARNING EXPERIMENT

1 Study the photograph on the right for one minute.

2 Draw a sketch of one of the people in the photograph.

3 Write two or three sentences describing this person.

4 Compare your drawing and description with those of your classmates by quickly passing them around the room.

THE RESULTS

No doubt, some sketches were much better than others. Some were detailed, accurate likenesses; others may have resembled stick figures. Likewise, some students wrote detailed descriptive sentences; others did not. You can conclude that some students have stronger artistic ability than others. Some students have stronger verbal abilities than others. Which students do you expect will do well in an art class? Who will do better on essay exams? Who might consider a career in graphic design?

LEARNING PRINCIPLE: WHAT THIS MEANS TO YOU

You have strengths and weaknesses as a learner; you should capitalize on your strengths and strive to overcome your weaknesses. In this chapter you will learn to identify strengths and weaknesses and choose study methods accordingly. You will also discover that instructors have unique teaching styles and discover how to adapt to them. Finally, you will learn what kinds of learning and thinking your instructors expect of you.

WHY ANALYZE YOUR LEARNING STYLE?

It is important to analyze you learning style because:

- You will understand your strengths and weaknesses as a learner and understand how to choose study methods accordingly.
- You will realize why you learn more easily from some instructors than from others.
- You will discover what kinds of learning and thinking are expected in college.

Goal ❶

Analyze your learning style

Tip If something is *unique*, it's the only one of its kind. But sometimes the word is used to describe something that is very unusual or that can't be duplicated. Note: the word part *uni-* means "one," as in *universe* and *united*.

ANALYZING YOUR LEARNING STYLE

Have you noticed that some types of tasks are easier to complete than others? Have you also discovered that some study methods work better than others? Have you ever found that a study method that works well for a classmate does not work as well for you? These differences can be explained by what is known as *learning style*. Just as you have a unique personality, you also have a unique learning style. People differ in how they learn and in the methods and strategies they use to learn. Your learning style can, in part, explain why some courses are easier than others and why you learn better from one instructor than from another. Learning style can also explain why certain assignments are difficult and other learning tasks are easy.

To begin to understand learning style, think of everyday tasks and activities that you have learned to do easily and well. Think of others that are always troublesome. For example, is reading maps easy or difficult? Is drawing or sketching easy or difficult? Can you assemble items easily? Are tasks that require physical coordination (such as racquetball) difficult? Can you easily remember the lyrics to popular songs? Just as some everyday tasks are easy and others are difficult, so are some academic tasks easy and others more challenging.

The following questionnaire will help you analyze how you learn and enable you to learn more efficiently. Complete the following Learning Style Questionnaire before continuing.

Learning Style Questionnaire

DIRECTIONS   Each item presents two choices. Select the alternative that best describes you. In cases where neither choice suits you, select the one that is closer to your preference. Write the letter of your choice on the line to the left of each item.

PART ONE

_____ 1. I would prefer to follow a set of
   a. oral directions.
   b. print directions.

_____ 2. I would prefer to
   a. attend a lecture given by a famous psychologist.
   b. read an online article written by the psychologist.

_____ 3. When I am introduced to someone, it is easier for me to remember the person's
   a. name.
   b. face.

_____ 4. I find it easier to learn new information using
   a. language (words).
   b. images (pictures).

_____ 5. I prefer classes in which the instructor
   a. lectures and answers questions.
   b. uses PowerPoint illustrations and videos.

_____ 6. To follow current events, I prefer to
   a. listen to the news on the radio.
   b. read the newspaper.

_____ 7. To learn how to repair a flat tire, I would prefer to
   a. listen to a friend's explanation.
   b. watch a demonstration.

PART TWO

_____ 8. I prefer to
   a. work with facts and details.
   b. construct theories and ideas.

_____ 9. I would prefer a job that involved
   a. following specific instructions.
   b. reading, writing, and analyzing.

_____ 10. I prefer to
   a. solve math problems using a formula.
   b. discover why the formula works.

_____ 11. I would prefer to write a term paper explaining
   a. how a process works.
   b. a theory.

_____ 12. I prefer tasks that require me to
   a. follow careful, detailed instructions.
   b. use reasoning and critical analysis.

_____ 13. For a criminal justice course, I would prefer to
   a. discover how and when a law can be applied.
   b. learn how and why it became law.

_____ 14. To learn more about the operation of a digital camera, I would prefer to
   a. work with several types of digital cameras.
   b. understand the principles on which it operates.

PART THREE

_____ 15. To solve a math problem, I would prefer to
   a. draw or visualize the problem.
   b. study a sample problem and use it as a model.

_____ 16. To remember something best, I
   a. create a mental picture.
   b. write it down.

_____ 17. Assembling a bicycle from a diagram would be
   a. easy.
   b. challenging.

_____ 18. I prefer classes in which I
   a. handle equipment or work with models.
   b. participate in a class discussion.

_____ 19. To understand and remember how a machine works, I would

    a. draw a diagram.

    b. write notes.

_____ 20. I enjoy

    a. drawing or working with my hands.

    b. speaking, writing, and listening.

_____ 21. If I were trying to locate an office on an unfamiliar university campus, I would prefer

    a. a map.

    b. a set of print directions.

PART FOUR

_____ 22. For a grade in biology lab, I would prefer to

    a. work with a lab partner.

    b. work alone.

_____ 23. When faced with a difficult personal problem, I prefer to

    a. discuss it with others.

    b. resolve it myself.

_____ 24. Many instructors could improve their classes by

    a. including more discussion and group activities.

    b. allowing students to work on their own more frequently.

_____ 25. When listening to a lecturer or speaker, I respond more to

    a. the person presenting the ideas.

    b. the ideas themselves.

_____ 26. When on a team project, I prefer to

    a. work with several team members.

    b. divide up tasks and complete those assigned to me.

_____ 27. I prefer to shop and do errands

    a. with friends.

    b. by myself.

_____ 28. A job in a busy office is

    a. more appealing than working alone.

    b. less appealing than working alone.

PART FIVE

_____ 29. To make decisions, I rely on

    a. my experiences and gut feelings.

    b. facts and objective data.

_____ 30. To complete a task, I

    a. can use whatever is available to get the job done.

    b. must have everything I need at hand.

_____ 31. I prefer to express my ideas and feelings through

    a. music, song, or poetry.

    b. direct, concise language.

_____ 32. I prefer instructors who

    a. allow students to be guided by their own interests.

    b. make their expectations clear and explicit.

_____ 33. I tend to

    a. challenge and question what I hear and read.

    b. accept what I hear and read.

_____ 34. I prefer

    a. essay exams.

    b. objective exams.

_____ 35. In completing an assignment, I prefer to

    a. figure out my own approach.

    b. be told exactly what to do.

To score your questionnaire, record the total number of times you selected choice *a* and the total number of times you selected choice *b* for each part of the questionnaire. Record your totals in the scoring grid provided.

SCORING GRID		
Part	**Total Number of Choice *a***	**Total Number of Choice *b***
Part One	_____ Auditory	_____ Visual
Part Two	_____ Applied	_____ Conceptual
Part Three	_____ Spatial	_____ Verbal
Part Four	_____ Social	_____ Independent
Part Five	_____ Creative	_____ Pragmatic

Now circle your higher score for each part of the questionnaire. The word below the score you circled indicates an aspect of your learning style. Scores in a particular row that are close to one another, such as a 3 and a 4, suggest that you do not exhibit a strong, clear preference for either aspect. Scores that are farther apart, such as a 1 and a 6, suggest a strong preference for the higher-scoring aspect. The next section explains how to interpret your scores and describes these aspects.

Interpreting Your Scores

The questionnaire was divided into five parts; each part identifies one aspect of your learning style. These five aspects are explained below.

PART ONE: AUDITORY OR VISUAL LEARNERS   This score indicates the sensory mode you prefer when processing information. Auditory learners tend to learn more effectively through listening, whereas visual learners process information by seeing it in print or other visual modes, including films, pictures, or diagrams. If you have a higher score in auditory than visual, you tend to be an auditory learner. That is, you tend to learn more easily by hearing than by reading. A higher score in visual suggests strengths with visual modes of learning.

PART TWO: APPLIED OR CONCEPTUAL LEARNERS   This score describes the types of learning tasks and learning situations you prefer and find easiest to handle. If you are an applied learner, you prefer tasks that involve real objects and situations. Practical, real-life learning situations are ideal for you. If you are a conceptual learner, you prefer to work with language and ideas; practical applications are not necessary for understanding.

PART THREE: SPATIAL OR VERBAL LEARNERS This score reveals your ability to work with spatial relationships. Spatial learners are able to visualize, or mentally see, how things work or how they are positioned in space. Their strengths may include drawing, assembling things, or repairing. Verbal learners tend to rely on verbal or language skills, rather than skills in positioning things in space.

PART FOUR: SOCIAL OR INDEPENDENT LEARNERS This score reveals your preferred level of interaction with other people in the learning process. If you are a social learner, you prefer to work with others—both peers and instructors—closely and directly. You tend to be people oriented and to enjoy personal interaction. If you are an independent learner, you prefer to work and study alone. You tend to be self-directed or self-motivated and often are goal oriented.

PART FIVE: CREATIVE OR PRAGMATIC LEARNERS This score describes the approach you prefer to take toward learning tasks. Creative learners are imaginative and innovative. They prefer to learn through discovery or experimentation. They are comfortable taking risks and following hunches. Pragmatic learners are practical, logical, and systematic. They seek order and are comfortable following rules.

Exercise 1

DIRECTIONS   Write a paragraph describing yourself as a learner. Include aspects of your learning style and give examples from everyday experience that confirm your profile. Explain any results of the Learning Style Questionnaire with which you disagree.●

Goal ②
Develop an action plan

DEVELOPING AN ACTION PLAN FOR LEARNING

Now that you know more about *how* you learn, you are ready to develop an action plan for learning what you read. Suppose you discovered that you are an auditory learner. You still have to read your assignments, which is a visual task. However, to learn the assignment you should translate the material into an auditory form. For example, you could repeat aloud, using your own words, information that you want to remember, or you could record key information and play it back. If you also are a social learner, you could work with a classmate, testing each other out loud.

Figure 2-1, on page 33, lists each aspect of learning style and offers suggestions for how to learn from a reading assignment. To use the figure:

1. Circle the five aspects of your learning style for which you received higher scores. Disregard the others.
2. Read through the suggestions that apply to you.
3. Place a check mark in front of those suggestions you think will work for you. Choose at least one from each category.
4. List the suggestions you chose in the following Action Plan for Learning box.

Auditory	Visual
1. Record review notes. 2. Discuss/study with friends. 3. Talk aloud when studying. 4. Record lectures.	1. Use mapping (see Chapter 16). 2. Use visualization. 3. Use online resources if available. 4. View videos when available. 5. Draw diagrams, charts, and maps.
Applied	**Conceptual**
1. Associate ideas with their application. 2. Take courses with a lab or practicum. 3. Think of practical situations to which learning applies. 4. Use case studies, examples, and applications to cue your learning.	1. Use outlining. 2. Focus on thought patterns (see Chapter 8). 3. Organize materials into rules and examples.
Spatial	**Verbal**
1. Draw diagrams; make charts and sketches. 2. Use outlining. 3. Use visualization. 4. Use mapping (see Chapter 16).	1. Record steps, processes, and procedures in words. 2. Write summaries. 3. Translate diagrams and drawings into language. 4. Write your interpretations next to textbook drawings, maps, and graphics.
Social	**Independent**
1. Interact with the instructor. 2. Find a study partner. 3. Form a study group. 4. Take courses involving class discussion. 5. Work with a tutor.	1. Use online tutorials if available. 2. Enroll in courses using a traditional lecture–exam format. 3. Consider independent study courses. 4. Purchase review books and study guides, if available.
Creative	**Pragmatic**
1. Take courses that involve exploration, experimentation, or discussion. 2. Use annotation to record impressions and reactions. 3. Ask questions about chapter content and answer them.	1. Write lists of steps, processes, and procedures. 2. Write summaries and outlines. 3. Use a structured study environment. 4. Focus on problem-solving and logical sequence.

Figure 2-1
Learning Strategies for Various Learning Styles

ACTION PLAN FOR LEARNING

Learning Strategy 1. _____

_____

Learning Strategy 2. _____

_____

Learning Strategy 3. _____

_____

Learning Strategy 4. _____

_____

Learning Strategy 5. _____

_____

Now that you have listed suggestions to help you learn what you read, the next step is to experiment with these techniques, one at a time. (You may need to refer to the chapters listed in parentheses in Figure 2-1 to learn or review how a certain technique works.) Use one technique for a while, then move on to the next. Continue using the techniques that seem to work; work on revising or modifying those that do not. Do not hesitate to experiment with other techniques listed in the figure; you may find other techniques that work well for you.

Developing Strategies to Overcome Limitations

You should also work on developing the weaker aspects of your learning style. Your learning style is not fixed or unchanging. You can improve areas in which you had low scores. Although you may be weak in auditory learning, for example, many of your professors will lecture and expect you to take notes. If you work on improving your listening and note-taking skills, you can learn to handle lectures effectively. Make a conscious effort to work on improving areas of weakness as well as taking advantage of your strengths.

Several Words of Caution

Ideally, through activities in this section and the use of the questionnaire, you have discovered more about yourself as a learner. However, several words of caution are in order.

1. The questionnaire is a quick and easy way to discover your learning style. Other more formal and more accurate measures of learning style are available. These include *Kolb's Learning Style Inventory* and the *Myers–Briggs Type Indicator*. These tests may be available through your college's counseling, testing, or academic skills centers.

2. There are many more aspects of learning style than those identified through the questionnaire in this chapter. To learn more about other factors affecting learning, see one or both of the tests listed in point 1.

3. Learning style is *not* a fixed, unchanging quality. Just as personalities can change and develop, so can learning style change and develop through exposure, instruction, or practice. For example, as you attend more college lectures, your skill as an auditory learner may be strengthened.

4. You probably will not be clearly strong or weak in each aspect. Some students, for example, can learn equally well spatially and verbally. If your scores on one or more parts of the questionnaire were quite close, then you may have strengths in both areas.

5. When students discover the features of their learning style, they usually recognize themselves. A frequent comment is "Yep, that's me." However, if for some reason you feel the description of yourself as a learner is incorrect, then do not make changes in your learning strategies on the basis of the outcome. Instead, discuss your style with your instructor or consider taking one of the tests listed in point 1.

TECH SUPPORT

Learning Style and Online Courses

Online courses require a great deal of independence, self-direction, and the ability to work alone. Independent learners, then, will find themselves well suited to online course work. If you are a social learner, it's wise to recognize that much of your work will have to be done independently. However, most instructors build activities into online courses that encourage or require interaction with classmates, creating a learning community of sorts. Regardless of whether you are an independent or social learner, use the following advice to succeed in online courses.

- **Avoid taking online courses during your first semester or first year.** It is better to learn what is expected in college classes by attending traditional classes. Once you are familiar with college expectations, you will be better prepared to take an online course.

- **Read, read, read.** Reading is your primary source of information. You read textbooks and communications from professors and other students. If you aren't a strong reader or feel as if you need personal contact and in-person support from other students, get in touch with a classmate or find a friend who will register for the same online course.

- **Keep up with the work.** Most students who fail online courses fail because they fall hopelessly behind with the required reading and written assignments and cannot catch up. Devote specific hours each week to the online course. Make a work/study schedule and follow it as you would for any other class.

- **Keep your focus.** Turn off music, instant messaging, and e-mail while working on your computer for your online course.

Goal ❸

Understand instructors' teaching styles

UNDERSTANDING YOUR INSTRUCTORS' TEACHING STYLES

Just as each student has his or her own learning style, each instructor also has his or her own teaching style. Some instructors, for example, have a teaching style that promotes social interaction among students. An instructor may organize small group activities, encourage class participation, or require students to work in pairs or teams to complete a specific task. Other instructors offer little or no opportunity for social interaction, as in a lecture class for example.

Some instructors are very applied; they teach by example. Others are more conceptual; they focus on presenting ideas, rules, theories, and so forth. In fact, the same five categories of learning styles identified on pages 31–32 can be applied to teaching styles as well.

To an extent, of course, the subject matter also dictates how the instructor teaches. A biology instructor, for instance, has a large body of factual information to present and may feel he or she has little time to schedule group interaction.

Comparing Learning and Teaching Style

Once you are aware of your learning style and consider the instructor's teaching style, you can begin to understand why you can learn better from one instructor than from another and why you feel more comfortable in certain instructors' classes than in others. When aspects of your learning style match aspects of your instructor's teaching style, you are on the same wavelength, so to speak: the instructor is teaching the way you learn. On the other hand, when your learning style does not correspond to an instructor's teaching style, you may not be as comfortable, and learning will be more of a challenge. You may have to work harder in that class by taking extra steps to reorganize or reformat the material into a form better suited to your learning style. The following section presents each of the five categories of learning–teaching styles and suggests how you might make changes in how you study to accommodate each.

AUDITORY–VISUAL   If your instructor announces essential course information (such as paper assignments, class projects, or descriptions of upcoming exams) orally and you are a visual learner, you should be sure to record as much information as possible in your notes. If your instructor relies on lectures to present new material not included in your textbook, taking complete lecture notes is especially important. If your instructor uses numerous visual aids and you tend to be an auditory learner, consider recording summaries of these visual aids.

APPLIED–CONCEPTUAL   If your instructor seldom uses examples, models, or case studies and you are an applied learner, you need to think of your own examples to make the course material real and memorable to you. Leave space in your class notes to add examples. Add them during class if they come to mind; if not, take time as you review your notes to add examples. If your instructor uses numerous demonstrations and examples and you are a conceptual learner, you may need to leave space in your class notes to write in rules or generalizations that state what the examples are intended to prove.

SPATIAL–VERBAL   If you are a spatial learner and your instructor has a verbal teaching style (he or she lectures and distributes printed study guides), then you will need to draw diagrams, charts, and pictures to learn the material. On the other hand, if you are a verbal learner and your instructor is spatial (he or she frequently uses diagrams, flowcharts, and so forth), then you may need to translate the diagrams and flowcharts into words in order to learn them easily.

SOCIAL–INDEPENDENT   If your instructor organizes numerous in-class group activities and you tend to be an independent learner, then you will need to spend time alone after class reviewing the class activity, making notes, and perhaps even repeating the activity by yourself to make it more meaningful. If your instructor seldom structures in-class group activities and you tend to be a social learner, try to arrange to study regularly with a classmate or create or join a study group.

CREATIVE–PRAGMATIC   Suppose your instructor is very systematic and structured in his or her lectures, and, as a creative learner, you prefer to discover ideas through experimentation and free-flowing discussion. In this case, you should consider creating a column in your class notes to record your responses and creative thoughts or reserve the bottom quarter of each page for such annotations. If your instructor is creative and tends to use a loose or free-flowing class format, and you tend to be a pragmatic learner, you may need to rewrite and restructure class notes. If he or she fails to give you specific guidelines for completing activities or assignments, you should talk with your instructor or ask for more information.

DIRECTIONS   Analyze your instructors' teaching styles by completing the following chart for the courses you are taking this semester. List as many teaching characteristics as you can, but do not try to cover every aspect of learning–teaching style.

Exercise 2

Course	Instructor's Name	Teaching-Style Characteristics
1.		
2.		
3.		
4.		
5.		
6.		

DIRECTIONS   After you have completed the chart in Exercise 2, select one of your instructors whose teaching style does not match your learning style. Write a paragraph describing the differences in your styles. Explain how you will change your study methods to make up for these differences.●

Exercise 3

Goal 4

Understand instructors' expectations

MEETING YOUR INSTRUCTORS' EXPECTATIONS

Learning in college is different from learning in high school or on-the-job training. Now that you have a profile of yourself as a learner, it is time to discover what kinds of learning are expected of you. Whether you have just completed high school or are returning to college with work experiences or family responsibilities, you will face new demands and expectations in college. The following sections describe your instructors' expectations.

Visual Thinking
APPLYING SKILLS

What does this student's comment reveal?

He only gave me a "C" on this paper.

Take Responsibility for Your Own Learning

In college, learning is mainly up to you. Instructors function as guides. They define and explain what is to be learned, but they expect you to do the learning. Weekly class time is far shorter than in high school. Often there isn't enough time in class for instructors to provide drills, practices, and reviews of factual course content. Instead, college class time is used primarily to introduce content that is to be learned and to discuss ideas. Instructors expect you to learn the material and to be prepared to discuss it in class. *When, where*, and *how* you learn are your choices. Be sure to take into account the five aspects of your learning style as you make these choices.

Focus on Concepts

Each course you take will require that you learn a great many facts, statistics, dates, definitions, formulas, rules, or principles. It is easy to become convinced that learning these is sufficient and to become a robot learner—memorizing facts from texts and lectures and then recalling them on exams and quizzes. Actually, factual information is only a starting point, a base from which to approach the real content of a course. Most college instructors expect you to go beyond facts to analysis—to consider what the collection of facts and details *means*. Many students, however, "can't see the forest for the trees"; they get caught up in specifics and fail to grasp the larger, more important concepts. To avoid this pitfall, be sure to keep the following questions in mind as you read and study:

- Why do I need to know this?
- Why is this important?
- What principle or trend does this illustrate?
- How can I use this information?
- How does this fit in with other course content?

Focus on Ideas, Not "Right Answers"

Through previous schooling, many students have come to expect their answers to be either right or wrong. They assume that learning is limited to memorizing a collection of facts and that their mastery of the course is measured by the number of "right answers" they have learned. Accordingly, they are lost when faced with an essay question such as:

> Defend or criticize the arguments that are offered in favor of capital punishment. Refer to any readings that you have completed.

There is no one right answer to this question. You can either defend the arguments or criticize them. The instructor who asks this question expects you to think and to provide a reasoned, logical, consistent response that draws on information you have acquired through your reading. Here are a few more examples of questions for which there are no single correct answers.

> Do animals think?
>
> Would you be willing to reduce your standard of living by 15 percent if the United States could thereby eliminate poverty? Defend your response.
>
> Imagine a society in which everyone has exactly the same income. You are the manager of an industrial plant. What plans, policies, or programs would you implement to motivate your employees to work?

Evaluate New Ideas

Throughout college you will continually encounter new ideas; you will agree with some and disagree with others. Don't make the mistake of accepting or rejecting a new idea, however, until you have really explored it and have considered its assumptions and implications. Ask questions such as:

- What evidence is available in support of this idea?
- What opposing evidence is available?
- How is my personal experience related to this idea?
- What additional information do I need in order to make a decision?

Tip An *assumption* is a firm belief that something is true even without all the evidence to prove it. An *implication* is an idea that's suggested but not stated directly. if your roommate says, "Take your umbrella today," you assume he or she is implying that it's going to rain soon.

Explore Ideas Using a Journal

As you begin college, you will encounter many new ideas and meet many new people, both classmates and instructors, from whom you will discover new approaches and conventions—new ways of looking at and doing things. You will also begin to explore many academic fields that you did not study in high school. It is easy to feel overwhelmed by it all. Sometimes you need to sort out ideas and your reactions to them. Many students find it helpful to keep a journal either in a notebook or in a computer file. A journal is an informal record of your thoughts, ideas, impressions, and reactions. Your journal may take any form you select and may contain whatever you choose. Some students record impressions and feelings; others record new ideas they want to explore. Writing about your ideas will focus them and clarify your response to them. Journal entries, by the way, are an excellent source of ideas when you have to choose a topic about which to write a paper.

Because learning is a major focus of college, and because you will be reading about new learning strategies throughout this book, consider including in your journal a record of each learning strategy you try and how it works. You will find it helpful to review your journal; often, doing so will suggest which strategies seem to work for each of your courses. A learning journal is discussed in more detail in Chapter 17, pages 376–77.

Goal 5

Use active learning skills

To practice using active learning skills, go to

> Active Reading Strategies

DEVELOPING ACTIVE LEARNING STRATEGIES

Your instructors also expect you to become an active learner, illustrated by the following situation. A first-year student who had always thought of himself as a B student was getting low C's and D's in his business course. The instructor gave weekly quizzes; each was a practical problem to solve. Every week the student memorized his lecture notes and carefully reread the assigned chapter in his textbook. When he spoke with his instructor about his low grades, the instructor told him that his study methods were not effective and that he needed to become more active and involved with the subject matter. Memorizing and rereading are passive approaches. The instructor suggested that he try instead to think about content, ask questions, anticipate practical uses, solve potential problems, and draw connections among ideas.

Active Versus Passive Learning

How did you learn to ride a bike, play racquetball, or change a tire? In each case you learned by doing, by active participation. College learning requires similar active involvement and participation. Active learning is expected in most college courses and can often make the difference between barely average grades and top grades. Figure 2-2 lists common college learning situations and contrasts the responses of passive and active learners. The examples in Figure 2-2 show that passive learners do not carry the learning process far enough. They do not go beyond what instructors tell them to do. They fail to think about, organize, and react to course content.

Figure 2-2
Characteristics of Passive and Active Learners

	Passive Learners	Active Learners
Class lectures	Write down what the instructor says	Decide what is important to write down
Textbook assignments	Read	Read, think, ask questions, try to connect ideas
Studying	Reread	Consider learning style, make and outlines study sheets, predict exam questions, look for trends and patterns
Writing class assignments	Only follow the professor's instructions	Try to discover the significance of the assignment, look for the principles and concepts it illustrates
Writing term papers	Do only what is expected to get a good grade	Try to expand their knowledge and experience with a topic and connect it to the course objective or content

Active Learning Strategies

When you study, you should be thinking about and reacting to the material in front of you. This is how:

1. **Ask questions about what you are reading.** You will find that this helps to focus your attention and improve your concentration.
2. **Consider the purpose behind assignments.** Why might a sociology assignment require you to spend an hour at the primate exhibit of the local zoo, for example?
3. **Try to see how each assignment fits with the rest of the course.** For instance, why does a section called "Amortization" belong in a business mathematics textbook chapter titled "Business and Consumer Loans"?
4. **Relate what you are learning to what you already know from the course and from your background knowledge and personal experience.** Connect a law in physics with how your car brakes work, for example.
5. **Think of examples or situations in which you can apply the information.**

Throughout the remainder of this text, you will learn many strategies for becoming an active learner. Active learning also involves active reading. In Chapter 6 you will learn specific strategies for becoming an active reader.

Exercise 4

DIRECTIONS   Consider each of the following learning situations. Answer each question by suggesting active learning approaches.

1. A graded exam is returned to you by your history professor. How could you use this as a learning device? _____

_____

_____

2. You have been assigned "Letter from Birmingham Jail" by Martin Luther King, Jr., for your English composition class. What questions would you try to answer as you read? _____

_____

3. Your biology course requires a weekly lab. How would you prepare for attending this lab? _____

_____

4. You have been assigned by your sociology instructor to read an article in *Newsweek* on crime in major U.S. cities. How would you record important ideas? _____

_____

THINKING CRITICALLY

Goal 6

Explain and illustrate critical thinking

In college, your instructors expect you to learn actively, and they also expect you to think critically. A first step in becoming a critical thinker is to become familiar with the types of thinking that college instructors demand. Figure 2-3 lists six levels of thinking in order of increasing complexity. Based on a progression of thinking skills developed by Benjamin Bloom and revised by Lorin Anderson, they are widely used by educators in many academic disciplines.

Figure 2-3
Levels of Thinking

Level	Examples
REMEMBERING: recalling information, repeating information with no changes	Recalling dates, memorizing definitions for a history exam
UNDERSTANDING: understanding ideas, using rules, and following directions	Explaining a mathematical law, knowing how the human ear functions, explaining a definition in psychology
APPLYING: applying knowledge to a new situation	Using knowledge of formulas to solve a new physics problem
ANALYZING: seeing relationships, breaking information into parts, analyzing how things work	Comparing two poems by the same author
EVALUATING: making judgments, assessing the value or worth of information	Evaluating the effectiveness of an argument opposing the death penalty
CREATING: putting ideas and information together in a unique way, creating something new	Designing a Web page

myreadinglab

To practice thinking critically, go to
> Critical Thinking

Tip *Synthesizing* means "combining." The word part *syn-* means "together" or "with."

The *remembering* level of thinking is basically memorization; this is something you've been doing for years. The *understanding* level is also familiar. If you are able to explain how to convert fractions to decimals, then you are thinking at the comprehension level. At the *applying* level, you apply to a new situation information that you have memorized and understood. When you use your knowledge of punctuation to place commas correctly in a sentence, you are functioning at the application level. The *analyzing* level involves examining what you have learned and studying relationships. When you explain how a microscope works, you are analyzing its operation. *Evaluating* involves making judgments. When you decide what is effective and what is ineffective in a classmate's presentation in a public speaking class, you are evaluating the presentation. The *creating* level requires you to put ideas together to form something new. When you write a paper by drawing on a variety of sources, you are synthesizing them.

APPLYING LEVELS OF THINKING

Reading and Levels of Thinking

As you read, be sure to think at each level. Here is a list of questions to help you read and think at each level.

Level of Thinking	Questions
REMEMBERING	What information do I need to learn?
UNDERSTANDING	What are the main points and how are they supported?
APPLYING	How can I use this information?
ANALYZING	How is this material organized? How are the ideas related?
	How are the data presented in graphs, tables, and charts related? What trends do they reveal?
EVALUATING	Is this information accurate, reliable, and valuable? Does the author prove his or her points?
CREATING	How does this information fit with other sources (class lectures, other readings, your prior knowledge)?

Using Levels of Thinking

The last three levels—analyzing, evaluating, and creating—involve critical thinking. Some exam questions require you to remember, understand, and apply. Many objective exams (multiple-choice, true/false) include items that focus on these levels. Essay exams, however, as well as some multiple-choice questions, require thinking at the three higher levels. Participating in class discussions, writing papers, making speeches, and artistic expression (music, painting, and the like) all require analyzing, evaluating, and/or creating. In later chapters, you'll learn more about these levels of thinking when preparing for and taking exams (see Chapters 18 and 19).

DIRECTIONS   Identify the level or levels of thinking that each of the following tasks demands.

Exercise 5

1. Retelling a favorite family story to your nieces and nephews

   _____

2. Using the principles of time management discussed in Chapter 1 to develop a weekly study plan

   _____

3. Learning the names of the U.S. presidents since World War II

   _____

4. Reorganizing your lecture notes by topic

   _____

5. Writing a letter to the editor of your hometown newspaper praising a recently passed city ordinance that restricts new toxic-waste disposal sites

   _____

6. Writing a term paper that requires library and online research

   _____

7. Using prereading techniques when reading your speech communication textbook

   _____

8. Listening to speeches by two candidates who are running for mayor and then deciding which one gets your vote

   _____

9. Watching several hours of TV programming to determine the amount of time given to commercials, to public service announcements, to entertainment programs, and to news

   _____

10. Writing an article for the campus newspaper explaining why on-campus parking is inadequate

   _____

Exercise 6

DIRECTIONS   Read "Dimensions of Nonverbal Communication" and answer the questions that follow.

Dimensions of Nonverbal Communication

In recent years, research has reemphasized the important role of physical, or nonverbal, behaviors in effective oral communication. Basically, three generalizations about nonverbal communication should occupy your attention when you are a speaker:

1. *Speakers reveal and reflect their emotional states through their nonverbal behaviors.* Your listeners read your feelings toward yourself, your topic, and your audience from your facial expressions. Consider the contrast between a speaker who walks to the front of the room briskly, head held high, and one who shuffles, head bowed and arms hanging limply. Communications scholar Dale G. Leathers summarized a good deal of research into nonverbal communication processes: "Feelings and emotions are more accurately exchanged by nonverbal than verbal means. . . . The nonverbal portion of communication conveys meanings and intentions that are relatively free from deception, distortion, and confusion."

2. *The speaker's nonverbal cues enrich or elaborate the message that comes through words.* A solemn face can reinforce the dignity of a funeral eulogy. The words "Either do this or do that" can be illustrated with appropriate arm-and-hand gestures. Taking a few steps to one side tells an audience that you are moving from one argument to another. A smile enhances a lighter moment in your speech.

3. *Nonverbal messages form a reciprocal interaction between speaker and listener.* Listeners frown, smile, shift nervously in their seats, and engage in many types of nonverbal behavior. . . . There are four areas of nonverbal communication that concern every speaker: (a) *proxemics*, (b) *movement and stance*, (c) *facial expressions*, and (d) *gestures*.

—Gronbeck et al., Principles of Speech Communication, pp. 217–218

1. **Remembering:** What are the three generalizations?

    _____

    _____

    _____

2. **Understanding:** Explain how a speaker can reveal his or her emotional state.

    _____

    _____

3. **Applying:** Give an example (not used in the excerpt) of how a speaker can reveal his or her emotional state.

    _____

    _____

4. **Analyzing:** If nonverbal communication is free of deception, is it possible to tell a lie using body language?

    _____

    _____

5. **Evaluating:** How is this information useful and important to me in a public speaking class?

_____

_____

_____

_____

6. **Creating:** To what extent is this information consistent with what I already know about nonverbal messages?

_____

_____

DIRECTIONS   Read "Communication Through Body Adornment," in Part Five, page 449. Then write two questions that require thinking at each of the levels we have discussed (a total of 12 questions). ●

Exercise 7

USING COLLEGE TEXTBOOKS
Considering Your Learning Style

Textbooks, unlike many other information sources, are designed to teach. Textbook authors, most of whom are professors, know what college students need in order to learn and include numerous features throughout their textbooks to help students read and learn actively. Your learning style will help you decide which features to focus on to help you learn. A sample textbook page from a textbook for a sociology marriage and family course is annotated on the next page to show features that appeal to various learning styles.

FURTHER PRACTICE WITH TEXTBOOK READING
Part A: Sample Textbook Chapter

Page through the sample chapter (pp. 489–502). Next, write a list of the features of the chapter that appeal to your learning style and explain how you will use each.

Part B: Your College Textbook

Choose a textbook that you have purchased for one of your other courses. Study its table of contents, read its preface, and page through the book. Write a list of features that appeal to your learning style and explain how you will use each.

Applied learners: Notice applications

▶▶▶ GO GLOBAL

World's Most Emotional Countries

What we might see as an "effective" communication style within families in the United States could be perceived as the exact opposite in other countries. A questionnaire by the Center for International Business Studies in the Netherlands identified different styles of communication among different countries.[26] Countries such as Mexico, Switzerland, China, Brazil, and Italy have been defined as **affective**, which means that people tend to rely a lot on nonverbal communication (such as hand gestures and physical contact) and openly expressed emotions.

In these countries, people are more likely to greet people with enthusiasm and talk more loudly when excited. In affective communication, the receiver must work harder to be able to decode these nonverbal signals.

Countries such as Japan, the United Kingdom, Indonesia, Argentina, and the United States emerged as "neutral" countries, meaning that people in these countries tend to keep their emotions in check and not express them publicly. Voice intonation, timing, and facial expressions all help communicate messages. Because of differences in cultures, there are variations among countries. The Japanese prefer a more indirect style of communication, whereas Americans communicate directly to convey a specific objective.[27]

Families in affective countries are more likely to have loud arguments and affectionate reconciliations than families in neutral countries. Because families in affective countries express their emotions, communication is not always effective. Receivers still need to pay attention to the real significance of nonverbal clues. Although America is considered a neutral country, it is also more personal; people are more likely to use first names in business, for example. This can carry over to how people interact inside the home.

Visual learners: Note the concepts these visuals emphasize

Spatial learners: Study this

making in marriages and families, such as the presence of children, gender roles, and individual interest in the outcome of the decision.[29] Families are also influenced by outside factors. If a student is burdened with tons of weekend homework, his or her family will find it difficult to plan a getaway during that time. The government's decision to promote or reject subsidies for low-income families can also be a relevant factor in the decision-making process of many families.

Different family types will also show different decision-making approaches. Studies reveal that gay couples strive for equality of power between the spouses, thus actively rejecting traditional gender roles of heterosexual couples.[30] Studies on stepfamilies show how parents often take the decision to join two families without involving their children.[31] Families also make decisions on the basis of their culture and ethnicity. A study revealed that Vietnamese women are mostly responsible for administering the family's economic resources to such a degree that they are referred to as "chiefs of domestic affairs."[32]

Conflict and Managing Conflict
WHAT IS CONFLICT?

Conceptual learners: Write an outline

Think about your relationship with your parents, your friends, or even your teachers. Despite the love, friendship, and/or respect you might feel for them, it is highly likely that at some point you've experienced some kind of conflict in these relationships. Conflict is an inescapable component of human relationships. Even those who are terrified of conflict and try avoiding it at all costs are still not immune to it. But how can we define *conflict*? Conflict happens when people differ in their feelings, thoughts, or behaviors. Conflict can be beneficial if it forces people to confront problems. However, when conflict is not resolved and does not enable personal growth, it can become harmful and may even lead to violence and abuse.

REACTIONS TO FAMILY CONFLICT

Auditory learners: Summarize with a classmate

How do you react to conflict? Do you voice every single thought that crosses your mind, no matter how hurtful? Do you try to keep calm and focus on the issue, not your ego? Do you avoid any kind of confrontation, staring into the distance with a frozen smile and murmuring to yourself that everything is great?

Conflict Styles

	Control	Solution Orientation	Non-Confrontation
Tactic	Uses blame and accusations.	Uses reasoning and compromise.	Uses withdrawal and avoidance.
More likely to say...	"You are always thinking about yourself!"	"This makes me feel unappreciated. Can we talk about it?"	"I just remembered I need to go out and buy some groceries."

<<< **The family in the hit TV series *The Sopranos* employed all conflict styles when dealing with the father's involvement in organized crime.** How do you think power structures within the family can influence conflict style within a family?

Creative learners: Create a similar situation

Verbal learners: Write interpretations

Sources: Turner, L.H., R. West. Perspectives of Family Communication, 165. McGraw Hill: New York, 2006.

53 — Communication, Power, and Conflict

SELF-TEST SUMMARY

Goal ①

Why is it useful to analyze your learning style?

Analyzing your learning style can help you to understand why you may learn better from one instructor than another and why some courses are easier for you than others. Building an awareness of how you learn best and what your limitations are can help you understand how to study more effectively and become a more efficient learner.

Goal 2 What is an action plan for learning?	An action plan is a strategy for capitalizing on each aspect of your learning style.
Goal 3 Why is it important to analyze your instructors' teaching styles?	You may need to make changes in how you learn to suit each instructor's teaching style.
Goal 4 What do instructors expect of college students?	In college, students are expected to set their own operating rules, take responsibility for their own learning, and focus on and evaluate ideas and concepts.
Goal 5 What does "becoming an active learner" mean?	Active learning is essential to success in college. To become a more effective learner, you should get actively involved with reading assignments, lectures, and class activities by (a) asking questions about class presentations and reading assignments, and (b) looking for the purpose behind learning the information presented.
Goal 6 What levels of thinking are expected of college students?	College instructors expect their students to read and think critically. There are six levels of thinking: remembering, understanding, applying, analyzing, evaluating, and creating. Many classroom activities, such as exams, papers, and discussions, require reading and thinking at these levels.

APPLYING YOUR SKILLS

DISCUSSING THE CHAPTER

1. What are the most common learning styles in your class? Discuss some subject-specific strategies that those with each style can apply to their studies.
2. How do learning styles relate to choice of major or choice of profession? Discuss majors and jobs that may be most appropriate or inappropriate for the various learning styles.
3. Take a look at the tests you've taken so far in college. Determine which of Benjamin Bloom's types of thinking are present in each exam question. Brainstorm some study strategies to help you prepare for questions in each category.

ANALYZING A STUDY SITUATION

DIRECTIONS   Working in groups of three or four students, analyze the following situation. Discuss answers to the questions that follow.

A history professor has just returned graded midterm exams to her class. One student looks at the grade on the first page, flips through the remaining pages while commenting to a friend that the exam was "too picky," and files it in her notebook. A second student reviews his exam for grading errors and notices one error. Immediately, he raises his hand and asks for an adjustment to his grade. The instructor seems annoyed and tells the student she will not use class time to dispute individual grades. A third student reviews her exam bluebook to identify a pattern of error; on the cover of the bluebook, she notes topics and areas in which she is weak.

1. Compare the three students' responses to the situation.
2. What does each student's response reveal about his or her approach to learning?
3. Analyze the student's response to the instructor's error in grading. What alternatives might have been more appropriate?
4. At what level(s) of thinking was each of the three students functioning?

WORKING ON COLLABORATIVE PROJECTS

DIRECTIONS   Working in groups of two or three, prepare a "Need to Know" list for new students on your campus. Include information you have discovered so far about learning and studying in college. Groups should compare and compile lists and may wish to prepare a handout for next semester's class, post information on the campus Web site, or submit the final list to the college newspaper for publication or to the director of student orientation for use with incoming students.

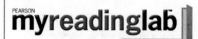 For support in meeting this chapter's goals, go to **MyReadingLab** and select **Critical Thinking**.

Quick **QUIZ**

DIRECTIONS   Write the letter of the choice that best completes each statement in the space provided.

CHECKING YOUR RECALL

_____ 1. Learning style can be defined as
   a. a person's mental ability and capacity for learning.
   b. the speed with which a person can grasp information.
   c. how much information a person remembers.
   d. the methods a person uses best in taking in information.

_____ 2. The primary value of identifying your learning style is that it can help you
   a. become interested in what you are studying.
   b. develop and maintain your concentration.
   c. become more efficient in how you study.
   d. increase your reading rate.

_____ 3. In order to meet your instructors' expectations, you should
   a. focus on "right answers."
   b. accept or reject ideas upon first being exposed to them.
   c. give the instructor responsibility for your learning.
   d. consider what facts and details mean, rather than devoting yourself to memorizing facts only.

_____ 4. After completing a reading assignment, an effective reader should
   a. connect the material to other assigned readings.
   b. decide how difficult the chapter was compared with others.
   c. memorize the vocabulary list.
   d. write down his or her opinion of the material.

_____ 5. An active learner would do all of the following _except_:
   a. read, think, ask questions, and try to connect ideas.
   b. predict exam questions and look for trends and patterns.
   c. do only what is expected to get a good grade.
   d. try to discover the significance of the assignment and look for the principles and concepts it illustrates.

APPLYING YOUR KNOWLEDGE

_____ 6. After completing the Learning Style Questionnaire, LaVon wanted to find out if she tends to learn better by hearing or by reading. She should look at her score on the
   a. auditory/visual section.
   b. applied/conceptual section.
   c. social/independent section.
   d. creative/pragmatic section.

_____ 7. Jens will graduate from high school in May and go on to college at the state university. He will probably find out that college learning is different from high school learning in that
   a. he will be spending more time each week in class.
   b. he will be expected to take responsibility for his learning.
   c. his instructors will place more emphasis on memorization of facts.
   d. his instructors will spend more time reviewing course content.

_____ 8. Craig learns best using diagrams, charts, and sketches. He frequently uses outlining, visualization, and mapping to help him organize the ideas presented in his classes. Craig can best be described as a
   a. verbal learner.
   b. auditory learner.
   c. spatial learner.
   d. applied learner.

_____ 9. On her physics test, Janiece will be expected to use her knowledge of formulas to solve a new physics problem. Janiece's test will require her to use which level of thinking?
   a. remembering   c. analyzing
   b. applying   d. evaluating

_____ 10. Amelia is taking a biology class in which the instructor relies on lectures to present information. Because the course covers so much material, the instructor does not have time to schedule group interaction. If Amelia were a social learner, it would be most helpful for her to
   a. drop the class immediately because it doesn't suit her learning style.
   b. spend time alone after class, reviewing the lecture.
   c. form a study group with students from her class.
   d. record lectures to listen to by herself later.

CHAPTER 3

Improving Learning and Memory

LEARNING GOALS

In this chapter you will learn to

1 Cope with forgetting

2 Understand how learning and memory work

3 Develop effective learning strategies

4 Review effectively

LEARNING EXPERIMENT

1 Suppose you wanted to become a better swimmer. What would you do? List some ideas here:

_____

_____

_____

2 Now read the following paragraph, which explains the physics of swimming, and examine the accompanying photograph.

For every action, there's an equal and opposite reaction. Swimmers move *forward* by pushing *back* against the water (instead of pushing *up* and *out* as many do). The greater the resistance of the water, the greater the forward thrust. And since still water provides greater resistance than water that's already moving backward, the old straight-arm pull isn't the most efficient way to swim. The most effective stroke, instead, is one that's curved so that you're always pushing against a column of "new" or still water. Resistance in the right places is a swimmer's friend. In the wrong places, though, it's an enemy, and it's known as drag. In order to move through water most efficiently, your body must pose as little resistance (drag) as possible. This is called streamlining. To streamline your body, keep it generally horizontal along the central axis (your spine) so that all your energy is used for propelling your body *directly forward*, and none is wasted by moving it vertically, to the side, or even backward.

—Katz, *Swimming for Total Fitness*, p. 99

3 Would the paragraph and/or photograph above help you become a better swimmer? Why or why not?

THE RESULTS

You probably agreed that the paragraph and photograph would be useful. Why? They explain how the process works and offer suggestions about how to position your body to move through the water more efficiently.

LEARNING PRINCIPLE: WHAT THIS MEANS TO YOU

By reading about the dynamics of swimming, you received an overview of the process. **If you understand how a process works, you will be able to put it to use more easily.** In this chapter you will learn how memory works and learn many practical suggestions for improving your memory. After you have completed this chapter you will be better prepared to learn from both lectures and textbooks.

Have you ever wondered why you can't remember what you have just read? Have you noticed students in your classes who seem to remember everything? Do you wonder how they do it? The answer is not that these other students are brighter than you are or that they have studied twice as long as you have. It is that they have learned *how* to learn and to remember; they have developed techniques for effective learning.

WHY IMPROVE YOUR LEARNING AND MEMORY TECHNIQUES?

It is important to improve your learning and memory techniques because:

- You will discover how to learn more efficiently.
- Learning is your primary job while in college; the more you know about it, the more confident and comfortable you will be.

FORGETTING

Forgetting, which is defined as the loss of information stored in memory, is a normal, everyday occurrence. Psychologists have extensively studied the rate at which forgetting takes place. For most people, forgetting occurs very rapidly right after learning and then levels off over time. Figure 3-1 illustrates just how fast forgetting normally occurs and how much information is lost. The figure shows what is known as the retention curve, and it shows how much you are able to remember over time.

Goal 1
Cope with forgetting

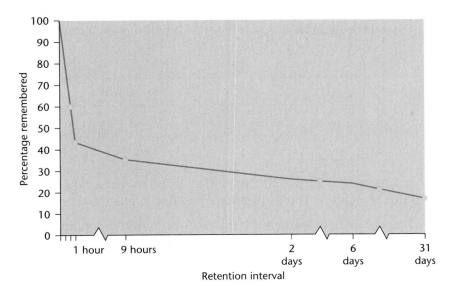

Figure 3-1
The Retention Curve

Tip *Retention* is the noun for the verb *retain*, which means "keep." *Recall* (with the stress on the first syllable) is a noun meaning "memory." The same word (but stressed on the second syllable) is a verb meaning "remember."

The retention curve is important to you as a learner. Basically, it suggests that unless you are one of the lucky few who remember almost everything they hear or read, you will forget a large portion of the information you learn unless you do something to prevent it. For instance, the graph shows that your recall of learned information drops to below 50 percent within an hour and to about 25 percent within two days.

Fortunately, certain techniques can prevent or slow down forgetting. These techniques are the focus of the remainder of this book. Throughout the book, you will learn techniques that will enable you to identify what to learn (pick out what is important) and to learn it in the most effective way. Each technique is intended to help you remember more and to slow down your rate of forgetting. For instance, in Chapter 4 you will learn how taking notes during class lectures can help you learn and remember what the lecture is about. In Chapter 17 you will learn a system for reading to learn and remember more.

Exercise 1

DIRECTIONS   Apply what you have learned about the rate of forgetting to each of the following study situations. Refer to Figure 3-1.

1. How much information from a textbook chapter can you expect to recall two days after you read it?

   _____

   _____

2. How much information from a lecture you attended last week can you expect to remember this week if you did not take any notes on the lecture?

   _____

   _____

3. What do you think your level of recall would be if you took notes on a particular lecture but did not review your notes for two weeks?

   _____

   _____

4. Why would it be necessary to take notes on a film shown in class if you had to write a reaction paper on it that evening?

   _____

   _____ ●

Why Forgetting Occurs

Suppose you have studied a topic but find that on an exam you are unable to remember much about it. There are several possible explanations:

- You never completely learned the information in the first place.
- You did not study the information in the right way.
- You are not asking the right questions or using the right means to remember the information.
- You have forgotten the information.

This chapter will describe how to learn information initially, how to study and review it, and how to use appropriate techniques to recall it.

There are two common reasons why forgetting occurs.

- **Disuse: Use it or lose it!** If you do not use information, you tend to forget it. For example, if you don't use a friend's address, you tend to forget it. If you use it frequently, you will remember it. To make sure you do not forget information you have learned, be sure to use it. Periodic review, discussed later in this chapter on page 62, will help keep information fixed in your memory.
- **Interference.** One type of interference occurs when something new you have learned prevents you from remembering something old you have already learned. If you start studying Spanish, you may find you have difficulty remembering the French you already learned. This type of interference occurs when the new learning is very similar to the old learning. To minimize the effects of interference, try not to study similar subjects back-to-back.

Another type of interference occurs when something you have already learned prevents you from learning something new. For example, you may call a local store, recently taken over by a large chain store, by its old name because you do not remember its new name. In a history course if you studied World War I and then World War II, you may have trouble remembering events in World War II. To prevent this type of interference, you may have to review the new learning to keep it fresh in your memory. Refer to the section of this chapter titled "How to Review," page 62.

Exercise 2

DIRECTIONS   For each of the following situations, use the information above on forgetting to explain why the student was experiencing difficulty.

1. Allan was taking both sociology and psychology. Why did he forget what he studied yesterday in sociology after he attended his psychology class today?

_____

_____

_____

2. Maria carefully read and highlighted each chapter in her business marketing text. She worked hard each week on the assigned chapters but never looked back at what she had already learned. When a exam was announced, she found she had to relearn much of the information. Why did she forget it?

_____

_____

_____

3. Kim was taking a history course. She reviewed her lecture notes each afternoon, right after class, and was confident she had learned the information. When an exam was announced, she found she had to relearn a great deal of information. Why did she forget it?

_____

_____

_____

Goal **2**

Understand how
learning and
memory work

myreadinglab

To practice using the
learning and memory
process to your
advantage, go to

> Memorization and
Concentration

AN OVERVIEW OF THE LEARNING AND MEMORY PROCESS

Three stages are involved in the memory process: encoding, storage, and retrieval. First, information enters the brain from a variety of sources. This process is known as **encoding**. In a learning situation, you take in information by reading or listening. This information lingers briefly in what is known as **sensory storage** and is then either stored or discarded. Momentary or brief storage is called **short-term memory**. Next, information in short-term memory is either forgotten or transferred into more lasting storage called **long-term memory**. Anything that is to be remembered for more than a few seconds must be stored in long-term memory. To place information in long-term memory, one must learn it in some way. Finally, information can be brought back, or remembered, through a process known as **retrieval**. Figure 3-2, below, is a visual model of the learning and memory processes. Refer to it frequently as you read the sections that explain each stage.

How Encoding Works

Every waking moment, your mind is bombarded with a variety of impressions of what is going on around you. Your five senses—hearing, sight, touch, taste, and smell—provide information about your surroundings. Think for a moment of all the signals your brain receives at a given moment. If you are reading, your eyes transmit the visual patterns of the words. But you may also hear a door slamming, a clock ticking, or a dog barking. Your sense of smell may detect perfume or cigarette smoke. Your sense of touch may signal that a pen you are using to underline will soon run out of ink or that the room is chilly. When you listen to a classroom lecture, you are constantly receiving stimuli—from the professor, from students around you, and from the lecture hall. All these environmental stimuli are transmitted to your brain for very brief sensory storage and interpretation. It is also easy to be distracted by competing stimuli.

Figure 3-2
A Model of Memory

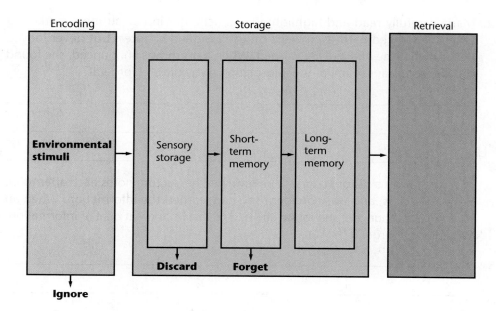

How Sensory Storage Works

Information received from your five senses is transmitted through the nervous system to the brain, which accepts and interprets it. The information stays briefly in the nervous system while the brain interprets it; this short period of interpretation is known as **sensory storage**.

How does your mind handle the barrage of information conveyed by your senses? Thanks to what is known as **selective attention**, your brain automatically sorts out the more important signals from the trivial ones. Trivial signals, such as insignificant noises around you, are ignored or discarded. Through the skills of concentration and attention, you can train yourself to ignore other, more distracting signals, such as a dog barking or people talking in the background.

Although your sensory storage accepts all information, data are kept there only briefly, usually less than a few seconds. Then the information either fades or decays or is replaced with new, incoming stimuli. The function of sensory storage, then, is to retain information long enough for you to selectively interpret it and send it to your short-term memory.

How Short-Term Memory Works

Short-term memory holds the information that was sent from your sensory storage system. It is used to store information you wish to retain for only a few seconds. If you look up a phone number on your computer, for example, it is stored in your short-term memory until you dial it. A lecturer's words are retained until you can record them in your notes. Most researchers agree that short-term memory lasts much less than a minute—perhaps 20 seconds or less. Information can be maintained longer if you practice or rehearse the information. When you are introduced to someone, you will not be able to remember the person's name unless you repeat it, thereby learning it, at the time of the introduction. Otherwise, incoming information will force it out of your short-term memory. Similarly, you will not be able to remember what you read in a textbook chapter or heard in a lecture unless you take action to learn and remember it.

Visual Thinking
APPLYING SKILLS

What types of sensory information compete for your attention in this lecture class? How can you ignore them?

Exercise 3

DIRECTIONS   Use your knowledge of the memory process to answer the following questions.

1. Observe and analyze the area in which you are sitting. What sensory impressions (sights, sounds, touch sensations) have you been ignoring as a result of selective attention?

   _____

   _____

2. Can you remember what you ate for lunch three Tuesdays ago? If not, why not?

   _____

3. Explain why two people are able to carry on a deep conversation at a crowded, noisy party.

   _____

4. Explain why someone who looks up an address and then walks into another room to write it on an envelope may forget the address.

   _____

   _____

5. Suppose you are reading a section of your history text. You come across an unfamiliar word and look up its meaning. Once you have looked up the word, you find that you must reread the section. Why?

   _____

   _____

   _____

How Long-Term Memory Works

Long-term memory is a relatively permanent store of information. Unlike short-term memory, long-term memory is nearly unlimited in both span (length) and capacity (size). It contains hundreds of thousands of facts, details, impressions, and experiences that you have accumulated throughout your life. For textbook reading, the key is deciding *what* information to store in your long-term memory. Textbooks do offer help. See "Using College Textbooks: Deciding What to Learn" at the end of this chapter, p. 66.

Once information is stored in your long-term memory, you recall it through a process known as **retrieval**. Academic tasks that require you to retrieve knowledge include math or science problems, quizzes and exams, and papers. Retrieval is tied to storage. The manner in which information is stored in your memory affects its availability and how easily you can retrieve it.

Goal ③

Develop effective learning strategies

LEARNING STRATEGIES

You have to learn something before you can remember it. The manner in which you take in information determines how well you can remember it. Use the following suggestions for learning information the first time.

Get Focused

You will learn more in less time if you get focused before you begin. Instead of jumping right into a new chapter or series of class notes, use the tips in the box below to zero in on the task.

HOW TO GET FOCUSED

Strategy	Why It Works
Avoid competing visual information. This includes a television, a computer screen, or a window overlooking a busy scene.	Any visual information pulls your eye and your mind away from the material you are trying to learn.
Identify your purpose. Is your purpose to prepare for an exam, write a research paper, or participate in a class discussion?	Knowing why you are learning creates a focused mind-set and will help you decide what to learn (see below).
Decide what types of information you need to learn. Are dates, events, definitions, statistics, or research findings important? What is less important? Use your syllabus to help you.	It is impossible to learn every fact in a textbook chapter or lecture. You are making the task doable by focusing on essential information.
Use previewing (see Chapter 6).	You will remember more of what you read if you are familiar with its content and organization before you begin.

Tip A *strategy* is a plan for an action or series of actions designed to achieve a specific goal, such as getting a good grade in biology.

Learn as Efficiently as Possible

Many students spend hours studying but do not get the grades they think they deserve. The key is not to simply spend time learning; it is important to use the right strategies to make the most of the time you spend. The strategies in the box below will help you optimize your study time.

HOW TO OPTIMIZE YOUR STUDY TIME

Strategy	Why It Works
Use numerous sensory channels. Don't just read. Use writing, listening, and speaking, as well. Take notes, repeat information aloud, listen to classmates talk about the material.	Processing the information through different channels gives your brain numerous ways to take in and organize the information.
Learn in your own words. When taking notes, avoid copying or repeating information word-for-word from textbooks or recording exactly what is said in a lecture.	By explaining ideas in your own words, you will test your understanding and create your own mental circuits for learning the information.
Connect new information with old information you have already learned. For example you might learn the steps in developing a business plan by associating them with how your family began its florist business.	The associations you build with old information work as links or springboards that lead you to and help you remember the new material.
Take advantage of your learning style (see Chapter 2).	Your learning style suggests your strengths as a learner. Its components point you toward the most efficient and best ways to learn (see Chapter 2).

Use Visualization

Even if you are not a visual learner, visualizing certain types of information is the best way to learn them. Visualizing means creating a mental picture of something in your mind. Your picture or image should be sufficiently detailed to include as much related information as possible. A student taking an anatomy and physiology class drew the sketch shown in Figure 3-3 to help her learn the parts of the human brain. She first drew it on paper and then she visualized, or mentally drew, the brain diagram to help her remember the parts.

Visualization makes remembering easier because related information is stored in one unified image, and, if you can recall any part of that mental picture, you will be able to retrieve the whole picture.

Figure 3-3
Sketch of Brain

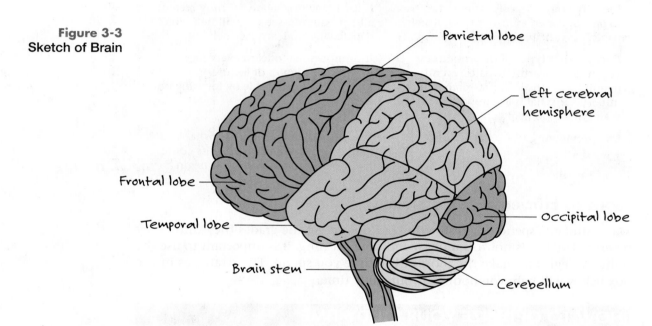

Organize Information by Chunking

Learning a large number of individual facts or pieces of information is often a difficult, frustrating task. Organize or reduce information into groups or chunks. Instead of overloading your memory with numerous individual facts, learn organized, meaningful sets of information that you can store as one chunk. Have you ever wondered why Social Security numbers and phone numbers have dashes? The dashes divide the information into chunks, making them easier to remember.

To organize information, keep the following suggestions in mind:

- **Discover how the material you are studying is connected.** Search for some organizing principle. In studying basic business management skills, for example, you may discover that you can chunk them into technical skills, interpersonal relations skills, and decision-making skills.
- **Look for similarities and differences.** If you are studying types of businesses, compare and contrast the following chunks: structure, operation, and efficiency of each type.

- **Look for sequences and for obvious divisions or breaking points within the sequences.** For example, if you are studying the overfishing of oceans as part of an environmental studies class, you could chunk the information into past practices, current policies, and unsolved problems.

TECH SUPPORT

Naming and Retrieving Computer Files

A computer is a great convenience for storing information, but it is convenient only if you can find a file once you have saved it! Think of the computer as an extension of your own brain's memory system. You put information in files and save them (storage), and later you attempt to locate the files (retrieval). As with human memory, if you store and organize (chunk) the information properly, retrieval is easier. Use the following tips to store computer files for easy retrieval.

- **Create folders for general categories of information.** Create one folder for each course you are taking, and other folders for social and personal information, such as tax returns, college loans, etc. The folders serve as chunks, grouping similar files together in an easily memorable way.
- **Name a file using a key word (retrieval clue) that describes its contents.** For example, if you are naming a set of psychology class notes to be placed in your psychology course folder, you could use the key word "Notes." If you need to distinguish notes taken in class from notes taken from textbook reading, then use designations such as CLSnotes and TXTnotes.
- **Add further information that distinguishes the file from other similar files.** For psychology class notes, you could include a date: CLSnotes09_17 has your notes from the September 17th class. Label drafts of a paper you are writing version 1 (PAPER9_18ver1), version 2 (PAPER9_18version2), and so forth.

Use Effective Study Strategies

You can learn more effectively and in less time if you use the right study methods. A major portion of this book is devoted to helping you learn and remember. Table 3-1 provides an easy reference guide to learning strategies.

TABLE 3-1 REFERENCE GUIDE TO LEARNING STRATEGIES	
Learning Strategy	**Chapter Reference**
Taking lecture notes, using the recall clue system to study lecture notes	Chapter 4
Previewing, active reading	Chapter 6
Recognizing thought patterns	Chapter 8
Highlighting in textbooks	Chapter 15
Outlining, summarizing, and mapping	Chapter 16
Using the SQ3R system	Chapter 17
Studying for exams	Chapter 18

Exercise 4

DIRECTIONS Use your knowledge of learning strategies to explain each of the following situations.

1. A business instructor plans to lecture on the process of analyzing job stress. Before class, she draws a diagram of this process on the chalkboard. During the lecture she refers to it frequently. Why did the instructor draw the diagram?

_____

_____

_____

_____

2. A political science instructor is discussing an essay on world terrorism. He begins the discussion by asking his students to recall recent terrorist acts and what the response to them was. How is the instructor helping his students learn the content of the essay?

_____

_____

_____

3. A student in a health care degree program was studying conflict resolution. She had to learn ten different resolution strategies. How could she learn them effectively?

_____

_____

_____

_____

_____

_____

4. One group of students read a psychology chapter and took notes on it. Another group read the chapter and took notes as well, but they also discussed the material in a study group. Why did the second group score higher on the exam that was based on that chapter?

_____

_____

_____

_____

5. A business management student was studying the decision-making process. She grouped the steps into three categories: data gathering, analysis, and resolution. What learning technique did she use?

_____

DIRECTIONS   Discuss techniques that might help you learn the following sets of information.

1. the process of amending the Constitution for an American government course

   _____

2. the factors that influence market price for an economics course

   _____

3. different forms of mental illness for a psychology course

   _____

4. ways to recognize and distinguish the different types of figurative language for a literature course

   _____

5. the process of cell division for a biology course

   _____

6. important terms for an introductory sociology course

   _____

7. the different types of white collar crimes and their cost to society for a criminology course

   _____

   _____

8. a comparison of the different kinds of psychoactive drugs for a health course

   _____

   _____ ●

REVIEW

Some students think that as long as they spend time studying they will get good grades. That is not necessarily the case. This section will teach you when to review and how to get the most out of your review time.

Goal 4

Review effectively

When to Review

While it is necessary to spend time studying, it is also very important to plan *when* to study and review so that you get the most out of the time you spend.

IMMEDIATE REVIEW   Forgetting occurs most rapidly right after learning. **Immediate review** means reviewing new information as soon as possible after you hear or read it. Think of immediate review as a way of fixing in your mind what you have just learned. Here are some ways to use immediate review:

- **Review your lecture notes as soon as possible after taking them.** This review will help the ideas stick in your mind.
- **Review a textbook chapter as soon as you finish reading it.** Do this by rereading each chapter heading and then rereading the summary.
- **Review all new course materials again at the end of each day of classes.** This review will help you pull together information and make it more meaningful.

PERIODIC REVIEW   Most college semesters are three or four months long. You cannot realistically expect to remember what you learned early in the semester, especially since you are continuing to learn more new information, unless you take active steps to do so. To keep from forgetting what you have learned, you will need to review it several times throughout the semester. **Periodic review**, then, means returning to and quickly reviewing previously learned material on a regular basis. Suppose you learned the material in the first three chapters of your criminology text during the first two weeks of the course. Unless you review that material regularly, you are likely to forget it and have to relearn it by the time your final exam is given. Therefore, you should establish a periodic review schedule in which you quickly review these chapters every three weeks or so.

FINAL REVIEW   **Final review** means making a last check of material before a test or exam. This should not be a lengthy session; instead, it should be a quick once-over of everything you have learned. A final review is helpful because it fixes in your mind what you have learned. Be sure to schedule your final review as close as possible to the exam in which you will need to recall the material.

How to Review

The worst way to review what you have learned is to simply reread it. Rereading textbook chapters and entire sets of lecture notes is time-consuming and produces very poor results. Use the following suggestions to improve how efficiently you review.

SCHEDULE SHORT REVIEW SESSIONS   While it is tempting to sit down and say you're not going to move until you can remember a set of information, you will learn more quickly if you schedule several short review sessions rather than one long one. If possible, spread your review over several days, with short sessions scheduled for each day.

TEST YOURSELF   If you study only by rereading chapters or notes, you will never know whether you can remember the material. Instead, test yourself. Make up questions and answer them. Study with another student and ask each other questions. Turn the headings in your textbook into questions and answer them. For more about these techniques, see the section on guide questions in Chapter 6, page 123. The recall system for note taking in Chapter 4, page 73, is another way you can test yourself.

DEVELOP RETRIEVAL CLUES   A **retrieval clue** is a tag that enables you to pull a piece of information from your memory. Think of your memory as having slots or compartments in which you store information. If you can name or label what is in the slot, you will know where to look to find information that is located in that slot. Think of memory slots as similar to the way kitchen cupboards are often organized, with specific items in specific places. If you need a knife to cut a pizza, you look in the utensil drawer. Similarly, if you have a memory slot labeled "environmental problems," in which you store information related to pollution and its problems, causes, and solutions, you can retrieve information on air pollution by locating the appropriate memory slot. Developing retrieval clues involves selecting a word or phrase that summarizes or categorizes several pieces of information. For example, you might use the phrase "motivation theories" to organize information for a psychology course on instinct, drive, cognitive, arousal, and opponent-process theories and the major proponents of each.

ANTICIPATE EXAM QUESTIONS   Information in a textbook appears in a different format and with different wording than the wording and format of exam questions. If you study simply by rereading, you have not practiced recognizing the information in different formats and may not realize what information an exam question is asking for. Instead, study for an exam by predicting exam questions and practicing writing answers to them. You will learn more about how to do this in Chapter 18.

SIMULATE TEST SITUATIONS   Practice retrieving learned information by simulating test conditions. If you are studying for a math exam, prepare by solving problems. In a horticulture class, if your exam requires you to identify certain plants, then study photos and characteristics of plants. Be sure to model your practice on the event for which you are preparing. It should be the same type of activity and the time limit should be similar.

Tip *Simulate* means "to produce something that is not real or original but seems to be." A *simulation is similar* to the original.

OVERLEARN   It is tempting to stop studying as soon as you feel you have learned a given body of information. However, to ensure complete, thorough learning, it is best to plan a few more review sessions. When you learned to drive a car, you did not stop practicing parallel parking after the first time you did it correctly. Similarly, for a botany course, you should not stop reviewing the process of photosynthesis and its place within the carbon cycle at the moment you feel you have mastered it. Instead, use additional review to make the material stick in your mind.

CONSIDER PHYSICAL SURROUNDINGS   It is easier to recall information when you are in the same setting in which you learned it. Consider reviewing your notes in the lecture hall in which you took them. Also, if possible, study in the room in which you will take a particular exam.

USE MEMORIZATION   Memorization is one of the least effective ways of learning, but there is plenty of material that must be learned this way. In chemistry, you have to memorize the periodic table. In history, you need to memorize dates and historical events. Here are some useful memorization techniques.

- *Mnemonics are memory tricks, or aids, that you can devise to help you remember information.* Mnemonics include rhymes, anagrams, words, nonsense words, sentences, and mental pictures that aid in the recall of facts. Do you remember this rhyme? "Thirty days hath September, /April, June, and November. /All the rest have thirty-one/except February, alone, / which has twenty-eight days clear/and twenty-nine in each leap year." The rhyme is an example of a mnemonic device. It is a quick and easy way of remembering the number of days in each month of the year. You may have learned to recall the colors of the rainbow by remembering the name *Roy G. Biv*; each letter in this name stands for one of the colors that make up the spectrum: *Red, Orange, Yellow, Green, Blue, Indigo, Violet*. Mnemonic devices are useful when you are trying to learn information that has no organization of its own. You will find them useful in reviewing texts and lecture notes as you prepare for exams.

• **Another memory device is called *method of loci*.** It involves selecting a familiar object, such as your home or car, and associating items to be remembered with areas in your home or parts of your car. For example, suppose you are trying to remember the four components of language: phonemes, morphemes, syntax, and semantics. Begin by picturing the first location, say the hood of your car. Place phonemes on the hood. Then move to the windshield; place morphemes on the windshield. Place syntax on the steering wheel and semantics on the dashboard. To learn the four components of language, visualize the first location and think of phonemes, associating them together, and so forth. To recall the components, take an imaginary tour of your car. When you think of the hood, you will think of phonemes.

Exercise 6

DIRECTIONS   Use your knowledge of the memory process to answer the following questions.

1. On many campuses, weekly recitations or discussions are scheduled for small groups to review material presented in large lecture classes. What learning function do these recitation sections perform?

   _____

   _____

2. After lecturing on the causes of domestic violence, a sociology instructor showed her class a video of an incident of domestic violence. What learning function(s) did the film perform? How would the video help students remember the lecture?

   _____

   _____

3. A student spends more time than anyone else in her class preparing for the midterm exam, yet she cannot remember important definitions and concepts at the time of the exam. Offer several possible explanations of her problem.

   _____

   _____

   _____

4. A sociology student is studying a chapter on age and the elderly. The exam based on that chapter will contain both multiple-choice items and an essay question. How should she test herself in preparation for the exam?

_____

_____

5. One student studied for his math exam for three hours the night before the exam. Another student studied for one hour on each of three days before the exam. He studied by creating and solving sample problems. Which student do you think did better on the exam? Why?

_____

_____

_____

_____

_____ ●

DIRECTIONS   Apply your knowledge of memorization techniques by completing each of the following activities.

1. Make up a rhyme or nonsense word to help you learn something you need to remember for one of your other courses.

2. Try the method of loci technique by trying to remember the last names of your classmates. Then try it out on material for one of your other courses. ●

Exercise 7

DIRECTIONS   Identify your most difficult course. Consider the material you are required to learn and review for the next major test. Spend some time organizing textbook and lecture material that you are sure will be on that test. Make a study plan that uses at least four of the techniques described in this chapter. Show your work to a classmate. Both of you should then offer each other suggestions to make studying more effective. ●

Exercise 8

DIRECTIONS   Select two or more learning strategies on pages 62–63 and apply them to the section of the sample textbook chapter titled "Nonverbal Emotional Expression" (p. 494). Use immediate review when you finish. Review the material periodically. Evaluate the effectiveness of the techniques you have chosen. ●

Exercise 9

USING COLLEGE TEXTBOOKS
Deciding What to Learn

One of the most challenging tasks facing college students is deciding what to learn in each of their textbooks. Let's face it: you cannot learn every fact in every one of your textbooks. Fortunately, your textbooks offer you plenty of guidance. They contain numerous features to help you pick out what is important.

One useful feature is chapter objectives. These may be labeled "Learning Objectives," "Chapter Objectives," or "Learning Goals," as they are called in this book. (In later chapters you will learn to use other aids, such as headings, summaries, focus questions, and self-tests that also help you know what to learn.)

Chapter objectives are a list of what you should know when you have finished reading a chapter. Often they correspond or relate to the course objectives that appear on your course syllabus. Read the objectives once before you read the chapter, as part of your preview. Then, after you have finished the chapter, use them to test yourself by writing notes that summarize what you have learned about each objective.

CHAPTER OBJECTIVES

After reading this chapter, you should be able to:

1. Discuss the unique design considerations of various accessories
2. Describe production methods for the major accessories
3. Explain accessory design and production centers
4. Discuss aspects of marketing for accessories
5. Explain fur garment production

—Frings, *Fashion*, p. 80

LEARNING OBJECTIVES

After studying this chapter, you will be able to:

1. Explain how to adapt to your audiences when writing reports and proposals, and provide an overview of the process of drafting report content
2. Provide an overview of the process of drafting proposal content, and list six strategies to strengthen proposal argument

—Thill and Bovee, *Excellence in Business Communication*, p. 355

UPON COMPLETING THIS CHAPTER, YOU WILL BE ABLE TO:

- Describe the scale of urbanization
- Assess urban and suburban sprawl
- Outline city and regional planning and land use strategies
- Evaluate transportation options
- Describe the roles of urban parks
- Analyze environmental impacts and advantages of urban centers
- Assess urban ecology, green building efforts, and the pursuit of sustainable cities

—Withgott and Brennan, *Environment*, p. 343

FURTHER PRACTICE WITH TEXTBOOK READING

Part A: Sample Textbook Chapter

Learning goals can take various forms. In the sample textbook chapter, the goals take the form of questions, appearing in the upper right-hand corner of page 490. Use these questions to guide you as you read the chapter; they are a list of what you need to learn. Answer each as you finish the section to which it corresponds. Then, when you have finished reading the chapter, answer all four questions again. Notice that the summary on page 501 provides answers to these four questions. Use this summary to verify that you have answered each question accurately and completely.

Part B: Your College Textbook

Choose a textbook that you are using in one of your other courses. Read a chapter. If it contains chapter objectives or learning goals, use them to test yourself by writing a set of notes summarizing the information you learned for each goal. If the chapter does not contain objectives or goals, use the chapter summary to write a set of goals. Then test yourself as described.

SELF-TEST SUMMARY

Goal 1 What is forgetting and why does it occur?	Forgetting is the loss of information stored in memory. It occurs through disuse or interference.
Goal 2 What are the steps in the learning process?	Encoding is the taking in of information. Information lingers briefly in short-term memory, and is either discarded or transferred to long-term memory. When information is remembered it is called retrieval.
Goal 3 What techniques can improve learning?	Avoid competing visual information, identify your purpose, decide what to learn, use prereading, use sensory channels, learn in your own words, connect new learning with old learning, take advantage of your learning style, use visualization, organize information, and use effective study strategies.
Goal 4 What strategies will help you review effectively?	Three types of review are immediate, periodic, and final. Use short review sessions, test yourself, use sensory channels, develop retrieval clues, anticipate exam questions, simulate test situations, overlearn, and consider physical surroundings.

APPLYING **YOUR SKILLS**

DISCUSSING THE CHAPTER

1. What strategies do you use to remember the following types of information: people's names, recipes, directions, steps in a process, a child's lullaby? Use the chapter's information to explain why different strategies are needed for these different types of information.
2. Imagine that you are learning about the culture of an African people, the artistic style of Monet, and the chemical differences between acids and bases. What could you do to learn the information in each of these situations?
3. Give some examples of mnemonic devices that you have used to help you store information.

ANALYZING A STUDY SITUATION

Carlos is having difficulty with his human anatomy and physiology course. He feels overwhelmed by the volume of facts and details, as well as the new terminology he must learn. His next assigned chapter is "The Skeletal System." It first discusses functions and types of bones and then describes all the bones in the human skeletal system, including the skull, vertebral column (spine), pelvis (hip), and extremities (arms, legs, feet, and hands). Carlos says that he understands the material as he reads it but cannot remember it later. His instructor gives weekly quizzes as well as hour-long exams.

1. Explain why Carlos understands information as he reads it but cannot recall it later.
2. What can Carlos do to correct his lack of recall?
3. What techniques would help Carlos learn the skeletal system?

WORKING ON COLLABORATIVE PROJECTS

DIRECTIONS   Form a pair with another student. If possible, choose a student who is taking or has taken one of the same courses you are taking, or is taking a course in the same field (science, mathematics, business, and so on). Together, prepare a list of strategies for learning the material initially and for reviewing it; give examples from the course or field of study you share. Include strategies that would be helpful to other students taking the course. Make your strategy list available to other class members who may take the course. Select two strategies and begin using them immediately.

For support in meeting this chapter's goals, go to **MyReadingLab** and select **Memorization and Concentration**.

Quick **QUIZ**

DIRECTIONS Write the letter of the choice that best completes each statement in the space provided.

CHECKING YOUR RECALL

_____ 1. All of the following are types of review *except*

    a. immediate review.
    b. purposeful review.
    c. periodic review.
    d. final review.

_____ 2. Information remains in your short-term memory for no longer than

    a. a minute.
    b. an hour.
    c. a day.
    d. a week.

_____ 3. Mnemonics involves

    a. making up rhymes or words to help you remember information.
    b. visualizing an event as it happened.
    c. connecting new information with already learned facts.
    d. grouping ideas together based on similar characteristics.

_____ 4. During selective attention, your brain

    a. classifies information into groups or sets.
    b. practices information to learn it.
    c. automatically sorts out important information from trivial signals.
    d. sends information to long-term memory.

_____ 5. If you are unable to explain information in your own words, it is a sign that

    a. you do not understand it.
    b. you did not review it properly.
    c. you did not connect new learning with previous learning.
    d. interference has occurred.

APPLYING YOUR KNOWLEDGE

_____ 6. Luis has just attended a chemistry lecture. According to the retention curve, if he does not transfer what he has learned into his long-term memory, he will forget more than half of what he has learned within

    a. an hour.
    b. a day.

    c. three days.
    d. a week.

_____ 7. Taylor is studying in his apartment while his roommates are home. He is concentrating on his studies and ignoring his roommates' chatter and laughter. Taylor is practicing

    a. overlearning.
    b. selective attention.
    c. retrieval.
    d. periodic review.

_____ 8. In her Introduction to Music elective, Katie uses the saying "Every good boy deserves fudge" to help her remember the line notes of the treble clef. This memory trick is an example of

    a. competing stimuli.
    b. a sensory channel.
    c. a visualization.
    d. a mnemonic device.

_____ 9. Zachary has just finished reading a textbook chapter on the causes of World War I. The most effective way for Zachary to store the information he has just learned is for him to

    a. immediately reread the chapter.
    b. move on to a completely different subject.
    c. read the next chapter.
    d. reread the chapter headings and the summary.

_____ 10. If Rosa wanted to develop retrieval clues to help her learn material for her geology class, she would specifically try to

    a. overlearn the material.
    b. store the information in one unified piece.
    c. choose a word or phrase that summarizes several pieces of information.
    d. connect the information with her personal experience.

Taking Notes in Class

LEARNING GOALS

In this chapter you will learn to

1. Sharpen your listening skills
2. Prepare for a class lecture
3. Take lecture notes
4. Edit your notes
5. Study your notes

LEARNING EXPERIMENT

1 Ask a friend to (or your instructor may choose to) read each of the following paragraphs aloud. (Each paragraph may be read aloud twice.) While paragraph 1 is read to you, just listen. While and after paragraph 2 is read to you, write a set of notes that contain its most important ideas.

Paragraph 1

Did you know that use of empty space is a form of communication? How humans use space can communicate as loudly as words and phrases. How close or how far away you stand from another person communicates a message. Research by Edward Hall identifies four types of distance, each of which defines the relationship you establish with others. The first, intimate distance, is not considered appropriate in public (except in crowded places, such as elevators). Family members and spouses may use the intimate distance. Personal distance is the space around you that no one invades unless invited, such as to shake hands. Social distance is the distance at which you operate in daily living—sitting in classrooms, attending a play, shopping, and so forth. The fourth type, public distance, is used when you are not involved with another person.

Paragraph 2

Communication occurs with words and gestures, but did you know it also occurs through sense of smell? Odor can communicate at least four types of messages. First, odor can signal attraction. Animal species give off scents to attract members of the opposite sex. Humans use fragrances to make themselves more appealing or attractive. Second, smell communicates information about tastes. The smell of popcorn popping stimulates the appetite. If you smell a chicken roasting you can anticipate its taste. A third type of smell communication is through memory. A smell can help you recall an event months or even years ago, especially if the event is an emotional one. Finally, smell can communicate by creating an identity or image for a person or product. For example, a woman may wear only one brand of perfume. Or a brand of shaving cream may have a distinct fragrance, which allows users to recognize it.

2 Wait 24 hours, or until the next class session; then, *without* reading either paragraph or looking at your notes, answer the following questions.

Paragraph 1

Name the four types of distances discussed in the paragraph.

Paragraph 2

Name the four messages that smell can communicate.

Check your answers using the Answer Key at the end of the chapter, page 89.

THE RESULTS

You probably got more information correct for paragraph 2 than you did for paragraph 1. Why? Because you listened to paragraph 2 and then you wrote. In doing this, you used three sensory modes: hearing (listening), touching (writing), and seeing (reading your notes). For paragraph 1, you used only one sensory mode: hearing.

LEARNING PRINCIPLE: WHAT THIS MEANS TO YOU

You have five senses—five ways of taking in information from the world around you: sight, touch, smell, sound, and taste. **The more senses you use to learn something, the easier it will be to learn.** When you listen to a college lecture, you are using only one sensory mode. If you take notes on the lecture as you listen, you are using your sense of touch as well as your sense of hearing. When you reread the notes after you have written them, you are employing a third sensory mode—sight. In this chapter you will learn how to take notes effectively, how to edit them, and how to develop a system to study them.

WHY TAKE NOTES ON LECTURES?

It is important to improve your note-taking techniques because:

- Taking notes focuses your attention and keeps your mind on the lecture.
- Taking notes helps you decide what is important to learn.
- Writing notes will help you understand ideas and see relationships among ideas.
- Taking notes will help you recall the lecture.
- Your notes will be a valuable study tool and can help you prepare for tests and exams.

SHARPENING YOUR LISTENING SKILLS

Goal

Sharpen your listening skills

The first step in taking good lecture notes is to sharpen your listening skills. The average adult spends 31 percent of each waking hour listening. By comparison, 7 percent is spent on writing, 11 percent on reading, and 21 percent on speaking. Listening, then, is an essential communication skill. During college lectures, listening is especially important: it is your primary means of acquiring information.

Have you ever found yourself not listening to a professor who was lecturing? Her voice was loud and clear, so you certainly could hear her, but you weren't paying attention—you tuned her out. This situation illustrates the distinction between hearing and listening. Hearing is a passive, biological process in which sound waves are received by the ear. Listening, however, is an intellectual activity that involves the processing and interpretation of incoming information. Listening must be intentional, purposeful, and deliberate. You must plan to listen, have a reason for listening, and carefully focus your attention. Use the suggestions in the box on the next page to sharpen your listening skills.

HOW TO IMPROVE YOUR LISTENING SKILLS

1. **Approach listening as a process similar to reading.** Listening, like reading, is a comprehension process in which you grasp ideas, assess their importance, and connect them to other ideas. All the reading comprehension skills you will develop in Part Two of this text are useful for listening as well.

2. **Focus on content, not delivery.** It is easy to become so annoyed, upset, charmed, or engaged with the lecturer as an individual that you fail to comprehend the message he or she is conveying. Force yourself to focus only on the content of the lecture.

3. **Focus on ideas as well as facts.** If you concentrate on recording and remembering separate, unconnected facts, you are doomed to failure. Instead, listen for ideas, significant trends, and patterns, as well as facts.

4. **Listen carefully to the speaker's opening comments.** As your mind refocuses from prior tasks and problems, it is easy to miss the speaker's opening remarks. However, these are among the most important. Here the speaker may establish connections with prior lectures, identify his or her purpose, or describe the lecture's content or organization.

5. **Attempt to understand the lecturer's purpose.** Is it to present facts, raise and discuss questions, demonstrate a trend or pattern, or present a technique or procedure?

6. **Fill the gap between rate of speech and rate of thinking.** Has your mind ever wandered back and forth during a lecture? The rate of speech is much slower than the speed of thought. The average rate of speech is around 125 words per minute, whereas the rate at which you can process ideas is more than 500 words per minute. To listen most effectively, use this gap to think about lecture content. Anticipate what is to follow, think of situations in which the information might be applied, or pose questions.

Tip *Anticipate* means "to predict, to state what you think will happen in the future."

Goal

Prepare for a class lecture

PREPARING FOR A LECTURE CLASS

Before you attend a lecture class, you should become familiar with the main topic of the lecture and be aware of important subtopics and related subjects.

Understanding the lecture and taking notes will be easier if you have some idea of what the lecture is about. If your instructor assigns a textbook chapter that is related to the lecture, try to read the assignment before attending. If you are unable to read the entire chapter before class, at least preview the chapter to become familiar with the topics it covers. (You will learn about previewing in Chapter 6.) If no reading assignment is given in advance, check your course outline to determine the topic of the lecture. Then preview the sections of your text that are about the topic.

Once you arrive at a lecture class, get organized before it begins. Take your coat off and have your computer or notebook and pen and your textbook chapter (if needed) ready to use. While waiting for class to begin, try to recall the content of the previous lecture: Think of three or four key points that were presented. Check your notes, if necessary. This process will activate your thought processes, focus your attention on course content, and make it easier for you to begin taking notes right away.

Visual Thinking
APPLYING SKILLS

Class is about to begin. What should this student be doing?

HOW TO TAKE LECTURE NOTES

A good set of lecture notes must accomplish three things. First, and most important, your notes must serve as a record or summary of the lecture's main points. Second, they must include enough details and examples so that you can recall the information several weeks later. Third, your notes must in some way show the relative importance of ideas presented and the organization of the lecture.

Record Main Ideas

The main ideas of a lecture are the points the instructor emphasizes and elaborates on. They are the major ideas that the details, explanations, examples, and general discussion support. Instructors can give clues to what is important in a lecture. The box on the next page suggests a few ways in which speakers show what is important.

Goal 3
Take lecture notes

To practice using active learning skills, go to

> Note Taking and Highlighting

HOW SPEAKERS GIVE CLUES

When the lecturer . . .	The lecturer means . . .
Slows down or speaks more loudly	This is important! Try to record the speaker's exact words.
Lists or numbers points ("There are five causes . . . ," "Six solutions are . . . ," etc.)	Each of the points is equally important.
Makes a direct announcement ("One important fact . . . ," "Be sure to remember . . .")	This is information you should learn. It may appear on an exam.
Uses nonverbal clues (pointing, pounding the desk, walking toward the audience, etc.)	He or she feels strongly about the idea or wants to emphasize its importance.
Writes on the whiteboard	He or she wants you to pay attention and copy the writing in your notes.
Uses PowerPoint slides	The information presented on the slides has been selected as particularly important.
Asks questions (either verbally or projected on a screen)	He or she is emphasizing the question's importance and may use this technique to provoke critical thinking (possible essay exam questions).
Distributes or posts online an outline of or note-taking guide for the lecture	The material is complex or he or she is aware that students may need help grasping the lecture's organization.

Exercise 1

DIRECTIONS   Select one of your instructors and analyze his or her lecture style. Attend one lecture, and, as you take notes, try to be particularly aware of how he or she lets you know what is important. After the lecture, write a paragraph analyzing your instructor's lecture technique. ●

Record Details and Examples

A difficult part of taking notes is deciding how much detail to include with the main ideas. Obviously, you cannot write down everything; lecturers speak at the rate of about 125 words per minute. Even if you could take shorthand, it would be nearly impossible to record everything the lecturer says. As a result, you have to be selective and record only particularly important details. As a rule of thumb, try to write down a brief phrase for each detail that directly explains or clarifies a major point.

    If an instructor gives you several examples of a particular law, situation, or problem, be sure to write down, in summary form, at least one example. Record more than one if you have time. Although at the time of the lecture it may seem that you completely understand what is being discussed, you will find that a few weeks later you really do need the example to boost your recall.

Tip A *rule of thumb* is a rough estimate based upon experience.

Record the Organization of the Lecture

As you write down the main ideas and important details of a lecture, try to organize or arrange your notes so that you can easily see how the lecture is organized. By recording the organization of the lecture, you will be able to determine the relative importance of ideas, and you will know what to pay the most attention to as you study and review for an exam.

A simple way to show a lecture's organization is to use indentation. Retain a regular margin on your paper or document. Start your notes on the most important of the topics at the left margin. For less important main ideas, indent your notes slightly. For major details, indent slightly more. Indent even more for examples and other details. The rule of thumb to follow is this: the less important the idea, the more it should be indented. Your notes might be organized like the sample that follows.

> **MAJOR TOPIC**
>   Main idea
>   detail
>   detail
>   example
>   Main idea
>   detail
>   detail
>   detail
> **MAJOR TOPIC**
>   Main idea
>   detail
>   example

Note that this sample looks like an outline but is missing the Roman numerals (I, II, III), capital letters (A, B, C), and Arabic numerals (1, 2, 3) that are usually included in an outline. Also note, however, that this system of note taking accomplishes the same major goal as an outline—it separates important information from less important information. This indentation system, like an outline, shows at a glance how important a particular fact or idea is. If the organization of a lecture is obvious, you may wish to use a number or letter system in addition to indenting.

Lectures are often organized using patterns: comparison–contrast, cause–effect, time sequence, classification, definition, or enumeration. Figure 4-1 lists tips for "customizing" your note taking to each of these patterns. An entire lecture may be organized using one pattern; a history lecture, for example, may use the time sequence pattern throughout. More often, however, several patterns will be evident at various points in a lecture. A psychology professor, for instance, may discuss definitions of *motivation* and compare and contrast different motivational theories. (Refer to Chapter 8 for a review of organizational patterns and the directional words that signal them.)

Tip *Classification* is a way of organizing ideas by dividing the general subject into its parts (for example, dividing sensory experience into its five sources).

Figure 4-1
Using Patterns in
Lecture Note Taking

PATTERN	NOTE-TAKING TIPS
Comparison–contrast	Record similarities, differences, and basis of comparison; use two columns or make a chart.
Cause–effect	Distinguish causes from effects; use diagrams.
Sequence or order	Record dates; focus on order and sequence; use a time line for historical events; draw diagrams; record in order of importance; outline events or steps in a process.
Classification	Use outline form; list characteristics and distinguishing features.
Definition	Record the general category or class; then list distinguishing characteristics; include several examples.
Listing, or Enumeration	Record in list or outline form; record the order of presentation.

The notes in Figure 4-2 and Figure 4-3 (p. 77) show that effective lecture notes should record main ideas, important details, and examples and that they should reflect the lecture's organization. Both sets of notes were taken on the same lecture. One set of notes is thorough and effective; the other is lengthy and does not focus on key ideas. Read and evaluate each set of notes.

Make Note Taking Easier

If you record main ideas, details, and examples using the indentation system to show the lecture's organization, your notes will be adequate. However, there are

Figure 4-2
Notes Showing
Lecture Organization

A. Social Stratification   Soc. 106
   Defs   9/16
   Soc. Strat. —hierarchy of ranks that exist in society
   Status   —criteria to find positions in soc.
        2 types
             1. ascribed status—handed down; inherited
                ex.: titles, race, wealth, ethnic background
             2. achieved status—things you control
                ex.: education, jobs
B. Social Mobility
   Def. —how indiv. moves in hierarchy
        —amt. of movement depends on society
   2 Types
             1. caste—ex.: India—no mobility—you inherit class +
                status
             2. open—large amt. of achieved status—great
                mobility—ex.: USA.

Social Stratification

    Social stratification—defined as the ranks that exist in society—the position that any person has—ascribed status—it is handed down—

    example: titles. A second kind is achieved—it is the kind you decide for yourself. Social stratification is important in understanding societies. How a person moves up and down + changes his social status is called mobility. Some societies have a lot of mobility. Others don't have any—example is India.

    There are 2 kinds of movement.
       1. Caste system is when everybody is assigned a class and they must stay there without any chance to change.
       2. Open—people can move from one to another. This is true in the United States.

Figure 4-3
**Less Effective,
Unfocused
Lecture Notes**

some tips you can follow to make note taking easier, to make your notes more complete, and to make study and review easier.

USE INK   Pencil tends to smear and is harder to read.

USE A STANDARD-SIZED NOTEBOOK OR A SIMPLE, CLEAR COMPUTER FONT   Paper smaller than 8½ by 11 inches doesn't allow you to write much on a page, and it is more difficult to see the overall organization of a lecture if you have to flip through a lot of pages.

KEEP A SEPARATE NOTEBOOK OR COMPUTER FOLDER FOR EACH COURSE   You need to have your notes for each course together so that you can review them easily.

DATE YOUR NOTES   For easy reference later, be sure to date your notes. Your instructor might announce that an exam will cover everything presented after, for example, October 5. If your notes are not dated, you will not know where to begin to study.

LEAVE BLANK SPACES   To make your notes more readable and to make it easier to see the organization of ideas, leave plenty of blank space. If you know you missed a detail or definition, leave additional blank space. You can fill it in later by checking with a friend or referring to your text.

MARK ASSIGNMENTS   Occasionally an instructor will announce an assignment or test date in the middle of a lecture. Of course you will jot it down, but be sure to mark "Assignment" or "Test Date" in the margin so that you can find it easily and transfer it to your assignment notebook.

MARK IDEAS THAT ARE UNCLEAR   If an instructor presents a fact or idea that is unclear, put a question mark in the margin. Later, ask your instructor or another student about this idea.

SIT IN THE FRONT OF THE CLASSROOM   Especially in large lecture halls, it is to your advantage to sit near the front. In the front you will be able to see and hear the instructor easily—you can maintain eye contact and observe his or her facial expressions and nonverbal clues. If you sit in the back, you may become bored, and it is easy to be distracted by all the people in front of you. The people seated between you and the instructor create a feeling of distance. You may feel that the instructor is not really talking to you.

DON'T PLAN TO RECOPY YOUR NOTES   Some students take each day's notes in a hasty, careless way and then recopy them in the evening. These students feel that recopying helps them review the information. Actually, recopying often becomes a mechanical process that takes a lot of time but very little thought. Time spent recopying can be better spent reviewing the notes in a manner that will be suggested later in this chapter. If, however, you are reorganizing and expanding upon your notes and not just copying them, then rewriting can be useful.

RECOGNIZE THAT RECORDING LECTURES IS TIME-CONSUMING   In an effort to get complete and accurate notes, some students record very detailed or complicated lectures. After the lecture, they play it back and edit their notes, starting and stopping the machine as needed. This is a time-consuming technique, but some students find it a helpful way to build their confidence, improve their note-taking techniques, and assure themselves that their notes are complete. If you decide to record, do so sparingly. Unless your notes are incomplete, listening to a recording requires a great deal of time and often yields little gain. *If you plan to record, be sure to ask your instructor for permission to do so.*

USE ABBREVIATIONS   To save time, try to use abbreviations instead of writing out long or frequently used words. If you are taking a course in psychology, you do not want to write out *p-s-y-c-h-o-l-o-g-y* each time the word is used. It would be much faster to use the abbreviation *psy*. Try to develop abbreviations that are appropriate for the subject areas you are studying. The abbreviations shown in Figure 4-4, devised by a student in business management, will give you an idea of the possibilities. Note that both common and specialized words are abbreviated.

Figure 4-4
Abbreviations for Use
in Note Taking

COMMON WORDS	ABBREVIATION	SPECIALIZED WORDS	ABBREVIATION
and	+	organization	org.
with	w/	management	man.
compare comparison	comp.	data bank	D.B.
		structure	str.
importance	imp't	evaluation	eval.
advantage	adv	management by objective	MBO
introduction	intro	management information system	M/S
continued	cont.	organizational development	OD
		communication simulations	comm/sim

As you develop your own set of abbreviations, be sure to begin gradually. It is easy to overuse abbreviations and end up with notes that are so cryptic as to be almost meaningless.

DIRECTIONS   Select one set of lecture notes from a class you recently attended. Reread your notes and look for words or phrases you could have abbreviated. Write some of these words and their abbreviations in the spaces provided.

Word	**Abbreviation**
_____	_____
_____	_____
_____	_____
_____	_____
_____	_____
_____	_____
_____	_____
_____	_____

CREATE A CODE SYSTEM   Devise a system by which you record or mark specific types of information in specific ways. For example, number the items in a list, write "ex" next to each example, or put question marks next to ideas you don't understand.

MAKE THE MOST OF YOUR LEARNING STYLE   Use your knowledge of your learning style preferences to guide your note taking. By adapting your note-taking strategies to take advantage of your learning style, you will also make study and review easier. Figure 4-5 offers some suggestions for tailoring your note taking to your learning style.

LEARNING CHARACTERISTICS	NOTE-TAKING STRATEGY
Auditory	Take advantage of your advantage! Take thorough and complete notes.
Visual	Work on note-taking skills; practice by recording a lecture; analyze and revise your notes.
Applied	Think of applications (record as annotations). Write questions in the margin about applications.
Conceptual	Discover relationships among ideas. Watch for patterns.
Spatial	Add diagrams and maps, as appropriate, during editing.
Nonspatial	Record lecture's diagrams and drawings—but translate into language during editing.
Social	Review and edit notes with a classmate. Compare notes with others.
Independent	Choose seating in close contact with the instructor; avoid distracting groups of students.
Creative	Annotate your notes, recording impressions, reactions, spinoff ideas, and related ideas.
Pragmatic	Reorganize your notes during editing. Pay attention to the lecturer's organization.

Figure 4-5
Adapting Note Taking to Your Learning Style

Overcoming Common Note-Taking Problems

Instructors present lectures differently, use various lecture styles, and organize their subjects in different ways. Therefore, students often have difficulty taking notes in one or more courses. Figure 4-6, page 80, identifies common problems associated with lecture note taking and offers possible solutions.

Goal

Edit your notes

HOW TO EDIT YOUR NOTES

After you have taken a set of lecture notes, do not assume that they are accurate and complete. Most students find that they missed some information and were unable to record as many details or examples as they would have liked. Even very experienced note takers face these problems. Fortunately, the solution is simple. Don't plan on taking a final and complete set of notes during the lecture. Instead, record just enough during the lecture to help you remember a main idea, detail, or example. Leave plenty of blank space; then, if possible, sit down immediately after the lecture and review your notes. Fill in the missing information. Expand, or flesh out, any details or examples that are not fully explained. If you took notes by hand, type them into a computer file and, as you go, fill in this additional information. This process is called **editing**. It is essentially a process of correcting, revising, and adding to your notes to make them complete and more accurate. Editing notes for a one-hour lecture should take no more than five or ten minutes.

Figure 4-6
Common Note-Taking Problems

PROBLEM	SOLUTION
"My mind wanders and I get bored."	Sit in the front of the room. Be certain to preview assignments. Think about questions you expect to be answered in the lecture.
"The instructor talks too fast."	Develop a shorthand system; use abbreviations. Leave blanks and fill them in later.
"The lecturer rambles."	Preview correlating text assignments to determine organizing principles. Reorganize your notes after the lecture.
"Some ideas don't seem to fit anywhere."	Record them in the margin or in parentheses within your notes, and think about them later during editing.
"Everything seems important."; "Nothing seems important."	You have not identified key concepts and may lack necessary background knowledge (see Chapter 6)—you do not understand the topic. Preview related text assignments.
"I can't spell all the new technical terms."	Write them phonetically, the way they sound. Fill in correct spellings during editing.
"The instructor uses terms without defining them."	Write the terms as they are used; leave space to record definitions later, when you can consult the text glossary or a dictionary.
"The instructor reads directly from the text."	Mark passages in the text; write the instructor's comments in the margin. Record page references in your notes.

If you are unable to edit your notes immediately after a lecture, it is critical that you edit them that evening. The more time that lapses between note taking and editing, the less effective editing becomes. Also, the greater the time lapse, the more facts and examples you will be unable to recall and fill in.

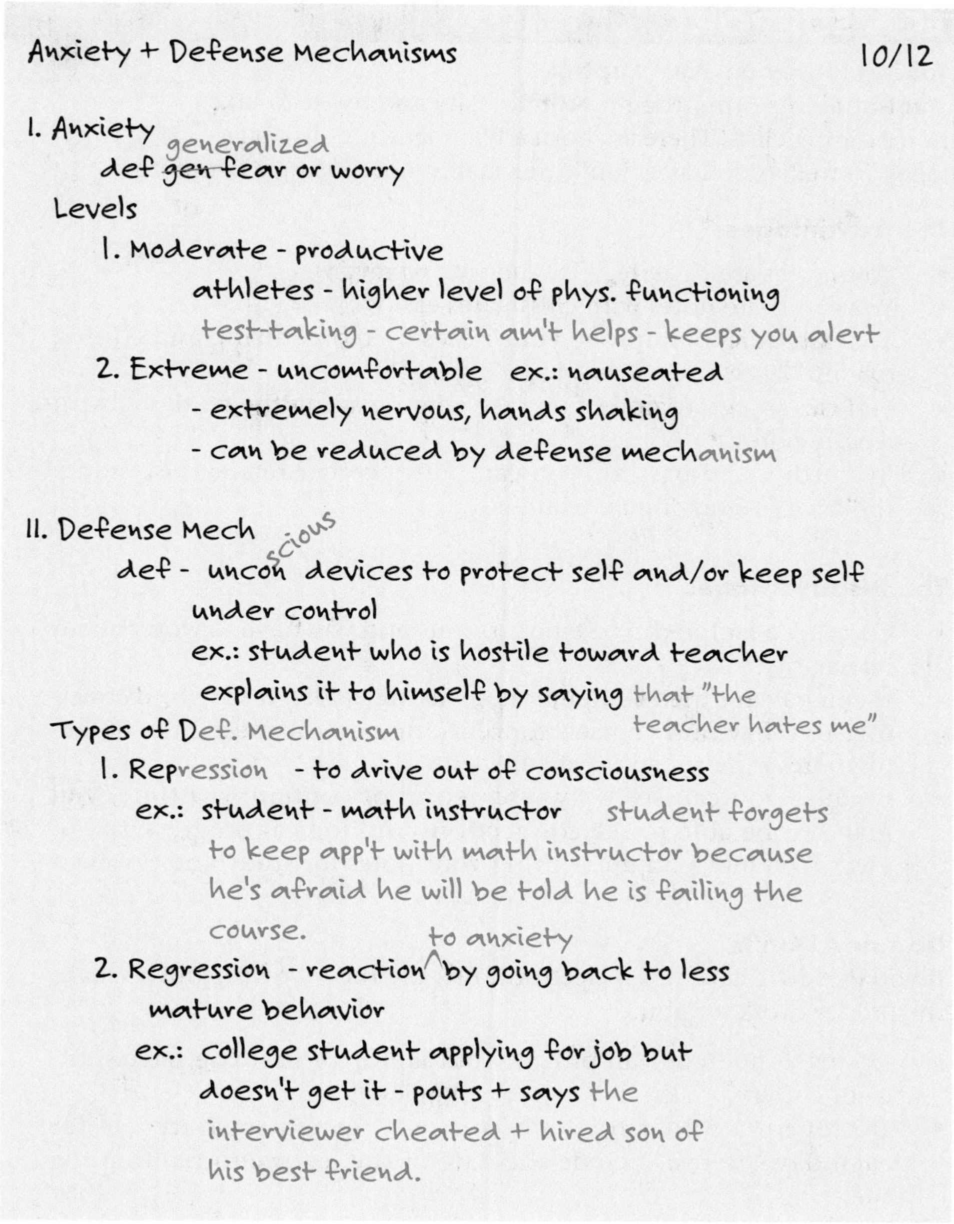

Figure 4-7
Edited Lecture Notes

Anxiety + Defense Mechanisms   10/12

I. Anxiety
     def ~~gen~~ *generalized* fear or worry
   Levels
      1. Moderate - productive
         athletes - higher level of phys. functioning
         test-taking - certain am't helps - keeps you alert
      2. Extreme - uncomfortable   ex.: nauseated
         - extremely nervous, hands shaking
         - can be reduced by defense mechanism

II. Defense Mech
     def - uncon*scious* devices to protect self and/or keep self
        under control
        ex.: student who is hostile toward teacher
        explains it to himself by saying *that "the*
   Types of Def. Mechanism   *teacher hates me"*
      1. Repression - to drive out of consciousness
        ex.: student - math instructor   *student forgets*
        to keep app't with math instructor because
        he's afraid he will be told he is failing the
        course.   *to anxiety*
      2. Regression - reaction ^ by going back to less
        mature behavior
        ex.: college student applying for job but
        doesn't get it - pouts + says *the*
        interviewer cheated + hired son of
        his best friend.

The sample set of lecture notes in Figure 4-7 has been edited. The notes taken during the lecture are in black; the additions and changes made during editing are in color. Read the notes, noticing the types of information added during editing.

Editing is also a time for you to think about the notes you've taken—to move beyond the literal knowledge and comprehension levels of thought to the levels that involve critical thinking.

Integrating Text and Lecture Notes

A continual problem students wrestle with is how to integrate lecture and text-book notes. The computer offers an ideal solution to the integration of text and

TECH SUPPORT

Taking Notes on Your Laptop

Some students bring their laptop to class and use it to take notes during class. There are both advantages and disadvantages, as well as do's and don'ts, for taking notes using a computer.

The Advantages

- Your notes are clear, legible, and easy to review.
- You can share notes with classmates easily.
- You can quickly improve your notes by reorganizing and editing (see pp. 79–81)
- You can integrate notes you take when reading the textbook with lecture notes.
- By cutting and pasting, you can pull together related notes on a topic when studying for exams.

The Disadvantages

- Carrying a laptop can be cumbersome, and you have to worry about its security.
- If you haven't tried computer note taking before, it may be distracting. You may find yourself concentrating on the mechanics of taking notes rather than on lecture content.
- Because you can see only a screenful of content at a time, you may not be able to see connections and logical progressions of ideas. You may end up printing your notes for study and review.

Do's and Don'ts

If you decide to take notes electronically, use the following tips to make the process work for you:

- Do make sure you can plug in your laptop or that you have sufficient battery power.
- Do set up a folder for each course. Create a separate file for each day's notes; include the date of the lecture in naming the file.
- Do save your document frequently, so you don't lose anything.
- Do keep a pen and paper handy to record diagrams, drawings, and figures.
- Don't allow distracting programs such as e-mail and instant messaging to compete for your attention.
- Don't risk interrupting class with annoying beeps and buzzes. Turn the sound off.

lecture notes. The cut-and-paste option enables you to move pieces (sections) of your notes to any desired place in the document. Thus, you can easily integrate text and lecture notes on each major topic.

If you are not working with a computer for note taking, you can annotate your textbook notes during or after class as described in "Using College Textbooks," page 86.

APPLYING LEVELS OF THINKING

Editing Notes and Levels of Thinking

As you edit your notes, keep the following questions in mind.

Level of Thinking	Questions
Applying	How can I use this information?
Analyzing	How do these notes fit with other lectures? With the textbook assignment?
Evaluating	How useful is this information? Was it clear and well presented? What additional information do I need? What don't I fully understand?
Creating	What does this all mean? How can I summarize it?

Do not hesitate to add marginal notes, jot down questions, add reactions, draw arrows to show relationships, and bracket sections that seem confusing.

HOW TO STUDY YOUR NOTES

Goal 5

Study your notes

Taking and editing lecture notes is only part of what must be done to learn from your instructor's lectures. You also have to learn and review the material in the notes in order to do well on an exam. To study lecture notes, try to apply the same principles that you use in learning material in your textbooks.

1. **Do not try to learn what is in your notes by reading them over and over.** Rereading is not an efficient review technique because it takes too much time relative to the amount you learn.
2. **As in reading textbook assignments, identify what is important.** You must sort out what you will learn and study from all the rest of the information you have written in your notes.
3. **Have a way of checking yourself—of deciding whether you have learned the necessary information.**

To study lecture notes, you can use a system called the recall clue system.

The Cornell Note-Taking Recall Clue System

Developed at Cornell University, the recall clue system helps make the review and study of lecture notes easier and more effective. To use the recall clue system, follow these steps:

1. **Leave a two-inch margin at the left side of each page of notes.**
2. **Write nothing in the margin while you are taking notes.**
3. **After you have edited your notes, fill in the left margin with words and phrases that briefly summarize the notes.**

The recall clues should be words that will trigger your memory and help you recall the complete information in your notes. These clues function as memory tags. They help you retrieve from your memory any information that is labeled with these tags. Figure 4-8 shows a sample of notes in which the recall clue system has been used. When you are taking an exam, the recall clues from your notes will work automatically to help you remember necessary information.

A variation on the recall clue system that students have found effective is to write questions rather than summary words and phrases in the margin (see Figure 4-9 on p. 85). The questions trigger your memory and enable you to recall the information that answers your question. The use of questions enables you to test yourself, simulating an exam situation.

**Figure 4-8
Lecture Notes with
Recall Clues Added**

	Chem 109
	Numerical Properties of Atoms 2/9
	I. Prop. related to Temperature + Heat
melting point	A. Melting Point
	- when particles in a solid move fast enough to overcome forces holding them together - temp at which this happens = melting point
freezing point	- Freezing Pt. -temp at which forces attracting particles to one another hold particles together
heat of fusion	- Heat of Fusion -amt. of heat req'd. to melt one gram of any substance at its melting pt.
boiling point	B. Boiling Point
	- Point at which molecules of a liquid begin to escape as gas
heat of vap.	- Heat of vaporization -amt. of heat req'd. to change one gram of liquid to a gas at its boiling pt.
condensation pt.	- Condensation Pt. - point at which gas, cooling, changes back to liquid
specific heat	C. Specific Heat
	ex. beach -sand hot, water cold- why? Sand + H_2O have different spec. heat
	def. -am't. of heat needed to raise temp. of a spec. mass of substance by a certain am't.
formula for s.h.	formula - s.h. = heat in cals.
	mass in grams × temp. diff. in °C
	$$s.h. = \frac{cal}{g \times °C}$$

Marketing
104

Role of Advertising

What is advertising?	Advertising —Widely used in our economy —Promotes competition; encourages open system definition—presentation of a product/service to broad segment of the population
What are its characteristics?	Characteristics 1. nonpersonal—uses media rather than person-to-person contact 2. paid for by seller 3. intended to influence the consumer
What is the ultimate objective?	Objectives Ultimate objective—to sell product or service
What are the immediate objectives?	Immediate objectives 1. to inform—make consumer aware ex. new product available 2. to persuade—stress value, advantages of product ex. results of market research 3. to reinforce—happens after 1 and 2—consumers need to be reminded about prod./service—even if they use it.—often done through slogans and jingles

Figure 4-9
Lecture Notes with Recall Questions Added

Using the Cornell Note-Taking Recall Clue System

To study your notes using the recall clue system, cover up the notes with a sheet of paper, exposing only the recall clues in the left margin. Next, read the first recall clue and try to remember the information in the portion of the notes beside it. Then slide the paper down and check that portion to see whether you remembered all the important facts. If you remembered only part of the information, cover up that portion of your notes and again check your recall. Continue checking until you are satisfied that you can remember all the important facts. Then move on to the next recall clue on the page, following the same testing–checking procedure.

To get into the habit of using the recall clue system, for handwritten notes mark off with a ruler a two-inch column on the next several blank pages in each of your notebooks. Then, when you open your notebook at the beginning of the class, you will be reminded to use the system.

If you take notes on your laptop, create a template that includes a two-column format.

Exercise 3

DIRECTIONS   Read the sample set of notes in Figure 4-2. Fill in the recall clues or formulate questions that would help you study and learn the notes. ●

Exercise 4

DIRECTIONS   For each course you are taking this semester, use the recall clue system for at least one week. Use the recall clues to review your notes several times. At the end of the week, evaluate how well the system works for you.

1. What advantages does it have?

_____

_____

2. Did it help you remember facts and ideas?

_____

_____

3. Are there any disadvantages?

_____

_____ ●

USING COLLEGE TEXTBOOKS
Taking Notes on Textbook Readings

In addition to taking notes on lectures and class discussions, you also need to take notes on your textbook reading assignments. Notes are valuable study tools, and the actual writing of the notes strengthens your retention and recall of the information. Be sure to include the following:

1. **Definitions.** Include definitions of important terms or concepts.
2. **Main ideas.** Write down the main idea of each paragraph.
3. **Examples.** Include examples for difficult concepts.
4. **Processes.** Outline processes that are described in the text.

You can take notes in the margins of your book, in a notebook, or on your computer. Be sure to label the pages the notes refer to. Refer to your notes during class or immediately after class, adding marginal notes or highlighting to indicate points your instructor emphasized.

On the next page is a textbook page showing the marginal notes a student made while reading. Also shown is a set of notes she took on this page, and then later edited.

TEXTBOOK EXCERPT

Why Do People Become Vegetarians?

When discussing vegetarianism, one of the most often-asked questions is why people would make this food choice. The most common responses are included here.

RELIGIOUS, ETHICAL, AND FOOD-SAFETY REASONS

Some make the choice for religious or spiritual reasons. Several religions prohibit or restrict the consumption of animal flesh; however, generalizations can be misleading. For example, while certain sects within Hinduism forbid the consumption of meat, perusing the menu at an Indian restaurant will reveal that some other Hindus regularly consume small quantities of meat, poultry, and fish. Many Buddhists are vegetarians, as are some Christians, including Seventh-Day Adventists.

Some religious sects may prohibit meat

Many vegetarians are guided by their personal philosophy to choose vegetarianism. These people feel that it is morally and ethically wrong to consume animals and any products from animals (such as dairy or egg products) because they view the practices in the modern animal industries as inhumane. They may consume milk and eggs but choose to purchase them only from family farms where they believe animals are treated humanely.

Personal choice based on moral outrage at inhumane treatment of animals.

There is also a great deal of concern about meat-handling practices, because contaminated meat is allowed into our food supply. For example, in 1982, there was an outbreak of severe bloody diarrhea that was eventually traced to bacteria burgers served at a fast-food restaurant. Several people became seriously ill and one child died after eating the hamburgers. Another concern surrounding beef is the possibility that it is tainted by the microbes that cause *mad cow disease*.

What is mad cow disease?

ECOLOGICAL REASONS

Many people choose vegetarianism because of their concerns about the effect of meat industries on the global environment They argue that cattle consume large quantities of grain and water, require grazing areas that could be used for plant food production, destroy vulnerable ecosystems including rain forests, and produce wastes that run off into surrounding bodies of water. Meat industry organizations argue that such effects are minor and greatly exaggerated. One area of agreement that has recently emerged focuses the argument not on *whether* we eat meat but on *how much* meat we consume. The environmental damage caused by the raising of livestock is due in part to the large number of animals produced. When a population reduces its consumption of meat, reduced reduction follows. In addition to the environmental benefits, eating less meat may also reduce our risk for chronic diseases such as heart disease and some cancers.

How much meat is too much?

—Thompson, *Nutrition for Life*, pp. 148–150

EXCERPT FROM NOTES

Page 148

A. Reasons for Vegetarianism
   1. Religious/spiritual: prohibitions/restriction on consumption of animal flesh
   2. Personal philosophy: belief that it is morally wrong to consume animals/animal products
   3. Safety concerns: contaminated meat that has made it into the food system, such as mad cow disease
   4. Ecological reasons: cattle negatively affect the environment
      a. Not whether we eat meat, but how much meat we eat is the issue now

emphasized this ———

seemed to disagree— oversimplification

FURTHER PRACTICE WITH TEXTBOOK READING

Part A: Sample Textbook Chapter

Read the section titled "Theories of Motivation" (p. 497) in the sample textbook chapter and take notes on it.

Part B: Your College Textbook

Choose a reading assignment you have been given in a textbook for another course. Take notes when you read the assignment.

SELF-TEST SUMMARY

Goal 1 How can you improve your listening skills?	Taking good lecture notes depends on good listening skills. To make your listening more intentional, purposeful, and deliberate, you should apply good reading skills to listening: Focus on content and ideas, not on the speaker's style or on facts alone; pay attention to opening statements; look for the speaker's purpose; and prevent your mind from wandering by focusing your concentration, attention, and thinking skills.
Goal 2 How should you prepare for a lecture?	Because many college instructors expect you to remember and apply the facts and ideas in their class lectures, it is a good idea to become familiar with the topic before the lecture. Be sure to read (or at least preview) the assignment. Get to class early enough to settle in and prepare to listen.
Goal 3 What are the characteristics of effective lecture notes?	Effective lecture notes should accomplish three things. First, good notes should summarize the main points of the lecture. Well-taken lecture notes are a valuable aid to study. Second, lecture notes should include enough details and examples so that you can recall and completely understand the information several weeks later. Third, the notes should show the relative importance of ideas and reflect the organization of the lecture.
Goal 4 Why should you edit your lecture notes?	After taking a set of lecture notes, it is necessary to correct, revise, fill in missing or additional information, and expand your notes. This editing process results in clearer, more accurate notes.
Goal 5 How should you study your lecture notes?	The recall clue system is a way of making study and review easier and more effective. During note taking, leave blank a two-inch margin at the left of each page of notes. Later, as you reread your notes, write in the margin words and phrases that briefly summarize the notes. These phrases, or recall clues, trigger your memory and help you recall information in the notes.

APPLYING YOUR SKILLS

DISCUSSING THE CHAPTER

1. What is the difference between hearing and listening? Is it similar to the distinction between reading and understanding?

2. What goals must a good set of lecture notes accomplish?

3. Why is the recall clue system effective in helping you study?

4. Use Figure 4-5 to determine note-taking strategies that are appropriate for your learning style. How can you use these strategies in this class?

ANALYZING A STUDY SITUATION

Jan is taking an American government course in which class lectures are very important. She has trouble following the lectures and knowing what is important because her instructor does not follow the textbook and often digresses from the topic. The instructor lectures at a fast pace, so Jan feels she is missing important information.

1. What advice would you give Jan for taking lecture notes?

2. How should she study and review her notes?

3. What thought patterns could she expect to find in an American government course?

4. Should Jan record the lectures?

5. Would rewriting or editing her notes be helpful? If so, what changes should she make?

Tip *Digress* means "to write or talk about a subject that's not related to the idea(s) being discussed."

WORKING ON COLLABORATIVE PROJECTS

DIRECTIONS Bring two sets of lecture notes to class. The first set should be notes taken *before* this chapter on note taking was assigned. The second should be a set of notes taken *after* this chapter was assigned and should contain editing and recall clues. Work with a partner to assess each other's progress and suggest areas for further improvement.

For support in meeting this chapter's goals, go to **MyReadingLab** and select **Note Taking and Highlighting**.

Answer Key for Learning Experiment
Paragraph 1: intimate, personal, social, public
Paragraph 2: attraction, taste, memory, identity

QUICK QUIZ

DIRECTIONS   Write the letter of the choice that best completes each statement in the space provided.

CHECKING YOUR RECALL

_____ 1. A speaker's opening comments typically
   a. identify the organization and purpose of the lecture.
   b. do not contain any important information.
   c. consist only of personal or humorous stories told to get the audience's attention.
   d. will be repeated at the conclusion of the lecture.

_____ 2. The gap between rate of speech and rate of thinking is such that the
   a. speaker has a distinct advantage.
   b. listener has to strain to follow along.
   c. speaker has to allow time for listeners to catch up.
   d. listener has time to think of other things.

_____ 3. One difference between listening and hearing is that listening is
   a. purely biological.
   b. passive.
   c. unintentional.
   d. purposeful.

_____ 4. Instructors often signal what is important during a lecture by doing all of the following _except_
   a. increasing their rate of speech.
   b. changing the tone or pitch of their voices.
   c. writing on the board.
   d. listing or numbering points.

_____ 5. Recall clues are intended primarily to
   a. aid your ability to retrieve information.
   b. identify the patterns used in a particular lecture.
   c. reduce the amount of information you must learn.
   d. organize your lecture notes.

APPLYING YOUR SKILLS

_____ 6. Pedro is reviewing the psychology notes he took in class today. The best way for Pedro to review his notes is to
   a. copy his notes over to make them more legible.
   b. expand on details that he didn't have time to write down.
   c. revise his notes while listening to a recording of the lecture.
   d. read his notes aloud over and over.

_____ 7. Craig is having trouble taking good notes because his instructor speaks too quickly for him. All of the following strategies might help him _except_
   a. recording the lectures.
   b. using abbreviations.
   c. sitting at the back of the class.
   d. leaving blanks in his notes for filling in missing information later.

_____ 8. Anwali is editing the notes she took during her biology class this morning. This means that Anwali is
   a. grouping the ideas in her notes into paragraphs.
   b. copying the notes over so that they are neater.
   c. memorizing the facts in the notes.
   d. correcting, revising, and adding to her notes to make them more complete and accurate.

_____ 9. Derek is trying to improve his listening skills during lectures. Derek should try to
   a. focus on delivery, not content.
   b. memorize unconnected facts.
   c. identify main ideas, relationships, and trends.
   d. come up with mnemonic devices.

_____ 10. Kimberly has arrived early for an English lecture. The most effective use of her time would be to
   a. review the homework assignment due that day.
   b. begin reading the next textbook chapter assignment.
   c. review her notes from the previous lecture.
   d. chat with friends until the class begins.

Communicating in the Classroom

CHAPTER

5

LEARNING GOALS

In this chapter you will learn to

1 Listen critically

2 Ask and answer questions during class

3 Participate in class discussions

4 Work on class activities

5 Make oral presentations

6 Communicate with your professor

LEARNING EXPERIMENT

1 Select two upcoming lectures for another course.

2 Use the strategies you learned in Chapter 4 to take notes on each lecture.

3 For one lecture, exchange your notes with a partner in that class. Take a few minutes to read each other's notes.

4 Develop three meaningful questions about your partner's notes. Take turns asking and answering each other's questions.

5 For the second lecture, reread your notes, but do not exchange notes with a classmate. Write three questions that could be asked about your notes.

6 After two days, review both sets of notes. Which set seems more familiar? For which do you recall

more information? Which would you feel more prepared to take a quiz on?

THE RESULTS

You probably felt better prepared with the first set of notes than with the second because you interacted with a classmate about their contents. You not only read the notes, you talked about them and exchanged ideas.

LEARNING PRINCIPLE: WHAT THIS MEANS TO YOU

By communicating with others about course content, you increase your understanding and learn more easily. Talking about course content and exchanging ideas facilitates learning. In this chapter you will learn to communicate with classmates in a variety of situations. You will also learn about asking and answering questions in class, participating in class discussions, working on group activities, and communicating with your professor.

WHY COMMUNICATE WITH CLASSMATES?

It is important to communicate with classmates because:

- Working with classmates reinforces what you learn from your instructors and your textbooks.
- Participation in class demonstrates that you are a serious student, enhances your academic image, and can improve your grade.
- Online or distance-learning classrooms offer an opportunity to practice communication skills.
- Communicating with classmates in a classroom setting—whether in person or online—prepares you for on-the-job teamwork.

Goal 1

Listen critically

LISTENING CRITICALLY

Listening is an important part of classroom communication. In order to respond to what is going on in class, you have to understand and evaluate it. Your first task, then, is to absorb and learn the information presented. (See Chapter 4 for information on taking lecture notes and developing recall clues to learn them.) However, another equally important task is to think critically about what your instructor presents and what other students say in class. Listening critically and constructively gives you the ability to respond thoughtfully and participate meaningfully. Avoid the following obstacles to critical listening:

1. **Closed-mindedness.** In your classrooms you will hear many ideas that you disagree with, and you will meet people who have different values than you do. What others may feel or believe is right, wrong, or important about the course subject matter—or about life in general—may not be the same as what you feel or believe. Avoid prejudging a speaker or his or her announced topic. Keep an open mind. Delay your judgment until the speaker has finished and you fully understand the speaker's message and intentions. If you are participating in an online course, you have the advantage of taking a few minutes to reread someone's posting before jumping in hastily with your own immediate reaction.

2. **Selective listening.** When listening to or reading ideas with which they disagree, some students hear only what they want to hear. That is, they pay attention to ideas they agree with and may misinterpret or even ignore ideas with which they disagree. Selective listening often occurs when discussing political, religious, or moral issues. To avoid selective listening, first recognize your own biases. A bias (as we'll discuss in Chapter 9) is a very strong feeling or inclination toward a particular point of view. Make a deliberate effort to recognize when a speaker's viewpoint conflicts with your own bias about an issue—and do not let your own bias block out your understanding of that opposing point of view. If your feelings are very strong, try taking notes or writing an outline of the speaker's viewpoints to keep yourself constructively engaged.

3. **Judging the speaker instead of the message.** Be sure to focus on the message, not the person delivering the message. Try not to be distracted by mannerisms, dress, or the method of delivery (pauses, tone of voice, grammatical errors in online postings, and so forth). Be sensitive to the feelings and viewpoints of other class members—try not to be bullying, argumentative, or overly emotional in your verbal responses or other reactions.

4. **Lack of audience awareness.** Don't get so caught up in what you're saying that you lose sight of your audience and their reactions. When making a point or offering a comment, watch both your instructor and others in the class. Their responses will show whether they understand you or need further information, whether they agree or disagree, whether you have accidentally caused offense, and whether they are interested or uninterested. You can then decide, based on their responses, whether you made your point effectively or whether you need to explain or defend your argument more carefully.

Exercise 1

DIRECTIONS   Working with a classmate, identify at least three or four class discussion topics for which it would be important to keep an open mind and avoid selective listening. ●

ASKING AND ANSWERING QUESTIONS

Goal 2

Ask and answer questions during class

Asking clear, direct questions is a skill you can develop and improve. Framing clear, direct answers to questions asked by your instructors or by fellow students is also a skill worth developing. Effective questioning is important in college classes, but it is also an important workplace skill. Use the following suggestions to strengthen your questioning and answering skills.

1. **Conquer the fear of asking questions.** Many students are hesitant to ask or answer questions, often because they are concerned about how their classmates and instructor will respond. They fear that their questions may seem dumb or that their answers may be incorrect. Asking questions is often essential to a complete and thorough understanding, and you will find that once you've asked a question, other students will be glad you asked because they had the same question in mind. Answering questions posed by your instructor gives you an opportunity to evaluate how well you have learned or understood course content as well as to demonstrate your knowledge.
2. **To get started, as you read an assignment, jot down several questions that might clarify or explain it better.** Bring your list to class. Refer to your list as you speak, if necessary.
3. **When you ask a question, state it clearly and concisely.** Don't ramble or make excuses for asking.
4. **Remember, most instructors invite and respond favorably to questions: if your question is a serious one, it will be received positively.** Don't pose questions for the sake of asking a question. Class time is limited and valuable.
5. **In answering questions, think your responses through before you volunteer them.**

Tip *Critiquing format* means "talking or writing about how good or bad the organization and/or design of something is" or "evaluating its method of presentation."

Exercise 2

DIRECTIONS   Select a reading assignment from one of your other courses. Practice asking and answering questions with a student from that class. Take turns critiquing format, content, and delivery of both questions and answers. ●

Exercise 3

DIRECTIONS   In one of your classes this week, pay attention to the types of questions and comments the students make. Which seem most helpful to the class as a whole? Which seem less important? Which seem to interrupt the class more than contribute to it? Why? ●

Goal ③

Participate in class discussions

PARTICIPATING IN CLASS DISCUSSIONS

Participation in class means more than being interested, prepared, and alert in class. To participate you must be actively involved in class discussions. Participating in class, even if it is not required, has a number of advantages.

1. **Participation will help you concentrate and stay focused.**
2. **Participation will help you sort out what you know and what you don't yet know.** By talking about ideas, you will discover which ideas you are knowledgeable about and which you need to study further.
3. **You will be better prepared for exams and quizzes because you have already put the course content into your own words.**
4. **Participation gives you practice in speaking before groups—a skill you will definitely need in the workplace.**

Class participation requires planning and preparation. Useful participation usually involves much more than offering an idea that comes to mind during a class discussion.

Finding Out What Your Instructor Expects

Before participating in a discussion, be sure to find out what your instructor expects. Your participation may count as part of your grade in the course. Check your syllabus or course management Web site to find out what percentage, if any, of your grade is determined by the level and quality of your participation. Regardless of whether participation counts in your grade, find out the following:

- Are you expected to react to assigned readings?
- Are you expected to respond to lecture content?
- Are you expected to react to the comments of other students?
- Are personal opinions welcome, or should you limit your response to factual information?
- Are online discussions part of the course? (See box on p. 95.)

Preparing for Class Discussions

Preparing for a class discussion demands more time and effort than getting ready for a lecture class does. In a lecture class, most of your work comes *after* the class, editing your notes and using the recall clue system to review them. The opposite is true for discussion courses, for which most of your work is done *before* you go to class. Be sure to spend considerable time reading, thinking, and making notes. You will perform better in a class discussion if you prepare in advance. Use the following strategies to be prepared:

1. **Read the assignment.** Usually a class discussion is about a particular topic. Frequently, instructors give textbook or library reading assignments that are intended to give you some background information or acquaint you with related issues. Read carefully; don't just skim through it.
2. **Mark and highlight important ideas as you read.** This will allow you review the material just before class begins and to locate ideas quickly during the discussion.

3. **Take notes.** Notes are essential to effective participation.
4. **Ask critical-thinking questions.** Class discussions seldom center around factual information. Instead, they usually focus on the application, analysis, synthesis, and evaluation of ideas and information. To prepare for discussions, then, start with the following critical-thinking questions:

- How can I use this information? To what situations is it applicable?
- How does this information compare with other information I have read or learned on the same topic?
- What is the source of the material?
- Is the material fact or opinion?
- What is the author's purpose?
- Is the author biased?
- Is relevant and sufficient evidence provided?

These questions will provoke thought and provide a base of ideas to use in discussions.

DIRECTIONS Working alone or with a classmate, develop a set of notes that contains a list of ideas and concepts presented in the sample textbook chapter in Part 6 that you could share in a group discussion. ●

Exercise 4

DIRECTIONS Prepare for one of your other classes as though it will take the form of a class discussion. Apply the critical-thinking questions above to the reading you do before the class meets, and make notes for the discussion. Whether the class actually takes the format of a lecture or a discussion, afterward think about how preparing in this way aided you in comprehending the class. ●

Exercise 5

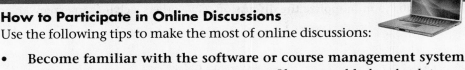

TECH SUPPORT

How to Participate in Online Discussions
Use the following tips to make the most of online discussions:

- **Become familiar with the software or course management system before you attempt to post messages.** If you need help, check to see whether there are print instructions or a model or demo to refer to. You can also get help from your campus computer center or ask classmates for help.
- **Be sure to read all previous posts before posting your comments.** You want to be sure someone else has not already said what you plan to say.
- **Plan ahead.** Unlike during in-class discussions, you have the luxury of thinking through what you want to say before you say it.
- **Show respect and consideration for your classmates and your instructor by making your comments easy to read.** Use correct spelling and grammar and format your comment using spacing, boldfaced print, numbered lists, etc.
- **Place your comments within a context.** Make it clear whether you are responding to another posting (if so, give date and name), a reading assignment (give chapter or page), or a lecture (give date).

Getting Involved in Class Discussions

Discussion classes require greater, more active involvement and participation than do lecture classes. In lecture classes, your main concern is to listen carefully and to record notes accurately and completely. In discussion classes, your responsibility is much greater. Not only do you have to take notes, but you also have to participate in the discussion. The problem many students experience in getting involved in discussions is that they do not know what to say or when to say it. Here are a few instances when it might be appropriate to speak. Say something when

- you can ask a serious, thoughtful question.
- someone asks a question that you can answer.
- you have a comment or suggestion to make about what has already been said.
- you can supply additional information that will clarify the topic under discussion.
- you can correct an error or clarify a misunderstanding.

PARTICIPATING CONSTRUCTIVELY IN CLASS DISCUSSIONS

- **Even if you are reluctant to speak before a group, try to say something early in the discussion.**
- **Make your comments brief and to the point.** Do not tell lengthy personal anecdotes.
- **Try to avoid getting involved in direct exchanges or disagreements with individual class members.**
- **Do not interrupt other speakers.** Signal to your instructor or moderator that you would like to be recognized to speak, if necessary.
- **Avoid talking privately with, IMing, or making comments to another student while the discussion is going on.**
- **Try not to monopolize the discussion.** Give others a chance to express their ideas.

To get more involved in classroom communication (both in person and online), try the strategies in the box above.

With careful preparation and attention, your classroom participation will be constructive and worthwhile.

Exercise 6

DIRECTIONS   Review the "Action Plan for Learning" you developed in Chapter 2 (p. 32). Which of your strategies could help you communicate more actively and constructively in the classroom? ●

Recording and Reviewing Classroom Communication

Class discussions contain important ideas and information. Some of the information may be included on tests or exams; other information may be useful in other discussions, when writing papers, or for completing class assignments.

Be sure to develop a note-taking system for keeping track of this information. Consider the following points:

- Taking notes while participating in the discussion leaves you less time to listen. Plan on recording only the main points during class and filling in the details later.
- It is a good idea to review your notes and fill in details as soon as possible after the discussion before forgetting occurs.
- Noting the speaker's name in the margin may help you recall his or her comments more vividly.
- While online discussions are always available for review by tracking back through the discussion, it is time-consuming to do so. Instead, write a brief summary of each topic, daily or weekly, depending on the number of posts.

WORKING ON CLASS ACTIVITIES

Goal 4
Work on class activities

Many assignments and class activities involve working with a small group of classmates. For example, a sociology instructor might divide the class into groups and ask each group to brainstorm solutions to the economic or social problems of the elderly. Your political science professor might create a panel to discuss ways to increase voter participation.

Group activities are intended to enable students to learn from one another by viewing each other's thinking processes and by evaluating each other's ideas and approaches. Group activities also develop valuable skills in interpersonal communication that will be essential in your career. Some students are reluctant to work in groups because they feel that they are not in control of the situation; they dislike having their grade depend on the performance of others as well as themselves. Use the following suggestions to help your group function effectively:

1. **Select alert, energetic classmates** if you are permitted to choose group members.
2. **Be an active, responsible participant.** Accept your share of the work and expect others to do the same. Approach the activity with a serious attitude, rather than joking or complaining about the assignment. This will establish a serious tone and cut down on wasted time.
3. **Take a leadership role.** Organization and direction are essential for productivity, and leadership roles are valuable experiences for your career.
4. **Take advantage of individual strengths and weaknesses.** For instance, a person who seems indifferent or is easily distracted should not be assigned the task of recording the group's findings. The most organized, outgoing member might be assigned the task of making an oral report to the class.

Exercise 7

DIRECTIONS   Suppose you are part of a five-member group that is preparing for a panel discussion on animal rights. One group member is very vocal and opinionated. You fear she is likely to dominate the discussion. Another group member is painfully shy and has volunteered to do double research if he doesn't have to speak much during the discussion. A third member appears uninterested and tends to sit back and watch as the group works and plans. How should the group respond to each of these individuals? List several possible solutions to each problem. ●

Goal **5**

Make oral
presentations

MAKING ORAL PRESENTATIONS

Oral presentations may be done in groups or individually. Groups may be asked to report their findings, summarize their research, or describe a process or procedure. Individual presentations are often summaries of research papers, reviews or critiques, or interpretations of literary or artistic works. Use the following suggestions to make effective oral presentations:

1. **Understand the purpose of the assignment.** Analyze it carefully before beginning to work.
2. **Research your topic thoroughly.** Collect and organize your information.
3. **Prepare outline notes.** Record only key words and phrases.
4. **Consider the use of visual aids.** Depending on the type of assignment as well as on your topic, diagrams, photographs, or demonstrations may be appropriate and effective in maintaining audience interest.
5. **Anticipate questions your audience may ask.** Review and revise your notes to include answers.
6. **Practice delivery.** This will build your confidence and help you overcome nervousness. First, practice your presentation aloud several times by yourself. Time yourself to be sure you are within any limits. Then practice in front of friends and ask for criticism. Finally, record your presentation. Play it back, looking for ways to improve it.
7. **Deliver your presentation as effectively as possible.** Engage your audience's interest by maintaining eye contact; look directly at other students as you speak. Make a deliberate effort to speak slowly; when you are nervous, your speech tends to speed up. Be enthusiastic and energetic.

Figure 5-1 answers some commonly asked questions about making oral presentations.

**Figure 5-1
Questions and
Answers About Oral
Presentations**

QUESTIONS	ANSWERS
1. How can I overcome the fear of public speaking?	• Be sure to practice delivering your speech before you actually make your presentation. Practice speaking slowly and distinctly, taking deep breaths, and pausing.
2. How can I make sure my presentation is interesting?	• Vary the content. For example, you could start off by telling an interesting story or engaging the class's attention by posing a thoughtful question. • Use visual aids such as a whiteboard, a projector, or a chart that you've designed to help you maintain the interest of your audience.
3. What if, during my presentation, the instructor and/or the class starts to show signs of boredom?	• Change the tone or pitch of your voice. • Maintain your audience's interest by engaging them in the presentation. Pose a question, for example. • Make eye contact with restless individuals.
4. What do I do if I "go blank"?	• Write brief notes. If you suddenly "go blank," all you need to do is look at your notes. • Ask whether there are any questions. Even if there aren't, this pause will give you time to think about what to say next.

Tip To *go blank* is to forget what you were going to say.

Visual Thinking
APPLYING SKILLS

Analyze the students in this lecture class. Which students seem to be serious active listeners? Which are not? Identify the behaviors that are not productive.

DIRECTIONS Develop a checklist of five to ten different criteria that you could use to evaluate how effective an oral presentation is. The next time you are asked to make an oral presentation, use your checklist to evaluate a practice session. ●

Exercise 8

COMMUNICATING WITH YOUR PROFESSOR

Goal 6
Communicate with your professor

Your instructors are valuable resources, and you can learn a great deal from them through communication other than through formal in-class attendance. Here are some options:

1. **Office hours.** Most professors announce office hours—times when they will be in their office and available to students. You can use them to discuss your progress in the course, ask for help, or seek advice. Don't hesitate to use office hours; they are an opportunity to get to know your professor and make yourself known to him or her.
2. **E-mail.** Many professors give students an e-mail address at which to contact them. Some professors check their e-mail daily; others do so as little as once or twice a week. Until you are certain a professor checks his or her e-mail frequently, do not send time-sensitive information.
3. **Phone.** Be especially cautious with professors' phone numbers, and always call at appropriate times. It's all right to call an office number at 2 A.M., but not a home number.
4. **Instant messaging.** Most professors do not communicate with students over IM. If you have one that does, treat his or her screen name like a home phone number; scrub your profile and other shared information.

TECH SUPPORT

Tips for Communicating by E-mail

- Use a more formal level of communication for professors than you would use for friends and family. Do not be overly friendly or familiar.
- Use correct grammar, spelling, and punctuation; avoid slang.
- Realize that some professors won't discuss grades or other personal information in e-mail.

Exercise 9

DIRECTIONS You are asked to make a three-minute oral presentation on how to study for a particular course you are taking this semester. Prepare a set of outline notes for your presentation, and practice delivery of your presentation. Then answer the following questions:

1. How did you organize your presentation?

2. Did preparation of your presentation force you to analyze how you learn in the course you chose?

3. How did you improve your presentation through practice? ●

USING COLLEGE TEXTBOOKS
Preparing for Class Discussions

Frequently instructors assign textbook readings that are intended to start you thinking about a topic, show you different points of view about an issue, or indicate some aspects of a problem. To prepare for a class discussion, make notes about the following, writing either in the margin of the text or on a separate sheet of paper or in a computer file:

- **Ideas, concepts, or points of view you do not understand.** Keep a list of these and use it as a guide to ask questions during class.
- **Ideas and points with which you disagree or strongly agree.** Making notes about these will give you some ideas to start with if your instructor asks you for a reaction to the reading.
- **Good and poor examples.** These will give you something concrete to point to when discussing your reactions to the reading.
- **Strong and weak arguments.** As you read, try to follow the line of reasoning, and evaluate any arguments presented. Make notes with your evaluations. These will remind you of points you may want to make during the discussion.

The following is an excerpt from a sociology textbook, along with sample marginal notes one student made in preparation for a class discussion.

Slaves in Tulsa

Could slavery still exist in the United States? According to Kevin Bales, the United States imports about *50,000 slaves* every year. In February 2002, the Midwestern city of Tulsa, Oklahoma, was shocked to learn that they had slaves working in their midst. Workers recruited by a Mumbai (formerly Bombay), India, company signed contracts for labor overseas. Many paid the company a fee of more than $2,000 to gain employment in the United States. Workers flew to Tulsa where they worked as welders for an industrial equipment manufacturer.

These workers left their country with a promise of long-term residency, good jobs, and high pay. What they found was significantly different. The group lived in barracks on the factory grounds, sometimes working 12-hour days and earning as little as $2.31 an hour. The company's food was substandard, and many workers had to share beds because of a shortage of space. In the dormitory, a sign stated that workers who left the grounds could be sent back to India and that armed guards patrolled the grounds. Many also reported verbal threats and deliberate intimidation to keep the workers on the property.

After the situation became public, many local community members helped the Indian workers find legitimate jobs, and immigration hearings allowed them to legally stay in the country. With new jobs, the workers now seek to make their American dream come true. This case has a happy ending, largely because it occurred in a country with a free press and a strong government. Unfortunately, most contract labor occurs in countries without either of these two important components.

Where are the rest of these slaves?

What is the definition of slaves? These people are not owned. How is this slavery? May be it is unlawful imprisonment instead.

Happy ending? What about their families? Were they allowed to come to the United States? What happened to workers who wanted to go back to their own country?

—adapted from Carl, *Think Sociology*, p. 143

FURTHER PRACTICE WITH TEXTBOOK READING
Part A: Sample Textbook Chapter

Read the section titled "Nonverbal Emotional Expression" in the sample textbook chapter on pages 494–96, and make notes to prepare for a class discussion on this section.

Part B: Your College Textbook

Choose an assignment given by one of your instructors and make notes on it as if you were preparing for a class discussion on the topic.

SELF-TEST
SUMMARY

Goal 1

Why is it important to listen critically in class?

Critical listening enables you to respond thoughtfully and participate meaningfully.

Goal 2

What strategies can be used to strengthen questioning and answering skills?

While reading an assignment, write down questions and bring the list to class. Be clear and concise. Ask serious questions, and think through your responses before volunteering them.

Goal 3

Why is participation in class discussions important and what strategies can improve your involvement in class discussions?

Participation improves concentration and focus. It gives you practice in speaking before groups. Try to say something early in the discussion. Be brief and concise, and avoid direct exchanges with individuals. Announce new topics, jot down ideas as the discussion is going on, and organize your remarks before speaking. Watch the group's responses as you speak.

Goal 4

For group activities, how can you help the group function most effectively?

Choose group members who are alert and energetic. Participate actively and responsibly and take a leadership role. Make the most of individual strengths and weaknesses.

Goal 5

How do you go about making an effective oral presentation?

Understand the purpose of the assignment. Research the topic thoroughly and prepare outline notes. Use visual aids if appropriate. Anticipate questions from the audience. Practice making the presentation, and deliver it as effectively as possible.

Goal 6

How can you communicate effectively with your professor?

Most professors hold office hours during which you can meet with them. Your professors are likely also available by e-mail or phone. Be sure to use a professional tone and call only at appropriate hours.

APPLYING YOUR SKILLS

DISCUSSING THE CHAPTER

1. Discuss what members of a class should or should not do when one class member continually dominates the class discussion or fills class time with unimportant questions.
2. Discuss what classmates could do to help a student who is afraid to make a required oral presentation.
3. Suppose you are a member of an assigned group that must prepare a group project and the group has chosen a topic that you are certain does not meet the instructor's requirements. What courses of action might you take?

ANALYZING A STUDY SITUATION

Martha is taking an interpersonal communication course in which the instructor allows students to select from a menu of activities that earn points that determine their final grade. Each student must choose at least three different activities. The activities include quizzes, final exams, oral reports, group projects, research papers, panel discussions, interviews with community leaders, and leading class discussions.

Because Martha is not confident about her writing skills and gets nervous when taking exams, she selected oral reports, group projects, and panel discussions. Martha is a shy, quiet, self-directed person. She is well organized and feels most comfortable when she knows exactly what to expect and is in control of details.

1. Evaluate her choice of activities.
2. What advice would you give her for how to be successful with each of her choices?

WORKING ON COLLABORATIVE PROJECTS

DIRECTIONS   Five or six class members should volunteer to participate in a panel discussion on a current controversial issue. The panel members should meet to plan their panel discussion while the rest of the class observes. The observers should critique the panel group's planning, efficiency, and interaction. Your instructor may "plant" problem panel members.

 For support in meeting this chapter's goals, go to **MyReadingLab** and select **Memorization and Concentration**.

Quick QUIZ

DIRECTIONS   Write the letter of the choice that best completes each statement in the space provided.

CHECKING YOUR RECALL

_____ 1. All of the following strategies can help you avoid obstacles to critical listening *except*

    a. keeping an open mind about a speaker or a topic.

    b. recognizing your own biases.

    c. practicing selective listening.

    d. observing the responses of the audience.

_____ 2. Preparing for and participating in class discussions allows you to do all of the following *except*

    a. avoid reading assigned material.

    b. practice speaking in front of groups.

    c. be better prepared for exams and quizzes.

    d. sort out what you know and what you need to study further.

_____ 3. The best way to prepare for a class discussion is to

    a. quickly skim through the reading assignment.

    b. talk to classmates about their views on the topic.

    c. focus on factual information about the topic.

    d. mark and highlight key ideas in the reading assignment.

_____ 4. In class discussions, you should use all of the following strategies *except*

    a. try to say something early in the discussion.

    b. try to involve other class members in direct exchanges.

    c. make your comments brief and to the point.

    d. watch the group's responses as you speak.

_____ 5. When you are preparing an oral presentation, your first step should be to

    a. understand the purpose of the assignment.

    b. decide on what kind of visual aid you will use.

    c. collect and organize your information.

    d. anticipate questions your audience may ask.

APPLYING YOUR SKILLS

_____ 6. Isaac is trying to improve his questioning and answering skills in class discussions. One strategy he should adopt is to

    a. wait until someone else in the class asks the question he is thinking of.

    b. answer a question only if he is positive his answer is correct.

    c. jot down questions as he is reading an assignment and bring the list to class.

    d. repeat a question that has already been asked.

_____ 7. Sydney will be participating regularly in online discussions for a health and nutrition class. She should plan to do all of the following *except*

    a. become familiar with the software before she posts messages.

    b. think through what she wants to say before she says it.

    c. avoid reading previous posts so she is not influenced by what others have said.

    d. indicate whether her comments are in response to an assignment or a lecture.

_____ 8. If your instructor asks the class to form small groups for a project, you can help your group function effectively by doing all of the following *except*

    a. taking a leadership role.

    b. selecting alert, energetic classmates for the group.

    c. joking with group members about the assignment to make it more fun.

    d. accepting your share of the work and expecting others to do the same.

_____ 9. Joanna is nervous about making an oral presentation for her sociology class. Her first step should be to

    a. practice her presentation aloud several times by herself.

    b. practice her presentation in front of her friends.

    c. practice by writing out the speech several times.

    d. practice answering possible questions about her presentation.

_____ 10. When you want to communicate with a professor outside of class, you should remember that

    a. most professors typically use IM to communicate with students.

    b. you can use your professor's office hours to ask for help in the course.

    c. e-mail is always best for sending your professors time-sensitive information.

    d. it is fine to use slang and other informal language in e-mails to professors.

SUCCESS
WORKSHOP

4 Read and Think Visually

Visuals are important in today's world, since Web sites, textbooks, television, and even academic journals contain more graphics than ever before. Visuals include graphics (such as charts, maps, and graphs) and photographs, as well as text that is made visually interesting by incorporating color, symbols, and design. You'll see visuals in every chapter of this book and explore them in detail in Chapter 13.

Analyzing . . .
The Importance of Visuals

Authors use visuals because they can convey a lot of information is a small space. Visuals are important for you because they are time savers, allowing you to understand main ideas, implied main ideas, and details very quickly. Because your brain stores visuals differently, they may be easier to retrieve, as well.

Examine the two sample textbook pages below. Which one would you rather read? List five things that are more appealing about the page you would rather read.

Example 1

which he defined as "the science of compelling men to use more and more things." Strauss felt that this was changing the nature of America by "bringing it about that the American citizen's first importance to his country is no longer that of citizen, but that of consumer."[34]

Vivre (www.vivre.com) offers a mail-order and online catalog aimed at "connecting luxury brands with affluent shoppers and providing material comfort for its customers." Consider a portion of how the company responds to the question "What is Vivre?" (taken from its Web site):

> One might consider Vivre to be a revival of the classic "first floor" of a department store, which traditionally displayed only the best of the best to a discriminating clientele. Likewise, Vivre presents only that which is deemed to be relevant, inspiring and exquisitely crafted. With a modern sensibility, the resulting treasure trove is delivered to doorsteps in the form of a glossy catalog . . . and to desktops via a full-service e-commerce website. Therein shoppers will find the best of the world at their fingertips.

> By presenting each season's collection in a lifestyle context, we create an emotional connection with our customers, who rely upon us to offer an edited collection of the very best of each season. By interspersing our selections with editorial and advice, we create an inspirational shopping experience—one where Vivre is considered to be a trusted advisor to "A Beautiful Life."[35]

Material comfort has often been associated with "bigger quantities of things" or "more of something." Recently, however, there has been a noticeable shift away from such a "more is better" viewpoint to a "better is better" vision—one that stresses better quality and better design. Americans today increasingly want *better*, and *better looking*, products. Such a state of affairs has been referred to as "the design economy"—that is, an economy that is based on the interaction of four elements: sustained prosperity, ongoing technology, a culture open to change, and marketing expertise.[36] Consider, for example, how the famous designer, Michael Graves, has helped Target (the mass-merchandise retailer) accomplish its goal of being a standout provider of finely designed products at mass-market prices.

INDIVIDUALISM

Americans value "being themselves." Self-reliance, self-interest, self-confidence, self-esteem, and self-fulfillment are all exceedingly popular expressions of *individualism*. Striving for individualism seems to be linked to the rejection of dependency; that is, it is better to rely on oneself than on others. Indeed, the opposite of *individualism* is *collectivism*, which implies that "being in a group is a basic human endeavor, so that self-concept involves group membership."[37]

American "rugged individualism" is a form of individualism. It is based on the notion of self-reliance with competition (i.e., we try to meet our needs through personal effort, and in a way that outperforms our peers). Still further, solo performance, to the rugged individualist, is more important than teamwork—tasks should be accomplished alone, and victory should be earned alone.[38] Table 11.4 presents an interesting elaboration of the concept of "rugged individualism."

In terms of consumer behavior, an appeal to individualism frequently takes the form of reinforcing the consumer's sense of identity with products or services that both reflect and emphasize that identity. For example, advertisements for high-style clothing and cosmetics usually promise that their products will enhance the consumer's exclusive or distinctive character and set him or her apart from others. Additionally, while the purchase of a well-known brand may reduce the perceived risk of the product not performing as expected (i.e., perceived performance risk), many consumers today exhibit enough self-confidence, optimism, and trust in their own ability to prefer modified or customized products, and are willing to pay a higher price for such goods.[39]

FREEDOM

Freedom is another very strong American value, with historical roots in such democratic ideals as freedom of speech, freedom of the press, and freedom of worship. As an outgrowth of these beliefs in freedom, Americans have a strong preference for *freedom of choice*, the opportunity to choose from a wide range of alternatives. This preference is reflected in the large number of competitive brands and product variations that can be found on the shelves of the modern supermarket or department store. For many products, consumers can select from a wide variety

Example 1

Example 2

Are You Really Listening?

Most of us have lamented the fact that someone "never listens" and seems to monopolize the entire conversation. Although we are quick to recognize such flaws in others, we are often less likely to spot listening problems of our own. What does it take to be an excellent listener? Try practicing the following skills and consciously using them on a daily basis:

❋ Be present in the moment. Good listeners participate and acknowledge what the other person is saying. Nodding, smiling, saying "yes" or "uh-huh," and asking questions at appropriate times all convey that you are attentive. Use positive body language and voice tone.
❋ Show empathy and sympathy. Watch for verbal and nonverbal clues to the other person's feelings and try to relate.
❋ Ask for clarification. If you aren't sure what the speaker means, indicate that you're not sure you understand, or paraphrase what you think you heard.
❋ Control that deadly desire to interrupt. Try taking a deep breath for 2 seconds, then hold your breath for another second and really listen to what is being said as you slowly exhale.
❋ Avoid snap judgments based on what other people look like or are saying.
❋ Resist the temptation to "set the other person straight."
❋ Try to focus on the speaker. Hold back the temptation to launch into your own rendition of a similar situation.
❋ Be tenacious. Stick with the speaker and try to stay on topic. If the person seems to wander, gently bring the topic back by saying, "You were just saying . . .".
❋ Offer your thoughts and suggestions, but remember that you should advise only up to a certain point. Clarify statements with "This is my opinion" as a reminder that it is only a viewpoint rather than a fact.

Becoming a Better Listener

Listening is a vital part of interpersonal communication; it allows us to share feelings, express concerns, communicate wants and needs, and let our thoughts and opinions be known. We must do the necessary work to improve both our speaking and listening skills, which will enhance our relationships, improve our grasp of information, and allow us to interpret more effectively what others say. We listen best when (1) we believe that the message is somehow important and relevant to us; (2) the speaker holds our attention through humor, dramatic effect, use of media, or other techniques; and (3)

nonverbal communication All unwritten and unspoken messages, both intentional and unintentional.

we are in the mood to listen (free of distractions and worries). When we really listen effectively, we try to understand what people are thinking and feeling from their perspective. We not only hear the words, but also try to understand what is really being said. How many times have you been caught pretending to listen when you were not? After several moments of nodding and saying, "Uh-huh," your friend finally asks you a question, and you haven't a clue what she has been saying. Sometimes this tuned-out behavior is due to lack of sleep, stress overload, being preoccupied, having had too much to drink, or being under the influence of drugs. Other times the reason is that the speaker is a motormouth who talks for the sake of talking, or that you find the speaker or topic of conversation boring. Some of the most common listening difficulties are things that we can work to improve. See the *Skills for Behavior Change* box at left for suggestions to improve your listening.

Using Nonverbal Communication

Understanding what someone is saying often involves much more than listening and speaking. Often, what is not actually said may speak louder than any words. Rolling the eyes, looking at the floor or ceiling rather than maintaining eye contact, making body movements and hand gestures—all these nonverbal clues influence the way we interpret messages. **Nonverbal communication** includes all unwritten and unspoken messages, both intentional and unintentional. Ideally, our nonverbal communication matches and

To what extent do people communicate without words?

Researchers have found that 93% of communication effectiveness is determined by nonverbal cues. Positive communication means using positive body language. Laughing, smiling, and gesturing all help convey meaning and assure your partner you are engaged.

(side tab) Skills for Behavior Change

Example 2

Discovering . . .

How Graphics Help You Learn

Look at the graphic below from a sociology textbook. Answer the following questions:

- What is the first thing you notice when you see this page?
- Without reading a single word in the graphic, what do you think this visual is going to be about?
- By looking at the graphic, what do you think this part of the textbook is about?
- Carefully examine the graphic. About how many facts do you think are contained in this graphic? Is it more effective to see all of this information in visual form than to read a long paragraph or textbook section listing all these facts? Why or why not?
- This graphic allows for comparison and contrast. Why is it more effective to see these comparisons and contrasts presented visually than to read about them?

The Gender Income Gap by Level of Education

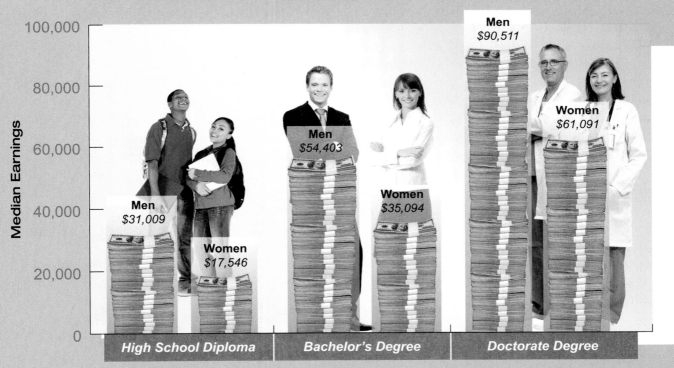

Carl, *Think: Sociology*, p. 197.

Changing . . .
How You Use Visuals

Because we live in such a visual society, it's important to learn how to get the most out of the visuals you are presented with. Examine them first before reading anything else. Look at them again after you have read the related textbook information.

Reflecting . . .

As you study your textbooks, ask yourself if you're paying attention to the visuals. Are you including information about them in your notes? Are you pulling out the main idea from each visual? Some visuals are easier to comprehend than others. Underlining and annotating will help you understand visuals more easily.

5 Manage Your Electronic Life

Why?

Technology is all around us. Computers, laptops, and tablets offer convenient ways of writing and revising, and give you access to all the information on the Internet. Cell phones, iPhones, and BlackBerries serve not only as communication devices but also as powerful, portable computers. Learning to make these fun tools work *for you* instead of *against you* is a challenge.

Discovering . . .

How Is Technology Affecting Your Ability to Concentrate?

Analyze the impact of technology on your daily life by answering the following questions.

EXAMINING DISTRACTIONS

Many electronic advances—such as text messages and social networking sites—are primarily forms of entertainment. Answer the following questions to get a sense of the type and number of distractions in your life and how they affect your ability to focus.

1. How many text messages do you send and receive per day? _____ How many of these are "important"? _____ Do you stop what you are doing to check your cell phone the second a text mesaage arrives? Have you ever "texted" while driving? _____

2. How many e-mails do you send and receive per day? _____ How many of these are valuable in terms of communicating important information? _____ How many are purely for entertainment or socializing? _____ How much time do you spend each day on e-mail unrelated to your college work or your job? _____

3. How many calls do you receive on your cell phone each day? _____ Do you leave your cell phone on all the time? _____ Do you answer it every time it rings, even when you're in class or studying? _____ Do you ever use your cell phone as a way to procrastinate? _____

4. How many hours a day do you spend surfing the Internet or posting on social networking sites like Facebook? _____ Does this socializing affect your studying, concentration, and grades? _____

Changing . . .
Making Technology Work for You

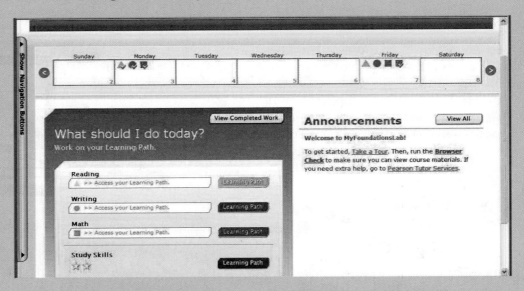

The benefits of technology are sometimes outweighed by the challenges. So how do you get rid of the *distractions* of technology and turn them to your advantage?

Cellphones. Turn off the ringer, vibrator, and text notifications while studying and attending class. Avoid the temptation to check for messages constantly. If you're writing at home, put the cell phone in a kitchen cupboard until you've finished your assignment. At school, leave it in your home, car, or dorm room while you visit the library.

E-mail. Set up two e-mail addresses: one for friends, another for "serious" matters. Communicate with classmates or teachers on the serious account. Check it occasionally during the day, because e-mails to this account can be valuable in terms of sharing ideas or important information. Check your "fun" e-mail only at night or during breaks.

Text Messages. In general, text messages are not effective for substantive communication. For most college students, text messages are almost purely social. Don't read or write text messages when you should be working on your writing assignments or during classes.

Apps. Many devices and phones offer applications, or "apps," that are helpful in your studies. You can download free (or inexpensive) dictionaries, encyclopedias, grammar guides, and a host of other apps that can help with your writing. Put these apps on your initial screen, and put your social apps (such as Facebook) on a later screen.

Webcams. In some classes, you will be expected to get together as a group to discuss topics or work together on projects. Programs like Skype make it easy for a group to "meet" when everyone is online at the same time. Leave your webcam off during all other study times.

Reflecting . . .
Does Limiting Social Technology Improve Your Work?

Commit to following the social media advice in this workshop for one week. At the end of the week assess your progress. Did you accomplish more and better quality work? Were you more focused in class? Did you get better grades on your assignments? Did you feel more in control of the technology in your life?

Remembering . . .
Take Charge

- Technology is a tool you use, not something that controls or directs your behavior.
- Create separate zones, school and social, to allow you to use technology more effectively.
- Reserve some time each day when you are technology free.

Active Reading Strategies

LEARNING GOALS

In this chapter you will learn to

1 Preview before you read

2 Discover what you already know about a topic

3 Define your purpose for reading

4 Check your comprehension

5 Strengthen your comprehension

LEARNING EXPERIMENT

1 In the space below, draw the front of a one-dollar bill.

2 Find a one-dollar bill and compare your drawing with it. Notice the features you did not include.

THE RESULT

Although hundreds of one-dollar bills have passed through your hands over the years, you probably did not recall very many features. Why? You did not recall these features because you did not plan to remember them. (No doubt you would have done better if the experiment directed you to study the face of a one-dollar bill for several minutes and then put it away and draw it.)

LEARNING PRINCIPLE: WHAT THIS MEANS TO YOU

We remember what we intend to remember. If you do not decide what you should remember before reading a textbook chapter, your recall is likely to be poor. On the other hand, if you decide what you need to know before you start, your recall will be much higher. This chapter will demonstrate several techniques that will help you decide what to learn in a textbook chapter. Specifically, you will learn to preview before reading, to discover what you already know about the topic, and to define your purposes for reading. You will also learn to monitor and strengthen your comprehension as you read.

WHY BECOME AN ACTIVE READER?

It is important to become an active reader because:

- Active reading stimulates your thinking.
- Active reading helps you get interested in and stay involved with what you read.
- It makes reading easier by providing you with a mental outline of the material.
- Active reading increases your recall.

myreadinglab

To practice using active learning skills, go to

> Active Reading Strategies

PREVIEWING AND PREDICTING

Do you check for traffic before crossing a street? Do you check the depth of a pool before diving in? What do you do with an article or chapter before you read it, before you "jump in"? In this section, you will become acquainted with the technique of previewing—a useful way of checking any written material before you read it. Just as most people check traffic before crossing a street or water depth before diving, to be an efficient reader you should check written materials before reading to become generally familiar with the overall content and organization.

Before reading, you should make predictions, or educated guesses, about the material. You might make predictions about how difficult or interesting the material will be, what topics will be discussed, or how the author will approach the subject. You might also anticipate how the material will be organized—how it progresses from one idea to another.

Goal 1

Preview before you read

How to Preview

Your overall purposes in previewing are to identify the most important ideas in the material and note their organization. You look only at specific parts and skip over the rest. The portions to look at in previewing a textbook chapter are described in the following box. Later you will learn how to adapt this procedure to other types of material.

PREVIEWING STEPS

1. **Read the title and subtitle.** The title provides the overall topic of the chapter; the subtitle suggests the specific focus, aspect, or approach toward the overall topic. Also note chapter objectives or chapter outlines, if provided.
2. **Read the introduction or first paragraph.** The introduction, or first paragraph if there is no introduction, serves as a lead-in to the chapter. It gives you an idea of where the material starts and where it is going.
3. **Read each major heading.** The headings function as labels or topic statements for what is contained in the sections that follow them. In other words, a heading announces the major topic of each section.
4. **Read the first sentence under each heading.** The first sentence frequently tells you what the passage is about or states the central thought. You should be aware, however, that in some types of material and in certain styles of writing, the first sentence does not function as a central thought. Instead,

(Continued)

the opening sentence may function as a transition or lead-in statement, or it may be designed to catch your interest. If the first sentence seems unimportant, read the last sentence; often this sentence states or restates the central thought.

5. **Note any typographical and graphical aids.** *Italic* (slanted) or **boldfaced** type is used to emphasize important terms and definitions by distinguishing them from the rest of the passage. Note any material that is numbered 1, 2, 3, lettered a, b, c, or presented in list form. Graphs, charts, pictures, and tables are other means of emphasis and usually signal something that is important in the chapter. Be sure to read the captions for pictures and the legends on graphs, charts, and tables. Also notice sidebars, marginal notes, boxed material, and annotations on figures and diagrams.

6. **Read the last paragraph or summary.** The summary or last paragraph gives a condensed view of the chapter and helps you identify key ideas. Often the summary outlines the key points in the chapter.

7. **Read quickly any end-of-chapter material.** This might include references, study questions, vocabulary lists, or biographical information about the author. These materials will be useful later as you read and study the article or chapter, and it is important, as part of your previewing, to note whether such materials are included. If there are study questions, it is useful to read them through quickly because they will indicate what is important in the chapter. If a vocabulary list is included, rapidly skim through it to identify terms you will need to learn as you read.

Demonstration of Previewing

The textbook chapter excerpt seen in Figure 6-1 below has been included to demonstrate what it is like to preview. This excerpt is taken from the textbook *Sociology*, by James M. Henslin. To illustrate how previewing is done, these pages have been specially marked. Everything that you should look at or read has been shaded. Preview this excerpt now, reading only the shaded portions of each page.

Figure 6-1
A Demonstration of Previewing

CREATING EFFECTIVE INSTANT MESSAGES

While e-mail is here to stay as a business medium, its disadvantages—including viruses, spam, and rampant overuse—are driving many people to explore alternatives. One of the most important of those alternatives is instant messaging (IM). For both routine communication and exchanges during online meetings, IM is now widely used throughout the business world and is beginning to replace e-mail for internal communication in many companies. Business-grade IM systems offer a range of capabilities, including basic chat, *presence awareness* (the ability to quickly see which people are at their desks and available to IM), remote display of documents, video capabilities, remote control of other computers, automated newsfeeds from blogs and websites, and the automated bot capabilities.

Figure 6-1
(*continued*)

Understanding the Benefits and Risks of Instant Messaging

The benefits of IM include its rapid response to urgent messages, lower cost than both phone calls and e-mail, ability to mimic conversation more closely than e-mail, and availability on a wide range of devices from PCs to mobile phones to PDAs. In addition, because it more closely mimics real conversation, IM doesn't get misused as a broadcast mechanism as often as e-mail does.

Of course, wherever technology goes, trouble seems to follow. The potential drawbacks of IM include security problems (both the risks of computer viruses and the worry that sensitive messages might be intercepted by outsiders), the need for *user authentication* (making sure that online correspondents are really who they appear to be), the challenge of logging messages for later review and archiving, and incompatibility between competing IM systems. Fortunately, with the growth of *enterprise instant messaging* (EIM), IM systems designed for large-scale corporate use, many of these problems are being overcome. Security remains an ongoing concern, however, with attacks on IM systems, both public and corporate, continuing to rise. A new breed of virus spread by bots is a particular concern. IM users who fall prey to these bots believe they are chatting with a trusted correspondent when in fact they are exchanging information with an automated bot that imitates human IM chat. The bot encourages the user to download a file or otherwise expose his or her computer to malicious software, then spreads the virus through the user's IM address book.

Adapting the Three-Step Process for Successful IM

Although instant messages are often conceived, written, and sent within a matter of seconds, the principles of the three-step process still apply:

- **Planning instant messages.** View every IM exchange as a conversation; while you may not deliberately plan every individual statement you make or question you pose, take a moment to plan the overall exchange. If you're requesting something, think through exactly what you need and the most effective way to ask for it. If someone is asking you for something, consider his or her needs and your ability to meet them before you respond. And although you rarely organize instant messages in the sense of creating an outline, try to deliver information in a coherent, complete way that minimizes the number of individual messages required.

- **Writing instant messages.** As with e-mail, the appropriate writing style for business IM is more formal than the style you may be accustomed to with personal IM or text messaging. In particular, you should generally avoid IM acronyms (such as "FWIW" for "for what it's worth" or "HTH" for "hope that helps") except when communicating with close colleagues. In the IM exchange in Figure A, notice how the participants communicate quickly and rather informally but still maintain good etiquette and a professional tone. This style is even more important if you or your staff use IM to communicate with customers and other outside audiences. In the coming years, business IM writing may become less formal, but for now, the best approach is to maintain a businesslike style and tone.

- **Completing instant messages.** One of the biggest attractions of IM is that the completing step is so easy. Once you've selected some basic font settings that apply to all your messages, you generally don't need to do anything in terms of producing each message, and distributing is as simple as clicking the Send button. However, don't skip over the revising and proofreading tasks. Take a second to scan each message before you send it to make sure you don't have any missing or misspelled words and that your message is clear and complete.

Figure 6-1
(*continued*)

To use IM effectively, all users need to pay attention to some important behavioral issues: the potential for constant interruptions, the ease of accidentally mixing personal and business messages, the risk of being out of the loop (if a hot discussion or impromptu meeting flares up when you're away from your PC or other IM device), and the "vast potential for wasted time" (in the words of MIT labor economist David Autor). On top of all that, users are at the mercy of other people's typing abilities, which can make IM agonizingly slow.

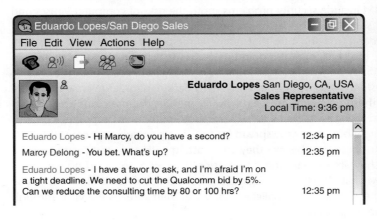

Eduardo Lopes/San Diego Sales

File   Edit   View   Actions   Help

Eduardo Lopes San Diego, CA, USA
Sales Representative
Local Time: 9:36 pm

Eduardo Lopes - Hi Marcy, do you have a second?	12:34 pm
Marcy Delong - You bet. What's up?	12:35 pm
Eduardo Lopes - I have a favor to ask, and I'm afraid I'm on a tight deadline. We need to cut the Qualcomm bid by 5%. Can we reduce the consulting time by 80 or 100 hrs?	12:35 pm

Figure A
Instant Messaging for Business Communication
Instant messaging is widely used in business, but it does not use the same informal style of communication you probably use to IM your friends and family.

Exercise 1

DIRECTIONS   Answer each of the following questions after you have previewed the reading titled "Creating Effective Instant Messages" in Figure 6-1 on pages 115–16. Do *not* read the entire selection. Mark *T* after statements that are true and *F* after those that are false. Do not look back in the reading to locate the answers. When you finish, check your answers in the answer key at the end of the chapter, page 135, and write your score in the space indicated.

1. The style of Instant Messaging (IM) used in business settings is the same as is used for friends and family.   _____

2. In the business world, IM is gradually replacing e-mail as a means of communication.   _____

3. One advantage of IM is lower cost than either e-mail or phone calls.   _____

4. There are no problems or trouble spots with the use of IM.   _____

5. There is no need to plan IMs before writing.   _____

Score (number right):   _____   ●

Look at your score on the quiz in Exercise 1. Probably you got at least half of the questions right, perhaps more. This quiz was a test of the main ideas that were presented in this excerpt. You can see, then, that previewing does familiarize you with the chapter and enables you to identify and remember many of the main ideas it contains. Actually, each part of the chapter that you read while previewing provided you with specific information about the organization and content of the chapter. The following exercise emphasizes how each step in the previewing process gives you useful information about the material to be read.

DIRECTIONS   Listed below are various parts of an actual textbook chapter or article to which you would refer in previewing. For each item, read the parts and then answer the question that follows.

1. *Sample text*

Section heading:	Culture and Technology
Subheadings:	Historical Roots and Trends
	Recent Technological Changes
	Predicted Long-Range Effects
Question:	What clues do you have about how the author arranged ideas in this section of the text?

_____

_____

_____

2. *Sample text*

Title:	*Diversity in Families*
Chapter title:	"The Social Construction of Intimacy"

Chapter introduction:

Intimacy, like other social relations, is shaped by our surroundings. Therefore, we cannot understand it in isolation from the rest of social life. This chapter is about intimate relationships and the ways in which they are embedded in social circumstances. Intimacy exists in relationships based on friendship, romantic love, and parenthood; it even exists among co-workers (Risman and Schwartz, 1989). Intimacy concerns both women and men, in homosexual as well as heterosexual relationships. Although intimacy need not include either sex or love, our focus is on relationships that encompass both.

In this chapter, we examine intimacy through a sociological lens. We begin by examining the changing historical and societal context giving rise to intimacy as it is defined today. We then look at patterns of courtship and mate selection by connecting them to historical developments. Turning to sexuality, we underscore the macro structural conditions that shape our most private behaviors. Here, we review the facts and trends pertaining to sex in contemporary U.S. society. We also consider some of the social connections between sexual practices and public health and policy issues. Finally, we turn our attention to the ways in which love and sex are patterned differently for various groups.

—Zinn and Eitzen, *Diversity in Families,* p. 205

Questions: a. List the topics the chapter will cover in the order in which you expect they will be covered.

_____

_____

_____

_____

_____

b. Which of the following will the chapter emphasize?

(1) how intimacy has changed over the past several decades

(2) that intimacy is affected by other aspects of social life

(3) the importance of intimacy in long-term relationships

(4) why courtship and mate selection depend on traditional values

3. *Sample text*

Title: *Conceptual Physical Science Explorations*

Subtitle:

Chapter title: "Fluid Mechanics"

Graphic aid: The chapter includes Figure 8.1

Density—A Measure of Compactness

An important property of materials is the measure of compactness: **density**. We think of density as the "lightness" or "heaviness" of materials of the same size. ✓ Density is a measure of how much mass occupies a given space, whether solid, liquid, or gas. Density is the amount of matter per unit volume:

$$\text{Density} = \frac{\text{mass}}{\text{volume}}$$

Question: How does the graphic help you understand the passage?

_____

_____

_____ •

FIGURE 8.1
When the volume of the bread is reduced, its density increases.

Previewing Specific Types of Material

Not all reading materials are organized in the same way, and not all reading materials have the same features or parts. Consequently, you must adjust the way you preview to the type of material you are working with. Figure 6-2 on next page offers suggestions on how to adapt the previewing method to suit what you are reading.

Why Previewing Works

Research studies suggest that previewing increases comprehension and improves recall. Several studies show that previewing is a useful technique for reading textbook chapters. Previewing is effective for several reasons.

1. **It helps you get interested in and involved with what you will read.** It activates your thinking. Because you know what to expect, reading the material completely is easier.

2. **It provides you with a mental outline of the material you are going to read.** You begin to anticipate the sequence of ideas; you see the relationships among topics; you recognize what approach and direction the author has taken in writing about the subject.

3. **It lets you apply several principles of learning.** You identify what is important, thus establishing an intent to remember.

4. **It functions as a type of rehearsal that enhances recall because it provides repetition of the most important points.**

Previewing is used best with factual material that is fairly well organized. Knowing this, you can see that previewing is not a good strategy to use when reading materials such as novels, poems, narrative articles, essays, or short stories.

TYPE OF MATERIAL	SPECIAL FEATURES TO CONSIDER
Textbooks	Title and subtitle Preface Table of contents Appendix Glossary
Textbook chapters	Summary Vocabulary list Review and discussion questions
Articles and essays	Title Introductory paragraphs Concluding paragraphs (see Chapter 8)
Research reports	Abstract
Articles without headings	First sentences of paragraphs
Tests and exams	Instructions and directions Number of items Types of questions Point distribution
Reference sources	Table of contents Index
Newspapers	Headline First few sentences Section headings

Figure 6-2
How to Adjust Previewing to the Material

Tip An *abstract* is a short written statement of the most important ideas in a piece of writing. Here, the word is a noun. Check your dictionary for different meanings of this word as a noun, adjective, and verb.

DIRECTIONS   Select a chapter from one of your textbooks. To be practical, choose a chapter that you will be assigned to read in the near future. After previewing it, answer the following questions.

Exercise 3

1. What is the major topic of the chapter?

   _____

2. How does the author subdivide, or break down, this topic?

   _____

3. What approach does the author take toward the subject? (Does he or she cite research, give examples, describe problems, list causes?)

   _____

4. Construct a brief outline of the chapter.

   _____

TECH SUPPORT

Previewing Online Sources

Previewing online sources is different from previewing written sources and is even more important to do, since online sources vary widely in content, format, and reliability (also see Chapter 13). Use the following tips:

- Get a sense of the layout of the page.
- Take note of advertisements and delete them, if possible.
- Locate the search box.
- Discover how to navigate through the site. Look for tabs, buttons, or links.
- Check to see whether the site has "Contact" and "About Us" tabs.

Making Predictions

Do you predict what a film will be about and whether seeing it will be worthwhile on the basis of a coming attractions preview? Do you anticipate what a party will be like before attending? This type of prediction or anticipation is typical and occurs automatically. Do you predict what a chapter will discuss before you read it?

Research studies of good and poor readers demonstrate that efficient readers frequently predict and anticipate the contents and organization of the material, both before reading and while they read. For example, from the title of a textbook chapter, you can predict the subject and, often, how the author will approach it. A business management textbook chapter titled "Schools of Management Thought: Art or Science?" indicates the subject—schools of management—but also suggests that the author will classify the various schools as artistic (creative) or scientific. Similarly, author, source, headings, graphics, photographs, chapter previews, and summaries, all of which you may check during previewing, provide additional information for anticipating content.

Making predictions is a way to expand and broaden your thinking beyond the Remembering and Understanding levels. Predicting is an opportunity for you to apply your knowledge to new situations (Applying), to examine how ideas fit together (Analyzing), and to put ideas together in unique ways (Creating). For a review of the Levels of Thinking, see Figure 2-3 on page 42.

Efficient readers frequently make predictions about organization as well as content. That is, they anticipate the order or manner in which ideas or information will be presented. For instance, from a chapter section title "The History of World Population Growth," you can predict that the chapter will be organized chronologically, moving ahead in time as the chapter progresses. A chapter titled "Behavioral vs. Situational Approaches to Leadership" suggests that the chapter will compare and contrast the two approaches to leadership.

As efficient readers read, they also confirm, reject, or revise their initial predictions. For example, a student who read the heading "Types of Managers" anticipated that the section would describe different management styles. Then he began reading:

Types of Managers

Now that you have an idea of what the management process is, consider the roles of managers themselves. It is possible to classify managers by the nature of the position they hold. This section will review some of the major categories of managers. The next section will identify how these differences affect a manager's job.

The student immediately revised his prediction, realizing that managers would be classified not by style but by the position they hold. Making predictions and anticipating content and organization are worthwhile because they focus your attention on the material. Further, the process of confirming, rejecting, or revising predictions is an active one—it helps you to concentrate and to understand. Once you know what to expect in a piece of reading, you will find it easier to read.

Exercise 4

DIRECTIONS Following are listed a textbook title, chapter title, and chapter headings. Place a check mark in front of the statements you predict will appear in the chapter. If possible, also indicate the section in which each statement is most likely to appear. (Indicate by marking 1, 2, 3, 4, or 5 to correspond to the headings.)

Textbook title: *America's Problems: Social Issues and Public Policy*
Chapter: "The Family"
Heading 1: Some Trends in Family Disruption
Heading 2: The Consequences of Family Disruption
Heading 3: Inequality in the Family: Division of Labor in the Home
Heading 4: Work, Family, and Social Supports
Heading 5: The Family as a Crucible of Violence
Statements:

_____ A. Divorce creates social and personal stress for both children and parents.

_____ B. Sex-role stereotypes dictate how much males contribute to housekeeping chores.

_____ C. Street crime takes an enormous toll on citizens and only rarely results in prosecution by the courts.

_____ D. Child and spouse abuse is aggravated by poverty and gender inequality.

_____ E. The continued concentration of minorities in lowpaying jobs is a reflection of inequality.

_____ F. Lack of day care for single-parent families creates insurmountable problems.

_____ G. Changing health care policies have reduced public responsibilities for family health care maintenance. ●

Exercise 5

DIRECTIONS Preview the textbook excerpt titled "Blogs and Democratization," in Part Five, page 474. Then make a list of topics you predict it will cover. Next, read the selection. Then review your list of predictions and place a check mark next to those that were correct. ●

Exercise 6

DIRECTIONS Select a chapter from one of your textbooks. Preview the chapter, and then write a list of predictions about the chapter's content or organization. ●

Goal 2

Discover what you already know about a topic

DISCOVERING WHAT YOU ALREADY KNOW

Discovering what you already know about a topic will make learning easier because you will be connecting new information to familiar information already in place. You will find, too, that reading material becomes more interesting once you have connected its topic with your own experience. Comprehension will be easier because you will have already thought about some of the ideas presented in the material.

Suppose you are studying a business textbook and are about to begin reading a chapter on advertising that discusses the objectives of advertising, the construction and design of ads, and the production of ads. Before you begin reading the chapter, you should spend a minute or two recalling what you already know about these topics. Try one or more of the following techniques.

1. **Ask questions and try to answer them.** You might ask questions such as "What are the goals of advertising?" In answering this question, you will realize you already know several objectives: to sell a product, to introduce a new product, to announce sales or discounts, and so on.
2. **Relate the topic to your own experience.** For a topic on the construction and design of ads, think about ads you have heard or read recently. What similarities exist? How do the ads begin? How do they end? This process will probably lead you to realize that you already know something about how ads are designed.
3. **Free-associate.** On a sheet of scrap paper, jot down everything that comes to mind about advertising. List facts and questions, or describe ads you have recently heard or seen. This process will also activate your recall of information.

At first, you may think you know very little—or even nothing—about a particular topic. However, by using one of the foregoing techniques, you will be surprised to find that there are very few topics about which you know nothing at all. For example, suppose you were about to read a biology chapter on genetics. At first you might think you know nothing about it. Complete Exercise 7 to discover what you do know about genetics.

Exercise 7

DIRECTIONS   For a chapter in a biology textbook titled "Medicine's Cutting Edge" write a list of questions, experiences, or associations that would help focus your mind on the topic. (Hint: Think of reasons, regulation, needs, processes, and so forth.) ●

Exercise 8

DIRECTIONS   In Exercise 5 you previewed the textbook excerpt titled "Blogs and Democratization." Discover what you already know about blogs using one of the techniques described in this section. ●

Exercise 9

DIRECTIONS   Select a chapter from one of your textbooks. Preview it, and use one of the techniques described in this section to discover what you already know about the subject of the chapter. ●

Goal 3

Define your purpose for reading

DEFINING YOUR PURPOSES FOR READING

Have you ever read a complete page or more and then not remembered a thing? Have you wandered aimlessly through paragraph after paragraph, section after section, unable to remember key ideas you have just read, even when you were really trying to concentrate? If these problems sound familiar, you probably began reading without a specific purpose in mind. That is, you were not looking for anything in particular as you read. Guide questions can focus your attention and help you pick out what is important.

Developing Guide Questions

Most textbook chapters use boldfaced headings to organize chapter content. The simplest way to establish a purpose for reading is to convert each heading into one or more questions that will guide your reading. These are called **guide questions**. As you read, you then look for the answers. For a section with the heading "The Hidden Welfare System," you could ask the questions "What is the hidden welfare system?" and "How does it work?" As you read that section, you would actively search for answers. For a section of a business textbook titled "Taxonomy of Organizational Research Strategies," you could pose such questions as "What is a taxonomy?" and "What research strategies are discussed and how are they used?"

DIRECTIONS   The excerpt that follows is taken from a nutrition textbook chapter on digestion. Before reading it, use the heading to formulate a guide question and list it here. Then read the passage to find the answer, and fill it in after your questions.

Question 1: _____

Answer: _____ •

Exercise 10

The Esophagus Propels Food into the Stomach

Once swallowed, a mass of food (a bolus) is pushed down your esophagus by the process of peristalsis (Figure A). The esophagus narrows at the bottom (just

Figure A

Blake, Nutrition and You: Core Concepts for Good Health, pp. 6–5

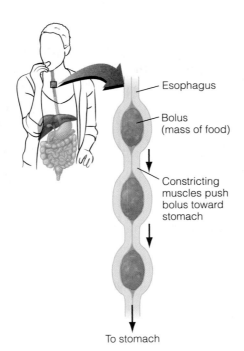

Esophagus

Bolus (mass of food)

Constricting muscles push bolus toward stomach

To stomach

Visual Thinking
ANALYZING IMAGES

How does this diagram help you understand the passage?

How could you use this diagram to study?

above the stomach) and ends at a sphincter, a circular muscle, called the *lower esophageal sphincter (LES)*. Under normal conditions, when you swallow food, the LES relaxes and allows the food to pass into the stomach, The stomach also relaxes to receive the food. After food enters the stomach, the LES should close. If it doesn't, hydrochloric acid from the stomach may flow back into the esophagus and irritate its lining. This is called *heartburn* because it causes a burning sensation in the middle of the chest. Chronic heartburn and the reflux of stomach acids are symptoms of gastroe sophageal reflux disease (GERD), which will be discussed later in this concept.

Did the guide question help you focus your attention and make the excerpt easier to read?

You may find it helpful to jot down your guide questions in the margins of your texts, next to the appropriate headings. These questions are then available for later study. Rereading and answering your questions is an excellent method of review.

Formulating the Right Guide Questions

Guide questions that begin with *What*, *Why*, and *How* are especially effective. *Who*, *When*, and *Where* questions are less useful, because they can often be answered through superficial reading or may lead to simple, factual, or one-word answers. *What*, *Why*, and *How* questions require detailed answers that demand more thought, so they force you to read in greater depth.

For example, "The Fall of the Roman Empire," the title of a section in a history text, could be turned into a question such as "When did the Roman Empire fall?" For this question, the answer is merely a date. This question, then, would not guide your reading effectively. On the other hand, questions such as "How did the Roman Empire fall?" and "What brought about the fall of the Roman Empire?" and "What factors contributed to the fall of the Roman Empire?" would require you to recall important events and identify causes.

Here are a few examples of effective guide questions:

Heading	Effective Guide Questions
Management of Stress in Organizations	What types of stress occur? How is stress controlled?
Theories of Leadership	What are the theories of leadership? How are they applied or used?
Styles of Leader Behavior	What are the styles of leader behavior? How do they differ? How effective are they?

Exercise 11

DIRECTIONS   Assume that each of the following is a boldfaced heading within a textbook chapter and that related textual material follows. In the space provided, write questions that would guide your reading.

1. **Operating System Aids to Efficient Merging of Computer Files**

   _____

   _____

2. **Natural Immunity and Blood Types**

   _____

   _____

3. **Production of Electromagnetic Waves**

   _____

   _____

4. **Physical Changes in Adolescence**

   _____

   _____

5. **Sociological Factors Related to Delinquency**

   _____

   _____ ●

Written Materials Without Headings

In articles and essays without headings, the title often provides the overall purpose, and the first sentence of each paragraph can often be used to form a guide question about each paragraph. In the following paragraph, the first sentence could be turned into a question that would guide your reading.

> Despite its recent increase in popularity, hypnotism has serious limitations that restrict its widespread use. First of all, not everyone is susceptible to hypnotism. Second, a person who does not cooperate with the hypnotist is unlikely to fall into a hypnotic trance. Finally, there are limits to the commands a subject will obey when hypnotized. In many cases, subjects will not do anything that violates their moral code.

From the first sentence you could form the question "What are the limitations of hypnotism?" In reading the remainder of the paragraph, you would easily find its three limitations.

Exercise 12

DIRECTIONS   Assume that each of the following sentences is the first sentence of a paragraph within an article that does not contain boldfaced headings. For each sentence, write a guide question.

1. Historically, there have been three branches of philosophical analysis.

   _____

   _____

2. Scientists who are studying earthquakes attribute them to intense pressures and stresses that build up inside the earth.

   _____

   _____

3. The way in which managers and employees view and treat conflict has changed measurably over the last 50 years.

_____

_____

4. Perhaps it will be easier to understand the nature and function of empathetic listening if we contrast it with deliberative listening.

_____

_____

5. In addition to the price of a good or service, there are dozens, perhaps hundreds, of other factors and circumstances that affect a person's decision to buy or not buy.

_____

_____ •

WHY GUIDE QUESTIONS WORK   A number of research studies have been conducted to test whether defining purposes for reading by forming guide questions improves understanding and recall of information. These studies confirm the effectiveness of guide questions and indicate that students who read with a purpose have a higher percentage of recall of factual information than students who read without a specific purpose.

Developing Connection Questions

Connection questions are those that require you to think about content. They force you to draw together ideas and to discover relationships between the material at hand and other material in the same chapter, in other chapters, or in class lectures. Here are a few examples:

- What does this topic have to do with topics discussed earlier in the chapter?
- How is this reading assignment related to the topics of this week's class lectures?
- What does this chapter have to do with the chapter assigned last week?
- What principle do these problems illustrate?

Connection questions enable you to determine whether your learning is meaningful—whether you are simply taking in information or are using the information and fitting it into the scheme of the course. The best times to ask connection questions are before beginning and after you have finished a chapter or each major section.

Exercise 13

DIRECTIONS   Turn to the Reading "Blogs and Democratization" in Part Five on page 474. Read the excerpt and form questions that would be useful in guiding your reading (see Exercise 17, page 129). •

Exercise 14

DIRECTIONS   Choose a three- to four-page selection from one of your textbooks. Select pages that have already been assigned or that you anticipate will be assigned. For each heading, form and record guide questions that establish a purpose for reading. Then read the selection and answer your questions. •

CHECKING YOUR COMPREHENSION

For many daily activities, you maintain an awareness, or check, of how well you are performing them. In sports such as racquetball, tennis, or bowling, you know if you are playing a poor game; you actually keep score and deliberately try to correct errors and improve your performance. When preparing a favorite food, you often taste it as you cook to be sure it will turn out as you want. When washing your car, you check to be sure that you have not missed any spots.

A similar type of monitoring or checking should occur as you read. You need to keep score of how well you understand. Comprehension, however, is difficult to assess, because it is not always either good or poor. You may understand certain ideas you read and be confused by others. At times, comprehension may be incomplete—you may miss certain key ideas and not know you missed them.

Recognizing Comprehension Signals

Think for a moment about what occurs when you read material you can understand easily, and then compare this with what happens when you read complicated material that is difficult to understand. When you read certain material, does it seem that everything clicks—that is, do ideas seem to fit together and make sense? Is that click noticeably absent at other times?

Read each of the following paragraphs. As you read, be alert to your level of understanding of each.

Paragraph 1

Marriages around the world are either monogamous or polygamous. In Western cultures, marriages are assumed to be **monogamous**—one person is married to another person and the relationship remains exclusive. In some parts of the world, **polygamous** marriages are the accepted form, in which one person is married to multiple husbands or wives. Polygamy is legally practiced in many parts of the world, including the Middle East, South America, Asia, and some parts of Africa. Polygamy is illegal in the United States, although it is still practiced in some states.

—Kunz, *THINK Marriages and Families*, p. 5

Paragraph 2

A pogonophoran lives within an upright tube of chitin and protein that it secretes around itself, with from one to many thousand tentacle-like branchiae protruding from the upper end of the tube. The branchiae are the "beard" of beard worms. Without their tubes many beard worms would look like threads that are badly frayed at one end. The branchiae are often called tentacles, but they absorb gases and are not used to capture solid food. In their typical cylindrical arrangement the branchiae resemble an intestine, complete with microvilli that increase the surface area.

—Harris, *Concepts in Zoology*, p. 573

Did you feel comfortable and confident as you read paragraph 1? Did ideas seem to lead from one to another and make sense? How did you feel while reading paragraph 2? Most likely you sensed its difficulty and felt confused. Unfamiliar words were used and you could not follow the flow of ideas, so the whole passage didn't make sense.

As you read paragraph 2, did you know that you were not understanding it? Did you feel confused or uncertain? Figure 6-3 on p. 128 lists and compares common signals that may help you assess your comprehension. Not all signals appear at the same time, and not all signals work for everyone. As you study

Figure 6-3
Comprehension
Signals

POSITIVE SIGNALS	NEGATIVE SIGNALS
Everything seems to fit and make sense; ideas flow logically from one to another.	Some pieces do not seem to belong; the material seems disjointed.
You understand what is important.	Nothing or everything seems important.
You are able to see where the author is leading.	You feel as if you are struggling to stay with the author and are unable to predict what will follow.
You are able to make connections among ideas.	You are unable to detect relationships; the organization is not apparent.
You read at a regular, comfortable pace.	You often slow down or reread.
You understand why the material was assigned.	You do not know why the material was assigned and cannot explain why it is important.
You can express the main ideas in your own words.	You must reread often and find it hard to paraphrase the author's ideas.
You recognize most words or can figure them out from the context.	Many words are unfamiliar.
You feel comfortable and have some knowledge about the topic.	The topic is unfamiliar, yet the author assumes you understand it.

the list, identify those positive signals you sensed as you read paragraph 1 on groups. Then identify the negative signals you sensed when reading paragraph 2 about pogonophorans.

Exercise 15

DIRECTIONS   For "Blogs and Democratization," which you read in Exercise 13, answer the following questions.

1. How would you rate your overall comprehension? What positive signals did you sense? Did you feel any negative signals? Did you encounter unfamiliar vocabulary?

2. Did you feel at any time that you had lost, or were about to lose, comprehension? If so, go back to that section now. What made that section difficult to read?

3. Do you think previewing and writing guide questions strengthened your comprehension? If so, how? ●

Exercise 16

DIRECTIONS   Select a three- to four-page section of a chapter in one of your textbooks. Read the section, and then answer questions 1 and 3 in Exercise 15. ●

Evaluating Your Comprehension

At times, signals of poor comprehension do not come through clearly or strongly enough. In fact, some students think they have understood what they read until they are questioned in class or take an exam. Only then do they discover that their comprehension was incomplete. Other students find that they understand material on a surface, factual level but that they do not recognize more complicated relationships and implied meanings or do not see implications and applications. Use the following process to determine whether you really understand what you read.

1. **Set checkpoints.** As you preview a textbook assignment, identify reasonable or logical checkpoints: points at which to stop, check, and (if necessary) correct your performance before continuing. Pencil a check mark in the margin to designate these points. These checkpoints should be logical breaking points where one topic ends and another begins or where a topic is broken down into several subtopics.

2. **Use your guide questions.** Earlier in this chapter, you learned how to form guide questions by using boldfaced headings. These same questions can be used to monitor your comprehension while reading. When you finish a boldface-headed section or reach a checkpoint, stop and take a moment to recall your guide question and answer it mentally or on paper. Your ability to answer your questions will indicate your level of comprehension.

3. **Ask connection questions.** To be certain that your understanding is complete and that you are not recalling only superficial factual information, ask connection questions.

4. **Use internal dialogue.** Internal dialogue—mentally talking to yourself—is another excellent means of monitoring your reading and learning. It involves rephrasing to yourself the message the author is communicating or the ideas you are studying. If you are unable to express ideas in your own words, your understanding is probably incomplete. Here are a few examples of the use of internal dialogue.

   • While reading a section in a math textbook, you mentally outline the steps to follow in solving a sample problem.
   • You are reading an essay that argues convincingly that the threat of nuclear war is real. As you finish reading each stage of the argument, you rephrase it in your own words.
   • As you finish each section in a psychology chapter, you summarize the key points.

DIRECTIONS   Read "Blogs and Democratization" in Part Five on page 474. Answer the guide questions you wrote in Exercise 13, page 126. ●   **| Exercise 17**

DIRECTIONS   Choose a section from one of your textbooks. Read it, and then check your understanding by using both guide questions and connection questions. List your questions on a separate sheet of paper. ●   **| Exercise 18**

DIRECTIONS   Select another section from one of your textbooks, and experiment with the technique of internal dialogue to assess your comprehension. In the space provided here, describe the technique you used and say whether or not it worked.   **| Exercise 19**

_____

_____

_____

_____ ●

Goal 5

Strengthen your
comprehension

STRENGTHENING YOUR COMPREHENSION

You have learned how to recognize clues that signal strong or weak understanding of reading material and how to assess your comprehension. This section offers some suggestions to follow when you realize you need to strengthen your comprehension.

1. **Analyze the time and place in which you are reading.** If you've been reading or studying for several hours, mental fatigue may be the source of the problem. If you are reading in a place with distractions or interruptions, you may not be able to understand what you're reading. (See the Success Workshop on page 320 for suggestions on how to monitor and improve your concentration.)
2. **Rephrase each paragraph in your own words.** You might need to approach complicated material sentence by sentence, expressing each in your own words.
3. **Read aloud sentences or sections that are particularly difficult.** Reading out loud sometimes makes complicated material easier to understand.
4. **Reread difficult or complicated sections.** At times, several readings, in fact, are appropriate and necessary.
5. **Slow down your reading rate.** On occasion, simply reading more slowly and carefully will provide you with the needed boost in comprehension.
6. **Write guide questions next to headings.** Refer to your questions frequently and jot down or underline answers.
7. **Write a brief outline of major points.** This will help you see the overall organization and progression of ideas. (See Chapter 16 for specific outlining techniques.)
8. **Highlight key ideas.** After you've read a section, go back and think about and highlight what is important. Highlighting forces you to sort out what is important, and this sorting process builds comprehension and recall. (Refer to Chapter 15 for suggestions on how to highlight effectively.)
9. **Write notes in the margins.** Explain or rephrase difficult or complicated ideas or sections.
10. **Determine whether you lack background knowledge.** Comprehension is difficult—at times, it is impossible—if you lack essential information that the writer assumes you have. Suppose you are reading a section of a political science text in which the author describes implications of the balance of power in the Third World. If you do not understand the concept of balance of power, your comprehension will break down. When you lack background information, take immediate steps to correct the problem:

    • Consult other sections of your text, using the glossary and index.
    • Obtain a more basic text that reviews fundamental principles and concepts.
    • Consult reference materials (encyclopedias, subject dictionaries, or biographical dictionaries).
    • Ask your instructor to recommend additional sources, guidebooks, or review texts.

Exercise 20

DIRECTIONS   The following three paragraphs have been chosen because they are difficult. Assess your comprehension as you read each, paying attention to both positive and negative signals (Figure 6-3, p. 128). After you have read each paragraph, list the signals you received, and indicate what you could do to strengthen your comprehension.

Paragraph 1

The extension of civil rights was not initiated by government act; civil rights were won through a long and bitter struggle of people determined to seize the citizenship that was their birthright. Deprived of political and business opportunities for a century, bright young black men and women turned to the black church to express their hopes, energies, and aspirations. This was particularly true in the segregated South. But during the 1950s the accumulation of change began to wear the edges of racial separation thin. When a young scholar, Martin Luther King, Jr., returned from Boston University to take up the ministry at Dexter Avenue Baptist Church in 1954 in Montgomery, Alabama, he had no hint that a nationwide civil rights movement would soon swirl around him or that his name would be linked with the great march on Washington of 1963 that would help open the floodgates of integration. What made King one of the most famous Americans of his day was the energy of a suppressed American culture, which he articulated into a momentous political and moral awakening. Its successes were his; its failures revealed his limitations and exposed the deepest barriers to equality in American life.

—Wilson et al., *The Pursuit of Liberty*, p. 422

Positive signals: _____

Negative signals: _____

Strengthen comprehension by: _____

Paragraph 2

In intermediary pricing, cost-plus pricing is the dominant mode among intermediaries in the marketing channel, wholesalers and retailers, where it is called *markup pricing*. These marketers deal with large assortments of products and do not have the resources to develop demand schedules for each item. Channel members' prices are not totally unrelated to demand; they do assign different percentage markups to different items based upon sales experience and estimates of consumer price sensitivity. Wholesalers and retailers will quickly lower prices if an item is not selling. Also, the intermediary's price is based upon a markup on manufacturer's selling price, or discount from manufacturer's suggested retail price. The manufacturer may have researched demand and conducted a competitive analysis before setting the price and discount schedules.

—Kinnear, Bernhardt, and Krentler, *Principles of Marketing*, p. 637

Positive signals: _____

Negative signals: _____

Strengthen comprehension by: _____

Paragraph 3

As noted previously, one of the main motivations for zoologists to study development is that it provides insights regarding taxonomic relationships among groups of animals. In the early 19th century the Estonian biologist Karl Ernst von Baer made a number of observations that suggest such a relationship, although he explicitly rejected any evolutionary implications. What is known as von Baer's law states that embryonic development in vertebrates goes from general forms common to all vertebrates to increasingly specialized forms characteristic of classes, orders, and lower taxonomic levels. Thus the early embryos of all vertebrates, whether fish, frog, hog, or human, all look alike. Later it is possible to tell the human embryo from the fish but not from the hog, and still later one can see a difference between these two mammals.

—Harris, *Concepts in Zoology*, p. 130

Positive signals: _____

Negative signals: _____

Strengthen comprehension by: _____ ●

Exercise 21

DIRECTIONS   Select three brief sections from your most difficult textbook. Choose three of the suggestions for strengthening your comprehension, and list them here. Try out each suggestion on one textbook section. Evaluate and describe the effectiveness of each.

Suggestion   **Evaluation**

1. _____   _____

2. _____   _____

3. _____   _____ •

USING COLLEGE TEXTBOOKS
Reading Difficult Textbooks

College textbooks vary in their levels of difficulty. As you advance in your studies in a particular field, you will likely encounter more difficult texts with more details and complicated concepts. Expressing the ideas of a difficult paragraph in your own words is a particularly useful strategy when dealing with difficult text. If you cannot express the main point of a paragraph in your own words, most likely you do not fully understand it.

The following excerpt shows how one student wrote a marginal summary of a particularly difficult concept from her consumer behavior textbook. Because the example makes the concept clear, as is often the case if one is provided, notice that the student bracketed the example.

Resolving Two Conflicting Attitudes

Attitude-change strategies
A way to help consumers understand that a negative attitude they have about a product may not be in conflict with another attitude, resulting in them thinking about the product more positively.

Attitude-change strategies can sometimes resolve actual or potential conflict between two attitudes. Specifically, if consumers can be made to see that their negative attitude toward a product, a specific brand, or its attributes is really not in conflict with another attitude, they may be induced to change their evaluation of the brand (i.e., moving from negative to positive). For example, Richard is an amateur photographer who has been thinking of moving from his point-and-shoot digital camera to a digital single lens reflex (DSLR) camera in order to take better pictures and to be able to change lenses. However, with the recent improvements in point-and-shoot cameras, Richard is unsure of whether his move to a DSLR camera will be worthwhile. Richard loves the idea of having the ability to change lenses (attitude 1), but he may feel that purchasing a DSLR camera is an unwise investment because these cameras may be supplanted in the near future by newer types of cameras (attitude 2). However, if Richard learns that Olympus and Panasonic are developing a "micro four-thirds format" small point-and-shoot size cameras that will offer interchangeable lenses, he might change his mind and thereby resolve his conflicting attitudes.

—Schiffman, *Consumer Behavior*, p. 246

FURTHER PRACTICE WITH TEXTBOOK READING

Part A: Sample Textbook Chapter

1. Preview the entire sample textbook chapter, pages 489–502. Predict what topics you expect to be covered in the chapter.
2. Use one of the strategies on page 122 to discover what you already know about the topics covered in the chapter.
3. Write at least five guide questions that would be useful in reading the chapter.
4. Read the section titled "Cognition and Emotion." Evaluate your comprehension, using the positive and negative signals on page 128.
5. Write marginal summaries of difficult ideas.

Part B: Your College Textbook

Choose a section from one of your most difficult textbooks. Read the section using the directions listed in Part A above.

SELF-TEST SUMMARY

Goal 1
What is previewing and how do you do it?

Previewing is a technique that allows you to become familiar with the material to be read before beginning to read it completely. Previewing makes the actual reading of the material easier and helps you understand and remember what you read. In previewing, you should note items such as the title and subtitle, the author and source, the introduction or first paragraph, each major heading and the first sentence under it, typographical aids (italics, maps, pictures, charts, graphs), the summary or last paragraph, and any end-of-chapter or end-of-article materials. Efficient readers make predictions about what they already know about the subject with the clues they pick up during previewing; they also continually revise and modify these predictions as they read.

Goal 2
Why is it valuable to discover what you already know before reading?

Discovering what you already know about a topic before you read will increase your comprehension. Three methods of discovery are questioning, relating to previous experience, and free association.

Goal 3
How can you define your purpose for reading?

Before reading, establish a purpose by developing guide questions built from boldfaced headings and from first sentences of articles or essays without headings. Ask *What*, *Why*, and *How* questions.

Goal 4 How can you keep track of comprehension while reading?	Keep track of both positive and negative signals by using these four techniques: establishing checkpoints, using guide questions, asking connection questions, and using internal dialogue.
Goal 5 How can you strengthen your comprehension?	Strengthen your comprehension by analyzing time and place, rephrasing, reading aloud, rereading, slowing down, writing guide questions, outlining, highlighting, writing marginal notes, and assessing background knowledge.

APPLYING **YOUR SKILLS**

DISCUSSING THE CHAPTER

1. How well does previewing work for you? If it does not work well, troubleshoot the problem with another student.
2. How do you know when you don't understand what you read? What strategies do you use to improve your understanding?
3. Among the strategies given for improving your comprehension, which seem most helpful? Why? Do you think the strategies should vary from course to course? If so, how?
4. What features do your textbooks offer to help you understand what you read? Which features are most helpful? Why?

ANALYZING A STUDY SITUATION

Malcolm's reading assignment this week for his sociology class consists of a newspaper article, a journal article that does not contain a summary, an essay, and a short story. The class is studying the changing structure of the family during the twentieth century.

1. Describe how Malcolm should preview the newspaper article. What should he be looking for?
2. Describe how Malcolm should preview the journal article.
3. What should Malcolm pay attention to in previewing the essay?
4. The short story was written in 1941 by an American writer. A short story is an unusual assignment in a sociology class. Realizing this, how should Malcolm preview it? What predictions can he make about the story? What should he be looking for as he reads it?
5. Which assignment is most likely to present comprehension problems?
6. How should Malcolm evaluate his comprehension for each?

WORKING ON COLLABORATIVE PROJECTS

DIRECTIONS   Choose another student with whom to work. Each student should select, from one of his or her textbooks, a chapter that he or she has already read. The students should exchange textbooks, and each should preview the selected chapter. The textbook owner should quiz the textbook previewer about what he or she learned from the chapter by previewing. Then the previewer should make predictions about chapter content and organization. Finally, the owner should confirm or deny each prediction.

For support in meeting this chapter's goals, go to **MyReadingLab** and select **Active Reading Strategies**.

Answer Key for Exercise 1
1. F   2. T   3. T   4. F   5. F

Quick **QUIZ**

DIRECTIONS   Write the letter of the choice that best completes each statement in the space provided.

CHECKING YOUR RECALL

_____ 1. The overall topic of a chapter is typically provided in the

a. title.
b. first paragraph.
c. summary.
d. references.

_____ 2. The first sentence under each boldfaced heading in a chapter typically

a. gives the author's qualifications.
b. tells what the section is about.
c. explains how the author will approach the topic.
d. announces the author's purpose for writing.

_____ 3. The primary purpose of free association while reading is to

a. establish your purpose for reading.
b. distinguish between important and unimportant information.
c. discover what you already know about the topic.
d. outline your beliefs about the topic.

_____ 4. The most useful type of guide questions begin with the word

a. *who.*
b. *when.*
c. *where.*
d. *why.*

_____ 5. Making predictions encourages you to do all of the following *except*

a. apply your knowledge to new situations.
b. examine how ideas fit together.
c. put ideas together in new ways.
d. memorize facts provided by the text.

APPLYING YOUR SKILLS

_____ 6. Lauren uses previewing a chapter to help her identify the most important ideas in the material. In previewing, Lauren

a. memorizes the important facts.
b. reads the introduction, each major heading, and the summary.
c. takes notes on the important points in the chapter.
d. reads the entire selection carefully.

_____ 7. For her British literature course this semester, Rima is required to read a novel, several poems, three short stories, and selected chapters from a textbook. Of these assignments, the most useful one for Rima to preview would be the

a. novel.
b. poems.
c. short stories.
d. textbook chapters.

_____ 8. Cory is trying to assess her comprehension of a chapter she has been reading in an anthropology textbook. One positive signal she should look for is whether

a. everything in the chapter seems important.
b. she often has to slow down or reread.
c. the vocabulary is unfamiliar.
d. she can paraphrase the author's ideas.

_____ 9. Antonio is evaluating his comprehension of a history text. To determine whether he really understands what he has read, Antonio should

a. read the entire chapter before stopping to assess his level of understanding.
b. answer guide questions and ask connection questions.
c. avoid mentally talking to himself in order to keep himself focused on the reading.
d. skip over information that seems difficult or boring.

_____ 10. Caleb has realized that he needs to strengthen his reading comprehension in his economics class. Caleb should do all of the following *except*

a. copy word for word sections of the text that are difficult to understand.
b. consult additional sources if he finds he does not have sufficient background knowledge.
c. rephrase each paragraph in his own words.
d. read in a quiet place at a time when he has the energy to concentrate.

Understanding Paragraphs

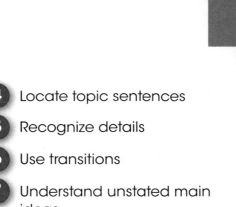

LEARNING GOALS

In this chapter you will learn to

1 Identify the essential elements of a paragraph

2 Identify the topic of a paragraph

3 Identify the main idea of a paragraph

4 Locate topic sentences

5 Recognize details

6 Use transitions

7 Understand unstated main ideas

LEARNING EXPERIMENT

1 Study list 1 below for a maximum of 15 seconds.

List 1	List 2	List 3	List 4
KQZ	BLT	WIN	DID
NLR	FBI	SIT	THE
XOJ	SOS	LIE	CAT
BTK	CBS	SAW	RUN
YSW	NFL	NOT	OFF

2 Now, cover list 1 with your hand or a piece of scrap paper and write down, in the space provided for list 1, as many items as you can remember.

List 1	List 2	List 3	List 4
____	____	____	____
____	____	____	____
____	____	____	____
____	____	____	____
____	____	____	____

3 Follow steps 1 and 2 for each of the other three lists.

4 Check to see how many items you had correct on each of the four lists.

THE RESULTS

Did you recall more items on list 2 than on list 1? Why? Did you remember more items on list 4 than on list 3? As you must now realize, after list 1, each list is more meaningful than the one before it. These lists progress from nonsense collections of letters to meaningful letter groups to words and, finally, to words that, when strung together, produce further meaning.

LEARNING PRINCIPLE: WHAT THIS MEANS TO YOU

You are able to remember information that is meaningful more easily than information that has no meaning. Once you understand how paragraphs are organized, they will become more meaningful and their contents easier to remember. In this chapter you will learn the three essential parts of a paragraph and how they work together to create meaning.

WHY STUDY PARAGRAPHS?

Paragraphs are the building blocks of textbooks and essays. Studying paragraphs has the following benefits:

- You will be able to identify the main point of each paragraph you read.
- You will learn to sort the more important details from those less important in paragraphs in your reading assignments.
- You will see how the ideas in each paragraph fit together.
- You will improve your own writing with more effective paragraphs.

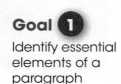

Goal 1

Identify essential elements of a paragraph

THREE ESSENTIAL ELEMENTS OF A PARAGRAPH

A **paragraph** can be defined as a group of related sentences about a single topic. This chapter focuses on knowledge and comprehension of paragraph structure. It will help you understand and remember what you read. It will also help you write paragraphs more effectively. Once you know how a paragraph is structured, you will be able to apply your knowledge to paragraph writing. Look for these three essential elements:

1. **Topic**   The one thing a paragraph is about. It is the unifying factor, and every sentence and idea contained in the paragraph is related to the topic.
2. **Main idea**   What the author wants to communicate about the topic. This is the central or most important thought in the paragraph. Every other sentence and idea in the paragraph is related to the main idea. The sentence that expresses this idea is called the **topic sentence**.
3. **Details**   The proof, support, explanation, reasons, or examples that explain the paragraph's main idea.

Each of the following examples contains a group of sentences, but only one has the three essential elements that make it a paragraph. Identify the paragraph.

1. Cats frequently become aggressive when provoked. Some plants require more light than others as a result of coloration of their foliage. Some buildings, because of poor construction, waste a tremendous amount of energy.
2. Some plants require more light than others as a result of coloration of their foliage. Some plants will live a long time without watering. Plants are being used as decorator items in stores and office buildings.
3. Some plants require more light than others as a result of coloration of their foliage. Plants with shades of white, yellow, or pink in their leaves need more light than plants with completely green foliage. For example, a Swedish ivy plant with completely green leaves requires less light per day than a variegated Swedish ivy that contains shades of white, yellow, and green in its leaves.

In the first example, the sentences were unrelated; each sentence was about a different thing, and there was no connection among them.

In the second example, each sentence was about plants—the common topic; however, the sentences together did not prove, explain, or support any particular idea about plants.

In the third example, each sentence was about plants, and all the sentences were about one main idea: that some plants need more light than others because of the coloration of their leaves. Thus, the third example is a paragraph: it has a topic—plants; a main idea—that plants require varying degrees of light due to coloration; and supporting details—the example of the Swedish ivy. The first sentence of the paragraph functions as a topic sentence.

In order to understand a paragraph, a reader must be able to identify the topic, main idea, and details. In the following paragraph, each of these parts is identified.

Topic sentence ⎡ As societies become industrialized, the distribution of workers among various economic activities tends to change in a pre-dictable way. In the early stages, the population is engaged in agriculture and the collection of raw materials for food and shelter. But as technology develops, agricultural workers are drawn into manufacturing and construction.

Topic: distribution of workers

Details

TECH SUPPORT

Paragraphs in Online Writing

Paragraphs are a way of organizing related thoughts and concepts. A well-organized paragraph helps readers under-stand a writer's main points. Online writing (such as e-mails, Web pages, e-portfolios, etc.) also requires paragraphs to include a topic, main idea, and details. However, research has shown that very long paragraphs are not as comfortable to read online as briefer paragraphs. When commu-nicating online, be sure that your text is clear and comfortable to read. Don't let paragraphs get too long. Consider changing font sizes or adding an additional line break between paragraphs to assist your reader.

This chapter will help you to identify these essential elements of the para-graph and read paragraphs more easily. Although the emphasis is on reading paragraphs, you will find this information useful in your own writing as well. Just as a reader must identify these elements, so must a writer structure his or her paragraphs by using these elements.

HOW TO IDENTIFY THE TOPIC

Goal 2
Identify the topic of a paragraph

The **topic** of a paragraph is the subject of the whole paragraph. It is the one thing that the whole paragraph is about. Usually, the topic of a paragraph can be expressed in two or three words. To find the topic of a paragraph, ask yourself this question: What is the one thing the author is discussing throughout the paragraph? Read the following example:

> For years, the loyal Dalmatian has been the trusted companion of firefighters. Few realize that this breed was originally chosen because of the strong bonds that the dogs formed with fire horses, protecting them and keeping them company at the station. The dogs were also expected to rouse the horses at the sound of the alarm bell, then run out and bark a warning at anyone who might be obstructing the fire house exit. The dogs would then chase the fire apparatus all the way to the scene, sometimes barking the whole way. They served the same function, essentially, as the emergency traffic signals located outside many fire stations today and the sirens on fire trucks. When horses were replaced by steam- or gasoline-driven fire engines,

many departments opted to keep their beloved mascots. It is not unusual even today to see a proud Dalmatian riding on a fire engine as it races to the scene of an emergency.

—Loyd and Richardson, *Fire and Emergency Services*, p. 12

In the example, the author is discussing one topic—Dalmation dogs—throughout the paragraph. Notice how many times the word *dogs* is repeated in the paragraph. Frequently, the repeated use of a word can serve as a clue to the topic of a paragraph.

Exercise 1

DIRECTIONS   Read each of the following paragraphs and then select the topic of the paragraph from the choices given.

1. Slavery has taken a number of different forms. War captives and their descendants formed a class of slaves in some societies; in others, slaves were a commodity that could be bought and sold. The rights granted to a slave varied, too. In ancient Greece, a slave could marry a free person, but in the stratified society of the southern United States before the Civil War, slaves were not allowed even to marry each other because they were not permitted to engage in legal contracts. Still, slaves in the South often lived together as husband and wife throughout their adult lives, forming nuclear families that remained tightly knit until they were separated at the auction block.

—Hicks and Gwynne, *Cultural Anthropology*, p. 270

     a. rights of slaves
     b. slavery in Greece
     c. forms of slavery
     d. slavery in the southern United States

2. Earth's magnetic field is known to have reversed polarity many times in our planet's history. The *geographic* North and South Poles have of course remained in place, but the *magnetic* north and south poles have changed polarity continually. Marine geophysicists interpreted the magnetic seafloor patterns as indicating that the rock either solidified during a time when Earth's magnetic field was like it is today (a "positive" value) or solidified at another time, when the field was reversed (a "negative" value). In a way, the formation of these magnetic patterns in rocks is similar to a tape recording: the changes in Earth's magnetic field are the signal, which is being recorded on two very slowly moving "tapes" that spread in opposite directions from the ridge.

—Ross, *Introduction to Oceanography*, p. 48

     a. polarity of the Earth's magnetic field
     b. patterns of rocks on the seafloor
     c. geographic poles of the Earth
     d. work carried out by marine geophysicists

3. By law, businesses cannot discriminate against people in any facet of the employment relationship. For example, a company cannot refuse to hire someone because of ethnicity or pay someone a lower salary than someone else on the basis of gender. A company that provides its employees with equal opportunities without regard to race, sex, or other irrelevant factors is meeting both its legal and its social responsibilities. Firms that ignore these responsibilities risk losing good employees and leave themselves open lawsuits.

     a. employment relationships
     b. employment discrimination
     c. employer ethics
     d. employee rights

4. Why is Buffalo, New York, so much snowier than frigid Winnipeg, Manitoba? Why is Miami, Florida, hot and humid while Tucson, Arizona, is hot and dry? Why does much of India experience monsoons? Why is the daily high temperature in tropical Pacific islands always near 80°F? The answers to all of these questions require an understanding of *climate*, the average weather of a place as measured over many years. The climate of a place includes various measures such as average temperature, average rainfall, and the average number of severe weather events in a given time period such as a month or a year. Climate should be distinguished from *weather*, which can be thought of as the current conditions in terms of temperature, cloud cover, and *precipitation* (rain or snowfall). Put another way, the weather in a place will tell you if you have to shovel snow tomorrow morning, while the climate in a place will tell you if you even need to own a snow shovel.

—Belk and Borden, *Biology: Science for Life,* pp. 392–393

   a. climate
   b. weather
   c. precipitation
   d. temperature

5. In today's technocentric world, cell phones, BlackBerries, computers, and other electronic goods quickly become outdated. However, while a cell phone might be outdated for you, it could be a lifeline for a family in need of protective services or an emergency 911 call. Before you donate your e-goods for general e-recycling, consider donating them to a violence prevention agency—it's an ecofriendly way to contribute to the safety of your community. Cell phones are particularly needed for domestic violence shelters and family violence prevention shelters around the nation. Check your regional and local violence prevention agencies to determine if and when they accept recycled cell phones.

—Donatelle, *Health,* p. 109

   a. donation of cell phones
   b. e-recycling
   c. domestic violence shelters
   d. speed of outdating in technology ●

DIRECTIONS   For each of the following paragraphs, read the paragraph and write the topic in the space provided. Be sure to limit the topic to a few words.

Exercise 2

1. Energy conservation in the short run and long run will require creative solutions in all areas of business. A few innovative solutions have already surfaced which indicate that business understands the importance of saving energy. The makers of Maxwell House coffee developed a method to save natural gas. The first step in making instant coffee is to brew the coffee just as people do at home, except in 1000-gallon containers. The heat to brew the coffee had come from burning natural gas, and the process left Maxwell House with tons of coffee grounds. The company then had to use trucks (that burned gasoline) to cart the coffee grounds away. Maxwell House realized it could save most of the cost of the natural gas (and the gasoline cost) by burning the grounds to get the heat to brew subsequent batches of coffee. Natural gas is now used only to start the coffee grounds burning.

—Kinnear, Bernhardt, and Krentler, *Principles of Marketing,* pp. 79–81

Topic: _____

2. The characteristic of speed is universally associated with computers. Power is a derivative of speed as well as of other factors such as memory size. What makes a computer fast? Or, more to the point, what makes one computer faster than

another? Several factors are involved, including microprocessor speed, bus line size, and the availability of cache. A user who is concerned about speed will want to address all of these. More sophisticated approaches to speed include flash memory, RISC computers, and parallel processing.

—Capron, *Computers*, p. 82

Topic: _____

3. A graduate student from the Medill School of Journalism at Northwestern University, Laura McGann, broke the story. The U.S. Department of Education had provided information from hundreds of student financial aid applications to the FBI, including Social Security and driver's license numbers. The data-mining operation, called "Project Strike Back," had begun just after the September 11 attacks as part of antiterror investigations. McGann had discovered her story in a reference to Project Strike Back in a document from the Government Accountability Office. She then filed a Freedom of Information Act request, and received heavily censored documents that allowed her to complete the research.

—Folkerts et al., *The Media in Your Life*, p. 257

Topic: _____

4. Earth is sometimes called the *blue* planet. Water more than anything else makes Earth unique. The **hydrosphere** is a dynamic mass of liquid that is continually on the move, evaporating from the oceans to the atmosphere, precipitating back to the land, and running back to the ocean again. The global ocean is certainly the most prominent feature of the hydrosphere, blanketing nearly 71 percent of Earth's surface to an average depth of about 3800 meters (12,500 feet). It accounts for about 97 percent of Earth's water. However, the hydrosphere also includes the freshwater found underground and in streams, lakes, and glaciers.

—Lutgens, Tarbuck, and Tasa, *Essentials of Geology*, p. 13

Topic: _____

5. Let's now deal with the fact that the human eye contains two distinctly different photoreceptor cells. Both rods and cones exist in our retinas, but they are not there in equal numbers. In one eye, there are approximately 120 million rods, but only 6 million cones; rods outnumber cones approximately 20 to 1. Not only are rods and cones found in unequal numbers, but they are not evenly distributed throughout the retina. Cones are concentrated in the center of the retina, at the fovea. Rods are concentrated in a band or ring surrounding the fovea, out toward the periphery of the retina. These observations have led psychologists to wonder if the rods and cones of our eyes have different functions.

—Gerow, *Essentials of Psychology*, p. 138

Topic: _____

6. Democracy is a means of selecting policymakers and of organizing government so that policy reflects citizens' preferences. Today, the term *democracy* takes its place among terms like *freedom, justice,* and *peace* as a word that seemingly has only positive connotations. Yet the writers of the U.S. Constitution had no fondness for democracy, as many of them doubted the ability of ordinary Americans to make informed judgments about what government should do. Roger Sherman, a delegate to the Constitutional Convention, said the people "should have as little to do as may be with the government." Only much later did Americans come to cherish democracy and believe that all citizens should actively participate in choosing their leaders.

—Edwards, Wattenberg, and Lineberry, *Government in America*, p. 16

Topic: _____

7. When a group is too large for an effective discussion or when its members are not well informed on the topic, a panel of individuals may be selected to discuss the topic for the benefit of others, who then become an audience. Members of a panel may be particularly well informed on the subject or may represent divergent views. For example, your group may be interested in UFOs (unidentified flying objects) and hold a discussion for your classmates. Or your group might tackle the problems of tenants and landlords. Whatever your topic, the audience should learn the basic issues from your discussion.

—Gronbeck et al., *Principles of Speech Communication*, p. 302

Topic: _____

8. It seems obvious that power inequality affects the quality of people's lives. The rich and powerful live better than the poor and powerless. Similarly, power inequality affects the quality of *deviant* activities likely to be engaged in by people. Thus the powerful are more likely to perpetrate profitable crimes, such as corporate crime, while the powerless are more likely to commit unprofitable crimes, such as homicide and assault. In other words, power—or lack of it—largely determines the type of crime people are likely to commit.

—Thio, *Sociology*, p. 181

Topic: _____

9. Automated radio has made large gains, as station managers try to reduce expenses by eliminating some of their on-the-air personnel. These stations broadcast packaged taped programs obtained from syndicates, hour after hour, or material delivered by satellite from a central program source. The closely timed tapes contain music and commercials, along with the necessary voice introductions and bridges. They have spaces into which a staff engineer can slip local recorded commercials. By eliminating disc jockeys in this manner, a station keeps its costs down but loses the personal touch and becomes a broadcasting automaton. For example, one leading syndicator, Satellite Music Network, provides more than 625 stations with their choice of seven different 24-hour music formats that include news and live disc jockeys playing records.

—Agee, Ault, and Emery, *Introduction to Mass Communications*, p. 225

Topic: _____

10. Bone is one of the hardest materials in the body and, although relatively light in weight, it has a remarkable ability to resist tension and other forces acting on it. Nature has given us an extremely strong and exceptionally simple (almost crude), supporting system without giving up mobility. The calcium salts deposited in the matrix give bone its hardness, whereas the organic parts (especially the collagen fibers) provide for bone's flexibility and great tensile strength.

—Marieb, *Essentials of Human Anatomy and Physiology*, p. 119

Topic: _____ •

HOW TO FIND THE MAIN IDEA

Goal

Identify the main idea of a paragraph

The main idea of a paragraph tells you what the author wants you to know about the topic. The main idea is usually directly stated by the writer in one or more sentences within the paragraph. The sentence that states this main idea is called the **topic sentence**. The topic sentence tells what the

inding the
go to
Idea

rest of the paragraph is about. In some paragraphs, the main idea is not directly stated in any one sentence. Instead, it is left to the reader to infer, or reason out.

To find the main idea of a paragraph, first decide what the topic of the paragraph is. Then ask yourself these questions: What is the main idea—what is the author trying to say about the topic? Which sentence states the main idea? Read the following paragraph:

> The Federal Trade Commission has become increasingly interested in false and misleading packaging. Complaints have been filed against many food packagers because they make boxes unnecessarily large to give a false impression of quantity. Cosmetics manufacturers have been accused of using false bottoms in packaging to make a small amount of their product appear to be much more.

In the preceding paragraph, the topic is false packaging. The main idea is that the Federal Trade Commission is becoming increasingly concerned about false or misleading packaging. The author states the main idea in the first sentence, so it is the topic sentence.

Goal 4

Locate topic sentences

WHERE TO FIND THE TOPIC SENTENCE

Although the topic sentence of a paragraph can be located anywhere in the paragraph, there are several positions where it is most likely to be found. Each type of paragraph has been diagrammed to help you visualize how it is structured.

First Sentence

The most common position of the topic sentence is first in the paragraph. In this type of paragraph, the author states the main idea at the beginning of the paragraph and then elaborates on it.

> The good listener, in order to achieve the purpose of acquiring information, is careful to follow specific steps to achieve accurate understanding. First, whenever possible, the good listener prepares in advance for the speech or lecture he or she is going to attend. He or she studies the topic to be discussed and finds out about the speaker and his or her beliefs. Second, on arriving at the place where the speech is to be given, he or she chooses a seat where seeing, hearing, and remaining alert are easy. Finally, when the speech is over, an effective listener reviews what was said and reacts to and evaluates the ideas expressed.

Usually, in this type of paragraph, the author is employing a deductive thought pattern in which a statement is made at the beginning and then supported throughout the paragraph.

Last Sentence

The second most common position of the topic sentence is last in the paragraph. In this type of paragraph, the author leads or builds up to the main idea and then states it in a sentence at the very end.

> Whenever possible, the good listener prepares in advance for the speech or lecture he or she plans to attend. He or she studies the topic to be discussed and finds out about the speaker and his or her beliefs. On arriving at the place where the speech is to be given, he or she chooses a seat where seeing, hearing, and remaining

alert are easy. And when the speech is over, he or she reviews what was said and reacts to and evaluates the ideas expressed. Thus, an effective listener, in order to achieve the purpose of acquiring information, takes specific steps to achieve accurate understanding.

The thought pattern frequently used in this type of paragraph is inductive. That is, the author provides supporting evidence for the main idea first and then states it.

Middle of the Paragraph

Another common position of the topic sentence is in the middle of the paragraph. In this case, the author builds up to the main idea, states it in the middle of the paragraph, and then goes on with further elaboration and detail.

> Whenever possible, the good listener prepares in advance for the speech or lecture he or she plans to attend. He or she studies the topic to be discussed and finds out about the speaker and his or her beliefs. An effective listener, then, takes specific steps to achieve accurate understanding of the lecture. Furthermore, on arriving at the place where the speech is to be given, he or she chooses a seat where it is easy to see, hear, and remain alert. Finally, when the speech is over, the effective listener reviews what was said and reacts to and evaluates the ideas expressed.

First and Last Sentences

Sometimes an author uses two sentences to state the main idea or states the main idea twice in one paragraph. Usually, in this type of paragraph, the writer states the main idea at the beginning of the paragraph, then explains or supports the idea, and finally restates the main idea at the very end.

> The good listener, in order to achieve the purpose of acquiring information, is careful to follow specific steps to achieve accurate understanding. First, whenever possible, the good listener prepares in advance for the speech or lecture he or she is going to attend. He or she studies the topic to be discussed and finds out about the speaker and his or her beliefs. Second, on arriving at the place where the speech is to be given, he or she chooses a seat where seeing, hearing, and remaining alert are easy. Finally, when the speech is over, he or she reviews what was said and reacts to and evaluates the ideas expressed. Effective listening is an active process in which a listener deliberately takes certain actions to ensure that accurate communication has occurred.

DIRECTIONS Read each of the following paragraphs and highlight the topic sentence.

Exercise 3

1. First, language consists of a large number of *symbols*. The symbols that make up a language are commonly referred to as *words*. They are the labels that we have assigned to the mental representation of our experiences. When we use the word *chair* as a symbol, we don't use it to label any one specific instance of a *chair*. We use it to represent our concept of what a chair is. Note that, as symbols, words do not have to stand for real things in the real world. With language, we can communicate about owls and pussycats in teacups; four-dimensional, time-warped hyperspace; and a cartoon beagle that flies his doghouse into battle against the Red Baron. Words are used to stand for our cognitions, our concepts, and we have a great number of them.

—Gerow, *Essentials of Psychology*, p. 289

2. Neanderthals first appeared in the European fossil record about 150,000 years ago. Contrary to the popular image of a hulking, stoop-shouldered "caveman," Neanderthals were quite similar to modern humans in many ways. Although more heavily muscled, Neanderthals walked fully erect, were dexterous enough to manufacture finely crafted stone tools, and had brains that, on average, were slightly larger than those of modern humans. Many European Neanderthal fossils show heavy brow ridges and a broad, flat skull, but others, particularly from areas around the eastern shores of the Mediterranean Sea, are somewhat more physically similar to *H. sapiens.*

—Audesirk, *Biology,* p. 337

3. Employers want proof that you have the skills to succeed on the job, but even if you don't have much relevant work experience, you can use your college classes to assemble that proof. Simply create and maintain an **employment portfolio,** which is a collection of projects that demonstrate your skills and knowledge. You can create both a *print portfolio* and an *e-portfolio;* both can help with your career effort. A print portfolio gives you something tangible to bring to interviews, and it lets you collect project results that might not be easy to show online, such as a handsomely bound report. An e-portfolio is a multimedia presentation of your skills and experiences. Think of it as a website that contains your résumé, work samples, letters of recommendation, articles you may have written, and other information about you and your skills.

—Thill and Bovée, *Excellence in Business Communication,* p. xxxiv

4. Potatoes that have been exposed to light and turned green, contain increased amounts of solanine, a toxin that can cause fever, diarrhea, paralysis, and shock. (Luckily, peeling potatoes usually removes the green layer and the potato can be safely eaten. If it tastes bitter, however, throw it out.) Wild lima beans contain high amounts of cyanogenic glycosides, which can be converted to the poison, cyanide. (Lima beans sold commercially have minimal amounts of this substance, so are safe to eat.) Cassava also contains cyanogenic glycosides and has been known to cause cyanide poisoning in people who eat large amounts of this root vegetable. Raw soybeans contain amylase inhibitors, which are inactivated when cooked or fermented. Thus, many plant foods naturally contain toxins in small amounts, so though they're generally safe to eat, consuming them in very large amounts could be harmful.

—adapted from Blake, *Nutrition and You,* p. 513

5. Nonverbal signals play three important roles in communication. The first is complementing verbal language. Nonverbal signals can strengthen a verbal message (when nonverbal signals match words), weaken a verbal message (when nonverbal signals don't match words), or replace words entirely. The second role for nonverbal signals is revealing truth. People find it much harder to deceive with nonverbal signals. You might tell a client that the project is coming along nicely, but your forced smile and nervous glances send a different message. In fact, nonverbal communication often conveys more to listeners than the words you speak—particularly when they're trying to decide how you really feel about a situation or when they're trying to judge your credibility and aptitude for leadership. The third role for nonverbal signals is conveying information efficiently. Nonverbal signals can convey both nuance and rich amounts of information in a single instant.

—Bovée and Thill, *Business Communication Today,* p. 54

6. The rate of cooling of an object depends on how much hotter the object is than the surroundings. The temperature change per minute of a hot apple pie will be

more if the hot pie is put in a cold freezer than if put on the kitchen table. When the pie cools in the freezer, the temperature difference between it and its surroundings is greater. A warm home will leak heat to the cold outside at a greater rate when there is a large difference in the inside and outside temperatures. Keeping the inside of your home at a high temperature on a cold day is more costly than keeping it at a lower temperature. If you keep the temperature difference small, the rate of cooling will be correspondingly low.

—Hewitt, *Conceptual Physics*, p. 279

7. The pawnshop industry has been in decline in most parts of the world. In Great Britain in 1900 there were 3,000 pawnshops; in the 1990s there are fewer than 150. In the United States, however, the pawnshop business actually grew during the same time period, from under 2,000 to more than 7,000 today. Pawnshops in this country currently make about 40 million loans a year with an aggregate dollar amount over $1 billion. Most of these pawnshops are in the Southeast and Rocky Mountain areas. One of the reasons for the growth of pawnshops is that many states have relaxed their restrictions (called *usury laws*) on the maximum interest rates that can be charged. Pawnshops in these states can now legally charge the high rates needed to stay in business. Further, the percentage of U.S. citizens classified as low-income has risen in recent decades. These individuals cannot get loans from mainstream financial institutions, such as banks and savings and loan associations, and so must turn to alternatives, one of which is the pawnshop.

—Miller, *Economics Today*, p. 213

> **Tip** A *pawnshop* is a shop that lends money to customers and in exchange holds some valuable personal property of theirs; unredeemed items may later be sold.

8. Because faces are so visible and so sensitive, you pay more attention to people's faces than to any other nonverbal feature. The face is an efficient and high-speed means of conveying meaning. Gestures, posture, and larger body movements require some time to change in response to a changing stimulus, whereas facial expressions can change instantly, sometimes even at a rate imperceptible to the human eye. As an instantaneous response mechanism, it is *the* most effective way to provide feedback to an ongoing message. This is the process of using the face as a regulator.

—Weaver, *Understanding Interpersonal Communication*, p. 220

9. As a result of casual dressing, the men's wear industry has changed. Men's suit sales have decreased, whereas sportswear has enjoyed tremendous growth. In the past, suits represented half of men's wardrobe purchases; now purchases are divided equally among suits, furnishings and accessories, and sportswear. As tailored clothing becomes more casual, the category distinctions become blurred. There is an intermixing of business and leisure wardrobes, such as an Armani suit jacket over jeans.

—Frings, *Fashion*, p. 80

10. During photosynthesis in green plants, as the energy of sunlight falls on the green pigment in the leaves, carbon dioxide and the hydrogens of water are used to make food, and water and oxygen are released. The release of oxygen by those first photosynthesizers was a critical step in the direction of life's development. In a sense, the production of oxygen falls into the "good news–bad news" category. It's good news for us, of course, since we need oxygen, but as oxygen began to become a prevalent gas in the atmosphere, it sounded the death knell for many of the early organisms. This is because oxygen is a disruptive gas, as demonstrated by the process of rusting metal. So, in the early days of life on the planet, many life forms were destroyed by the deadly and accumulating gas.

—Wallace, *Biology: The World of Life*, p. 167 ●

RECOGNIZING DETAILS

The **details** in a paragraph are those facts and ideas that prove, explain, support, or give examples of the main idea of the paragraph. Once you have identified the topic and main idea, recognizing the supporting details is a relatively simple matter. The more difficult job is selecting the few primary, or most important, details that clearly support the main idea.

All details in a paragraph are related to, and in some way expand, the paragraph's main idea, but not all these details are crucial to the author's central thought. Some details are just meant to describe; others are meant to provide added, but not essential, information; still others are intended merely to repeat or restate the main idea.

On the other hand, the primary supporting details within a paragraph are those statements that carry the primary supporting evidence needed to back up the main idea. To find the primary supporting details in a paragraph, ask yourself the question: What are the main facts the author uses to back up or prove what she or he said about the topic?

In the following paragraph, the topic sentence is highlighted in yellow; the key primary supporting details are highlighted in green. Notice how the highlighted details differ, in the type and importance of the information they provide, from the remaining details in the paragraph.

> Like many animals, humans mark both their primary and secondary territories to signal ownership. Humans use three types of **markers**: central, boundary, and ear markers. **Central markers** are items you place in a territory to reserve it for you. Examples include a drink at the bar, books on your desk, or a sweater over a library chair. **Boundary markers** serve to divide your territory from that of others. In the supermarket checkout line, the bar placed between your groceries and those of the person behind you is a boundary marker, as are fences, armrests that separate your chair from those on either side, and the contours of the molded plastic seats on a bus. **Ear markers**—a term taken from the practice of branding animals on their ears—are identifying marks that indicate your possession of a territory or object. Trademarks, nameplates, and initials on a shirt or briefcase are all examples of ear markers.
>
> —DeVito, *Essentials of Human Communication*, pp. 109–110

Each highlighted detail identifies and defines one type of marker. The details in the remainder of the paragraph offer examples or explain these markers.

Exercise 4

DIRECTIONS   Each of the following statements could function as the topic sentence of a paragraph. After each statement are sentences containing details that may be related to the main idea. Read each sentence and make a check mark beside those with details that can be considered primary support for the main idea statement.

1. *Topic sentence:*

    The development of speech in infants follows a definite sequence or pattern of development.

    Details:

    _____ a. By the time an infant is six months old, he or she can make 12 different speech sounds.

_____ b. Before the age of three months, most infants are unable to produce any recognizable syllables.

_____ c. During the first year, the number of vowel sounds a child can produce is greater than the number of consonant sounds he or she can make.

_____ d. During the second year, the number of consonant sounds a child can produce increases.

_____ e. Parents often reward the first recognizable word a child produces by smiling or speaking to the child.

2. *Topic sentence:*

In some parts of the world, famine is a constant human condition and exists for a variety of reasons.

Details:

_____ a. In parts of Africa, people are dying of hunger by the tens of thousands.

_____ b. Famine is partly caused by increased population.

_____ c. Advances in medicine have increased life expectancies, keeping more people active for longer periods of time.

_____ d. Agricultural technology has not made substantial advances in increasing the food supply.

_____ e. Because of the growth of cities, populations have become more dense, and agricultural support for these population centers is not available.

3. *Topic sentence:*

An individual deals with anxiety in a variety of ways and produces a wide range of responses.

Details:

_____ a. Anxiety may manifest itself in such physical symptoms as increased heart activity and labored breathing.

_____ b. Fear, unlike anxiety, is a response to real or threatened danger.

_____ c. Psychologically, anxiety often produces a feeling of powerlessness, or lack of direct control over the immediate environment.

_____ d. Temporary blindness, deafness, and loss of the sensation of touch are examples of extreme physical responses to anxiety.

_____ e. Some people cannot cope with anxiety and are unable to control the neurotic behavior associated with anxiety.

4. *Topic sentence:*

An individual's status or importance within a group affects his or her behavior in that particular group.

Details:

_____ a. High-status individuals frequently arrive late at social functions.

_____ b. Once a person achieves high status, he or she attempts to maintain it.

_____ c. High-status individuals demand more privileges.

_____ d. Low-status individuals are less resistant to change within the group structure than persons of high status.

_____ e. There are always fewer high-status members than low-status members in any particular group.

5. *Topic sentence:*

An oligopoly is a market structure in which only a few companies sell a certain product.

Details:

_____ a. The automobile industry is a good example of an oligopoly, although it gives the appearance of being highly competitive.

_____ b. The breakfast cereal, soap, and cigarette industries, although basic to our economy, operate as oligopolies.

_____ c. Monopolies refer to market structures in which only one company produces a particular product.

_____ d. Monopolies are able to exert more control and price fixing than oligopolies.

_____ e. In the oil industry, because there are only a few producers, each producer has a fairly large share of the sales. ●

Exercise 5

DIRECTIONS   Read each paragraph and identify the topic and the main idea. Write each in the space provided. Then underline the key supporting details.

1. Have you ever snacked on baby carrots? Did you know at the time that you were eating a functional food? A **functional food** is one that has been shown to have a positive effect on your health beyond its basic nutrients. Baby carrots are a functional food because they are rich in beta-carotene, which, in addition to being a key source of vitamin A, helps protect your cells from damaging substances that can increase your risk of some chronic diseases such as cancer. In other words, the beta-carotene's function goes beyond its basic nutritional role as a source of vitamin A, because it may also help fight cancer. Oats are another functional food

because they contain the soluble fiber beta-glucan, which has been shown to lower cholesterol levels. This can play a positive role in lowering the risk for heart disease.

—Blake, *Nutrition and You*, p. 52

Topic: _____

Main idea: _____

2. There are a number of reasons why there has been an increase in the demand for nurses, not the least of which is the aging of the U.S. population. Older people use hospitals more and have chronic ailments that require more nursing. Moreover, as hospitals reduce the length of stay of patients, people who are discharged earlier than in previous years need more home care, usually provided by nurses. At the same time as demand has been rising, the supply of nurses has decreased somewhat. The age distribution of women between 18 and 24 has decreased in the past decade. Because this is the group from which nurses traditionally come, there have been fewer potential nurses. In addition, women have more alternatives in the labor market than they did years ago.

—Miller, *Economics Today*, p. 84

Topic: _____

Main idea: _____

_____

3. Surveys by telephone, particularly those that are locally based, are used extensively by research firms. The telephone survey has four major advantages: (1) The feedback is immediate, (2) the telephone is a more personal form of communication, (3) it's less intrusive than interviewers going door to door, and (4) the response rate, if the survey is short and handled by skilled phone interviewers, can reach 80 to 90 percent. The major disadvantage of telephone surveys is the difficulty in getting access to telephone numbers. In many urban areas, as many as one-third to one-half of all numbers are unlisted. Although researchers can let a computer program pick numbers through random dialing, this method is not as effective as actually knowing who is being called. Another barrier is convincing respondents that a legitimate poll or survey is being taken. Far too many salespeople, and even charitable organizations, attempt to sell goods or get donations by posing as researchers.

—Wilcox and Camea, *Public Relations*, p. 145

Topic: _____

Main idea: _____

4. Put in simple terms, pronunciation means saying a word the way it should be said. Pronunciation is not always an easy task, and several characteristics of the English language make the task even harder. First, sometimes a letter in a word is silent; for instance, the *w* in *sword* and the *t* in *often*. Remember, you cannot always tell how to pronounce a word just by looking at it. When you are not sure you are saying a word correctly, consult a standard dictionary. Second, there are many ways to pronounce the same vowel in our language. For example, consider the six pronunciations of the letter *o* for the following words: *do, no, dot, oar, woman,* and *women*. Even some words that are spelled alike can require different pronunciations depending on the form they take. For instance, the word *read*

as in "Read the same passage you read yesterday." Third, correct pronunciation requires knowing how to accent words of more than one syllable. This is more difficult in some cases than in others. While the word *contact* is accented the same regardless of whether it is used as a noun, verb, adverb, or adjective, the similar word *contract* has the accent on the first syllable when used as a noun but on the second syllable when used as a verb.

—Koch, *Speaking with a Purpose*, p. 110

Topic: _____

Main idea: _____

5. The role of the pharmacist is extensive and varies significantly depending on the practice setting. For example, in a community pharmacy setting the pharmacist might counsel patients about over-the-counter remedies, whereas in a hospital pharmacy setting the pharmacist might advise physicians about the best drugs to prescribe for certain indications. The primary jobs of all pharmacists are to dispense medications prescribed by authorized medical professionals and provide vital information to patients about medications and their use. Pharmacists also monitor the health and progress of patients in response to drug therapy to ensure that the medications being used are safe and effective.

—Johnston, *Pharmacy Technician*, p. 13

Topic: _____

Main idea: _____

6. Most extinction occurs gradually, one species at a time. The rate at which this type of extinction occurs is referred to as the *background extinction rate.* However, Earth has seen five events of staggering proportions that killed off massive numbers of species at once. These episodes, called mass extinction events, have occurred at widely spaced intervals in Earth history and have wiped out 50–95% of our planet's species each time. The best-known mass extinction occurred 65 million years ago and brought an end to the dinosaurs (although birds are modern representatives of dinosaurs).

—Withgott and Brenna, *Environment*, p. 148

Topic: _____

Main idea: _____

7. In a public speaking situation, just as the speaker and the listener have ethical obligations, so does the critic. First, the ethical critic separates personal feelings about the speaker from the evaluation of the speech. A liking for the speaker should not lead you to give positive evaluations of the speech, nor should dislike for the speaker lead you to give negative evaluations. Second, the ethical critic separates personal feelings about the issues from an evaluation of the validity of the arguments. Recognize the validity of an argument even if it contradicts a deeply held belief; at the same time, recognize the flaws of an argument even if it supports a deeply held belief. Third, the ethical critic is culturally sensitive and doesn't negatively evaluate customs and beliefs simply because they differ from her or his own. Conversely, the ethical critic does not positively evaluate a speech just because it supports her or his own cultural beliefs and values.

—DeVito, *Essentials of Human Communication*, p. 278

Topic: _____

Main idea: _____

8. Each state is governed by a separate and unique constitution that spells out the basic rules of that state's political game. Every state elects a governor as its chief executive officer, and most states have a legislature with two chambers like Congress (except for Nebraska, which only has a senate). However, the states endow their governors with different powers and organize and elect their legislatures differently. Each state's constitution was written under unique historical conditions and with a unique set of philosophical principles in mind. Each is unique in its length and provisions. Some are modern documents; others were written over 100 years ago. The differences among these documents also reflect the diversity—social, economic, geographic, historic, and political—of the states.

—Edwards, Wattenberg, and Lineberry, *Government in America,* p. 653

Topic: _____

Main idea: _____

_____

9. **Spam**—junk e-mail sent to a mailing list or a newsgroup fan online discussion group)—is a greater nuisance than postal junk mail because the Internet is open to the public, e-mail costs are negligible, and massive mailing lists are accessible through file sharing or by theft. Spam operators send unwanted messages ranging from explicit pornography to hate mail to advertisements, and even destructive computer viruses. In addition to wasting users' time, spam also consumes a network's bandwidth, thereby reducing the amount of data that can be transmitted in a fixed amount of time for useful purposes. U.S. industry experts estimate spam's damage in lost time and productivity at more than $140 billion worldwide in 2008 alone.

—Ebert and Griffin, *Business Essentials,* pp. 211–212

Topic: _____

Main idea: _____

10. Gentrification refers to the movement of middle-class people into rundown areas of a city. They are attracted by the low prices for large houses that, although deteriorated, can be restored. A positive consequence is an improvement in the appearance of some urban neighborhoods—freshly painted buildings, well-groomed lawns, and the absence of boarded-up windows. However, a negative consequence is that the poor residents are displaced by the more well-to-do newcomers. Tension between the gentrifiers and those being displaced is widespread.

—Henslin, *Essentials of Sociology,* p. 402

Topic: _____

Main idea: _____

TRANSITIONS

Goal 6
Use transitions

Transitions are linking words or phrases used to lead the reader from one idea to another. Transitions make clear the connection between a paragraph's primary details. Figure 7-1 presents a list of commonly used transitions and

Figure 7-1
Common Transitions

TYPE OF TRANSITION	EXAMPLES	WHAT THEY TELL THE READER
Time sequence	first, later, next, finally	The author is arranging ideas in the order in which they happened.
Illustration	for example, for instance, to illustrate, such as	An example will follow.
Listing	first, second, third, last, another, next	The author is marking or identifying each major point (sometimes these may be used to suggest order of importance).
Continuation	also, in addition, and, further, another	The author is continuing with the same idea and is going to provide additional information.
Contrast	on the other hand, in contrast, however	The author is switching to a different, opposite, or contrasting idea than previously discussed.
Comparison	like, likewise, similarly	The writer will show how the previous idea is similar to what follows.
Cause–effect	because, thus, therefore, since, consequently	The writer will show a connection between two or more things, how one thing caused another, or how something happened as a result of something else.
Summation	thus, in short, to conclude	The writer will state or restate his or her main point.

indicates what they tell you. If you get in the habit of recognizing transitions, you will see that they often guide you through a paragraph, helping you to read it more easily.

In the following paragraph, notice how the highlighted transitions lead you from one important detail to the next.

> You need to take a few steps to prepare to become a better note-taker. First, get organized. It's easiest to take useful notes if you have a system. A loose leaf notebook works best because you can add, rearrange, or remove notes for review. If you use spiral or other permanently bound notebooks, use a separate notebook for each subject to avoid confusion and to allow for expansion. Second, set aside a few minutes each day to review the syllabus for your course, to scan the assigned readings, and to review your notes from the previous class period. If you do this just before each lecture, you'll be ready to take notes and practice critical thinking. Finally, prepare your pages by drawing a line down the left margin approximately two inches from the edge of the paper. Leave this margin blank while you take notes so that later you can use it to practice critical thinking.
>
> —Gronbeck et al., *Principles of Speech Communication*, pp. 32–33

Not all paragraphs contain such obvious transitions, and not all transitions serve as such clear markers of major details. Transitions may be used to alert you to what will come next in the paragraph. If you see the phrase *for instance* at the beginning of a sentence, then you know that an example will follow. When you see the phrase *on the other hand*, you can predict that a different, opposing idea will follow. In the next chapter, you will see that transitional words also signal the author's organization.

DIRECTIONS   Circle each transition used in the paragraphs in Exercise 5. ●

Exercise 6

UNSTATED MAIN IDEAS

Occasionally, a writer does not directly state the main idea of a given paragraph in a topic sentence. Instead, he or she leaves it up to the reader to infer, or reason out, what the main idea of the paragraph is. This type of paragraph is called **unstated main idea**. This type of paragraph contains only details or specifics that are related to a given topic and substantiate an unstated main idea. To read this type of paragraph, start as you would for paragraphs with stated main ideas. Ask yourself the question for finding the topic: What is the one thing the author is discussing throughout the paragraph? Then try to think of a sentence about the topic that all the details included in the paragraph would support.

Read the paragraph in the following example. First, identify the topic. Then study the details and think of a general statement that all the details in the paragraph would support or prove.

> Suppose a group of plumbers in a community decide to set standard prices for repair services and agree to quote the same price for the same job. Is this ethical? Suppose a group of automobile dealers agree to abide strictly by the used car blue book prices on trade-ins. Is this ethical? Two meat supply houses serving a large university submit identical bids each month for the meat contract. Is this ethical?

This paragraph describes three specific instances in which there was agreement to fix prices. Clearly, the author's main idea is whether price fixing is ethical, but that main idea is not directly stated in a sentence anywhere within the passage.

Goal 7

Understand unstated main ideas

myreadinglab

To practice recognizing the unstated main idea, go to

> Main Idea

Tip *Price fixing* is illegal agreement in which companies in the same industry charge the same price for specific items or services. (Note: Here, *fix* does *not* mean "repair.")

DIRECTIONS   In the following paragraphs the main idea is not directly stated. Read each paragraph, identify the topic, and write it in the space provided. Then write a sentence that expresses the main idea of the passage.

Exercise 7

1. What do a cast-iron skillet, the salt on an icy road, and the copper pipes in some houses have in common? They're made from some of the same minerals that play essential roles in your body. From iron to sodium to copper, these rocky substances occur as part of the earthen world around you and are necessary for your day-to-day functioning. Along with another essential nutrient, water, minerals help chemical reactions take place in your cells, help your muscles contract, and keep your heart beating.

   — Blake, *Nutrition and You*, p. 258

Topic: _____

Main idea: _____

2. According to the most recent statistics, more than 100,000 people in the United States were shot in murders, assaults, suicides, accidents, or by police intervention in 2007. Nearly 31,000 died from gun violence, whereas many who survived experienced significant physical and emotional repercussions. The presence of a gun in the home triples the risk of a homicide there. The presence of a gun in the home increases suicide risk by more than five times.

Topic: _____

Main idea: _____

Thinking Visually
ANALYZING IMAGES

What additional information does this graph contribute?

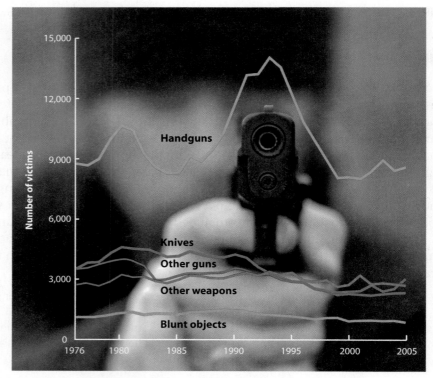

Homicide in the United States by Weapon Type, 1976–2005
Like the homicide rate generally, gun-involved incidents increased sharply in the late 1980s and early 1990s before falling to a low in 1999. The number of gun-involved homicides increased thereafter to levels experienced in the mid-1980s. During this same time period, homicides involving weapons other than firearms have declined slightly.

Source: Adapted from J. Fox and M. Zawitz, *Homicide Trends in the United States*, U.S. Department of Justice, Office of Justice Programs, Bureau of Justice Statistics, www.ojp.usdoj.gov/bjs/homicide/homtrnd.htm. Revised 2007.

3. A number of companies face the issue of religion in the workplace. On the one hand, some employees feel they should be able to express their beliefs in the workplace and not be forced to "check their faith at the door" when they come to work. On the other hand, companies want to avoid situations in which openly expressed religious differences cause friction between employees or distract employees from their responsibilities. To help address such concerns, firms such as Ford, Intel, Texas Instruments, and American Airlines allow employees to form faith-based employee support groups as part of their diversity strategies. In contrast, Procter & Gamble is among the companies that don't allow organized religious activities at their facilities.

—adapted from Thill and Bovée, *Excellence in Business Communication*, p. 73

Topic: _____

Main idea: _____

_____

4. The world population of domesticated animals raised for food rose from 7.2 billion animals to 24.9 billion animals between 1961 and 2008. Most of these animals are chickens. Global meat production has increased fivefold since 1950, and per capita meat consumption has doubled. The United Nations Food and Agriculture Organization (FAO) estimates that as more developing nations go through the

demographic transition and become wealthier, total meat consumption will nearly double by the year 2050.

—Withgott and Brennan, *Environment*, p. 267

Topic: _____

Main idea: _____

5. A number of ideas are being tested for how cancers get going in the first place, but a common thread that runs through these ideas is that, for cells to be brought to a cancerous state, two things are required: Their accelerators must get stuck and their brakes must fail. The control mechanisms that *induce* cell division must become hyperactive, and the mechanisms that *suppress* cell division must fail to perform. There are normal genes that induce cell division, but that when mutated can cause cancer; these are the stuck-accelerator genes, called oncogenes. Then there are genes that normally suppress cell division, but that can cause cancer by acting like failed brakes. These are tumor suppressor genes. Note that *both* kinds of genes must malfunction for cancer to get going.

—Krogh, *A Brief Guide to Biology*, p. 148

Topic: _____

Main idea: _____

6. Severe punishment may generate such anxiety in children that they do not learn the lesson the punishment was designed to teach. Moreover, as a reaction to punishment that they regard as unfair, children may avoid punitive parents, who therefore will have fewer opportunities to teach and guide the child. In addition, parents who use physical punishment provide aggressive models. A child who is regularly slapped, spanked, shaken, or shouted at may learn to use these forms of aggression in interactions with peers.

—Newcombe, *Child Development*, p. 354

Topic: _____

Main idea: _____

7. In 1920 there was one divorce for every seven marriages in the United States. Fifty years later the rate had climbed to one divorce for every three marriages, and today there is almost one divorce for every two marriages. The divorce rate in the United States is now the highest of any major industrialized nation, while Canada is in a rather distant second place.

—Coleman and Cressey, *Social Problems*, p. 130

Topic: _____

Main idea: _____

8. The use of the court system to resolve business and other disputes can take years and cost thousands, if not millions, of dollars in legal fees and expenses. In commercial litigation, the normal business operations of the parties are often disrupted. To avoid or lessen these problems, businesses are increasingly turning to methods of **alternative dispute resolution (ADR)** and other aids to resolving disputes. The most common form of ADR is *arbitration*. Other forms of ADR are *negotiation, mediation, conciliation, minitrial, fact-finding,* and using a *judicial referee*.

—Goldman, *Paralegal Professional*, p. 222

Tip *Induce* means "to cause a change."

Tip To *suppress* means "to prevent something from growing or developing."

Tip Something that is *mutated* is changed so that it is different from organisms of the same type (a genetic change).

Topic: _____

Main idea: _____

_____

9. People's acceptance of a product is largely determined by its package. The very same coffee taken from a yellow can was described as weak, from a dark brown can too strong, from a red can rich, and from a blue can mild. Even our acceptance of a person may depend on the colors worn. Consider, for example, the comments of one color expert: "If you have to pick the wardrobe for your defense lawyer heading into court and choose anything but blue, you deserve to lose the case. . . ." Black is so powerful it could work against the lawyer with the jury. Brown lacks sufficient authority. Green would probably elicit a negative response.

—DeVito, *Messages*, p. 153

Topic: _____

Main idea: _____

10. Most animals can survive for several weeks with no nutrition other than water. However, survival without water is limited to just a few days. Besides helping the body disperse other nutrients, water helps dissolve and eliminate the waste products of digestion. Water helps to maintain blood pressure and is involved in virtually all cellular activities.

—Belk and Borden, *Biology: Science for Life*, p. 46

Topic: _____

Main idea: _____ ●

Exercise 8

DIRECTIONS   Turn to the reading "You're Eating Genetically Modified Food." Read each paragraph and identify the topic and main idea. Then place brackets around the topic and underline the sentence that expresses the main idea. If the main idea is unstated, write a brief statement of the main idea in the margin. ●

Exercise 9

DIRECTIONS   Select a three-page section from a textbook that you have been assigned to read. After reading each paragraph, place brackets around the topic and then underline the sentence that states the main idea. If any paragraph has an unstated main idea, write a sentence in the margin that summarizes the main idea. Continue reading and marking until you have completed the three pages. ●

USING COLLEGE TEXTBOOKS
Locating Main Ideas

Textbook authors present their ideas clearly and directly in order to make them easy to understand and learn. You will find that paragraphs in college textbooks usually have clearly stated main ideas. Very often, too, the topic sentence is placed first or early in the paragraph to guide you through the paragraph.

Because textbooks are designed to teach, they contain numerous features to help you locate main ideas.

1. **Marginal labels.** Some textbooks, such as the one excerpted below, label key ideas. Others provide focus or review questions after major sections to enable you to check your recall of important information.

Key Concept

Music as a forum for rebellion Popular music has often served younger generations as a,way to express and encourage rebellion against existing social rules and norms. Music helps express the emotions people feel about their lives.

Social Meaning: Music and Rebellion

Music—particularly music as a form for mass media—has served each generation as a *forum for rebellion* against the status quo. As rock spread into a variety of subgroups defined by varying ethnic backgrounds, cultures, and classes, its breakthroughs and barriers in the recording industry represented cultural tension, not merely a change in musical form.

Donatelle, *Health*, p. 107

---

2. **Boldfaced headings and subheadings within a chapter.** These announce the topics to be discussed in each section and point you to main ideas. When you finish reading a headed section, turn each heading into a question and be sure you can recall the answer.

Here is a list of headings from a biology chapter on nutrients.

Nutrients of Life

13.1 Biomolecules Are Produced and Utilized in Cells
13.2 Carbohydrates Give Structure and Energy
13.3 Lipids Are Insoluble in Water

—Audesirk, *Biology*, p. 301

Notice that together these heads form an outline of the key ideas of the section, showing the progression of ideas. Here are a few questions you might ask based on the above headings:

- What are biomolecules and how are they produced?
- How do carbohydrates give structure and energy?
- What are lipids and why are they insoluble in water?

Answering these questions would lead you to the main ideas of the section.

3. **Chapter summary.** A chapter summary is a list of main ideas covered in a chapter. Notice that this book uses a chapter summary that provides a review of each of the chapter goals. Read the summary before you read the chapter to get an overview of the ideas you will be expected to learn. Study it after reading to review and to test your recall of main ideas. In this book, a question–answer format is used to enable you to test your mastery of the learning goals stated at the beginning of the chapter.

The sample below shows part of a chapter summary. Notice how each summary bullet clearly states a main idea.

15.2 What Causes Evolution?

Evolutionary change is caused by mutation, gene flow, small population size, nonrandom mating, and natural selection.

- Mutations are random, undirected changes in DNA composition. Although most mutations are neutral or harmful to the organism, some prove advantageous in certain environments. Mutations are rare and do not change allele frequencies very much, but they provide the raw material for evolution.
- Gene flow is the movement of alleles between different populations of a species. Gene flow tends to reduce differences in the genetic composition of different populations.

—Audesirk, *Biology*, p. 301

FURTHER PRACTICE WITH TEXTBOOK READING

Part A: Sample Textbook Chapter

Using the section called "Sleep Motivation," highlight the topic sentence of each paragraph. If the topic sentence is unstated, write a sentence stating the main idea.

Part B: Your College Textbook

Choose a textbook chapter that you have been assigned to read for one of your other courses. For the first five pages, highlight the topic sentence of each paragraph. If the topic sentence is unstated, write a sentence stating the main idea.

SELF-TEST SUMMARY

Goal 1 What are the essential elements of a paragraph?	A paragraph is a group of related sentences about a single topic. It provides explanation, support, or proof for a main idea (expressed or unexpressed) about a particular topic. A paragraph has three essential elements. a. Topic: the one thing the entire paragraph is about b. Main idea: a direct statement or an implied idea about the topic c. Details: the proof, reasons, or examples that explain or support the paragraph's main idea
Goal 2 How do you identify the topic?	The topic of a paragraph is the subject of the whole paragraph. Usually, the topic can be expressed in two or three words. To find the topic, ask yourself: What is the one thing the author is discussing throughout the whole paragraph?
Goal 3 How do you find the main idea?	The main idea tells you what the author wants you to know about the topic. It is often stated directly in the topic sentence. To find the main idea, ask yourself: What is the author trying to say about the topic?

Goal 4 Where is the topic sentence most likely to be found?	A topic sentence expressing the main idea of the paragraph may be located anywhere within the paragraph. It most commonly appears first or last but can also appear in the middle, or both first and last.
Goal 5 What are supporting details?	Supporting details are facts and ideas that explain, support, or give examples of the main idea.
Goal 6 What are transitions?	Transitions are linking words or phrases used to lead the reader from one idea to another. Transitions clarify the connections between ideas.
Goal 7 How do you recognize an unstated main idea?	To find an unstated main idea, read the paragraph while asking yourself: What is the one thing the author is discussing throughout the whole paragraph? Then, think of a general statement about the topic that covers all of the ideas that support it.

APPLYING YOUR SKILLS

DISCUSSING THE CHAPTER

1. Do newspaper articles use topic sentences? Why or why not?
2. Are topic sentences used in fiction? Why or why not?
3. Why would a writer choose not to explicitly state the main idea in his or her paragraph?
4. What are some guidelines a writer could use to know when to start a new paragraph?
5. How are the paragraphs typically organized in magazines? Web pages? Newspaper articles?

ANALYZING A STUDY SITUATION

Irina is having trouble distinguishing topic sentences from details in her sociology textbook. Imagine that you are Irina's study partner and that she has asked you for help. You have decided that the best way to help her is to explain by using some sample paragraphs.

1. Using "Tribal Identity Through Body Art" in Part Five, page 452, select several paragraphs you could use as samples.
2. Outline the advice you will give Irina about distinguishing topic sentences from details.

WORKING ON COLLABORATIVE PROJECTS

DIRECTIONS   Working in pairs, exchange the textbook sections you chose in Exercise 9. Review and critique each other's marking.

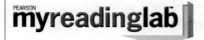

For support in meeting this chapter's goals, go to **MyReadingLab** and select **Main Ideas** and **Supporting Details**.

Quick QUIZ

DIRECTIONS   Write the letter of the choice that best completes each statement in the space provided.

CHECKING YOUR RECALL

_____ 1. The topic of a paragraph can be defined as the
   a. subject of the paragraph.
   b. most specific fact in the paragraph.
   c. noun that is the subject of the first sentence.
   d. author's point of view.

_____ 2. The three essential elements of a paragraph are its
   a. proof, reasons, and examples.
   b. topic, main idea, and details.
   c. main idea, topic sentence, and transitions.
   d. topic, transitions, and examples.

_____ 3. The best clue to the topic of a paragraph can be found in the paragraph's
   a. organization.
   b. transitional words.
   c. repeated use of a word.
   d. types of details.

_____ 4. The details of a paragraph are intended to
   a. restate the main idea.
   b. appear before the main idea.
   c. explain or support the topic sentence.
   d. indicate the topic of the next paragraph.

_____ 5. The phrase "to illustrate" indicates the type of transition known as
   a. cause and effect.
   b. example.
   c. comparison.
   d. summation.

APPLYING YOUR SKILLS

_____ 6. Erika is having difficulty identifying topic sentences in the paragraphs she reads. One helpful fact Erika should remember is that the topic sentence of a paragraph is most commonly the
   a. first sentence.
   b. second sentence.
   c. middle of the paragraph.
   d. last sentence.

_____ 7. Antonio is reading a paragraph in which the author has stated the main idea of the paragraph at both the beginning and the end of the paragraph. In this situation, Antonio should expect that
   a. the first statement is more important than the last.
   b. the last statement is more important than the first.
   c. the sentences in between are all examples.
   d. one sentence is a restatement of the other.

_____ 8. You are reading a paragraph in which the author has left the main idea unstated. Which of the following questions can help you find the main idea of the paragraph?
   a. Does the author reveal any bias?
   b. Does the author express an opinion?
   c. Are there any examples in the paragraph?
   d. What does the author want me to know about the topic?

_____ 9. Sofia is reading a paragraph with this topic sentence: "One unwelcome result of the increase in sexual activity is a high incidence of teenage pregnancies." Of the following sentences, the detail that does not belong in this paragraph is
   a. an epidemic of teenage pregnancies has captured national attention.
   b. nearly one million teenage girls become pregnant each year.
   c. about 30% of all teenage girls become pregnant once.
   d. teenage boys are traditionally unable to assume financial responsibility.

_____ 10. Diedre is reading a paragraph that arranges ideas in the order in which they happened. Diedre is correct if she identifies this type of pattern as
   a. comparison.
   b. time sequence.
   c. continuation.
   d. listing.

Following Thought Patterns

LEARNING GOALS

In this chapter you will learn to

1 Use textbook chapter organization

2 Recognize types of supporting information

3 Identify organizational patterns

LEARNING EXPERIMENT

1 Study the following five diagrams for a minute. Then cover the diagrams with your hand and draw as many of them as you can recall.

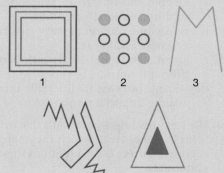

2 Compare your drawings with the original diagrams.

THE RESULTS

Did you get the first, second, third, or fifth drawing correct? Why didn't you get the fourth one correct?

Diagram 4 had no organization or pattern; the other four diagrams had an organization that you could identify.

LEARNING PRINCIPLE: WHAT THIS MEANS TO YOU

You are able to remember information better if it is organized or if you can detect a pattern. The experiment above demonstrated that you can recall a *diagram* more easily if you can detect a pattern. The same principle applies to ideas. If you can recognize how a writer has organized his or her ideas, you will be able to remember them more easily.

In college you will read a variety of materials; however, most of what you read will be textbooks, which are unique, highly organized information sources. If you become familiar with their organization and structure and learn to follow the author's thought patterns, you will find that you can read them more easily. This chapter focuses on important features of textbook chapters: (1) their overall structure or progression of ideas, (2) the types of details used to support each idea, and (3) organizational patterns (how the ideas fit together).

WHY LEARN ABOUT THOUGHT PATTERNS?

Thought patterns are important because they

- provide a framework for comprehending what you read.
- enable you to anticipate a writer's flow of thought.
- help you remember what you read.
- can help you organize your own thoughts.
- can improve your writing and speaking skills.

THE ORGANIZATION OF TEXTBOOK CHAPTERS

Goal ❶

Use textbook chapter organization

Reading a chapter can be compared to watching a football game. You watch the overall progression of the game from start to finish, but you also watch individual plays and notice how each is executed. Furthermore, you observe how several plays work together as part of a game strategy or pattern. Similarly, when reading a chapter, you are concerned with the progression of ideas. But you are also concerned with each separate idea and how it is developed and explained. This chapter focuses on important features of textbook chapters and essays.

myreadinglab

To practice learning from textbooks, go to

> Reading Textbooks

A textbook is made up of parts, each successively smaller and more limited in scope. As a general rule, the whole text is divided into chapters; each chapter may be divided by headings into sections and subsections, and each subsection is divided into paragraphs. Each of these parts has a similar structure. Just as each paragraph has a main idea and supporting information, each subsection, section, or chapter has its own key idea and supporting information.

Locate the Controlling Idea and Supporting Information

The controlling idea in a textbook section is the broad, general idea the writer is discussing throughout the section. It is the central, most important thought that is explained, discussed, or supported throughout the section. It is similar to the main idea of a paragraph but is a more general, more comprehensive idea that takes several paragraphs to explain. The controlling idea, then, is developed or explained throughout the section (see Figure 8-1 on p. 166).

Tip *Comprehensive* means "including everything that's necessary." A more comprehensive idea is broader than another one.

On page 167, read the section in Figure 8-2, "Learning," from a chapter in a biology book titled *Biology: The Network of Life*. (Note: Ellipses [. . .] indicate places where text has been omitted from the original.)

Note that paragraph 1 of the section introduces the subject: learning. The paragraph then defines learned behavior and states that only recently has it been studied in animals. The last sentence of the first paragraph states the controlling idea of the section: there are five categories of learning. The subheadings divide the remaining text, and each identifies one category of learning. Each group of paragraphs under a subheading explains one category of learning (its central thought). In the first subsection, on imprinting, the third sentence in paragraph 1 states the central thought of the section.

This example shows that the subheadings divided the section into five parts, or subsections. The section began with a general discussion of the subject and was divided into five smaller topics. This progression of ideas from large to

Figure 8-1
Organization of a
Textbook Section

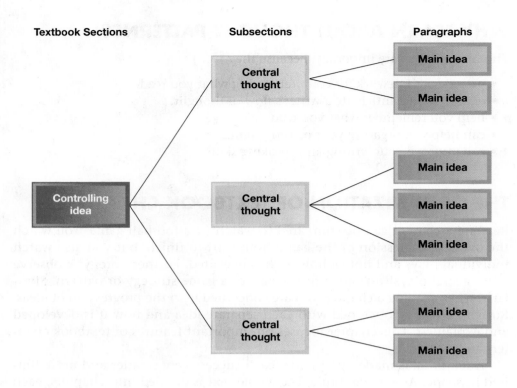

small, general to particular, is typical of most textbooks. When you are familiar with and can follow this progression, your textbooks will seem more logical and systematic and will be easier to read.

Exercise 1

DIRECTIONS   Turn to "Tribal Identity Through Body Art" in Part Five on page 452 of this text and complete the following instructions.

1. Where is the controlling idea of this article expressed? Underline it.
2. The dark-print headings divide the reading into three parts. Write a sentence expressing the main point of each part. ●

Exercise 2

DIRECTIONS   Read the excerpt "Blogs and Democratization" in Part Five on page 474 taken from a sociology textbook chapter. Complete the following activities.

1. Circle the subject the article discusses.
2. Highlight the controlling idea.
3. Underline the topic sentence of each paragraph. ●

Exercise 3

DIRECTIONS   From one of your textbooks, choose a three- to four-page section that you have already read, and answer the following questions.

1. What is the overall topic or subject discussed in this section?
2. What is the controlling idea?
3. Is the section divided by subheadings? If so, underline the central thought in each subsection. ●

Figure 8-2
Excerpt from *Biology: The Network of Life*

LEARNING

Learned behavior occurs when animals change their responses as a result of experience. Psychologists did a considerable amount of the early work on learning. They have primarily been concerned with human learning, and even when their research has been on animals, it has been with an eye toward using animals to understand human behavior. More recently, biologists have focused directly on animal learning. Although studies on learning have been carried out on a relatively small number of species, a vast amount of information has been generated. Scientists now recognize five major categories of learning: imprinting, habituation, associative learning, latent learning, and insight.

Imprinting

Imprinting is a highly specialized form of learning. In many species, it takes place during the early stages of an animal's life, when attachment to parents, the family, or a social group is critical for survival. Imprinting is a process whereby a young animal forms an association or identification with another animal, object, or class of items. . . .

Young animals are not completely indiscriminate in what they follow. For example, a mallard duckling will follow a moving object for the first two months after hatching. It will show a preference, however, for yellow-green objects . . .

Imprinting is an important form of learning because it has both short-term effects on the immediate parent–offspring relationship and long-term effects that become evident in adult animals. For example, lack of imprinting has been shown . . .

Habituation

Habituation is a simple form of learning . . .

Associative Learning

Habituation is learning that results in the loss of a response that is not relevant or useful to the animal. Associative learning, in contrast, is . . .

Latent Learning . . .

Insight . . .

TYPES OF SUPPORTING INFORMATION

Authors use various types of supporting information to explain the controlling idea of a textbook section. Recognizing these types of supporting information is the key to understanding *how* the author develops and connects his or her ideas.

Goal 2

Recognize types of supporting information

Examples

Usually a writer gives an example in order to make an idea practical and understandable. An example shows how a principle, concept, problem, or process works or can be applied in a real situation. In the following paragraph, notice how the writer explains the concept of objectivity by giving a specific example.

> The first concept in a sociologist's repertoire should be objectivity, the foundation for all sociological research. For sociologists, **objectivity** is the ability to conduct research without allowing personal biases or prejudices to influence them. They must put their own opinions and preconceived notions aside to study human behavior objectively. Being objective may seem simple, but it can be very difficult in practice. We all have our own opinions and prejudices, which can skew an objective point of view. For example, if you're studying the implication of ethics violations among NBA referees, your research might be swayed if you feel a particular referee has treated your favorite team unfairly. In that case, it's probably unwise to start this study after a bad call just cost your team a playoff game.
>
> —Carl, *Think Sociology*, p. 31

As you read examples, be sure to look for the connection between the example and the concept it illustrates. Remember that examples are important only for the ideas they illustrate.

Reasons

Certain types of main ideas are most easily explained by giving reasons. Especially in argumentative and persuasive writing, you will find that a writer supports an opinion, belief, or action by discussing why it is appropriate. In the following paragraph, the writer gives reasons *why* people postpone having children.

> Even more popular than a childfree lifestyle is the option to postpone having children. The National Survey of Families and Households (NSFH) found that the majority of 19- to 39-year-olds who didn't have children were planning to have them in the future. Postponing parenting often follows naturally from wanting to first complete higher education, establish one's self professionally, and achieve financial stability, all of which may also cause both women and men to postpone marriage.
>
> —Kunz, *Think Marriages and Families*, p. 134

You can see that the writer offers three reasons why people postpone having children: wanting to complete higher education, wanting to establish a career, and wanting to become financially stable.

Description

Tip *Composition* means "the different parts that make up a single thing." (Note the many other meanings of *composition* listed in your dictionary.)

An author uses description to help you visualize the appearance, organization, or composition of an object, a place, or a process. Descriptions are usually detailed and are intended to help you create a mental picture of what is being described. Read the following description of how movement is depicted in a particular thirteenth-century sculpture.

> To give lifelike feeling, artists often search for ways to create a sense of movement. Sometimes movement itself is the subject or a central quality of the subject. One of the world's most appealing depictions of movement is that of the Dancing Krishna, portraying a moment in India's ancient legend of the god Krishna when Krishna, as a playful child, has just stolen his mother's butter supply and now dances with glee. Bronze provides the necessary strength to hold the dynamic pose as the energy-radiating figure stands on one foot, counterbalancing arms, legs, and torso.
>
> —Preble, Preble, and Frank, *Artforms*, p. 60

You should be able to visualize the pose depicted in this bronze sculpture and even, perhaps, Krishna's facial expression. Each detail contributes to the description a bit of information that, when added to other bits, reveals its appearance.

Facts and Statistics

Another way to support an idea is to include facts or statistics that provide information about the main or controlling idea. Read the following paragraph, and notice how facts and statistics are used to support the idea that some people cannot digest milk products.

> Is it difficult for you to imagine life without milk, ice cream, or even pizza? Although some people consider these foods to be staples of the U.S. diet, they are not enjoyed by most of the world's population. Why? About 75% of people worldwide, including 25% of people in the United States, lose the ability to digest lactose, or milk sugar, in early childhood. Roughly 75% of African Americans, Hispanics, and Native Americans, as well as 90% of Asia Americans, experience **lactose intolerance**.
>
> —Audesirk, *Biology*, p. 106

When reading factual support or explanations, remember these questions: *What? When? Where? How?* and *Why?* They will lead you to the important facts and statistics contained in the passage.

Citation of Research

In many fields of study, authors support their ideas by citing research that has been done on the topic. Authors report the results of surveys, experiments, and research studies in order to substantiate theories or principles or to lend support to a particular viewpoint. The following excerpt from a psychology textbook reports the results of research conducted to evaluate the ability of chimpanzeees to learn numbers. The names and dates in parentheses in the first sentence are citations, or information that lets a reader know where to find the full research study. Complete source information for the research study appears in either an end-of-chapter or end-of-book reference list.

> More recent research suggests that chimpanzees may be able to learn numerical as well as linguistic symbols (Beran, 2004; Beran & Rumbaugh, 2001). Researchers trained two chimpanzees to use a joystick to move dots on a computer screen. Then, the chimps were taught to collect specific numbers of dots in association with Arabic numerals. In other words, when *3* was displayed on the screen, the chimp was supposed to use its joystick to move three dots from one location to another. Although the chimps learned the task, they tended to perform poorly with quantities in excess of six or seven. Afterward, the researchers ceased practicing with them because they wanted to find out whether the animals would remember the associations over extended periods of time. When they were restested 6 months later, the chimps were able to perform the task quite well, although they made more errors than when they were first trained. After 3 years, the researchers tested them again and found that they still remembered the symbol–quantity associations.
>
> —Wood, Wood, and Boyd, *Mastering the World of Psychology*, p. 210

When reading research reports, keep the following questions in mind. They will help you see the relationship between the research results and the author's controlling idea.

1. Why was the research done?
2. What did it show?
3. Why did the author include it?

Exercise 4

DIRECTIONS Read the following passages and identify the type of supporting information or detail that is used in each.

1. Three ceramic jars made in different villages in the late nineteenth and early twentieth centuries illustrate similarities and variations within the regional pottery style of the Pueblo peoples of New Mexico. The jars are similar in size and shape, but are different in surface decoration, with each bearing a design that is typical of the pottery produced by the artists of its Pueblo.

   The jar from Acoma Pueblo is decorated in large swaths—the brick-red elements seem to wander over the entire surface, draping over the shoulders of the jar like a garland. This undulating form divides the pot into irregularly shaped large areas.

   On the Zuni jar the design is divided by vertical lines into sections in which other lines define circular triangular areas.

   In San Ildefonso Pueblo, Maria Martinez and her husband developed another distinctive style. The San Ildefonso jar has contrasting curvilinear and rectilinear shapes. This jar also features the subtle contrast of matte black and shiny black areas.

   —Preble, Preble, and Frank, *Artforms*, pp. 98–99

   Type of detail: _____

2. For couples who have decided that biological childbirth is not an option, adoption provides an alternative. About 50,000 children are available for adoption in the United States every year. This is far fewer than the number of couples seeking adoptions. By some estimates, only 1 in 30 couples receives the child they want. On average, couples spend 2 years and $100,000 on the adoption process. Increasingly, couples are choosing to adopt children from other countries. In 2008, U.S. families adopted over 17,400 foreign-born children. The cost of intercountry adoption varies from approximately $10,000 to more than $30,000, including agency fees, dossier and immigration processing fees, and court costs. However, it may be a good alternative for many couples, especially those who want to adopt an infant rather than an older child.

   —Donatelle, *Health*, p. 186

   Type of detail: _____

Tip A *poll* is a survey of a selected group of people that is designed to reveal the opinion(s) of a much larger group. (Polls usually ask interviewees about political candidates, issues, or products.)

3. Polls help political candidates detect public preferences. Supporters of polling insist that it is a tool for democracy. With it, they say, policymakers can keep in touch with changing opinions on the issues. No longer do politicians have to wait until the next election to see if the public approves or disapproves of the government's course. If the poll results suddenly turn, government officials can make corresponding midcourse corrections. Indeed, it was George Gallup's fondest hope that polling could contribute to the democratic process by providing a way for public desires to be felt at times other than elections.

   Critics of polling, by contrast, think it makes politicians more concerned with following than leading. Polls might have told the constitutional convention delegates that the Constitution was unpopular, or told Jefferson that people did not want the Louisiana Purchase. Certainly they would have told William Seward not to buy Alaska, known widely at the time as "Seward's Folly." Polls may thus discourage bold leadership.

—Edwards, Wattenberg, and Lineberry, *Government in America*, p. 156

Type of detail: _____

4. Venetian portraitist Rosalba Carriera made dozens of works with pastels in the early eighteenth century. Her *Portrait of a Girl with a Bussola* shows her sensitivity to the medium. The hard, fine-grained pastels in common use at that time give the finished work a smooth surface that makes possible fine color shadings. Because of the artist's light, deft touch with short strokes of the pastel, the work resembles an oil painting in its appearance, an effect promoted by the very smooth paper. Carriera was in demand to make pastel portraits throughout Germany, France, and Noth Italy until poor eyesight forced her retirement in 1746.

Visual Thinking
ANALYZING IMAGES

How does the inclusion of the photograph make the paragraph easier to read?

Type of detail: _____

5. One reason why Americans seemed constantly on the move was their devotion to automobiles. In the postwar decades the automobile entered its golden age. During the booming 1920s, when the car became an instrument of mass transportation, about 31 million autos were produced by American factories. During the 1950s, 58 million rolled off the assembly lines; during the 1960s, 77 million. Gasoline consumption first touched 15 billion gallons in 1931; it soared to 35 billion gallons in 1950 and to 92 billion in 1970.

—Carnes and Garraty, *The American Nation*, p. 826

Type of detail: _____

6. A consumer's national origin is often a strong indicator of his preferences for specific magazines or TV shows, foods, apparel, and choice of leisure activities. Marketers need to be aware of these differences and sensitivities. Even overseas American restaurants must adapt to local customs. For example, in the Middle East, rules about the mixing of the sexes and the consumption of alcohol are quite strict. Chili's Grill & Bar is known simply as Chili's, and the chain offers a midnight buffet during Ramadan season, when Muslims are required to fast from dawn to dusk. McDonald's in Saudi Arabia offers separate dining areas for single men and women and children. Booths must have screens because women can't be seen eating meat.

—Solomon, Marshall, and Stuart, *Marketing: Real People, Real Choices*, p. 202

Type of detail: _____

7. The first stage of the purchase decision process is problem recognition. It occurs when a person perceives a difference between some ideal state and his or her actual state at a given moment. Consider, for example, a student who is in the market to rent an apartment. For her, the problem-recognition stage may have started when she decided that her dorm was too noisy or perhaps after an argument with her roommate. For a product like shampoo, problem recognition may occur when a consumer sees his favorite brand on sale, or it may be triggered when he notices that the bottle in his shower is almost empty.

Problem recognition may occur gradually. Several weeks may have passed before our student realized how much the noise in the dorm was bothering her. Sometimes, it occurs very quickly. When standing in the check-out line at the grocery store you see your favorite movie star on the cover of *People* and impulsively buy the magazine, you have experienced nearly instantaneous problem recognition. In fact, you have gone through virtually the entire purchase decision process in a matter of moments.

—Kinnear, Bernhardt, and Krentler, *Principles of Marketing*, p. 180

Type of detail: _____

8. Ice Age glaciers had significant effects on the landscape. For example, as the ice advanced and retreated, animals and plants were forced to migrate. This led to stresses that some organisms could not tolerate. Hence, a number of plants and animals became extinct. Other effects of Ice Age glaciers involved adjustments in Earth's crust due to the addition and removal of ice and sea-level changes associated with the formation and melting of ice sheets. The advance and retreat of ice sheets also led to changes in the routes taken by rivers. In some regions, glaciers acted as dams that created large lakes. When these ice dams failed, the effects on the landscape were profound.

—Lutgens, Tarbuck, and Tasa, *Essentials of Geology*, p. 261

Type of detail: _____

9. When the government sets out to measure the size of the labor force or the number of unemployed, its statisticians obviously cannot interview every single worker or potential worker. Survey data must be used. Although the survey technique is extensive—consisting of almost 60,000 households in almost 2,000 counties and cities in all 50 states and the District of Columbia—it is imperfect. One of the main reasons, argue some economists, is because of the *underground economy*. The underground economy consists of individuals who work for cash payments without paying any taxes. It also consists of individuals who engage in illegal activities such as prostitution, gambling, and drug trafficking.

Some who are officially unemployed and are receiving unemployment benefits do nonetheless work "off the books." Although they are counted as unemployed by the BLS, they really are employed. The same analysis holds for anyone who works and does not report income earned. The question, of course, is, How big is the underground economy? If it is small, the official unemployment statistics may still be adequate to give a sense of the state of the national economy. Various researchers have come up with different estimates of the size of the underground economy. Professor Peter Guttman believes that it is at least 10 percent of the size of the national economy. Other researchers have come up with estimates ranging from 5 to 15 percent. In dollars and cents that may mean that the underground economy represents between $300 billion and $900 billion a year. How many members of the true labor force work in this economy and their effect on the true unemployment rate is anyone's guess.

—Miller, *Economics Today*, p. 147

Type of detail: _____

10. Not only are older Americans living longer, healthier lives, they are also better educated, wealthier, and have achieved a higher standard of living than previous generations. *Baby boomers,* the generation born between 1946 and 1964, represent the majority of the aging population in the United States. Not only do the

78 million baby boomers make up the largest population group in the United States, they are also the wealthiest. Baby boomers, who in 2008 were between the ages of 44 and 62, have an estimated spending power of over $2 trillion a year. This makes baby boomers a large and lucrative target for businesses. Cosmetic company Revlon is eager to make a profit off the aging population by releasing an anti-aging beauty line called Vital Radiance that is aimed at baby boomer women. Revlon is hoping this new line will generate $200 million in new sales.

—Solomon, *Better Business*, p. 8

Type of detail: _____ ●

RECOGNIZING ORGANIZATIONAL PATTERNS

You have seen that textbook sections are structured around a controlling idea and supporting information and details. The next step in reading these materials effectively is to become familiar with how information is organized.

Recognition of organizational patterns is a useful learning device. It is based on the principle of meaningfulness, which states that things that are meaningful are easier to learn and remember than those that are not. When you fit details into a pattern, you connect them so that each one helps you recall the rest. By identifying how the key details in a paragraph or passage form a pattern, you are making them more meaningful to you and, as a result, making them easier to remember. Once you recognize that a paragraph or passage follows a particular pattern, its organization becomes familiar and predictable.

Six organizational patterns are commonly used in textbooks: definition, time sequence, comparison–contrast, cause–effect, classification, and listing. A chart that summarizes these patterns is shown in Figure 8-3.

To help you visualize each pattern, a diagram is presented for each. Later, in Chapter 16, you will see that these diagrams, also called maps, are useful means of organizing and retaining information.

For each pattern, particular words and phrases are used to connect details and lead from one idea to another. These words are called **transitional words** because they make a transition, or change, and indicate the direction or pattern of thought. A chart (Figure 8-13) giving examples of types of transitional words appears on page 186.

Goal ❸

Identify organizational patterns

myreadinglab

To practice recognizing organizational patterns, go to

> Patterns of
  Organization

TECH SUPPORT

Visualizing Organizational Patterns

Drawing maps to organize your ideas is an effective learning strategy; it can also help you with drafting writing assignments. Most word processing programs include tools that can help you visually organize your ideas. Look for "Diagram," "AutoShapes," and "Organization Charts" on the drop-down "Insert" menu of your word processing program.

Figure 8-3
Summary of
Organizational
Patterns

PATTERN	CHARACTERISTICS
Definition	Explains the meaning of a term or phrase; consists of class, distinguishing characteristics, and explanation
Time sequence/Process	Describes events, processes, procedures
Comparison–contrast	Discusses similarities and/or differences among ideas, theories, concepts, objects, or persons
Cause–effect	Describes how one or more things cause or are related to another
Classification	Explains by dividing a topic into parts or categories
Listing	Organizes lists of information: characteristics, features, parts, or categories

Definition

The definition pattern defines and explains the meaning of a term or concept. It is one of the most obvious patterns, and you will find it widely used in textbooks. Each academic discipline has its own language or specialized terminology (see Chapter 12).

Suppose you were asked to define the word *comedian* for someone unfamiliar with the term. First, you would probably say that a comedian is a person who entertains. Then you might distinguish a comedian from other types of entertainers by saying that a comedian is an entertainer who tells jokes and makes others laugh. Finally, you might mention as examples the names of several well-known comedians. Although you may have presented it informally, your definition would have followed the standard pattern. The first part of your definition tells what general class or group the term belongs to (entertainers). The second part tells what distinguishes the term from other items in the same class or category. The third part includes further explanation, characteristics, examples, or applications.

This pattern can be visualized as follows:

Figure 8-4
Typical Pattern of a
Definition

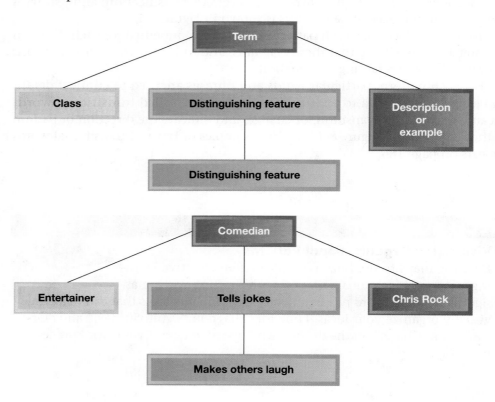

Read the following definition of *fossils* taken from a geology textbook.

Fossils are the remains or traces of prehistoric life. They are basic and important tools for interpreting the geologic past. Knowing the nature of the life forms that existed at a particular time helps researchers understand past environmental conditions. Further, fossils are important time indicators and play a key role in correlating rocks of similar ages that are from different places. Common examples of fossils include such objects as teeth, bones, and shells.

— Lutgens, Tarbuck, and Tasa, *Essentials of Geology,* p. 426

This definition has three parts: (1) the general class is stated first, (2) the distinguishing characteristics are then described, and (3) further explanation and examples are given. The first sentence states the general class—remains or traces of prehistoric life. The following sentences give distinguishing characteristics. The remainder of the passage gives further explanation of the term *fossils*, and the last sentence lists examples. When reading definitions, be sure to look for each of these parts. Passages that define often use transitional words and phrases such as:

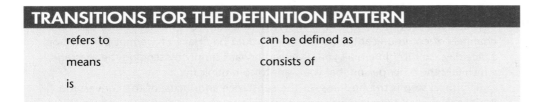

TRANSITIONS FOR THE DEFINITION PATTERN

refers to	can be defined as
means	consists of
is	

DIRECTIONS Define each of the following terms by identifying the class it belongs to and describing its distinguishing characteristics.

1. adolescence

2. automated teller machine (ATM)

3. cable television

4. computer

5. advertising ●

Exercise 5

Time Sequence and Process

One of the clearest ways to describe events, processes, procedures, and development of theories is to present them in the order in which they occurred. The event that happened first appears first in the passage; whatever occurred last is described last in the passage.

The time sequence pattern can be visualized as follows:

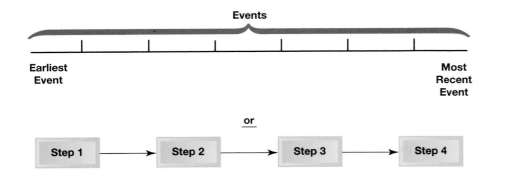

Figure 8-5
Typical Patterns of Time Sequence and Process

The first drawing is often called a **time line**, the second a **process diagram**. Time sequence focuses on events that may or may not be related, while process is concerned with the relationships among events as they progress through time.

Notice in the following example how the writer describes the process of communication among members of an organization.

> **Conversation,** whether face-to-face or online, takes place in five steps: opening, feedforward, business, feedback, and closing. Of course, there are variations in the process; when reading about the process of conversation, therefore, keep in mind the wide range of forms in which conversation can take place.
>
> The first step in conversation is the opening, which usually involves some kind of greeting. In face-to-face coversation, greetings can be verbal or nonverbal but are usually both. In most computer communication, the greetings are verbal with perhaps an emoticon or two thrown in. Verbal greetings include, for example, verbal salutes, initiation of the topic, and personal inquires. Nonverbal greetings include waving, smiling, shaking hands, and winking (and their emoticon equivalents).
>
> In the second step of conversation, you usually give some kind of feedforward in which you seek to accomplish a variety of functions. One function is to open the channels of communication. An example would be "Haven't we met before?" or "Nice day, isn't it?" In e-mail you give feedforward simply by sending the message, which tells the other person that you want to communicate.
>
> The third step is the business, or the substance and focus, of the conversation. Business is a good term for this stage, because it emphasizes that most conversations are directed at achieving some goal. You converse to fulfill the general purposes of interpersonal communication: to learn, relate, influence, play, or help.
>
> In the fourth step of conversation, feedback, you reflect back on the conversation. You normally do this immediately in face-to-face conversation and in your response to a previous e-mail. You say, for example, "So, you may want to send Jack a get-well card," or "Wasn't that the dullest meeting you ever went to?"
>
> The fifth and last step of the conversation process is the closing, the goodbye. Like the opening, the closing may be verbal or nonverbal but usually is a combination of both. Just as the opening signals access, the closing signals the intention to end access. The closing usually also signals some degree of supportiveness—for example, you express your pleasure in interacting ("Well, it was good talking with you").
>
> —DeVito, *Essentials of Human Communication,* pp. 131–133

Tip An *emoticon* is a symbol in an e-mail that shows the writer's feelings about a specific matter, such as a smiley face to indicate that the writer is kidding (making a joke).

This excerpt could be visualized as follows:

Material presented in terms of a time sequence is relatively easy to read because you know what order the writer will follow. When reading sequential, organized material, pay attention to the order of and connection between events. When studying this material, remember that the order is often as important as the events themselves. To test your memory and to prepare information for study, list ideas in this correct order, or draw a process diagram or time line.

The time sequence pattern uses transitional words to connect the events described or to lead you from one step to another. The most frequently used words are presented in the following box.

TRANSITIONS FOR THE TIME SEQUENCE AND PROCESS PATTERNS

first	before	following
second	after	last
later	then	during
next	finally	when
as soon as	meanwhile	until

DIRECTIONS For each of the following topic sentences, make a list of transitional words you expect to be used in the paragraph.

Exercise 6

1. Advertising has appeared in magazines since the late 1700s.

2. Large numbers of European immigrants first began to arrive in the United States in the 1920s.

3. The first step in grasping a novel's theme is reading it closely for literal content, including plot and character development.

4. After he left Spain, strong winds blew Columbus and his ships into the middle of the Atlantic.

5. The life cycle of a product consists of the stages a product goes through from when it is created to when it is no longer produced. ●

Comparison–Contrast

Many fields of study involve the comparison of one set of ideas, theories, concepts, or events with another. These comparisons usually examine similarities and differences. In anthropology, one kinship category might be compared with another; in literature, one poet might be compared with another; in biology, one species might be compared with another. You will find that the comparison–contrast pattern appears regularly in the textbooks used in these

TOPICS A AND B

Similarities	Differences
_____	_____
_____	_____
_____	_____

For example:

PROFESSOR MILLER AND PROFESSOR WRIGHT

Similarities	Differences
both require class attendance	Miller assigns term paper
both give essay exams	Wright demands class participation
both have sense of humor	age

fields. The comparison–contrast pattern can be visualized in several ways. For material that considers both similarities and differences, the maps below and on page 177 are effective.

For material that focuses primarily on differences, you might use the following:

	TOPIC A	TOPIC B
Feature 1	_____	_____
Feature 2	_____	_____
Feature 3	_____	_____
For example:		
Feature	*Professor Smith*	*Professor Jones*
teaching style	lecture	discussion
class atmosphere	formal	casual
type of exam	multiple choice	essay

A comparison–contrast pattern can be organized in one of three ways. A writer comparing two artists, X and Y, could use any of the following procedures:

1. Discuss the characteristics of artist X and those of artist Y, and then summarize their similarities and differences.
2. Consider their similarities first, and then discuss their differences.
3. Consider both X and Y together for each of several characteristics. For instance, discuss the use of color by X and Y, then discuss the use of space by X and Y, and then consider the use of proportion by X and Y.

Some comparison–contrast paragraphs focus primarily on similarities or concentrate on differences, as shown in the paragraph and map below.

In the battle to ratify the Constitution, proponents of the Constitution enjoyed great advantages over the unorganized opposition. Their most astute move was the adoption of the label **Federalist**. The term cleverly suggested that they stood for a confederation of states rather than for the creation of a supreme national authority. In fact, they envisioned the creation of a strong centralized national government capable of fielding a formidable army. Critics of the Constitution, who tended to be somewhat poorer, less urban, and less well educated than their opponents, cried foul, but there was little they could do. They were stuck with the name **Antifederalist**, a misleading term that made their cause seem a rejection of the very notion of a federation of the states.

The Federalists recruited the most prominent public figures of the day. In every state convention, speakers favoring the Constitution were more polished and better prepared than their opponents. The nation's newspapers threw themselves overwhelmingly behind the new government, whereas few journals even bothered to carry Antifederalist writings.

The Antifederalists were deeply suspicious of political power. They demanded direct, personal contact with their representatives and argued that elected officials should reflect the character of their constituents as closely as possible. According to the Antifederalists, the Constitution favored the wealthy.

Federalists mocked their opponents' localist perspective. The Constitution deserved support precisely because it ensured that future Americans would be represented by "natural aristocrats," those possessing greater insight, skills, and training than the ordinary citizen. These talented leaders were not tied to the selfish needs of local communities.

—Brands et al., *American Stories*, pp. 175–177

DIFFERENCES	
Federalists	**Antifederalists**
Name suggested federation of states	Misleading name suggested rejection
Well educated, richer, urban	Less well educated, poorer, less urban
Recruited popular public figures to speak	Speakers were less well prepared and less polished
Newspapers supported them	Few newspapers carried Antifederalist writings
Believed in natural aristocrats	Suspicious of political power

In comparison–contrast passages, the way ideas are organized provides clues to what is important. In a passage that is organized by characteristics, the emphasis is placed on the characteristics. A passage that groups similarities and then differences emphasizes the similarities and differences themselves rather than the characteristics.

Transitional words indicate whether the passage focuses on similarities, differences, or both.

TRANSITIONS FOR THE COMPARISON–CONTRAST PATTERN			
Similarities		**Differences**	
also	too	unlike	nevertheless
similarly	as well as	despite	however
like	both	instead	in spite of
likewise		on the other hand	

Exercise 7

DIRECTIONS   For each of the following topic sentences, predict the content of the paragraph. Will it focus on similarities, differences, or both? Also, if you predict that the passage will discuss both similarities and differences, predict the organization of the paragraph that will follow. (Identify the type of organization by its number in the list on page 178 for the comparison–contrast pattern.)

1. Two types of leaders can usually be identified in organizations: informal and formal.

   Content: _____   *Organization:* _____

2. The human brain is divided into two halves, each of which is responsible for separate functions.

   Content: _____   *Organization:* _____

3. Humans and primates, such as gorillas and New World monkeys, share many characteristics but are clearly set apart by others.

   Content: _____   *Organization:* _____

4. Interpersonal communication is far more complex than large group communication.

   Content: _____   *Organization:* _____

5. Sociology and psychology both focus on human behavior.

   Content: _____   *Organization:* _____ ●

Cause–Effect

Understanding any subject requires learning *how* and *why* things happen. In psychology it is not enough to know that people are often aggressive; you also need to know why and how people show aggression. In physics it is not enough to know the laws of motion; you also must understand why they work and how they apply to everyday experiences.

The cause–effect pattern arranges ideas according to why and how they occur. This pattern is based on the relationship between or among events. Some passages discuss one cause and one effect—the omission of a command, for example, causing a computer program to fail.

This relationship can be visualized as follows:

Figure 8-6
A Simple Cause–Effect Pattern

Most passages, however, describe multiple causes or effects. Some may describe the numerous effects of a single cause, such as unemployment producing an increase in crime, family disagreements, and a lowering of self-esteem.

Figure 8-7
A Complex Cause–Effect Pattern

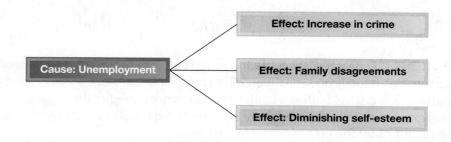

Others may describe the numerous causes of a single effect, such as increased unemployment and poverty along with decreased police protection causing a high crime rate.

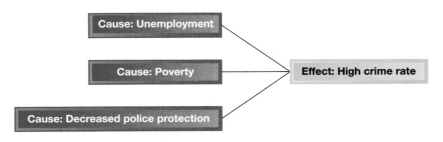

Figure 8-8
Multiple Causes of a
Single Effect

Still others may present multiple causes and effects, such as unemployment and poverty producing an increase in crime and in family disputes.

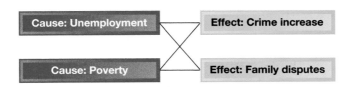

Figure 8-9
Multiple Causes and
Effects

Read the following passage, which is taken from a biology text, and determine which of the following patterns is used:

- single cause–single effect
- single cause–multiple effects
- multiple causes–single effect
- multiple causes–multiple effects

Then draw a diagram in the margin describing this relationship.

> Rabies is caused by a virus that spreads through animal saliva. In the "furious" form of the disease, the virus is passed on by means of one animal biting another, thus injecting its saliva into the second animal. Not surprisingly, one of the things the virus does is affect salivary tissue in an infected animal's head and neck. This ensures that there is plenty of saliva to be transmitted. The virus also inhibits swallowing in an infected animal, which ensures more saliva. Finally, the virus affects the animal's central nervous system in such a way as to bring about the famous behavioral change in infected animals—frenzied, unprovoked attacks on other animals.
>
> —Krogh, *A Brief Guide to Biology*, p. 406

The paragraph offers three effects of a rabid animal biting another. Numerous effects, then, result from a single cause.

When you read and study ideas organized in a cause–effect pattern, focus on the connection between or among events. To make relationships clearer, determine which of the four cause–effect patterns is used. Transitional words can help you determine the cause–effect relationship.

TRANSITIONS FOR THE CAUSE–EFFECT PATTERN	
Causes	**Effects**
because	consequently
because of	as a result
since	one result is
one cause is	therefore
one reason is	thus

Exercise 8

DIRECTIONS   From the following list of section headings from an American government textbook, predict which sections will be developed using the cause–effect pattern. Place a check mark in front of those you select.

_____ 1. How Public Policies Affect Income

_____ 2. Explaining the Decline of Isolationism in America

_____ 3. Tasks of Political Parties

_____ 4. The Affirmative Action Issue

_____ 5. Political Parties: How Party Loyalty Shifts

_____ 6. Why Bureaucracies Exist

_____ 7. The Organization of National Political Parties

_____ 8. How Lobbyists Shape Policy

_____ 9. Types of Special-Interest Groups

_____ 10. The Nature of the Judicial System ●

Classification

The classification pattern divides a broad topic into categories. If you were asked to describe types of computers, you might mention desktop, laptop, and tablet. By dividing computers into major categories, you are using a pattern known as **classification**.

This pattern is widely used in many academic subjects. For example, a psychology text might explain human needs by classifying them into two categories: primary and secondary. In a chemistry textbook, various compounds may be grouped and discussed according to common characteristics, such as the presence of hydrogen or oxygen. The classification pattern divides a topic into parts, on the basis of common or shared characteristics.

Here are a few examples of topics and the classifications or categories into which each might be divided:

- Movies: comedy, horror, mystery
- Motives: achievement, power, affiliation, competency
- Plant: leaves, stem, roots

You can visualize the classification patterns as follows:

Figure 8-10
A Classification Pattern

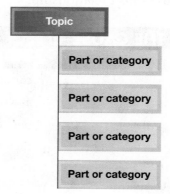

Note how the paragraph that follows classifies the various types of cancers.

> The name of the cancer is derived from the type of tissue in which it develops. Carcinoma (carc = cancer; omo = tumor) refers to a malignant tumor consisting of epithelial cells. A tumor that develops from a gland is called an adenosarcoma (adeno = gland). Sarcoma is a general term for any cancer arising from connective tissue. Osteogenic sarcomas (osteo = bone; genic = origin), the most frequent type of childhood cancer, destroy normal bone tissue and eventually spread to other areas of the body. Myelomas (myelos = marrow) are malignant tumors, occurring in middle-aged and older people, that interfere with the blood-cell-producing function of bone marrow and cause anemia. Chondrosarcomas (chondro = cartilage) are cancerous growths of cartilage.
>
> —Tortora, *Introduction to the Human Body*, p. 56

You can visualize this classification paragraph as follows:

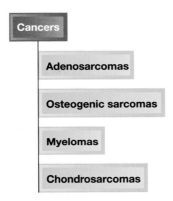

Figure 8-11
A Sample
Classification

TRANSITIONS FOR THE CLASSIFICATION PATTERN

several kinds	first	finally
one type	second	can be classified as
another type		

DIRECTIONS For each of the following topic sentences, supply three pieces of information that might be contained in the paragraph.

Exercise 9

1. There are magazines designed for almost every possible interest and every conceivable type of person.

2. Due, in part, to our complicated economic system, a number of different types of taxes are levied.

3. There are several different types of resources a person can turn to when experiencing financial difficulties.

4. There are many types of diet plans; the wise dieter evaluates the benefits of each.

5. Stress comes from a wide variety of situations; however, each situation falls into one of three primary sources. ●

Listing

Many types of information in textbooks have no inherent order or connection. Lists of facts, characteristics, parts, or categories can appear in any order; thus, writers use a pattern called **listing**, or **enumeration**. In this pattern, the information is often loosely connected with a topic sentence or controlling idea: "There are several issues to be considered . . ." or "There are three problems that may occur when . . ." and so forth. You can visualize the listing pattern as follows:

Figure 8-12
A Listing Pattern

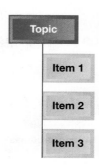

Read the following paragraph, observing how the pattern proceeds from one type of merger to another.

> The four types of mergers are the horizontal merger, vertical merger, congeneric merger, and conglomerate merger. A **horizontal merger** results when two firms *in the same line of business* are merged. An example is the merger of two machine tool manufacturers. This form of merger results in the expansion of a firm's operations in a given product line and at the same time eliminates a competitor. A **vertical merger** occurs when a firm acquires *a supplier or a customer*. For example, the merger of a machine tool manufacturer with its supplier of castings is a vertical merger. The economic benefit of a vertical merger stems from the firm's increased control over the acquisition of raw materials or the distribution of finished goods. A **congeneric merger** is achieved by acquiring a firm that is *in the same general industry* but is neither in the same line of business nor a supplier or customer. An example is the merger of a machine tool manufacturer with the manufacturer of conveyer systems. The benefit of a congeneric merger is the resulting ability to use the same sales and distribution channels to reach customers of both businesses. A **conglomerate merger** involves the combination of firms *in unrelated businesses*. The merger of a machine tool manufacturer with a chain of fast-food restaurants is an example of this kind of merger. The key benefit of the conglomerate merger is its ability to reduce risk by merging firms that have different patterns of sales and earnings.
>
> —Gitman, *Principles of Managerial Finance,* pp. 766–767

One key to reading and studying this pattern is to be aware of how many items are enumerated so you can check your recall of them. It is also helpful to note whether the information is listed in order of importance, frequency, size, or any other characteristic. This will help you organize the information for easier recall.

Transitional words are very useful in locating items in a list. As a writer moves from one item in a list to another, he or she may use transitional words to mark or identify each point.

TRANSITIONS FOR THE LISTING PATTERN

one	first
another	second
also	finally
too	for example
for instance	in addition

Exercise 10

DIRECTIONS For each of the following topic sentences, supply three pieces of information that might be contained in the paragraph.

1. There are a number of factors wise consumers must consider in deciding which credit card to apply for.

2. Humans have more than just five senses; within the broad category of touch, there are many different kinds of sensation that can be felt.

3. The species of mammals contains many widely different kinds of animals.

4. Scientists find life hard to define, except by describing its characteristics.

5. Because the purpose of a résumé is to sell the qualities of the person writing it, it should include several important kinds of information. ●

Mixed Patterns

In many texts, sections and passages combine one or more patterns. In defining a concept or idea, a writer might explain a term by comparing it with something similar or familiar. In describing an event or process, a writer might include reasons for or causes of an event or might explain why the steps in a process must be followed in the prescribed order.

Read the following paragraph and determine which two patterns are used.

Noise is anything that distorts the message and prevents the listeners from receiving your message as you intended it to be received. It's revealing to distinguish noise from "signal." In this context the term *signal* refers to information that is useful to you, information that you want. Noise, on the other hand, is what you find useless; it's what you do not want. So, for example, an e-mail list that contained lots of useful information would be high on signal an low on noise; if it contained lots of useless information, it would be high on noise and low on signal. Spam is high on noise and low on signal, as is static on the radio, television, or telephone. Noise may be physical (others talking loudly, cars honking, illegible handwriting), physiological (hearing or visual impairment, speech disorders), psychological (preconceived ideas, wandering thoughts), or semantic (misunderstood meanings).

—DeVito, *The Essential Elements of Public Speaking,* p. 8

This paragraph defines the terms *noise* and *signal*. The terms are also compared. Therefore, the paragraph combines a definition pattern with a comparison–contrast pattern.

When reading mixed patterns, do not be overly concerned with identifying or labeling each pattern. Instead, look for the predominant pattern that shapes the overall organization.

Figures 8-3 and 8-13 present a review of the organizational patterns and of transitional words commonly used with each pattern. Although this chapter has focused on the use of these patterns in textbook writing, you will find such patterns in other academic situations as well. For example, your professor may organize her or his lecture by using one or more of these patterns and may use transitional words to enable you to follow the line of thought. On exams, especially essay exams, you will find questions that require you to organize information in terms of one or more of the organizational patterns. (Refer to Chapter 19 for more information on essay exam questions.)

Organizational patterns and transitional words are also useful in organizing and presenting your own ideas. As you complete written assignments, these patterns will provide a basis for relating and connecting your ideas and presenting them in a clear and understandable form. The transitional words are useful for leading your reader from one idea to another.

Figure 8-13
Summary of Transitional Words

THOUGHT PATTERN		TRANSITIONAL WORDS
Definition		refers to, means, can be defined as, consists of, is
Time sequence/Process		first, second, later, before, next, as soon as, after, then, finally, meanwhile, following, last, during, when, until
Comparison–contrast	*Similarities:*	also, similarly, like, likewise, too, as well as, both
	Differences:	unlike, on the other hand, instead, despite, nevertheless, however, in spite of
Cause–effect	*Causes:*	because, because of, since, one cause is, one reason is
	Effects:	consequently, as a result, one result is, therefore, thus
Classification		several kinds, one type, another type, first, second, finally, can be classified as
Listing		one, another, also, too, for instance, first, second, finally, for example, in addition

Exercise 11

DIRECTIONS   Assume that each of the following sentences or groups of sentences is the beginning of a textbook section. On the basis of the information contained in each, predict what organizational pattern is used throughout the passage. Look for transitional words to help you identify the pattern.

1. In large businesses, clerical jobs are usually very specialized in order for the work to be accomplished in the most efficient manner. As a result, clerical work is very often routine and highly repetitive. _____

2. There are clear limitations to population growth and the use of natural resources. First, the food supply could be exhausted as a result of water, mineral, and soil depletion. _____

3. Unlike the statues of humans, the statues of animals found at Stone Age sites are quite lifelike. _____

4. When a patient enters a mental hospital, he is carefully tested and observed for 24 hours. Then a preliminary decision is made concerning medication and treatment. _____

5. One shortcoming of the clinical approach in treating mental illness is that definitions of normal behavior are subjective. Another shortcoming of the approach is that it assumes that when a patient has recovered, he will be able to return to his previous environment. _____

6. Most of the world's news is transmitted by Western news agencies. Third World nations regard this dominance as oppressive and feel that action must be taken to develop their communication networks. _____ ●

DIRECTIONS   Read each of the following passages, and identify the main organizational pattern used in each.

1. TAMPERING WITH GENES, OR GENETIC ENGINEERING?   Genetic engineering, as the name implies, involves manipulating genes to achieve some particular goal. Some people object to the entire idea of tailoring molecules with such profound implications for life. Where could it lead? Would we have the wisdom not to unleash something terrible on the earth?

   Perhaps the greatest threat of recombinant techniques, some would say, lies in [their] very promise. The possibilities of such genetic manipulation seem limitless. For example, we can mix the genes of anything—say, an ostrich and a German shepherd. This may bring to mind only images of tall dogs, but what would happen if we inserted cancer-causing genes into the familiar *E. coli* that is so well adapted to living in our intestines? What if the gene that makes botulism toxin, one of the deadliest poisons known, were inserted into the DNA of friendly *E. coli* and then released into some human population? One might ask, "But who would do such a terrible thing?" Perhaps the same folks who brought us napalm and nerve gas.

   Another, less cynical concern is that well-intended scientists could mishandle some deadly variant and allow it to escape from the laboratory. Some variants have been weakened to prevent such an occurrence; but we should remember that even though smallpox was "eradicated" from the earth, there were two minor epidemics in Europe caused by cultured experimental viruses that had escaped from a lab. One person died of a disease that technically didn't exist.

   —Ferl, Wallace, and Sanders, *Biology: The Realm of Life*, pp. 252–253

Organizational pattern: _____

2. SCHOOL ATTENDANCE AND NUTRITION   School attendance can affect a child's nutrition in several ways. In the hectic time between waking and getting out the door, many children minimize or skip breakfast completely. School children who don't eat breakfast are more likely to do poorly on schoolwork, have decreased attention spans, and have more behavioral problems than their peers who do eat breakfast. Public schools are required to offer low-cost school breakfasts; taking advantage of these

breakfasts can help children avoid hunger in the classroom. Another consequence of attending school is that, with no one monitoring what they eat, children do not always consume enough food. They may spend their lunch time talking or playing with friends rather than eating. They might not like the foods being served as part of the school lunch, and even homemade lunches that contain nutritious foods may be left uneaten or traded for less nutritious fare.

—Thompson and Manore, *Nutrition for Life*, p. 355

Organizational pattern: _____

3. There are three primary categories of stress that people report when they experience stage fright. *Physical sensations* make up the first category of stress that can occur when we are preparing to speak. The exact physical sensations vary from person to person, of course, but almost everyone experiences some degree of physical discomfort or uneasiness when speaking in front of others. The second category of stress includes *emotional responses* that can be experienced before, during, and after the speaking performance. They can include feelings of fear, loss of control, panic, anxiety, shame, and anger. The final category is the *psychological responses* of stress that can be experienced when delivering a speech. They include loss of memory, negative self-talk, jumbled thought patterns, nervous repetition of words or phrases, and the use of verbal pauses, such as "ah," "um," and "you know."

—Fujishin, *The Natural Speaker*, p. 21

Organizational pattern: _____

4. Many will contests involve written wills. The contesters allege things such as mental incapacity of the testator at the time the will was made, undue influence, fraud, or duress. To prevent unwarranted will contests, a testator can use a **videotaped will** to supplement a written will. Videotaping a will that can withstand challenges by disgruntled relatives and alleged heirs involves a certain amount of planning. A written will should be prepared to comply with the state's Statute of Wills. The video session should not begin until after the testator has become familiar with the document. The video should begin with the testator reciting the will verbatim. Next, the lawyer should ask the testator questions to demonstrate the testator's sound mind and understanding of the implications of his or her actions. The execution ceremony—the signing of the will by the testator and the attestation by the witnesses—should be the last segment on the film. The videotape then should be stored in a safe place.

—Goldman, *Paralegal Professional*, p. 561

Organizational pattern: _____

5. In a two-year study of more than 25 different communities, Jonathan Kozol observed public schools in the United States and noted that not all schools are created equal. Kozol saw that urban schools frequently lacked basic supplies necessary to teach: Playgrounds often had little or no equipment, chemistry labs were missing beakers and test tubes, and students had to share textbooks. Meanwhile, suburban schools often had a surplus of supplies and staff. Kozol pointed out that while these two systems often turned out different qualities of education, the major cause for this disparity rested in the structures that supported the educational systems. Property values and taxes are higher in the suburbs, so their schools receive more funding than urban schools. This extra financial support allows suburban schools to purchase up-to-date materials and hire ample staff for the students. Unfortunately, because most urban schools are underfunded, the students who need the most help actually

get the least, which adds to the endless cycle of educational inequality. Is this really "equal opportunity"?

—Carl, *Think Sociology*, p. ____

Organizational pattern: _____

6. COUNCILS AND COMMITTEES   Councils and committees are advisory groups found in many different kinds of societies. We have briefly mentioned councils among the Shavante, Tetum, and Qashgai. They meet in public and are usually made up of informally appointed elders. *Committees* differ from councils in that they meet privately. Moreover, whereas councils are typical of simpler political organizations, committees are more characteristic of states. But the two kinds of groups can and often do coexist within the same political organization. When this occurs, councils are superior to committees, whose tasks and powers are delegated to them by councils.

Councils tend to be consensus-seeking bodies, while committees are more likely to achieve agreement by voting (although either kind of body may reach decisions in either way). Consensus seeking is typical of small social groups whose members have frequent personal interaction. Once a council or committee increases to more than about 50 members, decision by consensus is no longer possible. Voting is typical of larger groups whose members do not see much of one another in daily life and who owe their main allegiance not to other group members but to people (perhaps many millions) outside the council or committee. Members may in fact represent these outside people, as is the case with the U.S. Congress.

—Hicks and Gwynne, *Cultural Anthropology*, p. 304

Organizational pattern: _____

7. Sociologist Louis Wirth defined a **minority group** as people who are singled out for unequal treatment and who regard themselves as objects of collective discrimination. Worldwide, minorities share several conditions: Their physical or cultural traits are held in low esteem by the dominant group, which treats them unfairly, and they tend to marry within their own group. These conditions tend to create a sense of identity among minorities (a feeling of "we-ness"). In many instances, a sense of common destiny emerges.

Surprisingly, a minority group is not necessarily a *numerical* minority. For example, before India's independence in 1947, a handful of British colonial rulers discriminated against tens of millions of Indians. Accordingly, sociologists usually refer to those who do the discriminating not as the majority but, rather, as the **dominant group,** for they have the greater power, privileges, and social status.

—Henslin, *Essentials of Sociology*, p. 226

Organizational pattern: _____

8. The Founders selected a presidential system of government for the United States. Most democracies in developed countries, however, have chosen a parliamentary system. In such a system the chief executive, the prime minister, is selected by the legislature, not the voters. The prime minister is a member of the legislature, elected from one district as a member of parliament. The majority party, or the largest bloc of votes in the legislature if there is no majority party, votes its party leader to be prime minister. Unlike the president, the prime minister may remain in power for a long time—as long as his or her party or coalition has a majority of the seats and supports the leader.

Presidents and prime ministers govern quite differently. Prime ministers never face divided government, for example. Since they represent the majority party or coalition, they can almost always depend on winning on votes. In addition, party discipline is better in parliamentary systems than in the U.S. Parties know that if the prime minister should lose on an important vote, the government might have to call elections under circumstances unfavorable to the majority. As a result, members of parliament almost always support their leaders.

So why does the United States maintain a presidential system? The Founders were concerned about the concentration of power, such as that found in the prime minister. Instead, they wanted to separate power so that the different branches could check each other.

—Edwards, Wattenberg, and Lineberry, *Government in America*, p. 398

Organizational pattern: _____

9. A **hangover** is your body's way of saying, "Don't do that to me again." After heavy drinking, individuals can experience the unpleasant symptoms of a hangover, ranging from a pounding headache, fatigue, nausea, and increased thirst to a rapid heartbeat, tremors, sweating, dizziness, depression, anxiety, and irritability. Alcohol contributes to the symptoms of a hangover in several ways. Alcohol is a diuretic, so it can cause dehydration, and thus, electrolyte imbalances. It inhibits the release of antidiuretic hormone from your pituitary gland, which in turn causes your kidneys to excrete water, as well as electrolytes, in your urine. Vomiting and sweating during or after excessive drinking will further contribute to dehydration and electrolyte loss. Dehydration also increases your thirst and can make you feel lightheaded, dizzy, and weak. Increased acid production in the stomach and secretions from the pancreas and intestines can cause stomach pain, nausea, and vomiting.

—Blake, *Nutrition and You*, p. 318

Organizational pattern: _____

10. Blood is critical to maintaining life, as it transports virtually everything in our bodies. Blood is actually a tissue, the only fluid tissue in our bodies. It is made up of four components. **Erythrocytes,** or red blood cells, are the cells that transport oxygen. **Leukocytes,** or white blood cells, protect us from infection and illness. **Platelets** are cell fragments that assist in the formation of blood clots and help stop bleeding. **Plasma** is the fluid portion of the blood and enables blood to flow easily through the blood vessels.

—Thompson and Manore, *Nutrition for Life*, p. 205

Organizational pattern: _____

USING COLLEGE TEXTBOOKS
Identifying Patterns

Because patterns can help you comprehend and recall what you read, it is especially helpful to identify them when reading textbooks. Both textbook chapter titles and the major headings within a chapter provide important clues about the pattern(s) used in the chapter.

1. **Chapter titles.** Chapter titles often suggest how the writer will organize the ideas contained in the chapter. For example, for a chapter titled "Islam: From Its Origins to 1300" in a Western civilization textbook, you can predict that, overall, a chronological order will be used. Here are a few more chapter titles. Can you predict the pattern?

6 Your Reproductive Choices

—Donatelle, *Health*, p. 158

Pattern? cause / effect _____

The Process of Fitting *into* Society

—Carl, *Think Sociology*, pp. 82–83

Pattern? process _____

The History of Life   Chapter 17

—Audesirk, *Biology*, p. 317

Pattern? time sequence _____

2. **Chapter heading.** Headings within a chapter form an outline of the chapter content. Headings can also often suggest the pattern of the material to follow. If you see a heading "Events Leading Up to the Thirty Years War" you expect a cause and effect pattern to be used. Below are a variety of headings from different textbooks. Can you identify the pattern each suggests?

Consumer Involvement and Passive Learning   211

Definitions and Measures of Involvement   211

—Schiffman, *Consumer Behavior*, p. xi

Pattern? definition _____

Types of Business Ownership   19–21

Sole Proprietorship   19
Partnership   20
Corporation   20

—Poatsy, *Better Business*, p. v

Pattern? classification _____

CULTURAL DIFFERENCES
Individualist and Collectivist Cultures
High- and Low-Context Cultures
Masculine and Feminine Cultures
High- and Low-Power-Distance Cultures
High- and Low-Ambiguity-Tolerant Cultures

—DeVito, *Interpersonal Messages*, p. v

Pattern? compare / contrast _____

FURTHER PRACTICE WITH TEXTBOOK READING

Part A: Sample Textbook Chapter

Identify the pattern(s) used in the section titled "Comparing Specific Emotions" on page 493.

Part B: Your College Textbook

Choose a textbook chapter that you have been assigned to read for one of your other courses. Analyze its title and study the headings. After you have read the chapter, make a list of the patterns used in the chapter.

SELF-TEST
SUMMARY

Goal ❶ Why is it important to become familiar with the organization of your textbooks?	Textbooks are unique, highly organized sources of information. Becoming familiar with their organization and structure and learning to follow the writer's thought patterns are important textbook reading skills. A textbook is divided into parts: chapters, sections, subsections, and paragraphs. Although each is successively smaller in size and more limited in scope, each follows a similar organization and is built around a single idea with details that support and explain it.
Goal ❷ What types of supporting information are used in textbooks?	Textbook writers explain ideas by providing various types of supporting information: examples, reasons, description, facts and statistics, and citation of research.
Goal ❸ Why is it helpful to recognize the pattern or organization of a paragraph or passage you are reading?	The organizational patterns are definition, time sequence/process, comparison–contrast, cause–effect, classification, and listing. By paying close attention to transitional words and phrases a writer uses to connect ideas and lead from one idea to another, you can usually identify the pattern being used. When you recognize that what you are reading follows a specific pattern, you will be better able to follow the ideas being presented and to predict what will be presented next. You will find that you have connected the important details so that recalling one idea will help you recall the others, and as a result, it will be easier to learn and remember them.

APPLYING YOUR SKILLS

DISCUSSING THE CHAPTER

1. Choose a particular academic discipline, such as biology or psychology. Which organizational patterns do you think are used most frequently in that discipline? Why?
2. Think about the various essay examinations you've taken in recent months. Which types of supporting information did you use to explain the controlling idea of your answer? How can you improve your ability to organize an essay question on an examination?
3. Compare the organization of several textbooks. How are the texts organized similarly? How are they different? Which style seems best suited for the topic each text presents?
4. How do Web sites, television shows, radio programs, and documentary films organize information presented? Which type of organization is most typical in each medium?
5. What type of supporting evidence is typically found in each of the media listed in question 4? How do you know when supporting evidence is sufficient?

ANALYZING A STUDY SITUATION

Suzanne is writing a research paper on "male and female language" for her sociology class. She has collected a great deal of information through research and interviews, but she is having difficulty organizing it. Some of the subtopics on which she has collected information are listed below.

Subject of Paper:
Male and Female Language

Subtopics:
- Research studies on use of language in adolescent, sex-separate peer groups
- Men's language patterns
- Women's language patterns
- Stages of language development in infants and children
- Physical differences in areas of men's and women's brains that control language functioning
- Types of games children play and how they involve language

1. What possible *overall* organizational pattern could her paper follow?
2. What organizational pattern(s) might she follow in developing the section of her paper that deals with each of the topics above?
3. What types of details do you anticipate that Suzanne will include to develop each subtopic?

WORKING ON COLLABORATIVE PROJECTS

DIRECTIONS   Locate and mark, in one of your textbooks or in Part Five of this text, several paragraphs that are clear examples of thought patterns discussed in this chapter. Write the topic sentence of each paragraph on a separate index card. Once your instructor has formed small groups, choose a group "reader" who will collect all the cards and read each sentence aloud. Groups should discuss each and predict the pattern of the paragraph from which the sentence was taken. The "finder" of the topic sentence should then confirm or reject the prediction and quote sections of the paragraph if necessary.

 PEARSON

For support in meeting this chapter's goals, go to **MyReadingLab** and select **Reading Textbooks, Supporting Details,** and **Patterns of Organization.**

QUICK QUIZ

DIRECTIONS Write the letter of the choice that best completes each statement in the space provided.

CHECKING YOUR RECALL

_____ 1. The controlling idea in a textbook section is similar to the main idea of a paragraph *except* that the

    a. paragraph's main idea is more general.
    b. paragraph's main idea is more comprehensive.
    c. textbook section's controlling idea relies on fewer supporting details.
    d. textbook section's controlling idea takes several paragraphs to explain.

_____ 2. The supporting ideas and information are usually presented in an essay's

    a. thesis statement.
    b. introduction.
    c. body.
    d. summary.

_____ 3. The type of supporting information that is used primarily to create a mental picture consists of

    a. research evidence.
    b. comparisons.
    c. reasons.
    d. description.

_____ 4. The primary purpose of an example is to

    a. support ideas with facts and statistics.
    b. highlight differences between two ideas.
    c. illustrate how an idea can be applied to a real situation.
    d. help the reader visualize a process.

_____ 5. Transitional words and phrases such as "on the other hand" and "however" suggest the organizational pattern called

    a. comparison–contrast.
    b. cause–effect.
    c. listing.
    d. time sequence.

APPLYING YOUR SKILLS

_____ 6. For Louise's biology paper, she wants to explain the various stages that a polliwog goes through before becoming a frog. The best way for her to present this information would be to use a

    a. time sequence pattern.
    b. cause–effect pattern.
    c. classification pattern.
    d. definition pattern.

_____ 7. Dean is writing a research paper using the cause–effect organizational pattern. Of the following topics, the one most likely to be written by Dean is

    a. measurement of personality traits.
    b. sources of stress.
    c. limitations of objective tests.
    d. classification of mental disorders.

_____ 8. Mykaela is attempting to identify organizational patterns in articles she is reading for her economics class. To help her identify the comparison–contrast pattern, Mykaela should look for

    a. the meaning of a term or phrase.
    b. events, processes, and procedures.
    c. differences among similar situations.
    d. "if . . . then" relationships.

_____ 9. Miguel wrote a paper in which he stated that several factors, including unemployment, poverty, and decreased police protection, were responsible for the current high crime rate in his city. The cause–effect pattern that Miguel used in his paper was

    a. single cause–single effect.
    b. multiple causes–single effect.
    c. single cause–multiple effects.
    d. multiple causes–multiple effects.

_____ 10. Kelli is writing an article for the college newspaper listing the wide variety of activities available on campus. Kelli is using listing as the organizational pattern for this information because the list

    a. has no inherent order or connection.
    b. is based on the relationship between events.
    c. has its own specialized terminology.
    d. focuses primarily on why and how things happen.

Evaluating the Author's Message

LEARNING GOALS

In this chapter you will learn to

1. Make valid inferences

2. Evaluate publication sources

3. Examine qualifications

4. Distinguish between fact and opinion

5. Identify the author's purpose

6. Recognize bias

7. Analyze tone

8. Analyze arguments

9. Evaluate evidence

LEARNING EXPERIMENT

1 Read the following paragraph on school voucher systems and highlight important ideas.

In the late 1960s, a new idea began to receive considerable publicity. It was vintage USA: If there were more competition among schools, perhaps schools would be better. After all, people were entitled to more freedom in choosing where their children would be educated. This idea inspired proposals for voucher plans. Public schools have a virtual monopoly on public funds for education, and children attend schools depending, for the most part, on where they live. A voucher plan can change this situation. In a sense, parents, not schools, receive public money. They receive it in the form of a *voucher*, which they use to pay for their children's attendance at the schools of their choice. The schools receive money from the government in return for the vouchers. The greater the number of parents who choose a particular school, the more money it receives. The idea is to force the public schools to compete with each other, and with private and parochial schools, for

"customers." Presumably, good schools would attract plenty of students, and poor schools would be forced either to improve or close.

—Thio, *Sociology*, pp. 376–377

2 Read the following paragraph on homeschooling and then answer the questions that follow, either alone, as part of a classroom discussion group, or with a friend or classmate.

There has been phenomenal growth in the number of children who receive their formal education at home. In the late 1970s there were only about 12,500 such children, but today the number has soared to more than 500,000 and is still increasing rapidly. Before 1994, most of the home-schooling parents were fundamentalist Christians who believed that religion was either abused or ignored in the public school. But today two thirds of the families reject public education for secular reasons: poor teaching, crowded classrooms, or lack of safety. Many of the older children, though, enroll in public schools part time, for a math class or a chemistry lab, or for after-school activities such as football or volleyball. Most home-schooling parents have some college education, with median incomes between $35,000 and $50,000. Over 90 percent are white.

—Thio, *Sociology*, p. 377

1. What are the advantages and disadvantages of homeschooling for the child?
2. What credentials should parents be required to demonstrate in order to teach their own children?
3. Do you think a home-schooled child would learn as much or more than a traditionally schooled child? Why?

3 On which topic—voucher systems or home-schooling—do you feel you would be better prepared to write a paper, make a speech, or lead a discussion group?

THE RESULTS

You most likely feel better prepared to work with the topic of homeschooling. Why? Probably because the discussion questions that you answered after reading provoked your thinking and opened up your mind to new ideas. By discussing the topic of homeschooling, you used the principle of elaboration.

LEARNING PRINCIPLE: WHAT THIS MEANS TO YOU

Elaboration or thinking about and reacting to what you read helps you to remember more of what you read and prepares you to write about and discuss the ideas. This chapter will show you how to improve your critical reading skills by reacting to and analyzing what you read. You will learn to make inferences, ask critical questions, and analyze arguments effectively. You will learn to handle exam questions, class discussions, and written assignments that demand critical reading and thinking more effectively.

WHY LEARN TO EVALUATE WHAT THE AUTHOR SAYS?

Evaluating what the author says is important because:

- You will understand your reading assignments more fully if you become a critical thinker. Textbook reading requires critical thinking.
- You will write more effective papers if you apply critical thinking skills.
- With so much information available both in print and online, you need to develop skills to help you distinguish reliable and useful sources from those that are misleading and inappropriate.
- You will learn to recognize both effective arguments and those that are flawed.

MAKE INFERENCES AS YOU READ

The photograph shown on page 198 was taken from a psychology textbook. What do you think is happening? Where is it happening? How do the participants feel about one another?

To answer these questions, you used what you saw in the photo to make reasonable guesses. The process you went through is called making an inference. An **inference** is a reasoned guess about what you don't know based on what you do know. We all make inferences throughout our daily lives. If a friend is late, you may predict that she was delayed in traffic, especially if you know she often is so delayed. If you see a seated man frequently checking his watch, you can infer that he is waiting for someone who is late.

Goal 1

Make valid inferences

To practice making inferences as you read, go to
> Inference

As you read, you also need to make inferences frequently. Authors do not always directly state exactly what they mean. Instead, they may only hint at or suggest an idea. You have to reason out or infer the meaning an author intends (but did not say) on the basis of what he or she did say. For instance, suppose a writer describes a character as follows:

> As Agatha studied Agnes, she noticed that her eyes appeared misty, her lips trembled slightly, and a twisted handkerchief lay in her lap.

From the information the author provides, you may infer that Agnes is upset and on the verge of tears. Yet the writer does not say any of this. Instead, the author implies her meaning through the description she provides.

How to Make Inferences

There are no specific steps to follow in making inferences. Each inference depends on the situation and the facts provided as well as on your knowledge and experience with the situation. Below are a few general guidelines for making inferences.

MAKING INFERENCES

Steps	Make Inference by Asking these Questions
Understand the directly stated meaning first.	• What is the topic? • What is the main idea? • What are the supporting details? • What is the organizational pattern?
Add up the facts.	• What is the author trying to suggest through the stated information? • What do all the facts and ideas point to or add up to? • For what purpose did the author include these facts and details?

Use clues provided by the writer.	• Is descriptive language used? • Do you notice emotionally charged words? • Do certain words have positive or negative connotations?
Make a logical inference.	• Is your inference consistent with all available facts? • It is logical and plausible?
Verify your inference.	• Do you have sufficient evidence to support your inference? • Have you overlooked equally possible or more likely inferences?

DIRECTIONS Read the following passages and then answer the questions. The answers are not directly stated in the passage; you will have to make inferences in order to answer the questions.

Exercise 1

Passage A

The Lion's Share

The lion, the jackal, the wolf, and the hyena had a meeting and agreed that they would hunt together in one party and share equally among them whatever game they caught.

They went out and killed an antelope. The four animals then discussed which one of them would divide the meat. The lion said, "Whoever divides the meat must know how to count."

Immediately the wolf volunteered, saying, "Indeed, I know how to count."

He began to divide the meat. He cut off four pieces of equal size and placed one before each of the hunters.

The lion was angered. He said, "Is this the way to count?" And he struck the wolf across the eyes, so that his eyes swelled up and he could not see.

The jackal said, "The wolf does not know how to count. I will divide the meat."

He cut three portions that were small and a fourth portion that was very large. The three small portions he placed before the hyena, the wolf, and himself. The large portion he put in front of the lion, who took his meat and went away.

"Why was it necessary to give the lion such a large piece?" the hyena said. "Our agreement was to divide and share equally. Where did you ever learn how to divide?"

"I learned from the wolf," the jackal answered.

"Wolf? How can anyone learn from the wolf? He is stupid," the hyena said.

"The jackal was right," the wolf said. "He knows how to count. Before, when my eyes were open, I did not see it. Now, though my eyes are wounded, I see it clearly."

—Courlander, *The King's Drum and Other African Stories*, pp. 110–111

1. What did the jackal learn from the wolf?
2. Although "The Lion's Share" is a folktale, it does make a point. Summarize the message this story offers.

Passage B

Is laughter the best medicine?

Lucy went to the hospital to visit Emma, a neighbor who had broken her hip. The first thing Lucy saw when the elevator door opened at the third floor was a clown, with an enormous orange nose, dancing down the hall, pushing a colorfully decorated cart. The clown stopped in front of Lucy, bowed, and then somersaulted to the nurses' station. A cluster of patients cheered. Most of them were in wheelchairs or on crutches. Upon asking for directions, Lucy learned that Emma was in the "humor room," where the film *Blazing Saddles* was about to start.

Since writer Norman Cousins's widely publicized recovery from a debilitating and usually incurable disease of the connective tissue, humor has gained new respectability in hospital wards around the country. Cousins, the long-time editor of the *Saturday Review,* with the cooperation of his physician, supplemented his regular medical therapy with a steady diet of Marx brothers movies and *Candid Camera* film clips. Although he never claimed that laughter alone effected his cure, Cousins is best remembered for his passionate support of the notion that, if negative emotions can cause distress, then humor and positive emotions can enhance the healing process.

—Zimbardo and Gerrig, *Psychology and Life,* p. 501

1. In paragraph one, the author states that Lucy ran into the clown. For what reason is the author suggesting the clown is there?
2. What kind of movie is *Blazing Saddles*?
3. What kind of treatment did Emma's hospital use?
4. How does the author imply that humor assists in healing? ●

Goal **2**
Evaluate publication sources

EVALUATE THE PUBLICATION SOURCE

Textbook information can usually be accepted as reliable and well researched. Not all other sources, however, are as worthy of your trust. Not all authors and publishers apply equally high standards of research and verification of information. Not all sources are equal in their levels of detail and technical accuracy, which depend in part on their intended audience. Consequently, checking the source can help you evaluate the accuracy and completeness of the information it contains. Suppose you were doing a research paper on the economic advantages of waste recycling. You found that each of the following sources contained information on recycling. Which do you predict would contain the type of information that would be most useful in writing a term paper?

• An article in *USA Today* titled "Stiffer Laws for Waste Recycling"
• A newspaper opinion piece titled "Why I Recycle"
• A brochure published by the Waste Management Corporation explaining the benefits of recycling to its potential customers
• An article on BusinessWeek.com titled "Factors Influencing an Economic Boom: Recycling and Waste Management"

The *USA Today* article is limited to discussing laws that regulate recycling and will not focus on its advantages. The newspaper opinion piece is likely to contain a single, personal viewpoint rather than factual information. The brochure may be biased (see p. 206), because it was written to convince potential customers that they need the company's services. The best source will be the article on BusinessWeek.com. It is concerned with economic effects of recycling and is likely to contain fairly detailed factual information.

HOW TO EVALUATE SOURCES

1. **Consider for whom the source is intended.** Its audience will suggest the level of detail, as well as the standards used to prepare it.
2. **Identify the author.** Do online research to determine whether the author is an authority on the topic he or she is writing about.
3. **Check the date of publication or Web page.** Be sure that the source is recent and up-to-date.
4. **Look for footnotes, endnotes, or a list of references.** These suggest the author consulted other sources and is presenting reliable information.
5. **Verify the information by checking additional sources.** Note whether the information in the source you are evaluating is consistent with other sources.
6. **Check with your college librarians.** They are familiar with a variety of sources and may help you assess a particular source's reliability.

Online sources, in particular, should be carefully evaluated since anyone can place information on the Internet, whether it is accurate and reliable, or not. Refer to Chapter 13 for more on evaluating online sources.

Exercise 2

DIRECTIONS   For each situation described, predict how useful and appropriate the following sources will be. Rate each as "very appropriate," "possibly useful," or "not appropriate."

1. *Situation:* You are collecting information for a research paper on food cravings for your health and nutrition class.
   Source: A *Time* magazine article on American eating habits
2. *Situation:* You are preparing a presentation on flea markets for your public speaking class.
   Source: A book titled *Junk and Collectibles: The History of Flea Markets*
3. *Situation:* You are writing a letter to the editors of your local newspaper opposing the construction of a chemical waste treatment plant in your neighborhood; you need evidence about possible dangers.
   Source: The Human Ecologist, a periodical dealing with environmental health issues
4. *Situation:* You are shopping for a used car.
   Source: A classified ad for a Toyota
5. *Situation:* You are writing a paper evaluating whether the lumber industry acts responsibly toward the environment.
   Source: A newsletter published by the Sierra Club, a group devoted to environmental protection ●

EXAMINE THE AUTHOR'S QUALIFICATIONS

Goal 3
Examine qualifications

To evaluate printed material, you must also consider the competency of the author. If the author lacks expertise in or experience with the subject, the material he or she produces may not meet an acceptable level of scholarship and accuracy.

Depending on the type of material you are using, you have several means of checking the qualifications of an author. In textbooks, the author's credentials may be described in one of two places. The author's college or university affiliation, and possibly his or her title, may appear on the title page beneath the author's name. Second, in the preface of the book, the author may indicate or summarize his or her qualifications for writing the text. In nonfiction books and general market paperbacks, a synopsis of the author's credentials and experiences may be included on the book jacket or the back cover. However, in other types of material, little effort is made to identify the author or his or her qualifications. In newspapers, magazines, and reference books, the reader is given little or no information about the writer. You are forced to rely on the judgment of the editors or publishers to assess an author's authority.

If you are familiar with an author's work, then you can anticipate the type of material you will be reading and predict the writer's approach and attitude toward the subject. If, for example, you found an article on world banking written by former President Clinton, you could predict it will have a political point of view. If you were about to read an article about Yankee's player Alex Rodriguez written by Hank Steinbrenner, a co-owner of the team, you could predict the article might possibly include details of their working relationship from Steinbrenner's point of view.

Goal 4
Distinguish between fact and opinion

myreadinglab

To practice distinguishing between fact and opinion, go to
> Critical Thinking

DISTINGUISH BETWEEN FACT AND OPINION

When working with any source, try to determine whether the material is factual or an expression of opinion. Facts are statements that can be verified—that is, proved to be true or false. Opinions are statements that express feelings, attitudes, or beliefs and are neither true nor false. Here are a few examples of each:

Facts

1. More than one million teenagers become pregnant every year.
2. The costs of medical care increase every year.

Opinions

1. Government regulation of our private lives should be halted immediately.
2. By the year 2025, most Americans will not be able to afford routine health care.

Facts that are taken from a reputable source or verified can be accepted and regarded as reliable information. Opinions, on the other hand, are not reliable sources of information and should be questioned and carefully evaluated. Look for evidence that supports the opinion and indicates that it is reasonable. For example, opinion 2 above is written to sound like a fact, but look closely. What basis does the author have for making that statement?

Some authors are careful to signal the reader when they are presenting an opinion. Watch for words and phrases such as:

apparently	this suggests	in my view	one explanation is
presumably	possibly	it is likely that	according to
in my opinion	it is believed	seemingly	

Other authors do just the opposite; they try to make opinions sound like facts, as in opinion 2 above.

In the following excerpt from a psychology textbook, notice how the author carefully distinguishes factual statements from opinion by using qualifying words and phrases (highlighted).

> Some research has suggested that day care can have problematic effects on children's development. For example, studies indicate that children who begin day care as infants are more aggressive, more easily distracted, less considerate of their peers, less popular, and less obedient to adults than children who have never attended day care or haven't attended for as long.
>
> Other studies have found that day care is associated with adaptive behaviors. For example, researchers have reported that children who attend day care develop social and language skills more quickly than children who stay at home, although the children who don't attend day care catch up in their social development in a few years. Poor children who go to day care are likely to develop better reading and math skills than poor children who stay at home.
>
> —Uba and Huang, *Psychology*, p. 323

Other authors, however, mix fact and opinion without making clear distinctions. This is particularly true in the case of informed opinion, which is the opinion of an expert or authority. Thomas Friedman represents expert opinion on globalization, for example. Textbook authors, too, often offer informed opinion, as in the following statement from an American government text:

> The United States is a place where the pursuit of private, particular, and narrow interests is honored. In our culture, following the teachings of Adam Smith, the pursuit of self-interest is not only permitted but actually celebrated as the basis of the good and prosperous society.
>
> —Greenberg and Page, *The Struggle for American Democracy*, p. 186

The authors of this statement have reviewed the available evidence and are providing their expert opinion on what the evidence indicates about American political culture. The reader, then, is free to disagree and offer evidence to support an opposing view.

Exercise 3

DIRECTIONS Read each of the following statements and identify whether it sounds like fact, opinion, or informed opinion.

_____ 1. United Parcel Service (UPS) is the nation's largest deliverer of packages.

_____ 2. United Parcel Service will become even more successful because it uses sophisticated management techniques.

_____ 3. UPS employees are closely supervised; new drivers are accompanied on their rounds, and time logs are kept.

_____ 4. The best way to keep up with world news is to read the newspaper.

_____ 5. A community, as defined by sociologists, is a collection of people who share some purpose, activity, or characteristic.

_____ 6. The mayor of our city is an extraordinarily honest person.

_____ 7. To a dieter, food is a four-letter word.

_____   8. According to a leading business analyst, most television advertising is targeted toward high-spending consumer groups.

_____   9. Americans spend $13.7 billion per year on alternative medicine and home remedies.

_____ 10. A survey of Minnesota residents demonstrated that lotteries are played most frequently by those who can least afford to play. ●

Exercise 4

DIRECTIONS   Read or reread "Medicine's Cutting Edge" in Part Five on page 468. Underline four statements of informed opinion contained in the excerpt. ●

Exercise 5

DIRECTIONS   Using one of your own textbooks from another course, identify three statements of fact and three statements of informed opinion. ●

Goal 5

Identify the author's purpose

myreadinglab

To practice identifying the author's purpose, go to

> Purpose and Tone

IDENTIFY THE AUTHOR'S PURPOSE

Author's purpose refers to the reason(s) a writer has for writing. Here are a few examples: Textbook authors write to inform and present information. Advertising copy writers write to sell products or services. Comic strip writers write to amuse, entertain, or provide social commentary. Essay writers write to inform, describe, or persuade.

Recognizing an author's purpose can help you decide what critical questions to ask. It can also provide a means of evaluating the material. Ask yourself: How effectively did the author accomplish what he or she set out to accomplish?

For many types of material, the author's purpose is obvious. You know, for example, that the directions on a toy carton are written to tell you how to assemble it and that an advertisement is written to sell a product or service. Other times, the author's purpose is less obvious. To find the author's purpose, use the suggestions in the following table:

HOW TO IDENTIFY THE AUTHOR'S PURPOSE

What to Consider	Questions to Ask	Example
Consider the source of the material.	• Is the source specific and detailed? • To whom do the examples appeal? • Are the ideas complex and sophisticated or obvious and straightforward? • Is the language simple or difficult?	A review of a rock concert that appeared in *Rolling Stone* would be quite different in style, content and purpose than an article that appeared in *Popular Music & Society*.
Consider the intended audience.	• To what interest level, age, sex, occupational, or ethnic groups would this material appeal?	An article about a musical rock group appearing in *Teen Vogue* may be written to encourage concert attendance or increase its popularity.

| Consider the point of view (the perspective from which the material is written). | • Is the point of view objective (factual) or subjective (showing emotion and feeling)?
• Are both sides of an issue shown, or does the writer present or favor only one side? | A rock concert may be described quite differently by a music critic, a teenager, and a classical music fan, each with different attitudes and opinions expressed. |
| Consider what the writer may be trying to prove. | • Is the material written to persuade you to accept a particular viewpoint or take a particular action? | A rock concert promoter may write to encourage concert attendance; a music critic may argue that the group has copied the style of another group. |

DIRECTIONS   For each of the following passages, identify the author's purpose.

Exercise 6

Passage 1

Quotation by Jay Leno

For the first time ever, overweight people outnumber average people in America. Doesn't that make overweight the average then? Last month you were fat, now you're average—hey, let's get a pizza!

— Jay Leno, www.workinghumor.com/quotes/jay_leno.shtml

Purpose: _____

_____

Passage 2

Shawn Fanning

Shawn Fanning grew up in a welfare family. Brothers and sisters were in and out of foster homes. His break came when an uncle brought Shawn to his Cape Cod computer game company and gave him a computer. Fascinated, the teenager found new direction. It didn't make him rich, though. When it came time for college, Fanning, with only $80, could afford to apply to only two colleges.

In freshman year at Northeastern University in Boston, Fanning listened to his roommates' complaints that they couldn't find the music they wanted to download from the Internet, Fanning decided to write a program to help. He obsessed about the project. He wrote code day and night until he had a system that would allow people to tap into each other's hard drives for MP3 downloads.

That was in 1998. The rest is history. Fanning dropped out of college, found a venture capitalist, moved to Silicon Valley and went into business. His program, called **Napster** after his childhood nickname, almost instantly attracted thousands of music fans, who began trading millions of songs online.

—Vivian, *The Media of Mass Communication*, p. 136

Purpose: _____

_____

Passage 3

Life in the Universe

What about the existence of intelligent life that could communicate with us? Some scientists argue that as a result of natural selection, the evolution of intelligence is inevitable wherever life arises. Others point to the history of life on Earth—consisting of at least 2.5 billion years, during which all life was made up of single-celled organisms—to argue that most life in the universe must be "simple and dumb." It is clear from our explorations of the solar system that none of the sun's other planets host intelligent life. The nearest sun-like stars that could host an Earth-like planet, Alpha Centauri A and B, are over 4 light years away—nearly 40 trillion miles. With current technologies, it would take nearly 50,000 years to reach the Alpha Centauri stars, and there is certainly no guarantee that intelligent life would be found on any planets that circle them. For all practical purposes, at this time in human history, we are still unique and alone in the universe.

—Belk and Borden, *Biology: Science for Life*, p. 41

Purpose: _____

_____

Goal 6
Recognize bias

BE ALERT FOR BIAS

Bias refers to an author's partiality, inclination toward a particular viewpoint, or prejudice. A writer is biased, for example, if she or he takes one side of a controversial issue and does not recognize opposing viewpoints. Perhaps the best example of bias occurs in advertising. A magazine advertisement for a new snack cracker, for instance, describes only positive selling features: taste, low cholesterol, convenience, and crunch. The ad does not recognize the cracker's negative features: that it's high in calories, high in fat, and so on. In some material, the writer is direct and forthright in expressing his or her bias; at other times, the bias is less obvious and is left for the reader to discover through careful analysis.

Read the following passage about global warming:

Al Gore's "The ice is melting!" rant deserves as much attention as Chicken Little's "The sky is falling!" The problem is he and other global-warming alarmists are getting as much attention as Chicken Little did. And while the fabled fowl was only trying to be helpful, the unscrupulous intent of global-warming alarmists is to set up an energy-regulating global government and an international carbon-trading market worth billions. Even though polar ice conditions are far from unusual or dangerous, these climate tycoons have far too much at stake to ever admit the sky isn't falling and humans aren't to blame. The public would do well to remember when Chicken Little's friends joined in her hysteria, they ended up as dinner in the fox's den. Unless countered through sound facts and reasoning, global-warming hysteria will end with much the same fate.

—Terrell, "Are the Polar Ice Caps Melting," *The New American*

In this passage, the author's bias against the belief in global warming is clear. The author's choice of words—*rant, Chicken Little, alarmists, unscrupulous, tycoons,* and *hysteria*—reveals a negative attitude. Note, too, that the author's selection of detail is biased; no evidence confirming global warming is offered.

RECOGNIZING BIAS

To identify bias, apply the following steps:

1. **Pay attention to emotional language.** Does the author use numerous positive or negative terms to describe the subject?
2. **Notice descriptive language.** What impression is created? How does the author make you feel?
3. **Look for opposing viewpoints.** Does the author present or ignore disadvantages, limitations, and alternative solutions?

DIRECTIONS Read each of the following statements, and place a check mark in front of any that reveal bias.

Exercise 7

_____ 1. Hydrogen is by far the best choice for an alternative fuel.

_____ 2. Intelligent design should not be taught in schools along with evolution.

_____ 3. In 1913, Arthur Whynne created the first crossword puzzle.

_____ 4. The Swim to Stay Fit Program gives students an excellent way to get in shape.

_____ 5. A third of all students today buy their back-to-school items online. ●

DIRECTIONS Describe the author's bias in each of the following statements.

Exercise 8

1. Those clamoring to shut down the farmers, however, should look hard at the prospect of a prairie full of subdivisions and suburban pollution: car exhaust, lawn and garden fertilizers, woodstoves, sewage. Certainly, the smoke from field burning is an annoyance, particularly to the hard-hit Sandpoint area, and to some it's a health hazard. But the benefits the sturdy farmers produce 50 weeks of the year shouldn't be dismissed casually.

   —Oliveria, "Burning Will Go; That's Not All Good," _Spokesman Review_

2. Cruises are one of the best buys in vacationing today. Prices have not increased in over a decade yet the amenities on board have improved year after year. And the service is second to none. Passengers are pampered by employees at every turn; by the pool, in the many dining rooms, in the casino, and in their cabins, with a steward on call 24 hours a day.

   —Adapted from Cook, Yale, Marqua, _Tourism: The Business of Travel,_ p. 245

3. While world leaders once again pledged to help Africa, the many poor people in another part of the developing world, Latin America, attract little notice. There is a reason for that oversight: all but a wretched pair (Haiti and Nicaragua) of Latin American countries are officially classed as "middle-income" and all (except Cuba) are democracies. Latin America is less of a stain on the world's conscience.

   —"Not Always With Us," _The Economist_

4. NASCAR can't make vague rules. This bunch of young race-car drivers is high-strung and emotional. They're hot-headed, and they react to everything quickly. They don't have the wisdom and patience of an older driver. They are young men who are wired to the max. They're coiled up like a snake all the time, and they're ready to strike at anybody or anything.

   —Waltrip, "Calling Dr. Phil: NASCAR Needs Black-and-White Penalties,"
   FOXSports.com ●

Exercise 9

DIRECTIONS   Read the following passage. Underline words and phrases that reveal the author's bias.

Jerry's Got to Be Kidding
Why Disabled People Aren't Laughing

People with disabilities are outraged by the backward practices of telethons, the worst of which is the Jerry Lewis Muscular Dystrophy Association (MDA) Telethon. Some of us demonstrated against last fall's Labor Day telethon. As a writer–activist and a severely disabled person who must use a power wheelchair to get around, I helped lead a vigil outside the telethon in Los Angeles, as did others in Chicago, Denver, and other cities.

Do I watch the telethon? Yes, on tape, in manageable doses to avoid a stroke. Jerry Lewis' comedy career began with crude imitations of disabled people. He continues with smarmy, self-glorifying performances of songs like "The Wind Beneath My Wings" while mugging, beaglelike, at the camera or one of his disabled "kids." He encapsulates everything that disabled people wish to escape.

I have polio, not muscular dystrophy. Nevertheless, the stigma created by the telethon smears *all* physically disabled people. And those without muscular dystrophy do not even receive any of the MDA's stingy services.

—Bolte, *In These Times* ●

Goal ❼
Analyze tone

myreadinglab

To practice analyzing tone, go to
> Purpose and Tone

ANALYZE THE AUTHOR'S TONE

In speech, a speaker's tone of voice often reveals his or her attitude toward the subject and contributes to the overall message. Tone is also evident in a piece of writing, and it also contributes to meaning. Recognizing an author's tone is often important because tone can reveal feelings, attitudes, or viewpoints not directly stated by the author. An author's tone is achieved primarily through word choice and stylistic features such as sentence pattern and length.

Tone, then, often reveals feelings. Many human emotions can be communicated through tone—disapproval, hate, admiration, disgust, gratitude, and forcefulness are examples.

A list of words frequently used to identify tone are shown in the table below.

WORDS FREQUENTLY USED TO DESCRIBE TONE				
abstract	condemning	flippant	irreverent	playful
absurd	condescending	forgiving	joyful	reverent
amused	convincing	formal	loving	righteous
angry	cynical	frustrated	malicious	sarcastic
apathetic	depressing	gentle	melancholic	satiric
arrogant	detached	grim	mocking	sensational
assertive	disapproving	hateful	nostalgic	serious
awestruck	disrespectful	humorous	objective	solemn
bitter	distressed	impassioned	obsequious	sympathetic
caustic	docile	incredulous	optimistic	tragic
celebratory	earnest	indignant	outraged	uncomfortable
cheerful	excited	indirect	pathetic	vindictive
comic	fanciful	intimate	persuasive	worried
compassionate	farcical	ironic	pessimistic	

Read the following passage, paying particular attention to the feeling it creates.

What You Don't Know About Indians: Native American Issues Are Not History

Most Americans, even those deeply concerned about issues of justice, tend to speak of Indian issues as tragedies of the distant past. So ingrained is this position that when the occasional non-Indian does come forward on behalf of *today's* Indian cause—Marlon Brando, William Kunstler, Robert Redford, Jane Fonda, David Brower—they are all dismissed as "romantics." People are a bit embarrassed for them, as if they'd stepped over some boundary of propriety.

The Indian issue is *not* part of the distant past. Many of the worst anti-Indian campaigns were undertaken scarcely 80 to 100 years ago. Your great-grandparents were already alive at the time. The Model-T Ford was on the road.

And the assaults continue today. While the Custer period of direct military action against Indians may be over in the United States, more subtle though equally devastating "legalistic" manipulations continue to separate Indians from their land and their sovereignty.

—Mander, *Utne Reader*

Here the author's tone is concerned and serious. He is concerned about Native American issues and current legal manipulations.

IDENTIFYING TONE

Use the following tips and questions to identify the author's tone:

1. **Consider how the material makes you feel.** What emotions surface?
2. **Study the author's word choice.** Does he or she use words that provoke strong feelings? Which words and phrases have positive or negative associations or connotations? (See p. 224 for more about connotative language.)
3. **Study how the author writes.** Is the material straightforward and factual or does the writer play with language, use sarcasm or humor, or use figurative language?

DIRECTIONS   Describe the tone of each of the following passages.

Exercise 10

1. The caller's voice does not hold together well. I can tell he is quite old and not well. He is calling from Maryland.

    "I want four boxes of the Nut Goodies," he rasps at me after giving me his credit card information in a faltering hurry.

    "There are 24 bars in each box," I say in case he doesn't know the magnitude of his order. Nut Goodies are made here in St. Paul and consist of a patty of maple cream covered with milk chocolate and peanuts. Sort of a Norwegian praline.

    "OK, then make it five boxes but hurry this up before my nurse gets back."

    He wants the order billed to a home address but sent to a nursing home.

    "I've got Parkinson's," he says. "I'm 84."

    "OK, sir. I think I've got it all. They're on the way." I put a rush on it.

    "Right. Bye," he says, and in the pause when he is concentrating God knows how much energy on getting the receiver back in its cradle, I hear a long, dry chuckle.

One hundred and twenty Nut Goodies.
Way to go, buddy.

—Swardson, *City Pages*

Tone: _____

_____

2. **Gleanings**

So these three economists are on one of those Washington week-in-review shows.
You know, the kind where reliable gray men with bad haircuts wear sincere
gray suits and everybody talks to each other with pained grimaces like they're
reunited school chums harboring a deadly secret ("She's *all* of our problem now,
Finchley"). At prediction time, the grayest of the men says the economy is about
to shoot toward unprecedented growth, the slate-colored one warns of triple-
dip recession-sugar cone extra and the steely guy says "no change." Three different pointy heads, one economy, three totally different predictions. These are the
experts? What the hell kind of job is that?

—Durst, "We Don't Know Squat"

Tone: _____

_____

3. **What You Need**

You need a large wooden frame and enough space to accommodate it. Put
comfortable chairs around it, allowing for eight women of varying ages, weight,
coloring, and cultural orientation. It is preferable that this large wood frame be
located in a room in a house in Atwater or Los Banos or a small town outside
Bakersfield called Grasse. It should be a place that gets a thick, moist blanket of
tule fog in the winter and be hot as blazes in the summer. Fix plenty of lemonade.
Cookies are a nice complement.

When you choose your colors, make them sympathetic to one another.
Consider the color wheel of grammar school—primary colors, phenomena of light
and dark; avoid antagonism of hues—it detracts from the pleasure of the work.
Think of music as you orchestrate the shades and patterns; pretend that you are a
conductor in a lush symphony hall; imagine the audience saying *Ooh* and *Ahh* as
they applaud your work.

—Otto, *How to Make an American Quilt*

Tone: _____

_____

Exercise 11

DIRECTIONS   Read the article titled "Getting Found Out, Web 2.0 Style" in Part
Five on p. 480 and complete the following items.

1. Evaluate the source of the article and the author's credentials.
2. Identify two statements of fact and two statements expressing opinion.
3. What was the author's purpose in writing the article?
4. Is the author biased?
5. Write two or three words that describe the author's tone. ●

ANALYZE ARGUMENTS

An argument has three essential parts:

- **issue**
- **claim**
- **support**

First, an argument must address an **issue**—a problem or controversy about which people disagree. Abortion, gun control, animal rights, capital punishment, and drug legalization are all examples of issues. Second, an argument must take a position on an issue. This position is called a **claim**. An argument may claim that capital punishment should be outlawed or that medical use of marijuana should be legalized. Finally, an argument offers **support** for the claim. Support consists of reasons and evidence that the claim is reasonable and should be accepted. An argument may also include a fourth part—a **refutation**. A refutation considers opposing viewpoints and attempts to disprove or discredit them.

Here is an example: baseball players' use of steroids is an issue. A claim could be made that baseball players' use of steroids is unhealthy and unfair and that owners and players need to take the issue seriously. Support for the claim could include reasons why steroid use is unhealthy and unfair. An opposing viewpoint to the author's argument may be that steroid use creates enhanced performance, which makes the game more fun and competitive for fans. This argument could be refuted by providing evidence that fans dislike extraordinary feats of performance and would prefer to see the game played without the use of performance-enhancing drugs.

For most issues, more than one claim is possible. For example, on the issue of gun control, here are three possible claims:

- All handguns should be legal.
- No handguns should be legal.
- Some handguns should be legal for certain individuals.

Consider the issue of recycling. Here are three possible claims:

- Recycling should be mandatory.
- Recycling should be optional.
- Recycling should be required for industries with large amounts of recyclable waste.

An **argument**, then, takes one position on an issue and provides reasons and evidence that its claim is sound or believable.

Goal 8

Analyze arguments

PEARSON
myreadinglab

To practice analyzing arguments, go to
> Critical Thinking

DIRECTIONS For each of the following issues, identify at least two claims and write a sentence expressing each.

1. Immigration laws restricting entry into the United States

   _____

   _____

2. Drug testing in the workplace

   _____

   _____

Exercise 12

3. Smoking in public places

_____

_____ ●

Exercise 13

DIRECTIONS   For each of the following essay titles, predict the issue and claim that the essay addresses.

1. "Organic Farming: Quality and Environmental Care"
2. "Park Neighbors Applaud Curfew"
3. "Limited Access Limits Votes of Disabled"
4. "Global Warming Linked to Hurricanes"
5. "Solar Energy: An Energy Alternative Whose Time Has Come" ●

Types of Support

Three common types of support for arguments are reasons, evidence, and emotional appeals. A **reason** is a general statement that supports a claim. It explains why the writer's viewpoint is reasonable and should be accepted. In an argument opposing steroid use by baseball players, two primary reasons are

- It is unhealthy.
- It is unfair.

Evidence consists of facts, statistics, experiences, comparisons, and examples that demonstrate why the claim is valid. To support the claim that steroids are unhealthy, a writer could offer medical facts that demonstrate that steroids are dangerous to one's health. Alternatively, the writer could provide an example of a player who used steroids and describe his health problems.

Emotional appeals are ideas that are targeted toward needs or values that readers are likely to care about. Needs include physiological needs (food, drink, shelter) and psychological needs (sense of belonging, sense of accomplishment, sense of self-worth, sense of competency). In an argument against steroid use, the writer could appeal to a reader's sense of fairness—players should not be allowed to succeed by using drugs rather than natural talent. The writer could also appeal to the reader's sense of nostalgia by mentioning baseball traditions that are being corrupted. An argument favoring gun control, for example, may appeal to a reader's need for safety, while an argument favoring restrictions on sharing personal or financial information may appeal to a reader's need for privacy and financial security.

Exercise 14

DIRECTIONS   Identify the type(s) of evidence used to support each of the following brief arguments.

1. Many students have part-time jobs that require them to work late afternoons and evenings during the week. These students are unable to use the library during the week. Therefore, library hours should be extended to weekends.
2. Because parents have the right to influence their children's sexual attitudes, sex education should take place in the home, not at school.

3. No one should be forced to inhale unpleasant or harmful substances. That's why the ban on cigarette smoking in public places was put into effect in our state. Why shouldn't there be a law to prevent people from wearing strong colognes or perfumes, especially in restaurants, since the sense of smell is important to taste? ●

EVALUATE THE DATA AND EVIDENCE

Goal 9
Evaluate evidence

Once you have understood a writer's argument by identifying what is asserted and how, the next step is to evaluate the soundness, correctness, and worth of the reasons and evidence that support the assertion. As a critical reader, your task is to assess whether the evidence is sufficient to support the claim. Let's look at a few types of evidence that are often used.

FACTS   Be sure the facts are taken from a reliable source and are verifiable.

PERSONAL EXPERIENCE   Writers often substantiate their ideas through experience and observation. Although a writer's personal account of a situation may provide an interesting perspective on an issue, personal experience should not be accepted as proof. The observer may be biased or may have exaggerated or incorrectly perceived a situation.

EXAMPLES   Examples can illustrate or explain a principle, concept, or idea. To explain what aggressive behavior is, your psychology instructor may offer several examples: fighting, punching, and kicking. Examples should not be used by themselves to prove the concept or idea they illustrate, as is done in the following passage:

> The American judicial system treats those who are called for jury duty unfairly. It is clear from my sister's experience that the system has little regard for the needs of those called as jurors. My sister was required to report for jury duty the week she was on vacation. She spent the entire week in a crowded, stuffy room waiting to be called to sit on a jury and never was called.

The sister's experience does sound unfair, but it, by itself, does not prove anything about the entire judicial system.

STATISTICS   Many people are impressed by statistics—the reporting of figures, percentages, averages, and so forth—and assume that they are irrefutable proof. Actually, statistics can be misused, misinterpreted, or used selectively to give other than the most objective, accurate picture of a situation. Always approach statistical evidence with a critical, questioning attitude.

Statistics are often presented in graphical form. Writers use graphs to make points dramatically. At times they may exaggerate certain data by manipulating how the graph is drawn or by their choice of what scale to use. For more information on how to read graphs, see pp. 275–89.

COMPARISONS AND ANALOGIES   Comparisons and analogies (extended comparisons) serve as illustrations and are often used in argument. Their reliability depends on how closely the comparison corresponds, or how similar it is, to the situation to which it is being compared. For example, Martin Luther King, Jr., in his famous letter from the Birmingham jail, compared nonviolent protesters to a robbed man. To evaluate this comparison, you would need to consider how the two are similar and how they are different.

APPEAL TO AUTHORITY   A writer may quote a well-known person or expert on the issue. Unless the well-known person is knowledgeable or experienced with the issue, his or her opinion is not relevant. Whenever an expert is cited, be certain that the expert offers support for her or his opinion.

CAUSE–EFFECT RELATIONSHIPS   A writer may argue that when two events occurred in close sequence, one caused the other. In other words, a writer may assume a cause–effect relationship when none exists. For example, suppose unemployment decreased the year a new town mayor was elected. The mayor may claim she brought about the decrease in unemployment. However, the decrease may have been caused by factors the mayor was not involved with, such as a large corporation opening a branch within the town and creating new jobs.

Relevancy and Sufficiency of Evidence

Once you have identified the evidence used to support an argument, the next step is to decide whether the writer has provided enough of the right kind of evidence to lead you to accept his or her claim. This is always a matter of judgment; there are no easy rules to follow. You must determine (1) whether the evidence provided directly supports the statement and (2) whether sufficient evidence has been provided.

Suppose an article in your campus newspaper urges the elimination of mathematics as a required course at your college. As evidence, the student offers the following:

> Mathematics does not prepare us for the job market. In today's world, calculators and computer programs have eliminated the need for the study of mathematics.

This evidence neither directly supports the statement nor provides sufficient evidence. First, calculators and computer programs do not substitute for an understanding of mathematical principles. Second, the writer does nothing to substantiate his idea that mathematics is irrelevant to the job market. The writer should provide facts, statistics, expert opinion, or other forms of documentation.

Exercise 15

DIRECTIONS   For each of the following statements, discuss the type or types of evidence that you would need in order to support and evaluate the statement.

1. Individuals must accept primary responsibility for the health and safety of their children.
2. Apologizing is often seen as a sign of weakness, especially among men.
3. There has been a steady increase in illegal immigration over the past 50 years.
4. More college women than college men agree that euthanasia should be legal.
5. Car advertisements sell fantasy experiences, not a means of transportation. ●

Reading an Argument

When reading arguments, use the following steps:

READING ARGUMENTS

1. **Identify the issue.** What controversial question or problem does the argument address?
2. **Identify the claim/position, idea, or action the writer is trying to persuade you to accept.** Often, a concise statement of this key point appears early in the argument or in the introduction of a formal essay. The author often restates this key point.
3. **Read the entire article or essay completely, more than once if necessary.** Underline key evidence that supports the author's claim.
4. **Evaluate the types of evidence the author provides.** Does he or she offer statistics, facts, or examples? Is the evidence relevant and sufficient?
5. **Watch for conclusions.** Words and phrases such as *since, thus, therefore, accordingly, it can be concluded, it is clear that, it follows that,* and *hence* are signals that a conclusion is about to be given.
6. **Reread the argument and examine its content and structure.** What is stated? What is implied or suggested?
7. **Write a brief outline of the argument, listing its key points.**

Now read the following brief argument, applying the steps listed above.

Misstep on Video Violence
USA Today

In the booming world of video games, there are more than a few dark corners: Murder and mayhem. Blood and gore. Explicit sex and abuse of women. In one of the best-selling series, *Grand Theft Auto*, car stealing is accompanied by drug use, shootouts that kill police and bystanders, and simulated sex with comely prostitutes who are beaten with baseball bats afterward.

> **Tip** *Booming* means "growing, increasing."

Small wonder some parents are concerned over what game-crazed teens may be up to. And small wonder, too, that legislators in several states are playing to these concerns by trying to outlaw the sale of violent and sexually explicit games to minors. A bill banning the sale of such games to anyone younger than 18 is awaiting the governor's signature in Illinois. A similar proposal is moving in the Michigan Legislature. The issue has been raised this year in at least nine other states and the District of Columbia. But to what useful end?

> **Tip** *Small wonder* means "it isn't surprising."

This is the latest chapter in a very old story. When teenage entertainment offends adult sensibilities—think Elvis Presley's pulsating hips or the arrival on newsstands of Hugh Hefner's *Playboy*—the first response is to see the new phenomenon as a threat to social order. The second is to attempt to ban it. Parents—former teenagers all—seem to forget history's lesson: The bans never work. And they're probably not constitutional, anyway. Courts have ruled that today's sophisticated video games are protected as creative expression. If communities want to limit access, they must show overriding evidence that the games pose a public threat. That evidence does not exist.

Lawmakers and activist groups assert that the thrill of engaging in virtual criminal activity will spur teens to try the real thing. But the violent crime rate has gone down nearly 30% since the first bloody shoot-'em-up games debuted in the early 1990s. Youth crime rates have dropped even more. And a Federal Trade Commission

survey found parents already involved in 83% of video-game purchases and rentals for minors.

Judges have repeatedly rejected as flawed the studies that advocates say show a link between fantasy violence and anti-social behavior. To the extent there is a threat, it is mainly to the individual, vulnerable teenager, and it can be addressed only by parents.

Unknown to many parents, they're getting some help. The game industry's rating system classifies games in six categories from "early childhood" to "adults only" and requires detailed content descriptions. Also, newer models of popular games include parental controls that can block their use for age-inappropriate games. Manufacturers have announced an expanded ratings-education program, and major retailers are tightening their restrictions on sales to minors.

There will always be a market for the dark, tasteless, even the outrageous, and parents ought to keep kids away from it. But even with the best intentions of legislators, the problem is beyond their reach. New laws are likely to give parents only the false impression that someone else is solving that problem for them.

—*USA Today,* June 6, 2005

The issue discussed in the argument is legislation banning video violence. The author takes the position that legislation is not effective in controlling video violence.

The author offers the following reasons:

- The bans never work. He cites the examples of Elvis Presley and *Playboy* magazine.
- The bans may not be constitutional.
- The games do not pose a public threat. He or she offers statistics that violent crime is dropping since video games came on the market.
- Many parents already monitor video game use.
- The game industry already classifies the games, gives details of their content, and plans a ratings education program.
- Retailers are tightening restrictions on sales to minors.

DIRECTIONS   Read the argument below, paying particular attention to the type(s) of evidence used. Then answer the questions that follow.

Is a border fence the answer to the illegal immigration problem?

I am acutely aware of the challenges of securing our borders, having served for more than 26 years with the U.S. Border Patrol. I have not only patrolled the U.S.-Mexican border but also supervised thousands of hard-working, dedicated Border Patrol agents and initiated a successful deterrence strategy called Operation Hold the Line. I also supported fencing certain strategic areas to augment enforcement. I strongly feel, however, that erecting nearly 700 miles of fencing on our Southern border is wasteful, irresponsible and unnecessary, and I voted against the Secure Fence Act.

Hundreds of miles of fencing will do little to curb the flow of undocumented immigrants and could even increase demand for human smuggling. It will only provide a false sense of security for supporters of a hard line on immigration reform. With construction expected to exceed $1.2 billion and lifetime maintenance of up to $50 billion, the exorbitant cost of this border fence would be better invested in additional Border Patrol agents, equipment and technology.

As the only member of Congress with a background in border control, I have worked to educate my colleagues that existing policies and the border fence will do little to honor our legacy as a nation of immigrants and will threaten our nation's security. I have worked with the Department of Homeland Security (DHS), hosted many leaders at annual border conferences and have emphasized that border communities must be consulted in fencing decisions.

Unfortunately, DHS Secretary Michael Chertoff recently made the troubling announcement that he intends to waive more than 30 federal environmental laws to expedite construction of the fence. This approach continues DHS's continued disregard for border communities and undermines decades-old policies that have preserved many of our region's most valuable environmental assets, cultural sites and endangered wildlife.

After Secretary Chertoff's decision, I joined 13 of my colleagues in submitting an *amicus* brief to the U.S. Supreme Court, asking the justices to hear an appeal challenging the secretary's waiver authority.

Our nation needs comprehensive immigration reform with three main components: strengthened border security; an earned path to legalization along with tough, strictly enforced sanctions against employers who hire undocumented immigrants; and a guest worker program. Hundreds of miles of border fencing is not the answer.

—Silvestre Reyes, Former El Paso Sector Chief,
U.S. Border Patrol. Written for *CQ Researcher,* September 2008

1. What is the issue? _____

_____

2. What is the claim? _____

_____

3. What types of evidence are used? _____

_____

4. Is the evidence convincing? _____

_____

5. Is there sufficient evidence? Why or why not? _____

_____

6. What action is called for? _____

_____ ●

USING COLLEGE TEXTBOOKS
Critical Thinking Questions

Textbooks contain information on a variety of topics and issues, many of which demand critical thinking and evaluation. Many textbook authors include features in their textbooks that guide students to think critically, evaluate chapter content, and make connections to their other coursework and their own lives. For instance, critical thinking questions are designed to help you process and apply the information you have learned. In the excerpt below from an environmental studies textbook, the question requires readers to fully understand factors that influence population growth.

> **5. THINK IT THROUGH**   India's prime minister puts you in charge of that nation's population policy. India has a population growth rate of 1.6% per year, a TFR of 2.7, a 49% rate of contraceptive use, and a population that is 71% rural. What policy steps would you recommend, and why?

—Withgott, *Environment*, p. 222

Use critical thinking questions to broaden your understanding of what you have read. The example below, taken from a communication textbook, requires the reader to understand how groups function and then apply the information to real situations in his or her own life. By thinking about the information in terms of real examples, students get a deeper understanding of chapter content.

> **THINKING CRITICALLY   About Members and Leaders**
> 1. **Group Role in Interpersonal Relationships.** Can you identify roles that you habitually or frequently serwve in certain groups? Do you serve these roles in your friendship, love, and family relationships as well?
> 2. **Groupthink.** Have you ever been in a group when groupthink was operating? If so, what were its symptoms? What effect did groupthink have on the process and conclusions of the group?

—DeVito, *Human Communication*, p. 240

FURTHER PRACTICE WITH TEXTBOOK READING
Part A: Sample Textbook Chapter

Read the quote on pages 495 and 497. Then, answer the questions based on your understanding of the sections.

Part B: Your College Textbook

Choose a textbook chapter that you have been assigned to read for one of your other courses. Read the chapter, and then answer the critical thinking questions at the end. If your textbook chapter does not have any, then write your own questions and answer them.

SELF-TEST
SUMMARY

Goal 1 What is an inference?	An inference is a reasoned guess about what you do not know based on information that you do have.
Goal 2 Why is it important to check the source of material?	Not all sources are reliable or trustworthy.
Goal 3 Why should you check the author's qualifications?	Not all authors are qualified to write about their subjects. From an unqualified author you may get incomplete or incorrect information.
Goal 4 What is the difference between facts and opinions?	Facts are statements that can be verified as correct. Opinions express feelings, attitudes, and beliefs and are neither true nor false.
Goal 5 How can you identify an author's purpose?	You can identify an author's purpose by considering the source and point of view of the author's writing, as well as any persuasive statements he or she makes.
Goal 6 What is author bias?	Author bias refers to an author's partiality or inclination to express only one viewpoint.
Goal 7 What is tone?	Tone is an expression of the author's attitude toward his or her subject.
Goal 8 What are the three parts of an argument?	An argument addresses an issue, takes a position or makes a claim, and presents reasons and evidence to support the position.
Goal 9 What are seven types of evidence?	Evidence includes facts, personal experience, examples, statistics, comparisons and analogies, appeals to authority, and cause–effect relationships.

APPLYING   YOUR SKILLS

DISCUSSING THE CHAPTER

1. Think about editorials that you've read in your school or local paper. What makes a great editorial? What makes a poor editorial? What techniques can an author use to present his or her argument and supporting evidence in an editorial?
2. Why is making inferences helpful in college studies? What subjects most frequently require you to make inferences?
3. What types of evidence are typically used in articles related to the topics you are studying? What types of questions should you ask when dealing with these various types of evidence?

ANALYZING A STUDY SITUATION

Ian is taking a business course in which he is studying forms of business ownership: sole proprietorships, partnerships, corporations, cooperatives, syndicates, and joint ventures. He read and highlighted his textbook and attended all class lectures. To prepare for an essay exam, Ian made a study sheet summarizing the characteristics of each form of ownership. When Ian read the following exam question, he knew he was in trouble.

Exam Question

Suppose you are the sole proprietor of a successful car wash. The owner of a competing car wash suggests that you form a partnership. Another competitor suggests that you enter into a joint venture to explore expansion opportunities. And a major car wash chain offers you a management position and stock in the corporation if you sell out. Write an essay explaining what factors you would consider in making a decision.

1. What levels of thinking did Ian use in preparing for the exam?
2. Why was Ian in trouble? That is, what types of thinking does the question demand?
3. How should Ian have prepared for the exam?

WORKING ON COLLABORATIVE PROJECTS

DIRECTIONS   Bring to class a brief (two- or three-paragraph) newspaper article, editorial, film review, etc. Working in groups of three or four students, each student should read his or her piece aloud or distribute copies. The group should discuss and evaluate (1) the source of the material,

(2) the author's qualifications, (3) whether more facts or opinions are represented, (4) the author's purpose, (5) any bias, and (6) the tone of the passage. Your group should choose one article and submit your findings to the class or instructor.

| | For support in meeting this chapter's goals, go to **MyReadingLab** and select **Inference, Purpose and Tone,** and **Critical Thinking.** |

Quick **QUIZ**

DIRECTIONS   Write the letter of the choice that best completes each statement in the space provided.

CHECKING YOUR RECALL

_____ 1. A fact is a statement that
  a. can be verified.
  b. is true.
  c. has no proof.
  d. expresses an opinion.

_____ 2. Statistics must be evaluated primarily because they may
  a. include too many facts.
  b. have appeared in another source first.
  c. have been manipulated.
  d. be based on another person's research.

_____ 3. All of the following questions indicate a higher level of thinking *except:*
  a. What are the author's qualifications?
  b. Is the material fact or opinion?
  c. What is the literal meaning of the material?
  d. What is the author's purpose?

_____ 4. One characteristic of biased writing is that it
  a. analyzes examples in great detail.
  b. favors a particular viewpoint.
  c. presents evidence objectively.
  d. consists primarily of untrue statements.

_____ 5. The author's position in an argument can best be described as the
  a. author's paraphrase of the issue.
  b. author's collection of relevant evidence.
  c. idea the author wants you to agree with.
  d. concept the author is refuting.

APPLYING YOUR SKILLS

_____ 6. Antonio arrived several minutes late for his sociology class and discovered the room empty and dark. He decided that the class must have been canceled and went to the library instead. In this situation, Antonio reached his decision by making
  a. an informed opinion.
  b. an inference.
  c. a generalization.
  d. a connotation.

_____ 7. In her research on homeschooling, Raquel has encountered the following statements. The one that is an example of an opinion is:
  a. Over half a million children are home-schooled annually.
  b. Homeschooled children completely miss out on all those normal social advantages that a child in public school gets every day.
  c. Most parents who homeschool their children have had at least one year of college.
  d. Most homeschooling parents are middle-class, with median incomes between $35,000 and $50,000.

_____ 8. Robert has a literature assignment in which he has to identify Jane Austen's tone in *Persuasion.* In this assignment, he will be looking specifically for Austen's
  a. feelings about her subject.
  b. purpose for writing.
  c. style of writing.
  d. use of historical information.

_____ 9. Analise wants to identify bias in the articles she has found while researching the need for increased security in courtrooms. Analise can assume an article is biased when the author
  a. presents both sides of a controversial issue.
  b. includes numerous facts and statistics as evidence.
  c. attempts to appeal to a general-interest audience.
  d. uses primarily positive or negative terms to describe the subject.

_____ 10. Trevor has been asked to evaluate the argument presented by the author of an article on the use of the atomic bomb in World War II. As a critical reader, Trevor should evaluate an argument primarily by deciding whether the
  a. author's ideas agree with his own.
  b. evidence is relevant and sufficient.
  c. author's personal experience is interesting and believable.
  d. supporting details are presented dramatically.

Evaluating Authors' Techniques

LEARNING GOALS

In this chapter you will learn how to

1 Recognize and interpret connotative language

2 Recognize and interpret figurative language

3 Identify missing information

4 Identify generalizations

5 Analyze assumptions

6 Recognize manipulative language

LEARNING EXPERIMENT

1 Read each of the following statements.

_____ 1. The governor of our state is a loose cannon.

_____ 2. They say that the economy is booming and will show further improvement over the next year.

_____ 3. The tendency to prefer products and people from one's own culture over those from other cultures is known as ethnocentrism.

_____ 4. Politicians are a greedy, lazy bunch.

_____ 5. People in glass houses shouldn't throw stones.

_____ 6. Senator Whiner's foreign policies were criticized and then defeated.

2 Place a check mark in front of each of the above statements that you think is true, for which you do not need further information, and which you could safely use in a research paper, provided that it came from a reliable source and you documented that source.

THE RESULTS

Did you check only statements 3 and 6? If so, this shows that you are a questioning, critical thinker. All of the other statements are not usable. You need further explanation, evidence, or more information before you can accept them as reliable.

LEARNING PRINCIPLE: WHAT THIS MEANS TO YOU

Reading with a critical eye and a questioning attitude is an important skill. This chapter will show you how to recognize the various techniques writers can use to mislead, misguide, or even deceive a reader. You will learn how to spot emotional language, interpret figurative language, spot missing information, examine generalizations and assumptions, and study manipulative language.

WHY EVALUATE AUTHORS' TECHNIQUES?

Evaluating an author's techniques is important because:

- You will become more successful in reading and evaluating a wide range of authors and sources.
- You will be able to select accurate, reliable information to include in many different kinds of assignments.
- You will learn to recognize misleading and manipulative language.

Goal ❶

Recognize and interpret connotative language

PAY ATTENTION TO CONNOTATIVE LANGUAGE

If you were wearing a jacket that looked like leather but was made out of man-made fibers, would you prefer it be called *fake* or *synthetic?* Would you rather be part of a *crowd* or a *mob?* Would you rather be called *thin* or *skinny?*

Each of the pairs of words above has basically the same meaning. A *crowd* and a *mob* are both groups of people. Both *fake* and *synthetic* refer to something manmade. If the words have similar meanings, why did you choose *crowd* rather than *mob* and *synthetic* rather than *fake?* While the pairs of words have similar primary meanings, they carry different shades of meaning; each creates a different image or association in your mind. This section explores these shades of meaning, called connotative meanings.

All words have one or more standard meanings. These meanings are called **denotative meanings.** Think of them as those meanings listed in the dictionary. They tell us what the word names. Many words also have connotative meanings. **Connotative meanings** include the feelings and associations that may accompany a word. For example, the denotative meaning of *sister* is a female sibling. However, the word carries many connotations. For some, *sister* suggests a playmate with whom they shared their childhood. For others the term may suggest an older sibling who watched over them.

Connotations can vary from individual to individual. The denotative meaning for the word *flag* is a piece of cloth used as a national emblem. The American flag itself is a symbol, but to many people the word connotes patriotism and love of one's country. To some people, though, it may connote an interesting decoration to place on their clothing. The word *dog* to dog lovers suggests a loyal and loving companion. To those who are allergic to dogs, however, the word *dog* connotes discomfort and avoidance—itchy eyes, a runny nose, and so forth.

Writers and speakers use connotative meanings to stir your emotions or to bring to mind positive or negative associations. Suppose a writer is describing how someone drinks. The writer could choose words such as *gulp, sip, slurp,* or *guzzle.* Each creates a different image of the person drinking. Connotative meanings, then, are powerful tools of language. When you read, be alert for meanings suggested by the author's word choice. When writing or speaking, be sure to choose words with appropriate connotations.

Exercise 1

DIRECTIONS   For each of the following pairs of words, underline the word with the more positive connotation.

1. suspicious   curious
2. simple   plain
3. shove   nudge

4. immature   youthful
5. mistake   blunder
6. welcome   allow
7. junk   salvage
8. enthusiastic   fanatic
9. timid   shy
10. easygoing   lazy ●

DIRECTIONS For each word listed, write a word that has similar denotative meaning but a negative connotation. Then write a word that has a positive or neutral connotation. Consult a dictionary or thesaurus, if needed.

Exercise 2

Word	Negative Connotation	Positive or Neutral Connotation
Example: slow	sluggish	gradual
1. large	_____	_____
2. persuade	_____	_____
3. characteristic	_____	_____
4. uncommon	_____	_____
5. work	_____	_____
6. protect	_____	_____
7. toss	_____	_____
8. lecture	_____	_____
9. obtain	_____	_____
10. smart	_____	_____ ●

DIRECTIONS Discuss the differences in the connotative meanings of each of the following sets of words. Consult a dictionary, if necessary.

Exercise 3

1. **refuge:** retreat—shelter—hideout
2. **original:** unusual—strange—creative
3. **sensitive:** responsive—thin-skinned—emotional
4. **enemy:** adversary—opponent—rival
5. **tolerant:** permissive—liberal—soft
6. **routine:** regular—predictable—boring
7. **trick:** prank—feat—hoax
8. **complaint:** protest—criticism—gripe
9. **fascinate:** charm—hypnotize—seduce
10. **careful:** cautious—particular—fussy ●

EXAMINE FIGURATIVE LANGUAGE

Goal 2

Recognize and interpret figurative language

Figurative language makes a comparison between two unlike things that share one common characteristic. If you say that your apartment looked as if it had been struck by a tornado, you are comparing two unlike things—your apartment and the effects of a tornado. Figurative language makes sense creatively or imaginatively, but not literally. You mean that the apartment is messy and disheveled, not that a tornado appeared in your living room. Figurative language is a powerful tool that allows writers to create images or paint pictures in the reader's mind. Figurative language also allows writers to suggest an idea without directly stating it. If you say the mayor bellowed like a bear, you are suggesting that the mayor was animal-like, loud, and forceful, but you have not said so directly. By planting the image of bearlike behavior, you have communicated your message to your reader.

There are three primary types of figurative language—similes, metaphors, and personification. A **simile** uses the words *like* or *as* to make the comparison:

The computer hums like a beehive.

After 5:00 P.M. our downtown is as quiet as a ghost town.

A **metaphor** states or implies the relationship between the two unlike items. Metaphors often use the word *is*.

The computer lab is a beehive of activity.

After 5:00 P.M. our downtown is a ghost town.

Personification compares humans and nonhumans according to one characteristic, attributing human characteristics to ideas or objects. If you say "the wind screamed its angry message," you are giving the wind the humanlike characteristics of screaming, being angry, and communicating a message. Here are some other examples:

The sun mocked us with its relentless glare.

After two days of writer's block, her pen started dancing across the page.

Because figurative language is a powerful tool, be sure to analyze the author's motive for using it. Often, a writer uses figurative language as a way of describing rather than telling. A writer could say "The woman blushed" (telling) or "The woman's cheeks filled with the glow of a fire" (describing). Other times, however, figurative language is a means of suggesting ideas or creating impressions without directly stating them. When evaluating figurative language, ask the following questions:

- Why did the writer make the comparison?
- What is the basis or shared characteristic of the comparison?
- Is the comparison accurate?
- What images does the comparison suggest? How do these images make you feel?
- Is the comparison positive or negative?
- Are several different interpretations possible?

Exercise 4

DIRECTIONS   Label each statement as a simile, metaphor, or personification. Then, explain the comparison made in each.

1. The rain moved like a curtain across the lake.
2. At the busy playground, the child was glued to her mother's side.
3. Every time the locker room door opened, a pungent bouquet of dirty socks, wet towels, and sweaty boys smacked us in the face.
4. The roast beef was as tough as an old boot.
5. After hours of delays, the weary passengers were herded like sheep through the airport and onto a hotel shuttle bus. ●

DIRECTIONS Discuss how the writer of each of the following passages uses figurative language to create a specific impression.

1. Aliens have invaded Hollywood. Helped by new computer graphics technology that has simplified the creation of weird-looking extraterrestrials, the silver screen is now crawling with cosmic critters eager to chow down on us, abduct us, or just tick us off as they total our planet. Why are aliens suddenly infesting the local multiplex? Partly it's because after the collapse of the Soviet Union, Hollywood had to hunt around for a new source of bad guys. But our own space program has also convinced many among the popcorn-eating public that visiting other worlds will be a walk in the park for any advanced species.

—Bennett, Shostak, and Jakosky, *Life in the Universe*, p. 2

2. A frequent objection is that poetry ought not to be studied at all. In this view, a poem is either a series of gorgeous noises to be funneled through one ear and out the other without being allowed to trouble the mind, or an experience so holy that to analyze it in a classroom is as cruel and mechanical as dissecting a hummingbird.

—Kennedy and Gioia, *Literature: An Introduction to Fiction, Poetry, and Drama*, p. 454

3. Thick as a truck at its base, the Brazil-nut tree rises 10 stories to an opulent crown, lord of the Amazon jungle. It takes the tree a century to grow to maturity; it takes a man with a chain saw an hour to cut it down. "It's a beautiful thing," nods Acelino Cardoso da Silva, a 57-year-old farmer. "But I have six hungry people at home. If the lumberman turns up, I'll sell."

—Margolis, "A Plot of Their Own," *Newsweek* ●

DIRECTIONS Convert each of the following statements to an expression of figurative language.

Example: The daffodils bloomed. The daffodils covered the hillside like a bright yellow blanket.

1. People cried at the movie.
2. I was embarrassed.
3. We ate too much.
4. The fireworks were beautiful.
5. It snowed a lot last night. ●

WATCH FOR MISSING INFORMATION

Goal 3
Identify missing information

Most writers are honest and straightforward in conveying their meaning; however, some writers use techniques that are intended to mislead or manipulate the reader. Writers mislead by omission. Writers may omit essential details, ignore contradictory evidence, or selectively include only details that favor their position. They may also make incomplete comparisons, use the passive voice, or use unspecified nouns and pronouns.

Suppose, in describing homeschooling, an author states, "Many children find homeschooling rewarding." But what is the author not telling us? If the author does not tell us that some children find homeschooling lonely and feel isolated from their peers, the author is not presenting a fair description of homeschooling. The writer has deliberately omitted essential details that a reader needs to understand homeschooling.

Suppose the same writer describes a research study that concludes that homeschooled children excel academically. The writer, to be fair, should also report that other studies have demonstrated that homeschooled children do not differ in academic achievement from traditionally educated students. In this case, the writer has ignored contradictory evidence, reporting only evidence that he or she wants the reader to know.

One way writers avoid revealing information is to use a particular sentence structure that does not identify who performed a specified action. In the sentence *The bill was paid,* you do not know who paid the bill. This sentence pattern is called the passive voice. Here are a few more examples of the passive voice. In each, notice what information is missing.

> The tax reform bill was defeated.
>
> The accounting procedures were found to be questionable.
>
> The oil spill was contained.

Another way writers avoid revealing information is to use nouns and pronouns that do not refer to a specific person or thing. The sentence *They said it would rain by noon* does not reveal who predicted rain. The sentence *It always happens to me* does not indicate what always happens to the writer. Here are a few more examples:

> They say the enemy is preparing to attack.
>
> Anyone can get rich with this plan; many people have already.
>
> Politicians don't care about people.

To be sure you are getting full and complete information, ask the questions in the box below.

HAS ANYTHING BEEN OMITTED?

Be sure to ask . . .	To find out if . . .	Then you may need to . . .
What hasn't the author told me?	The author has deliberately omitted important information in an attempt to cover up or mislead.	Do additional research on the topic.
Did the author report details selectively?	The author favors a particular viewpoint.	Determine the author's bias. Compare the source with a source presenting an alternative viewpoint.
Is there contradictory evidence that was not reported?	The author has presented both sides of an issue fairly.	Obtain additional sources that discuss both sides of an issue. If the writer presents only one viewpoint, read sources presenting the opposite or alternative viewpoints.
What additional information may be helpful or important?	The author has covered all aspects of the problem or issue, or given just a quick overview.	Read a source that is more comprehensive and detailed.

DIRECTIONS For each of the following statements, indicate what information might be missing.

1. They were denied health insurance.
2. Ticket prices have doubled this year.
3. Anyone can get a fake I.D.
4. Our schools are safer.
5. Real estate prices are inflated in parts of the country. ●

BE ALERT FOR GENERALIZATIONS

Goal 4

Identify generalizations

Suppose you are reading an article that states that "Artists are temperamental people." Do you think that every artist who ever painted a portrait or composed a song is temperamental? Can you think of exceptions? This statement is an example of a generalization. A **generalization** is a statement about an entire group (artists) based on known information about part of the group (artists the writer has met or observed). A generalization requires a leap from what is known to a conclusion about what is unknown. Generalizations may be expressed using words such as *all, always, none,* or *never.* Some statements may imply but not directly state that the writer is referring to the entire group or class. The statement "Artists are temperamental people" suggests but does not directly state that all artists are temperamental. Here are a few more generalizations:

Rich people are snobs.

Chinese food is never filling.

Pets are always troublesome.

The ability to generalize is a valuable higher-level thinking skill. Many generalizations lead to valuable insights and creative problem-solving. However, generalizations made without sufficient evidence may be dangerous and misleading. The key to evaluating generalizations is to evaluate the type, quality, and amount of evidence given to support them. Here are a few more generalizations. What type of evidence would you need to be convinced that each is or is not true?

College students are undecided about future career goals.

All fast food lacks nutritional value.

Foreign cars always outperform similar American models.

For the generalization about college students, you might need to see research studies about college students' career goals, for example. And then, even if studies did conclude that many college students are undecided, it would not be fair to conclude that every single student is undecided. If no evidence is given, then the generalization is not trustworthy and should be questioned.

You can also evaluate a generalization by seeing whether the author provides specifics about the generalization. For the statement "Pets are always troublesome," ask what kind of pets the author is referring to—a pet potbellied pig, an iguana, or a cat? Then ask what is meant by troublesome—does it mean the animal is time-consuming, requires special care, or behaves poorly?

Another way to evaluate a generalization is to try to think of exceptions. For the generalization *Medical doctors are aloof and inaccessible,* can you think of a doctor you have met or heard about who was caring and available to his or her patients? If so, the generalization is not accurate in all cases.

Exercise 8

DIRECTIONS   Read each of the following statements and place a check mark before each generalization.

_____ 1. Motorcyclists are thrill-seekers.

_____ 2. Houses are not built like they used to be.

_____ 3. In the United States, hurricane season lasts from June 1 to November 30.

_____ 4. Cars equipped with diesel engines are about 25 percent more efficient than regular cars.

_____ 5. People who visit online chat rooms are looking for trouble. ●

Exercise 9

DIRECTIONS   Read each of the following paragraphs and underline each generalization.

1. Students who attend coeducational middle and high schools are at a disadvantage. Teenage boys and girls always learn better in single-sex classrooms, without the constant distraction of the opposite sex.
2. Travelers are fed up with their treatment by the airlines. Flight delays occur even in good weather, and the constant overbookings leave passengers scrambling to find another flight. On top of the inconvenience, tickets cost a fortune.
3. Motorists never give pedestrians the right of way. Once they get behind the wheel of a car, people believe that they own the road; yielding to someone on foot would never occur to someone driving a car. ●

Exercise 10

DIRECTIONS   For each of the following generalizations, indicate what questions you would ask and what types of information you would need to evaluate the generalization.

1. No one writes letters anymore.
2. The weather is always perfect in San Diego.
3. All of the instructors at the college are dedicated to helping students.
4. People who work at home have a better quality of life.
5. Cosmetic surgery is only for the very wealthy and the very vain. ●

EXAMINE THE AUTHOR'S ASSUMPTIONS

Suppose a friend asked you, "Have you stopped cheating on your girlfriend?" This person, perhaps not a friend after all, is making an assumption. He or she is assuming that you already have been cheating. An **assumption** is an idea or principle the author accepts as true and makes no effort to prove or substantiate. Usually, it is a beginning or premise on which he or she bases the remainder of the statement. Assumptions often use words such as *since, if,* or *when.* Here are a few more examples:

Goal ⑤

Analyze assumptions

- You're not going to make that mistake again, are you? (The assumption is that you have already made the mistake at least once.)
- When you're mature, you'll realize you made a mistake. (The assumption is that you are not mature now.)
- You are as arrogant as your sister. (The assumption is that your sister is arrogant.)

Each of the previous statements makes no attempt to prove or support the hidden assumption; it is assumed to be true.

Authors who make assumptions often fail to prove or support them. For example, an author may assume that television encourages violent behavior in children and proceed to argue for restrictions on TV viewing. Or a writer may assume that protests against a government are wrong and suggest legal restrictions on how and when protests may be held. If a writer's assumption is wrong or unsubstantiated, then the statements that follow from the assumption should be questioned. If television does not encourage violent behavior, for example, then the suggestion to restrict viewing should not be accepted unless other reasons are offered.

DIRECTIONS   Read each of the following statements and then circle those choices that are assumptions made by the writer of the statement.

1. Since fossil-fuel resources are dwindling, it is imperative that we begin converting to nuclear energy now.
   a. It can be accurately predicted when fossil fuels will run out.
   b. People who oppose nuclear power are not realistic.
   c. Nuclear power is the only alternative to fossil fuels.
2. Many cultural treasures, such as paintings and other artifacts, were wrenched from their country of origin during times of war; these national treasures should be returned and displayed in their rightful homes.
   a. These artifacts were taken forcibly and illegally.
   b. Some artifacts were taken in an effort to safeguard them from damage.
   c. There is an appropriate and safe place for such artifacts to be displayed in their country of origin.
3. Hip-hop music and gangsta rap encourage violence and criminal behavior; therefore, these types of music should be subject to government censorship.
   a. It is the government's responsibility to censor music.
   b. Criminal behavior is a result of hip-hop music and gangsta rap.
   c. Other forms of entertainment feature violence and criminal behavior. ●

Exercise 11

Tip *Dwindling* means "decreasing."

Imperative means "very important to do immediately."

Converting means "changing."

Visual Thinking
ANALYZING IMAGES

Why would the author have chose this image to support her assertion?

Figure A   Noted rapper Ja Rule awaits a hearing.

DIRECTIONS   For each statement listed below, identify at least one assumption.

1. Musicians should let their songs be downloaded for free. The profits they make more than make up for any losses they may have from fans' file sharing.
2. Adding essay items to standardized tests will make the tests impossible to grade objectively.
3. Sports teams should be banned from using Native American names or references; teams such as the Braves and the Redskins are showing extreme disrespect to Native Americans.
4. Shopping online is the most efficient way to purchase clothing and other household items.
5. Sodas and other carbonated beverages have no place in our schools; school vending machines should contain bottled water, juice, or sports drinks only. ●

Exercise 12

WATCH FOR MANIPULATIVE LANGUAGE

Authors can shape their readers' thinking and response to their message by the language they choose to express that message. Writers use a variety of language manipulation techniques to achieve a particular effect, to communicate their message in a particular way, and to appeal to specific groups of people. These techniques include clichés, allusions, and euphemisms.

Clichés

A **cliché** is a tired, overused expression. Here are a few examples:

> Curiosity killed the cat.
>
> Bigger is better.
>
> Absence makes the heart grow fonder.
>
> He is as blind as a bat.

These everyday expressions have been overused; they are so frequently used that they no longer carry a specific meaning. They have become pat expressions, often used by authors without much thought or creativity. Because the expressions are so common, many readers tend to accept them at face value rather than to evaluate their meaning and appropriateness. When you recognize a cliché, ask yourself the following questions:

- Why did the writer use the cliché?
- Why did the writer not use a fresh, original expression instead?

Numerous clichés used throughout a piece of writing may suggest that the author has not thought in depth about the topic or has not made the effort to express his or her ideas in an interesting and unique way. When evaluating a writer's use of cliché, ask the following questions:

- **Is the author trying to gloss over or skip over details by using a cliché?** Clichés often oversimplify a situation that is complex. In trying to decide which courses to register for, a student may say, "Don't put off till tomorrow what you can do today." Actually the student *could* register today, but it may be better to wait until he or she has had time to think, do research, and talk to others about course selection.
- **Is the author trying to avoid directly stating an unpopular or unpleasant idea?** After describing recent acts of terrorism, suppose a writer concludes with the cliché, "What will be, will be." What does this cliché really say? In this context, the cliché suggests (but does not directly state) that nothing can be done about terrorism.
- **Is the cliché fitting and appropriate?** A writer may admonish students not to spend their financial aid loan before they receive it, by saying, "Don't count your chickens before they are hatched." The writer's audience would be better served if the writer had explained that loan checks are often delayed, and that spending money before it is received may cause serious financial problems.
- **What does the use of clichés reveal about the author?** A writer who packs an article full of clichés is not aware that his or her readers prefer fresh, descriptive information, rather than standard clichés.

TECH SUPPORT

Use a Grammar Checker to Watch for Clichés
The grammar and spell-checking functions of word process-
ing programs include optional features that can help you
check your own writing for clichés, colloquialisms, and jargon. From the
"Tools" menu, select "Spelling and Grammar," "Options," and "Settings."
You'll find these options under "Style."

DIRECTIONS   For each of the following clichés, explain its meaning and then think
of a situation in which it would be untrue or inappropriate.

Exercise 13

1. There's no time like the present.
2. No pain, no gain.
3. Don't judge a book by its cover.
4. Every cloud has a silver lining.
5. If you can't take the heat, get out of the kitchen. ●

DIRECTIONS   Replace each of the following clichés with more specific information
that fits the context of the sentence.

Exercise 14

1. Joe had worked at the firm for a year but he was still low man on the totem
   pole.
2. The councilman promised to turn over a new leaf after he was convicted of
   bribery and extortion.
3. We wanted to sell our house quickly, so when our agent brought a prospective
   buyer we put all our cards on the table.
4. The caterers were two hours late and the band was awful, but the straw that
   broke the camel's back was seeing the guest of honor's name misspelled on the
   cake.
5. The new teacher may seem strict but she has a heart of gold. ●

Allusions

Allusions are references to well-known religious, literary, artistic, or historical
works or sources. A writer may refer to a biblical verse, a character in a famous
poem or novel, a line in a well-known song, or a historical figure such as Napoleon or George Washington. An allusion makes a connection or points to similarities between the author's subject and the reference. Writers usually assume
that educated readers will recognize and understand their allusions. Here are a
few examples of allusions:

- A writer describes a person as having the patience of Job. In the Bible, Job is
  a righteous man whose faith was tested by God.
- An article on parental relationships with children refers to the Oedipus complex. Oedipus was a figure in Greek mythology who unknowingly killed his
  father and married his mother. He blinded himself when he discovered what
  he had done. The Oedipus complex is controversial but refers to a child's
  unconscious sexual desires.

If you encounter an allusion you do not understand, check it on the Internet using a search engine such as Google or a reference such as Wikipedia by typing in the key words of the allusion.

Allusions can make writing interesting and connected to the past. Some authors, however, may include numerous literary or scholarly allusions to give their writing the appearance of scholarship. Do not be overly impressed by a writer's use of allusions, particularly obscure ones. A writer may use allusions to divert readers' attention from the lack of substantive detail or support. When evaluating a writer's use of allusions, ask the following questions:

- What does the allusion mean?
- Why did the author include the allusion?
- What does the allusion contribute to the overall meaning of the work?

Exercise 15

DIRECTIONS   For each of the following statements, explain the meaning of the allusion.

1. The investigation into city politics has opened a Pandora's box.
2. The cruise ship appeared Brobdingnagian next to the fishing boat.
3. Thanks to a good samaritan, our flat tire was changed and we were on our way again in less than an hour.
4. The latest cell phones have a Big Brother aspect to them, allowing parents to constantly monitor their children's locations and activities.
5. When it comes to investing, my brother-in-law certainly has the Midas touch. ●

Euphemisms

What do these sentences have in common?

He suffered combat fatigue.

The company is downsizing.

Capital punishment is controversial.

Each uses an expression called a **euphemism**, a word or phrase that is used in place of a word that is unpleasant, embarrassing, or otherwise objectionable. The expression *combat fatigue* is a way to refer to the psychological problems of veterans caused by their experiences in war, *downsizing* replaces the word *firing*, and *capital punishment* is a substitute for *death penalty*.

Euphemisms tend to downplay something's importance or seriousness. They are often used in politics and advertising. They can be used to camouflage actions or events that may be unacceptable to readers or listeners if bluntly explained. For example, the phrase *casualties of war* may be used instead of the phrase *dead soldiers* to lessen the impact of the attack. To say that a politician's statement was *at variance with the truth* has less impact and is less forceful than to say that the politician lied.

Use the following questions to evaluate an author's use of euphemisms:

1. **What is the subject being discussed?** State it in everyday, straightforward, and direct language.
2. **How does the euphemism alter your perception of the situation?** Does it seem less harsh, severe, ugly, or serious?
3. **Why did the author use the euphemism?** Determine how the euphemism advances the writer's position and whether it reveals bias.

DIRECTIONS   For each of the underlined euphemisms, write a substitution that does not minimize or avoid the basic meaning of the term.

1. Her grandmother <u>passed away</u> after a long illness.
2. Several ferryboat passengers experienced severe <u>motion discomfort</u> and became violently ill.
3. They finally made the difficult decision to have their dog <u>put to sleep</u>.
4. Because of our financial status, we bought a <u>pre-owned</u> vehicle. ●

DIRECTIONS   Read "Tattoos Honor Marines Killed in Iraq and Help the Survivors" in Part Five on page 457 and complete each of the following tasks.

1. Identify at least five words that have strong connotative meanings.
2. Identify at least three generalizations.
3. Is there any information the author might have purposefully omitted?
4. What assumptions does the author make? ●

USING COLLEGE TEXTBOOKS
Using Critical Thinking Boxes

Many textbooks contain boxed information or boxed inserts that discuss issues and problems related to chapter content. Their purposes are to demonstrate how chapter content can be applied to practical situations and to ask thought-provoking questions that will lead students to think critically. Here is a sampling of such titles.

TAKING A CLOSER LOOK

What does it say about American cultural values and norms when it is assumed that if a baby is left unattended it will be abducted and harmed? Can you think of other behaviors that might be considered deviant by American cultural standards, but perfectly acceptable in another country?

—Thompson and Hickey, *Society in Focus*, p. 167

STOP AND STRETCH

One possible consequence of global warming is a decrease in the overall ice cover at the North Pole. Less ice is not only an effect of warming, it is likely to increase the rate of warming. Why?

—Belk, *Biology*, p. 399

What Do You Think?

What implications do developments in global health have for people living in the United States today? What international programs, policies, or services might help control the world's health problems in the next decade? Are there actions that individuals can take to help?

—Donatelle, *Health*, p. 12

FURTHER PRACTICE WITH TEXTBOOK READING

Part A: Sample Textbook Chapter

Read the box titled "Imagine" (p. 490), in the sample textbook chapter. Then write a list of questions that apply chapter content to your own life or to real-life situations.

Part B: Your College Textbook

Choose a textbook chapter that you have been assigned to read for one of your other courses. Read any boxes and summarize their content. If your textbook chapter does not have any, then write a proposal for one.

SELF-TEST SUMMARY

Goal ❶ What is connotative language?	Connotative language refers to the feelings and associations that may accompany a word.
Goal ❷ What is figurative language? What are three types of figurative language?	Figurative language is a comparison that makes sense imaginatively but not literally. Similes make comparisons using the words *like* or *as*. Metaphors make the comparison more directly, often using the word *is*. Personification compares humans and nonhumans according to one characteristic.
Goal ❸ What information might an author purposefully omit?	An author may omit essential information or contradictory evidence that doesn't support his or her argument.
Goal ❹ What is a generalization?	A generalization is a statement about an entire group based on known information about only part of the group.
Goal ❺ What is an assumption?	An assumption is an idea or principle that the author accepts as true and makes no effort to prove or substantiate.
Goal ❻ What are clichés, allusions, and euphemisms?	A cliché is a tired, overused expression. An allusion is a reference to well-known religious, literary, artistic, or historical works or sources. A euphemism is a word or phrase used in place of a word that is unpleasant, embarrassing, or otherwise objectionable.

APPLYING YOUR SKILLS

DISCUSSING THE CHAPTER

1. Discuss the types of publications in which you might expect a writer to purposefully omit information.
2. Create a figurative expression to describe one characteristic of a close friend.
3. Brainstorm a list of clichés that you are tired of hearing and would like to avoid using in your speech and writing.
4. Create a list of connotative meanings that may exist for one of the following words: *birthday, patriotism, paycheck,* or *dinner.*

ANALYZING A STUDY SITUATION

Analyze the following situation and answer the questions below.

An English instructor gave his class the following assignments:

Locate three articles on a current controversial issue. One of the three must express a different viewpoint from the other two. Write a two-page paper that critically evaluates each article.

One student in the class located three articles on censorship but did not know how to approach the assignment. He summarized each article and then wrote a paragraph describing how one article differed from the other two. The instructor refused to accept and grade this student's paper, saying that he had not completed the assignment.

1. Why was the student's paper unacceptable?
2. How should he have approached the assignment?
3. On what bases or using what criteria might the student have evaluated the articles?

WORKING ON COLLABORATIVE PROJECTS

DIRECTIONS   Each student should bring a copy of a current popular magazine to class. Choose a feature article and examine it for each of the topics covered in this chapter. Analyze why each was included and its possible effect on unsuspecting readers.

For support in meeting this chapter's goals, go to **MyReadingLab** and select **Critical Thinking.**

Quick **QUIZ**

DIRECTIONS   Write the letter of the choice that best completes each statement in the space provided.

CHECKING YOUR RECALL

_____ 1. The standard, dictionary meaning of a word is known as its

    a. connotative meaning.
    b. denotative meaning.
    c. figurative meaning.
    d. inferred meaning.

_____ 2. A generalization can be defined as a

    a. principle or idea that an author accepts as true and makes no effort to prove.
    b. comparison between two unlike things that share one common characteristic.
    c. statement expressing feeling, attitudes, or beliefs that are neither true nor false.
    d. statement about a whole group based on information about part of the group.

_____ 3. An author who uses the passive voice may be trying to avoid

    a. identifying who performed a particular action.
    b. explaining incomplete comparisons.
    c. including contradictory evidence.
    d. revealing details that favor one position.

_____ 4. An assumption can be defined as an idea or principle that the author

    a. attempts to disprove.
    b. approaches logically.
    c. disagrees with.
    d. accepts as true without attempting to prove.

_____ 5. Figurative language compares

    a. several images.
    b. two unlike things.
    c. many similar things.
    d. several descriptive images.

APPLYING YOUR LEARNING

_____ 6. The statement "The cousins fought like cats and dogs" is a example of

    a. an allusion.
    b. a cliché.
    c. a euphemism.
    d. jargon.

_____ 7. The statement "She's got the Midas touch when it comes to making money" is an example of

    a. a euphemism.
    b. denotative language.
    c. jargon.
    d. an allusion.

_____ 8. The statement "The soldier was wounded by friendly fire" is an example of

    a. a euphemism.
    b. a cliché.
    c. jargon.
    d. a generalization.

_____ 9. An expression that describes a person who is intelligent but which also has a negative connotation is

    a. intellectual.
    b. scholar.
    c. egghead.
    d. wise guy.

_____ 10. Of the following statements, the one that expresses a generalization is

    a. "I learned more than I ever expected to in this course."
    b. "That course was my favorite."
    c. "Dr. Fassell is a biology professor."
    d. "All of the instructors at the college are dedicated to helping students."

Using Context and Word Parts

LEARNING GOALS

In this chapter you will learn to

1 Learn unfamiliar words

2 Use context clues

3 Analyze word parts

LEARNING EXPERIMENT

1 Here are five words and their meanings.

> **List A**
>
> **turmoil:** complete confusion, uproar
>
> **subjective:** involving judgment or feelings; not objective
>
> **eccentric:** odd, strange
>
> **devious:** shifty; not straightforward; deceptive
>
> **corroborate:** to strengthen or support with other evidence

Study the list until you have memorized it.

2 When *hyper* is placed in front of a word it means "more than normal."

Using the information above, learn the meaning of each of the following words.

List B

hyperactive: overly active

hypersensitive: overly sensitive

hypertension: abnormally high blood pressure

hyperextension: extension of a bodily joint beyond its normal range

hyperventilate: to breathe overly fast

THE RESULTS

Which list was easier and faster to learn? Probably the second list. Why? In list A, you had to learn five unrelated words; in list B, the words all began with the prefix (word beginning) *hyper-*.

LEARNING PRINCIPLE: WHAT THIS MEANS TO YOU

You can learn things more easily if they are meaningful and related to one another (as the words in list B are). In this chapter you will learn two methods for finding and connecting the meanings of unfamiliar words.

WHY LEARN TO USE CONTEXT AND WORD PARTS?

Use context and word parts to:

- dramatically improve your reading, writing, speaking, and listening vocabularies.
- learn more words faster than by simply memorizing individual meanings.
- save time by not having to look up as many unfamiliar words in the dictionary.

Goal 1

Learn unfamiliar words

PEARSON
myreadinglab

To practice learning unfamiliar words, go to

> Vocabulary

A STRATEGY FOR LEARNING UNFAMILIAR WORDS

What should you do when you are reading a passage and you come to a word you don't know?

Despite what you might expect, looking up a word in a dictionary is not the first thing to do when you encounter a word you don't know. In fact, a dictionary is your last resort—somewhere to turn when all else fails. Instead, first try pronouncing the word aloud. Hearing the word may help you recall its meaning. If pronouncing the word does not help, try to figure out the meaning of the word from the words around it in the sentence, paragraph, or passage that you are reading. Very often, these surrounding words include various clues that enable you to reason out the meaning of the unknown word. The words around an unknown word that contain clues to its meaning are referred to as the context. The clues themselves are called context clues. You can use four basic types of context clues in determining word meanings in textbook material: definition, example/illustration, contrast, and logic of the passage.

If a word's context does not provide clues to its meaning, you might try breaking the word into parts. Analyzing a word's parts, which may include its prefix, root, and suffix, also provides clues to its meaning. Finally, if word parts do not help, look up the word in a dictionary. Regardless of the method you use to find a word's meaning, be sure to record its meaning in the margin of the page. Later, transfer its meaning to your vocabulary log (see Chapter 12, p. 267).

Goal 2

Use context clues

Tip *Synonyms are words that mean the same or almost the same (in the same language).*

USING CONTEXT CLUES
Definition and Synonym Context Clues

The most obvious type of context clue is an author's direct statement of the meaning of a new term. A textbook author does this when he or she is aware that a word is new to the reader and therefore takes the time to give an accurate definition of the term. Fox example, in the first chapter of a chemistry book, the term *chemical reaction* is defined.

> A chemical reaction is an interaction involving different atoms, in which chemical bonds are formed, or broken, or both.

Some writers signal you directly that they are presenting a definition with expressions such as "Mass is . . ." or "Anthropology can be defined as . . ." Other writers, however, are less direct and obvious when they include a definition.

Parentheses may be used to give a definition or partial definition of a word, as in the following sentence:

> Deciduous trees (trees bearing leaves that are shed annually) respond differently to heat and cold than coniferous trees (trees bearing cones).

An author may use commas or dashes to set off a brief definition within the sentence.

> Mendel needed true-breeding plants, plants that showed little variation from generation to generation.
>
> The mean—the mathematical average of a set of numbers—will determine whether grades will be based on a curve.

Finally, an author may simply insert a synonym (a word with a similar meaning) directly within the sentence.

> Another central issue, that of the right of a state to withdraw or secede from the Union, was simply avoided.

Exercise 1

DIRECTIONS   In each sentence, locate the part of the sentence that gives a definition or synonym of the underlined word. Underline this portion of the sentence.

1. A <u>democracy</u> is a form of government in which the people effectively participate.
2. The amount of heat that it takes to melt one gram of any substance at its melting point is called the <u>heat of fusion</u>.
3. <u>Linoleic acid</u> is an essential fatty acid necessary for growth and skin integrity in infants.
4. When a gas is cooled, it <u>condenses</u> (changes to a liquid) at its condensation point.
5. But neither a monkey nor an ape has thumbs long enough or flexible enough to be completely <u>opposable</u>, able to reach comfortably to the tips of all the other fingers, as is required for our delicate yet strong precision grip. ●

Example/Illustration Context Clues

Authors frequently explain their ideas and concepts by giving specific, concrete examples or illustrations. Many times, when an example is given that illustrates or explains a new term, you can figure out the meaning of the term from the example. Suppose, for instance, that you frequently confuse the terms *fiction* and *nonfiction* and you are given the following assignment by your instructor: *Select any nonfiction book and write a critical review; you can choose from a wide range of books, such as autobiographies, sports books, how-to manuals, commentaries on historical periods, and current consumer-awareness paperbacks.* From the examples given, you can easily see that *nonfiction* refers to books that are factual, or true.

Writers sometimes give you an advance warning or signal that they are going to present an example or illustration. Phrases that signal an example or illustration to follow include *for example, for instance, to illustrate, such as, included are,* and so on. Read the following examples:

> Some everyday, common solutions include gasoline, antifreeze, soda water, seawater, vodka, and ammonia.

Tip A *critical review* is a piece of writing that includes an evaluation, statements about the strengths and/or weaknesses, of a movie, written work, concert, art exhibit, and so on.

Specifically, management of a New York bank developed a strategic plan to increase its customers by making them see banks as offering a large variety of services rather than just a few specialized services (cashing checks, putting money into savings accounts, and making loans).

Exercise 2

DIRECTIONS   Read each sentence and write a definition or synonym for each underlined word. Use the illustration/example context clue to help you determine word meanings.

1. Maria enjoys all equestrian sports, including jumping, riding, and racing horses.

   _____

2. Murder, rape, and armed robbery are reprehensible crimes.

   _____

3. Psychological disturbances are sometimes traceable to a particular trauma in childhood. For example, the death of a parent may produce long-range psychological effects.

   _____

4. To substantiate his theory, Watson offered experimental evidence, case study reports, testimony of patients, and a log of observational notes.

   _____

5. Many phobias can seriously influence human behavior; the two most common are claustrophobia (fear of confined spaces) and acrophobia (fear of heights).

   _____

6. Homogeneous groups, such as classes made up entirely of boys, social organizations of people with high IQs, country clubs, and wealthy families, have particular roles and functions.

   _____ ●

Contrast Context Clues

It is sometimes possible to figure out the meaning of an unknown word from a word or phrase in the context that has an opposite meaning. To use a simple example, in the sentence "Sam was thin, but George was obese," a contrast of opposites is set up between George and Sam. The word *but* signals that an opposite or contrasting idea is to follow. By knowing the meaning of *thin* and knowing that George is the opposite of thin, you figure out that *obese* means "not thin," or "fat."

Most often when an opposite or contrasting meaning is given, a signal word or phrase in the sentence indicates a change in the direction of the thought. Most commonly used are these signal words or phrases: *on the other hand, however, although, whereas, but, nevertheless, on the contrary.* Note the following example:

The Federalists, from their pessimistic viewpoint, believed the Constitution could protect them by its procedures, whereas the more positive Anti-Federalists thought of the Constitution as the natural rights due to all people.

In the preceding example, if you did not know the meaning of the word *pessimistic,* you could figure it out because a word appears later in the sentence that gives you a clue. The sentence is about the beliefs of two groups, the Federalists and the Anti-Federalists. The prefix *anti-* tells you that they hold opposite or differing views, and *whereas* also signals a contrast. If the Federalists are described as pessimistic and their views are opposite those of the Anti-Federalists, who are described as more positive, you realize that *pessimistic* means "the opposite of positive," or "negative."

Here is another example:

> Most members of Western society marry only one person at a time, but in other cultures polygamy is common and acceptable.

In this sentence, by the contrast established between Western society and other cultures, you can infer that *polygamy* refers to the practice of marriage to more than one person at a time.

DIRECTIONS   Read each sentence and write a definition or synonym for each underlined word. Use the contrast context clue to help you determine the meaning of the word.

Exercise 3

1. The philosopher was <u>vehement</u> in his objections to the new grading system; the more practical historian, on the other hand, expressed his views calmly and quietly.

   _____

2. The mayor was <u>dogmatic</u> about government policy, but the assistant mayor was more lenient and flexible in his interpretations.

   _____

3. Instead of evaluating each possible solution when it was first proposed, the committee decided it would <u>defer</u> judgment until all possible solutions had been proposed.

   _____

4. The two philosophical theories were <u>incompatible</u>: One acknowledged the existence of free will; the other denied it.

   _____

5. Cultures vary in the types of behavior that are considered socially acceptable. In one culture, a man may be <u>ostracized</u> for having more than one wife, whereas in other cultures, a man with many wives is an admired and respected part of the group.

   _____ ●

Context Clues in the Logic of a Passage

One of the most common ways in which context provides clues about the meaning of an unknown word is through logic or general reasoning about the content of a sentence or about the relationship of ideas within a sentence. Suppose that before you read the following sentence you did not know the meaning of the word *empirical.*

Some of the questions now before us are empirical issues that require evidence directly bearing on the question.

From the way *empirical* is used in the sentence, you know that an empirical issue is one that requires direct evidence, and from that information you can infer, or reason, that *empirical* has something to do with proof or supporting facts.

Now suppose that you did not know the meaning of the term *cul-de-sac* before reading the following sentence:

A group of animals hunting together can sometimes maneuver the hunted animal into a cul-de-sac: out onto a peak of high land, into a swamp or river, or into a gully from which it cannot escape.

From the mention of the places into which a hunted animal can be maneuvered—a gully, a peak, or a swamp—you realize that the hunters have cornered the animal and that *cul-de-sac* means a blind alley or a situation from which there is no escape.

Exercise 4

Tip *Convictions* are strong beliefs or opinions.

DIRECTIONS   Read each of the following sentences and write a synonym or definition for each underlined word or term. Look for context clues in the logic of the passage to help you figure out the meaning of each word.

1. Religious or ethical convictions make the idea of capital punishment, in which a life is willingly, even legally, extinguished, a repugnant one.

   _____

2. The former Berlin Wall, originally built with enough force and strength to separate East and West Germany, was impervious to attack.

   _____

3. When the judge pronounced the sentence, the convicted criminal shouted execrations at the jury.

   _____

4. The police officer was exonerated by a police review panel of any possible misconduct or involvement in a case of police bribery.

   _____

Tip *Bribery* means "the offering of a benefit (money, gifts, etc.) to get someone to do something that he or she shouldn't do."

5. The editor would not allow the paper to go to press until certain passages were expunged from an article naming individuals involved in a political scandal.

   _____   ●

Exercise 5

DIRECTIONS   Each of the following sentences contains an underlined word or phrase whose meaning can be determined from the context. Underline the part of the sentence that contains the clue to the meaning of the underlined words. Then, in the blank below, identify what type of context clue you used.

1. Separation of powers is the principle that the powers of government should be separated and put in the care of different parts of the government.

   _____

2. Samples of moon rock have been analyzed by <u>uranium dating</u> and found to be about 4.6 billion years old, or about the same age as the earth.

_____

3. Like horses, human beings have a variety of <u>gaits</u>; they amble, stride, jog, and sprint.

_____

4. In the past, <u>malapportionment</u> (large differences in the populations of congressional districts) was common in many areas of the country.

_____

5. Tremendous <u>variability</u> characterizes the treatment of the mentally retarded during the medieval era, ranging from treatment as innocents to being tolerated as fools to persecution as witches.

_____ ●

Exercise 6

DIRECTIONS   Read each of the following paragraphs. For each underlined word, use context to determine its meaning. Write a synonym or brief definition in the space provided.

1. In the laboratory, too, nonhuman primates have accomplished some surprising things. In one study, chimpanzees compared two pairs of food wells containing chocolate chips. One pair might contain, say, five chips and three chips, the other four chips and three chips. Allowed to choose which pair they wanted, the chimps almost always chose the one with the higher combined total, showing some sort of <u>summing ability</u>. Other chimps have learned to use <u>numerals</u> to label quantities of items and simple sums. Two rhesus monkeys, named Rosencrantz and Macduff, learned to <u>order</u> groups of one to four symbols according to the number of symbols in each group (e.g., one square, two trees, three ovals, four flowers). Later, when presented with pairs of symbol groups containing five to nine symbols, they were able to point to the group with more symbols, without any further training. This is not exactly algebra, but it does suggest that monkeys have a <u>rudimentary</u> sense of number.

—Wade & Tavris, *Psychology*, p. 337

   a. summing ability _____

   b. numerals _____

   c. order _____

   d. rudimentary _____

2. Many animals communicate by chemical signals, which have the unique advantage of <u>persisting</u> for some time after the messenger has left the area. They also have the advantage that they will be detected only by those with receptors that respond to the chemical, so they are less likely to attract predators. Some chemical messages have a hormone-like ability to <u>induce</u> specific behavioral responses in recipients in the same species. Such

Visual Thinking
ANALYZING IMAGES

How is this animal releasing pheromones?

chemical messages are called pheromones. The best-known pheromones are insect sex attractants, many of which have been isolated and chemically analyzed. The first such pheromone to be studied was bombykol, which is produced in minute amounts by glands near the anus of the female silk moth *Bombyx mori*. The glands from half a million females had to be processed to yield 12 mg of pheromone. (One lab worker was reportedly overheard complaining, "The end is always in sight, but the work is never done.") A single molecule of bombykol is enough to evoke an action potential from the antenna of a male silk moth, and several hundred molecules are enough to make the male fly upwind, toward the female.

—Harris, *Concepts in Zoology*, pp. 408–409

a. persisting _____

b. induce _____

c. pheromones _____

d. evoke _____

3. Certain personal characteristics may explain who among the extremely poor are more likely to become homeless. These characteristics have been found to include chronic mental problems, alcoholism, drug addiction, serious criminal behavior, and physical health problems. Most of the extremely poor do not become homeless because they live with their relatives or friends. But those who suffer from any of the personal disabilities just mentioned are more likely to wear out their welcome as dependents of their parents or as recipients of aid and money from their friends. After all, their relatives and friends are themselves likely to be extremely poor and already living in crowded housing. We should be careful, though, not to exaggerate the impact of personal disabilities on homelessness. To some degree, personal disabilities may be the consequences rather than the cause of homelessness.

—Thio, *Sociology*, p. 235

a. characteristics _____

b. disabilities _____

c. dependents _____

d. recipients _____

e. exaggerate _____

f. impact _____

g. consequences _____ ●

Goal ❸

Analyze word parts

myreadinglab

To practice analyzing word parts, go to

> Vocabulary

ANALYZING WORD PARTS

The purpose of this section is to present a system of vocabulary learning. This system works for specific courses in which a great deal of new terminology is presented, as well as for building your overall, general vocabulary. The approach is based on analyzing word parts. Many words in the English language are made up of word parts called **prefixes**, **roots**, and **suffixes**. Think of these as beginnings, middles, and endings of words. These word parts have specific meanings, and when added together, they can help you figure out the meaning of the word as a whole. Let's begin with a few words from biology.

poikilotherm homeotherm endotherm ectotherm

You could learn the definition of each term separately, but learning would be easier and more meaningful if you could see the relationship among the terms.

Each of the four words has as its root *therm,* which means "heat." The meaning of the prefix, or beginning, of each word is given below.

poikilo-	=	changeable
homeo-	=	same or constant
endo-	=	within
ecto-	=	outside

Knowing these meanings can help you determine the meaning of each word.

poikilotherm	=	organism with variable body temperature (i.e., cold-blooded)
homeotherm	=	organism with stable body temperature (i.e., warm-blooded)
endotherm	=	organism that regulates its temperature internally
ectotherm	=	organism that regulates its temperature by taking in heat from the environment or giving off heat to the environment

When you first start using this method, you may not feel that you're making progress; in this case, you had to learn four prefixes and one root to figure out four words. However, what may not yet be obvious is that these prefixes will help unlock the meanings of numerous other words, not only in the field of biology but also in related fields and in general vocabulary usage. Here are a few examples of words that include each of the word parts we have analyzed:

therm	poikilo-	homeo- (homo-)	ecto-	endo-
thermal	poikilocyte	homeostasis	ectoparasite	endocytosis
thermodynamics	poikilocytosis	homogeneous	ectoderm	endoderm

The remainder of this section will focus on commonly used prefixes, roots, and suffixes that are used in a variety of academic disciplines. In various combinations, these will unlock the meanings of thousands of words. For example, more than 10,000 words begin with the prefix *non-.*

Once you have mastered the prefixes, roots, and suffixes given in this chapter, you should begin to identify word parts that are commonly used in each of your courses. For example, Figure 11-1 shows a partial list made by one student for a psychology course. Keep these lists in your course notebooks or use index cards, as described in Chapter 12.

**Figure 11-1
A Sample List of
Prefixes**

Psychology

neuro– nerves, nervous system   path– feeling, suffering

phob– fear   homo– same

auto– self   hetero– different

Before learning specific prefixes, roots, and suffixes, it is useful to be aware of the following points:

1. **In many cases, a word is built on at least one root.**
2. **Words can have more than one prefix, root, or suffix.**

   - Words can be made up of two or more roots (*geo / logy*).
   - Some words have two prefixes (*in / sub / ordination*).
   - Some words have two suffixes (*beauti / ful / ly*).

3. **Words do not always have both a prefix and a suffix.**

   - Some words have neither a prefix nor a suffix (*view*).
   - Others have a suffix but no prefix (*view / ing*).
   - Others have a prefix but no suffix (*pre / view*).

4. **Roots may change in spelling as they are combined with suffixes.** Some common variations are noted on page 251.
5. **Sometimes you may identify a group of letters as a prefix or root but find that it does not carry the meaning of the prefix or root.** For example, in the word *internal*, the letters *inter* should not be confused with the prefix *inter-*, meaning "between." Similarly, the letters *mis* in the word *missile* are part of the root and are not the prefix *mis-*, which means "wrong" or "bad."

Prefixes

Prefixes, appearing at the beginning of many English words, alter or modify the meaning of the root to which they are connected. In Figure 11-2 (p. 249), common prefixes are grouped according to meaning.

Exercise 7

DIRECTIONS   Use the prefixes listed in Figure 11-2 to help determine the meaning of the underlined word in each of the following sentences. Write a brief definition or synonym for each. If you are unfamiliar with the root, you may need to check a dictionary.

1. The instances of <u>abnormal</u> behavior reported in the mass media are likely to be extreme.

   _____

2. The two theories of language development are not fundamentally <u>incompatible</u>, as originally thought.

   _____

3. When threatened, the ego resorts to <u>irrational</u> protective measures, which are called defense mechanisms.

   _____

4. Freud viewed the <u>interplay</u> among the id, ego, and superego as of critical importance in determining behavioral patterns.

_____

5. The long-term effects of continuous drug abuse are <u>irreversible</u>.

_____ ●

PREFIX	MEANING	SAMPLE WORD
Prefixes indicating direction, location, or placement		
circum-	around	circumference
com-, col-, con-	with, together	compile
de-	away, from	depart
ex-/extra-	from, out of, former	ex-wife
hyper-	over, excessive	hyperactive
inter-	between	interpersonal
intro-/intra-	within, into, in	introduction
mid-	middle	midterm
post-	after	posttest
pre-	before	premarital
re-	back, again	review
retro-	backward	retrospect
sub-	under, below	submarine
super-	above, extra	supercharge
tele-	far	telescope
trans-	across, over	transcontinental
Prefixes referring to amount or number		
bi-	two	bimonthly
equi-	equal	equidistant
micro-	small	microscope
mono-	one	monocle
multi-	many	multipurpose
poly-	many	polygon
semi-	half	semicircle
tri-	three	triangle
uni-	one	unicycle
Prefixes meaning "not" (negative)		
a-, an-, ab-	not	asymmetrical
anti-	against	antiwar
contra-	against, opposite	contradict
dis-	apart, away, not	disagree
mis-	wrong, bad	misunderstand
non-	not	nonfiction
pseudo-	false	pseudoscientific
un-	not	unpopular

Figure 11-2
Common Prefixes

DIRECTIONS Write a synonym or brief definition for each of the following underlined words. Check a dictionary if the root is unfamiliar.

Exercise 8

1. a <u>substandard</u> performance _____

2. to <u>transcend</u> everyday differences _____

3. telecommunications equipment _____

4. a hypercritical person _____

5. a retroactive policy _____

6. superconductive metal _____

7. extracurricular activities _____

8. postoperative nursing care _____

9. a blood transfusion _____

10. antisocial behavior _____

11. to misappropriate funds _____

12. a microscopic organism _____

13. a monotonous speech _____

14. a pseudointellectual essay _____

15. a polysyllabic word _____ ●

Roots

Roots carry the basic or core meaning of a word. Hundreds of root words are used to build words in the English language. Thirty of the most common and most useful are listed in Figure 11-3. Knowing the meanings of these roots will assist you in unlocking the meanings of many words. For example, if you know that the root *dic-* or *dict-* means "tell" or "say," then you have a clue to the meanings of such words as *predict* (to tell what will happen in the future), *contra-diction* (a statement that is contrary or opposite), and *diction* (wording or manner of speaking).

Exercise 9

DIRECTIONS   Write a synonym or brief definition for each of the underlined words. Consult Figures 11-2 and 11-3 as necessary.

1. a monotheistic religion _____

2. a subterranean tunnel _____

3. a chronicle of events _____

4. a conversion chart _____

5. exportation policies _____

6. leading an introspective life _____

7. to speculate on the results _____

8. sensuous music _____

9. a versatile performance _____

10. an incredible explanation _____

11. infant mortality rates _____

12. the tensile strength of a cable _____

13. a <u>vociferous</u> crowd _____

14. a logical <u>deduction</u> _____

15. a <u>corporate</u> earnings report _____ •

ROOT	MEANING	SAMPLE WORD
aster, astro	star	astronaut
aud, audit	hear	audible
bio	life	biology
cap	take, seize	captive
chron(o)	time	chronology
corp	body	corpse
cred	believe	incredible
dict, dic	tell, say	predict
duc, duct	lead	introduce
fact, fac	make, do	factory
geo	earth	geophysics
graph	write	telegraph
log, logo, logy	study, thought	psychology
mit, miss	send	dismiss
mort, mor	die, death	immortal
path	feeling, disease	sympathy
phone	sound, voice	telephone
photo	light	photosensitive
port	carry	transport
scop	seeing	microscope
scribe, script	write	inscription
sen, sent	feel	insensitive
spec, spic, spect	look, see	retrospect
tend, tent, tens	stretch, strain	tension
terr, terre	land, earth	territory
theo	god	theology
ven, vent	come	convention
vert, vers	turn	invert
vis, vid	see	invisible
voc	call	vocation

**Figure 11-3
Common Roots**

Suffixes

Suffixes are word endings that often change the part of speech of a word. For example, adding the suffix *-y* to a word changes it from a noun to an adjective and shifts the meaning—for example, *cloud, cloudy.*

Often several different words can be formed from a single root word with the addition of different suffixes. Here is an example:

Root: *class*
        classify
        classification
        classic

Common suffixes are grouped according to meaning in Figure 11-4.

Figure 11-4
Common Suffixes

SUFFIX	SAMPLE WORD
Suffixes that refer to a state, condition, or quality	
-able	touchable
-ance	assistance
-ation	confrontation
-ence	reference
-ible	tangible
-ic	aerobic
-ion	discussion
-ity	superiority
-ive	permissive
-ment	amazement
-ness	kindness
-ous	jealous
-ty	loyalty
-y	creamy
Suffixes that mean "one who"	
-ee	employee
-eer	engineer
-er	teacher
-ist	activist
-or	editor
Suffixes that mean "pertaining to" or "referring to"	
-al	autumnal
-hood	brotherhood
-ship	friendship
-ward	homeward

Exercise 10

DIRECTIONS   Write a synonym or brief definition of each of the underlined words. Consult a dictionary if necessary.

1. acts of <u>terrorism</u> _____

2. a <u>graphic</u> description _____

3. a <u>materialistic</u> philosophy _____

4. <u>immunity</u> to disease _____

5. <u>impassable</u> road conditions _____

6. a speech <u>impediment</u> _____

7. <u>intangible</u> property _____

8. <u>instinctive</u> behavior _____

9. <u>interrogation</u> techniques _____

10. the communist <u>sector</u> _____

11. obvious <u>frustration</u> _____

12. <u>global</u> conflicts _____

13. in <u>deference</u> to _____

14. <u>piteous</u> physical ailments _____

15. Supreme Court <u>nominee</u> _____ •

DIRECTIONS From a chapter in one of your textbooks, make a list of words with multiple word parts. Using Figures 11-2, 11-3, and 11-4, define as many as you can. Check the accuracy of your definitions using your book's glossary or a dictionary. •

Exercise 11

USING COLLEGE TEXTBOOKS
Locating Word Meanings

Because textbooks are written by professors, they often contain words that may be difficult or unfamiliar. However, to understand the paragraph in which they are used, you need to figure out their meanings.

Textbooks offer the following features to help you figure out and learn the unfamiliar words they contain.

1. **Context clues.** Because textbook authors know much of the terminology they use is unfamiliar, they often provide obvious context clues. Definition, synonym, and example clues are the most common.

   Definition

   When it comes to production, **scheduling** refers to the efficient organization of equipment, facilities, labor, and materials.

   —Solomon, *Better Business*, p. 323

   Synonymn

   Granulated sugar or crystalline sucrose, called *table sugar*, plays a variety of roles in food systems.

   —Bennion, *Scheule.*

2. **Marginal definitions.** Many textbooks include the meanings of unfamiliar terms in the margin next to where each word is first used.

Proteins are one of the three macronutrients and are found in a wide variety of foods. Our bodies are able to manufacture (or *synthesize*) all of the macronutrients. But **DNA**, the genetic material in our cells, dictates the structure only of protein molecules, not of carbohydrates or lipids. We'll explore how our bodies synthesize proteins and the role that DNA plays in this process shortly.

proteins Large, complex molecules made up of amino acids and found as essential components of all living cells.

DNA A molecule present in the nucleus of all body cells that directs the assembly of amino acids into body proteins.

—Thompson, *Manore*

Highlight these definitions as you read. Be sure to check them again as you review and study for exams. If there is a lot of terminology to learn, use the index card system described on p. 266.

FURTHER PRACTICE WITH TEXTBOOK READING

Part A: Sample Textbook Chapter

The following words appear in "Nonverbal Emotional Expression" (pp. 494–95). For each word, use context or a dictionary to write a definition of the word as it is used in the excerpt.

a. coyly (para. 2) _____

b. universal (para. 3) _____

c. innate (para. 3) _____

d. zygomatic (para. 4) _____

e. morphology (para. 6) _____

Part B: Your College Textbook

Choose a textbook chapter that you have been assigned to read for one of your other courses. Identify ten previously unknown words that you are able to determine the meaning of using the textbook's aids, context clues, or a dictionary.

SELF-TEST
SUMMARY

Goal 1 What are the strategies for learning unfamiliar words?	The strategies are (1) saying the word aloud, (2) analyzing the context, (3) breaking the word into parts, and (4) using a dictionary.
Goal 2 What is a context clue and what are the four basic types of context clues? Define each.	The context—the words around an unknown word—frequently contains clues that help you figure out the meaning of the unknown word. There are four basic types of context clues. a. *Definition:* A brief definition or synonym of an unknown word may be included in the sentence in which the word is used. b. *Example/illustration:* Writers may explain their words and ideas by giving specific, concrete examples. c. *Contrast:* The meaning of an unknown word can sometimes be determined from a word or phrase in the context that has the opposite meaning. d. *Logic of the passage:* The meaning of an unknown word can sometimes be determined through reasoning or by applying logic to the content of the sentence or paragraph.
Goal 3 How can learning word parts improve your vocabulary?	Learning word parts enables you to figure out the meaning of an unknown word by analyzing the meanings of its parts—prefixes, roots, and suffixes.

APPLYING YOUR SKILLS

DISCUSSING THE CHAPTER

1. Discuss in which academic courses learning word parts would be most useful. In which courses would it be less useful?
2. Which types of context clues are used most frequently in college textbooks?
3. In which of your textbooks do you find the definition context clue most commonly used?
4. In classroom lectures, how do instructors explain the meaning of unfamiliar terms?

ANALYZING A STUDY SITUATION

Imagine that Jon is taking one of your courses with you. He is having difficulty figuring out and remembering new terms presented in the text and in lectures.

1. Photocopy several pages from your notes and from your text where new terms are introduced.
2. Explain to Jon what context clues the professor and the author are using.
3. Share with Jon your system for building up a content-specific vocabulary.

WORKING ON COLLABORATIVE PROJECTS

DIRECTIONS   Your instructor will choose a reading selection from Part Five and divide the class into groups. In your group, locate and underline at least five difficult words in the selection that can be defined by analyzing word parts and/or using context clues. Work together with group members to determine the meaning of each word, checking a dictionary to verify and expand meanings.

 For support in meeting this chapter's goals, go to **MyReadingLab** and select **Vocabulary**.

Quick QUIZ

DIRECTIONS   Write the letter of the choice that best completes each statement in the space provided.

CHECKING YOUR RECALL

_____ 1. If you encounter an unfamiliar word when you are reading, the *first* strategy you should try is to
   a. look it up in a dictionary.
   b. pronounce it out loud.
   c. analyze its parts.
   d. figure out its meaning from the words around it.

_____ 2. Teresa read this sentence in her biology class syllabus: "We will study fission—the act of splitting into parts—during our unit on cells." The type of context clue in this situation is
   a. definition.
   b. example.
   c. illustration.
   d. contrast.

_____ 3. The word or phrase that signals an example context clue is
   a. *on the other hand.*
   b. *however.*
   c. *for instance.*
   d. *nevertheless.*

_____ 4. All of the following statements about word parts are true *except*
   a. words always have at least one prefix, one root, and one suffix.
   b. roots may change in spelling as they are combined with suffixes.
   c. some words have more than one root.
   d. words can have more than one prefix or suffix.

APPLY YOUR SKILLS

DIRECTIONS   Each of the following sentences contains a word whose meaning can be determined from the context. Select the choice that most clearly states the meaning of the underlined word as it is used in the sentence.

_____ 5. The tour guide assured us that the trail was safe for travel, but it looked <u>precarious</u> to the rest of the group.
   a. unknown
   b. unsafe
   c. narrow
   d. messy

_____ 6. The comedian <u>satirized</u> the tourists in the front row, making fun of the way they were dressed.
   a. complimented
   b. ridiculed
   c. ignored
   d. spoke to

_____ 7. The actor often portrayed <u>taciturn</u> characters, but in the television <u>interview</u> he was quite chatty.
   a. talkative
   b. relaxed
   c. quiet
   d. unpleasant

DIRECTIONS   Each of the following underlined words contains a root and a prefix and/or suffix. Using your knowledge of roots, prefixes, and suffixes, choose the best definition for each word.

_____ 8. Martin is <u>hypersensitive</u> about his mother's health.
   a. considerate
   b. complimentary
   c. overly concerned
   d. indifferent

_____ 9. The scientist used a <u>chronograph</u> as part of her experiment.
   a. sound system
   b. light-sensitive film
   c. scale
   d. time-measuring instrument

_____ 10. To treat the inflammation, the patient must receive shots <u>intramuscularly</u>.
   a. within the muscle
   b. next to the muscle
   c. between muscles
   d. away from the muscle

Expanding Your Vocabulary

LEARNING GOALS

In this chapter you will learn to

1 Expand your vocabulary

2 Use reference sources

3 Handle specialized vocabulary

4 Use systems to build your vocabulary

LEARNING EXPERIMENT

1 Study the following list of words and meanings (list A) for one to two minutes.

List A

contrive: to plan with cleverness; to devise

comprise: to consist of

revulsion: feeling of violent disgust

retaliate: to return in kind, to get even with

repertoire: a collection of skills or aptitudes; a collection of artistic or musical works to be performed

2 Study list B for one to two minutes. Then, for each word, write a sentence using the word.

List B

ambivalent: uncertain or undecided about a course of action

infallible: incapable of making a mistake

mundane: commonplace, ordinary

relentless: unyielding, unwilling to give in

déjà vu: the impression of having seen or experienced something before

3 Wait two days and then take the following quiz. Cover the two lists above before you begin the quiz.
Match each word in column A with its meaning in column B. Write the letter from column B in the blank provided.

Column A	Column B
_____ 1. revulsion	a. to return in kind
_____ 2. comprise	b. undecided
_____ 3. repertoire	c. feeling of violent disgust
_____ 4. contrive	d. feeling of experiencing something again
_____ 5. retaliate	e. collection of skills or aptitudes
_____ 6. ambivalent	f. to consist of

(Continued)

(Continued)

_____	7.	relentless	g. ordinary
_____	8.	infallible	h. incapable of error
_____	9.	déjà vu	i. to create a clever plan
_____	10.	mundane	j. unwilling to give in

4 Check your answers using the key at the end of the chapter, page 271.

THE RESULTS

Questions 1–5 were based on list A; Questions 6–10 were based on list B. You probably got more questions right for list B than for list A. Why? For list B, you used each word in a sentence. By using each word in a sentence you were practicing it. Practice is a part of a technique known as rehearsal, which means going back over material you are attempting to learn.

LEARNING PRINCIPLE: WHAT THIS MEANS TO YOU

Rehearsal improves both your ability to learn and your ability to recall information. To expand your vocabulary, be sure to practice using words you identify as important to learn, whether they are part of your general vocabulary or the specialized terminology of your courses. This chapter will help you to identify the words you need to add to your vocabulary and to use the resources that can expand your vocabulary.

WHY EXPAND YOUR VOCABULARY?

Expanding your vocabulary is important because:

- Your vocabulary is a reflection of you, and a strong vocabulary creates a positive image.
- Broadening your vocabulary will improve the clarity of your thinking.
- Your reading and writing skills will improve as your vocabulary improves.
- A strong vocabulary will contribute to both academic and career success.

Goal ❶

Expand your vocabulary

myreadinglab

To practice expanding your vocabulary, go to

> Vocabulary

Tip *Succinctly* means "expressed well in as few words as possible; concisely."

GENERAL APPROACHES TO VOCABULARY EXPANSION

Expanding your vocabulary requires motivation, a positive attitude, and skills. Of these, motivation is the most important. To improve your vocabulary, you must be willing to work at it, spending both time and effort to notice and learn new words and meanings. This chapter will focus on the skills you need to build your vocabulary. Before you continue, however, read the following suggestions for expanding your vocabulary.

Read Widely

One of the best ways to improve your vocabulary is by reading widely and diversely, sampling many different subjects and styles of writing. Through reading, you encounter new words and new uses for familiar words. You also see words used in contexts that you have not previously considered.

College is one of the best places to begin reading widely. As you take elective and required courses, you are exposed to new ideas as well as to the words that express them clearly and succinctly. While you are a student, use your required and elective reading to expand your vocabulary.

Use Words You Already Know

Most people think they have just one level of vocabulary and that this can be characterized as large or small, strong or weak. Actually, everyone has at least four levels of vocabulary, and each varies in strength.

1. Words you use in everyday speech or writing
   Examples: *laptop, leg, lag, lead, leave, lost*
2. Words you know but seldom or never use in your own speech or writing
   Examples: *lethal, legitimate, lawful, landscape, laid-back*
3. Words you've heard or seen before but cannot fully define
   Examples: *logistics, lament, lackadaisical, latent, latitude*
4. Words you've never heard or seen before
   Examples: *lanugo, lagniappe, laconic, lactone, lacustrine*

DIRECTIONS In the spaces provided below, list five words that fall under each of these four categories. It will be easy to think of words for category 1. Words for categories 2 through 4 may be taken from the following list.

Exercise 1

activate	delicate	impartial
alien	delve	impertinent
attentive	demean	liberate
congruent	focus	logic
connive	fraught	manual
continuous	garbanzo	meditate
contort	gastronome	osmosis
credible	havoc	resistance
deletion	heroic	voluntary

Category 1	*Category 2*	*Category 3*	*Category 4*
_____	_____	_____	_____
_____	_____	_____	_____
_____	_____	_____	_____
_____	_____	_____	_____
_____	_____	_____	_____

To build your vocabulary, try to shift as many words as possible from a less familiar to a more familiar category. This task is not easy. You start by noticing words. Then you question, check, and remember their meanings. Finally, and most important, you use these new words often in your speech and writing.

Look for Five-Dollar Words to Replace One-Dollar Words

Some words in your vocabulary are general and vague. Although they convey meaning, they are not precise, exact, or expressive. Try to replace these one-dollar words with five-dollar words that convey your meaning more directly. The word *good* is an example of a much-overused word that has a general, unclear meaning in the following sentence:

The movie was so good, it was worth the high admission price.

Try substituting the following words for *good* in the preceding sentence: *exciting, moving, thrilling, scary, inspiring.* Each of these gives more information than the word *good.* These are the types of words you should strive to use in your speech and writing.

Build Your Word Awareness

One of the first steps in expanding your vocabulary is to develop a word awareness. Get in the habit of noticing new or unusual words when reading and listening. Learn to pay attention to words and notice those that seem useful. Once you begin to notice words, you will find that many of them automatically become part of your vocabulary.

Your instructors are a good resource for new words. Both in formal classroom lectures and in more casual discussions and conversations, many instructors use words that students understand but seldom use. You will hear new words and technical terms that are particular to a specific discipline.

Other good sources are textbooks, reading assignments, and reference materials. If you are like most students, you understand many more words than you use in your own speech and writing. As you read, you will encounter many words you are vaguely familiar with but cannot define. When you begin to notice these words, you will find that many of them become part of your vocabulary.

Frank and Ernest

© 2011 Thaves. Reprinted with permission.

Visual Thinking
ANALYZING IMAGES

What point does this cartoon make about choice of words and their appropriateness?

Goal 2
Use reference sources

USING REFERENCE SOURCES

Once you have developed a sense of word awareness and have begun to identify useful words to add to your vocabulary, the next step is to become familiar with the references you can use to expand your vocabulary.

Dictionaries: Which One to Use

Many dictionaries of different types are available on the Internet. Two of the most widely used English print dictionaries, those by Merriam-Webster and American Heritage, have Internet versions. Other dictionary sites, such as Wiktionary.org. and Dictionary.com, do not have a print version. Specialized dictionaries in all fields also have places in cyberspace. From medical terminology to foreign languages, Web searchers can find vocabulary help for almost all their needs.

There are several types of print dictionaries, each with its own purpose and use. A pocket or paperback dictionary is an inexpensive, shortened version of a standard dictionary. It is small enough to carry with you to your classes and is relatively inexpensive.

A collegiate dictionary is a larger, more inclusive dictionary. Although a pocket dictionary is convenient, it is also limited. A pocket edition lists about

TECH SUPPORT

Using Online Dictionaries

Online dictionaries have several important advantages over print dictionaries.

- **Audio component.** Some online dictionaries such as Merriam-Webster and American Heritage feature an audio component that allows you to hear how the word is pronounced.
- **Multiple dictionary entries.** Some sites, such as Dictionary.com, display entries from several dictionaries at once for a particular word.
- **Tolerance for misspellings.** If you aren't sure of how a word is spelled or you mistype it, several suggested words will be returned.

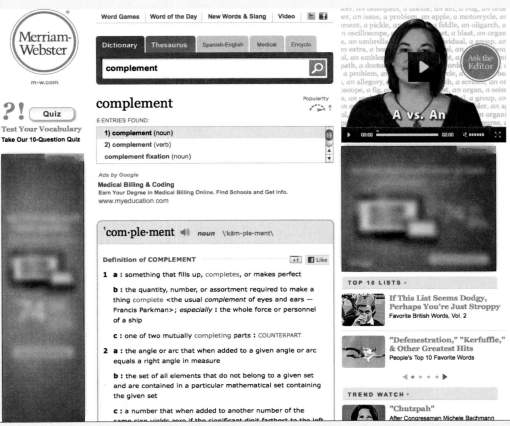

—By permission. From *Merriam-Webster Online* ©2007 by Merriam-Webster, Incorporated (www.Merriam-Webster.com).

Tip Something (a piece of writing, music, etc.) that is *unabridged* is not shortened; it is complete. (An unabridged dictionary contains several hundred thousand words, nearly all of the general words in English.)

55,000 words, whereas a collegiate dictionary lists up to 150,000 words. The collegiate edition also provides much more information about each word.

Another type is the unabridged dictionary, which can be found in the reference section of any library. The unabridged edition provides the most information on each word in the English language.

Whether you purchase a collegiate or a pocket dictionary will depend on your needs as well as on what you can afford. It would be ideal to have both. A pocket dictionary is sufficient for checking spelling and for looking up common meanings of unfamiliar words. To expand your vocabulary by learning additional meanings of words or to do any serious word study, you need a desk dictionary.

If you are an ESL student, be sure you purchase an ESL dictionary. Numerous ones are available in print and in paperback editions, including *The Longman Advanced American Dictionary.*

Using the Dictionary

Dictionaries offer a wide variety of information, as shown in this sample entry.

Pronunciation

Parts of speech

Meanings

Specialized meanings

Etymology

Spelling of other forms of the entry word

curve (kûrv) *n.* **1a.** A line that deviates from straightness in a smooth, continuous fashion. **b.** A surface that deviates from planarity in a smooth, continuous fashion. **c.** Something characterized by such a line or surface, especially a rounded line or contour of the human body. **2.** A relatively smooth bend in a road or other course. **3a.** A line representing data on a graph. **b.** A trend derived from or as if from such a graph: *"Once again, the politicians are behind the curve"* (Ted Kennedy). **4.** A graphic representation showing the relative performance of individuals as measured by each other, used especially as a method of grading students in which the assignment of grades is based on predetermined proportions of student. **5.** *Mathematics* **a.** The graph of a function on a coordinate plane. **b.** The intersection of two surfaces in three dimensions. **c.** The graph of the solutions to any equation of two variables. **6.** *Baseball* A curve ball. **7.** *Slang* Something that is unexpected or designed to trick or deceive. ❖*v.* **curved, curv•ing, curves** —*intr.* To move in or take the shape of a curve: *The path curves around the lake.* —*tr.* **1.** To cause to curve. See synonyms at **bend**[1]. **2.** *Baseball* To pitch a curve ball to. **3.** To grade (students, for example) on a curve. [From Middle English, *curved*, from Latin *curvus*; see **sker-**[2] in Appendix I. N., sense 6, short for CURVE BALL.] —**curv′ed•ness** *n.* —**curv′y** *adj.*

—"Curve," *American Heritage Dictionary of the English Language,* p. 447

Exercise 2

DIRECTIONS   Use the sample dictionary entry above to complete the following items.

1. What is the origin of the word *curve?*

_____

2. Find three meanings for *curve* and write a sentence using each.

_____

3. Explain what *curve* means when used in baseball.

_____

Thesauruses

A thesaurus, or dictionary of synonyms, is a valuable reference for locating a precise, accurate, or descriptive word to fit a particular situation. Suppose you are searching for a more precise term for the expression *looked over,* as used in the following sentence:

My instructor looked over my essay exam.

The thesaurus lists the synonyms of the phrase and you can choose from the list the word that most closely suggests the meaning you want to convey. Choices include *scrutinized, examined, skimmed,* and so forth. The easiest way to do this is to test out, or substitute, various choices in your sentence to see which one is most appropriate; check the dictionary if you are not sure of a word's exact meaning.

Many students misuse the thesaurus by choosing words that do not fit the context. *Be sure to use words only when you are familiar with all their shades of meaning.* Remember, a misused word is often a more serious error than a wordy or imprecise expression.

The most widely used print thesaurus is *Roget's Thesaurus;* it is readily available in an inexpensive paperback edition. Online thesauruses are available at

- Roget's Thesaurus   http://thesaurus.com/Roget-Alpha-Index.html
- Merriam-Webster   http://merriam-webster.com/
  (Pick Browse the Thesaurus.)

Exercise 3

DIRECTIONS   Replace the underlined word or phrase in each sentence with a more descriptive word or phrase. Use a thesaurus to locate your replacement.

1. When Sara learned that her sister had committed a crime, she was <u>sad</u>.
2. Compared with earlier chapters, the last two chapters in my chemistry text are <u>hard</u>.
3. The instructor spent the entire class <u>talking about</u> the causes of inflation and deflation.
4. The main character in the film was a <u>thin</u>, talkative British soldier.
5. We went to see a <u>great</u> film that won the Academy Award for best picture. ●

Subject Area Dictionaries

Many academic disciplines have specialized dictionaries that list important terminology used in that field. They give specialized meanings and suggest how and when to use a word. For the field of music there is the *New Grove Dictionary of Music and Musicians,* which lists and defines the specialized vocabulary of music. Other subject area dictionaries include *Taber's Cyclopedic Medical Dictionary, A Dictionary of Anthropology,* and *A Dictionary of Economics.*

Be sure to find out whether there is a subject area dictionary for your courses and area of specialization. Most of these dictionaries are available only in hardbound copies, and they are likely to be expensive. Many students, however, find them to be worth the initial investment. You will find that most libraries have copies of specialized dictionaries in their reference section.

Exercise 4

DIRECTIONS   List below each course you are taking this term. Using your campus library or the Internet, find out whether a subject area dictionary is available for each discipline. If so, list their titles below.

Course   **Subject Area Dictionary**

_____   _____

_____   _____

_____   _____

_____   _____ •

E-books and Other Electronic Sources

Electronic textbooks (e-books, e-readers, etc.) offer very useful ways to build vocabulary. Many offer a feature that allows you to click on a word so its definition pops up. You can also highlight terminology that is important to learn. You can use this feature to test yourself. For a word you have highlighted, try to recall its definition, and then click on the word and compare your definition with the one that pops up.

Various Web sites are useful for vocabulary building. The Merriam-Webster Web site (http://www.m-w.com), for example, offers a word of the day on its site. Wordsmith (http://www.wordsmith.org) allows you to sign up to receive a word of the day in your e-mail. A variety of other Web sites offer assistance with idioms, frequently confused words, and so forth. Do a Google search to locate currently available sites.

Goal ❸
Handle specialized
vocabulary

LEARNING SPECIALIZED TERMINOLOGY

Each subject area can be said to have a language of its own—its own set of specialized words that makes it possible to describe and accurately discuss topics, principles and concepts, problems, and events related to the subject area.

One of the first tasks that both college instructors and textbook authors face is the necessity of introducing and teaching the specialized language of an academic field. Often the first few class lectures in a course are introductory. They are devoted to acquainting students with the nature and scope of the subject area and to introducing the specialized language.

Tip *Scope* means the range of topics (or other matters) that a course, textbook, etc. covers from beginning to end.

The first few chapters in a textbook are introductory, too. They are written to familiarize students with the subject of study and acquaint them with its specialized language. In one economics textbook, 34 new terms were introduced in the first two chapters (40 pages). In the first two chapters (28 pages) of a chemistry book, 56 specialized words were introduced. A sample of the words introduced in each of these texts is given below. Some of the terms are common, everyday words that take on a specialized meaning; others are technical terms used only in that subject area.

New Terms: Economics Text	**New Terms: Chemistry Text**
capital	matter
ownership	element
opportunity cost	halogen

New Terms: Economics Text	**New Terms: Chemistry Text**
distribution	isotope
productive contribution	allotropic form
durable goods	nonmetal
economic system	group (family)
barter	burning
commodity money	toxicity

Recognition of specialized terminology is only the first step in learning the language of a course. More important is the development of a systematic way of identifying, marking, recording, and learning the specialized terms. Because new terminology is introduced in both class lectures and course textbooks, it is necessary to develop a procedure for handling the specialized terms in each.

Exercise 5

DIRECTIONS   Turn to the reading "You're Eating Genetically Modified Food" in Part Five, page 461. Identify as many new terms as you can, and record them in the space provided below.

Total number of specialized words: _____

Examples of specialized vocabulary: _____

_____

_____

_____

_____ ●

Exercise 6

DIRECTIONS   Select any two textbooks you are currently using. In each, turn to the first chapter and check to see how many specialized terms are introduced. List the total number of such terms. Then list several examples.

Textbook 1: _____   Textbook 2: _____
title   *title*

Total number of specialized words: _____   Total number of specialized words: _____

Examples of Specialized Words   **Examples of Specialized Words**

1. _____   1. _____

2. _____   2. _____

3. _____   3. _____

4. _____   4. _____

5. _____   5. _____

6. _____   6. _____

7. _____   7. _____ ●

Specialized Terminology in Class Lectures

Tip Something that is *consistent* is the same or similar repeatedly; not contradictory. (Consistent behavior can be good or bad, but, either way, it's predictable.)

As a part of your note-taking system, develop a consistent way of separating new terms and definitions from other facts and ideas. You might circle or draw a box around each new term; or, as you edit your notes (make revisions, changes, or additions to your notes after taking them), underline each new term in red; or mark "def." in the margin each time a definition is included. The mark or symbol you use is a matter of preference. Be sure to use a system to organize the terms for efficient study. One such system will be suggested later in this chapter.

Specialized Terminology in Textbooks

Textbook authors use various means to emphasize new terminology; these include italics, boldfaced type, colored print, marginal definitions, and a new-terms list or vocabulary list at the beginning or end of each chapter.

While you are reading and highlighting important facts and ideas, you should also mark new terminology. Be sure to mark definitions and to separate them from other chapter content. (The mark or symbol you use is your choice.)

If you encounter a new term that is not defined or for which the definition is unclear, check the glossary at the back of the book for its meaning. Make a note of the meaning in the margin of the page.

At the end of the course, use the glossary to test yourself; read an entry, cover up the meaning, and try to remember it; then check to see whether you were correct.

Goal 4

Use systems to build your vocabulary

SYSTEMS FOR LEARNING VOCABULARY

Here are two effective ways to organize and learn specialized or technical vocabulary for each of your courses.

The Vocabulary Card System

Once you have identified and marked new terminology, both in your lecture notes and in your textbook, the next step is to organize the words for study and review. One of the most efficient and practical ways to accomplish this is the vocabulary card system. Use a 3-by-5-inch index card for each new term. Record the word on the front and its meaning on the back. If the word is particularly difficult, you might also include a guide to its pronunciation. Underneath the correct spelling of the word, indicate in syllables how the word sounds. For the word *eutrophication* (a term used in chemistry to mean "overnourishment"), you could indicate its pronunciation as "you-tro-fi-kay'-shun." On the back of the card, along with the meaning, you might want to include an example to help you remember the term more easily. A sample vocabulary card, front and back, is shown in Figure 12-1.

Use these cards for study, for review, and for testing yourself. Go through your pack of cards once, looking at the front and trying to recall the meaning on the back. Then reverse the procedure; look at the meanings and see whether you can recall the terms. As you go through the pack in this way, sort the cards into two piles: words you know and words you don't know. The next time you review the cards, use only cards in the "don't know" pile for review. This sorting

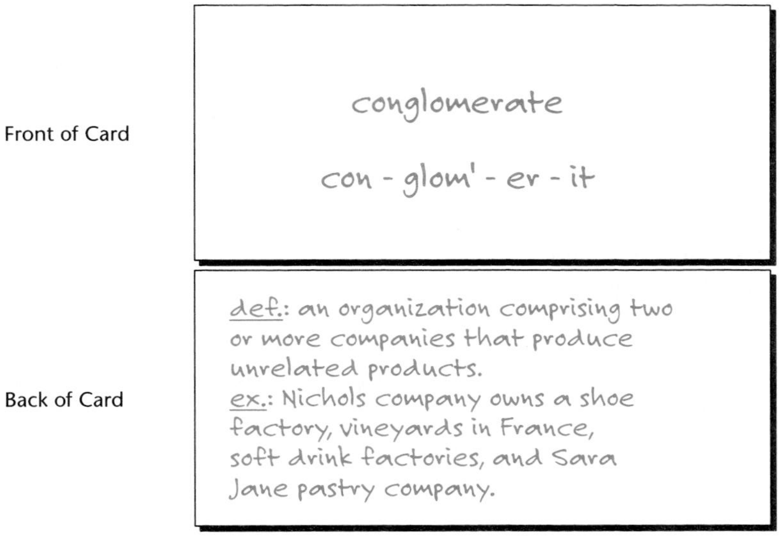

Front of Card

conglomerate

con - glom' - er - it

Back of Card

def.: an organization comprising two or more companies that produce unrelated products.
ex.: Nichols company owns a shoe factory, vineyards in France, soft drink factories, and Sara Jane pastry company.

Figure 12-1
A Sample Vocabulary Card

procedure will help you avoid wasting time reviewing words you have already learned. Continue to review the cards until you are satisfied that you have learned each new term. To prevent forgetting, review the entire pack of cards periodically.

The Computerized Vocabulary Log

Using a word processing program, create a computer log for each of your courses. Daily or weekly, review both textbook chapters and lecture notes and enter specialized and technical terms that you need to learn. Use a three-column format, entering the word in one column, its meaning in the second, and a page reference in the third. You might subdivide or code your file by textbook chapter so that you can review easily when exams or quizzes on particular chapters are announced. A sample is shown below.

Word	Meaning	Page
intraspecific aggression	attack by one animal upon another member of its species	310
orbitofrontal cortex	region of the brain that aids in recognition of situations that produce emotional responses	312
modulation	an attempt to minimize or exaggerate the expression of emotion	317
simulation	an attempt to display an emotion that one does not really feel	319

Figure 12-2
Sample Vocabulary Log for a Psychology Course

Your files can be used in several different ways. If you alphabetize the words, you have created a glossary that will serve as a handy reference. Keep a print copy handy as you read new chapters and review lecture notes. When studying the words in your file, try scrambling the words to avoid learning them in a fixed order.

Exercise 7

DIRECTIONS   Select two or three sets of notes on a particular topic from any course you are taking. Prepare a set of vocabulary cards for the new terms introduced. Review and study the cards. ●

Exercise 8

DIRECTIONS   Select one chapter from any of the textbooks you are currently using. Prepare a vocabulary card for each new term introduced in the chapter. Review and study the cards. ●

USING COLLEGE TEXTBOOKS
Learning Specialized Language

Each discipline has its own language. Textbook authors realize that students need to learn the language of their discipline in order to be successful; so, they use a variety of methods to help you learn this specialized language.

Textbooks contain useful features that help you learn specialized vocabulary.

1. **Chapter vocabulary review.** This list identifies key terms introduced in the chapter, often followed by page numbers indicating where the terms were first used. This list may appear either at the beginning or at the end of the chapter. Check this list before you read the chapter so you will know what key words to look for.

> ### Key Terms
> absolute temperature, p. 100
> absolute zero, p. 99
> atom, p. 94
> backdraft event, p. 112
> British thermal unit, p. 99
> caloric (or calorific) value, p. 102
> chain reaction of self-sustained combustion, p. 96
> electron, p. 95
> endothermic reactions, p. 103
> energy, p. 99
> exothermic, p. 96
> fire flow, p. 102

—Loyd, *Fundamentals of Fire and Emergency Services*, p. 93

As you read, highlight each term and its definition. Use the list as a study aid later: test yourself to be sure you can define each term. You might use the vocabulary card system shown on page 267.

2. **Glossaries.** Appearing at the end of a text, a glossary is an alphabetical list of new terms introduced in the text. Use it to check the meanings of words not defined in the text or those you may have forgotten. If all the chapters in a text have been assigned, you can use the glossary to review for a final exam. Scan the glossary; look for words that are unfamiliar or that you are unable to give a complete definition for, and learn their meanings.

covenant marriage   is a type of marriage that requires a couple to commit to a more strenuous set of legal requirements in an effort to strengthen their relationship and reduce the possibility of divorce. (211)

crisis   is an unstable condition in which there is a lack of sufficient resources to manage the situation. (221)

cross-cultural study   is a research study in which subjects from two or more cultures are observed. (35)

crude birth rate   is the annual number of childbirths for every 1,000 people in a given population. (104)

crude divorce rate   is the number of divorces per 1,000 people. (251)

—Kunz, *Think Marriages and Families*, p. 291

FURTHER PRACTICE WITH TEXTBOOK READING

Part A: Sample Textbook Chapter

Preview and read "Incentives," (pp. 497–98), and then create your own vocabulary review list of terms and definitions that would be important to learn for an exam covering that material.

Part B: Your College Textbook

Choose a textbook chapter that you have been assigned to read for one of your other courses. Locate the vocabulary review list. After you have read the chapter, write a definition for each term listed. (If your textbook does not contain a vocabulary list, prepare your own.)

SELF-TEST
SUMMARY

Goal ❶ What can you do to expand your overall vocabulary?	Develop a sense of word awareness; pay attention to and notice words. Wide reading can expose you to new words and new uses of familiar words. In your speech and writing, you should try to use more exact and expressive words to convey your meaning more clearly and directly.
Goal ❷ Which reference sources are helpful in vocabulary building?	Online, pocket, or desk dictionaries are helpful for quick reference and serious word study. A good thesaurus is an indispensable reference for selecting the best word for a particular situation. Subject area dictionaries are very helpful in locating meanings and uses of specialized terms for the different academic disciplines.

Goal How can you identify which specialized terms to learn?	While taking notes and reading textbooks, pay special attention to specialized words. When taking lecture notes, distinguish new terms and definitions by circling them, highlighting them in a coded color, or labeling them in the margins of your notes. Your textbooks make special terms stand out by using italics, bold print, or color. Mark any other terms that are new to you. Consult each chapter's vocabulary list for terms to learn and use your text's glossary as a study aid.
Goal How can you use the vocabulary card system to help you learn new vocabulary?	The vocabulary card system provides an easy and efficient way to learn words. It involves using 3-by-5-inch cards for study, review, and self-testing. Each card should contain a word and its pronunciation on one side and its meaning and an example on the other. Study these cards by looking at one side and then at the other and then reversing the process. Sort them into piles: "words learned" and "words to be learned." Concentrate on the words you haven't learned until you master them all. Keep them fresh in your memory by reviewing them often and testing yourself frequently.

APPLYING **YOUR SKILLS**

DISCUSSING THE CHAPTER

1. What are some ways that you learn new vocabulary? Explain the methods that are particularly effective for you in various classes and subject areas.
2. What are the advantages of using a large vocabulary when you write?
3. What are an author's responsibilities related to vocabulary when writing for various audiences?
4. One challenge of accepting a new job is learning the specialized vocabulary used by the people who work in a chosen field, company, or department. What are some ways that a new employee can most effectively deal with new vocabulary?

ANALYZING A STUDY SITUATION

Erika is taking a human anatomy course and is having difficulty understanding and learning all the new vocabulary items. Her instructor uses many specialized words in lectures. Often Erika is unable to spell the words correctly, and sometimes she cannot write down the entire definition.

1. Is there a dictionary you would recommend that Erika use?
2. How can Erika separate out these new terms in her lecture notes?
3. How can Erika use the glossary in her textbook to help her study for exams?
4. How can she use the vocabulary card system to study?

WORKING ON COLLABORATIVE PROJECTS

DIRECTIONS After listing 20 unfamiliar words and their meanings on the chalkboard, the instructor will divide the class into two groups. Group 1 should record each word on an index card, writing the word on the front and its meaning on the back. Group 2 should copy the words in a list on a sheet of notebook paper, writing the meaning to the right of each word. Both groups will be given five minutes to study the words (which have been erased from the chalkboard). Members of Group 1 should study by testing themselves using their index cards. Members of Group 2 should study by rereading their lists. During the next class, both groups will take a test on the words. Tally and compare scores of each group, and discuss what this experiment demonstrates about vocabulary learning.

For support in meeting this chapter's goals, go to **MyReadingLab** and select **Vocabulary.**

Answer Key for Learning Experiment
1. c 2. f 3. e 4. i 5. a 6. b 7. j 8. h 9. d 10. g

Quick QUIZ

DIRECTIONS   Write the letter of the choice that best completes each statement in the space provided.

CHECKING YOUR RECALL

_____ 1. A thesaurus lists a word's

    a. synonyms.
    b. translations.
    c. abbreviations.
    d. history.

_____ 2. In a textbook, the glossary is typically located

    a. in the margin of each page.
    b. at the beginning of each chapter.
    c. at the end of each chapter.
    d. at the end of the book.

_____ 3. Specialized vocabulary includes words and phrases that

    a. have a different meaning in another language.
    b. are used in a particular subject area.
    c. must be defined each time they are used.
    d. are used casually in speech.

_____ 4. All of the following characterize a strong vocabulary *except*

    a. substituting long words for short words.
    b. speaking with precise, descriptive language.
    c. using unusual meanings for common words.
    d. applying technical terms in specific disciplines.

_____ 5. In most dictionaries, you can find all of the following information about a word *except* its

    a. pronunciation.
    b. origin.
    c. part of speech.
    d. opposite meaning.

APPLYING YOUR SKILLS

_____ 6. Preston wants to expand his vocabulary and has asked his friends for advice. All of the following suggestions are efficient ways for Preston to expand his vocabulary *except*

    a. reading a wide range of subjects and styles.
    b. developing an awareness of new or unusual words.
    c. replacing the general words in his vocabulary with more descriptive words.
    d. avoiding the use of specialized terminology.

_____ 7. Olivia needs detailed information about a variety of words for a project in her English class. The source that will provide her with the most information on each word in the English language is

    a. a pocket dictionary.
    b. a collegiate dictionary.
    c. a subject area dictionary.
    d. an unabridged dictionary.

_____ 8. Davis needs to determine the meaning of some technical engineering terms. The best sources for the meanings of the technical terms include all of the following *except*

    a. his instructor's presentations.
    b. a subject area dictionary.
    c. his textbook.
    d. a thesaurus.

_____ 9. Detra plans to use the vocabulary card system to help her learn material for a botany course. When she creates her cards, she should be sure to

    a. record as many definitions on each card as possible.
    b. keep the cards in alphabetical order at all times.
    c. include a pronunciation guide for difficult words.
    d. review the whole set of cards every time.

_____ 10. Ron has noticed that his economics instructor often introduces specialized vocabulary in class lectures. When this happens, Ron should

    a. find the term in his text and highlight it.
    b. record it on a separate list.
    c. disregard it if he doesn't know what it means.
    d. record and mark it in his notes.

Reading Graphics and Evaluating Visual and Online Sources

CHAPTER 13

LEARNING GOALS

In this chapter you will learn to

1 Read and analyze graphics

2 Interpret various types of graphics

3 Read online text

4 Evaluate Internet sources

5 Avoid plagiarism

LEARNING EXPERIMENT

1 Read the following paragraph and answer the question that follows.

Of all living things, 75.7 percent are animals; 15.4 percent are plants; 4.6 percent are protists; 4.1 percent are fungi; 2 percent are bacteria. Within the animal kingdom, the largest group is insects comprising 72.7 percent of all animal species. Vertebrates represent 3.9 percent, while Arachnids represent 5.7 percent of animal species. Mollusks represent 5.3 percent, Crustaceans represent 3.0 percent, roundworms represent 1.9 percent, and miscellaneous species represent 7.5 percent. Among the vertebrates, fishes comprise 48 percent, reptiles comprise 14 percent, birds comprise 19 percent, mammals comprise 9 percent, and amphibians comprise 10 percent.

Question: What single category comprises the smallest percentage of vertebrates?

2 Study the circle graphs in Figure 13-1 and answer the question that follows.

Question: What single category comprises the smallest percentage of vertebrates?

THE RESULTS

For which question was it easier to locate the answer? Which took less time to answer? Why? The second question was easier because the graphs presented a visual representation. You could easily see which portion of the circle labeled Vertebrates was the smallest.

SPECIES DIVERSITY

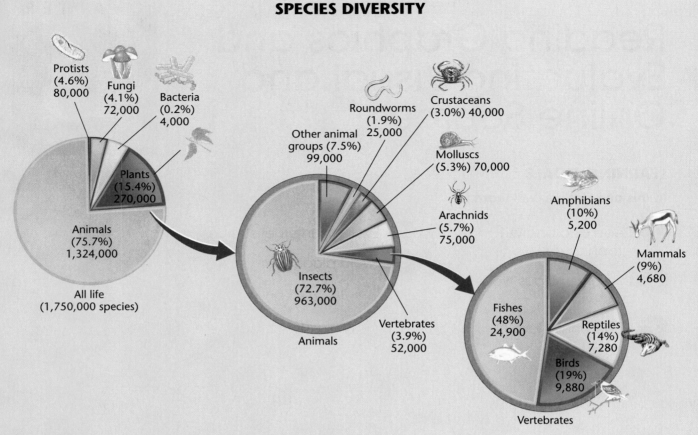

Figure 13-1
Circle Graphs
—Withgott, *Environment: The Science Behind the Stories*, p. 461

LEARNING PRINCIPLE: WHAT THIS MEANS TO YOU

Visualization enables you to grasp ideas, see relationships, and recall information easily. At times, textbook authors will present information visually; other times you may have to create your own visual images. In this chapter you will learn to use visual aids as a learning tool.

WHY LEARN TO READ GRAPHICS AND ONLINE SOURCES?

Graphics and online sources are important for the following reasons:

- Graphics—pictures of information—help you study complex ideas quickly and efficiently.
- Graphics condense and organize information that may be complicated and difficult to remember.
- Graphics display trends and patterns in a clear form so you can better see differences or changes.
- Online information is different from the information on a printed page and needs to be approached differently.

- An increasing number of college instructors expect their students to use electronic sources.
- Computers are an important means of communication and source of information in the workplace.
- Some useful sources of information are available only online.

READING GRAPHICS

Highly detailed specific information is often an integral part of course content. For instance, a sociology course may include crime-rate statistics, a chemistry course is concerned with the characteristics of atomic particles, and an art history course focuses on historical periods.

These kinds of highly specialized information are often presented in graphic form. The term *graphic* refers to all forms of visual representation of information, including maps, charts, tables, and diagrams. Textbooks in many academic disciplines use graphics to organize and present information. Although in most courses your textbook is still your primary source of information, more and more instructors are expecting their students to use the Internet to supplement their textbooks or obtain additional, more current information by visiting Web sites. (Textbooks, no matter how up-to-date they may be, often do not contain information from the year prior to their publication.) Other instructors expect their students to consult Internet sources in researching a topic for a paper. Many students, too, are finding valuable information on personal or special interests on the Internet. The purpose of this chapter is to present strategies for reading graphics and for using online sources of information.

Below is a general strategy for reading graphics. More specific suggestions for each type of graphic will follow.

Goal 1

Read and analyze graphics

myreadinglab

To practice reading graphics, go to

> Graphics and Visuals

HOW TO READ A GRAPHIC

1. **Read the title or caption.** The title will identify the subject and may suggest what relationship is being described.
2. **Determine how the graphic is organized.** Read a table's column headings or the labels on the horizontal and vertical axes of a graph.
3. **Identify the variables.** Decide what is being compared with what or what relationship is being described.
4. **Anticipate the purpose.** On the basis of what you have seen, predict what the graphic is intended to show. Is its purpose to show change over time, describe a process, compare costs, or present statistics?
5. **Determine scale, values, or units of measurement.**
6. **Study the data to identify trends or patterns.** Note changes, unusual statistics, and any unexplained variations.
7. **Draw connections with the chapter content.** Take a moment to figure out why the graphic was included and what concepts or key points it illustrates or explains.
8. **Make a brief summary note.** In the margin, jot a brief note about the trend or pattern the graphic emphasizes. Writing will crystallize the idea in your mind, and your note will be useful when you review.

Tip

A *variable* is something that may be different in different situations; for example, in Figure 13-2, the variables are the populations of the different regions in different years.

Goal 2

Interpret various types of graphics

TYPES OF GRAPHICS

There are many types of graphics; each accomplishes specific purposes for the writer, and each describes a particular relationship.

APPLYING LEVELS OF THINKING

Graphics and Levels of Thinking

Reading graphics involves several levels of thinking. Your first task is to comprehend the information presented in the graphic. Then you move to analysis, synthesis, and evaluation by focusing on what the graph means or how it can be interpreted. Here is a list of questions to guide your thinking about graphics.

Level of Thinking	Question
REMEMBERING AND UNDERSTANDING	What factual information does the graphic present?
APPLYING	How can this information be applied to ideas presented in the chapter or to my own experience?
ANALYZING	What changes or variations occur in the data?
EVALUATING	Of what use or value are these trends or patterns?
CREATING	What trends or patterns are evident?

Tables

A table is an organized display of factual information, usually numbers or statistics. Its purpose is to present large amounts of information in a condensed and systematically arranged form. Tables often classify information and allow readers to compare and contrast various categories. (See the classification and comparison–contrast thought patterns on p. 182 and p. 177.) It's easy to make comparisons among data. Take a few minutes to study the table in Figure 13-2. Then use the tips listed below.

HOW TO READ A TABLE

1. **Determine how the data are classified or divided.** The table shown in Figure 13-2 classifies population growth by year and subdivides it by region (developing or developed).

2. **Make comparisons and look for trends or patterns.** This step involves looking at the rows and columns, noting how each compares with the others. Look for similarities, differences, and sudden changes or variations. Underline or highlight unusual or outstanding data. Try to note increases or decreases that seem unusually high or low. Also note trends in the data. For example, in Figure 13-2, you might note that population growth is projected to slow down in the twenty-first century in developed regions.

3. **Draw conclusions.** Decide what the data mean and what they suggest about the subject at hand. Examine the paragraphs that correspond to the table for clues, or sometimes direct statements, about the purpose of the graph. You can conclude from Figure 13-2 that the world population in general has grown tremendously since 1900 and that a vast majority of the growth has occurred in developing countries.

Tip

Data is the irregular plural of *datum*, a noun meaning "information collected in order to be analyzed."

Figure 13-2
A Table

HUMAN POPULATION TRENDS, 1900–2100					
Population (Millions)					
	1900	1950	2000	2025	2100
Developing regions (total)	1,070	1,681	4,837	6,799	8,748
Africa	133	224	872	1,617	2,591
Asia[a]	867	1,292	3,419	4,403	4,919
Latin America	70	165	546	779	1,238
Developed regions (total)	560	835	1,284	1,407	1,437
Europe, USSR, Japan, Oceania[b]	478	669	987	1,062	1,055
Canada, United States	82	166	297	345	382
World total	1,630	2,516	6,121	8,206	10,185

[a]Excludes Japan.
[b]Includes Australia and New Zealand.

—Mix, Farber, and King, *Biology: The Network of Life*, p. 165.

Exercise 1

DIRECTIONS   Study the table in Figure 13-2 and answer the following questions.

1. Which region has the highest population in every year?
2. Which region will nearly double its population from 2000 to 2025?
3. Which developing region had the lowest population in 1900?
4. What was the total world population in 1950?
5. What year shows the greatest difference in *total* population between developing regions and developed regions? ●

Graphs

There are two primary types of graphs: bar graphs and line graphs. Each plots a set of points on a set of axes. These graphs show relationships among variables.

BAR GRAPHS   A bar graph makes comparisons between quantities or amounts. It is particularly useful in showing changes that occur with passing time. Bar graphs usually are designed to emphasize differences. The graph shown in Figure 13-3 (p. 278) displays the percentage of the world's population living in urban areas. It makes it easy to see at a glance how the percentage of city dwellers will increase until the year 2025.

Tip
On a line graph, axes are the horizontal and vertical lines along which the positions of points are marked. *Axes* is the irregular plural of *axis*.

Exercise 2

DIRECTIONS   Study the bar graph in Figure 13-3 (p. 278) and answer the following questions.

1. Between which years did the percentage of people living in cities increase the most?
2. Between which years did the percentage of people living in cities increase the least?
3. What was the last year in which more people lived outside of cities than in cities?
4. In what year was the percentage of people *not* living in cities the highest? ●

Figure 13-3
Bar Graph

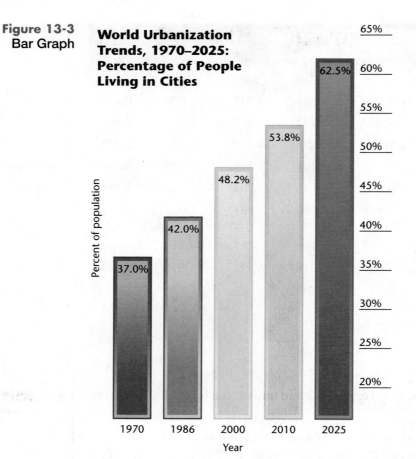

World Urbanization Trends, 1970–2025: Percentage of People Living in Cities

—Kaufman and Franz, *Biosphere 2000: Protecting the Global Environment*, p. 143

MULTIPLE BAR GRAPHS A multiple bar graph displays at least two or three comparisons simultaneously. Figure 13-4 compares male and female preferences for private brands of food products by age group.

Figure 13-4
Multiple Bar Graph

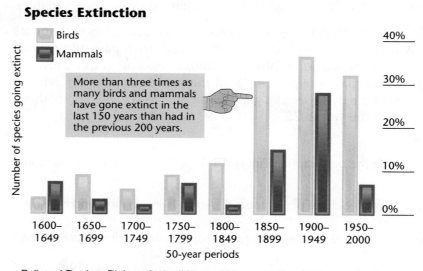

Species Extinction

More than three times as many birds and mammals have gone extinct in the last 150 years than had in the previous 200 years.

—Belk and Borden, *Biology*, 2nd edition, p. 363

DIRECTIONS   Study the multiple bar graph in Figure 13-4 and answer the following questions.

Exercise 3

1. What two groups are shown on this graph?
2. In which 50-year periods did more than 30% of bird species go extinct?
3. In which 50-year periods did the largest number of mammals go extinct?
4. In which 50-year periods did the rate of extinction for birds exceed that of mammals?
5. What major trend is shown on this graph? ●

STACKED BAR GRAPHS   In a stacked bar graph, instead of being arranged side by side, bars are placed one on top of another. This variation is often used to emphasize whole/part relationships—that is, to show what part of an entire group or class a particular item accounts for. Stacked bar graphs also make numerous comparisons possible. The graph in Figure 13-5 enables you to compare responses to a question about care of elderly parents by religion and race and shows a national response as well.

Figure 13-5
Stacked Bar Graph

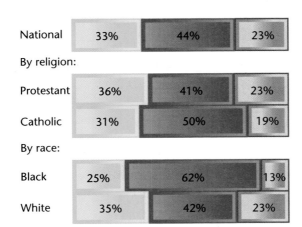

Care of Elderly Parents

Question: Do you think it is better for most older Americans who cannot live alone to live in a home for the aged or with their children?

For older Americans who cannot live alone, it is better for them to live in a home for the aged.

It is better for them to live with their children.

Don't know

National	33%	44%	23%

By religion:

Protestant	36%	41%	23%
Catholic	31%	50%	19%

By race:

Black	25%	62%	13%
White	35%	42%	23%

—Skolnick, *The Intimate Environment: Exploring Marriage and Family,* p. 443

DIRECTIONS   Study the stacked bar graph in Figure 13-5 and answer the following questions.

Exercise 4

1. What living arrangement do most people think is preferable for elderly Americans who cannot live alone?

2. What percentage of Catholics think that older Americans should live with their children?
3. What percentage of Protestants think that older Americans should live in a home for the aged?
4. Which racial group feels more strongly that older Americans should live with their children?
5. Among white people, what percentage think that older Americans should live in a home for the aged? ●

LINE GRAPHS   In a line graph, or linear graph, points are plotted along a vertical and a horizontal axis and then connected to form a line. A line graph allows more data points than a bar graph. Consequently, it is used to present more detailed and/or larger quantities of information. A line graph may represent the relationship between two variables; if so, it consists of a single line. More often, however, line graphs are used to compare relationships among several variables, and multiple lines are included. The graph shown in Figure 13-6 shows the changes in population percentages for various minority groups from 1995 to 2050.

Line graphs are generally used to display continuous data—data that are connected in time or events that occur in sequence. The data in Figure 13-6 go from 1995 to 2050.

The line graph in Figure 13-6 shows an overall positive relationship between year and all three nonwhite groups. Between 1995 and 2025, we can see a steady increase in the percentage of the population each group comprises, indicating a positive relationship between decade and percentage of the population. Once you know the trend and the nature of the relationship that a linear graph describes, jot them down in the margin next to the graph. These notes will be valuable time-savers as you review the chapter.

Figure 13-6
Line Graph

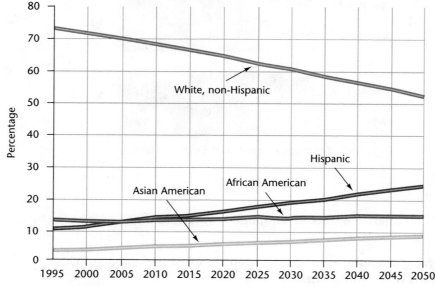

Population Change in Minority Populations

United States Census Bureau

—Edwards, Wattenberg, and Lineberry, *Government in America*, p. 180

DIRECTIONS Study the line graph in Figure 13-6 and answer the following questions.

1. Which two minority groups made up the same percentage of the population in 2005?
2. Which minority group represents the smallest percentage of the population in every year shown?
3. Which minority group appears to be increasing its share of the population at the highest rate?
4. Between which years will the Hispanic minority group reach 20% of the population?
5. In the year 2000, which minority group comprised the largest percentage of the population? ●

TECH SUPPORT

Creating Graphics

Learning to present data in a visual format will help you in many college writing assignments (especially in social sciences and business courses), and will also be useful in workplace writing. It's easy to create simple bar graphs, line graphs, pie charts, and other basic graphs in most word processing programs. In Word, choose "Object" from the drop-down "Insert" menu, and click the "Create New" tab. Enter your data in the "Datasheet" and select "Chart Type" to plot the data. If your graphic uses color, be sure that you have access to a color printer before printing a final copy of your paper to turn in to your professor.

Charts

Four types of charts are commonly used in college textbooks: pie charts, organizational charts, flowcharts, and pictograms. Each is intended to display a relationship, either quantitative or cause–effect.

PIE CHARTS Pie charts, sometimes called circle graphs, are used to show whole/part relationships or to show how given parts of a unit have been divided or classified. They let the reader compare the parts with each other as well as compare each part with the whole. Figure 13-7, taken from an American

Figure 13-7
Pie Charts

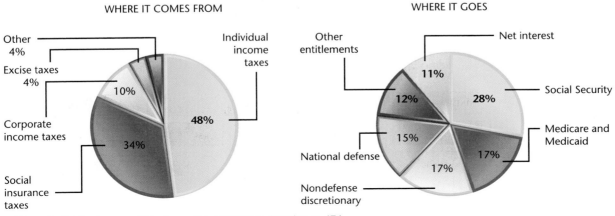

THE FEDERAL GOVERNMENT DOLLAR

WHERE IT COMES FROM

Other 4%
Excise taxes 4%
Corporate income taxes
Social insurance taxes
10%
34%
48%
Individual income taxes

WHERE IT GOES

Other entitlements
National defense
Nondefense discretionary
Net interest
11%
12%
15%
17%
17%
28%
Social Security
Medicare and Medicaid

—Edwards, Wattenberg, and Lineberry, *Government in America*, p. 474

government textbook, shows the federal budget in terms of where government dollars come from and how they are spent. Each pie chart provides a clear visual for understanding and comparing the different parts of the federal budget.

HOW TO READ A PIE CHART

1. **Determine the subject of the chart.** What is being divided into parts or slices?
2. **Notice how the subject is divided and how the slices are arranged.** Are they arranged from largest to smallest? What labels or headings are used?
3. **Notice trends and patterns.** What does the chart reveal about the subject?

Exercise 6

DIRECTIONS   Study the pie charts in Figure 13-7 (p. 281) and answer the following questions.

1. How many different sources of federal government dollars are compared?
2. Which source provides the biggest percentage of the federal budget?
3. How many different expenditures of federal government dollars are compared?
4. What percentage of the federal budget is spent on Medicare and Medicaid?
5. Are the pie charts more or less effective than a bar graph containing the same data? Why? ●

ORGANIZATIONAL CHARTS   An organizational chart divides an organization, such as a corporation, a hospital, or a university, into its administrative parts, staff positions, or lines of authority. Figure 13-8 shows the structure of a company organized by function. It indicates that there are four major subdivisions and depicts divisions of responsibility for each.

HOW TO READ AN ORGANIZATIONAL CHART

1. **Identify the organization being described.**
2. **Study its organization.** What do various boxes and arrows represent?
3. **Identify lines of authority and responsibility.** Determine who is in charge of what and what each office or person or department is responsible for.

Figure 13-8
Organizational Chart

Thompson Manufacturing Group Corporation

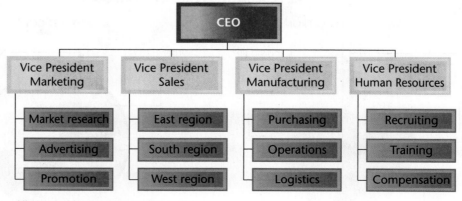

—Hitt et al., *Management*, p. 241

DIRECTIONS Study the organizational chart in Figure 13-8 and answer the following questions.

Exercise 7

1. What type of organization is depicted on the chart?
2. What four major subdivisions are depicted for this organization?
3. To whom does the purchasing department report?
4. What activities are included within the marketing function?
5. Which vice president is responsible for recruiting, training, and compensation? ●

FLOWCHARTS A flowchart is a specialized type of chart that shows how a process or procedure works. Lines or arrows are used to indicate the path (route or routes) through the procedure. Various shapes (boxes, circles, rectangles) enclose what is done at each stage or step. You could draw, for example, a flowchart to describe how to apply for and obtain a student loan or how to locate a malfunction in your car's electrical system. The flowchart shown in Figure 13-9, taken from a consumer behavior textbook, describes how consumers make decisions. The chart reveals a multistage process and describes the parts of each step.

STAGES IN CONSUMER DECISION MAKING

Figure 13-9
Flowchart

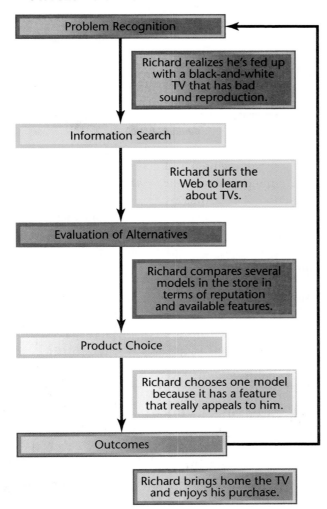

—Solomon, *Consumer Behavior*, p. 293

HOW TO READ A FLOWCHART

1. **Determine what process the flowchart shows.**
2. **Next, follow the chart, using the arrows and reading each step.** Start at the top or far left of the chart.
3. **When you've finished, describe the process in your own words.** Try to draw the chart from memory without referring to the text. Compare your drawing with the chart, and take note of anything you forgot or misplaced.

Exercise 8

DIRECTIONS   Study the flowchart in Figure 13-9 (p. 283) and answer the following questions.

1. What process does this flowchart describe?
2. What is the purpose of the boxes that mention Richard?
3. Invent another situation and another person that could be used to replace the boxes describing Richard's behavior.
4. What other outcomes are possible for Richard? ●

PICTOGRAMS   A combination of a chart and a graph, a pictogram uses symbols or drawings (such as books, cars, or buildings), instead of bars or lines, to represent specified amounts. This type of chart tends to be visually appealing, makes statistics seem realistic, and may carry an emotional impact. For example, a chart that uses stick-figure drawings of pregnant women to indicate the number of abortions performed each year per state may have a greater impact than statistics presented in numerical form. The pictogram shown in Figure 13-10 uses a garbage can to represent the types of trash and a truck to represent what happens to the trash.

HOW TO READ A PICTOGRAM

1. **Identify the subject.** What is the purpose of the pictogram?
2. **Identify what symbols are used and what they stand for.**
3. **Determine the numeric value of each symbol.**
4. **Figure out whether the various symbols are drawn proportionally.** It is easy to misrepresent a value by drawing a symbol larger than it should be in comparison to other figures.
5. **Examine the pictogram to determine what trends or patterns the arrangement of symbols suggests.**

Figure 13-10
Pictogram

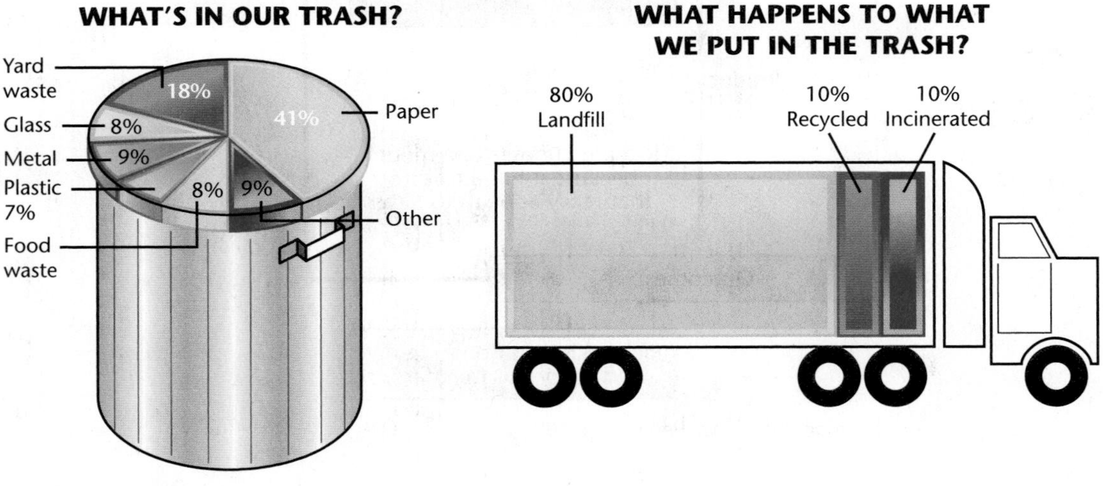

WHAT'S IN OUR TRASH?

Yard waste 18%
Glass 8%
Metal 9%
Plastic 7%
Food waste 8%
9%
Paper 41%
Other

WHAT HAPPENS TO WHAT WE PUT IN THE TRASH?

80% Landfill
10% Recycled
10% Incinerated

—Donatelle, *Health: The Basics*, p. 386

Copyright © 2013 by Pearson Education, Inc.

DIRECTIONS   Study the pictogram in Figure 13-10 and answer the following questions.

1. What item makes up the largest percentage of trash?
2. What item makes up the smallest percentage of trash?
3. What percentage of trash is made up of yard waste?
4. What happens to most of what is put in the trash?
5. What percentage of trash is recycled? ●

Diagrams

Diagrams often are included in technical and scientific as well as business and social science texts to explain processes. Diagrams are intended to help you see relationships between parts and understand what follows what. Figure 13-11, taken from a government textbook, explains the process of amending the Constitution.

Figure 13-11
Diagram

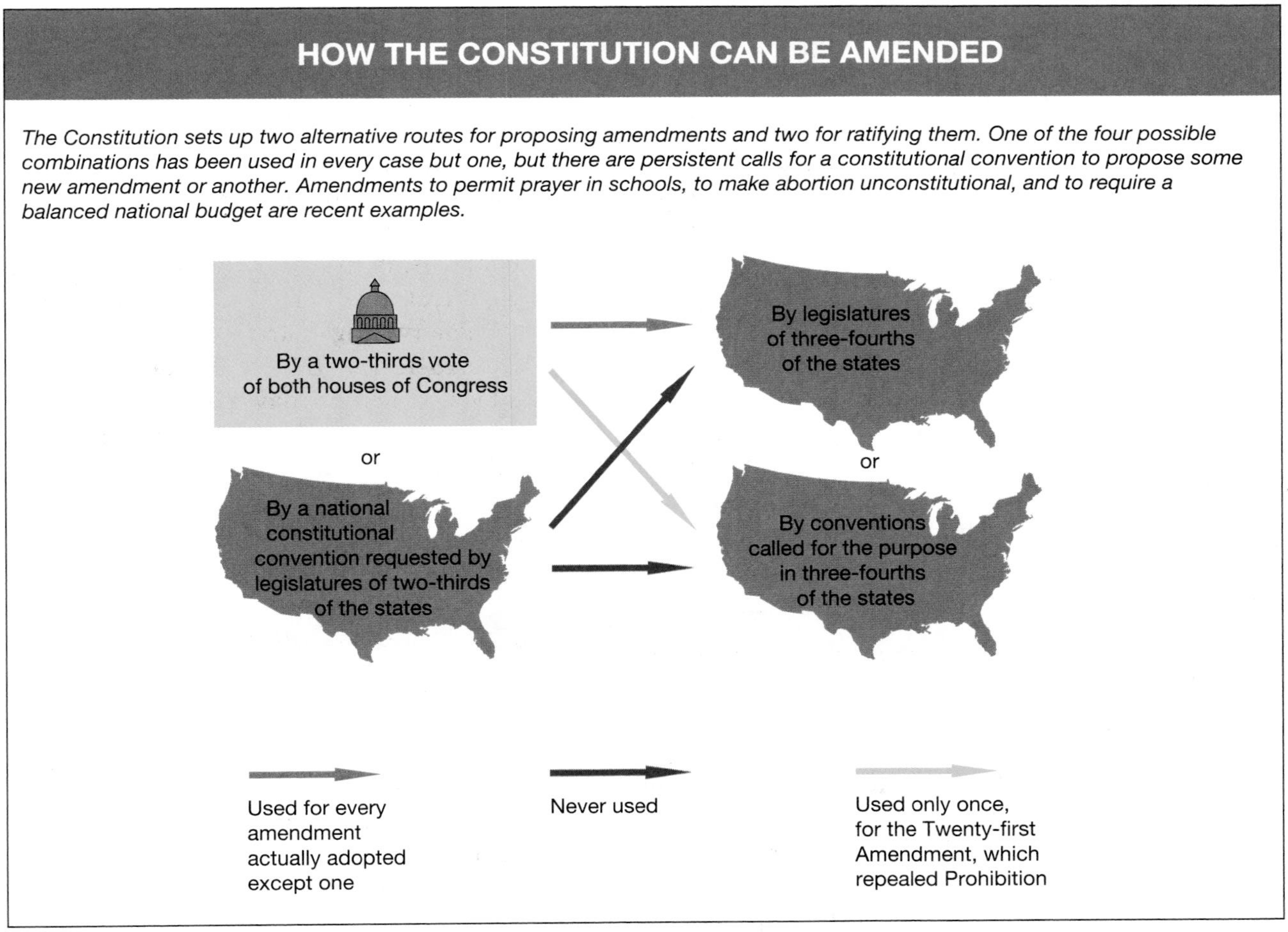

HOW THE CONSTITUTION CAN BE AMENDED

The Constitution sets up two alternative routes for proposing amendments and two for ratifying them. One of the four possible combinations has been used in every case but one, but there are persistent calls for a constitutional convention to propose some new amendment or another. Amendments to permit prayer in schools, to make abortion unconstitutional, and to require a balanced national budget are recent examples.

By a two-thirds vote of both houses of Congress

or

By a national constitutional convention requested by legislatures of two-thirds of the states

By legislatures of three-fourths of the states

or

By conventions called for the purpose in three-fourths of the states

Used for every amendment actually adopted except one

Never used

Used only once, for the Twenty-first Amendment, which repealed Prohibition

—Edwards, Wattenberg, and Lineberry, *Government in America*, p. 47

HOW TO READ A DIAGRAM

1. **Plan on switching back and forth between the diagram and the text paragraphs that describe it.**
2. **Get an overview.** Study the diagram and read the corresponding text paragraphs once to discover what process it is describing. Pay particular attention to the heading of the textbook section and the title of the diagram.
3. **Read both the diagram and text several more times, focusing in the details of the process.** Examine each step or part and understand the progression from one step or part to the next.
4. **Study the diagram by trying to redraw it without referring to the original.** Include as much detail as possible.
5. **Test your understanding and recall by explaining the process, step-by-step, using your own words.**

Exercise 10

DIRECTIONS   Study the diagram shown in Figure 13-11 (p. 285) and answer the following questions.

1. What is the purpose of the diagram?
2. What amendment process is most commonly used?
3. Name two processes that have never been used.
4. Explain the process by which Prohibition was repealed. ●

Maps

Maps describe relationships and provide information about location and direction. They are commonly found in geography and history texts, and they also appear in ecology, biology, and anthropology texts. Although most of us think of maps as describing distances and locations, maps also are used to describe placement of geographical and ecological features such as areas of pollution, areas of population density, and political data (voting districts).

Now look at the map shown in Figure 13-12 (p. 287). Its key depicts boxes with various numbers of days in a school year; the more days per year, the larger the box. Using this code, you can quickly locate those countries with the most and fewest school days by looking for the largest and smallest boxes. You can also observe which parts of the world tend to have the most and the fewest school days in general.

HOW TO READ MAPS

1. **Read the caption.** This identifies the subject of the map.
2. **Use the legend or key to identify the symbols or codes used.**
3. **Note distance scales.**
4. **Study the map, looking for trends or key points.** Often the text that accompanies the map states the key points that the map illustrates.
5. **Try to create a mental picture of the map.**
6. **As a learning and study aid, write, in your own words, a statement of what the map shows.**

Figure 13-12
Map

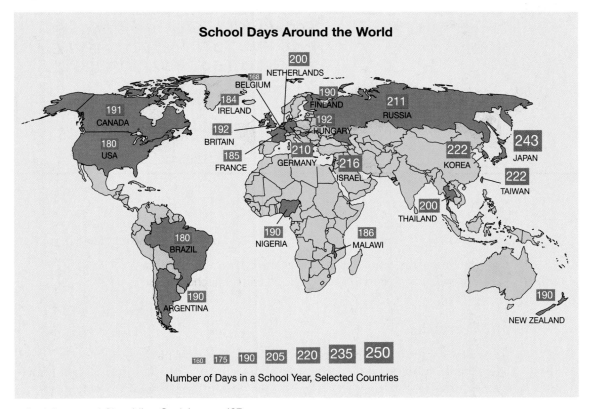

—Applebaum and Chambliss, *Sociology,* p. 427

DIRECTIONS   Study the map in Figure 13-12 and answer the following questions.

Exercise 11

1. Which country has the most school days? Which country has the fewest school days?
2. Name the four countries in which students attend school 190 days per year.
3. In which part of the world do countries tend to have the most school days?
4. How many days a year do students in Malawi attend school? ●

Cartoons

Cartoons are included in textbooks to make a point quickly or simply to lighten the text by adding a touch of humor about the topic at hand. Cartoons usually appear without a title or legend and there is often no reference within the text to the cartoon.

Cartoons can make abstract ideas and concepts concrete and real. Pay close attention to cartoons, especially if you are a visually oriented learner. They may help you remember ideas easily by serving as a recall clue that triggers your memory of related material.

The cartoon shown in Figure 13-13 (p. 288) appears in a sociology textbook chapter titled "Socialization and Gender." It appears on a page that dicusses gender roles learned during childhood.

Figure 13-13
Cartoon
Frank and Ernest

Exercise 12

DIRECTIONS   Study the cartoon in Figure 13-13 and answer the following questions.

1. What message or main point does the cartoon make?
2. Why was it included in the sociology textbook chapter? ●

Photographs

Although sometimes considered an art form instead of a graphic, photographs, like other graphics, can be used in place of words to present information. Photographs also are used to spark your interest and, often, to draw out an emotional response or feeling. The caption on a photograph often provides a clue to its intended meaning. As you study a photograph, ask "What is my first overall impression?" and "What details did I notice first?" These questions will lead you to discover the purpose of the photograph.

Exercise 13

DIRECTIONS   Indicate what type(s) of graphic(s) would be most useful in presenting each of the following sets of information:

1. Damage done to ancient carved figures by sulfur dioxide in the air
2. A comparison of the types of products the United States imports with those it exports
3. Changes in worker productivity each year from 1970 through 2005 in Japan, France, Germany, and the United States
4. The probabilities of being murdered, broken down by various racial and ethnic groups in the United States
5. Foreign revenue, total revenue, foreign operating profit, foreign assets, and total assets for the ten largest American multinational corporations
6. Living arrangements (one parent, two parents, neither parent) for white, black, and Hispanic-origin children under 18 years of age in 1970, 1980, 1990, 2000, and 2010
7. The basic components of a robot's manipulator arm
8. A description of how the AIDS virus affects the immune system
9. Sites of the earliest Neanderthal discoveries in Western Europe
10. Number of receipts of, and profits for, three types of businesses: sole proprietorships, partnerships, and corporations ●

Figure 13-14
Photographs

DIRECTIONS   Study the photographs from a sociology text that are shown in Figure 13-14 and answer the following questions.

1. What are the photographs intended to emphasize?
2. What does this pair of photographs show that a paragraph could not easily describe?
3. List details in the photographs that are particularly compelling. ●

Exercise 14

Goal 3

Read online text

READING ONLINE TEXT

Reading online text is not only different from reading print sources, but it also tends to be slower. In a book your eyes can see the layout of two full pages. From the two pages you can see headings, division of ideas, and sub-topics. By glancing at a print page, you can make an initial assessment of what it contains. You can tell, for example, if a page is heavily statistical (your eye will see numbers, dates, symbols) or is anecdotal (your eye will see capitalized proper names, quotation marks, and numerous indented paragraphs for dialogue, for example). Because you have a sense of what the page contains and how it is organized, you can read somewhat faster. Because a screen holds fewer words, you get far less information before you begin to read.

Here is the site map for exploratorium, an online science museum. The site map is like a table of contents for an entire Web site.

Exercise 15

DIRECTIONS   In groups of two or three students, consider one aspect of learning style. For each, discuss the tendencies, limitations, and implications this particular learning style may have for reading online text. How would a pragmatic learner approach a Web site? How might this differ from how a creative learner might approach it? ●

Developing New Ways of Thinking and Reading

Reading online sources demands a different type of thinking from reading print sources. A print source is linear—it progresses in a straight line from idea to idea. Online sources, due to the presence of links, tend to be multidirectional; you can follow numerous paths.

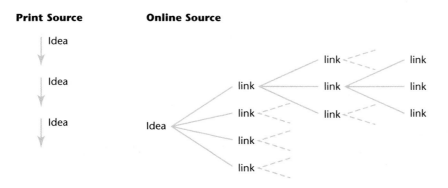

Reading online also requires new strategies. To read online easily and effectively you must adapt how you read.

HOW TO READ ONLINE

1. **Focus on your purpose.** Focus clearly on your purposes for visiting the site. What information do you need?
2. **Spend a few minutes discovering how the site is organized.** Scroll through it quickly to determine how it is organized and what information is available.
3. **Use the site map, if provided, to discover what information is available and how it is organized.**
4. **Expect the first screen to grab your attention and make a main point.** Web site authors know that many people who read a Web page do not scroll down to see the next screenful.
5. **Get used to the Web site's design before you attempt to obtain information from the site.** Your eye may have a tendency to focus on color or movement, rather than on print. Because some Web sites are highly visual, they require visual as well as verbal thinking. The author intends for you to respond to photos, graphics, and animation.
6. **Consider the order in which you want to take in information.** Choose an order in which to explore links; avoid randomly clicking on them. Doing so is somewhat like randomly choosing pages to read out of a reference book.
7. **Expect shorter, less detailed sentences and paragraphs.** Much online communication tends to be briefer and more concise than in traditional sources. as a result, you may have to mentally fill in transitions and make inferences about the relationships among ideas. For example, you may have to infer similarities and differences or recognize cause–effect connections.

Goal

Evaluate Internet
sources

EVALUATING INTERNET SOURCES

Although the Internet contains a great deal of valuable information and resources, it also contains rumor, gossip, hoaxes, and misinformation. In other words, not all Internet sources are trustworthy. You must evaluate a source before accepting it. Here are some guidelines to follow when evaluating Internet sources.

Discover the Purpose of a Web Site

There are millions of Web sites and they vary widely in purpose. Table 13-1 summarizes five primary types of Web sites.

Exercise 16

DIRECTIONS   Using the information in Table 13-1, determine the purpose of five of the following Web sites. Some sites may have more than one purpose. Be sure to investigate the whole site carefully and explain your choices.

1. College Finder: http://www.college-finder.com
2. Israel—A Country Study: http://lcweb2.loc.gov/frd/cs/iltoc.html
3. Senator Chuck Schumer: http://schumer.senate.gov/
4. Center for Science in the Public Interest: http://www.cspinet.org/
5. Dr. Kary Mullis: http://www.karymullis.com ●

TABLE 13-1 TYPES OF WEB SITES			
Type	**Purpose and Description**	**Domain**	**Sample Sites**
Informational	To present facts, information, and research data. May contain reports, statistical data, results of research studies, and reference materials.	.edu or .gov	http://www.haskins.yale.edu/ http://www.census.gov/
News	To provide current information on local, national, and international news. Often supplements print newspapers, periodicals, and television news programs.	.com or .org	http://news.yahoo.com/ http://www.theheart.org
Advocacy	To promote a particular cause or point of view. Usually concerned with a controversial issue; often sponsored by nonprofit groups.	.com or .org	http://www.goveg.com/ http://www.bradycampaign.org/
Personal	To provide information about an individual and his/her interests and accomplishments. May list publications or include the individual's résumé.	Varies . . . may contain .com, .org, .biz, .edu, .info May contain a tilde (~)	http://www.jessamyn.com/ http://www.johnfisher.biz/resume.html http://www.maryrussell.info/ http://www.plu.edu/~chasega/
Commercial	To promote goods or services. May provide news and information related to products.	.com, .biz, .info	http://websitebuilding.biz/ http://www.alhemer.com/ http://www.vintageradio.info/

Evaluate the Content of a Web Site

When evaluating the content of a Web site, evaluate its appropriateness, its source, its level of technical detail, its presentation, its completeness, and its links.

Evaluate Appropriateness   To be worthwhile a Web site should contain the information you need. That is, it should answer one or more of your search questions. If the site only touches upon answers to your questions but does not address them in detail, check the links on the site to see if they lead you to more detailed information. If they do not, search for a more useful site.

Evaluate the Source   Another important step in evaluating a Web site is to determine its source. Ask yourself "Who is the sponsor?" and "Why was this site put up on the Web?" The sponsor of a Web site is the person or organization who paid for its creation and placement on the Web. The sponsor will often suggest the purpose of a Web site. For example, a Web site sponsored by Nike is designed to promote its products, while a site sponsored by a university library is designed to help students learn to use its resources more effectively.

If you are uncertain who sponsors a Web site, check its URL, its copyright, and the links it offers. Another way to check the ownership of a Web site is to try to locate the site's home page.

Evaluate the Level of Technical Detail   A Web site's level of technical detail should be suited to your purpose. Some sites may provide information that is too sketchy for your search purposes; others assume a level of background knowledge or technical sophistication that you lack. For example, if you are writing a short, introductory-level paper on global warming, information on the University of New Hampshire's NASA Earth Observing System site (http://www.eos-ids.sr.unh.edu/) may be too technical and contain more information than you need, unless you have some previous knowledge in that field.

Evaluate the Presentation   Information on a Web site should be presented clearly; it should be well written. If you find a site that is not clear and well written, you should be suspicious of it. If the author did not take time to present ideas clearly and correctly, he or she may not have taken time to collect accurate information, either.

Evaluate Completeness   Determine whether the site provides complete information on its topic. Does it address all aspects of the topic that you feel it should? For example, if a Web site on important twentieth-century American poets does not mention Robert Frost, then the site is incomplete. If you discover that a site is incomplete, search for sites that provide a more thorough treatment of the topic.

Evaluate the Links   Many reputable sites supply links to other related sites. Make sure that the links are current. Also check to see if the sites to which you are sent are reliable sources of information. If the links do not work or the sources appear unreliable, you should question the reliability of the site itself. Also determine whether the links provided are comprehensive or only present a representative sample. Either is acceptable, but the site should make clear the nature of the links it is providing.

Exercise 17

DIRECTIONS Evaluate the content of two of the following sites. Explain why you would either trust or distrust the site for reliable content.

1. http://www.innercircleofpoets.com
2. http://www.earlham.edu/~peters/knotlink.htm
3. http://www.age-of-the-sage.org/psychology/ ●

Evaluate the Accuracy and Timeliness of a Web Site

When using information on a Web site for an academic paper, it is important to be sure that you have found accurate and up-to-date information. One way to determine the accuracy of a Web site is to compare it with print sources (periodicals and books) on the same topic. If you find a wide discrepancy between the Web site and the printed sources, do not trust the Web site. Another way to determine a site's accuracy is to compare it with other Web sites that address the same topic. If discrepancies exist, further research is needed to determine which site is more accurate.

The site itself will also provide clues about the accuracy of its information. Ask yourself the following questions:

- **Are the author's name and credentials provided?** A well-known writer with established credentials is likely to author only reliable, accurate information. If no author is given, you should question whether the information is accurate.
- **Is contact information for the author included on the site?** Sites often provide an e-mail address where the author may be contacted.
- **Is the information complete or in summary form?** If it is a summary, use the site to find the original source. Original information has less chance of error and is usually preferred in academic papers.
- **If opinions are offered, are they presented clearly as opinions?** Authors who disguise their opinions as facts are not trustworthy.
- **Does the writer make unsubstantiated assumptions or base his or her ideas on misconceptions?** If so, the information presented may not be accurate.
- **Does the site provide a list of works cited?** As with any form of research, sources used to put information up on a Web site must be documented. If sources are not credited, you should question the accuracy of the Web site.

It may be helpful to determine whether the information is available in print form. If it is, try to obtain the print version. Errors may occur when an article or essay is put up on the Web. Web sites move, change, and delete information, so it may be difficult for a reader of an academic paper to locate the Web site that you used in writing it. Also, page numbers are easier to cite in print sources than in electronic ones.

Although the Web is well known for providing up-to-the-minute information, not all Web sites are current. Evaluate a site's timeliness by checking the following dates:

- The date on which the Web site was published (put up on the Web)
- The date when the document you are using was added
- The date when the site was last revised
- The date when the links were last checked

This information is usually provided at the end of the site's home page or at the end of the document you are using.

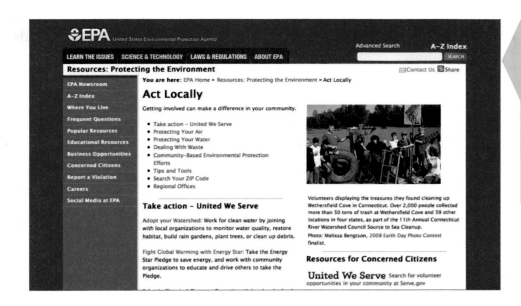

Copyright © 2013 by Pearson Education, Inc.

Visual Thinking
APPLYING SKILLS

Imagine you are writing a paper on protecting your local environment. Would this website be an appropriate source? Why or why not?"

DIRECTIONS   Complete each of the following items.

Exercise 18

1. Evaluate the accuracy of two of the following Web sites:
   a. http://www.nlf.net/
   b. http://www.krysstal.com/democracy.html
   c. http://www.idausa.org/facts/pg.html
2. Evaluate the timeliness of two of the following Web sites, using the directions given for each site.
   a. http://www.hwg.org/resources/?cid=30
      See when these links were last checked. Find out the consequences by checking the links yourself.
   b. http://www.chebucto.ns.ca/Urbancap/
      Evaluate whether this site contains up-to-date information and links for the Community Access Program in Nova Scotia.
   c. http://conference.journalists.org/2004conference/
      Explain what information on this site might be useful even though the event is over. How would you find out current information for this conference? ●

AVOIDING PLAGIARISM

Goal 5

Avoid plagiarism

As you write papers for college classes, you will probably use online sources to locate the information you need. As you read and take notes, and later, as you write the paper, you need to know the rules for indicating that you have taken information or ideas from the work of other people. You identify your sources in order to help readers find a source if they want to look into the ideas of that author further, as well as to give credit to the person who originally wrote the material or thought of the idea.

Plagiarism means borrowing someone else's ideas or exact wording without giving that person credit. If you take information on Frank Lloyd Wright's architecture from a reference source, but do not indicate where you found it, you have plagiarized. If you take the six-word phrase "Martinez, the vengeful, despicable drug czar" from an online news article on the war on drugs without putting quotation marks around it and noting the source, you have plagiarized. Plagiarism is intellectually dishonest because you are taking someone else's ideas or wording and passing them off as your own.

The Internet, while a tremendous source of information, has unfortunately contributed to an increase in plagiarism by students—both accidental and

WHAT CONSTITUTES PLAGIARISM

- Plagiarism is the use of another person's words without giving credit to that person.
- Plagiarism uses another person's theory, opinion, or idea without listing where the information was taken from.
- Plagiarism results when another person's exact words are not placed inside quotation marks. Both the quotation marks and a citation (reference) to the original source are needed.
- Paraphrasing (rewording) another person's words without giving credit to them is plagiarism.
- Using facts, data, graphs, charts, and so on without stating where they were taken from is plagiarism.
- Using commonly known facts or information is not plagiarism and you need not give a source for your information. For example, the fact that Neil Armstrong set foot on the moon in 1969 is widely known and so does not require documentation.
- Plagiarism is treated very seriously by authors, publishers, instructors, and academic departments.

deliberate. The Internet makes it easy to copy something from an Internet document and paste it into your own paper without giving credit to the source posting the information. Numerous Web sites offer student papers for sale on the Internet. Using these papers and submitting them as one's own is also considered plagiarism.

There are academic penalties for plagiarism. You may receive a failing grade on your paper or you may fail the entire course. At some institutions you can even be academically dismissed. Plagiarism is treated very seriously by authors, publishers, instructors, and acadmic departments.

AVOIDING ONLINE PLAGIARISM

Use the following suggestions to avoid unintentional plagiarism.

- If you copy exact words from any source, put them in quotation marks in your notes, along with the publication information: the author, title, publisher, date of publication, and page number of the source, or, for Web sites, the author, name of the site or page, date of publication, and URL. Be sure to consult a style manual for details on how to indicate in your paper which material is borrowed and how to set up a list of the works you used in your paper.
- List sources for all the information you include in your notes regardless of whether it takes the form of direct quotations, paraphrases, or summaries of someone else's ideas.
- Never copy and paste directly from a Web site into your paper without enclosing the words in quotation marks and listing the source.
- List the source for any information, facts, ideas, opinions, theories, or data you use from a Web site.
- When paraphrasing someone else's words, change as many words as possible and try not to follow the exact same organization. Credit where the information came from.
- Write paraphrases without looking at the original text so you will rephrase it in your own words.

DIRECTIONS   Read the following passage from *Sociology for the Twenty-First Century* by Tim Curry, Robert Jiobu, and Kent Schwirian, p. 207. Then place a check mark next to each statement that is an example of plagiarism.

Currently, Mexican Americans are the second-largest racial or ethnic minority in the United States, but by early in the next century they will be the largest group. Their numbers will swell as a result of continual immigration from Mexico and the relatively high Mexican birth rate. Mexican Americans are one of the oldest racial-ethnic groups in the United States. Under the terms of the treaty ending the Mexican-American War in 1848, Mexicans living in territories acquired by the United States could remain there and were to be treated as American citizens. Those that did stay became known as "Californios," "Tejanos," or "Hispanos."

_____ a. Mexican Americans are the second-largest minority in the United States. Their number grows as more people immigrate from Mexico.

_____ b. After the Mexican-American War, those Mexicans living in territories owned by the United States became American citizens and were called "Californios," "Tejanos," and "Hispanos" (Curry, Jiobu, and Schwirian, 207).

_____ c. "Mexican Americans are one of the oldest racial-ethnic groups in the United States."

_____ d. The Mexican-American War ended in 1848. ●

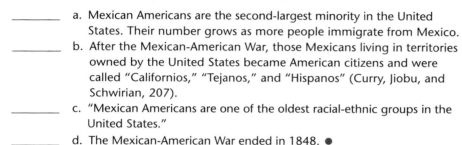

USING COLLEGE TEXTBOOKS
Finding Implied Main Ideas in Visuals

Photographs, images, and graphics are visual ways of communicating information. Usually visuals are included in a textbook chapter to clarify or emphasize important concepts. Most photographs, images, and graphics, however, do not directly state their main point in words. Instead, the main point is implied through their visual content and form.

Your job as a reader is to study and add up the details presented in the visual and determine its implied main idea. Use the following suggestions to help you:

1. **Look at photographs and other images and identify what they are intended to illustrate.** These visual elements often suggest but do not directly state ideas about chapter content. Photographs and images convey details that usually add up to a single impression. That impression is often the implied main idea.

   Study the photograph and visual on the next page, taken from the textbook chapters indicated. What point does each make about the chapter content?

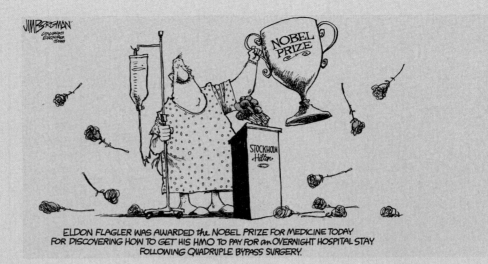

Chapter Title: "Policy Making for Health Care and the Environment"
—from Edwards et al., *Government in America*, p. 602

Implied Main Idea: _____

The Luen Thai Factory in Dongguan, China, with 14,000 Workers in 15 Buildings *(Courtesy of Liz Claiborne)*

Chapter Title: "Apparel Production and Global Sourcing"
—Baird, *THINK Psychology*, p. 26

Implied Main Idea: _____

2. **Analyze graphs, tables, and diagrams.** To find the implied main idea, look for trends or patterns. Ask yourself: What do all the details, when taken together, show?

    Study the following graphics, taken from the textbook chapters indicated. What point does each make about its topic?

Divorce Rates Around the World
(Percentages of new marriages that end in divorce in selected countries, 2002)

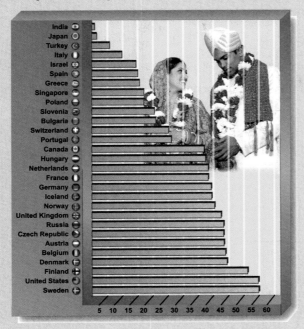

Chapter Title: "Single Parent Families, Remarriage, and Step Families"

—from Kunz, *THINK Marriage and Families,* p. 241

Implied Main Idea: _____

_____

The Importance of Religion in People's Lives

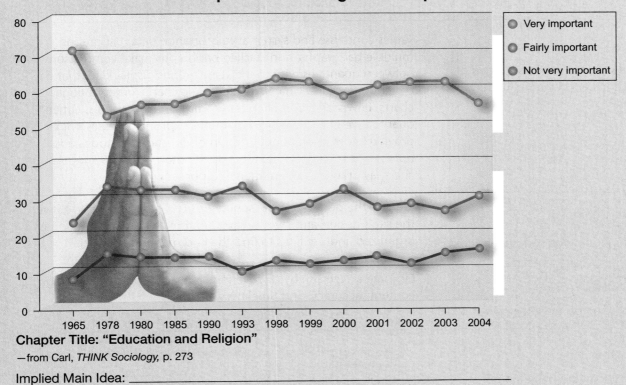

Chapter Title: "Education and Religion"

—from Carl, *THINK Sociology,* p. 273

Implied Main Idea: _____

_____

FURTHER PRACTICE WITH TEXTBOOK READING

Part A: Sample Textbook Chapter

Read "Theories of Emotion" (p. 491) and consider what information the photograph and graph contribute to the reading that is not directly stated in the chapter.

Part B: Your College Textbook

Choose a textbook chapter that you have been assigned to read for one of your other courses that contains photographs and/or graphics. Choose one photo and one graphic. For each, determine what information it contributes to the text and write a sentence explaining its main point.

SELF-TEST
SUMMARY

Goal 1	
What steps can you take to read graphic material more effectively?	Graphics condense information and enable the reader to see patterns, identify trends, observe variations, and interpret information. To get the most from all types of graphics, you should begin by reading the title or caption and determining how the graphic is organized, what its purpose is, what variables are being presented, and what scale, values, or units of measurements are being used. You should then study the data to identify trends and patterns and to draw connections with the content of the chapter. Finally, making marginal notes will aid your further reading and review.
Goal 2 What are the common types of graphics and what is the function of each?	Tables condense and systematically arrange data. Bar graphs, multiple bar graphs, and stacked bar graphs make comparisons between quantities or amounts. Line graphs display data that have continuous values. Charts, including pie charts, organizational charts, flowcharts, and pictograms, display relationships, either quantitative or cause–effect. Diagrams explain processes. Maps provide information about location or direction. Cartoons add humor or may make a point quickly. Photographs spark interest and may draw out an emotional response.
Goal 3 How should you read online text?	Identify the purpose of the source or site. Familiarize yourself with the site's design and layout. Pay attention to how information is organized and use links to find the information you need.
Goal 4 How can you evaluate a Web site?	Evaluate a Web site by discovering its purpose and considering its content, accuracy, and timeliness.
Goal 5 What is online plagiarism?	Online plagiarism refers to the borrowing of information from the Internet without giving credit to the source posting the information.

APPLYING YOUR SKILLS

DISCUSSING THE CHAPTER

1. What are the characteristics of good graphic material? When creating graphics, which of these characteristics are most important to consider? Bring some examples of good and bad graphics to class to review and critique.
2. Do you prefer to read essays and texts with or without graphics? Which learning styles are best suited for graphics use?
3. What are some of the risks when using the Internet for research or information? How can you minimize these risks?

ANALYZING A STUDY SITUATION

Elaine is a liberal arts major who is taking a biology class to fulfill her science requirement. Her reading assignment for this week includes a chapter on plant reproduction and development. It includes numerous complicated diagrams of reproductive life cycles of conifers (a type of evergreen tree) and flowering plants. Elaine is unsure how to approach reading and understanding the material. She is also frustrated because some of the diagrams appear before the part of the chapter that explains them. The chapter also describes, but does not illustrate, the reproductive stages of ferns, mosses, and algae.

1. Give some suggestions to help Elaine read and study the chapter.
2. How should she read and study the diagrams in the chapter?
3. How can Elaine learn and understand the life cycles not illustrated in the chapter?
4. What general suggestions would you offer to help Elaine succeed in a science course that contains a great deal of technical material?

WORKING ON COLLABORATIVE PROJECTS

DIRECTIONS   Working with another student, select a topic of mutual interest. Discuss it, narrow it down, and write two or three specific research questions. Working independently, use the Internet to locate answers to your research questions. When you have finished, compare your answers and the sources from which you obtained them.

For support in meeting this chapter's goals, go to **MyReadingLab** and select **Graphics and Visuals**.

Quick QUIZ

DIRECTIONS Write the letter of the choice that best completes each statement in the space provided.

CHECKING YOUR RECALL

_____ 1. All of the following strategies are effective for reading graphics *except*

   a. predicting what the graphic is intended to show.
   b. identifying the variables.
   c. ignoring titles or captions.
   d. drawing connections with chapter content.

_____ 2. The primary purpose of tables is to

   a. elicit an emotional response.
   b. display events that occur in a specific sequence.
   c. illustrate parts of a process.
   d. present factual information, such as numbers or statistics, in a condensed form.

_____ 3. All of the following statements about graphs are true *except*

   a. bar graphs usually are designed to emphasize similarities.
   b. multiple bar graphs display two or three comparisons simultaneously.
   c. stacked bar graphs show bars placed one on top of another.
   d. linear graphs present more detailed information than bar graphs.

_____ 4. Which of the following is *not* a clue to the timeliness of a Web site?

   a. the date the Web site was put on the Web.
   b. the date the Web site was last revised.
   c. the date the author's biography was last revised.
   d. the date when the links were last checked.

_____ 5. The sponsorship of a Web site may provide clues about its

   a. purpose.
   b. timeliness.
   c. structure.
   d. user-friendliness.

APPLYING YOUR SKILLS

_____ 6. Gabriel is writing a paper about the American judicial system. The best way for him to show the levels of the federal court system,

from the Supreme Court on down, would be in

   a. a pictogram.
   b. a process diagram.
   c. a pie chart.
   d. an organizational chart.

_____ 7. As Philip previews his economics assignment, he notices that there are many diagrams in this lesson. Philip can assume the diagrams are designed to

   a. situate events in time.
   b. clarify causes and effects.
   c. illustrate parts of a process.
   d. make statistics seem more realistic.

_____ 8. Kevin is interested in examining the death penalty issue and wants to compare both pro and con viewpoints. Kevin should check a number of different

   a. commercial Web sites.
   b. personal Web sites.
   c. advocacy Web sites.
   d. news Web sites.

_____ 9. Which of the following questions will help you evaluate the accuracy of a Web site?

   a. Does the author state his or her purpose?
   b. Are the author's name and credentials provided?
   c. Who designed the Web site?
   d. Does the URL end in .com?

_____ 10. Sam is writing a research paper using various Web pages as resources. To avoid online plagiarism, Sam should avoid all of the following *except*

   a. reading information provided by Web sites and not listing them as sources.
   b. writing a paper on a topic already found on the Internet.
   c. cutting and pasting information from the Internet into his own paper without crediting the source.
   d. writing a paper that consists mostly of quotations and paraphrased information.

Reading Other Academic Sources

LEARNING GOALS

In this chapter you will learn to

1 Read nontextbook assignments

2 Read periodicals

3 Read nonfiction and scholarly works

4 Read academic sources

5 Evaluate academic sources

LEARNING EXPERIMENT

1 Select and summarize a chapter from one of your textbooks.

2 At the library, find a periodical article and a chapter in a nonfiction or scholarly book that cover the same topic as your textbook chapter.

3 Summarize the article and the book chapter, and evaluate the author's tone and use of data and evidence (see p. 208, Chapter 9).

4 Compare how each of these three different sources covers the same basic topic. What are the strengths and weaknesses of each source? How does consulting all three sources give you a more complete picture of your topic?

THE RESULTS

Textbooks give a straightforward, basic overview of information necessary to learn about a discipline or skill. Writers for nonstudent audiences have more flexibility when it comes to tone, data, and evidence, and complement the basic understanding you get from a textbook.

LEARNING PRINCIPLE: WHAT THIS MEANS TO YOU

Applying your critical reading skills to other sources in addition to textbooks will broaden your understanding of an academic subject area. Knowing how to identify useful and authoritative sources will encourage you to keep learning about topics that interest you.

WHY LEARN TO READ OTHER ACADEMIC SOURCES?

It is important to learn to read other academic sources because:

- Textbooks are written for students and are a good introduction to a field; however, many professors expect you to go beyond your textbook to find further information or explore related issues.
- Reading serious and scholarly books and periodicals about your field of study introduces you to what professionals in the field are thinking about and working on.
- Textbooks are not generally accepted as sources for research papers. You will need to consult other kinds of sources when you do research for your course work.

Goal 1

Read nontextbook assignments

BEYOND TEXTBOOKS: OTHER KINDS OF ACADEMIC SOURCES

Your political science professor assigns a five-page research paper. Your psychology professor assigns a text and ten related readings—research articles from *Science Digest*. Your marketing professor requires that you read and summarize two articles per week on topics related to her weekly lectures. You probably have discovered that your reading assignments are not limited to textbooks; many of your professors require that you read magazine, journal, and newspaper articles. Some professors distribute reading lists and direct you to read a specified number of articles or write a specified number of abstracts. Others post links to readings on your class course management system or place materials to be read on reserve in the library.

Reading academic sources is very different from reading textbooks. It differs in the following ways:

- **Level of retention and recall.** When reading textbooks, your goal is usually a high level of retention and recall of all assigned material. In reading other sources, however, complete retention is not always necessary. You may be searching for evidence to support an argument, reading widely to gain overall familiarity with a subject, or locating a particular statistic.
- **Format and organization.** Also, while textbooks follow a consistent format and organization, research and reference sources differ widely in these characteristics. Consequently, you must adapt your reading strategy to suit the nature of the material.

This chapter presents a systematic approach to locating, reading, and evaluating academic sources. Often your instructor assigns or guides you to specific academic sources.

HOW TO LOCATE SOURCES

When it is up to you to locate your own sources, use the following general guidelines:

1. **Consult with your reference librarian to find out whether computerized searches are available.** Many libraries have access to data banks that identify all possible sources on a given topic. (Some libraries charge a fee for this service.) Consult with your reference librarian to find out where to start. The

librarian can show you all the main sources, both print and online, for your topic. Check the library's Web site; there might be an online guide or tutorial for undertaking research in your subject.

2. **Read an encyclopedia entry to get an overview of the subject.** Both general and specialized encyclopedias for specific subjects are available in print and online.

3. **Check the library's online catalog to see how your topic is subdivided.** Start your search by using keywords. Once you find one subtopic that looks useful, check the subject headings for that item. Use those subject headings to do a more specific search that narrows in on your topic.

4. **Consider your purpose and the type of information you need.** If you need an overview of a topic, choose a more general source. If you need detailed information, choose a specialized source.

5. **Consult your instructor if you're not sure whether your source is appropriate.** Your reference librarian can then direct you toward more suitable sources if necessary.

There is a wide variety of academic sources, each with a specified purpose and use. These are summarized in the table below.

TABLE 14-1   TYPES OF REFERENCE SOURCES

Source	Purpose and Use
Reference book (encyclopedia, directory)	Provides authoritative background and overview; useful when starting out on a new topic to become familiar with the key names, dates, and concepts; usually lists sources for further reading
Scholarly nonfiction book—monograph	One author's detailed treatment of a subject using his own research, ideas, and informed opinions supported with those of others. Often it refutes opposing viewpoints and offers future considerations.
Scholarly nonfiction book—edited collection	A group of essays centered around a common theme or idea, each providing a specific point of view or theory
Periodical: magazine	Provides articles on current topics of interest for a broad audience; can give a simplified treatment of a scholarly topic
Periodical: scholarly journal	Provides articles written by experts and researchers in a specific field; often contains original research studies
Primary sources	Original documents that give a first-person account of an era or event (e.g., letters and diaries)

DIRECTIONS   Using Table 14-1 as a guide, identify what type of source would be useful in each of the following situations.

Exercise 1

1. You are giving a presentation on the Oregon Trail and you want to include a firsthand account from one of the pioneers traveling West.

2. For your political science class, you need to prepare for a debate on the United States' use of the atomic bomb in WWII, but you hardly know anything about this topic.

3. You need a lot of in-depth information and analysis from an expert on Abraham Lincoln for your history class research paper.

4. An online class requires you to contribute your thoughts on current events once per week; you need a source that will keep you up-to-date on a variety of topics without overwhelming you with too much detail.

5. One of your professors has assigned a research paper for which you need studies that show how a vegan diet affects diabetes. ●

Goal 2
Read periodicals

PERIODICALS: MAGAZINES AND SCHOLARLY JOURNALS

Periodicals include both popular press magazines, such as *Time, Sports Illustrated,* and *In Style,* and scholarly publications, such as *The Journal of Sociology* and *Marine Ecology.* Magazines and scholarly journals differ in the ways shown in Table 14-2.

Visual Thinking
APPLYING SKILLS

Which of these periodicals are trustworthy and reliable sources of information?

What standards would you use to evaluate them?

In many classroom situations, magazines are not considered appropriate sources because the articles are written by journalists for a general audience and do not provide the depth necessary for academic investigation. For example, an article in a magazine about healthy eating may mention a study about eating pomegranates for good health. The actual original study described the

TABLE 14-2 COMPARING MAGAZINES AND SCHOLARLY JOURNALS	
Magazines	**Scholarly Journals**
Broad audience, often the general public	Specialized audience, such as professionals
Information and entertainment	Research, theories, ideas, detailed analysis
Colorful, photographs, graphics	Black and white, charts, graphs, tables
Advertising	Little or no advertising
Commercial publisher	Published by a professional organization or educational institute
Writers are journalists or enthusiasts; they are paid for their articles.	Authors are experts in the field—researchers, professors; they are not paid for their articles.

details of the method, participants, data, and findings. Perhaps it was a study of only five senior citizens in Sweden who only ate pomegranates for a month and didn't get a cold during that time. Looking at the original study would help the student to discover firsthand how relevant the data are, whereas the journalist takes the data and makes his own interpretation to fit his article.

On the other hand, a magazine article might be appropriate when you need an easy-to-read overview of a complicated topic before you start your research.

For example, there are many specific, complicated technical studies that deal with aspects of climate change, but a magazine article might give a good overview of all the issues so you know where you want to concentrate your efforts.

The Structure of Articles and Essays

An article or essay begins with a **title** and is usually followed by an **introduction** that presents the thesis statement (or controlling idea). Then one or more paragraphs are devoted to each supporting idea. The main part of the essay, often called the **body**, presents ideas and information that support the thesis statement. A **conclusion** makes a final statement about the subject and draws the article or essay to a close.

You can visualize the organization of an article or essay as follows.

The Structure of an Essay

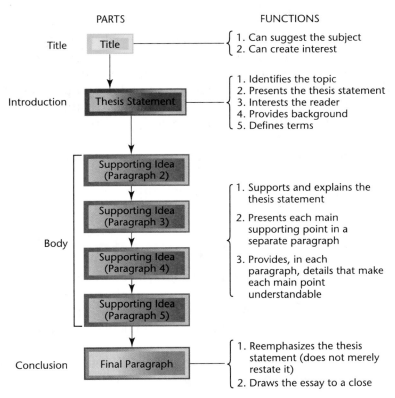

Note: There is no set number of paragraphs that an essay contains. This model shows six paragraphs, but in actual essays the number will vary greatly.

DIRECTIONS Assume you have been assigned the essay "You're Eating Genetically Modified Food." (Part Five, p. 461) by your sociology instructor. Read it and then answer the following questions.

Exercise 2

Introduction:
1. How does the author try to interest you in the subject?
2. What is the subject of the essay?
3. What is the author's thesis?

Body:
4. What main supporting ideas does the author offer to support the thesis?

Conclusion:
5. How does the author conclude the essay? ●

The Structure of Scholarly Articles

Many scholarly articles, especially those that report research conducted by the author, follow a similar format and often include the following parts. Different journals may use different headings to organize their articles, or they may not label all sections with headings.

- **Abstract.** An abstract is a brief summary of the article and its findings and is sometimes labeled "Summary." It usually appears at the beginning of the article, following the title and author. Read the abstract to get an overview of the article. It can help you determine whether the study or report contains the information you need.

Tip *Cite* means "to mention as an example."

- **Summary of Related Research.** Many research articles begin by summarizing research that has already been done on the topic. Authors will cite other studies and briefly report their findings. This summary brings you up to date on the most current research and may suggest why the author's study or research is necessary. In some journals this rationale may appear in a section titled "Statement of the Problem."
- **Methodology.** In this section the author describes his or her research. For experimental research, you can expect it to include purpose, description of the population studied, sample size, procedures, and statistical tests applied.
- **Results.** Results and findings of the research are presented in this section.
- **Implications, Discussion, and Conclusion.** Here the author explains what the results mean and presents possible implications and conclusions.
- **Further Research.** Based on their findings, some authors conclude the article by suggesting additional research that is needed to further explain the problem or issue being studied.

Goal **3**

Read nonfiction and scholarly work

NONFICTION AND SCHOLARLY BOOKS

Many professors will assign papers that require you to analyze a topic deeply and with reference to its history. For example, you might be asked to evaluate the way that Russia has developed into a country with a market economy. This topic will require the use of several scholarly nonfiction books that deal with different aspects of the topic, such as the history of Russia and the Soviet Union, the political and social factors that led to the change, the political and economic theories in play, and the current situation. Another typical use of scholarly nonfiction is in the subject of literary criticism. Many students have assignments for which they need to find critical examinations of works of literature or specific authors. To make sure you are using appropriate scholarly nonfiction, use the guidelines below.

HOW TO IDENTIFY APPROPRIATE SCHOLARLY NONFICTION SOURCES

1. **What are the author's credentials?** Look for information on the author. What are his or her educational background and current college or university affiliation? What awards has he or she won and what other books has he or she written?
2. **Who is the publisher?** Look at who published the book. Is it an educational institution or a professional organization?
3. **Is the writing style serious and high level?** Skim through a few chapters.
4. **Does the author cite his or her sources?** Is there a bibliography or list for further reading? Do these sources seem scholarly?

Finding What You Need in a Serious Nonfiction or Scholarly Book

Textbooks have lots of useful features to help you find, summarize, memorize, and work with information, such as chapter-review questions, glossaries, etc. Books written for the serious general reader or for a scholarly audience do not have most of these helpful features. To find the information you need in a nonfiction or scholarly book, look for the following:

- Table of contents
- Index
- Notes, bibliographies, lists of works cited
- Illustrations

Exercise 3

DIRECTIONS   You have located each of the following books for a research paper on how diet affects cancer risk. Explain why you think each book is or is not a serious or scholarly work.

1. *Nutrition and Cancer Prevention: New Insights into the Role of Phytochemicals*
2. *Health Education Ideas and Activities: 24 Dimensions of Wellness for Adolescents*
3. *Nutrition in the 21st Century*
4. *Nutrition for Dummies*
5. *The Clinical Guide to Oncology Nutrition* ●

HOW TO READ ACADEMIC SOURCES

Goal 4
Read academic sources

Let's assume you have located five articles and books for a psychology assignment on the psychological effects of terrorism on its victims. How should you proceed?

1. **Analyze the assignment.** Listen carefully as your professor announces the assignment; he or she often provides important clues about how to read the sources you locate. If the purpose of an assignment is to present new and important topics not covered in your text, then you know that a high level of recall is required. If, on the other hand, an assignment's purpose is to expose you to alternative points of view on a controversial issue, then key ideas are needed but highly factual recall is not as important.

Tip An *issue* is a problem or subject that people discuss and have different opinions about.

2. **Preview the sources.** Use previewing to determine which sources are useful for your assignment. (Previewing is discussed in detail in Chapter 6.) Eliminate any sources that are outdated. Next, glance through the table of contents to get an overall idea of the material covered by each source. Check the index to determine how extensively the source treats your specific topic. Select only those sources that provide a comprehensive treatment of your topic. Once you have identified these sources, randomly select a sample page in each and skim it to get a "feel" for the source. Pay particular attention to the level of difficulty. Is the source too basic, containing little more information than is in your course textbook? Or is the source too complicated? Does it assume extensive background knowledge of the subject, such as an extensive knowledge of psychoanalysis, for example?

3. **Determine how the sources are organized.** Use the sections titled "The Structure of Articles and Essays" (p. 307) and "The Structure of Scholarly Articles" (p. 308) to guide you.

TABLE 14-3 LEVELS OF COMPREHENSION		
Level of Comprehension	**Percentage of Recall**	**When Used**
Complete	100%	Reading critical analysis; reading directions or procedures
High	90–100%	Reading a primary reference source
Moderate	70–90%	Reading for an overview of a subject
Low	50–70%	Reading to obtain background information; reading only for key ideas
Selective	50% or below	Looking up a statistic in an almanac; checking a date in a biographical dictionary

4. **Select a level of comprehension that suits your purpose.** Comprehension is not an either/or situation. Rather, comprehension is a continuum, and many levels of understanding are possible. An extremely high level of comprehension is necessary if you are reading a critical interpretation of a poem for an English literature paper, for example. Each detail is important. However, a lower level of comprehension is appropriate for reading excerpts from a biography assigned for an American history course. Here, you would not be expected to recall each descriptive detail or bit of conversation.

5. **Select a level of comprehension that suits the task.** The reading strategy you select is also shaped by the tasks that will follow your reading. Comprehension can, somewhat arbitrarily, be divided into five levels: complete, high, moderate, low, and selective, as described in Table 14-3.

6. **Choose a reading strategy.** Depending on the purpose of the assignment and the necessary level and type of recall, your reading choices range from a careful, thorough reading to skimming to obtain an overview of the key ideas presented. Table 14-4 lists examples of assignments and their purposes and suggests possible reading and retention strategies for each. The table shows how strategies vary widely to suit the material and the purpose for which it was assigned.

TABLE 14-4 STRATEGIES FOR READING ACADEMIC SOURCES			
Assignment	**Purpose**	**Reading Strategies**	**Retention Strategies**
Historical novel for American history course.	To acquaint you with living conditions of the period being studied.	Read rapidly, noting trends, patterns, characteristics; skip highly detailed descriptive portions.	Write a brief synopsis of the basic plot; make notes (including some examples) of lifestyles and living conditions (social, religious, political, as well as economic).
Essay on exchange in Moroccan bazaars (street markets) for economics course.	To describe system of barter.	Read for main points, noting process, procedures, and principles.	Underline key points.
Article titled "What Teens Know About Birth Control" assigned in a maternal care nursing course.	To reveal attitudes toward, and lack of information about, birth control.	Read to locate topics of information, misinformation, and lack of information; skip details and examples.	Prepare a three-column list: information, misinformation, and lack of information.

DIRECTIONS Working with a classmate, select a level of comprehension that seems appropriate for each of the following research situations.

Exercise 4

1. Reading a biographical entry on Ella Fitzgerald in *The Encyclopedia of Jazz* for a term paper on the history of jazz
2. Locating names of leaders of Third World countries in the *International Yearbook* and *Statesman's Who's Who*
3. Reading the directions for using an online card catalog
4. Reading a source to verify that you have not missed any key information in sources you have already used
5. Reading a review of a performance of *The Lion King* in preparation for a drama class discussion on audience responsiveness ●

DIRECTIONS Summarize how you would approach each of the following academic assignments. What would be your purpose? What reading and study strategies would you use?

Exercise 5

1. Reading a *Time* magazine article about a recent incident of terrorism for a discussion in your political science class
2. Reading two articles that present opposing opinions and evidence about the rate of the spread of AIDS throughout Third World countries
3. Reading a recent journal article on asbestos control to obtain current information for a research paper on the topic
4. Reading a case study of a child with autism for a child psychology course
5. Reading Microsoft's end-of-the-year statement for stockholders for a business class studying public relations strategies ●

Using Skimming and Scanning to Read Academic Sources

For reading assignments that require lower levels of comprehension, you can afford to read some parts and skip others. Two reading strategies, in particular, will be helpful—skimming and scanning. (Refer to Chapter 20 for more information on both skimming and scanning techniques.)

Skimming is a technique in which you selectively read and skip in order to find only the most important ideas. Here are a few situations in which you might skim academic sources.

- Reading a section of a reference book that you are using to complete a research paper. If you have already collected most of your basic information, you might skim through additional references, looking only for new information not discussed in sources you have used before.
- Sampling a 15-item supplementary reading list for a sociology class. Your instructor has encouraged you to review as many of the items as possible. You anticipate that the final exam will include one essay question that is related to these readings. Clearly, you cannot read every entry, but you can skim a reasonable number.

Scanning is a technique for quickly looking through reading material to locate a particular piece of information—a fact, a date, a name, a statistic. Every time you use a dictionary to find a particular word, you are scanning. If you look up the population of the United States, you are scanning.

Exercise 6

DIRECTIONS   Choose one of the nontextbook readings in Part Five, beginning on p. 448. Skim the reading and write a brief summary including the main point and most important information. Then check the accuracy of your summary by reading the selection more closely. ●

Goal 5

Evaluate academic sources

EVALUATING ACADEMIC SOURCES

You usually assume that your course textbook is timely, reliable, and authoritative—but you can't assume that about other sources you read. Not all sources are equal in accuracy, scholarship, or completeness. In fact, some sources may be inaccurate, and some may be purposely misleading. Other sources that were once respected are now outdated and have been discredited by more recent research. Part of your task as a serious reader is to evaluate available sources and select those that seem the most reliable and appropriate. Use the following suggestions in evaluating sources:

1. **Assess the authority of the author.** In standard reference books such as encyclopedias and biographical dictionaries, you can assume the publisher has chosen competent authors. However, when using individual source materials, it is important to find out whether the author is qualified to write on the subject. Does he or she have a degree or experience in the field? What is the author's present position or university affiliation? This information may appear in the preface or on the title page of a book. In journal articles, a brief paragraph at the end of the article or on a separate page in the journal may summarize the author's credentials. By appraising the sources the author cites (footnotes and bibliography), you also can judge the competence of the author.

> **Tip** *Affiliation* means "association with or membership in an organization, such as a school, political group, or religious institution."

2. **Check the copyright date.** The date the source was published or revised is indicated on the back of the title page. Especially in rapidly changing fields such as computer science, the timeliness of your sources is important. Using outdated sources can make a research paper incomplete or incorrect. Consult at least several current sources, if possible, to discover recent findings and new interpretations.

3. **Identify the intended audience.** For whom is the work intended? Some sources are written for children, others for young adults, and others for a general-interest audience. The work should suit the audience in format, style, complexity of ideas, and amount of detail.

4. **Verify one source against another.** If you find information that seems questionable, unbelievable, or disputable, verify it by locating the same information in several other reputable sources. Ask your reference librarian for assistance, if necessary. If you do verify the information in other sources, then you can be reasonably confident that the information is acceptable. You cannot, however, assume that it is correct—only that it is one standard or acceptable approach or interpretation.

> **Tip** *Consensus* means "an opinion that everyone in a group can agree with or accept."

5. **Look for a consensus of opinion.** As you read differing approaches to or interpretations of a topic, sometimes it is difficult to decide what source(s) to accept. When you encounter differing opinions or approaches, the first thing to do is locate additional sources; in other words, do more reading. Eventually, you will discover the consensus.

6. **Ask critical questions.** Consider whether the article is fact or opinion. Question the author's purpose, the use of generalizations, any basic assumptions, and the type of evidence presented. For a review of these criteria, refer to the sections in Chapters 9 and 10.

DIRECTIONS   What questions would you ask when evaluating each of the following sources?

1. An article in *Newsweek* reporting a dramatic increase in domestic violence in the United States

_____

_____

2. An article written by an executive of a large home mortgage company describing effective and ineffective business management strategies

_____

_____

3. An essay on juvenile street gangs reporting a high incidence of emotional disturbance among gang members (Other articles, using other sources, report a much lower rate.)

_____

_____

4. An article, published in an advertising trade journal, titled "Teenage Drinking: Does Advertising Make a Difference?"

_____

_____

5. An article in *TV Guide* focusing on TV reality shows titled "Should Producers Pay More Attention to the Moral Messages?"

_____

_____

USING COLLEGE TEXTBOOKS
Adapting Your Learning Style By Reading Further

Textbooks often include additional material to assist you in studying or exploring topics of interest. These are particularly useful for adapting your textbook reading and study to suit your learning style.

1. **For Further Reading.** Authors sometimes include lists of books or articles related to a chapter's content so that you can learn more about it or explore a topic in greater detail. You can also use the references as a starting point for research when choosing a topic to write a paper about or for researching a chosen topic.

FOR FURTHER READING

Baum, Matthew A. *Soft News Goes to War: Public Opinion and American Foreign Policy in the New Media Age.* Princeton, NJ: Princeton University Press, 2003. A path-breaking examination of how people learn about major foreign policy events from entertainment news shows like *Oprah* and *Dateline*.

Davis, Richard. *Typing Political: The Role of Blogs in American Politics.* New York: Oxford University Press, 2009. A comprehensive assessment of the growing role played by political blogs and their relationship with the mainstream media.

—Edwards, *Government in America*, p. 223

2. **Web Site Links.** Many textbooks have Web sites associated with them that include videos, MP3 files, study guides, sample tests, and more. These offer different methods of learning as well as additional information and valuable study aids.

Succeed with MySocLab

Experience, Discover, Observe, Evaluate

MySocLab is designed just for you. Each chapter features a pre-test and post-test to help you learn and review key concepts and terms.

Experience sociology in action with dynamic visual activities, videos and readings to enhance your learning experience. Complete the following activities at www.mysoclab.com.

—Thompson, *Society in Focus*, p. 325

RELEVANT WEB SITES

http://alcoholism.about.com/od/abuse/
   Comprehensive domestic abuse site that provides a potential abuse screening quiz, various personalized stories of abuse by victims, and information on the association of drinking and spousal abuse and the effect on children and adults of witnessing repeated domestic abuse.
http://www.elderabusecenter.org/
   National Center on Elder Abuse site that is a gateway for information on elder abuse, neglect, and exploitation.

—Withgott, *Environment*, p. 106

FURTHER PRACTICE WITH TEXTBOOK READING

Part A: Sample Textbook Chapter

Visit the Web site referenced on page 502 the sample textbook chapter. Go to the site and click on the book title, *THINK PSYCHOLOGY*, then click on Chapter 13. Explore the additional materials that are offered. Which, if any, are particularly well suited to your learning style?

   How do they help you understand the material in the chapter? Are they useful to you? Why or why not? How would you use them to study the chapter?

Part B: Your College Textbook

Choose a textbook that you are using in one of your other courses. Use one of the additional materials the textbook offers to correspond with a current assignment. Evaluate how effective and helpful these materials are. Which, if any, are particularly well suited to your learning style?

SELF-TEST
SUMMARY

Goal ❶ How is reading other academic sources different from reading textbooks?	The high level of retention and recall usually needed for textbooks may not be necessary for other academic sources. Consult with a reference librarian first to find the main print and online sources for your topic. Read an encyclopedia entry for an overview of the subject. Check the library's online catalog to see how the subject is subdivided. Consider your purpose and the type of information you need, and consult your instructor to verify the appropriateness of a source.
Goal ❷ How do scholarly and popular periodicals differ?	Popular periodicals, such as magazines, target a broad audience, often the general public. Scholarly articles focus on a specialized audience, usually including an abstract; a summary of related research; methodology; results; implications, discussion, and conclusion; and suggestions for further research.
Goal ❸ What are common uses of scholarly nonfiction sources?	Scholarly nonfiction sources are often used to research context and analyze literary criticism.
Goal ❹ How should you read academic sources?	Analyze the purpose of the assignment. Use previewing to determine which sources are useful for the assignment. Determine how each source is organized. Select a level of comprehension that suits both your purpose and the tasks that will follow your reading. Choose a reading strategy appropriate to the assignment. Record useful information and keep track of your sources.
Goal ❺ How do you evaluate academic sources?	Assess the author's authority (his or her competence and qualifications). Check the copyright date to be sure the source is timely. Identify the intended audience of the work. Verify questionable information against other sources. Look for a consensus of opinion, locating more sources if necessary. Ask critical questions.

APPLYING **YOUR SKILLS**

DISCUSSING THE CHAPTER

1. Suppose you were asked to write a paper for a sociology class on the effects of social media (Facebook, Twitter, Digg, etc) Would you use popular magazines or scholarly sources, or both, to learn about the topic? Explain your answer.
2. In what situations or for what topics would a scholarly journal be a more appropriate source than a magazine article?
3. When researching a topic, when might you consider locating a nonfiction book on your topic, instead of journal or magazine articles?

ANALYZING A STUDY SITUATION

Kerry has been assigned a four-page research paper for her business class, and she has decided to write about ethics in the workplace. For this class, she also has to read and summarize two articles on current events in business each week. In addition, she is expected to read a case study on public relations strategies, which was the topic of this week's lecture, and be prepared to discuss it in class.

1. For Kerry's research paper, she went to the library and found several print and online sources, including magazine and journal articles, encyclopedia entries, and reference books. In fact, she found too many sources and now she feels overwhelmed. What should she do to narrow her topic and determine which sources are appropriate for her paper?
2. Kerry found four articles that seem to fit the current events assignment, but they are all from popular press magazines. What steps should Kerry take to evaluate the quality of the sources? Where else should she look for material for this assignment?
3. To prepare for the class discussion on the case study, what reading strategies would you suggest for Kerry? What level of retention would be most appropriate for this assignment?

WORKING ON COLLABORATIVE PROJECTS

DIRECTIONS   Working with another student, select and skim one of the readings in Part Five of this text. Then question each other on the main ideas the article presents.

PEARSON myreadinglab	For support in meeting this chapter's goals, go to **MyReadingLab** and select **Critical Thinking**.

Quick QUIZ

DIRECTIONS Write the letter of the choice that best completes each statement in the space provided.

CHECKING YOUR RECALL

_____ 1. One way that reading other academic sources is different from reading textbooks is that academic sources

a. follow a consistent format.
b. always require a high level of recall and retention.
c. differ widely in format and organization.
d. can only be found online.

_____ 2. In comparison to magazines, scholarly journals typically feature

a. a broad audience made up of the general public.
b. an emphasis on information and entertainment.
c. unpaid authors who are experts in the field.
d. colorful photographs and graphics.

_____ 3. An abstract can be defined as a

a. group of essays centered around a common theme.
b. brief summary of an article and its findings.
c. statement of related research that has already been done on a topic.
d. description of the procedures and tests used in an author's research.

_____ 4. The technique for looking quickly through reading material to locate a particular piece of information is known as

a. skimming.
b. sampling.
c. scanning.
d. previewing.

_____ 5. When you are evaluating academic sources, you should do all of the following *except*

a. verify the author's qualifications.
b. check the copyright date for timeliness.
c. look for a consensus of opinion.
d. accept statistical figures without question.

APPLYING YOUR SKILLS

_____ 6. Gus is writing a research paper on the theme of family in *The Adventures of Huckleberry Finn*. The reference source that would provide him with a group of critical essays centered around Mark Twain's work is

a. a monograph.
b. a specialized encyclopedia.
c. a popular press magazine.
d. an edited collection in a scholarly nonfiction book.

_____ 7. For a research paper in biology, Tashayla chose to write about wildlife migration and located a scholarly article on the subject. The section of the article that would give Tashayla a detailed description of the author's research is the

a. summary.
b. statement of the problem.
c. methodology.
d. conclusion.

_____ 8. As part of a sociology project, Claire has located several articles and reference books on language and communication in animals. Her first step in reading these academic sources should be to

a. analyze the purpose of the assignment.
b. eliminate any sources that seem outdated.
c. determine how each source is organized.
d. create a bibliography for each of her sources.

_____ 9. Edie wants to verify several biographical dates for a research paper. The appropriate level of comprehension for her task is

a. selective.
b. complete.
c. moderate.
d. high.

_____ 10. Javier has found several interesting articles about carbon offsetting that he plans to use in a research paper. In evaluating the sources, it is important that he ask all of the following questions *except*

a. Is the author qualified to write on the subject?
b. Which sources share my opinions on the subject?
c. For whom is the work intended?
d. How current is the source?

SUCCESS WORKSHOP

6 Communicate and Network with Other Students

Why?

In college, as in life and in the workplace, success is often determined by your ability to build a support network and to communicate and work with others. Developing strong networks with fellow students can help you in even the most challenging courses.

Analyzing . . .
How You Network

Place a check mark in front of the type of networking you use most often to communicate with classmates about class assignments. For each method you use, estimate how much time per week you spend on each.

___E-mail _____

___Texting _____

___Facebook messaging _____

___Cell phone_____

Discovering . . .
How to Be a Better Networker

Some people find it easy to get to know fellow students, while others find it challenging. Make a point to sit next to a different person once a week and exchange contact information. Once you know two or three people, suggest meeting as a study group on campus once a week, or before big tests. The more people you get to know in your class, the more resources you will have when you need help understanding something.

Changing . . .
The Way You Network

For each class, keep a list in your notebook or a file on your computer listing the name and cell phone number of every person you meet. Friend each of them on Facebook.

Class Name: _____

Professor name, e-mail, and phone:

_____

Contacts:

Name	Number
_____	_____
_____	_____
_____	_____
_____	_____

Improving . . .
Your Use of Technology to Communicate

Texting is an excellent way to get a quick answer to a question such as "What is today's assignment?" but it's not useful for in-depth discussions of course materials and sample problems. Facebook is a great way to organize study sessions, exchange information about assignments, and keep in touch about what you missed. Use e-mail to exchange class notes. Meet in person or via Skype for study sessions.

Learning . . .
Use Professor-Created Message Boards

Some professors set up message boards for their classes so students can communicate together in one forum. Remember that anything you post here is public and available for anyone to read. Avoid posting complaints about assignments, the professor, or the workload. Instead, use the message board positively. Get other students' points of view on topics and issues, or share study tips, information sources, or course deadlines.

Evaluating . . .
Methods of Communication

Suppose you are preparing for an exam that will take place next week. You have decided to assemble a study group of five students. You have identified five possible ways of getting together to study:

- Meeting at the library for a two-hour study session
- Sitting in front of your computers with Skype
- Texting each other on your cell phones
- Setting up a chat room that you all attend
- Starting an e-mail chain in which one person asks a question and everyone else answers

What are the pros and cons of each method?

7 Strengthen Your Concentration

Why?

Strengthening your concentration is important. No matter how intelligent you are, or what skills and talents you possess, if you can't keep your mind on the task at hand, studying will be difficult and frustrating. But it doesn't have to be.

What Is Wrong with This Picture?

Why could this student be having trouble concentrating? List as many reasons as you can think of below.

_____

_____

_____

Have You Ever Made Comments Like These?

"I just can't seem to concentrate!"

"I've got so much reading to do; I'll never be able to catch up!"

"I try to study, but nothing happens."

"I waste a lot of time just trying to get started."

If you have, consider the following suggestions for improving your study surroundings and focusing your attention.

Learning . . .
Improve Your Surroundings

Make sure you create a workable study environment.

- Choose a place with minimal distractions.
- Establish a study area with a table or desk that is yours alone for study.
- Control noise levels. Determine how much background noise, if any, you can tolerate, and choose a place best suited to you.
- Eliminate distracting clutter. Get rid of photos, stacks of bills, mementos, and so forth.
- Have necessary supplies at your fingertips: for example, dictionaries, pens, calculator, calendar, clock.

Changing . . .
Plan a Better Study Area

Put a check mark next to each suggestion in the previous section that you could use to improve your surroundings. Plan how you will improve each area, assigning one task to do on each of the next three days.

Learning . . .
Focus Your Attention

Once your study area is set up, use these ideas to focus your attention.

- Establish goals and time limits for each assignment. Deadlines will keep you motivated and create a sense of urgency in which you are less likely to daydream or become distracted.
- Reward yourself. Use rewards such as checking your messages or ordering a pizza when you complete an evening of study.
- Use writing to keep mentally and physically active. Highlighting, outlining, or note taking will force you to keep your mind on the material you are reading.
- Vary your activities. Avoid working on one type of activity for a long period of time. Instead, alternate between writing, reading, reviewing, and solving math problems, for example.

Changing . . .
Plan Ways to Focus Your Attention

How many of the ideas above would help you focus your attention while studying? Make a plan here for trying out each idea for a week to see which you find most helpful.

Week 1 _____

_____

_____

Week 2 _____

_____

_____

Week 3 _____

_____

_____

Week 4 _____

_____

_____

Week 5 _____

_____

_____

- Keep a distractions list. As distracting thoughts enter your mind, jot them on a notepad. You may, for example, think of your mother's upcoming birthday as you're reading psychology. Writing it down will help you remember it and will eliminate the distraction.
- End on a positive note. For long-term projects, stop at a point at which it will be easy to pick up again.
- Check your own concentration. Each time your mind wanders, place a light check mark on the page. When the number of check marks increases, you'll know it is time to take a break or vary your activities.

Reflecting . . .
What Worked, and What Didn't?

In order to learn from what you do, you need to keep track of what worked and what did not.

Of the various ideas you have tried, which were the most helpful? Which weren't as helpful? For the ideas that didn't seem to work as well, can you think of different ways to put them into action that might work better for you? Keep experimenting until you think you have made full use of all suggestions.

Remember . . .
Focus

- Figure out how to make your study area work for you.
- Organize your assignments to vary your activities.
- Concentrate on one task at a time.
- Use writing to stay actively engaged in study.
- Set goals and time limits for each assignment.
- Use textbook features that are designed to help you learn.

Textbook Highlighting and Marking

LEARNING GOALS

In this chapter you will learn to

1 Study and review textbooks

2 Highlight textbooks

3 Recognize effective highlighting

4 Mark textbooks

LEARNING EXPERIMENT

1 Study the following diagram of the human brain. Estimate how long it would take you to learn all the parts of the brain shown in the diagram.

2 Now, using the same diagram, estimate how long it would take you to learn only the four principal parts of the brain.

Principal Parts of the Human Brain

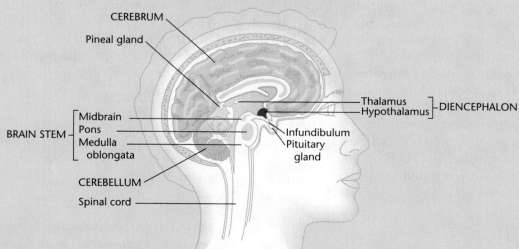

CEREBRUM

Pineal gland

Thalamus — DIENCEPHALON
Hypothalamus

Midbrain
BRAIN STEM — Pons
Medulla
oblongata

Infundibulum
Pituitary
gland

CEREBELLUM

Spinal cord

THE RESULTS

No doubt your estimate was much lower for step 2. Why? You had less information to learn.

LEARNING PRINCIPLE: WHAT THIS MEANS TO YOU

You can make studying textbooks easier if you are selective about what to learn. In most courses, you are not expected to learn and recall every detail and example in your textbook.

Instead, you are responsible for learning the more important ideas. In this chapter you will learn how to identify what is important in a textbook chapter and develop a system of highlighting and marking what is important.

WHY LEARN TO HIGHLIGHT AND MARK YOUR TEXTBOOKS?

Highlighting and marking are important because:

- They force you to decide what is important and what is not.
- They keep you physically active while you read and help focus your attention on the material.
- They help you remember what you read.
- They help you see the organization of facts and ideas and connections between them.

THE CHALLENGE OF TEXTBOOK REVIEW

Goal 1
Study and review textbooks

As you have already discovered, most college courses involve lengthy and time-consuming reading assignments. Just completing the reading assignments is a big job. Have you begun to wonder how you will ever go back over all those textbook chapters when it's time for an exam?

Let's suppose that it takes you at least four hours to carefully read a 40-page chapter for one of your courses. Assume that your text has ten chapters of approximately 40 pages each. It would take a total of 40 hours, then, to read completely through the text once. Suppose that your instructor is giving a final exam that will cover the entire text. If the only thing you did to prepare for the final was to reread the whole text, then it would take close to another 40 hours to study for the exam; and one additional reading is no guarantee that you will pass the exam.

Now consider this: If you had highlighted and marked important ideas and facts as you were first reading the chapters, when you were ready to review, you would have to read and study only what you marked. If you had marked or highlighted 15 to 20 percent of the chapter material, you would have cut your rereading time by 80 to 85 percent, or 32 hours! Of course, to prepare effectively for the exam, you would have to review in other ways besides rereading, but you would have time left to do this.

Goal 2

Highlight textbooks

PEARSON
myreadinglab

To practice using highlighting, go to

> Note Taking and Highlighting

HOW TO HIGHLIGHT TEXTBOOKS

To learn how to highlight textbooks effectively, start with the following guidelines:

1. **Read first; then highlight.** As you are reading to develop skill in high-lighting, it is better to read a paragraph or section first and then go back and highlight what is important to remember and review. Later, when you've had more practice highlighting, you may be able to highlight while you read.
2. **Read the boldfaced headings.** Headings are labels, or overall topics, for what is contained in that section. Use the headings to form questions that you expect to be answered in the section.
3. **After you have read the section, go back and highlight the parts that answer your questions.** These will be parts of sentences that express the main ideas, or most important thoughts, in the section. In reading and highlighting the following section, you could form questions like those suggested and then highlight as shown.

Questions to Ask

What are primary groups?

What are secondary groups?

Primary and Secondary Groups

It is not at all surprising that some students used their families as a reference group. After all, families are the best examples of the groups Charles Cooley called *primary* chiefly because they "are fundamental in forming the social nature and ideals of the individual." In a primary group the individuals interact informally, relate to each other as whole persons, and enjoy their relationship for its own sake. This is one of the two main types of social groups. In the other type, a secondary group, the individuals interact formally, relate to each other as players of particular roles, and expect to profit from each other.

—Thio, *Sociology,* p. 100

4. **As you identify and highlight main ideas, look for important facts that explain or support the main idea, and highlight them too.**
5. **When highlighting main ideas and details, do not highlight complete sentences.** Highlight only enough so that you can see what is important and so that your highlighting makes sense when you reread. Note how only key words and phrases are highlighted in the following passage.

Gossip

There can be no doubt that everyone spends a great deal of time gossiping. In fact, gossip seems universal among all cultures, and among some it's a commonly accepted ritual. Gossip refers to third party talk about another person; the word gossip "now embraces both the talker and the talk, the tattler and the tattle, the newsmonger and the news mongering." Gossip is an inevitable part of daily interactions; to advise anyone not to gossip would be absurd. Not gossiping would eliminate one of the most frequent and enjoyable forms of communication.

In some instances, however, gossip is unethical. First, it's unethical to reveal in-formation that you've promised to keep secret. Although this principle may seem too obvious to even mention, it seems violated in many cases. For example, in a

Tip *Unethical* means "not morally right."

study of 133 school executives, board presidents, and superintendents, the majority received communications that violated an employee's right to confidentiality. When it is impossible to keep something secret (Bok offers the example of the teenager who confides a suicide plan), the information should be revealed only to those who must know it, not to the world at large. Second, gossip is unethical when it invades the privacy that everyone has a right to, for example, when it concerns matters that are properly considered private and when the gossip can hurt the individuals involved. Third, gossip is unethical when it's known to be false and is nevertheless passed on to others.

—DeVito, *The Interpersonal Communication Book*, p. 191

Tip *Confidentiality* means "trust that secret or private information told to one person will not be revealed to anyone else."

ASPECTS OF EFFECTIVE HIGHLIGHTING

For your highlighting to be effective and useful to you as you study and review, it must follow four specific guidelines.

1. **The right amount of information must be highlighted.**
2. **The highlighting must be regular and consistent.**
3. **It must be accurate.**
4. **It must clearly reflect the content of the passage.**

Suggestions for implementing these guidelines and examples of each are given in the following paragraphs.

Goal 3

Recognize effective highlighting

Highlight the Right Amount

Students frequently make the mistake of highlighting either too much or too little. If you highlight too much, the passages you have marked will take you too long to reread when you are studying later. If you highlight too little, you won't be able to get any meaning from your highlighting as you review it.

TOO MUCH HIGHLIGHTING

Iran, which had served as an area of competition between the British and the Russians since the nineteenth century, became a bone of contention between the United States and the Soviet Union after World War II. As the result of an agreement between the British and the Russians in 1941, Shah Mohammad Reza Pahlavi (1919–1980) gained the Iranian throne. After the war he asked foreign troops to withdraw from his country, but following the slow return of the Soviet army to its borders, aggressive activities of the Iranian Communist party (Tudeh), and an assassination attempt on the Shah's life, Iran firmly tied itself to the West.

—Wallbank et al., *Civilization Past and Present*, pp. 1012–1013

Tip A *bone of contention* is an idiom referring to something people disagree about and are arguing about.

TOO LITTLE HIGHLIGHTING

Iran, which had served as an area of competition between the British and the Russians since the nineteenth century, became a bone of contention between the United States and the Soviet Union after World War II. As the result of an agreement between the British and the Russians in 1941, Shah Mohammad Reza Pahlavi (1919–1980) gained the Iranian throne. After the war he asked foreign troops to withdraw from his country, but following the slow return of the Soviet army to its borders, aggressive activities of the Iranian Communist party (Tudeh), and an assassination attempt on the Shah's life, Iran firmly tied itself to the West.

EFFECTIVE HIGHLIGHTING

Iran, which had served as an area of competition between the British and the Russians since the nineteenth century, became a bone of contention between the United States and the Soviet Union after World War II. As the result of an agreement between the British and the Russians in 1941, Shah Mohammad Reza Pahlavi (1919–1980) gained the Iranian throne. After the war he asked foreign troops to withdraw from his country, but following the slow return of the Soviet army to its borders, aggressive activities of the Iranian Communist party (Tudeh), and an assassination attempt on the Shah's life, Iran firmly tied itself to the West.

Almost all of the first passage is highlighted. To highlight nearly all of the passage is as ineffective as not highlighting at all, because it does not distinguish important from unimportant information. In the second passage, only the main point of the paragraph is highlighted, but very sketchily—not enough detail is included. The highlighting in the third passage is effective; it identifies the main idea of the paragraph and includes enough details to make the main idea clear and understandable.

As a rule of thumb, try to highlight no more than one-quarter to one-third of each page. This figure will vary, of course, depending on the type of material you are reading.

Develop a Regular and Consistent System of Highlighting

As you develop your textbook highlighting skills, you should focus on this second guideline: Develop a system for deciding what type of information you will highlight and how you will mark it. First, decide what type of information you want to mark. Before marking anything, decide whether you will mark only main ideas or mark main ideas and details. You should also decide whether you will highlight or mark definitions of new terminology and, if so, how you will distinguish them from other information marked in the paragraph. Second, it is important to use consistently whatever system and type of highlighting you decide on so that you will know what your highlighting means when you review it. If you sometimes mark details and main ideas and other times highlight only main ideas, at review time you will find that you are unsure of what passages are marked in what way, and you will be forced to reread a great deal of material.

You may decide to develop a system for separating main ideas from details, major points from supporting information. When you review highlighting done this way, you will immediately know what is the most important point of the paragraph or section, and you will not get bogged down in the details—unless you need to. One such system uses one color of marker for main points and a different color for details. Another approach is to use asterisks and brackets to call attention to the main points.

Each of the following paragraphs has been highlighted using one of the suggested systems. You will notice that the paragraphs vary in the type of information marked in each.

VERSION 1: USE OF COLOR

Monochronism and Polychronism

Another important cultural distinction exists between **monochronic** and **polychronic time orientations**. Monochronic peoples or cultures such as those of the United States, Germany, Scandinavia, and Switzerland schedule one thing at a time. These cultures compartmentalize time and set sequential times for different activities. Polychronic peoples or cultures such as those of Latin America, the Mediterranean, and the Arab world, on the other hand, schedule multiple things at the same time. Eating, conducting business with several different people, and taking care of family matters may all go on at once. No culture is entirely monochronic or polychronic; rather, these are general or preponderant tendencies. Some cultures combine both time orientations; in Japan and in parts of American culture, for example, both orientations can be found.

—DeVito, *Essentials of Human Communication*, p. 125

VERSION 2: USE OF BRACKETS AND ASTERISKS

Monochronism and Polychronism

Another important cultural distinction exists between **monochronic** and **polychronic time orientations**. Monochronic peoples or cultures such as those of the United States, Germany, Scandinavia, and Switzerland schedule one thing at a time. These cultures compartmentalize time and set sequential times for different activities. Polychronic peoples or cultures such as those of Latin America, the Mediterranean, and the Arab world, on the other hand, schedule multiple things at the same time. Eating, conducting business with several different people, and taking care of family matters may all go on at once. No culture is entirely monochronic or polychronic; rather, these are general or preponderant tendencies. Some cultures combine both time orientations; in Japan and in parts of American culture, for example, both orientations can be found.

DIRECTIONS   Read the following passage. Then evaluate the effectiveness of the highlighting, making suggestions for improvement.

Exercise 1

Scarcity of Human Fossils

Unfortunately humans are a maddeningly poor source of fossils. In 1956, the paleontologist G. H. R. von Koenigswald calculated that if all the then-known fragments of human beings older than the Neanderthal people were gathered together they could be comfortably displayed on a medium-sized table. Although many more fossils of early hominids have been found since then, discoveries are still rare.

Why are human fossils so scarce? Why can one go to good fossil sites almost anywhere in the world and find millions of shell remains or thousands of bones of extinct reptiles and mammals, while peoples earlier than Neanderthal are known from only a handful of sites at which investigators, working through tons of deposits, pile up other finds by the bushel basket before recovering a single human tooth?

There are many reasons. First, the commonness of marine fossils is a direct reflection of the abundance of these creatures when they were alive. It also reflects the tremendous span of time during which they abounded. Many of them swarmed through the waters of the earth for hundreds of millions of years. When they died, they sank and were covered by sediments. Their way of life—their life in the water—preserved them, as did their extremely durable shells, the only parts of them that now remain. Humans, by contrast, have never been as numerous as oysters and clams. They existed in small numbers, reproduced slowly and in small numbers, and lived a relatively long time. They were more intelligent than, for example, dinosaurs and were perhaps less apt to get mired in bogs, marshes, or quicksands. Most important, their way of life was different. They were not sea creatures or exclusively riverside browsers but lively, wide-ranging food-gatherers and hunters. They often lived and died in the open, where their bones were gnawed by scavengers, were trampled on, and were bleached and decomposed by the sun and rain. In hot climates, particularly in tropical forests and woodlands, the soil is likely to be markedly acid. Bones dissolve in such soils, and early humans who lived and died in such an environment had a very poor chance of leaving remains that would last until today. Finally, human ancestors have been on earth only a few million years. There simply has not been as much time for them to leave their bones as there has been for some of the more ancient species of animals.

—Campbell and Loy, *Humankind Emerging,* pp. 22–23 ●

Exercise 2

DIRECTIONS Read each passage and then highlight the main ideas and important details in each. You may want to try various systems of highlighting as you work through this exercise.

1. Why We Worry About the Wrong Things

Nowadays we often worry about things that have a low probability of killing us and ignore things that have a much higher probability of doing us in. We worry more, for example, about being murdered by others than about killing ourselves, even though twice as many Americans commit suicide every year than are murdered. We worry about being struck by lightning during a thunder storm, while more than 10 times as many Americans die from falling out of bed. We are more afraid of dying in an airline accident than on the highway, although more than 500 times as many people die in car wrecks as in plane crashes. We are not shaken up over the likelihood of getting the common flu, which annually contributes to 36,000 deaths in the United States. We are not scared, either, by the cholesterol in our hamburger that contributes to heart disease killing 700,000 Americans a year.

Why, then, do we worry so much about those things that threaten us less than other things? One reason is the dread of prolonged pain or suffering. Thus we are more afraid of AIDS than heart disease because AIDS may take years for the patient to die but heart disease can kill in seconds. Another reason is that unfamiliar threats such as avian flu appear more fightening than familiar ones like the common flu. A third reason is the lack of control, which may explain the decision to drive rather than fly. Behind the wheel, you are in charge, but as an airline passenger, you are at the mercy of the pilot.

—adapted from Thio, *Sociology,* p. 105

2. DNA Fingerprinting and Forensics

DNA fingerprinting has become a vital tool in forensic medicine (the application of medical knowledge to questions of law). For example, DNA fingerprinting is used to identify "John and Jane Does," unknown human remains. The U.S. military takes blood and saliva samples from every recruit so it can identify soldiers killed in the line of duty. DNA fingerprinting can also identify victims of mass disasters such as airplane crashes. The World Trade Center tragedy called for genetic analysis on an unprecedented scale.

DNA fingerprinting can prove that a suspect was actually at the scene of a crime. In the United States, some communities now require certain criminal offenders to provide DNA samples, which are classified and stored. DNA profiles can also establish innocence. At least 10 people in the United States have been released from death row after genetic evidence exonerated them.

DNA fingerprinting can also verify relationships in cases of disputed

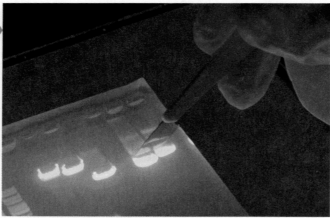

Scientist using DNA electrophoresis.
"DNA retrieval can become a race against time."

This process involves cutting DNA into fragments and sorting them by length. Scientists then search for a repeating sequence or pattern, which constitutes a person's unique DNA profile. A person's known DNA is then compared with DNA samples collected at crime scenes.

(adapted from same source as passage—Marieb)

Visual Thinking
ANALYZING IMAGES

What would you high-light or what notes would you make after studying the photo-graph and caption?

property, identify long-lost relatives, and establish paternity, even in paternity cases that are centuries old. For example, historians have fiercely debated whether Thomas Jefferson, our third president, fathered any children by his slave Sally Hemings. Modern DNA researchers entered the fray by profiling Jefferson's Y chromosome. A comparison of 19 genetic markers on the Jefferson Y chromosomes and those of Hemings' descendants found indentical matches between the Jefferson line and Hemings' youngest son. Could it be chance? Hardly!

—Marieb, *Essentials of Human Anatomy & Physiology*, p. 58 ●

Tip *Entered the fray means "joined the argument."*

Highlight Accurately

A third guideline for marking textbooks is to be sure that the information you highlight accurately conveys the content of the paragraph or passage. In a rush, students often overlook the second half of the main idea expressed in a paragraph, miss a crucial qualifying statement, or mistake an example or (worse yet) a contrasting idea for the main idea. Read the following paragraph and evaluate the accuracy of the highlighting.

It has long been established that the American legal court system is an open and fair system. Those suspected to be guilty of a criminal offense are given a jury trial in which a group of impartially selected citizens are asked to determine, based upon evidence presented, the guilt or innocence of the person on trial. In actuality, however, this system of jury trial is fair to everyone except the jurors involved. Citizens are expected and, in many instances, required to sit on a jury. They have little or no choice as to the time, place, or any other circumstances surrounding their participation. Additionally, they are expected to leave their job and accept jury duty pay for each day spent in court in place of their regular on-the-job salary. The jury must remain on duty until the case is decided.

In the preceding paragraph, the highlighting indicates that the main idea of the paragraph is that the legal system that operates in American courts is open and fair. The paragraph starts out by saying that the legal system has long been established as fair, but then it goes on to say (in the third sentence) that the system is actually unfair to one particular group—the jury. In this case, the student who did the highlighting missed the real main statement of the paragraph by mistaking the introductory contrasting statement for the main idea.

Make Your Highlighting Understandable for Review

As you highlight, keep the fourth guideline in mind: Be certain that your highlighting clearly reflects the content of the passage so that you will be able to reread and review it easily. Try to highlight enough information in each passage so that the passage reads smoothly when you review it.

Read these two examples of highlighting of the same passage. Which highlighting is easier to reread?

VERSION 1

Capital may be thought of as manufactured resources. Capital includes the tools and equipment that strengthen, extend, or replace human hands in the production of goods and services. Hammers, sewing machines, turbines, bookkeeping machines, and component parts of finished goods—all are capital goods. Even the specialized skills of trained workers can be thought of as a kind of human capital. Capital resources permit "roundabout" production: producing goods indirectly with a kind of tool rather than directly by physical labor.

To construct a capital resource requires that we postpone production of consumer goods and services today so that we can produce a tool that will enable us to produce more goods and services in the future. To postpone production of wanted goods and services is sometimes a painful decision, particularly when people are poor and in desperate need of goods and services today.

—McCarty, *Dollars and Sense*, pp. 213–214

VERSION 2

Capital may be thought of as manufactured resources. Capital includes the tools and equipment that strengthen, extend, or replace human hands in the production of goods and services. Hammers, sewing machines, turbines, bookkeeping machines, and component parts of finished goods—all are capital goods. Even the specialized skills of trained workers can be thought of as a kind of human capital. Capital resources permit "roundabout" production: producing goods indirectly with a kind of tool rather than directly by physical labor.

To construct a capital resource requires that we postpone production of consumer goods and services today so that we can produce a tool that will enable us to produce more goods and services in the future. To postpone production of wanted goods and services is sometimes a painful decision, particularly when people are poor and in desperate need of goods and services today.

A good way to check to see if your highlighting is understandable for review is to reread only your highlighting. If parts are unclear right away, you can be sure it will be more confusing when you reread it a week or a month later. Be sure to fix ineffectual highlighting in one paragraph before you continue to the next paragraph.

Exercise 3

DIRECTIONS   Read or reread the first six paragraphs of "Tribal Identity Through Body Art" in Part Five on p. 452. Highlight the main ideas and important details. When you have finished, test your highlighting by asking the four questions in the box below. Make any changes that will make your highlighting more consistent, accurate, or understandable. ●

Exercise 4

DIRECTIONS   Choose a three- to four-page passage from one of your textbooks. Read the selection and highlight the main ideas, the important details, and any key terms that are introduced. When you have finished, test your highlighting by asking the four questions listed below, and make any changes that will improve your highlighting. ●

CHECKING YOUR HIGHLIGHTING

As you are learning highlighting techniques, it is important to check to be certain that your highlighting is effective and will be useful for review purposes. To test the effectiveness of your highlighting, ask yourself the following questions:

1. **Have I highlighted the right amount or do I have too much or too little information highlighted?**
2. **Have I used a regular and consistent system for highlighting?**
3. **Does my highlighting accurately reflect the meaning of the passage?**
4. **As I reread my highlighting, is it easy to follow the train of thought or does the passage seem like a list of unconnected words?**

MARKING A TEXTBOOK

As you were highlighting paragraphs and passages in the earlier part of this chapter, you may have realized that highlighting alone is not sufficient, in many cases, to separate main ideas from details and both of these from new terminology. You may have seen that highlighting does not easily show the relative importance of ideas or indicate the relationship between facts and ideas. Therefore, it is often necessary to mark, as well as highlight, selections that you are reading. Suggestions for marking are shown in Figure 15-1.

Goal 4

Mark textbooks

To practice using marking as you read, go to

> Note Taking and Highlighting

Figure 15-1
Textbook Marking

Type of Marking		Example
Circling unknown words	def	. . . redressing the apparent (asymmetry) of their relationship . . .
Marking definitions	def	To say that the balance of power favors one party over another is to introduce a disequilibrium
Marking examples	ex	. . . concessions may include negative sanctions, trade agreements . . .
Numbering lists of ideas, causes, reasons, or events		. . . components of power include ①self-image, ②population, ③natural resources, and ④geography
Placing asterisks next to important passages	*	Power comes from three primary sources . . .
Putting question marks next to confusing passages	?→	. . . war prevention occurs through institutionalization of mediation . . .
Making notes to yourself	check def in soc text	. . . power is the ability of an actor on the international stage to . . .
Marking possible test items	T	There are several key features in the relationship . . .
Drawing arrows to show relationships		. . . natural resources . . . control of industrial manufacturing capacity
Writing comments, noting disagreements and similarities	Can terrorism be prevented through similar balance?	. . . war prevention through balance of power is . . .
Marking summary statements	Sum	. . . the greater the degree of conflict, the more intricate will be . . .

TECH SUPPORT

Annotating and Highlighting E-books

Many of the same highlighting tips and strategies discussed in this chapter apply to online versions of college textbooks (e-books). For example, if you are using an e-book of *College Reading and Study Skills* in MyReadingLab, your e-book includes "Highlighter" and "Note" tools in the toolbar. Your annotations and highlighting are saved when you log out of your account, and will still be there when you log back in.

Critical Comments

When you highlight, you are operating at the knowledge and comprehension levels of thinking (see Chapter 2, p. 42). Marking is an opportunity to record your thinking at other levels.

APPLYING LEVELS OF THINKING

Marking and Levels of Thinking
Here are some examples of the kinds of marginal notes you might make.

Level of Thinking	Marginal Notes
Applying	Jot notes about how to use the information.
Analyzing	Draw arrows to link related material.
Evaluating	Comment on the worth, value, relevance, and timeliness of ideas.
Creating	Record ideas about how topics fit together; make notes connecting material to lectures; condense ideas into your own words.

Writing Summary Notes

Writing summary words or phrases in the margin of your textbook is one of the most valuable types of textbook marking. It involves pulling ideas together and summarizing them in your own words. This process forces you to think and evaluate as you read and makes remembering easier. Writing summary phrases is also a good test of your understanding. If you cannot state the main idea of a section in your own words, you probably do not understand it clearly. This realization can serve as an early warning signal that you may not be able to handle a test question on that section.

The following sample passage has been included to illustrate effective marking of summary phrases. First, read through the passage. Then look at the marginal summary clues.

Under-the-Radar Advertising

Inundated with advertisements, 6,000 a week on network television, double since 1983, many people tune out. Some do it literally with their remotes. Ad people are concerned that traditional modes are losing effectiveness. People are overwhelmed. Consider, for example, that a major grocery store carries 30,000 items, each with packaging that screams "buy me." More commercial messages are there than a human being can handle. The problem is ad clutter. Advertisers are trying to address the clutter in numerous ways, including stealth ads, new-site ads and alternative media. Although not hidden or subliminal, stealth ads are subtle—even covert. You might not know you're being pitched unless you're attentive, really attentive.

3 new forms of advertising

- **Stealth Ads.** So neatly can *stealth ads* fit into the landscape that people may not recognize they're being pitched. Consider the Bamboo lingerie company, which stenciled messages on a Manhattan sidewalk: "From here it looks like you could use some new underwear." Sports stadiums like FedEx Field outside of Washington, D.C., work their way into everyday dialogue, subtly reinforcing product identity.

hidden ads

ads built into TV shows

- **Product Placement.** In the 1980s advertisers began wiggling brand-name products into movie scripts, creating an additional although minor revenue stream for moviemakers. The practice, **product placement,** stirred criticism about artistic integrity, but it gained momentum. Fees zoomed upward. For the 2005 release of *The Green Hornet,* Miramax was seeking an automaker willing to pay at least $35 million for its products to be written into the script, topping the $15 million that Ford paid for its 2003 Thunderbird, Jaguar and Aston Martin lines to be in the James Bond movie *Die Another Day.*

ad made to look like a TV program

- **Infomercials.** Less subtle is the **infomercial**, a program-length television commercial dolled up to look like a newscast, a live-audience participation show or a chatty talk show. With the proliferation of 24-hour television service and of cable channels, airtime is so cheap at certain hours that advertisers of even offbeat products can afford it. Hardly anybody is fooled into thinking that infomercials are anything but advertisements, but some full-length media advertisements, like Liz Taylor wandering through CBS sitcoms, are cleverly disguised.

magazines published by advertisers

A print media variation is the *'zine*—a magazine published by a manufacturer to plug a single line of products with varying degrees of subtlety. 'Zine publishers, including such stalwarts as IBM and Sony, have even been so brazen as to sell these wall-to-wall advertising vehicles at newsstands. One example was a splashy new magazine called *Colors,* for which you paid $4.50. Once inside, you probably realized it was a thinly veiled ad for Benetton casual clothes. *Guess Journal* may look like a magazine, but guess who puts it out as a 'zine: The makers of the Guess fashion brand.

—Vivian, *The Media of Mass Communication,* pp. 336–338

Omnipresent Ads.
Like many advertisers worried that their messages are lost in ad-crammed traditional media, this salon has struck out for nontraditional territory to be noticed. Regina Kelley, director of strategic planning for the Saatchi & Saatchi agency in New York, said: "Any space you can take in visually, anything you can hear, in the future will be branded."

Summary notes are most effectively used in passages that contain long and complicated ideas. In these cases, it is simpler to write a summary phrase in the margin than to highlight a long or complicated statement of the main idea and supporting details.

To write a summary clue, try to think of a word or phrase that accurately states, in brief form, a particular idea presented in the passage. Summary words should trigger your memory of the content of the passage.

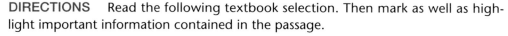

DIRECTIONS Read the following textbook selection. Then mark as well as highlight important information contained in the passage.

Exercise 5

Children as Consumers-in-Training

Anyone who has had the "delightful" experience of grocery shopping with children in tow knows that kids often have a say (sometimes a loud, whiney one) in what their parents buy. Children make up three distinct markets:

Primary Market. Kids spend a lot on their own wants and needs that include toys, apparel, movies, and games. When marketers at M&Ms candy figured out who was actually buying a lot of their products, they redesigned vending machines with coin slots lower to the ground to accommodate shorter people, and sales rose dramatically. Most children choose their own brands of toothpaste, shampoo, and adhesive bandage.

Influence Market. Parental yielding occurs when a parental decision maker surrenders to a child's request. Yielding drives many product selections because about 90 percent of requests to a parent are by brand name. Researchers estimate that children directly influence about $453 billion worth of family purchases in a year. They report that on average children weigh in with a purchase request every 2 minutes when they shop with parents. In recognition of this influence, *Mrs. Butterworth*'s Syrup created a $6 million campaign to target kids directly with humorous ads that show the lengths to which adults will go to get the syrup bottle to talk to them. An executive who worked on the campaign explained, "We needed to create the *nag factor* [where kids demand their parents buy the product]."

Future Market. Kids have a way of growing up to be adults and savvy marketers try to lock in brand loyalty at an early age. That explains why **Kodak** encourages kids to become photographers. Currently, only 20 percent of children aged 5 to 12 own cameras, and they shoot an average of only one roll of film a year. The company produces ads that portray photography as a cool pursuit and as a form of rebellion. It packages cameras with an envelope to mail the film directly back so parents can't see the photos.

—Solomon, *Consumer Behavior,* pp. 465–466 ●

Exercise 6

DIRECTIONS Turn to the reading on page 330 in Part Five that you highlighted to complete Exercise 3. Review the section and add marking and summary words that would make the section easier to study and review. ●

Exercise 7

DIRECTIONS Choose a three- to four-page excerpt from one of your textbooks. Highlight and mark main ideas, important details, and key terms. Include summary words, if possible. ●

USING COLLEGE TEXTBOOKS
Knowing What Is Important and Identifying Supporting Details

Textbook authors often help you identify main ideas and their major supporting details, and thereby know what to highlight and mark, by using in-chapter focus questions and end-of-chapter review questions. Here are some ways to use each.

1. **Focus Questions.** Focus questions appear at the beginning of the chapter or before or after each major section of a chapter. Their purpose is to focus your attention on what is important and provide a way for you to test your recall. They may be labeled in a variety of ways: "Learning Checks," 'Spotlight on Key Ideas," and so forth. Here are two ways to use them:
   - **Read focus questions before you read the chapter.** It is sometimes helpful to read the questions that correspond to a section before you read the section. The questions often serve as a list of what you are supposed to know when you finish reading.
   - **Answer focus questions as you come to them.** Some students answer them mentally; others annotate the chapter; others answer them in their

notes. It is usually better to write the answers than to just mentally think them through. You will remember more, and you will also have a written record to use for later review.

Here are a few samples from various textbooks.

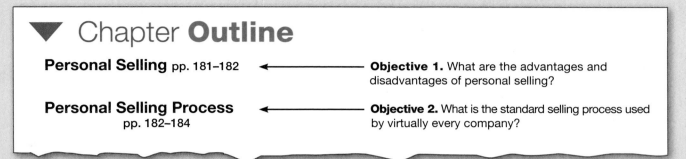

▼ Chapter **Outline**

Personal Selling pp. 181–182 ⟵ **Objective 1.** What are the advantages and disadvantages of personal selling?

Personal Selling Process pp. 182–184 ⟵ **Objective 2.** What is the standard selling process used by virtually every company?

—Levens, *Marketing*, p. 180

SECTION **13.4 Review Questions**

1. Describe the three layers of tissue that make up the heart.
2. What is an aneurysm?
3. What are actions that people can take to prevent myocardial infarction?

—Thomson, *Nutrition*, p. 39

TEST YOURSELF

Are these statements true or false? Circle your guess.

1 Your stomach is the primary organ responsible for telling you when you are hungry.   **TRUE** or **FALSE**

2 The entire process of digestion and absorption of one meal takes about 24 hours.   **TRUE** or **FALSE**

3 Some types of bacteria actually help keep our digestive system healthy.   **TRUE** or **FALSE**

4 Most ulcers result from a type of infection.   **TRUE** or **FALSE**

5 Irritable bowel syndrome is a rare disease that mostly affects older people.   **TRUE** or **FALSE**

Test Yourself answers can be found at the end of the chapter.

—Badasch, *Health Science Fundamentals*, p. 356

2. **Review Questions.** These end-of-chapter questions may be in the form of simple questions; other authors use a multiple-choice format. They are designed to help you discover what is important to learn in the chapter and to test your recall. Here is how to use them:

- **Carefully read the end-of-chapter review questions.** If the questions are in a question-and-answer format, it may be useful to read through them before you begin reading the chapter. Multiple-choice format questions usually are not as useful as a preview.

- **Write answers to these questions when you finish the chapter.** These types of questions are included to help you self-test your understanding of the chapter and increase your comprehension of its content.
- **Use both the questions and your written answers when reviewing for exams.** Cover your answers, read the questions, and test yourself to see if you can recall the answers.

Here are a few samples of review questions from textbooks:

Questions for Review

1. How have textile imports taken such a big market share in the United States?

2. What has been the textile industry's response to imports?

3. How does modern marketing differ from textile marketing in the past, when only natural fabrics were available?

—Frings, *Fashion*, p. 158

Learning the Basics

1. Define the term *metabolism*.
2. List three common cellular substances that can pass through cell membranes unaided.
3. Macronutrients _____.

A. include carbohydrates and vitamins; **B.** should comprise a small percentage of a healthful diet; **C.** are essential in minute amounts to help enzymes function; **D.** include carbohydrates, fats, and proteins; **E.** are synthesized by cells and not necessary to obtain from the diet

—Belk, *Biology*, p. 78

MORE TOPICS FOR WRITING

1. Choose a story from this chapter. Describe your experience of reading that story, and of encountering its symbols. At what point did the main symbol's meaning become clear? What in the story indicated the larger importance of that symbol?

2. From any story in this book, select an object, or place, or action that seems clearly symbolic. How do you know? Now select an object, place, or action from the same story that clearly seems to signify no more than itself. How can you tell?

—Kennedy, *Literature*, p. 258

FURTHER PRACTICE WITH TEXTBOOK READING

Part A: Sample Textbook Chapter

Read the section titled "Hunger" (p. 499). This textbook author did not include focus questions. Write and answer several focus questions that would help other students learn and remember the content of this section.

Part B: Your College Textbook

Choose a textbook chapter that you have been assigned to read for one of your other courses. When you have completed the chapter, answer the review questions at the end to test your knowledge of the material. Make note of the questions you did not answer correctly and review that material.

SELF-TEST SUMMARY

Goal 1 Why should you highlight and mark chapters when you read them?	Reading textbook chapters is a long and time-consuming process. As you read, you encounter a great deal of information that you know you will need to study and review for your next exam or quiz. To be able to locate this information quickly when you study, it is necessary to highlight and mark important information as you read. Without a system of highlighting and marking, you need to reread an entire chapter in order to review it effectively.
Goal 2 Why should you highlight as a way to prepare for study?	Highlighting is an effective way to prepare yourself for study because it takes advantage of a number of learning principles. This method challenges you to focus your concentration by keeping you physically active, makes you think about and evaluate the information, helps you grasp the organization of the material, and provides you with a way to check your understanding.
Goal 3 What guidelines should you follow for effective highlighting?	Highlight the right amount. Develop a regular and consistent system of highlighting. Highlight accurately. And make your highlighting understandable for later review. It is also wise to have a system for marking as well as highlighting.
Goal 4 Why should you supplement your textbook highlighting with marking?	Marking involves the use of marginal notes, summary words, and symbols that can make a passage easier to review. Marking can help you to organize the information you have highlighted by showing the relative importance of, or the relationships between, facts and ideas.

APPLYING YOUR SKILLS

DISCUSSING THE CHAPTER

1. Highlighting becomes more challenging as the density of the material increases. Discuss the systems you use to highlight and mark texts in various subject areas.
2. Why is highlighting frequently a new skill learned in college? Why do many college students tend to highlight too much? Why is a regular and consistent highlighting system important?
3. Evaluate your own ability to highlight effectively. What are your strengths? What are your weaknesses?

ANALYZING A STUDY SITUATION

Jin Lon always highlights her psychology textbook but often wonders whether her highlighting is effective. She usually highlights complete sentences because she is afraid she will miss something important. Sometimes she uses just one marker, and other times she uses two different colored markers. She usually highlights about half of each paragraph. As she reads, she notices things that she thinks could be on an exam, makes a mental note, and continues reading. She doesn't make any notes in the margins because she is unsure what to write.

1. How could Jin Lon determine whether her highlighting is effective?
2. Evaluate Jin Lon's highlighting technique.
3. Should she continue to use two highlighting systems?
4. How could she make better note of possible exam questions?
5. What advice could you give her on marking her textbooks?

WORKING ON COLLABORATIVE PROJECTS

DIRECTIONS   Your instructor will choose a reading from Part Five and divide the class into two groups for an out-of-class assignment. One group should highlight the reading but make no other markings. The second group should both highlight and mark the reading. During the next class session, students may quiz each other to determine which group is better prepared for (1) an essay exam, (2) a multiple-choice exam, and (3) a class discussion.

 **myreadinglab**   For support in meeting this chapter's goals, go to **MyReadingLab** and select **Note Taking and Highlighting.**

Quick QUIZ

DIRECTIONS Write the letter of the choice that best completes each statement in the space provided.

CHECKING YOUR RECALL

_____ 1. In general, you should highlight no more than about

 a. one-tenth of each page.
 b. one-third of each page.
 c. one-half of each page.
 d. three-fourths of each page.

_____ 2. The primary purpose of highlighting is to

 a. increase your reading rate.
 b. make review and study more efficient.
 c. learn to highlight the right amount.
 d. increase your review time.

_____ 3. When you are reading a textbook assignment, you should try to highlight all of the following *except*

 a. main ideas.
 b. important definitions.
 c. complete sentences.
 d. possible exam questions.

_____ 4. You should highlight for all of the following reasons *except* to

 a. help you remember what you read.
 b. keep you physically active while you read.
 c. make you decide which ideas are important.
 d. guarantee that you'll understand the material the first time you read it.

_____ 5. One difference between highlighting and marking is that, typically,

 a. highlighting shows the relative importance of ideas.
 b. highlighting indicates the relationship between facts and ideas.
 c. marking requires you to operate at higher levels of thinking.
 d. marking can be done without reading the text.

APPLYING YOUR SKILLS

_____ 6. Jameson has read and highlighted a text assignment. To study for his upcoming examination, he should

 a. review his highlighting.
 b. reread the chapter.
 c. go back and revise his highlighting.
 d. never need to look at it again.

_____ 7. Oliver is trying to decide what he should highlight in his psychology text. In making his decision, he should pay particular attention to

 a. paragraph length.
 b. page layout.
 c. graphics.
 d. boldfaced headings.

_____ 8. Caitlyn wants to test the effectiveness of her highlighting. She should ask herself all of the following questions *except:*

 a. Have I highlighted the right amount of information?
 b. Does my highlighting accurately reflect the meaning of the passage?
 c. Have I varied my system for highlighting to make it more interesting?
 d. Is my highlighting understandable for review?

_____ 9. Rashida has finished highlighting and marking a chapter in her physics text and is now writing summary notes. If Rashida is working effectively, she is most likely

 a. pulling ideas together and summarizing them in her own words.
 b. taking notes based only on the summary of a chapter.
 c. highlighting a long or complicated section first.
 d. recording her impression of the material's value.

_____ 10. Your friend Danae is struggling with learning to mark information in her textbooks. You can suggest that she should

 a. mark only the information that has not been highlighted.
 b. include comments on the author's style.
 c. make sure someone else can understand her notes.
 d. think about the information and evaluate it as she reads.

Methods of Organizing Information

LEARNING GOALS

In this chapter you will learn to

1 Outline to organize information

2 Summarize to condense information

3 Map to visualize ideas

LEARNING EXPERIMENT

1 Read the following description of the steps involved in a conversation.

Conversation takes place in at least five steps: opening, feedforward, business, feedback, and closing. It is convenient to divide any act—and conversation is no exception—into chunks or stages and view each stage as requiring a choice of what to say and how to say it. In this model the conversation process is divided into five stages, each of which requires that you make a choice as to what you'll do. The first step is to open the conversation, usually with some kind of greeting: "Hi. How are you?" "Hello, this is Joe." It is a message that establishes a connection between two people and opens the channels for more meaningful interaction. At the second step, you usually provide some kind of feedforward, which gives the other person a general idea of the conversation's focus: "I've got to tell you about Jack," "Did you hear what happened in class yesterday?" or "We need to talk about our vacation plans." At the third step, you talk "business," the substance or focus of the conversation. The term "business" is used to emphasize that most conversations are goal directed; you converse to fulfill one or several of the general purposes of interpersonal communication: to learn, relate, influence, play or help. The fourth step is the reverse of the second. Here you reflect back on the conversation to signal that as far as you're concerned the business is completed: "So you want to send Jack a get-well card," "Wasn't that the craziest class you ever heard of?" or "I'll call for reservations, and you'll shop for what we need."

—DeVito, *The Interpersonal Communication Book*, p. 266

2 Now, draw a diagram or write an outline that explains the process of conversation.

THE RESULTS

Did drawing the diagram or writing the outline help you learn or understand the steps in conversation? Why? In order to diagram or outline, you had to grasp the process and make it fit within a framework. Through these activities you were consolidating, or putting together, the information.

You organized it and made connections among the ideas presented.

LEARNING PRINCIPLE: WHAT THIS MEANS TO YOU

Consolidation is a process in which information settles, gels, or takes shape. The key to learning large amounts of information is to organize and consolidate it. Basically, this involves looking for patterns, differences, similarities, or shared characteristics and then grouping, rearranging, and reducing the information into manageable pieces. In this chapter you will learn three methods of consolidating information from either textbooks or lectures: outlining, summarizing, and mapping.

WHY ORGANIZE INFORMATION FROM YOUR TEXTBOOKS?

It is important to organize textbook information because:

- You will learn the material as you organize it.
- Outlining helps you understand the relationships among ideas.
- Summarizing enables you to express ideas in a condensed form.
- Mapping forces you to discover how ideas are connected.
- You will increase the amount of material you can remember by organizing it.

ORGANIZING BY OUTLINING

Outlining is an effective way of organizing the relationships among ideas. From past experiences, many students think of an outline as an exact, detailed, organized listing of all information in a passage; they consider outlining as routine copying of information from page to page and, therefore, avoid doing it.

Actually, an outline should *not* be a recopying of ideas. Think of it, instead, as a means of pulling together important information and showing how ideas interconnect. It is a form of note taking that provides a visual picture of the structure of ideas within a textbook chapter.

Outlining has many advantages, one being that you learn while you do it. Outlining allows you to think about the material you read and to sort out the important ideas from those that are less important. Because it requires you to express ideas in your own words and to group them, outlining reveals whether you have understood what you read. Finally, thinking about, sorting, and expressing ideas in your own words is a form of repetition that helps you to remember the material.

Goal ❶

Outline to organize information

To practice using outlining, go to

> Outlining and Summarizing

WHEN TO USE OUTLINING

Outlining is useful in a variety of situations.

- **When you are using reference books or reading books you do not own, outlining is an effective way of taking notes.**
- **When you are reading material that seems difficult or confusing, outlining forces you to sort ideas, see connections, and express them in your own words.**

(Continued)

- **When you are asked to write an evaluation or critical interpretation of an article or essay, it is helpful to briefly outline the factual content.** The outline will reflect the development and progression of thought and will help you analyze the writer's ideas.
- **In courses where order or process is important, an outline is particularly useful.** In a data processing course, for example, in which various sets of programming commands must be performed in a specified sequence, making an outline is a good way to organize the information.
- **In the natural sciences, in which classifications are important, outlines help you record and sort information.** In botany, for example, one important focus is the classification and description of various plant groups. Making an outline will enable you to list subgroups within each category and to keep track of similar characteristics.

How to Develop an Outline

Tip *Relative* means "having a particular quality when compared to something else." (Here, it means deciding which ideas are more important and which less important.)

To be effective, an outline must show (1) the relative importance of ideas and (2) the relationship between ideas. The easiest way to achieve this is to use the following format.

> I.   First major topic
>   A. First major idea
>   1. First important detail
>   2. Second important detail
>   B. Second major idea
>   1. First important detail
>   a. Minor detail or example
>   2. Second important detail
> II. Second major topic
>   A. First Major Idea

Note that the more important ideas are closer to the left margin, whereas less important details are indented toward the middle of the page. A quick glance at an outline indicates what is most important and how ideas support or explain one another.

DEVELOPING AN OUTLINE

Here are a few suggestions for developing an effective outline.

1. **Don't get caught up in the numbering and lettering system.** Instead, concentrate on showing the relative importance of ideas. How you number or letter an idea is not as important as showing what other ideas it supports or explains. Don't be concerned if some items don't fit exactly into outline format.
2. **Be brief; use words and phrases, never complete sentences.** Abbreviate words and phrases where possible.
3. **Use your own words rather than lifting most of the material from the text.** You can use the author's key words and specialized terminology.
4. **Be sure that all information underneath a heading supports or explains it.**
5. **All headings that are aligned vertically should be of equal importance.**

Now study the sample outline in Figure 16-1, which is based on the first three paragraphs of "Communication Through Body Adornment" in Part Five on page 449.

Figure 16-1
A Sample Outline

I. Communication Through Body Adornment

    A. Body Language –can function as text

        1. Actions include body movements and inscriptions

            a. movements: eye movement, posture, walking style, standing and sitting style.

            b. inscriptions: tattoos, hairstyles, dress, shoes, jewelry

        2. Follows rules similar to verbal language

            a. rules and meanings are learned

            b. without learning the rules, errors occur

    B. Type of body language used is culturally determined

        1. Some emphasize touch; some emphasize facial expressions

        2. Eye contact- valued by Euro-Americans; considered rude by Asians

    C. Body language conveys messages

        1. modification and marks give messages about age, gender, sexual interest or availability, wealth, emotions

        2. Color of clothing gives messages about identity, class, gender

            a. In US gender differentiation begins at birth; blue=boys, pink=girls.

            b. In Middle East men wear white, women black.

How Much Information to Include

Before you begin to outline, decide how much information to include. An outline can be very brief and cover only major topics, or, at the other extreme, it can be very detailed, providing an extensive review of information.

TECH SUPPORT

Outlining Using a Computer

Use the following tips for outlining using your computer:

- Use the tab key to make indenting easy and systematic.
- Devise a system for using different typefaces to designate the relative importance of ideas (caps for major topics, lowercase for details, for example).
- Use symbols, such as asterisks or brackets to mark important information and definitions.
- Use the cut and paste function to rearrange information and group together ideas on a specific topic.

Tip *Collateral* means *additional* or *aside,* so a *collateral assignment* would be one that comes from a source other than your main text.

How much detail you include in an outline should be determined by your purpose in making it. For example, if you are outlining a collateral reading assignment for which your instructor asked that you be familiar with the author's viewpoint and general approach to a problem, then little detail is needed. On the other hand, if you are outlining a section of an anatomy and physiology text for an upcoming objective exam, a much more detailed outline is needed. To determine the right amount of detail, ask yourself: What do I need to know? What type of test situation, if any, am I preparing for?

Exercise 1

DIRECTIONS   Read each of the following passages and complete the outline that follows it.

1. Fibromyalgia

Although there are many diseases today that seem to defy our best medical tests and treatments, one that is particularly frustrating is fibromyalgia, a chronic, painful, rheumatoid-like disorder that affects as many as 5 to 6 percent of the general population. Persons with fibromyalgia experience an array of symptoms including headaches, dizziness, numbness and tingling, itching, fluid retention, chronic joint pain, abdominal or pelvic pain, and even occasional diarrhea. Suspected causes have ranged from sleep disturbances, stress, emotional distress, and viruses, to autoimmune disorders; however, none have been proven in clinical trials. Because of fibromyalgia's multiple symptoms, it is usually diagnosed only after myriad tests have ruled out other disorders. The American College of Rheumatology identifies the major diagnostic criteria as:

Tip *Autoimmune disorders* are conditions in which substances that normally prevent illness in the body instead attack and harm parts of it.

Tip *Myriad* means "a great many."

- History of widespread pain of at least 3 months' duration in the axial skeleton as well as in all four quadrants of the body.
- Pain in at least 11 of 18 paired tender points on digital palpitation of about 4 kilograms of pressure.

—adapted from Donnatelle, *Health: The Basics,* p. 346

I. Fibromyalgia—chronic rheumatoid-like disorder

   A. Affects _____ % of population

   B. Symptoms

      1. headaches, _____, numbness, tingling, itching, _____, joint pain, abdominal or _____ pain, diarrhea

   C. Suspected _____

      1. Sleep disturbances, _____, _____, viruses, autoimmune disorders

   D. Major diagnostic criteria

      1. _____

      _____

      2. _____

2. Gathering Data in Foreign Countries

Conducting market research around the world is big business for U.S. firms. Among the top 50 U.S. research firms, over 40 percent of revenues come from projects outside the United States. However, market conditions and consumer preferences vary widely in different parts of the world, and there are big differences in the sophistication of market research operations and the amount of data available to global marketers.

For these reasons, choosing an appropriate data collection method is difficult. In some countries many people may not have phones, or low literacy rates may interfere with mail surveys. Local customs can be a problem as well. Offering money for interviews is rude in Latin American countries. Saudi Arabia bans gatherings of four or more people except for family or religious events, and it's illegal to stop strangers on the street or knock on the door of someone's house! Cultural differences also affect responses to survey items. Both Danish and British consumers, for example, agree that it is important to eat breakfast, but the Danish sample may be thinking of fruit and yogurt whereas the British sample is thinking of toast and tea. Sometimes these problems can be overcome by involving local researchers in decisions about the research design, but even so care must be taken to ensure that they fully understand the study's objectives and can relate what they find to the culture of the sponsoring company.

Another problem with conducting marketing research in global markets is language. It is not uncommon for researchers to mistranslate questionnaires, or for entire subcultures within a country to be excluded from research. For example, there are still large areas in Mexico where native Indian tribes speak languages other than Spanish, so researchers may bypass these groups in surveys. To overcome these difficulties, researchers use a process called *back-translation*, which requires two steps. First, a questionnaire is translated into the second language by a native speaker of that language. Second, this new version is translated back into the original language to ensure that the correct meanings survive the process. Even with precautions such as these, however, researchers must interpret data obtained from other cultures with care.

—Solomon, *Marketing,* p. 135

Tip *Sophistication* means "the quality of being advanced and perhaps complicated (when discussing equipment, procedures, etc., not people)."

Tip *Market research* means "the collection of information about what products and services people buy, whether they like them, and why."

I. Market research in foreign countries

  A. Big business for U.S. firms

    1. _____ of U.S. research firms' revenue comes from foreign projects

    2. _____ and consumer preferences vary widely

    3. differences in sophistication and _____

  B. Choice of data collection methods

    1. no _____

    2. _____

    3. _____ customs

    4. cultural differences affect _____

    5. problems may be overcome by using _____

  C. Language problems

    1. _____

    2. _____

    3. overcome problems using back-translation

      a. _____

      b. _____ ●

Exercise 2

DIRECTIONS   Turn to the article titled "The Genetic Crystal Ball" in Part Five on page 464. Write a brief outline of the article. ●

Exercise 3

DIRECTIONS   Choose a section from one of your textbooks and write a brief outline that reflects the organization and content of that section. ●

Goal ❷

Summarize to condense information

---

myreadinglab

To practice using summarizing, go to
> Outlining and Summarizing

SUMMARIZING: CONDENSING IDEAS

A **summary** is a brief statement or list of ideas that identifies the major concepts in a textbook section. Its main purpose is to record the most important ideas in an abbreviated and condensed form. A summary is briefer and less detailed than an outline. It goes one step beyond an outline by pulling together the writer's thoughts and making general statements about them. In writing a summary or making summary notes, you may indicate how the writer makes his or her point or note the types of supporting information the writer provides.

In writing a summary you go beyond separate facts and ideas and consider what they mean as a whole. Summarizing encourages you to consider such questions as "What is the writer's main point?" and "How does the writer prove or explain his or her ideas?" It is also a valuable study technique that will clarify the material.

WHEN TO USE SUMMARIES

Summaries are particularly useful in learning situations in which factual, detailed recall is not needed.

- **Use summaries to prepare for essay exams.** Because essay exam questions often require you to summarize information you have learned on a particular topic, writing summaries is a good way to practice taking the exam.

- **Use summaries when you read literature.** Writing a plot summary (describing who did what, when, and where) for fiction and a content summary for nonfiction will help you be certain you have mastered the literal content.

- **A brief summary is a useful study aid for collateral reading assignments.** In many undergraduate courses, instructors give additional reading assignments to supplement information in the text, to present a different or opposing viewpoint, to illustrate a concept, or to show practical applications.

- **Summarize laboratory reports or demonstrations.** Laboratory reports often include a summary. Writing and reviewing your summaries is an efficient way of recalling the purposes, procedures, and outcomes of lab and classroom experiments conducted throughout the semester.

How to Summarize

Although most students think of a summary as a correctly written paragraph, a summary written for your own study and review purposes may be in either paragraph or note format. If you choose a note format, however, be sure that you record ideas and not just facts. The box on page 348 lists tips for writing summaries. Before reading them, read the selection titled "Causes of Ulcers" and the sample summary shown in Figure 16-2.

Causes of Ulcers

For decades, physicians believed that experiencing high levels of stress, drinking alcohol, and eating spicy foods were the primary factors responsible for ulcers. But in 1982, Australian gastroenterologists Robin Warren and Barry Marshall detected the same species of bacteria in the majority of their patients' stomachs. Treatment with an antibiotic effective against the bacterium, *Helicobacter pylori (H. pylori),* cured the ulcers. It is now known that *H. pylori* plays a key role in development of most peptic ulcers. The hydrochloric acid in gastric juice kills most bacteria, but *H. pylori* is unusual in that it thrives in acidic environments. Approximately 40% of people have this bacterium in their stomach, but most people do not develop ulcers. The reason for this is unknown.

Prevention of infection with *H. pylori,* as with any infectious microorganism, includes regular hand-washing and safe food-handling practices. Because of the role of *H. pylori* in ulcer development, treatment usually involves antibiotics and acid-suppressing medications. Special diets and stress-reduction techniques are no longer typically recommended because they do not reduce acid secretion. However, people with ulcers should avoid specific foods that cause them discomfort.

Although most peptic ulcers are caused by *H. pylori* infection, some are caused by prolonged use of nonsteroidal anti-inflammatory drugs (NSAIDs); these drugs include pain relievers such as aspirin, ibuprofen, and naproxen sodium. They appear to cause ulcers by suppressing the secretion of mucus and bicarbonate, which normally protect the stomach from its acidic gastric juice. Ulcers caused by NSAID use generally heal once a person stops taking the medication.

—Thompson and Manore, *Nutrition for Life,* p. 59

Stress, alcohol, and spicy foods used to be blamed for causing ulcers, but in 1982, gastroenterologists identified the bacterium Helicobacter pylori (H. pylori) as key to most peptic ulcers. H. pylori thrives in acidic environments. About 40% of people have H. pylori in their stomach, but for unknown reasons most people do not get ulcers. Infection with H. pylori can be prevented by regular hand-washing and safe food handling. Infections are treated with antibiotics and acid-suppressing medications. People with ulcers should avoid foods that cause discomfort. Peptic ulcers may also be caused by prolonged use of nonsteroidal anti-inflammatory drugs (NSAIDs), such as aspirin, ibuprofen, and naproxen sodium, which suppress the secretion of protective mucus and bicarbonate in the stomach. These ulcers usually heal once a person stops taking the NSAID.

Figure 16-2
A Sample Summary

HOW TO SUMMARIZE

1. **Define your purpose.** Before writing a summary, take a moment to consider your purpose for writing it. Your purpose will help you determine how much and what kind of information you want to include in your summary. Gear your summary toward what you are trying to learn from the selection. In the sample summary in Figure 16-2, the student's purpose is to understand the causes of ulcers.

2. **Identify the main point.** When you begin to write a summary, first identify the author's main idea. Once you find it, write a statement that expresses it. This statement will help you to focus your summary. In the summary in Figure 16-2, the main point is that spicy foods used to be thought to cause ulcers, but now a strain of bacteria has been identified as the cause.

3. **Include key supporting information.** After you have located the main point, look for the most important information used by the author to support his or her main idea. Include only key reasons, facts, or events. In Figure 16-2, why the bacteria thrive in the stomach and how infections can be prevented are included.

4. **Identify key definitions.** Make a point to include definitions of key terms, new principles, theories, or procedures that are explained in the text. As you write the summary, underline or highlight essential words or phrases as you define them so that you will be able to locate them easily when reviewing.

5. **Evaluate the importance of details.** You will probably want to include some details in your summary; however, the amount of detail needed will vary depending on the type and amount of recall you need.

   It can be useful to include details such as examples in a summary when you have difficulty understanding or remembering a concept.

6. **Consider the author's attitude and approach.** It may be appropriate to include the author's attitude and approach toward the subject, depending on the type of material you are summarizing. Additionally, you may want to include the author's purpose for writing the passage.

Tip *Boil down* means "reduce a speech, piece of writing, idea, etc. to its most important elements."

GENERAL SUMMARY WRITING TIPS   Keep your summary objective and factual. Think of it as a brief report that reflects the writer's ideas and does not include your own evaluation of them. You are not writing an analysis of the passage, you're simply trying to boil down the basic facts and information presented in the passage.

Exercise 4

DIRECTIONS   After reading each selection, circle the letter of the choice that best summarizes it.

1. Learning Influences Our Food Choices

Pigs' feet, anyone? What about blood sausage, stewed octopus, or tripe? These are delicacies in various European cultures, whereas the meat of horses, dogs, monkeys, and snakes are enjoyed in different regions of Asia. Would you eat grasshoppers? If you'd grown up in certain parts of Africa or Central America, you probably would. That's because our preference for particular foods is largely a *learned* response: The cultures in which we are raised teach us what plant and animal products are appropriate to eat. If your parents fed you cubes of plain tofu throughout your toddlerhood, then you are probably still eating tofu now.

That said, early introduction to foods is not essential: we can learn to enjoy new foods at any point in our lives. Immigrants from developing nations settling in the United States or Canada often adopt a typical Western diet, especially when their traditional foods are not readily available. This happens temporarily when we travel: the last time you were away from home, you probably enjoyed sampling a variety of dishes that were not normally part of your diet.

We can also "learn" to dislike foods we once enjoyed. For example, if we experience an episode of food poisoning after eating undercooked scrambled eggs, we may develop a strong distaste for all types of cooked eggs. Many adults who become vegetarians do so after learning about the treatment of animals in slaughterhouses: they may have eaten meat daily when they were young but could not imagine ever eating it again.

—Thompson and Manore, *Nutrition for Life,* pp. 42–43

a. We make our food choices depending on what we grew up eating and on our experiences as an adult. We learn from our culture what foods are good to eat. We can also learn to enjoy different foods, whether we are new to a country or simply traveling there.

b. Our preference for certain foods is mostly learned from the cultures in which we are raised. However, we can learn to like or dislike new foods at any time in our lives as a result of exposure to new foods or information or experiences.

c. People have different food preferences because their cultures teach them what is appropriate to eat. Pigs' feet, blood sausage, stewed octopus, and tripe are delicacies in some European cultures. People in different areas of Asia eat the meat of horses, dogs, monkeys, and snakes, and grasshoppers are food in certain parts of Africa and Central America. Similarly, if you grew up eating tofu, you probably still eat it.

d. We learn to prefer certain foods because of how we were raised. We learn to dislike other foods because we have bad experiences, such as food poisoning, or because we learn new information, such as finding out about the treatment of animals at slaughterhouses.

2. Designing Your Fitness Program

Once you commit yourself to becoming physically active, you must decide what type of fitness program is best suited to your needs. Good fitness programs are designed to improve or maintain cardiorespiratory fitness, flexibility, muscular strength and endurance, and body composition. A comprehensive program could include a warm-up period of easy walking followed by stretching activities to improve flexibility, then selected strength development exercises, followed by performance of an aerobic activity for 20 minutes or more, and concluding with a cool-down period of gentle flexibility exercises.

The greatest proportion of your exercise time should be spent developing cardiovascular fitness, but you should not exclude the other components. Choose an aerobic activity you think you will like. Many people find cross training—alternate-day participation in two or more aerobic activities (i.e., jogging and swimming)—less monotonous and more enjoyable than long-term participation in only one aerobic activity. Cross training is also beneficial because it strengthens a variety of muscles, thus helping you avoid overuse injuries to muscles and joints.

—Donatelle, *Health: The Basics,* p. 282

a. A good fitness program includes a warm-up period of easy walking, stretching, strength development exercises, a 20-minute aerobic activity, and a cool-down period of flexibility exercises.

b. Good fitness programs improve or maintain cardiorespiratory fitness, flexibility, muscular strength and endurance, and body composition. A program's focus should be on cardiovascular fitness but should include other components.

Cross training, alternate-day participation in two or more aerobic activities, strengthens a variety of muscles.

c. It is important to choose a fitness program that is best suited to your needs. You should choose an aerobic activity you like. Cross training reduces boredom and is more enjoyable than just one aerobic activity. It helps avoid overuse injuries to muscles and joints as well.

d. Cardiovascular fitness is the most important component of a fitness program. A cool-down period is recommended. Jogging and swimming are two aerobic activities that can be done together in cross training. A comprehensive fitness program will include the different components of body composition. ●

Visual Thinking
ANALYZING IMAGES

How does this graphic enhance the passage "Designing Your Fitness Program"?

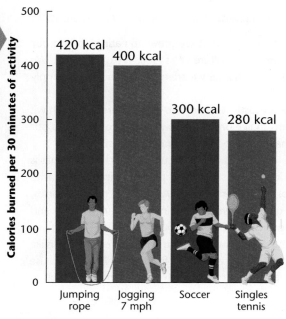

Figure A
Calories Burned by Different Activities
The harder you exercise, the more energy you expend. Estimated calories burned for various moderate and vigorous activities are listed for a 30-minute bout of activity.

Exercise 5

DIRECTIONS   Read each of the following selections and then complete the summaries that follow them by filling in the blanks.

1. Tsunami or Seismic Sea Wave

An occasional wave that momentarily but powerfully influences coastlines is the tsunami. Tsunami is Japanese for "harbor wave," named for its devastating effect where its energy is focused in harbors. Tsunami often are reported incorrectly as "tidal waves," but they have no relation to the tides. They are formed by sudden, sharp motions in the sea floor, caused by earthquakes, submarine landslides, or eruptions of undersea volcanoes. Thus, they properly are called *seismic sea waves*.

—Christopherson, *Geosystems,* p. 470

Summary: A _____ (also called a tsunami) is a wave that powerfully influences coastlines and is formed by _____

caused by _____.

It has devastating effects on _____.

2. Types of Evidence Presented in Court

The outcome of a trial usually hinges on the presentation of evidence. Attorneys for the prosecution and defense have two major types of evidence they can offer in support of their case: demonstrative evidence and testimonial evidence. Demonstrative evidence consists of physical objects—for example, the bloody glove presented in the O.J. Simpson trial, a weapon, fingerprints, blood samples, DNA, stolen property, tire or shoe prints, business records, computer files, and written or videotaped confessions. Testimonial evidence consists of oral evidence given under oath either in the courtroom or in depositions taken before attorneys for both sides and recorded by a court reporter.

—Barlow, *Criminal Justice in America*, p. 439

Summary: Two types of _____ can be presented in court. _____ is physical objects. Testimonial evidence is _____ or _____ .

3. Store Image

When people think of a store, they often have no trouble portraying it in the same terms they might use in describing a person. They might use words like *exciting, depressed, old-fashioned, tacky,* or *elegant.* Store image is how the target market perceives the store—its market position relative to the competition. For example, Bloomingdale's department store is seen by many as chic and fashionable, especially compared to a more traditional competitor such as Macy's. These images don't just happen. Just as brand managers do for products, store managers work hard to create a "personality."

—Solomon, *Marketing*, p. 418

Summary: _____ is how the target market perceives _____ and is its market position relative to _____ . Store managers must work hard to create _____ .

4. Hay Fever

Perhaps the best example of a chronic respiratory disease is hay fever. Usually considered to be a seasonally related disease (most prevalent when ragweed and flowers are blooming), hay fever is common throughout the world. Hay fever attacks, which are characterized by sneezing and itchy, watery eyes and nose, cause a great deal of misery for countless people. Hay fever appears to run in families, and research indicates that lifestyle is not as great a factor in developing hay fever as it is in other chronic diseases. Instead, an overzealous immune system and an exposure to environmental allergens including pet dander, dust, pollen from various plants, and other substances appear to be the critical factors that determine vulnerability. For those people who are unable to get away from the cause of their hay fever response, medical assistance in the form of injections or antihistamines may provide the only possibility of relief.

—Donatelle, *Health: The Basics*, p. 338

Summary: Hay fever is a _____ that is seasonally related and common _____ . It is characterized by _____ . It runs in families and is not affected by _____ . Overzealous immune systems and

_____ determine vulnerability. It can be

treated with _____ .

5. Aging and Culture

Culture shapes how we understand growing old. In low-income countries, old age gives people great influence and respect because they control most land and have wisdom gained over a lifetime. A preindustrial society, then, is usually a gerontocracy, a form of social organization in which the elderly have the most wealth, power and privileges.

But industrialization lessens the social standing of the elderly. Older people typically live apart from their grown children, and rapid social change renders much of what seniors know obsolete, at least from the point of view of the young. A problem of industrial societies, then, is ageism, prejudice and discrimination against the elderly.

—Macionis, *Society: The Basics,* p. 77

Summary: _____ affects how we regard aging. _____

societies are usually gerontocracies, where the elderly have the most

_____ . In _____ societies, the elderly

live apart from their families and have obsolete knowledge. _____ ,

which means prejudice and _____ against older people, be-

comes a problem. ●

Exercise 6

DIRECTIONS   Read the following selection and then complete the summary by filling in the blanks.

Catalogs

A catalog is a collection of products offered for sale in book form, usually consisting of product descriptions accompanied by photos of the items. Catalogs came on the scene within a few decades of the invention of moveable type in the fifteenth century, but they've come a long way since then. The early catalogs pioneered by Montgomery Ward and other innovators such as Sears were designed for people in remote areas who lacked access to stores.

Today the catalog customer is likely to be an affluent career woman with access to more than enough stores but who does not have the time or desire to go to them. According to the Direct Marketing Association, over two-thirds of the U.S. adult population orders from a catalog at least once in a year. Catalog mania extends well beyond clothing and cosmetics purchases. Dell and Gateway 2000, direct-selling computer companies, each have annual sales of over $1 billion. Recent catalog entries by computer giants IBM and Compaq are signs that ordering even a complex and expensive purchase such as a computer by mail is becoming common for many shoppers.

Although established retailers such as Bloomingdale's or JCPenney publish catalogs, others are start-ups by ambitious entrepreneurs who cannot afford to open a store. For example, a housewife named Lillian Hochberg began by selling handbags through the mail. Today the Lillian Vernon catalog mails out more than 137 million copies each year. As we saw with Neiman-Marcus, many stores use catalogs to complement their in-store efforts. In fact, more than half of the top 50 department stores use this selling technique. This allows the store to reach people who live in areas too small to support a store. Although catalogs can be an efficient way to reach shoppers, they can also be an expensive way to do business. Catalog retailers must expect to mail out 10 to 20 books for every order they receive, and paper and printing costs are rising steadily.

—Solomon, *Marketing*, p. 427

Summary: A catalog is _____

_____. Typical catalog customers are

_____. Two-thirds of the U.S. population

_____. Catalog sales of _____ are

becoming common. Fifty percent of all department stores use cata-

logs to _____. Catalogs allow stores to reach

people who _____. Catalogs can be an

_____ way to do business since _____

_____. ●

DIRECTIONS Write a summary of reading "Impact of the Internet on Thinking" which begins on page 484 in Part Five. ●

Exercise 7

DIRECTIONS Refer to the section from one of your textbooks that you used to complete Exercise 3 on page 346. Write a summary of the information presented in this section. ●

Exercise 8

MAPPING: A VISUAL MEANS OF ORGANIZING IDEAS

Goal 3

Map to visualize ideas

Mapping is a visual method of organizing information. It involves drawing diagrams to show how ideas or concepts in an article or chapter are related. Mapping provides a visual representation of how ideas are developed and connected.

HOW TO DRAW MAPS

Think of a map as a picture or diagram that shows how ideas are connected. Use the following steps in drawing a map:

1. Identify the overall topic or subject, and write it in the center or at the top of the page.
2. Identify the major supporting information that is related to the topic. Write each fact or idea on a line connected to the central topic.
3. When you discover a detail that further explains an idea already mapped, draw a new line branching from the idea it explains.

How you arrange your map will depend on the subject matter and how it is organized. Like an outline, it can be either quite detailed or very brief, depending on your purpose.

**Figure 16-3
A Model Map**

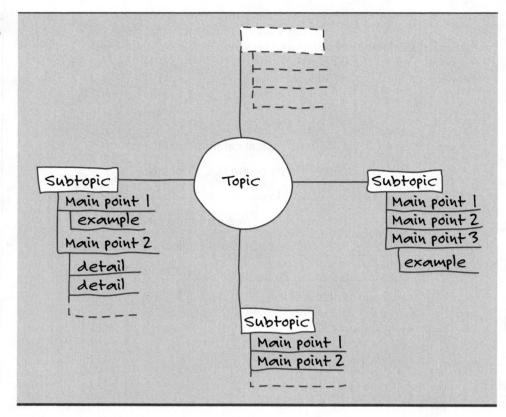

Maps can take numerous forms. You can draw them in any way that shows the relationships among ideas. They can be hand drawn or drawn using a word processor's capability to box and block type. Figure 16-3 shows the types of information to include in a map, depending on the desired level of detail. Figure 16-4 on the next page shows two sample maps. Each was drawn to show the organization of the section "Checking Your Comprehension" in Chapter 6 of this book. Refer to pages 127–129; then study each map.

WHEN TO USE MAPS

Maps are particularly well suited to the following situations:

- **Use maps if you are a visual learner.** You will be able to close your eyes and visualize the map.
- **Use maps for complicated processes and procedures that contain numerous steps.**
- **Use maps for material that is difficult to organize.** Constructing the map will help you see connections between ideas.
- **Use maps for physical objects.** Drawing a diagram of a piece of equipment or of the skeletal system of the human body is an effective study method.

Exercise 9

DIRECTIONS   Draw a map showing the organization of any section of Chapter 1 in this text. ●

Exercise 10

DIRECTIONS   Turn to the reading "You're Eating Genetically Modified Food" on page 461 in Part Five. Draw a map showing how the article is organized. ●

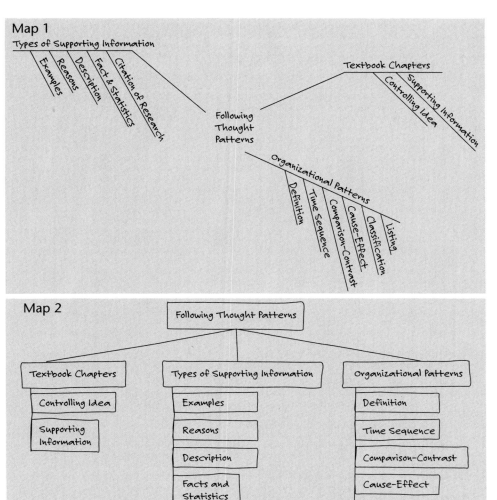

Figure 16-4
Two Maps for the
Same Information,
Organized in Different
Styles

DIRECTIONS Select a section from one of your textbooks. Draw a map that reflects its organization. ●

Exercise 11

LEARNING STYLE TIPS

Use the following tips to help you choose strategies that suit your learning style:

- If you are a social learner, work together in creating summaries, outlines, and maps using computer file sharing or exchanging edited versions.
- If you are a spatial learner, mapping will help you visualize the material.
- If you are a pragmatic learner, outlines provide a systematic, orderly format to work with.

Specialized Types of Maps

Maps may take numerous forms. This section presents five types of maps useful for organizing specific types of information: time lines, process diagrams, part/function diagrams, organizational charts, and comparison–contrast charts.

**Figure 16-5
A Time Line**

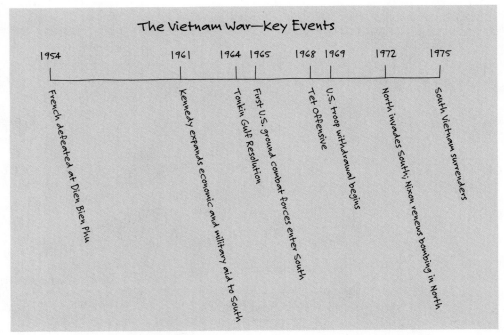

TIME LINES   In a course in which chronology of events is the central focus, a time line is a useful way to organize information. To visualize a sequence of events, draw a single horizontal line and mark it off in yearly intervals, just as a ruler is marked off in inches, and then write events next to the appropriate year. The time line in Figure 16-5, for example, was developed for an American history course in which the Vietnam War was being studied. It shows the sequence of events and helps you to visualize the order in which things happened.

Exercise 12

DIRECTIONS   The following passage reviews the ancient history of maps. Read the selection, and then draw a time line that helps you visualize these historical events. (Remember that B.C.E. refers to time before the common era, and such numbers increase as time moves back in history.)

In Babylonia, in approximately 2300 B.C.E., the oldest known map was drawn on a clay tablet. The map showed a man's property located in a valley surrounded by tall mountains. Later, around 1300 B.C.E., the Egyptians drew maps that detailed the location of Ethiopian gold mines and that showed a route from the Nile Valley to the mines. The ancient Greeks were early mapmakers as well, although no maps remain for us to examine. It is estimated that in 300 B.C.E. they drew maps showing the earth to be round. The Romans drew the first road maps, a few of which have been preserved for study today. Claudius Ptolemy, an Egyptian scholar who lived around 150 C.E., drew one of the most famous ancient maps. He drew maps of the world as it was known at that time, including 26 regional maps of Europe, Africa, and Asia. ●

PROCESS DIAGRAMS   In the natural sciences, as well as in other courses such as economics and data processing, processes are an important part of course content. A diagram that visually presents the steps, variables, or parts of a process will aid learning. A biology student, for example, might use Figure 16-6, which describes the food chain and shows how energy is transferred through food consumption. Note that this student included an example, as well as the steps in the process, to make the diagram clearer.

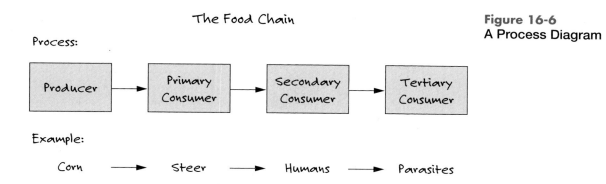

The Food Chain

Process:

Figure 16-6
A Process Diagram

DIRECTIONS   The following paragraph describes the process through which malaria is spread by mosquitoes. Read the paragraph, and then draw a process diagram that shows how this process occurs.

Exercise 13

> Malaria, a serious tropical disease, is caused by parasites, or one-celled animals, called protozoa. These parasites live in the red blood cells of humans as well as in female anopheles mosquitoes. These mosquitoes serve as hosts to the parasites and carry and spread malaria. When an anopheles mosquito bites a person who already has malaria, it ingests the red blood cells that contain the malaria parasites. In the host mosquito's body, these parasites multiply rapidly and move to its salivary glands and mouth. When the host mosquito bites another person, the malaria parasites are injected into the victim and enter his or her bloodstream. The parasites again multiply and burst the victim's blood cells, causing anemia. ●

PART/FUNCTION DIAGRAMS   In courses that deal with the use and description of physical objects, labeled drawings are an important learning tool. In a human anatomy and physiology course, for example, the easiest way to study the parts and functions of the inner, middle, and outer ear is to use a drawing of the ear. You can study the material and make a sketch of the ear, then test your recall of ear parts and their function. Refer to Figure 16-7 for a sample part/function diagram.

Figure 16-7
A Part/Function Diagram

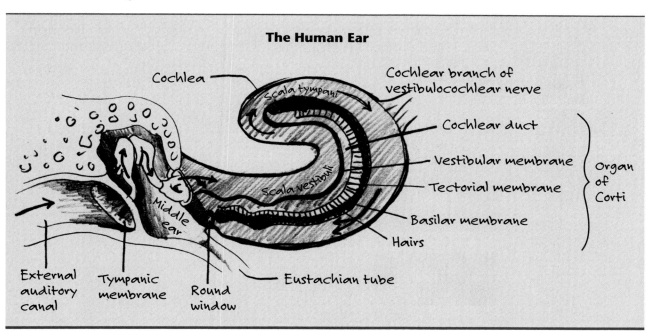

Exercise 14

DIRECTIONS   The following paragraph describes the Earth's structure. Read the paragraph, and then draw a diagram that will help you visualize how the Earth's interior is structured.

At the center is a hot, highly compressed inner core, presumably solid and composed mainly of iron and nickel. Surrounding the inner core is an outer core, a molten shell primarily of liquid iron and nickel with lighter liquid material on the top. The outer envelope beyond the core is the mantle, of which the upper portion is mostly solid rock in the form of olivine, an iron–magnesium silicate, and the lower portion chiefly iron and magnesium oxides. A thin coat of metal silicates and oxides (granite), called the crust, forms the outermost skin.

—Berman and Evans, *Exploring the Cosmos,* p. 145 ●

ORGANIZATIONAL CHARTS   When you are reviewing material that is composed of relationships and structures, organizational charts are useful study aids. Suppose that in a business management course, you are studying the organization of a small temporary clerical employment agency. If you drew and studied the organizational chart shown in Figure 16-8 below, the structure would become apparent and easy to remember.

Exercise 15

DIRECTIONS   The following paragraph describes one business organizational structure that is studied in management courses. Read the paragraph, and then draw a diagram that will help you visualize this type of organization.

It is common for some large businesses to be organized by *place,* with a department for each major geographic area in which the business is active. Businesses that market products for which customer preference differs from one part of the country to another often use this management structure. Departmentalization allows each region to focus on its own special needs and problems. Often the president of such a company appoints several regional vice presidents, one for each part of the country. Then each regional office is divided into sales districts, each supervised by a district director. ●

COMPARISON–CONTRAST CHARTS   A final type of visual aid that is useful for organizing factual information is the comparison–contrast chart. Based on the categorization principle of learning, this method of visual organization divides

Figure 16-8
An Organizational
Chart

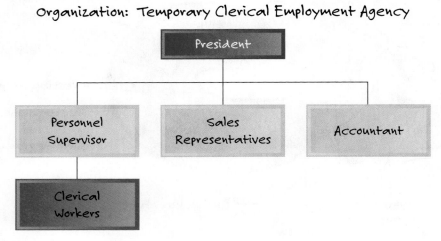

Organization: Temporary Clerical Employment Agency

and groups information according to similarities or common characteristics. Suppose that in a marketing and advertising course, you are studying three types of market survey techniques: mail, telephone, and personal interview surveys. You are concerned with factors such as cost, level of response, time, and accuracy. In your text, this information is discussed in paragraph form. To learn and review this information in an efficient manner, you could draw a chart such as the one shown in Figure 16-9.

Market Survey Techniques

Type	Cost	Response	Accuracy
Mail	usually the cheapest	higher than phone or personal interview	problems with misunderstanding directions
Phone	depends on phone service	same as personal interview	problems with unlisted phones and homes w/out phones
Personal interview	most expensive	same as phone	problems with honesty when asking personal or embarrassing questions

Figure 16-9
A Comparison–Contrast Chart

DIRECTIONS   The following passage describes the major physical differences between humans and apes. Read the selection, and then arrange the information into a chart that would make the information easy to learn.

Exercise 16

Numerous physical characteristics distinguish humans from apes. While apes' bodies are covered with hair, the human body has relatively little hair. While apes often use both their hands and feet to walk, humans walk erect. Apes' arms are longer than their legs, while just the reverse is true for humans. Apes have large teeth, necessary for devouring coarse, uncooked food, and long canine teeth for self-defense and fighting. By comparison, human teeth are small and short. The ape's brain is not as well developed as that of the human being. Humans are capable of speech, thinking, and higher-level reasoning skills. These skills enable humans to establish culture, thereby placing the quality and level of human life far above that of apes.

Humans are also set apart from apes by features of the head and face. The human facial profile is vertical, while the ape's profile is *prognathous,* with jaw jutting outward. Humans have a chin; apes have a strong lower jaw, but no chin. Human nostrils are smaller and less flaring than those of the ape. Apes also have thinner, more flexible lips than human beings.

Man's upright walk also distinguishes him from apes. The human spine has a double curve to support his weight, while an ape's spine has a single curve. The human foot is arched both vertically and horizontally but, unlike the ape's, is unable to grasp objects. The human torso is shorter than that of apes. It is important to note that many of these physical traits, while quite distinct, differ in degree rather than in kind. ●

USING COLLEGE TEXTBOOKS
Using Chapter Summaries

Chapter summaries appear at the end of textbook chapters and are brief paragraphs, lists, or outlines of the important information in the chapter. To use these:

1. Read the summary before you read the chapter to get a preview of what is important and what you have to learn.
2. Review the summary after you read the chapter to be certain you understood the material and found the important points.
3. Compare your notes on the textbook chapter with the summary to be sure you included everything in the summary in your notes.
4. Study the summaries when preparing for tests.

Here are a few sample summaries:

> 2. **What are the principles of supply and demand and the factors that affect each principle? (pp. 35–41)**
>
> - **Supply** (p. 36) refers to how much of a product or service is available. The amount supplied will increase as price increases. Supply is affected by:
>   - technology changes
>   - changes in resource prices
>   - price expectations
>   - price of substitute goods
>   - number of suppliers

—Solomon, *Better Business*, p. 56

> The six categories of drugs are prescription drugs, over-the-counter (OTC) drugs, recreational drugs, herbal preparations, illicit (illegal) drugs, and commercial preparations. Routes of administration include oral ingestion, inhalation, injection (intravenous, intramuscular, and subcutaneous), inunction, and suppositories.

—Donatelle, Health, p. 218

PEACE ORGANIZATIONS AND PEACE MOVEMENTS

Some believe the best chances for peace exist outside of the nation-state in emerging global political organizations and peace movements that seek to demilitarize society and remove the conditions that contribute to conflict and violence. Just as the media and technomedia have taken on an expanded role in promoting and sustaining peace.

—Thompson, *Society in Focus*, p. 481

FURTHER PRACTICE WITH TEXTBOOK READING

Part A: Sample Textbook Chapter

Draw a map or create an outline of the section "Theories of Emotion" on page 491 then compare this with the first chapter summary on page 501.

Part B: Your College Textbook

Choose a textbook you are using in one of your classes that has end-of-chapter summaries. Read the chapter, and then review the summary. Compare your notes on the chapter with the summary to be sure you included all the information.

SELF-TEST
SUMMARY

Goal **1** What is an outline and what are its advantages?	Outlining is a way to organize information to indicate the relative importance of ideas and the relationships among them. When done correctly, it helps you to sort ideas, test your understanding, and recall the material.
Goal **2** What is a summary and what are its advantages?	Summarizing is the process of recording a passage's most important ideas in a condensed, abbreviated form. A summary not only helps you to organize the facts and ideas presented in the text but also enables you to go beyond the facts and react to them critically.
Goal **3** What is mapping and what are its advantages?	Mapping creates a visual representation of the information and shows relationships. Five types of concept maps are time lines, process diagrams, part/function diagrams, organizational charts, and comparison–contrast charts. Mapping is versatile in that it enables you to adjust to both the type of information you are recording and its unique organization. Grouping and consolidating information in different ways makes it easier to learn and remember.

APPLYING   YOUR SKILLS

DISCUSSING THE CHAPTER

1. Why is it important to determine what type of test situation, if any, you are preparing for before you begin to outline?
2. In what types of learning situations are summaries most helpful to you? How and when have you used summaries in the past? What makes a particularly effective summary?
3. Share some maps that you have created for various classes. What makes the maps particularly effective?
4. List some learning situations in which time lines, process diagrams, part/function diagrams, organizational charts, and comparison–contrast charts can be most helpful to you and your classmates.

ANALYZING A STUDY SITUATION

Ken's courses this semester include History of the British Empire, Business Management, Biology, and Introduction to Anthropology. The history course requirements include several reading assignments from books placed on reserve in the library and an essay final exam. The anthropology course content includes several textbook chapters and lectures explaining how humans evolved and the relationships of other species to humans; a short-answer and essay final exam will be given. The biology course involves textbook reading, lectures, labs, and multiple-choice exams. The business management course focuses, in part, on the organization and structure of corporations; two multiple-choice and true/false exams will be given.

1. In which course(s) do you think Ken will need to use outlining? Why?
2. In which course(s) do you think Ken will need to use summarizing? Why?
3. Recommend a mapping strategy Ken might use for each course. Explain why each recommended approach is appropriate.

WORKING ON COLLABORATIVE PROJECTS

DIRECTIONS   Your instructor will choose a reading from Part Five and divide the class into three groups. Members of one group should outline the material, another group should draw maps, and the third should write summaries. When the groups have completed their tasks, the class members should review each other's work. Several students should read their summaries aloud, draw their maps, and write their outlines on the chalkboard. Discuss which of the three methods seemed most effective for the material and how well prepared each group feels for (1) an essay exam, (2) a multiple-choice exam, and (3) a class discussion.

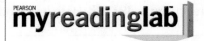

PEARSON
myreadinglab   For support in meeting this chapter's goals, go to **MyReadingLab** and select **Outlining and Summarizing**.

Quick **QUIZ**

DIRECTIONS   Write the letter of the choice that best completes each statement in the space provided.

CHECKING YOUR RECALL

_____ 1. Outlining can best be described as

    a. listing information to be learned.
    b. recopying detailed ideas and examples.
    c. recording facts in alphabetical order.
    d. organizing ideas to show relationships.

_____ 2. Outlining requires you to do all of the following *except*

    a. think about the material you read.
    b. decide the relative importance of ideas.
    c. put ideas into your own words.
    d. include your opinion of the information.

_____ 3. The main purpose of a summary is to

    a. reflect the organization of ideas.
    b. present a brief review of information.
    c. raise questions about the material.
    d. provide a detailed record of content.

_____ 4. A summary should always include

    a. the author's main point.
    b. examples.
    c. a list of graphics.
    d. your own opinion.

_____ 5. The most useful type of map for organizing information according to similarities of common characteristics is

    a. an organizational chart.
    b. a process diagram.
    c. a comparison–contrast chart.
    d. a time line.

APPLYING YOUR SKILLS

_____ 6. Four students created outlines from a chapter in their economics text. Which student probably created the most effective outline?

    a. Ron included only the information that fit into the outline format he chose.
    b. Emily focused on outlining the author's attitudes.
    c. Michel ensured that his outline expressed at least four levels of ideas.
    d. Li-Min showed the relative importance of ideas.

_____ 7. Dominique needs to complete the following tasks. The task for which writing a summary would be most helpful would be

    a. preparing for an essay exam in sociology.
    b. keeping track of the steps to follow in solving calculus problems.
    c. learning a list of terms and definitions for a biology course.
    d. learning the characteristics of different types of mental illness for a psychology class.

_____ 8. In Yolanda's music class, she drew a diagram showing the various parts of an electric guitar and what each part does. The type of concept map she created in this situation is called

    a. an organizational chart.
    b. a time line.
    c. a process diagram.
    d. a part/function diagram.

_____ 9. Mimi is taking a sociology course in which the focus is social problems. Her instructor has distributed a list of articles, of which she is expected to read ten. The most effective way for her to record the information from her reading would be to prepare

    a. a detailed outline of each article.
    b. index cards for each article.
    c. a summary of each article.
    d. a time line to organize the articles.

_____ 10. In a course on child development, James is studying the development and changes in the human brain prior to birth. The most effective method of study in this situation would be for him to

    a. write a brief summary.
    b. draw a process diagram.
    c. create an organizational chart.
    d. draw a part/function diagram.

SUCCESS WORKSHOP

8 Polish Your Academic Image

Why?

Imagine that you are a teacher meeting a class of students for the first time. Look at the students in the photos below from the **teacher's point of view**. Next to each photo, write your first impressions of how each student will approach his or her course work. For example:

- Who do you think will participate in class?
- Who will turn in careful, neatly organized work?

- Who will be early, on time, or late for class?
- Who will come to your office to ask questions when he or she doesn't understand an assignment? Who will you never see there?
- Who will tell you the dog ate his or her homework?

Be prepared to discuss your reasoning.

Discovering . . .

How Do You Rate Your Academic Image?

	Always	Sometimes	Never
1. I ask and answer questions in class.	❑	❑	❑
2. I make eye contact with my instructor during class.	❑	❑	❑
3. I speak to my instructors when I see them on campus.	❑	❑	❑
4. I turn in neat, carefully done assignments.	❑	❑	❑
5. I make myself known to instructors by speaking to them before or after class.	❑	❑	❑
6. I attend all classes and explain any necessary lengthy absences to my instructors.	❑	❑	❑
7. I avoid talking with classmates while the instructor is talking.	❑	❑	❑
8. I come to class before the instructor and stay until class is dismissed.	❑	❑	❑
9. I try to stay alert to show that I am interested.	❑	❑	❑
10. I sit in class with other students who demonstrate a positive academic image.	❑	❑	❑

If you answered "Sometimes" or "Never" to more than one or two questions, you should improve your academic image.

Think About It!

When you meet someone new, how do you figure out what he or she is like? You can't read people's minds to know what they are thinking, so, normally, you try to understand others by the way they act—their behavior. Your instructors do the same.

How can your instructor tell that you are interested in the course material? She can watch for behaviors that usually go along with interest—asking questions when you want to know more or don't understand something, answering questions that the instructor poses, paying attention to what she says, and taking notes. She can also see if you ever visit her office for help or if you seem to need extra help.

Suppose you were introduced to a new person, but she only glanced at you and mumbled a quick "hi" while continuing her conversation with someone else. You might think that she didn't want to get to know you or that she was rude. If you talk to your classmates instead of paying attention to your instructor, she will likely make the same judgment about you.

On the other hand, if you meet someone who looks you in the eye, repeats your name, shakes your hand, and spends a few minutes talking with you, you'll have quite a different impression. Which classroom behaviors from the questionnaire above are similar to this example?

You can also tell a lot about people from the pride they take in their work. If you took your car to a mechanic to fix the brakes, and the brakes worked again but made a terrible screeching noise, what judgment would you make about the mechanic's pride of work? What is a similar situation in college classes that can affect your academic image?

Think about it.

Changing . . .

Planning a More Successful Academic Image

For each response of "Sometimes" or "Never" you gave in the questionnaire on page 365, write a new statement about how you can change your everyday behavior in class and on campus to improve your academic image. What will help your instructors think of you as a serious, hard-working, responsible student? (Remember what things look like from the front of the room!)

1. I will _____
   _____

2. I will _____
   _____

3. I will _____
   _____

4. I will _____
   _____

Reflecting . . .

Every Week or Two, Check Again

- Am I communicating with my instructors?
  - Do I talk to instructors before or after class?
  - Do I take advantage of my instructor's office hours?
  - Have I explained any problems to my instructor?
- Am I participating in my classes?
  - Am I making eye contact with my instructor?
  - Do I ask and answer questions in class?
  - Do I show my interest and motivation in class?
- Am I turning in good quality work?
  - Do I submit neat and complete assignments?
  - Do I always include my name and the date, course title, and section number on my assignments?
  - Do I word process all my papers?
- Am I projecting a successful academic image?

Interest

Motivation

Attention

Good Work

Energy

9 Stay Healthy and Manage Stress

Why?

Learning to handle the many demands of college life can be stressful, especially if you are trying to raise a family or work a job at the same time. If you stay healthy and learn to manage stress, you will find that your life becomes more enjoyable and fun.

Discovering . . .
Think About Your General Health

1. How much sleep do you usually get each night?
2. How much time do you spend exercising each week?
3. How often do you eat regular, healthy meals?
4. Do you smoke or drink alcohol? If so, how much?

Analyzing . . .
Think About Your Stress Level

1. Do you spend most of your time either studying or worrying about not studying?
2. Have you ever noticed that you get sick when you can least afford it?
3. Do you have a tendency to skip meals, eat junk food, stay up late, or skip exercise when you are overworked?
4. Do you often feel impatient or irritable without knowing why?
5. Do you feel stressed out?

Focus on the elements of this workshop that will help you the most in moving toward a healthier, more relaxed lifestyle.

Reflecting . . .
Do Your Habits Work for You?

Regardless of how busy you are, be sure to:

Get enough sleep.   The amount of sleep a person needs is highly individual. Discover how much you need by noticing patterns. For several weeks, analyze how well your day went and consider how much sleep you had the night before. Then adjust your schedule to make sure you get the right amount of sleep for you each night.

Exercise regularly.   Exercising three times a week for about 15 minutes each time is a good way to get started on a regular fitness program. Whenever you find yourself getting tense, for example when your shoulders or neck start tensing, take a few minutes immediately to stretch or go for a brief walk.

Eat regular, healthy meals.   Give yourself time to eat three meals a day. For snacks in between, eat fruit or vegetables. Avoid a diet heavy in fats, and try to eat balanced meals rather than junk food.

Reduce or eliminate smoking and drinking alcohol.   Check with a counselor at the student health center for a program that will help you.

Learn to say "No" to unreasonable requests from friends and family.   Explain your schedule to your family, and make sure they understand your academic goals. Then when you need to turn down unreasonable requests, they will understand why.

Take breaks.   Constantly pushing yourself compounds stress. Slow down and do nothing for a brief period, even if just for five minutes. If you practice deep breathing on your breaks, you will relax even more. Breathe in through your nose; then breathe out completely through your mouth.

Planning . . .
How Can You Improve Your Habits?

Examine your weekly schedule of classes, study, work, and family activities. Look for short time periods that you could use for exercise, better meals, and breaks. Look for ways to increase the amount of sleep you're getting, if that's an issue. Make a plan for improving your health and relaxation by writing the necessary changes into your schedule.

Changing . . .
Does Your Thinking Help You?

When you feel as if you don't have enough time in your day to get everything done, don't think negatively—"I'll never be able to get all this done!" This leads to unnecessary stress. Instead think positively—"It's going to feel great to accomplish this!"

- Visualize success. Imagine yourself getting everything done in an orderly, systematic way.

- Focus on the benefits of completing each task. How will completing each task help you or others?

- Develop a plan or schedule that will allow you to get everything done (refer to Chapter 1 for tips on time management).

Discovering . . .
Using Your Senses for Success

Success follows from working productively. Keeping your senses trained on the world around you, rather than on your personal thoughts, can help you focus on the task at hand and increase your productivity. Use this brief exercise to refocus your senses when you take a break from your work.

Stand up and move around your study area for three to five minutes. Look closely at the colors, shapes, and images in the room. As you are looking, listen carefully for all the sounds that you can hear: traffic sounds, music playing, appliances humming, people talking. While looking and listening, notice what you can feel around you: touch different objects, notice the air temperature, feel the floor under your feet. Examine what you are seeing, hearing, and feeling as if the sights, sounds, and sensations are all new to you.

When you return to your work, you will find that you are more able to put aside unrelated thoughts and complete your task more efficiently. During long study periods, repeat this exercise every 50 minutes and notice how much more you can accomplish!

Reflecting . . .
Every Week or Two, Check Again

- Am I getting enough sleep?
- Am I exercising regularly?
- Am I eating regular, healthy meals?
- Am I taking brief breaks when I start to feel stressed?
- Am I focusing my senses on success?
- Am I focusing on the benefits of completing each task?
- Is my schedule allowing me to get everything done?

Study and Review Strategies

LEARNING GOALS

In this chapter you will learn to

1 Use paraphrasing to restate ideas

2 Test yourself to evaluate your learning

3 Use a learning journal

4 Use the SQ3R system

5 Adapt the SQ3R system to fit your needs

LEARNING EXPERIMENT

1 Make a list of five to ten tasks (sports, hobbies, household duties, etc.) you can perform well. For each, indicate how you know you are proficient at the task.

2 Make a list of two to five things you might want to learn to do at some point in your lifetime (write a novel, ride horseback, race cars, etc.). For each, indicate how you will measure your success.

THE RESULTS

For each task, either those at which you are proficient or those you would like to learn, you were able to suggest some measure or yardstick by which you can evaluate your proficiency or success.

LEARNING PRINCIPLE: WHAT THIS MEANS TO YOU

To know whether you have accomplished something, you need some measurement standard. To know whether you have learned something, you also need to test or measure your learning. **For academic learning, self-testing, often through writing, is an effective way to measure what you have learned.** In this chapter you will discover several learning strategies that involve review and self-testing. Even though you have read a textbook chapter and highlighted or outlined it, you cannot be certain that you have learned the material or will be able to apply it on exams. Study and review must follow reading and organizing.

WHY LEARN REVIEW STRATEGIES?

Review strategies are important because:

- You will forget material rapidly unless you review it.
- If you review what you have learned regularly, you won't have to cram before exams.
- By using effective study strategies, you will get more out of the time you spend studying.
- You will earn better grades.

PARAPHRASING

A paraphrase is a restatement of a passage's ideas in your own words. The author's meaning is retained, but your wording, *not* the author's, is used. We use paraphrasing frequently in everyday speech. For example, when you relay a message from one person to another, you convey the meaning but do not use the person's exact wording. A paraphrase can be used to make a passage's meaning clearer and often more concise. A paraphrase, then, moves you from a knowledge level in which you can recall information to a comprehension level in which you understand the ideas presented. Paraphrasing is also an effective learning and review strategy in several situations.

Goal 1

Use paraphrasing to restate ideas

WHEN TO PARAPHRASE

Paraphrase when . . .

- **Exact detailed comprehension is required.** Working through a passage line by line will strengthen your comprehension. You might paraphrase the steps in solving a math problem or a process in biology, for example.
- **Reading material is difficult or complicated.** If you can express the author's ideas in your own words, you can be sure you understand it. If you cannot paraphrase it, you will know your comprehension is incomplete. See Figure 17-1.
- **Material is stylistically complex or uses obsolete or unfamiliar language.** Paraphrasing will help you break though the language barrier and express the content as simply as possible.

Tip *Obsolete* means "no longer generally used; out-of-date."

HOW TO PARAPHRASE EFFECTIVELY

Use the following suggestions to paraphrase effectively:

1. Read slowly and carefully, and read the material through entirely before writing anything.
2. As you read, pay attention to exact meanings and relationships among ideas.
3. Read each sentence and express the key idea in your own words.
4. Reread the original sentence; look away and write your own sentence; then reread the original and add anything you missed.
5. Don't try to paraphrase word by word; instead, work with ideas.
6. For words or phrases that you are unsure of or are not comfortable using, check a dictionary to locate a more familiar meaning.
7. You may combine several original sentences into a more concise paraphrase.
8. When finished, reread your paraphrase and compare it with the original for completeness and accuracy.

Figure 17-1
A Comparison of
Paraphrases of
Difficult, Complicated
Material

Tip *Trillion* means
1,000,000,000,000.

Quadrillion means
1,000,000,000,000,000.

PASSAGE: NEURONS

Individual neurons do not form a continuous chain, with each neuron directly touching another, end to end. If they did, the number of connections would be inadequate for the vast amount of information the nervous system must handle. Instead, individual neurons are separated by a minuscule space called the synaptic cleft, where the axon terminal nearly touches a dendrite or the cell body of another. The entire site—the axon terminal, the cleft, and the membrane of the receiving dendrite or cell body—is called a synapse. Because a neuron's axon may have hundreds or even thousands of terminals, a single neuron may have synaptic connections with a great many others. As a result, the number of communication links in the nervous system runs into the trillions or perhaps even the quadrillions.

Although we seem to be born with nearly all the neurons we will ever have, many synapses have not yet formed at birth. Research with animals shows that axons and dendrites continue to grow as a result of both physical maturation and experience with the world, and tiny projections on dendrites called spines increase both in size and in number. Throughout life, new learning results in the establishment of new synaptic connections in the brain, with stimulating environments producing the greatest changes (Greenough & Anderson, 1991; Greenough & Black, 1992). Conversely, some unused synaptic connections are lost as cells or their branches die and are not replaced (Camel, Withers, & Greenough, 1986). The brain's circuits are not fixed and immutable; they are continually developing and being pruned in response to information and to challenges and changes in the environment.

—Wade and Tavris, *Psychology*, pp. 124–125

Paraphrase 1: Demonstrates Lack of Understanding

Neurons don't connect with each other because it would be too much information for the nervous system. They have trillions or even quadrillions of links and hundreds or thousands of terminals. They also have clefts, membranes, and synapses—the receiving dendrite or cell body. We seem to be born with all of them that we will ever have. Spines or dendrites become more and bigger, and some of their branches aren't replaced. The brain's circuits cannot be fixed, but are pruned.

Paraphrase 2: Demonstrates Understanding

Neurons are separated from each other by tiny spaces or clefts between the axon of one and the dendrite of another. These three parts make up a synapse. Because of synapses, neurons can make more connections with each other than if they had to touch. This allows for trillions of links in the nervous system. The number of synapses we have is constantly changing. Unused connections vanish, and learning causes our axons and dendrites to grow and make new synaptic connections.

Exercise 1

DIRECTIONS   Write a paraphrase for each of the following excerpts.

1. The tides are important for several reasons. Tidal mixing of nearshore waters removes pollutants and recirculates nutrients. Tidal currents also move floating animals and plants to and from their usual breeding areas in estuaries to deeper waters. People who fish frequently follow tidal cycles to improve their catch, because strong tidal currents concentrate bait and smaller fish, thus attracting larger fish. When sailing ships were more common, departures or arrivals in a harbor had to be closely linked to the tidal cycle.

   —Ross, *Introduction to Oceanography*, p. 239

2. The *stomach* is a muscular sac that churns the food as it secretes mucus, hydrochloric acid, and enzymes that begin the digestion of proteins. The food is meanwhile sealed in the stomach by two sphincters, or rings of muscles, one at

either end of the stomach. After the mixing is completed, the lower sphincter opens and the stomach begins to contract repeatedly, squeezing the food into the small intestine. A fatty meal, by the way, slows this process and makes us feel "full" longer. This is also why we're hungry again so soon after a low-fat Chinese dinner.

The *small intestine* is a long convoluted tube in which digestion is completed and through which most nutrient products enter the bloodstream. Its inner surface is covered with tiny, fingerlike projections called *villi*, which increase the surface area of the intestinal lining. Furthermore, the surface area of each villus is increased by about 3000 tiny projections called *microvilli*. Within each villus is a minute lymph vessel surrounded by a network of blood capillaries. While the digested products of certain fats move directly into the lymph vessel, the products of protein and starch digestion move into the blood capillaries.

—Wallace, *Biology: The World of Life*, p. 443

> **Tip** *Minute* means "very small." The word is pronounced [my-noot] and stressed on the second syllable. Don't confuse it with *minute* [min-nut], meaning 60 seconds.

3. *Section 7.* (1). All bills for raising revenue shall originate in the House of Representatives; but the Senate may propose or concur with amendments as on other bills.

(2). Every bill which shall have passed the House of Representatives and the Senate, shall, before it become a law, be presented to the President of the United States; if he approve he shall sign it, but if not he shall return it, with his objections to that House in which it shall have originated, who shall enter the objections at large on their journal, and proceed to reconsider it. If after such reconsideration two thirds of that House shall agree to pass the bill, it shall be sent, together with the objections, to the other House, by which it shall likewise be reconsidered, and if approved by two thirds of that House, it shall become a law. But in all such cases the votes of both Houses shall be determined by yeas and nays, and the names of the persons voting for and against the bill shall be entered on the journal of each House respectively. If any bill shall not be returned by the President within ten days (Sundays excepted) after it shall have been presented to him, the same shall be a law, in like manner as if he had signed it, unless the Congress by their adjournment prevent its return, in which case it shall not be a law.

—U.S. Constitution ●

DIRECTIONS Write a paraphrase of the first paragraph of "You're Eating Genetically Modified Food" in Part Five, on page 461. ●

Exercise 2

DIRECTIONS Write a paraphrase of a two- or three-paragraph excerpt from one of your textbooks. Choose a passage that is difficult or stylistically complex. ●

Exercise 3

SELF-TESTING

Have you ever taken an exam for which you studied hard and felt prepared, only to find out you earned just an average grade? Although you spent time reviewing, you did not review in the right ways; you probably focused on recalling factual information. Many college professors demand much more of their students than factual recall of textbook and lecture content. They expect their students to react, evaluate, and apply ideas. They require their students to be able to compare and synthesize sources and integrate ideas.

Self-testing is a study strategy that uses writing to discover and relate ideas. It involves writing possible exam questions and drafting answers to them. This activity combines the use of factual recall with interpretation and evaluation.

Goal ②

Test yourself to evaluate your learning

myreadinglab

To practice studying and reviewing, go to
> Test Taking

Visual Thinking

This photograph shows students studying a chapter for their criminal justice course. Members of the group compare their highlighting of the chapter and then discuss how the chapter compares to lecture content. What else should the group do to make sure they have learned chapter content? Make specific suggestions.

Constructing potential test questions is fun and challenging and can be done with a classmate or in groups. It is usually best to write answers yourself, however, to get maximum benefit from the technique. After writing, compare and discuss your answers with classmates. If you prefer to work alone, be sure to verify your answers by referring to your text and/or lecture notes.

What kinds of questions you ask depends on the type of material you are learning as well as on the type or level of analysis your instructor expects. Sample questions for various types of material that you may be required to study are listed in Figure 17-2 on the next page.

Many students who use self-testing as a review strategy are pleasantly surprised when they take their first exam: they discover that some (or many!) of their questions actually appear on the exam. This discovery boosts their confidence during the exam and saves them time as well.

Exercise 4

DIRECTIONS   Write a list of questions that might be asked on an exam covering one of the chapters that you have already read in this book. Answer them and then verify the correctness of your answers by consulting the chapter. ●

TECH SUPPORT

Creating Electronic Flash Cards

Flash cards are a quick and easy way to learn anything from new vocabulary words for your Spanish class to the symbols on the periodic table of elements. While flash cards are most effective for learning brief, objective facts, you can also create flash cards to help you with self-testing. The software program PowerPoint, which can be found on most computers, can help you create flash cards that can be edited and expanded as you learn more about a subject. In addition, free online services such as Flash Card Machine allow you to create and share Web-based flash cards with your classmates. Use the hints in the box "Creating Effective Self-Testing Questions" to create your PowerPoint flash cards.

Figure 17-2
Questions to Provoke Thought

TYPE OF MATERIAL	QUESTIONS
Reports of research studies and experiments	What was the purpose of the study? What are the important facts and conclusions? What are its implications? How can these results be used?
Case studies	What is the case intended to illustrate? What problems or limitations does it demonstrate? To what other situations might this case apply?
Models	How was the model derived? What are its applications? What are its limitations? Do other models of the same process exist?
Current events	What is the significance of the event? What impact will this have in the future? Is there historical precedent?
Supplementary readings	Why did your instructor assign the reading? How is it related to course content? What key points or concepts does the reading contain? Does the reading present a particular viewpoint?
Sample problems	What processes or concepts does the problem illustrate? What is its unique feature? How is it similar to and different from other problems?
Historical data (historical reviews)	Why were the data presented? What trends or patterns are evident? How is this information related to key concepts in the chapter or article?
Arguments	Is the argument convincing? How is the conclusion supported? What persuasive devices does the author use? Do logical flaws exist? Is the author's appeal emotional?
Poetry	What kinds of feelings does the poem evoke? What message or statement is the poet making? How does the poet use language to create feelings?
Essays	What is the author's purpose? What thought patterns are evident? How does the author support his or her key point (thesis)?
Short stories	What does the title mean? Beyond the plot, what does the story really mean? (What is the theme?) What kinds of comments does it make about life? How do the plot, setting, and tone contribute to the overall meaning?

CREATING EFFECTIVE SELF-TESTING QUESTIONS

To construct and answer possible test questions, use the following hints:

1. Do not waste time writing multiple-choice or true/false questions. They are time-consuming to write, and you know the answer before you start.
2. Matching tests are useful, but they are limited to information that requires only factual recall.
3. Open-ended questions that require sentence answers are best because they tend to require more levels of thought.
4. Consult Figure 17-2 for ideas on how to word your questions.
5. You are interested in long-term retention of information, so it is best to write the questions one day and answer them a day or two later.
6. As you answer your questions, respond in complete sentences. Writing complete sentences usually involves more careful and deliberate thought and therefore leads to more effective learning.
7. Take time to review and critique your answers. This process will also contribute to learning.
8. Rewrite any answers that you found to be poor or incomplete. This repetition will facilitate learning.
9. Save your answers, and review them once again the evening before the exam.

Exercise 5

DIRECTIONS   Write a list of questions for an upcoming exam in one of your courses. Answer each one. Save your questions, and after you have taken the exam, mark those that appeared on the exam. (Do not expect the actual questions to use the same wording or format as those you constructed.) ●

Goal 3

Use a learning journal

KEEPING A LEARNING JOURNAL

Some students find it effective to keep a learning journal—an informal written record of the techniques they have tried, how well these techniques worked, and what problems they encountered. Writing the journal helps you to sort and evaluate techniques. The journal also serves as a record and is useful to reread as you revise or consider new approaches. Keep a separate journal (a notebook or computer file) for each of your most challenging courses.

A sample learning journal entry is shown in Figure 17-3. It was written as the student applied several of the techniques in this chapter to her biology textbook.

Figure 17-3
Sample Learning Journal

<u>Paraphrasing</u>   It is difficult not to use the same words. I was unable to find a paraphrase for scientific words. I learned the material very well, though, because I spent so much time thinking about it.

<u>Self-testing</u>   This was very helpful and helped me to focus on important parts of the chapter. I'm going to keep the questions I wrote and use them while studying for the final exam.

<u>SQ3R</u>   This was really effective, and I improved on it by highlighting the answer I found to the question I asked. This helped to focus my reading. Asking and answering the question out loud also helped since i'm an auditory learner. I also drew maps and diagrams and i reread them out loud.

APPLYING LEVELS OF THINKING

Self-Testing and Levels of Thinking

When you use the strategy of self-testing, be sure to ask questions at all six levels of thinking.

Level of Thinking	Types of Questions to Ask
Knowing	What is . . . ? When did . . . ? Who was . . . ?
Understanding	Explain how . . . Define . . . Describe the process by which . . .
Applying	Give an example of how . . . Think of a situation in which . . . How can you use . . . ?
Analyzing	Why does . . . ? What trends are evident?
Evaluating	What is the value, importance, or significance of _____ ? How effectively does . . . ?
Creating	How is _____ related to _____ ? What are the similarities or differences between _____ and _____ ?

WHAT TO INCLUDE IN A LEARNING JOURNAL

Your journal may include a wide range of observations, comments, and reactions. Consider including the following:

1. General reactions to course content
2. Unique features of assignments
3. What you like and what you don't like about the course
4. Problems encountered with a particular assignment
5. Techniques that worked (and *why*)
6. Techniques that didn't work (and *why*)
7. New ideas for approaching the material
8. Changes you made in using various techniques
9. Analysis and reactions to exams after you take them and again when they are returned

HOW TO KEEP A LEARNING JOURNAL

1. Be sure to date your entries and indicate the particular chapters or assignments to which they apply.
2. Record the amount of time spent on each assignment.
3. Once you've made several entries for a particular course, reread your entries and look for patterns. Try to discover what you are doing right, what needs changing, and what changes you'll make.
4. Write an entry summarizing your findings.

DIRECTIONS   For each course you are taking this semester, create a learning journal. Experiment with self-testing as a means of reviewing a particular chapter in each course. Then write a journal entry describing how you used self-testing, how you modified the technique to suit the course, and how effective you felt it to be. ●

Exercise 6

Goal

Use the SQ3R system

A CLASSIC SYSTEM: SQ3R

Psychologist Francis P. Robinson developed a study-reading system called SQ3R that integrates study and review with reading. The SQ3R system, which is based on principles of learning theory, was carefully researched and tested and has been used ever since by millions of students. Continuing experimentation has confirmed its effectiveness. Since that time, SQ3R has been taught to thousands of college students and has become widely recognized as the classic study-reading system.

As a step toward developing your own personalized system, look at SQ3R as a model. Once you see how and why SQ3R works, you can modify or adapt it to suit your own academic needs.

Steps in the SQ3R System

The SQ3R system involves five basic steps that integrate reading and study techniques. As you read the following steps, some of them will seem similar to the skills you have already learned.

S—SURVEY   Try to become familiar with the organization and general content of the material you are to read.

1. **Read the title.**
2. **Read the lead-in or introduction.** (If it is extremely long, read just the first paragraph.)
3. **Read each boldfaced heading and the first sentence that follows it.**
4. **Read titles of maps, charts, or graphs; read the last paragraph or summary.**
5. **Read the end-of-chapter questions.**
6. **After you have surveyed the material, you should know generally what it is about and how it is organized.**

The Survey step is the technique of previewing that you learned in Chapter 6.

Q—QUESTION   Try to form questions that you can answer as you read. The easiest way to do this is to turn each boldfaced heading into a question. (The section of Chapter 6 titled "Defining Your Purposes for Reading" discusses this step in depth.)

R—READ   Read the material section by section. As you read each section, look for the answer to the question you formed from the heading of that section.

R—RECITE   After you finish each section, stop. Check to see whether you can answer your question for the section. If you can't, look back to find the answer. Then check your recall again. Be sure to complete this step after you read each section.

R—REVIEW   When you have finished the whole reading assignment, go back to each heading; recall your question and try to answer it. If you can't recall the answer, be sure to look back and find the answer. Then test yourself again.

The SQ3R method ties together much of what you have already learned about active reading. The first two steps activate your background knowledge and establish questions to guide your reading. The last two steps provide a means of monitoring your comprehension and recall.

Why SQ3R Works

Results of research studies overwhelmingly suggest that students who are taught to use a study-reading system understand and remember what they read much better than students who have not been taught to use such a system.

If you consider for a moment how people learn, it becomes clear why study-reading systems are effective. One major way to learn is through repetition. Consider the way you learned the multiplication tables. Through repeated practice and drills, you learned $2 \times 2 = 4$, $5 \times 6 = 30$, $8 \times 9 = 72$, and so forth. The key was repetition. Study-reading systems provide some of the repetition necessary to ensure learning. Compared with the usual once-through approach to reading textbook assignments, which offer one chance to learn, SQ3R provides numerous repetitions and increases the amount learned.

SQ3R has many psychological advantages over ordinary reading. First, surveying (previewing) gives you a mental organization or structure—you know what to expect. Second, you always feel that you are looking for something specific rather than wandering aimlessly through a printed page. Third, when you find the information you're looking for, it is rewarding; you feel you have accomplished something. And if you can remember the information in the immediate- and long-term recall checks, it is even more rewarding.

DIRECTIONS Read the article titled "Getting Found Out, Web 2.0 Style" beginning on page 480, using the SQ3R method. The following SQ3R worksheet will help you get started. Fill in the required information as you go through each step.

Exercise 7

SQ3R Worksheet

S—Survey: Read the title of the article, the introduction, and each boldfaced heading, and look at any pictures that appear.

1. What is the article about?

   _____

2. What major topics are included?

   _____

Q—Question 1: Turn the first heading into a question.

_____

_____

R—Read: Read the material that follows the first heading, looking for the answer to your question.

R—Recite: Reread the heading and recall the question you asked. Briefly answer this question in your own words without looking at the section. Check to see whether you are correct.

_____

_____

Q—Question 2: Turn the second heading into a question.

_____

_____

R—Read: Read the material that follows the second heading, looking for the answer to your question.

R—Recite: Briefly answer the question.

_____

_____

Q—Question 3: Turn the third heading into a question.

_____

_____

R—Read: Read the material that follows the third heading, looking for the answer to your question.

R—Recite: Briefly answer the question.

_____

_____

Now complete the review step.

R—Review: Look over the entire article by rereading the headings. Try to answer the question you made from each heading.

Answer to Question 1:

_____

_____

Answer to Question 2:

_____

_____

Answer to Question 3:

_____

_____

Check to see that your answers are correct. ●

Goal ⑤

Adapt the SQ3R system to fit your needs

ADAPTING AND REVISING THE SQ3R SYSTEM

Now that you are familiar with the basic SQ3R system, it is time to modify it to suit your specific needs. Figure 17-4 lists the steps in the SQ3R method and indicates how you can expand each step to make it work better for you. Most of the techniques listed have been described in previous chapters, as indicated in the table.

As shown in Figure 17-4, the Survey step is really a get-ready-to-read step, along with the Question step. The Read step becomes much more than simply the see-words step. It involves interacting with the text, thinking, anticipating, and reacting. The Recite step can involve much more than answering the

SQ3R STEPS	ADDITIONAL STRATEGIES
Survey	Preview (Chapter 6) Activate your background and experience (Chapter 6) Predict (Chapter 6)
Question	Ask guide questions (Chapter 6)
Read	Check your understanding (Chapter 6) Highlight and mark (Chapter 15) Anticipate thought patterns (Chapter 8)
Recite	Outline (Chapter 16) Summarize (Chapter 16) Map (Chapter 16)
Review	Paraphrase (Chapter 17) Self-test (Chapter 17) Review highlighting, outlines, and maps (Chapters 15 and 16)

Figure 17-4
Expanding SQ3R

questions posed in the Question step. As you identify important information, grasp relationships, and understand key concepts, you might change your highlighting, add to your marking, write notes or questions, self-test, summarize, outline, or draw maps. The final step, Review, can be expanded to include paraphrasing, self-testing, and the review of highlighting, annotation, outlines, and maps.

One popular modification of the SQ3R system is the addition of a fourth R—"Rite"—creating an SQ4R system. SQ4R recognizes the importance of writing, note taking, outlining, and summarizing in the learning process.

Because critical thinking is an important part of learning, many students add an Evaluate step to the SQ3R system. The Review step assures you that you have mastered the material at the knowledge and comprehension levels of thinking. An Evaluate step encourages you to sit back and *think* about what you have read. To get started, ask yourself questions such as:

- Why is this information important?
- How can I use it?
- How does it fit with the class lectures?
- How is this chapter related to previously assigned ones?
- Does the author provide enough evidence to support his or her ideas?
- Is the author biased?
- What are the author's tone and purpose?

CONSIDERING YOUR LEARNING STYLE

Use the characteristics of your learning style to make SQ3R work for you.

- If you are a visual or spatial learner, draw maps or diagrams that show the chapter organization.
- If you are an auditory learner, record your questions as part of the Question step and Recite your answers to them out loud.
- If you are a social learner, study with a classmate and quiz each other during the Recite step.

Exercise 8

DIRECTIONS   Review the results of the Learning Style Questionnaire on page 28–31. Then write a list of the changes you might make to the SQ3R method for one of your courses. ●

Adapting Your System for Different Academic Disciplines

Various academic disciplines require different kinds of learning. In an English composition and literature class, for example, you learn skills of critical interpretation, whereas in a chemistry course you learn facts, principles, and processes. A history course focuses on events, their causes, their significance, and their long-term trends.

Because different courses require different types of learning, they also require different types of reading and study; therefore, you should develop a specialized study-reading approach for each subject. The following chart lists some of the academic disciplines most commonly studied by beginning college students for which changes in a study-reading system are most important. For each, possible modifications in a study-reading system are suggested.

USING A STUDY-READING SYSTEM ACROSS THE CURRICULUM

Discipline	Kind of Learning	Step(s) to Add	What to Do
Mathematics	Sample problems	1. Study the Problems	• Understand what theory or process the problem illustrates. • Work through and review additional practice problems.
Social Sciences	Basic principles and theories, key terminology, problems and viewpoints	1. Highlight/ Write 2. Vocabulary Review	• Highlight reading assignments. • Write outlines. • Create a vocabulary log of new terms.
Sciences	Facts, principles, formulas, and processes	1. Vocabulary Review 2. Write/ Diagram	• Learn common prefixes, roots, and suffixes. • Write study sheets to summarize information. • Draw diagrams of processes; create part/function diagrams.
Literature	Interpreting, reacting to, and writing about literature	1. Interpret (replaces Recite) 2. React	• Analyze characters, their actions, writer's style, point of view, and theme. • Ask questions such as "What meaning does this have for me?" How effectively did the writer communicate his or her message?" and "Do I agree with this writer's view of life?"

Other Academic Disciplines

This brief chapter does not permit discussion of modifications for every academic discipline. Probably you are taking one or more courses that have not been mentioned. To adapt your study-reading system to these courses, ask yourself the following questions:

1. What type of learning is required? What is the main focus of the course? (Often the preface or the first chapter of your text will answer these questions. The instructor's course outline or objectives may be helpful.)
2. What must I do to learn this type of material?

Learn to "read" the instructor of each course. Find out what each expects, what topics and types of information each feels are important, and how your grades are determined. Talk with other students in the course or with students who have already taken the course to get ideas for useful ways of studying.

DIRECTIONS Three textbook excerpts appear in Part Five (pp. 449, 464, and 474). Each represents a different academic discipline: Discuss how you would modify the SQ3R system to study-read each textbook excerpt. ●

Exercise 9

DIRECTIONS For each of the courses you are taking, explain how you will change your study-reading system to meet its characteristics and requirements. ●

Exercise 10

USING COLLEGE TEXTBOOKS
Adapting SQ3R

SQ3R is an effective way to read and learn the material in college textbooks. Most textbooks use plenty of headings and subheadings. The Q step, "Question," involves using chapter headings to form questions to guide your reading. Be sure to ask questions that will help you focus on the type of information that is important to learn. You have to learn different types of information in different academic disciplines. Be sure to adapt the kinds of questions you ask to suit each discipline. Here are a few examples:

Careers: Focus on Process and Procedures

Textbook Title: *The Paralegal Professional*

CONSTRUCTING A COMPUTER SEARCH QUERY	
Creating a Computer Search ⟵	How do you create a computer search?
Search Method and Query ⟵	What search method should be used?
Creating the Query ⟵	How is the query created?

—Goldman, *Paralegal Professional*, p. 393

History: Focus on Events and Time Sequence, Significance of Events

Textbook Title: *America Past and Present*

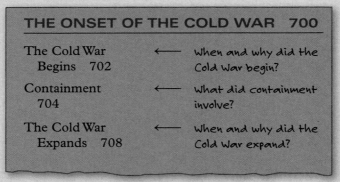

THE ONSET OF THE COLD WAR   700

The Cold War Begins 702	⟵ When and why did the Cold War begin?
Containment 704	⟵ What did containment involve?
The Cold War Expands 708	⟵ When and why did the Cold War expand?

—Divine et al., *America Past and Present*, p. xv

Biology: Focus on Terminology, Characteristics, Cause–Effect Relationships

Textbook Title: *Biology*

The Properties of Water	⟵ What are the properties of water?
The Structure of Water	⟵ What is the structure of water?
Water Is a Good Solvent	⟵ What is a solvent and why is water a good solvent?
Water Facilitates Chemical Reactions	⟵ What are chemical reactions? How does water facilitate chemical reactions?

—Belk, *Biology*, pp. 30–31

FURTHER PRACTICE WITH TEXTBOOK READING

Part A: Sample Textbook Chapter

Use the section titled "Emotion and the Body" and turn each heading into a question. Then read the section and write answers to each of your questions. Ask the kind of questions you expect your instructor to ask you on an exam.

Part B: Your College Textbook

Choose a textbook you are currently using. Choose a section of the textbook and turn each heading into a question. Then read the section and write answers to the questions. Ask the kind of questions you expect your instructor to ask you on an exam.

SELF-TEST
SUMMARY

Goal 1 Why is paraphrasing a useful study strategy?	Paraphrasing, the restatement of a passage's ideas in your own words, is a particularly useful strategy for recording the meaning and checking your comprehension of detailed, complex, precise, or poorly or unusually written passages. When you use your own words rather than the author's, the meaning of the passage is expressed in a clearer and more concise way than the original, making it easier to study and review.
Goal 2 What are the advantages of self-testing?	Self-testing emphasizes interpretation and application of the information being learned. Writing possible exam questions and drafting answers to them causes you to think about and organize ideas and to express them in your own words. It also gives you a way to practice for an upcoming exam.
Goal 3 How can a learning journal help you find the study techniques that work for you?	By keeping a written record of your reactions, comments, and assessments of learning strategies for individual courses, you can discover which strategies work best for you and how to modify them to be even more useful. Rereading your journal entries periodically and summarizing your impressions can help you see what is working, as well as what needs changing and how to change it.
Goal 4 What is the SQ3R study-reading system and why is it effective?	The SQ3R method is a classic five-step method of study and review. The steps are Survey, Question, Read, Recite, and Review. The SQ3R study method has several advantages over ordinary reading. By building a mental framework on which to fit information, searching actively for important facts, going through the repetitions involved in the three Rs, and feeling rewarded when you find the answers to your questions, you can improve your comprehension and recall of study material.
Goal 5 How can you adapt your study-reading system for different academic disciplines?	The SQ3R method should be adapted to suit the unique characteristics of various academic disciplines. The system can also be expanded to include additional and/or newer techniques and strategies. Considering the focus of the course, the type of learning required, and what you must do to learn the material will guide you in adapting and expanding your study-reading system.

APPLYING YOUR SKILLS

DISCUSSING THE CHAPTER

1. In what everyday situations have you used paraphrasing?
2. What makes paraphrasing and self-testing particularly effective?
3. What questions can you ask your professors to improve the effectiveness of self-testing in specific classes?
4. Discuss your use of SQ3R. What worked? What do you need to change?
5. What types of study-reading systems are effective for each learning style represented in your class? Why are these systems effective for each group?

ANALYZING A STUDY SITUATION

Sharon is a visual, conceptual, and pragmatic learner. She is taking an astronomy course and is finding the textbook complicated. She is having difficulty understanding and completing reading assignments. Exams in astronomy are a combination of multiple-choice and essay. She is also taking Introduction to African Americans' Studies. Many of the readings are articles from Web sites about current events and essays about the history of roles. The exam will be an essay exam.

1. What reading techniques and learning strategies using writing would you recommend to Sharon to help her with her astronomy text?
2. How can Sharon prepare for her essay exam? What specific suggestions can you make on the basis of the types of readings assigned for the course?
3. How might Sharon adapt SQ3R for her astronomy course?
4. How might Sharon adapt SQ3R for Introduction to African Americans' Studies?

WORKING ON COLLABORATIVE PROJECTS

DIRECTIONS   Your instructor will divide the class into three groups and select one of the readings in Part Five. As an out-of-class assignment, the members of one group should *only* read the assignment (they should not use SQ3R or preview or review). A second group should preview (see Chapter 6) but should not review. A third group should use the SQ3R system. During the next class meeting, your instructor will quiz you and will report which group earned the highest scores. The class should evaluate their scores and draw conclusions about the relative effectiveness of the study methods used.

PEARSON
myreadinglab   For support in meeting this chapter's goals, go to **MyReadingLab** and select **Test Taking.**

Quick **QUIZ**

DIRECTIONS   Write the letter of the choice that best completes each statement in the space provided.

CHECKING YOUR RECALL

_____ 1. Self-testing is a study strategy that involves
   a. writing and answering possible exam questions.
   b. taking a graded exam at home or in another location outside the class.
   c. rewriting the end-of-chapter questions in a textbook.
   d. using old exams and quizzes to study for an exam.

_____ 2. Of the following self-test questions, the one that requires the highest level of thinking is:
   a. Who were the major literary figures during the Great Depression?
   b. When did Allen Ginsberg write "Howl"?
   c. How does Walt Whitman connect poetic devices and emotion in "To a Locomotive in Winter"?
   d. Where was Langston Hughes born?

_____ 3. The "S" step of SQ3R is similar to
   a. summarizing.
   b. previewing.
   c. outlining.
   d. categorizing.

_____ 4. The Recite step of SQ3R primarily involves
   a. becoming familiar with the organization and general content of the material you are about to read.
   b. forming questions that you can answer as you read.
   c. checking to see if you can answer the questions you formed for each section.
   d. going back over the material once you have read it.

_____ 5. When you are developing your own study-reading system, it is most important to consider
   a. your learning style.
   b. what you dislike most about studying.
   c. how much time each of your assignments requires.
   d. how many of the SQ3R steps you can eliminate.

APPLYING YOUR SKILLS

_____ 6. As part of a music theory assignment, Joshua has been asked to paraphrase an article describing the evolution of the blues. To paraphrase effectively, Joshua should do all of the following *except*
   a. read slowly and carefully.
   b. follow the author's arrangement of ideas.
   c. read the material before writing anything.
   d. paraphrase word by word.

_____ 7. Nora has decided to use paraphrasing to help her learn a chapter in her linguistics textbook. Her primary focus in paraphrasing should be on
   a. evaluating the material for relevance.
   b. recording her reactions to the author's point of view.
   c. thinking of practical applications for the material.
   d. restating the author's meaning in her own words.

_____ 8. Garrett's academic advisor recommends that Garrett begin using a learning journal. Garrett's advisor most likely wants him to
   a. keep track of each week's assignments.
   b. transcribe recorded lectures.
   c. record and evaluate learning strategies.
   d. outline difficult textbook chapters.

_____ 9. Emma is using the SQ3R system to study a chapter in her physics textbook. She should do the Review step of SQ3R
   a. while she is reading the chapter.
   b. while she is forming questions.
   c. after she has completed a section.
   d. after she has completed the assignment.

_____ 10. Luis is creating a study-reading system for a modern fiction course. In this situation, he should probably add a
   a. Study Problems step.
   b. Vocabulary Review step.
   c. Paraphrase step.
   d. React and Interpret step.

Preparing for Exams

LEARNING GOALS

In this chapter you will learn to

1 Organize how you study

2 Figure out what to study

3 Pull together information

4 Review for objective and essay exams

LEARNING EXPERIMENT

Imagine you are taking a statistics class and must learn to calculate the median of a set of numbers.

1 Read the following paragraph defining the term *median*.

Because it can be affected by extremely high or low numbers, the mean is often a poor indicator of central tendency for a list of numbers. In cases like this, another measure of central tendency, called the **median**, can be used. The *median* divides a group of numbers in half; half the numbers lie above the median, and half lie below the median.

Find the median by listing the numbers *in order* from *smallest* to *largest*. If the list contains an *odd* number of items, the median is the *middle number*.

If a list contains an *even* number of items, there is no single middle number. In this case, the median is defined as the mean (average) of the *middle two* numbers.

2 Applying the definition above, find the median of each of the following groups of numbers.

17, 24, 6, 9, 10, 2, 44
7, 13, 9, 4

Which step was more useful in helping you learn the formula?

THE RESULTS

Most students find step 2 more useful. Why? In step 1 all you do is read. In step 2 you apply the explanation to two sets of numbers. Step 2 forces you to use and apply the information contained in step 1. By practicing computing the median, you come to understand it.

LEARNING PRINCIPLE: WHAT THIS MEANS TO YOU

One of the best ways to prepare for a test is to simulate the test conditions. To prepare for an exam, then, practice answering the types of questions you think will be on the test. Do not just read or reread as step 1 required you to do. This chapter will offer many ideas on preparing for exams and will show you ways to study by simulating test conditions for both objective and essay tests. You will also learn how to organize your review, identify what to study, analyze and synthesize information, prepare study sheets, and learn and remember what is important.

WHY LEARN TO PREPARE FOR EXAMS?

Preparing carefully for exams is important because:

- Preparing well for exams helps you tie together the facts and concepts you have learned.
- It helps you achieve better grades.
- It minimizes stress.

ORGANIZING YOUR STUDY AND REVIEW

Studying is the most important thing you can do to increase your chance of passing an exam. When grades are posted you may hear comments like "I spent at least ten hours studying. I went over everything, and I still failed the exam!" Students frequently complain that they spend large amounts of time studying and do not get the grades they think they deserve. Usually the problem is that although they did study, they did not study effectively. The first thing to do, well in advance of the exam, is to get organized. The timing of your review sessions is crucial to achieving good test results. Organize your review sessions, using the suggestions discussed in the following sections.

Goal 1

Organize how you study

myreadinglab

To practice preparing for exams, go to

> Test Taking

Organize Your Time

1. **Schedule several review sessions at least a week in advance of an exam.** Set aside specific times for daily review, and incorporate them into your weekly schedule. If you are having difficulty with a particular subject, set up extra study times.
2. **Spend time organizing your review.** Make a list of all chapters, notes, and handouts that need to be reviewed. Divide the material, planning what you will review during each session.
3. **Reserve time the night before the exam for a final, complete review.** Do not study new material during this session. Instead, review the most difficult material, checking your recall of important facts or information for possible essay questions.

Find Out About the Exam

To prepare effectively for an exam, you need to know as much as possible about it.

1. **Find out whether it will be objective, essay, or a combination of both.** If your instructor does not indicate the type of exam when he or she announces the date, ask during or after class.
2. **Be sure you know what material the exam will cover.** Usually your instructor will either announce the exam topics or give the time span that the exam will cover.
3. **Find out what your instructor expects of you and how he or she will evaluate your exam.** Some instructors expect you to recall text and lecture material; others expect you to agree with their views on a particular subject; still others encourage you to recall, discuss, analyze, or disagree with the ideas and information they have presented. You can usually tell what to expect by the way quizzes have been graded or classes have been conducted.

Attend the Class Before the Exam

Be sure to attend the class prior to the exam. Cutting class to spend the time studying, though tempting, is a mistake. During this class, the instructor may give a brief review of the material to be covered or offer last-minute review suggestions. Have you ever heard an instructor say "Be sure to look over . . ." prior to an exam? Also, listen carefully to how the instructor answers students' questions; these answers will provide clues about what the exam will emphasize.

Consider Studying with Others

Depending on your learning style, it may be helpful to study with another person or with a small group of students from your class. Be sure to weigh the following advantages and disadvantages of group study. Then decide whether group study suits your learning style.

Group study can be advantageous for the following reasons:

1. **Group study helps you to become actively involved with the course content.** Talking about, reacting to, and discussing the material aids learning. If you have trouble concentrating or staying focused when studying alone, group study may be useful.
2. **One of the best ways to learn something is to explain it to someone else.** By using your own words and thinking of the best way to explain an idea, you are analyzing it and testing your own understanding. The repetition involved in explaining something you already understand also strengthens your learning.

Group study can, however, have disadvantages.

1. **Unless everyone is serious, group study sessions can turn into social events in which very little studying occurs.**
2. **Studying with the wrong people can produce negative attitudes that will work against you.** For example, the "None of us understands this and we can't all fail" attitude is common.
3. **By studying with someone who has not read the material carefully or attended classes regularly, you will waste time reviewing basic definitions and facts that you already know, instead of focusing on more difficult topics.**

Exercise 1

DIRECTIONS   Plan a review schedule for an upcoming exam. Include material you will study and when you will study it. ●

Figure out what to study

IDENTIFYING WHAT TO STUDY

In preparing for an exam, review every source of information—textbook chapters and lecture notes—as well as sources sometimes overlooked, such as old exams and quizzes, the instructor's handouts, course outlines, and outside assignments. Talking with other students about the exam can also be helpful.

Textbook Chapters

You must review all chapters that were assigned during the period covered by the exam or that are related to the topics covered by the exam. Review of textbook chapters should be fairly easy if you have kept up with weekly assignments, used your own variation of a study-reading system, and marked and underlined each assignment.

Lecture Notes

In addition to textbook chapters, review all relevant notes. This, too, is easy if you have used the note-taking and editing system presented in Chapter 4.

Previous Exams and Quizzes

Be sure to keep all old tests and quizzes, which are valuable sources of review for longer, more comprehensive exams. Most instructors do not repeat the same test questions, but old quizzes list important facts, terms, and ideas. The comprehensive exam will probably test your recall of the same information through different types of questions.

Visual Thinking
APPLYING SKILLS

What should the student do with this graded assignment to prepare for his or her next exam?

LOOK FOR PATTERNS OF ERROR Pay particular attention to items that you got wrong; try to see a pattern of error.

1. **Are you missing certain types of questions?** If so, spend extra time on these questions.
2. **Are there certain topics on which you lost most of your points?** If so, review these topics.
3. **Are you missing questions at a particular level of thinking?** Use a grid like the one shown in Figure 18-1 to analyze what type of questions you are getting wrong. If you discover, for example, that you are getting knowledge and comprehension questions wrong, include more factual review in your study plans. On the other hand, if you are missing numerous synthesis questions, you need to focus more on drawing connections between and among your study topics.

Level of Question	Exam 1 Wrong Answers	Exam 2 Wrong Answers	Exam 3	Exam 4	Exam 5
Remembering	0	1			
Understanding	2	0			
Applying	7	5			
Analyzing	1	2			
Evaluating	1	0			
Creating	0	0			

Figure 18-1
Sample Grid for Analysis of Errors

IDENTIFY THE LEVELS OF THINKING YOUR INSTRUCTOR EMPHASIZES The grid shown in Figure 18-2 can be used to identify the level of thinking your instructor requires on exams. For example, some instructors may emphasize

Figure 18-2
Sample Grid for Determining Your Instructor's Emphasis

Level of Thinking	Exam 1 Question Numbers	Exam 2 Question Numbers
Remembering	5, 8, 25	
Understanding	1, 3, 18, 19, 21, 22, 24	
Applying	2, 6, 7, 10, 11, 12, 14, 16, 20	
Analyzing	4	
Evaluating	13, 17	
Creating	9, 15, 23	

application; others may focus on analysis and synthesis of information. You can see that the exam analyzed in Figure 18-2 emphasized understanding and application questions. To discover your instructor's emphasis, go through a previous exam, question by question, identifying and marking each question's type in the grid. Once you have discovered your instructor's emphasis, adjust your study methods accordingly. Include more factual review if knowledge and comprehension are emphasized. Be sure to consider practical situations and uses if application questions are frequently asked.

Instructors' Handouts

Instructors frequently distribute duplicated sheets of information, such as summary outlines, lists of terms, sample problems, maps and charts, or explanations of difficult concepts. Any material that an instructor prepares for distribution is bound to be important. As you review these sheets throughout the course, date them and label the lecture topic to which they correspond. Keep them together in a folder or in the front of your notebook so that you can refer to them easily.

Outside Assignments

Out-of-class assignments might include problems to solve, library research, written reactions or evaluations, or lectures or movies to attend. If an instructor gives an assignment outside of class, the topic is important. Because of the limited number of assignments that can be given in a course, instructors choose only those that are most valuable. You should therefore keep your notes on assignments together for easy review.

Talk with Other Students

Talking with classmates can help you identify the right material to learn. By talking with others, you may discover a topic that you have overlooked or recognize a new focus or direction.

Exercise 2

DIRECTIONS   Construct a grid like the one shown in Figure 18-2. Use it to analyze the level(s) of thinking your instructor emphasized on one of your previous exams. ●

Goal 3

Pull together information

ANALYZING AND SYNTHESIZING INFORMATION

Once you have identified what material to learn, the next step is to draw together, analyze, and synthesize the information. Synthesis is an important critical-thinking skill because it forces you to see connections among ideas. In your close study of chapters and lecture notes, it is easy to get lost in details and lose sight of major themes or processes. When concentrating on details, you can miss significant points and fail to see relationships. Exams often measure your awareness of concepts and trends as well as your recall of facts, dates, and definitions. The following suggestions will help you learn to synthesize information.

Get a Perspective on the Course

To avoid focusing too narrowly on details and to obtain perspective on the course material, step back and view the course from a distance. Imagine that all your notes, textbook chapters, outlines, and study sheets are arranged on a table and that you are looking down on them from a peephole in the ceiling. Then ask yourself: What does all that mean? When put together, what does it all show? Why is it important?

Tip *Perspective* means "a way of thinking about something, influenced by one's experiences." The word is similar to *point of view*.

Look for Relationships

Study and review consist of more than just learning facts. Try to see how facts are related. In learning the periodic table of chemical elements, for example, you should do more than just learn names and symbols. You should understand how elements are grouped, what properties the elements in a group share, and how the groups are arranged.

Look for Patterns and the Progression of Thought

Try to see why the material was covered in the order in which it was presented. How is one class lecture related to the next? To what larger topic or theme are several lectures connected? For class lectures, check the course outline or syllabus that was distributed at the beginning of the course. Because it lists major topics and suggests the order in which they will be covered, your syllabus will be useful in discovering patterns.

Similarly, for textbook chapters, try to focus on the progression of ideas. Study the table of contents to see the connection between chapters you have read. Often chapters are grouped into sections based on similar content.

Watch for the progression or development of thought. Ask yourself: What is the information presented in this chapter leading up to? What does it have to do with the chapter that follows? Suppose that in psychology you had covered a chapter on personality traits and next were assigned a chapter on abnormal and deviant behavior. You would want to know what the two chapters have to do with each other. In this case, the first chapter on personality establishes the standards or norms by which abnormal and deviant behavior are determined.

Tip *Deviant* is similar to *abnormal* but sometimes less extreme.

Interpret and Evaluate

Do not let facts and details camouflage important questions. Remember to ask yourself: What does this mean? How is this information useful? How can this be applied to various situations? Once you have identified the literal content, stop, react, and evaluate its use, value, and application.

Tip *Camouflage* means "to hide someone or something by making the person, animal, or thing look like the surroundings or like something different." The word can be a verb or a noun.

Prepare Study Sheets

The study sheet system is a way of organizing and summarizing complex information by preparing a mini-outline. It is most useful for reviewing material that is interrelated, or connected, and needs to be learned as a whole rather than as

Figure 18-3
A Sample Study Sheet

	Problem-Focused Approach	Emotion-Focused Approach
Purpose	solving the problem causing stress	changing or managing the emotions the problems caused
Example	learning about a disability and how to live with it	expressing grief and anger to get them out of your system
How it is accomplished	1. define the problem 2. learn about the problem and how to fix it 3. take steps to fix the problem	1. reappraisal 2. comparisons 3. avoidance 4. humor

separate facts. Types of information that should be reviewed on study sheets include:

1. **Theories and principles**
2. **Complex events with multiple causes and effects**
3. **Controversial issues—pros and cons**
4. **Summaries of philosophical issues**
5. **Trends in ideas or data**
6. **Groups of related facts**

Look at the sample study sheet in Figure 18-3, which was made by a student preparing for a psychology exam that would cover a chapter on stress. Note that the study sheet organizes information on two approaches to coping with stress and presents that information in a form that permits easy comparison.

To prepare a study sheet, first select the information to be learned. Then outline the information, using as few words as possible. Group together important points, facts, and ideas related to each topic.

Exercise 3

DIRECTIONS   Prepare a study sheet for the selection "Impact of the Internet on Thinking"; which begins on page 484 in Part Five. You might use the headings Pro and Con. ●

Exercise 4

DIRECTIONS   Prepare a study sheet for a topic you are studying in one of your courses. Include all the information you need to learn in order to prepare for an exam. ●

LEARNING AND MEMORIZING

Goal **4**

Review for objective
and essay exams

The methods and procedures you use to learn and to remember information depend on the type of exam for which you are preparing. You would study and learn information differently for a multiple-choice test than for an essay exam.

Exams can be divided into two basic types: objective and essay. Objective tests include short-answer questions in which you choose one or more answers from several that are given, or supply a word or phrase to complete a statement. Multiple-choice, true/false, matching, and fill-in-the-blank questions appear on objective tests. In each of these, the questions are constructed so that the answers you choose are either right or wrong; scoring is completely objective, or free from judgment.

Essay tests require you to answer questions in your own words. You have to recall information, organize it, and present it in an acceptable written form. This is different from recognizing the correct answer among several choices or recalling a word or phrase. Because essay exams differ from objective tests, you must use different methods in preparing and reviewing for them.

Review for Objective Tests

Objective tests usually require you to recognize the right answer. On a multiple-choice test, for example, you have to pick the correct answer from the choices given. On matching tests, you have to recognize which two items go together. One goal in reviewing for objective tests, then, is to become so familiar with the course material that you can recognize and select the right answers.

USE HIGHLIGHTING AND MARKING   Your highlighting of reading assignments can be used in several ways for review.

1. **Reread your highlighting in each chapter.**
2. **Read the chapter's boldfaced headings and form a question for each, as you did in the Question step in the SQ3R system.**
3. **Try to answer your question; then check your highlighting to see whether you were correct.**
4. **Review special marks you may have included**. If, for example, you marked new or important definitions with a particular symbol, then you should go through the chapter once and note these terms, checking your recall of their meanings.

USE THE RECALL CLUES IN YOUR LECTURE NOTES   Your recall clues are an important tool for reviewing lecture content.

1. **Go back through each set of lecture notes and check your recall by using the marginal recall clue system.**
2. **Test yourself by asking questions and trying to remember answers.** Mark in red ink things you have trouble remembering.
3. **Use ink of a different color the second time you go through your notes, marking information you still can't recall.**

USE STUDY AIDS Use all study sheets, outlines, summaries, and organizational charts and diagrams that you have prepared to review and learn course content. To learn the information on a study sheet or outline, follow these steps:

1. **Read through it several times.**
2. **Take the first topic, write it on a sheet of paper, and see whether you can fill in the information under the topic on your study sheet or outline.**
3. **If you can't recall all the information, test yourself until you have learned it.**
4. **Continue in this way with each topic.**

USE THE INDEX CARD SYSTEM The index card system is an effective way of reviewing for objective tests. Using 3-by-5-inch index cards (or just small sheets of paper), write part of the information on the front, the remainder on the back. To review the dates of important events, write the date on the front, the event on the back; to review vocabulary, put each term on the front of a card and its definition on the back. See the sample index cards shown in Figure 18-4, which were made by a student preparing for an objective exam in biology.

To study these cards, follow these steps:

1. **Look at the front of each and try to remember what is written on the back.** Then turn the card over to see whether you are correct.
2. **As you go through your pack of cards, sort them into two stacks—those you know and those you don't remember.**
3. **Then go back through the stack of those you don't know, study each, and retest yourself, again sorting the cards into two stacks.**
4. **Continue this procedure until you are satisfied that you have learned all the information.**

Figure 18-4
Sample Study Cards

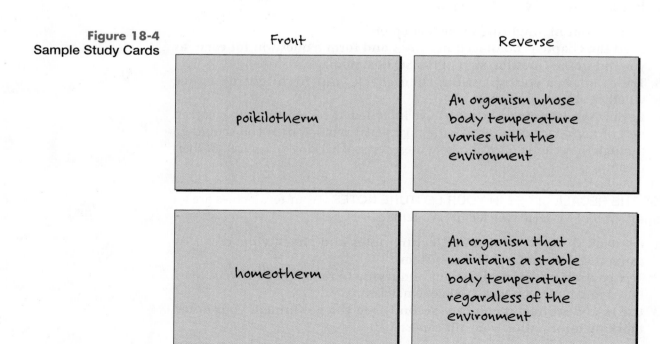

Front   Reverse

poikilotherm

An organism whose body temperature varies with the environment

homeotherm

An organism that maintains a stable body temperature regardless of the environment

5. **Go through your cards in this manner two or three times a day for three or four days before the exam.**
6. **On the day of your exam, do a final, once-through review so that the information is fresh in your mind.**

The index card system is more appropriate for learning brief facts than for reviewing concepts, ideas, and principles or for understanding sequences of events, theories, and cause–effect relationships. For this reason, it works best when you are studying for objective tests that include short-answer questions such as fill-in-the-blanks.

TEST YOURSELF   Check to be sure you have learned all the necessary facts and ideas. By testing yourself before the instructor tests you, you are preparing in a realistic way for the exam. If you were entering a marathon race, you would prepare for the race by running—not by playing golf. The same is true of test taking; you should prepare for a test by testing yourself—not by simply rereading chapters or pages of notes. You can test yourself in any of the following ways:

1. **Use recall clues for your lecture notes.** (See Chapter 4, p. 83.)
2. **Draw and label maps.** (See Chapter 16, p. 353.)
3. **Write partially completed outlines.** Fill in the blanks from memory.
4. **Use vocabulary cards.** (See Chapter 12, p. 266.)
5. **Work with a classmate, testing each other by making up sample questions and answering them.**

DIRECTIONS   Prepare a set of index cards (at least 20) for a chapter or section of a chapter you are studying in one of your courses. Then learn the information on the cards, using the sorting technique described in this section. ●

Exercise 5

Review for Essay Exams

Essay exams demand extensive recall. Starting with a blank sheet of paper, you are required to retrieve from your memory all the information that answers the question. Then you must organize that information and express your ideas about it in acceptable written form.

To review for an essay exam, first identify topics that may be included in the exam. Then predict actual questions and write outline or rough-draft answers.

SELECT PROBABLE TOPICS   In choosing topics to study, you attempt to predict what questions will be included on the exam. There are several sources from which you can choose topics:

1. **Boldfaced textbook headings usually identify important topics or subtopics.**
2. **End-of-chapter discussion questions and recall clues written in the margins of your lecture notes may also suggest topics.**
3. **The course outline distributed by your instructor at the beginning of the course frequently contains a list of major topics.**

STUDY THE TOPICS SELECTED   To effectively study the topics you have chosen, do the following:

1. **Identify aspects of each topic that might be tested.**
2. **Use clues from your instructor as a guideline.** What does he or she emphasize? Causes and effects? Events? Research? Theories? Historical significance? Similarities and differences?

WRITE POSSIBLE QUESTIONS   Next, write actual questions that you think your instructor might ask. Study the sample essay questions in Figure 19-1 on page 416 to get an idea of how they are written. Be sure to predict questions at all levels of thinking.

APPLYING LEVELS OF THINKING

Preparing for Essay Exams and Levels of Thinking

Level of Thinking	What to Ask
Knowing and Understanding	These levels require recall of facts; remembering dates, names, definitions, and formulas falls into these categories. The five "W" questions—Who? What? Where? When? and Why?—are useful to ask.
Applying	This level of thinking requires you to use or apply information. The following two questions best test this level: In what practical situations would this information be useful? What does this have to do with what I already know about the subject?
Analyzing	Analysis involves seeing relationships. Ask questions that test your ability to take ideas apart, find cause–effect relationships, and discover how things work.
Evaluating	This level involves making judgments and assessing value or worth. Ask questions that challenge sources, accuracy, long-term value, importance, and so forth.
Creating	This level involves pulling ideas together. Ask questions that force you to look at similarities and differences.

WRITE OUTLINE OR ROUGH-DRAFT ANSWERS   Once you have identified possible exam questions, the next step is to practice answering them.

1. **Collect and organize the information you would include in your answer.**
2. **Do not take the time to write out full, complete sentences.**
3. **Write your answer in brief note or outline form, listing the information you would include.**

USE KEY-WORD OUTLINES   As a convenient way to remember what your draft answer includes, make a key-word outline of your answer. For each item in your draft, identify a key word that will trigger your memory of that idea. Then list and learn these key words. Together, these words form a mini-outline of topics and ideas to include in an essay on this topic. A key-word outline is shown in Figure 18-5. It is a mini-outline for the study sheet shown on p. 394.

TECH SUPPORT

Organizing Textbook and Lecture Notes
To pull together information on each topic you identified as a possible exam question, you need to integrate text and lecture information.

- Use your computer to create a study sheet for each question.
- Cut and paste sections of lecture notes and textbook chapter outlines or maps into a separate file for each topic.
- Test your recall of the information you have collected by writing rough draft outlines from memory, without referring to the study sheet.

> Problem vs. Emotion
> Purpose
> Example
> how accomplished

Figure 18-5
A Sample Key-Word Outline

Predicting and answering possible examination questions is effective for several reasons. Predicting forces you to analyze the material, not just review it. Drafting answers forces you to express ideas in written form. Through writing, you will recognize relationships, organize your thoughts, and discover the best way to present them.

Exercise 6

DIRECTIONS Assume you are preparing for an essay exam in one of your courses. Predict several questions that might be asked for one textbook chapter and write them in the space provided. Try to write questions that require different levels of thinking.

_____

_____

_____

_____

_____ ●

Exercise 7

DIRECTIONS Choose one of the essay exam questions that you wrote in Exercise 6. Prepare a study sheet that summarizes the information on the topic. Then reduce that information on your study sheet to a key-word outline. ●

USING COLLEGE TEXTBOOKS
Using Self-Test Questions

Just because you have read a textbook chapter does not mean you have learned it. To help you learn chapter content, many textbooks include self-test questions interspersed throughout the chapters and/or at the end of chapters. Here are some suggestions for how to use them.

1. **Answer in-chapter questions *while* you are reading.** If you are unable to answer the question, this is a signal that you need to go back and reread the section. Mark in your notes that this is a section you had difficulty with.

SO FAR . . .

1. Under the biological species concept, species are defined by their _____ behavior.

2. The critical factor leading to speciation is reduced _____ between two _____ of the same species.

3. Two factors always play a part in allopatric speciation: first, the development of _____ and second, the development of one or more _____.

—Krogh, *Biology,* p. 334

CONCEPT CHECK

1. Fission and fusion are opposite processes, yet each releases energy. Isn't this contradictory?

2. To get a release of nuclear energy from the element iron, should iron undergo fission or fusion?

CHECK YOUR ANSWERS

1. No, no, no! This is contradictory only if the same element is said to release energy by both fission and fusion. Only the fusion of light elements and the fission of heavy elements result in a decrease in nucleon mass and a release of energy.

2. Neither, because iron is at the very bottom of the "energy valley." Fusing a pair of iron nuclei produces an element to the right of iron on the curve, in which the mass per nucleon is higher. If you split an iron nucleus, the products will lie to the left of iron on the curve and again have a higher mass per nucleon. So no energy is released. For energy release, "decrease mass" is the name of the game—any game, chemical or nuclear.

—Suchocki, *Conceptual Chemistry,* p. 145

2. **Read end-of-chapter questions through before you begin the chapter.** These will serve as a list of what you should pay particular attention to as you read.

3. **Answer end-of-chapter questions once you have completed the chapter.** If you are unable to answer the questions, go back and review the section in question. After answering a question, find the relevant section in your notes and make sure you have answered the question correctly.

TESTING YOUR COMPREHENSION

1. In what ways are campus sustainability efforts relevant to sustainability efforts in the broader society?

2. Describe one way in which campus sustainability proponents have addressed each of the following areas: (1) recycling and waste reduction, (2) "green" building, and (3) water conservation.

—Withgott, *Environment*, p. 688

SAMPLE TEST QUESTIONS

MULTIPLE CHOICE

These multiple-choice questions are similar to those found in the test bank that accompanies this textbook.

1. Which of these statements is TRUE of marriages in all cultures?

   a. Marriage is a legal union between one man and one woman.
   b. Marriage is a voluntary union between two parties.
   c. Marriage establishes rights and obligations related to gender.
   d. Marriage is only legally recognized if individuals are over the age of 16.

2. Which of these is NOT a current trend in modern households?

   a. fewer marriages
   b. fewer children
   c. delayed marriage
   d. more nuclear families

—Kunz, *Think Marriage and Families*, p. 21

FURTHER PRACTICE WITH TEXTBOOK READING
Part A: Sample Textbook Chapter

After reading the entire chapter, answer the "Test Your Understanding" questions on page 501 to evaluate your understanding.

Part B: Your College Textbook

Choose a textbook you are currently using. Read a chapter and then answer the self-test questions throughout the chapter or at the end to evaluate your understanding of the material. If the chapter does not have questions, write questions and then answer them.

SELF-TEST SUMMARY

Goal 1

How can you get organized to study and review for exams?

Organizing for study and review requires planning and scheduling your time so that you can review all the material carefully and thoroughly. You should begin at least a week before the exam to plan what material you will study each day and at what specific times you will study, and you should plan time for a complete review the evening before the exam. Attending the last class before the exam can provide you with useful hints, and group study can be helpful for certain individuals and circumstances.

Goal 2

How can you identify what to study?

In order to identify what to study, it is important to review all of your sources of information. To determine what material is to be learned, you should review all textbook chapters assigned, your lecture notes, exams and quizzes you have taken, classroom handouts, and notes on outside assignments. From these sources and discussion with other students, you will arrive at the topics most likely to be covered on the exam.

Goal 3

How can you organize these facts and ideas and synthesize them into a meaningful body of information to be studied?

To synthesize the information presented in a course, it is helpful to "step back" and look at the larger picture of the meaning of the course. Look at relationships between ideas, note patterns in the course syllabus and your textbook's table of contents, and see past the details to the important questions regarding the use, value, and application of this information. Preparing study sheets or mini-outlines can help in this process.

Goal 4

How can you best learn and memorize the information for objective and essay exams?

Learning and memorizing, the final steps in preparing for exams, require learning the material in a manner that is appropriate for the type of exam you will take. For objective exams, you should review all highlighting and marking, the recall clues in your lecture notes, and any study aids you have prepared throughout the course. By using the index card system and testing yourself, you can be sure you have learned all the important facts and ideas. For essay exams, you should begin by predicting probable exam questions. Next, you should study the topics selected by preparing a study sheet from which you can review and write a clear, concise essay. Finally, prepare a key-word outline or mini-outline that will guide you when writing answers to the questions you predicted earlier.

APPLYING YOUR SKILLS

DISCUSSING THE CHAPTER

1. Under what conditions have study groups been effective in helping you study?
2. What are some ground rules your group could establish to help ensure your valuable time is spent well?
3. Review several previous exams, quizzes, or tests from one of your other courses. Discuss whether this review was beneficial.

ANALYZING A STUDY SITUATION

Kimberly is taking a psychology course in which grades are based on four multiple-choice exams. Each exam contains 50 items worth two points and is machine scored. When exams are returned, students receive their answer sheets but do not receive the questions themselves. On the first exam, Kimberly earned 68 points, which is a high D grade. For the second exam, she spent more time studying but only earned 72, a C–. When Kimberly visited her instructor in her office and asked for advice on how to improve her grade, the instructor handed Kimberly copies of the first two exams and said, "Spend a half hour or so with each of these; I'm sure you'll discover what's going wrong."

1. What things should Kimberly look for in the exams?
2. What kinds of notes should she make, if any, about the exams?
3. How should Kimberly use each of the following in preparing for her next multiple-choice exam?
   - index cards
   - lecture notes
   - summaries of textbook chapters

WORKING ON COLLABORATIVE PROJECTS

DIRECTIONS   Each student should write five essay questions based on one of the readings included in Thematic Group C, "Technology and the Internet," in Part Five, pages 473–86. Working in groups of three or four students, compare and evaluate your questions, revise several strong ones, and categorize each question using the levels of thinking described in Chapter 2 on page 42. Finally, choose one question to submit to the class. After each group has presented its question, the class will identify the level(s) of thinking that each question demands and discuss which is the hardest and which is the easiest.

For support in meeting this chapter's goals, go to **MyReadingLab** and select **Test Taking**.

Quick **QUIZ**

DIRECTIONS Write the letter of the choice that best completes each statement in the space provided.

CHECKING YOUR RECALL

_____ 1. As you prepare for an exam, you should do all of the following *except*
   a. spend time organizing your review.
   b. skip the class prior to the exam so you can study.
   c. find out what type of exam it will be.
   d. set aside specific times for daily review.

_____ 2. The best reason to review previous exams and quizzes before an exam is to
   a. try to identify important facts, terms, and ideas.
   b. look for questions that will be repeated on the exam.
   c. eliminate some areas of study.
   d. replace extensive textbook review.

_____ 3. A common mistake students make when studying for an exam is to
   a. begin reviewing too far ahead of the exam.
   b. study with other students.
   c. look for relationships among ideas.
   d. fail to interpret facts and details.

_____ 4. A study sheet is most similar to
   a. a mini-outline.
   b. an organizational chart.
   c. a self-test.
   d. a learning journal.

_____ 5. Of the following review situations, index cards would be most useful for
   a. comparing Thoreau and Whitman for a literature class.
   b. studying the theory of relativity in physics.
   c. learning definitions for an anatomy and physiology class.
   d. studying the events leading up to America's involvement in Vietnam for a history class.

APPLYING YOUR SKILLS

_____ 6. By looking at old exams, Evan has determined that his marketing instructor tends to emphasize essay questions at the application level of thinking. Therefore, Evan should predict essay questions that ask students to
   a. recall facts, dates, names, and definitions.
   b. use information in practical situations.
   c. find cause–effect relationships.
   d. assess the long-term value of the information.

_____ 7. Alicia is studying her American government textbook before an exam. If she wanted to find out the textbook's progression of ideas, she would probably consult the text's
   a. appendix.
   b. preface.
   c. table of contents.
   d. first chapter.

_____ 8. Sheri has analyzed her patterns of error on history exams and discovered that she frequently gets knowledge and comprehension questions wrong. One way she should adjust her study methods is to focus more on
   a. connections between topics.
   b. factual review.
   c. practical situations and uses.
   d. out-of-class assignments.

_____ 9. Keith is preparing for an essay exam in his world history class. The first step Keith should take is to
   a. identify topics that may be included on the exam.
   b. predict actual questions.
   c. write sample essay answers.
   d. create a key-word outline.

_____ 10. Spencer is preparing for an essay test. He should use a key-word outline to
   a. trigger his memory of ideas he wants to include in an essay.
   b. serve as a guide for study and review.
   c. organize his study.
   d. test his understanding of a topic.

Taking Exams

LEARNING GOALS

In this chapter you will learn to

1 Use tips for taking exams

2 Use strategies to perform better on objective exams

3 Use strategies to perform better on standardized tests

4 Use strategies to perform better on essay exams

5 Control test anxiety

LEARNING EXPERIMENT

1 Here is a multiple-choice test item from a psychology exam:

Modern psychological researchers maintain that the mind as well as behavior can be scientifically examined primarily by

   a. observing behavior and making inferences about mental functioning.
   b. observing mental activity and making inferences about behavior.
   c. making inferences about behavior.
   d. direct observation of behavior.

If you know the correct answer, circle it now.

2 If you did not know the correct answer, use your reasoning skills to determine the best answer and circle it.

Hints:
1. Which choices do *not* refer to both the mind and behavior? (Answer: choices c and d)

2. Which choice contains an activity that cannot be easily done? (Answer: b—mental activity cannot be observed without specialized medical equipment.)

THE RESULTS

Using the hints above, you probably were able to eliminate choices b, c, and d.

LEARNING PRINCIPLE: WHAT THIS MEANS TO YOU

Although you probably did not know the correct answer, you were able to figure it out. **When taking exams, trust your reasoning skills to help you figure out correct answers.** In this chapter you will learn how to sharpen your reasoning skills for all types of exams. The manner in which you approach an exam, how you read and answer objective questions, and how carefully you read, organize, and write your answers to an essay exam can influence your grade. This chapter discusses each of these aspects of becoming test-wise and also considers a problem that interferes with many students' ability to do well on exams: test anxiety.

WHY LEARN HOW TO TAKE EXAMS?

Learning how to take exams is important because:

- You will be required to take plenty of exams in your college career.
- Exams may be an important part of admission to graduate school, the job application process, and licensing and certification for various careers.
- Knowing how to approach an exam can earn you extra grade points.

Goal **1**

Use tips for taking exams

GENERAL SUGGESTIONS FOR TAKING EXAMS

The following suggestions will help you approach classroom exams in an organized, systematic way.

To practice taking exams, go to

> Test Taking

Bring Necessary Materials

When going to any exam, be sure to take along any materials you might be asked or allowed to use. Be sure you have an extra pen, and take a pencil in case you must make a drawing or diagram. Take paper—you may need it for computing figures or writing essay answers. Take along anything you have been allowed to use throughout the semester, such as a pocket calculator, conversion chart, or dictionary. If you are not sure whether you may use them, ask the instructor.

Get There on Time

It is important to arrive at the exam room on time, or a few minutes early, to get a seat and get organized before the instructor arrives. If you are late, you may miss instructions and feel rushed as you begin the exam.

If you arrive too early (15 or more minutes ahead), you risk anxiety induced by panic-stricken students questioning each other, trading last-minute memory tricks, and worrying about how difficult the exam will be.

Sit in the Front of the Room

If you have a choice, the most practical place to sit in an exam room is at the front. There you often receive the test first and get a head start. There, also, you are sure to hear directions and corrections and can easily read any changes written on the board. Finally, it is easier to concentrate at the front of the room. At the back, you are exposed to distractions, such as a student dropping papers or cheating, or the person in front who is already two pages ahead of you.

Preview the Exam

Before you start to answer any of the questions, take a minute or two to quickly page through the exam, noting the directions, the length, the types of questions, and the general topics covered. Previewing provides an overview of the whole exam. Previewing also helps eliminate the panic you may feel if you go right to the first few questions and find that you are unsure of the answers.

Plan Your Time

After previewing the exam, you will know the number and types of questions included. You should then estimate how much time you will spend on each part of the exam. The number of points each section is worth (the point distribution) should be your guide. If, for example, one part of an exam has 20 multiple-choice questions worth one point each and another part has two essays worth 40 points each, you should spend much more time answering the essay questions than working through the multiple-choice items. If the point distribution is not indicated on the test booklet, you may want to ask the instructor what it is.

As you plan your time, be sure to allow three to four minutes at the end of the exam to review what you have done, answering questions you skipped and making any necessary corrections or changes.

To keep track of time, wear a watch. Many classrooms do not have wall clocks, or you may be sitting in a position where the clock is difficult to see.

If you were taking an exam with the following distribution of questions and points, how would you divide your time? Assume the total exam time is 50 minutes.

Type of Question	Number of Questions	Total Points
Multiple-choice	25 questions	25 points
True/false	20 questions	20 points
Essay	2 questions	55 points

You should probably divide your time like this:

Previewing	1–2 minutes
Multiple-choice	15 minutes
True/false	10 minutes
Essay	20 minutes
Review	3–4 minutes

Because the essays are worth twice as many points as either of the other two parts of the exam, it is necessary to spend twice as much time on the essay portion.

DIRECTIONS For each of the exams described below, estimate how you would divide your time.

Exercise 1

1. Time limit: 75 minutes

Type of Question	Number of Questions	Total Points
Multiple-choice	20 questions	40 points
Matching	10 questions	10 points
Essay	2 questions	50 points

How would you divide your time?

Previewing	_____ minutes
Multiple-choice	_____ minutes

Matching   _____ minutes

Essay   _____ minutes

Review   _____ minutes

2. Time limit: 50 minutes

Type of Question	Number of Questions	Total Points
True/false	15 questions	30 points
Fill in the blank	15 questions	30 points
Short answer	10 questions	40 points

How would you divide your time?

Previewing   _____ minutes

True/false   _____ minutes

Fill in the blank   _____ minutes

Short answer   _____ minutes

Review   _____ minutes ●

Read the Questions Carefully

Most instructors word their questions so that what is expected is clear. A common mistake students make is to read more into the question than is asked for. To avoid this error, read the question several times, paying attention to how it is worded. If you are uncertain what is asked for, try to relate the question to the course content. Don't anticipate hidden meanings or trick questions.

TECH SUPPORT

Taking an Exam on a Computer
Use the following tips for taking computerized exams:

1. Don't wait until the due date to take the exam. Last minute computer problems or connection issues may force you to miss the deadline.
2. Avoid technical problems and glitches by taking the exam on a computer you are familiar with. Close all other programs so nothing interferes with the exam's operation or interrupts your thought.
3. Wait until the exam is fully loaded on your computer before you start working on it.
4. Read the instructions closely to be sure you move forward and backward correctly, use the right format for entering responses, and submit your final answers properly.
5. If you are uncomfortable with computerized exams, ask if a print exam is available.

Goal ②

Use strategies to perform better on objective exams

HINTS FOR TAKING OBJECTIVE EXAMS

When taking objective exams—usually true/false, matching, short answer, fill in the blank, or multiple choice—remember the following hints, which may net you a few more points.

General Hints for Objective Exams

1. **Read the directions.** Before answering any questions, read the directions. Often an instructor may want the correct answer marked in a particular way (underlined rather than circled). The directions may contain crucial information that you must know in order to answer the questions correctly. If you were to ignore directions such as the following and assume the test questions were of the usual type, you could lose a considerable number of points.

   True/False Directions

   Read each statement. If the statement is true, mark a T in the blank to the left of the item. If the statement is false, add and/or subtract words in such a way as to make the statement true.

   Multiple-Choice Directions

   Circle all the choices that correctly complete the statement.

   Without reading the true/false directions, you would not know that you should correct incorrect statements. Without reading the multiple-choice directions, you would not know that you are to choose more than one answer.

2. **Leave nothing blank.** Before turning in your exam, be sure you have answered every question. If you have no idea about the correct answer to a question, guess—you might be right. On a true/false test, your chances of being correct are 50 percent; on a four-choice multiple-choice question, your odds are 25 percent.

   Students frequently turn in tests with some items unanswered because they leave difficult questions blank, planning to return to them later. Then, in the rush to finish everything, they forget to go back to them. The best way to avoid this problem is to enter what look like the best answers and mark the question numbers with an X or a check mark; then, if you have time at the end of the exam, you can give them more thought. If you run out of time, at least you will have attempted to answer them.

3. **Look for clues.** If you encounter a difficult question, choose what seems to be the best answer, mark the question so that you can return to it, and keep the item in mind as you go through the rest of the exam. Sometimes you will see some piece of information later in the exam that reminds you of a fact or idea. At other times you may notice information that, if true, contradicts an answer you have already chosen.

4. **Don't change answers without good reason.** When reviewing your exam answers, don't make a change unless you have a specific reason for doing so. If a later test item made you remember information for a previous item, by all means make a change. If, however, you are just having second thoughts about an answer, leave it alone. Your first guess is usually the best one.

Hints for Taking True/False Tests

1. **Watch for words that qualify or change the meaning of a statement; often, just one word makes it true or false, as in the following oversimplified example.**

   All dogs are white.

   Some dogs are white.

On college true/false exams, you will find that one word often determines whether a statement is true or false.

All paragraphs must have a stated main idea.

Spelling, punctuation, and handwriting *always* affect the grade given to an essay answer.

When taking notes on a lecture, try to write down *everything* the speaker says.

Also watch for words that specific degree (**usually, commonly**), quantity, (**most, several**) or change in amount (**increase, reduce**).

Overlooking these words may cost you several points on an exam.

2. **Read two-part statements carefully.** Occasionally, you may find a statement with two or more parts. In answering these items, remember that both or all parts of the statement must be true in order for it to be correctly marked true. If part of the statement is true and another part is false, then mark the statement false.

The World Health Organization (WHO) has been successful in its campaign to eliminate smallpox and malaria.

Although it is true that WHO has been successful in eliminating smallpox, malaria is still a world health problem and has not been eliminated. Because only part of this statement is true, it should be marked false.

3. **Look for negative and double-negative statements.** Test items that use negative words or word parts can be confusing. Words such as *no, none, never, not,* and *cannot* and beginnings of words such as *in-, dis-, un-, it-,* and *ir-* are easy to miss and always alter the meaning of the statement. Make it a habit to underline or circle negative statements in items as you read.

Statements that contain two negatives, such as the following, are even more confusing.

It is not unreasonable to expect returning veterans to continue to suffer post-traumatic stress disorder years after their discharge.

In reading these statements, remember that two negatives balance or cancel out each other. "Not unreasonable," then, can be interpreted to mean "reasonable."

If you encounter such statements, rephrase them in your own words; then you will probably know the correct answer.

4. **Make your best guess.** When all else fails and you are unable to reason out the answer to an item, use these three last-resort rules of thumb:

- **Absolute statements tend to be false.** Because there are very few things that are always true and for which there are no exceptions, your best guess is to mark statements that contain words such as *always, all, never,* or *none* as false.
- **Mark any item that contains unfamiliar terminology or facts as false.** If you've studied the material thoroughly, trust that you would recognize as true anything that was a part of the course content.
- **When all else fails, it is better to guess true than false.** It is more difficult for instructors to write false statements than true statements. As a result, many exams have more true items than false.

DIRECTIONS   The following true/false test is based on content presented in the reading "The Genetic Crystal Ball" in Part Five on page 464. Read each item. In the space provided at the left, indicate whether the statement is true or false by marking T for true and F for false. "Then find and underline the single word that, if changed or deleted, could change the truth or falsity of the statement."

Exercise 2

——— 1. Society is already struggling with questions about the proper use of our expanding knowledge of human genetics.

——— 2. Human DNA always consists of 23 chromosones.

——— 3. All parents will want to use genetic testing to evaluate the health (or even the eye color) of their future children.

——— 4. Some people urge caution in genetic research, warning that genetic information can easily be abused.

——— 5. Genetic screening could let people know their medical destiny and allow doctors to manipulate segments of DNA to prevent diseases before they appear. ●

Hints for Taking Matching Tests

Matching tests require you to select items in one list that can be paired with items in a second list. Use the following tips to complete matching tests:

1. **Before answering any items, glance through both lists to get an overview of the subjects and topics the test covers.** Next, try to discover a pattern. Are you asked to match dates with events, terms with meanings, people with accomplishments?
2. **Answer the items you are sure of first, lightly crossing off items as you use them.**
3. **Don't choose the first answer you see that seems correct; items later in the list may be better choices.**
4. **If the first column consists of short words or phrases and the second is made up of lengthy definitions or descriptions, save time by "reverse matching."** That is, look for the word or phrase in column 1 that fits each item in column 2.

Hints for Taking Short-Answer Tests

Short-answer tests require you to write a brief answer, usually in list or sentence form. Here is an example:

List three events that increased U.S. involvement in the Vietnam War.

In answering short-answer questions, be sure to:

1. **Use point distribution as a clue to how many pieces of information to include.** For a nine-point item asking you to describe the characteristics of a totalitarian government, give at least three ideas.
2. **Plan what you will say before starting to write.**
3. **Use the amount of space provided, especially if it varies for different items, as a clue to how much you should write.**

Hints for Taking Fill-in-the-Blank Tests

Items that ask you to fill in a missing word or phrase within a sentence require recall of information rather than recognition of the correct answer. It is important, therefore, to look for clues that will trigger your recall.

1. **Look for key words in the sentence, and use them to decide what subject matter and topic the item covers.**
2. **Decide what type of information is required.** Is it a date, name, place, or new term?
3. **Use the grammatical structure of the sentence to determine the type of word called for.** Is it a noun, verb, or qualifier?

Hints for Taking Multiple-Choice Tests

Multiple-choice exams are among the most frequently used types of exams and are often the most difficult. The following suggestions should improve your success in taking multiple-choice tests.

1. **Read all choices first, considering each.** Do not stop with the second or third choice, even if you are sure that you have found the correct answer. Remember, on most multiple-choice tests, your job is to pick the *best* answer, and the last choice may be better than the preceding answers.
2. **Be alert for questions that include combinations of previously listed choices.** See the following test item:

   Among the causes of slow reading is (are)

   a. lack of comprehension.
   b. reading word by word rather than in phrases.
   c. poorly developed vocabulary.
   d. making too few fixations per line.
   e. a and b
   f. a, b, and c
   g. a, b, c, and d

   The addition of choices that are combinations of previous choices tends to be confusing. Treat each choice, when combined with the stem, as a true or false statement. As you consider each choice, mark it true or false. If you find more than one true statement, select the choice that contains the letters of all the true statements you identified.
3. **Use logic and common sense.** Even if you are unfamiliar with the subject matter, it is sometimes possible to reason out the correct answer. The following item is taken from a history exam on Japanese–American relations after World War II:

   Prejudice and discrimination are

   a. harmful to our society because they waste our economic, political, and social resources.
   b. helpful because they ensure against attack from within.
   c. harmful because they create negative images of the United States in foreign countries.
   d. helpful because they keep the majority pure and united against minorities.

Through logic and common sense, it is possible to eliminate choices b and d. Prejudice and discrimination are seldom, if ever, regarded as positive, desirable, or helpful, because they are inconsistent with democratic ideals. Having narrowed your answer to two choices, a or c, you can see that choice a offers a stronger, more substantial reason why prejudice and discrimination are harmful. What other countries think of the United States is not as serious as the waste of economic, political, and social resources.

4. **Study any items that are very similar.** When two choices seem very close and you cannot choose between them, stop and examine each. First, try to express each in your own words. Then analyze how they differ. Often this process will lead you to recognize the correct answer.

5. **Look for qualifying words.** As in true/false tests, the presence of qualifying words is important. Because many statements, ideas, principles, and rules have exceptions, you should be careful in selecting items that contain such words as *best, always, all, no, entirely,* and *completely,* all of which suggest that something is always true, without exception. Also be careful of statements that contain such words as *none, never,* and *worst,* which suggest things that without exception are never true. Items containing words that provide for some level of exception or qualification are more likely to be correct; a few examples are *often, usually, less, seldom, few, more,* and *most.*

   In the following example, note the use of italicized qualifying words:

   In most societies

   a. values are *highly* consistent.
   b. people *often* believe and act on values that are contradictory.
   c. *all* legitimate organizations support the values of the majority.
   d. values of equality *never* exist alongside prejudice and discrimination.

In this question, items c and d contain the words *all* and *never,* suggesting that those statements are true without exception. Thus, if you did not know the answer to this question based on content, you could eliminate items c and d on the basis of the level of qualifiers.

6. **Be alert for questions that require application of knowledge or information.** You may be asked to analyze a hypothetical situation or to use what you have learned to solve a problem. Here is an example taken from a psychology test:

   Carrie is uncomfortable in her new home in New Orleans. When she gets dressed up and leaves her home and goes to the supermarket to buy the week's groceries, she gets nervous and upset and thinks that something is going to happen to her. She feels the same way when walking her four-year-old son Jason in the park or playground.
      Carrie is suffering from

      a. shyness.
      b. a phobia.
      c. a personality disorder.
      d. hypertension.

Tip A *hypothetical* situation is one that hasn't happened, but it or something similar could happen.

In answering questions of this type, start by crossing out unnecessary information that can distract you. In the preceding example, distracting information includes the woman's name, her son's name, where she lives, why she goes to the store, and so forth.

7. **Answer the items using your own words.** If a question concerns steps in a process or the order in which events occur, or any other information that is likely to confuse you, ignore the choices and use the margin or scrap paper to jot down the information as you can recall it. Then select the choice that matches what you wrote.

8. **Avoid selecting answers that are unfamiliar or that you do not understand.** A choice that looks complicated or uses difficult words is not necessarily correct. If you have studied carefully, a choice that is unfamiliar to you is probably incorrect.

9. **Pick the choice that seems most complete.** As a last resort, when you do not know the answer and are unable to eliminate any of the choices as wrong, guess by picking the one that seems complete and contains the most information. This is a good choice because instructors are always careful to make the best answer completely correct and recognizable. Such a choice often becomes long or detailed.

10. **Make educated guesses.** In most instances, you can eliminate one or more of the choices as obviously wrong. Even if you can eliminate only one choice, you have increased your odds of being correct on a four-choice item from 1 in 4 to 1 in 3. If you can eliminate two choices, you have improved your odds to 1 in 2, or 50 percent. Don't hesitate to play the odds and make a guess—you may gain points.

Tip *Play the odds* means "make the choice most likely to be successful." (The term is commonly used in making bets when gambling.)

Goal 3

Use strategies to perform better on standardized tests

HINTS FOR TAKING STANDARDIZED TESTS

At various times in college, you may be required to take a standardized test, which is a commercially prepared, timed test used nationally or statewide to measure skills and abilities. Your score compares your performance with that of large numbers of other students throughout the state or the country. The SAT and ACT are examples of standardized tests; many graduate schools require a standardized test as part of their admission process. Following are a few suggestions for taking this type of test:

1. **Most standardized tests are timed, so the pace you work at is a critical factor.** You need to work at a fairly rapid rate, but not so fast as to make careless errors.

2. **Don't plan on finishing the test.** Many of the tests are designed so that no one finishes.

3. **Don't expect to get everything right.** Unlike classroom tests or exams, you are not expected to get all of the answers correct.

4. **Find out if there is a penalty for guessing.** If there is none, then use the last 20 or 30 seconds to randomly fill in an answer for each item that you have not had time to answer. The odds are that you will get one item correct for every four items that you guess.

5. **Get organized before the timing begins.** Line up your answer sheet and test booklet so you can move between them rapidly without losing your place.

Goal 4

Use strategies to perform better on essay exams

HINTS FOR TAKING ESSAY EXAMS

Essay questions are usually graded on two factors: what you say and how you say it. It is not enough, then, simply to include the correct information. The information must be presented in a logical, organized way that demonstrates your understanding of the subject you are writing about. There can be as much as one whole letter grade difference between a well-written and a poorly written essay, although both contain the same basic information. This section offers suggestions for getting as many points as possible on essay exams.

Read the Question

For essay exams, reading the question carefully is the key to writing a correct, complete, and organized answer.

READ THE DIRECTIONS FIRST. The directions may tell you how many essays to answer and how to structure your answer, or they may specify a minimum or maximum length for your answer.

STUDY THE QUESTION FOR CLUES. The question usually includes three valuable pieces of information. First, the question tells you the *topic* you are to write about. Second, it contains a *limiting word* that restricts and directs your answer. Finally, the question contains a *key word* or phrase that tells you how to organize and present answers. Read the essay question in this example.

(key word)	(limiting word)	(topic)	(limiting word)	(topic)
↓	↓		↓	

Compare the *causes* of the *Vietnam War* with the *causes* of the *Korean War.*

In this example you have two topics—the Vietnam War and the Korean War. The question also contains a limiting word that restricts your discussion of these topics and tells you what to include in your answer. In this sample question, the limiting word is *causes*. It tells you to limit your answer to a discussion of events that started, or caused, each war. Do not include information about events of the war or its effects. The key word in the sample question is *compare*. It means you should consider the similarities, and possibly the differences, between the causes of the two wars. When directed to compare, you already have some clues as to how your answer should be written. One possibility is to discuss the causes of one war and then the causes of the other and finally to make an overall statement about their similarities. Another choice is to discuss one type of cause for each of the wars, and then go on to discuss another type of cause for each. For instance, you could discuss the economic causes of each and then the political causes of each.

There are several common key words and phrases used in essay questions. They are listed in Figure 19-1 on page 416. Some questions require only knowledge and comprehension, but most require the higher-level thinking skills of applying, analyzing, evaluating, and creating.

Watch for Questions with Several Parts

A common mistake that students make is to fail to answer all parts of an essay question, perhaps because they get involved with answering the first part and forget about the remaining parts. Questions with several parts come in two forms. The most obvious form is as follows:

For the U.S. invasion of Afghanistan, discuss the

a. causes.
b. immediate effects.
c. long-range political implications.

A less obvious form that does not stand out as a several-part question is the following:

Discuss *how* the Equal Rights Amendment was developed and *why* it has aroused controversy.

When you find a question of this type, underline or circle the limiting words to serve as a reminder.

Figure 19-1
Key Words Used in
Essay Questions

KEY WORDS	EXAMPLE	INFORMATION TO INCLUDE
Understanding		
Discuss	Discuss Tamoxifen as a treatment for cancer.	Consider important characteristics and main points.
Enumerate	Enumerate the reasons for U.S. withdrawal from Vietnam.	List or discuss one by one.
Define	Define thermal pollution and include several examples.	Give an accurate meaning of the term with enough detail to show that you really understand it.
Applying		
Illustrate	State Boyle's law and illustrate its use.	Explain, using examples that demonstrate or clarify a point or idea.
Analyzing		
Compare	Compare the causes of air pollution with those of water pollution.	Show how items are similar as well as different; include details or examples.
Contrast	Contrast the health-care systems in the United States with those in England.	Show how the items are different; include details or examples.
Explain	Explain why black Americans are primarily city dwellers.	Give facts, details, or reasons that make the idea or concept clear and understandable.
Describe	Describe the experimentation that tests whether plants are sensitive to music.	Tell how something looks or happened, including how, who, where, and why.
Justify	Justify former President Carter's attempt to rescue the hostages in Iran.	Give reasons that support an action, event, or policy.
Evaluating		
Evaluate	Evaluate the strategies our society has used to treat mental illness.	React to the topic in a logical way. Discuss the merits, strengths, weaknesses, advantages, or limitations of the topic.
Criticize	Criticize the current environmental controls to combat air pollution.	Make judgments about quality or worth; include both positive and negative aspects.
Prove	Prove that ice is a better cooling agent than water.	Demonstrate or establish that a concept or theory is correct, logical, or valid.
Creating		
Trace	Trace the history of legalized prostitution in Nevada.	Describe the development or progress of a particular trend, event, or process in chronological order.
Summarize	Summarize the arguments for and against offering sex education courses in public schools.	Cover the major points in brief form; use a sentence-and-paragraph form.

Make Notes As You Read

As you read a question the first time, you may begin to formulate an answer. When this occurs, jot down a few key words that will bring these thoughts back when you are ready to organize your answer.

DIRECTIONS Read each of the following essay questions. For each question, underline the topic, circle the limiting word, and place a box around the key word.

Exercise 3

1. Discuss the long-term effects of the trend toward a smaller, more self-contained family structure.

2. Trace the development of monopolies in the late nineteenth and early twentieth centuries in America.

3. Explain one effect of the Industrial Revolution on each of three of the following:
   a. transportation
   b. capitalism
   c. socialism
   d. population growth
   e. scientific research

4. Discuss the reason why, although tropical plants have very large leaves and most desert plants have very small leaves, cactus grows equally well in both habitats.

5. Describe the events leading up to the War of 1812.

6. Compare and contrast the purpose and procedures in textbook marking and lecture note taking.

7. Briefly describe a complete approach to reading and studying a textbook chapter that will enable you to handle a test on that material successfully.

8. List four factors that influence memory or recall ability and explain how each can be used to make study more efficient.

9. Summarize the techniques a speaker or lecturer may use to emphasize the important concepts and ideas in a lecture.

10. Explain the value and purpose of the prereading technique and list the steps involved in prereading a textbook chapter. ●

DIRECTIONS Write ten possible essay questions for a course you are taking. *Be sure to write at least one question at each level of thinking.* ●

Exercise 4

Organize Your Answer

As mentioned earlier, a well-written, organized essay often gets a higher grade than a carelessly constructed one. Read each of these sample responses to an essay question and notice how they differ. Each essay was written in response to this instruction on a psychology final exam: Describe the stages involved in the memory process.

Example 1

Memory is important to everybody's life. Memory has special ways to help you get a better recollection of things and ideas. Psychologists believe that memory has three stages: encoding, storage, and retrieval.

In the encoding stage, you are putting facts and ideas into a code, usually words, and filing them away in your memory. Encoding involves preparing information for storage in memory.

The second stage of memory is storage. It is the stage that most people call memory. It involves keeping information so that it is accessible for use later in time. How well information is stored can be affected by old information already stored and newer information that is added later.

The third step in memory is retrieval, which means the ability to get back information that is in storage. There are two types of retrieval—recognition and recall. In recognition, you have to be able to identify the correct information from several choices. In recall, you have to pull information directly from your memory without using the recognition type of retrieval.

Example 2

Memory is very complicated in how it works. It involves remembering things that are stored in your mind and being able to pull them out when you want to remember them. When you pull information out of your memory it is called retrieval. How well you can remember something is affected by how you keep the information in your mind and how you put it in. When keeping, or storing, information you have to realize that this information will be affected by old information already in your memory. Putting information in your memory is called encoding, and it means that you store facts and ideas in word form in your memory. Information stored in your memory can also be influenced by information that you add to your memory later.

There are two ways you can retrieve information. You can either recognize it or recall it. When you recognize information you are able to spot the correct information among other information. When you recall information you have to pull information out of your head. Recall is what you have to do when you write an essay exam.

While these two essays contain practically the same information, the first will probably receive a higher grade. In this essay, it is easy to see that the writer knows that the memory process has three stages and knows how to explain each. The writer opens the essay by stating that there are three stages and then devotes one paragraph to each of the three stages.

In the second essay, it is not easy to identify the stages of memory. The paragraphs are not organized according to stages in the memory process. The writer does not write about one stage at a time in a logical order. Retrieval is mentioned first; then storage and retrieval are discussed further. At the end, the writer returns to the topic of retrieval and gives further information.

Here are a few suggestions to help you organize your answer.

1. **Think before you start to write.** Decide what information is called for and what you will include.
2. **Make a brief word or phrase outline of the ideas you want to include in your answer.**
3. **Study your word outline and rearrange its order.** You may want to put major topics and important ideas first and less important points toward the end, or you may decide to organize your answer chronologically, discussing events early in time near the beginning and mentioning more recent events near the end. The topic you are discussing will largely determine the order of presentation.
4. **If the point value of the essay is given, use that information as a clue to how many separate points or ideas may be expected.** For an essay worth 25 points, for example, discussion of five major ideas may be expected.

5. **Use correct paragraph form.** Be sure to write your answers in complete, correct sentences and include only one major point in each paragraph. Each paragraph should have a main idea, usually expressed in one sentence. The remainder of the paragraph should explain, prove, or support the main idea you state. Also, use correct spelling and punctuation.

6. **Begin your answer with a thesis statement.** Your first sentence should state what the entire essay is about and suggest your approach to it. If a question asks you to discuss the practical applications of Newton's three laws of motion, you might begin by writing, "Newton's laws of motion have many practical applications." Then you should proceed to name the three laws and their practical applications, devoting one paragraph to each law.

7. **Make your main points easy to find.** State each main point at the beginning of a new paragraph. For lengthy answers or multipart questions, you might use headings or the same numbering used in the question. Use space (skip a line) to divide your answers into different parts.

8. **Include sufficient explanation.** Instructors often criticize essay answers because they fail to explain or support ideas fully. Make sure your answers convince your instructor that you have learned the material: Remember to explain, define, and give examples. Too much information is better than too little.

9. **Avoid opinions and judgments.** Unless the question specifically asks you to do so, do not include your personal reaction to the topic. When you are asked to state your reactions and opinions, include reasons to support them.

10. **Make your answer readable.** An instructor cannot help having personal reactions to your answer. Try to make those reactions positive by handing in a paper that is as easy to read as possible. It is annoying to an instructor to try to read poor handwriting and carelessly written answers.

11. **Proofread your answer.** Before rereading your essay, read the question again. Then check to see that you have included all necessary facts and information and that you have adequately explained each fact. Add anything you feel improves your answer. Next reread the essay a second time, checking and correcting all the mechanical aspects of your writing.

If You Run Out of Time

Despite careful planning of exam time, you may run out of time before you finish writing one of the essays. If this happens, try to jot down the major ideas that you would discuss fully if you had time. Often, your instructor will give you partial credit for this type of response, especially if you mention that you ran out of time.

If You Don't Know the Answer

Despite careful preparation, you may forget an answer. If this should happen, do not leave a blank page; write something. Attempt to answer the question—you may hit upon some partially correct information. The main reason for writing something is to give the instructor a chance to give you a few points for trying. If you leave a blank page, your instructor has no choice but to give you zero points. Usually when you lose full credit on one essay, you are automatically unable to get a high passing grade.

Exercise 5

DIRECTIONS   Organize and write a response to one of the following essay questions.

1. Six organizational patterns are commonly used in textbook writing: comparison–contrast, definition, time sequence, cause–effect, classification, and enumeration. Discuss the usefulness of these patterns in predicting and answering essay exam questions.
2. Describe three strategies that have improved your reading skills. Explain why each is effective.
3. Describe your approach to time management. Include specific techniques and organizational strategies that you have found effective. ●

Visual Thinking
APPLYING SKILLS

The nursing students in this photograph are taking a hands-on exam called a practicum exam.

Discuss how students should prepare for and take this type of exam.

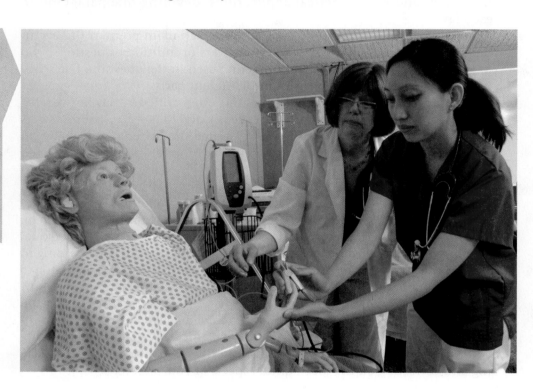

Goal ⑤
Control test anxiety

CONTROLLING TEST ANXIETY

Do you get nervous and anxious just before an exam begins? If so, your response is normal; most students feel some level of anxiety before an exam. In fact, research indicates that some anxiety is beneficial and improves your performance by sharpening your attention and keeping you alert. However, very high levels of anxiety can interfere with test performance.

Test anxiety is a complicated psychological response to a threatening situation, and it may be related to other problems and past experiences. The following suggestions are intended to help you ease test anxiety. If these suggestions do not help, the next step is to discuss the problem with a counselor.

Be Sure Test Anxiety Is Not an Excuse

Many students say they have test anxiety when actually they have not studied and reviewed carefully or thoroughly. The first question, then, that you must answer honestly is this: Are you in fact *unprepared* for the exam, and do you therefore have every reason to be anxious?

Get Used to Test Situations

Psychologists who have studied anxiety use processes called "systematic desensitization" and "simulation" to reduce test anxiety. Basically, these are ways of becoming less sensitive to or disturbed by tests by putting yourself in testlike conditions. These techniques are complicated processes often used by trained therapists, but here are a few ways you can use these processes to reduce test anxiety:

1. **Become familiar with the building and room in which the test will be given.** Visit the room when it is empty and take a seat. Visualize yourself taking a test there.
2. **Develop practice or review tests.** Treat them as real tests, and work on them in situations as similar as possible to real test conditions.
3. **Practice working with time limits.** Set an alarm clock and work only until it rings.
4. **Take as many tests as possible, even though you dislike them.** Always take advantage of practice tests and make-up exams. Buy a review book for the course you are taking or a workbook that accompanies your text. Treat each section as an exam, and have someone else correct your work.

Control Negative Thinking

Major factors that contribute to test anxiety are self-doubt and negative thinking. Just before and during an exam, test-anxious students often think, "I won't do well." "I'm going to fail." "What will my friends think of me when I get a failing grade?" This type of thinking predisposes you to failure; you are telling yourself that you expect to fail. By thinking in this way, you undermine your own chances for success.

One solution to this problem is to send yourself positive rather than negative messages, such as, "I have studied hard and I deserve to pass." "I know that I know the material." "I know I can do it!" And remember, being well prepared is one of the best ways to reduce test anxiety.

Compose Yourself Before the Test Begins

Don't take an exam on an empty stomach; you will feel queasy. Have something light or bland to eat. Some students find that a brisk walk outside before going to an exam helps to reduce tension.

Before you begin the test, take 30 seconds or so to calm yourself, to slow down, and to focus your attention. Take several deep breaths, close your eyes, and visualize yourself calmly working through the test. Remind yourself that you have prepared carefully and have every reason to do well.

Answer Easy Questions First

To give yourself an initial boost of confidence, begin with a section of the test that seems easy. This will help you to work calmly, and you will prove to yourself that you can handle the test.

USING COLLEGE TEXTBOOKS
Using Headings to Create Practice Tests

Before you take a test in class, it is helpful to prepare yourself by taking practice tests. If your textbook does not contain sample essay questions or detailed review questions, you can create practice essay tests on your own.

To write your own practice essay exam questions, study the headings in the chapter you will be tested on. Think about the topics and concepts presented and write some possible questions that require you to understand, apply or analyze the facts contained in the section. You can write actual answers, or create an outline of your answer. Here is an example of the questions one student wrote for a section of his sociology textbook.

TEXTBOOK: THINK SOCIOLOGY

Headings

AGING AND HEALTH

The Graying of Society 208

Health Defined 211
    Social Epidemiology 211
Health in the United States: Living
    off the Fat of the Land 213
    Childhood Obesity 213 •
    Stigmatization of the Obese 214
    Obesity and Race 214
Health Care 215
    The Uninsured 215 • Costs of
    Services 215 • Health Care:
    An International Comparison
    215 • Health Care and the
    Elderly—Medicare 216
Aging: The Graying of the United
    States 216
    Aging and Demographic
    Change in the United State 216
    The "Sandwiched" Generation 217
    Concerns About Aging 219

Essay Questions

Discuss the impacts of obesity on the United States. How have these changed in recent years?

Explain how the aging population in the United States is affecting society.

Describe the ways that health care and health insurance affect the economy.

—Carl, *Think Sociology*, p. vii

FURTHER PRACTICE WITH TEXTBOOK READING

Part A: Sample Textbook Chapter

For the section titled "Perspectives on Motivation, Drives, and Incentives," predict two possible essay questions.

Part B: Your College Textbook

Choose a textbook that you are currently using in one of your other courses and select a chapter. Predict an essay question for each main heading in the chapter.

SELF-TEST SUMMARY

Goal 1 How can you improve the way you take most exams?	You can improve your exam grades by approaching tests in a systematic, organized manner. This involves taking the necessary materials, arriving on time, deliberately choosing a seat in a nondistracting section of the room, previewing the exam, planning the time you will devote to various sections of the exam, and reading the questions carefully.
Goal 2 What can you do to improve the way you take most objective exams?	When taking any type of objective exam, read the directions carefully, leave nothing blank, and look for clues that will help you recall the information. When taking true/false tests, you should also read two-part statements carefully and be aware of negative words or word parts. When you have no idea of the answer, make your best guess by marking extreme statements and those that contain unfamiliar terms as false and all others as true. For multiple-choice tests, you should make educated guesses by reading the choices carefully, narrowing them down by using reasoning power, paying attention to qualifying words, and considering the choices in light of what you know about the topic. When all else fails, eliminate unfamiliar or confusing items and choose an answer that seems complete. When taking short-answer tests, use the point distributions and the amount of space provided to determine how much to write, and plan what to write beforehand. For fill-in-the-blank tests, decide what kind of information is being asked for by the key words in, and grammatical structure of, the sentence.
Goal 3 How should you approach standardized tests?	When taking a standardized test, maintain a rapid but careful pace and don't be upset if you don't finish the test or don't know all the answers. Before testing, find out if there is a penalty for guessing. Get organized before you begin the test.

Goal ④ What can you do to improve the way you take essay exams?	When taking an essay exam, it is important to read the question carefully, reading the directions, noting all parts, and looking for clues in the question to determine exactly what type of response your instructor wants. Essay answers should be carefully organized and written in an easy-to-read form. This can be achieved by including a topic sentence in each paragraph, using numbering and headings, including enough information to prove your point, and stating opinions and judgments only when the question asks for them. Take pains to make your answer readable, and carefully proofread for accuracy, grammar, and mechanics. If you run out of time or your memory fails, you may be able to earn some credit by jotting down an outline or writing something relevant to the subject of the essay on the page.
Goal ⑤ How can you control test anxiety?	Too much test anxiety can seriously affect your performance on exams. You can relieve it by being prepared for the exam; becoming familiar with the testing location, conditions, and time limits; controlling negative thoughts; taking time to compose yourself near the time of the exam; and beginning with the easy questions for an initial boost of confidence.

APPLYING YOUR SKILLS

DISCUSSING THE CHAPTER

1. What techniques do you use to overcome test anxiety? What techniques are particularly effective for various types of examinations?
2. What types of exams are the least stressful for people with each learning style? What can people do to become more relaxed when taking various types of examinations?
3. Why do professors use various types of objective and essay tests in order to evaluate student learning? From the professor's perspective, what are the advantages and disadvantages of using each type of examination?
4. Why do you think a person's first guess on a multiple-choice test item is usually the best one?

ANALYZING A STUDY SITUATION

Maria is taking an American history course. The instructor announced that the next exam will cover only three chapters on the Constitution—its origins, history, and current applications and interpretations. Further, students are allowed to bring their textbook and both lecture and study notes to class and use them during the exam. As most students breathed a sigh of relief, the instructor cautioned, "It's not as easy as you think!" Still, many students in the class are not preparing for this exam at all. Maria knows she should prepare, but she is uncertain about what to do.

1. What type of questions (multiple-choice, true/false, short-answer, or essay) do you think Maria's exam will contain?

2. Why would the instructor allow students to bring materials to the exam? What types of learning is she emphasizing? What is she not emphasizing?
3. How should Maria prepare for this exam?

WORKING ON COLLABORATIVE PROJECTS

DIRECTIONS   Each member of the class should write an answer to the following essay question, which is based on the reading "The Genetic Crystal Ball" in Part Five, page 464.

Discuss the ethical issues raised by human genetic engineering. Identify the issues and explain why it is controversial.

Working in pairs, compare your answers, noting the strengths and weaknesses of the essays. Then rewrite and combine your answers to produce a stronger or more nearly complete response.

 For support in meeting this chapter's goals, go to **MyReadingLab** and select **Test Taking**.

Quick **QUIZ**

DIRECTIONS   Write the letter of the choice that best completes each statement in the space provided.

CHECKING YOUR RECALL

_____ 1. The best way to approach an exam is to
   a. plan to arrive at least 30 minutes before the exam begins.
   b. sit near the back of the class.
   c. bring only a pencil with you.
   d. preview the exam before you answer any questions.

_____ 2. Neil's history exam has a total of 100 points, divided as follows: ten multiple-choice questions worth 20 points, five short-answer questions worth 20 points, five true/false questions worth 10 points, and one essay question worth 50 points. Based on this information, Neil should plan to spend most of his time on the
   a. true/false questions.
   b. short-answer questions.
   c. multiple-choice questions.
   d. essay question.

_____ 3. One thing to remember when taking an objective exam is that
   a. the directions for all objective tests are the same.
   b. you should leave difficult questions blank.
   c. absolute statements tend to be true.
   d. your first guess is usually the best one.

_____ 4. An example of a limiting word in a true/false statement is
   a. _always._
   b. _however._
   c. _when._
   d. _because._

_____ 5. On a multiple-choice test, the qualifying word most likely to indicate a correct statement is
   a. _always._
   b. _usually._
   c. _best._
   d. _worst._

APPLYING YOUR SKILLS

_____ 6. All of the following suggestions can help improve your performance on multiple-choice exams _except_
   a. choosing the answer that seems most complete.
   b. using logic and common sense.
   c. answering the item first in your own words.
   d. choosing the answer that is unfamiliar to you.

_____ 7. Graham is taking a standardized test for admission to college. One thing he should know about this type of test is that
   a. it is most important that he finish the test.
   b. he is expected to get most of the answers correct.
   c. he should guess on all the items he doesn't know, regardless of how the test is scored.
   d. he should work at a fairly quick rate because the test is probably timed.

_____ 8. In order to reduce test anxiety, you should try to do all of the following _except_
   a. become familiar with the testing location.
   b. avoid taking practice tests and make-up exams.
   c. control negative thinking.
   d. practice working within time limits.

_____ 9. Of the following essay exam questions, the one that asks you to give reasons that support an idea is:
   a. Define symbiosis and give several examples.
   b. Enumerate the strategies our society uses to deal with homelessness.
   c. Justify President George W. Bush's invasion of Iraq.
   d. State Boyle's law and illustrate its use.

_____ 10. When you are writing an essay exam answer, you should typically try to do all of the following _except_
   a. begin with a thesis statement.
   b. use correct paragraph form.
   c. provide sufficient explanation.
   d. include your personal reaction to the topic.

Improving Your Reading Rate and Flexibility

CHAPTER 20

LEARNING GOALS

In this chapter you will learn to

1 Build your reading rate

2 Develop your reading flexibility

LEARNING EXPERIMENT

1 The following paragraph discusses one method by which new products are developed. Read the paragraph only until you get to the words "STOP HERE."

Me-toos are products that are new to a firm but not new to the marketplace. Companies create "me-toos" because they believe there is room in the market for another competitor, and the projected returns outweigh the risks. For example, STOP HERE when McDonald's decided to enter the fast-food breakfast business, its product was new to the company even though a fast-food breakfast was not new to the market. Procter & Gamble has entered the "me-too" game with both disposable training pants and ultra-thin diapers—two offerings that enable the firm to play catch-up with diaper developments by Kimberly-Clark.

2 Based on what you read, predict what the remainder of the paragraph will contain and write it below.

_____

_____

_____

_____

3 Now, go back and check: Did you predict accurately?

THE RESULTS

You have probably discovered that you can predict the content of paragraphs from their topic sentences. The experiment above demonstrates that some parts of a paragraph are more important than others.

LEARNING PRINCIPLE: WHAT THIS MEANS TO YOU

Successful students read and learn selectively. You should not read every paragraph in the same way. Instead, you should vary your technique and approach depending on the nature of the assignment and what you are expected to learn from it. This chapter will show you how to adjust your reading rate and reading technique to suit the material you are reading and your purpose for reading it. You will also learn how to skim and scan, alternatives to reading a text in its entirety.

WHY LEARN TO IMPROVE YOUR READING RATE?

Improving your reading rate is important because:

- Reading takes time; if you can learn to read faster, you will save time.
- Not everything on a page is equally important. If you can learn to read selectively, you will save time.

Goal ❶

Build your reading rate

myreadinglab

To practice improving your reading rate, go to

> Reading Rate

BUILDING YOUR READING RATE

Reading rate, the speed at which you read, is measured in words per minute (wpm). What should your reading rate be? Is it better to be a fast reader or a slow reader? Does a good reader read every word? You should be able to read at 100, 200, 300, and 400 wpm; you should be both a fast *and* a slow reader; good readers are often "word skippers." These answers may seem strange or even contradictory, but they are nevertheless true. You should strive to improve your reading rate in order to become a more efficient reader, but you should also be able to change your rate and method of reading to fit different situations and different types of reading material.

To read faster, you must improve your capacity to process information rapidly. Instead of thinking about your eyes and how they move, concentrate on getting information quickly from the printed page. Reading at a faster rate involves understanding ideas and how they interrelate.

By working through this book, you have learned skills and techniques that have improved your comprehension. Many techniques that improve comprehension also improve rate. Reading faster is often a combination of pushing yourself to higher reading speeds on different types of materials and learning and applying several new techniques. The following suggestions will help you to read faster.

Avoid Roadblocks to Reading Efficiency

Tip Literally, a *roadblock* is an obstruction that prevents passage on a road; figuratively, it is something that prevents progress.

Certain poor reading habits often carry over from when you first learned to read. These are (1) moving your head as you read, (2) moving your lips as you read, and (3) using your finger or pen to keep your place on the line. Each of these habits can slow you down and contribute to poor comprehension.

MOVING YOUR HEAD   Moving your head rather than just your eyes across the line of print prevents you from reading at even a normal rate and also creates strain and muscle fatigue. Ask someone to check to see whether you move your head while reading; this person should check when you are not consciously thinking about the problem. One of the easiest ways to break this habit is to sit with your elbow up on your desk with your hand cupping your chin. If you start to move your head, you will feel your hand and forearm move, and this will remind you to correct the habit.

MOVING YOUR LIPS   Moving your lips limits your reading rate. The average adult rate of speech (pronouncing words out loud) is 125 words per minute, whereas the average adult rate for silent reading is 250 to 300 words per minute. Thus, moving your lips can really slow your silent reading down—by as much as half. However, there is one situation in which lip movement may be appropriate. When you are reading something that is extremely difficult or complicated, you may find that moving your lips or even whispering aloud as you read helps you to understand the material.

To eliminate this habit, sit in a position in which part of your hand or your fingers touch your lips. If you move your lips while reading, you will feel the movement on your hand or fingers.

KEEPING YOUR PLACE ON THE LINE   Another bad habit is keeping your place on a line of print by moving your finger or a pen or pencil across the line as you read. Online readers often use the cursor to keep the place on the page. These practices cause very slow, word-by-word reading. The solution is simple—tightly grasp the book with both hands. This will prevent you from following across the line with your finger or another object. Don't cheat and slide your thumb down the margin as a guide to where you are on the page. If you have tried unsuccessfully to control this habit, an eye exam is advisable. Inability to keep one's place on the line is one symptom of a need for corrective lenses.

Preview to Familiarize Yourself with the Material

In Chapter 6, you learned that previewing is a means of improving your comprehension by becoming familiar with the organization and content of material before you begin to read it. In addition to improving your comprehension, previewing increases your reading speed. Because previewing enables you to anticipate the flow of ideas, you will find yourself able to read the material more rapidly.

Eliminate Regressions

As your eyes move across a line, they normally proceed from left to right. Occasionally, instead of moving to the next word, your eyes move backward, or regress, to a word in the same line or in a line already read. Regressions (backward movements) scramble word order, thus creating confusion that slows your pace. Although even very good readers make regressions, your rate and comprehension will improve if you can reduce the number of regressions. The following suggestions will help you eliminate or reduce regressions:

1. **Be conscious of the tendency to regress, and force yourself to continue reading.** Do not allow yourself to regress until you have finished a sentence. Then, if the meaning is still unclear, reread the entire sentence.
2. **If you frequently regress to a word or phrase on a previous line, you might try sliding a 5-by-8-inch index card down the page as you read.** Use the card to cover the lines you have finished reading. This technique will help you break the habit of regression because when you look back, the line will be covered.
3. **For online reading, continue scrolling down the page as you read.** You will hide from view previously read lines.

Read in Meaning Clusters

Most college students read word by word, looking at each word and then moving to the next one. A more efficient way to read is to combine words that naturally go together. Try not to think of a sentence as a string of single words.

Instead, think of it as several word clusters, or phrases. Look at the following sentence:

The math instructor told her class about the quiz.

"The" does not convey any meaning by itself. While "math" does have meaning, it is intended to describe the next word, "instructor." Rather than reading the first three words separately, try to think of them together as a meaningful phrase—"the math instructor." The remainder of the sentence could then be read as two additional phrases: "told her class" and "about the quiz."

The following brief paragraph has been divided into meaningful word groups separated by slashes. Read the paragraph; as you read, try to see and think of each cluster as a unit of thought rather than as two or three separate words.

In order / to protect themselves / against loss / drivers purchase / liability insurance. / There are / two types of / liability insurance. / Bodily injury liability / provides payment / if you / are injured / in an accident. / Property damage liability / covers you / when your car / damages the property / of others.

Note that words that make sense together are grouped together. Words are grouped with the words they explain or modify. Once you begin reading in word clusters, you will find that meaning falls into place more easily, thus enabling you to read somewhat faster.

Exercise 1

DIRECTIONS To see whether you can group words into meaning clusters, divide the following paragraph with slashes. The first two lines have been done for you.

The United States / has changed / in the past one hundred years / from an agricultural economy / to an industrial economy / and has become / the world's first / service economy. What does the term *service* mean? There is no widely accepted definition in marketing. In fact, there is no clear distinction between those firms that are part of / a marketing channel for products and those firms that market services. Restaurants / are often classified as food distributors because they compete with supermarkets, but restaurants also provide services to customers.

—Kinnear, Bernhardt, and Krentler, *Principles of Marketing,* p. 654 ●

Learn to Pace Yourself

An established method of improving your reading rate is *pacing,* which requires maintaining a preestablished rate. Pacing means pushing yourself to read faster than your normal speed while maintaining your level of comprehension. There are numerous ways to pace yourself in order to increase your speed; the following are among the most common methods:

1. **Use an index card.** Slide a 5-by-8-inch card down the page as you read, moving it so that it covers up lines as you read them. This technique will force you along and keep you moving rapidly. Move the card down the page at a fixed pace, and try to keep up while reading. How fast you move the card will depend on the size of the print and the length of the line, so it will vary for each new piece of material you read. At first you will need to experiment to find an appropriate pace. Try to move at a pace that is slightly uncomfortable and that you are not sure you can maintain.

2. **Use a timer or clock.** Start by measuring what portion of a page you can read in a minute. Then set a goal for yourself: Determine how many pages

you will attempt to read in a given period of time. Set your goal slightly above what you could read at your current rate.

3. **Use the scroll key when reading online.** You can force yourself to move rapidly by pressing the down arrow key at a rate that is slightly uncomfortable.

Exercise 2

DIRECTIONS   Select a magazine or newspaper article that you are interested in or a section of a novel you are reading. Using one of the pacing techniques described in this section, try to increase your current reading speed by approximately 50 wpm. Record your results in the space provided.

Article title: _____   Reading time: _____

Estimated number of words:* _____   Words per minute: _____

Finishing time: _____   Estimated level
of comprehension: _____
Starting time: _____

*If you are reading online, you can get a word count by cutting and pasting the article into Word and choosing "Word Count" from "Tools." •

Use Rereading to Build Speed

Although rereading is not an effective way to learn, it is an effective method of building your reading speed. Rereading at a slightly faster pace prepares you for reading new material faster. Rereading gets you moving at a faster rate and serves as a practice or trial run for reading new material faster.

To reread for speed increase, use the following steps:

1. **Select an article or passage and time yourself.** Read it as you normally would for careful or leisure reading.
2. **Compute your speed in words per minute after you finish reading.**
3. **Take a break (five minutes or so).** Then reread the same selection, timing yourself again. Push yourself to read faster than you read the first time.
4. **Compute your speed again.** You should be able to reread the selection at a faster rate than you read it initially.
5. **Read a new selection, pushing yourself to read almost as fast as you** *re*read the first selection.

Exercise 3

DIRECTIONS   Choose two magazine or newspaper articles that you are interested in reading. Follow the preceding steps for rereading to build speed. Record your results below.

Article 1
Title: _____   Estimated number of words: _____

First reading
Time: _____   Words per minute: _____

Second reading
Time: _____   Words per minute: _____

Article 2
Title: _____   Estimated number of words: _____

First (only) reading
Time: _____   Words per minute: _____ •

Goal **2**

Develop your reading
flexibility

myreadinglab

To practice improving
your reading rate, go to
> Reading Rate

DEVELOPING YOUR READING FLEXIBILITY

Your purpose for reading is an important factor related to both rate and comprehension. As you can see from Figure 20-1, no one should have just one reading rate. Instead, your reading rate should vary according to *what* you are reading and *why* you are reading it. Adjusting your rate in response to the material and to your purpose for reading is called *reading flexibility.*

Learning to adjust your rate according to style, content, and purpose will require a conscious effort at first. If you are now in the habit of reading everything at the same pace, as most college students are, then you will need to force yourself to make an assessment of the particular reading material before deciding how fast you can read it. Previewing can help you adjust your rate as you read. Pay particular attention to the overall difficulty of the material, as well.

Deciding how much to speed up or slow down for a particular article is a matter of judgment. It is important to develop *flexibility.* Here is a step-by-step procedure you can follow that will help you build the habit of varying your reading rate:

1. **Choose a time and place for reading that will help rather than hinder your concentration.** Choose a time when you are alert and your state of mind is conducive to study.
2. **Preview the material.** As you preview, assess the difficulty of both the writing style and the content. Are there a lot of difficult words? Are the sentences long and complicated? How factual is the material? How much background information do you have on the subject?
3. **Define your overall purpose for reading.** Your purpose will determine the level of comprehension and the degree of retention that you require. Are you reading for enjoyment, looking up facts, or reading a text chapter to prepare for an exam?
4. **Decide what rate would be appropriate for reading this particular material.**
5. **After you've finished the first page of the reading material, stop and evaluate.** Can you understand and remember what you are reading? Can you summarize the ideas in your own words?

Figure 20-1
Types of Reading

METHOD OF READING	RANGE OF SPEED	PURPOSE OF READING	TYPES OF MATERIAL
Analytical reading	Under 100 wpm	Detailed comprehension: analysis, evaluation, critique	Poetry, argumentative writing
Study reading	150–250 wpm	High comprehension and high recall	Textbooks, library research
Casual reading	250–400 wpm	Moderate comprehension of main ideas, entertainment, enjoyment, general	Novels, newspapers, Web sites, magazines
Accelerated reading	Above 600 wpm	Overview of material; rapid location of a specific fact	Reference material, magazines, novels, nonfiction

You Don't Have to Read Everything

Before you begin to read flexibly, you must recognize that the importance and value of printed information are determined by whether you need to learn it or whether you can use it in a practical way. Depending on the kind of material and on your purpose for reading it, many times you may only need to read some parts and skip over others. You might read selectively in the following situations:

1. **A high level of comprehension is not needed.** If you are not trying to remember a major portion of the facts and details, then you might concentrate on reading only main ideas. This method of reading only main ideas is called *skimming.* Specific techniques for skimming are presented later in the chapter.

2. **You are searching for specific information.** If you are looking up the date of a historical event in your history text, you skip over everything in the chapter except the exact passage that contains the information. This technique of skipping everything except the specific information for which you are looking is called *scanning.* Practice in scanning techniques is included later in the chapter.

3. **You are familiar with what you are reading.** In a college chemistry course, for example, you might find that the first few chapters of your text are very basic if you have already studied high school chemistry. You can therefore afford to skip basic definitions and explanations and examples of principles that you already know. Do not, however, decide to skip an entire chapter or even large sections within it; there just may be some new information included. You may find that more exact and detailed definitions are given or that a new approach is taken toward a particular topic.

4. **The material does not match your purpose in reading.** Suppose that, in giving an assignment in your physics text, your instructor told you to concentrate only on theories, laws, and principles presented in the chapter. As you begin reading the chapter, you find that the first topic discussed is Newton's law of motion, but the chapter also contains a biographical sketch of Newton giving detailed information about his life. Because your purpose in reading the chapter is to focus on theories, laws, and principles, it is appropriate to skip over much of the biographical information.

5. **The writer's style allows you to skip information (portions).** Some writers include many examples of a particular concept or principle. If, after reading two or three examples, you are sure that you understand the idea being explained, just quickly glance at the remaining examples. Unless they present a new aspect or different point of view, skip over them. Other writers provide detailed background information before getting into a discussion of the intended topic. If a chapter starts out by summarizing information that was covered in a chapter you just read last week, it is not necessary to read this information again carefully unless you feel you need to review.

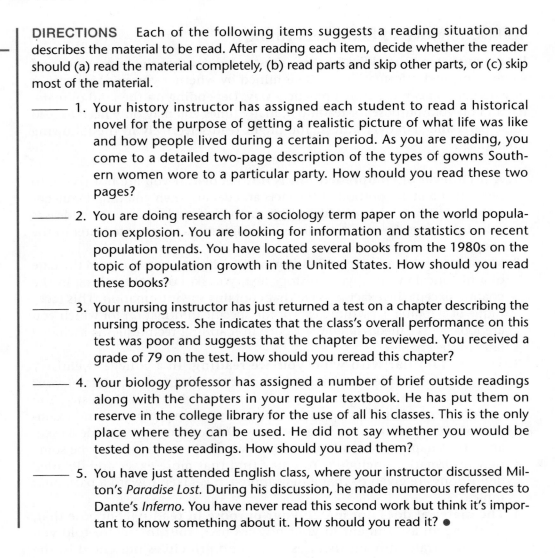

Exercise 4

DIRECTIONS   Each of the following items suggests a reading situation and describes the material to be read. After reading each item, decide whether the reader should (a) read the material completely, (b) read parts and skip other parts, or (c) skip most of the material.

———— 1. Your history instructor has assigned each student to read a historical novel for the purpose of getting a realistic picture of what life was like and how people lived during a certain period. As you are reading, you come to a detailed two-page description of the types of gowns Southern women wore to a particular party. How should you read these two pages?

———— 2. You are doing research for a sociology term paper on the world population explosion. You are looking for information and statistics on recent population trends. You have located several books from the 1980s on the topic of population growth in the United States. How should you read these books?

———— 3. Your nursing instructor has just returned a test on a chapter describing the nursing process. She indicates that the class's overall performance on this test was poor and suggests that the chapter be reviewed. You received a grade of 79 on the test. How should you reread this chapter?

———— 4. Your biology professor has assigned a number of brief outside readings along with the chapters in your regular textbook. He has put them on reserve in the college library for the use of all his classes. This is the only place where they can be used. He did not say whether you would be tested on these readings. How should you read them?

———— 5. You have just attended English class, where your instructor discussed Milton's *Paradise Lost*. During his discussion, he made numerous references to Dante's *Inferno*. You have never read this second work but think it's important to know something about it. How should you read it? ●

Skimming Techniques

As you know, the term **skimming** refers to the process of reading only main ideas within a passage and simply glancing at the remainder of the material. Skimming is used to get an overall picture of the material, to become generally familiar with the topics and ideas presented, or to get the gist of a particular work. Usually skimming is an end in itself; that is, skimming is all you intend to do with the article. You do not intend to read it more intensively later. You are willing to settle for an overview of the article, giving up a major portion of the details.

At this point, you may be thinking that skimming seems similar to the technique of previewing. If so, you are correct. Previewing is actually a form of skimming. To be more precise, there are three forms of skimming: *preview skimming, skim-reading,* and *review skimming.* Preview skimming assumes that you plan to read the entire article or chapter and that you are previewing as a means of getting ready to read. Skim-reading refers to situations in which skimming is the only coverage you plan to give the material. Review skimming assumes that you have already read the material and are going back over it as a means of study and review.

We discussed previewing in Chapter 6. Skimming to review after reading is part of the reading-study systems, such as SQ3R, discussed in Chapter 17. This chapter will focus on skim-reading techniques.

Demonstration of Skimming

The sample article in Figure 20-2 has been included to demonstrate what skimming is like. The parts of the passage that should be read while skimming are shaded.

How to Skim-Read

Your purpose in skimming is to get an overall impression of the content of a reading selection. The technique of skimming involves selecting and reading those parts of the selection that contain the most important ideas and merely glancing at the rest of the material. Below is a step-by-step procedure to follow in skimming for main ideas.

1. **Read the title.** If the piece is an article, check the author, publication date, and source.
2. **Read the introduction.** If it is very long, read only the first paragraph completely. Read the first sentence of each paragraph. Usually the first sentence is a statement of the main idea of that paragraph.
3. **Read any headings and subheadings.** When taken together, the headings form an outline of the main topics that are covered in the material.
4. **Notice any pictures, charts, or graphs.** These are usually included to emphasize important ideas, concepts, or trends.
5. **If you do not get enough information from the headings or if you are working with material that does not have headings, read the first sentence of each paragraph.**
6. **Glance at the remainder of the paragraph.**

   - Notice any italicized or boldfaced words or phrases. These are key terms used throughout the selection.
   - Look for any lists of ideas within the text of the material. The author may use numerals, such as 1, 2, and 3, to organize the list or may include signal words such as *first, second, one major cause, another cause,* and the like.
   - Look for unusual or striking features of the paragraph. You may notice a series of dates, many capitalized words, or several large-figure numbers.

7. **Read the summary or last paragraph.**

FROM A VEGETARIAN: LOOKING AT HUNTING FROM BOTH SIDES NOW

Deer hunting season opened Nov. 18, and as the gunfire resumes in our woodlands 1 and fields so will the perennial sniping between hunters and animal rights supporters. I always feel caught in the cross-fire on this matter, because I have been a vegetarian and animal rights advocate for over 25 years, but I also have friends I respect who are hunters. I've learned the issue is not as black-and-white as I once believed.

(continued)

Figure 20-2
An Example of Skimming

Growing up with many beloved pets and no hunters in my life, I assumed these people were bloodthirsty animal haters. When, in my 20s, I read the great humanitarian Albert Schweitzer's writings on reverence for life, I became a vegetarian and even more contemptuous of hunters.   2

But I had to revise my opinion after seeing the classic 1981 African film, "The Gods Must Be Crazy." The hero, a good-hearted bushman, slays a small gazelle, then tenderly strokes her, apologizing for taking her life. He explains his family is hungry and thanks her for providing food. I was stunned: a hunter practicing reverence for life! Later, I learned that Native American tradition has the same compassionate awareness about life lost so another life may be sustained.   3

My position softened further several years ago when Alex Pacheco, a leading animals-rights activist, spoke here. Detailing inhumane practices at meat-packing plants and factory farms, he said the most important thing anyone could do to lessen animal suffering was to stop eating meat. I decided to work toward being vegan (eating no animal products) and reluctantly admitted that hunters were not the animal kingdom's worst enemies. However, I still disliked them.   4

What really changed my perspective was getting to know some hunters personally, through my job at a Red Cross blood-donation center. Some of my co-workers and a number of our donors are civic-minded people who donate blood (which most people don't) but also shed animal blood with their guns and arrows. Confronting this paradox brought me some realizations.   5

First, hunters are like any group that differs from me: lacking personal experience of them made it easier to demonize them. They aren't monsters. I don't know if any of them apologizes to or thanks his kill as the hungry bushman did but I do know they aren't cruel, sadistic or bloodthirsty—quite the opposite, as I later discovered.   6

Tip *Demonize* means "describe as evil (immoral) like a demon."

Second, these people aren't just amusing themselves by ending a life; they are acquiring food. This death that sustains another life has a meaning that, for example, fox hunting does not. To the animal, this distinction may mean little. But it is significant when considering a person's intentions.   7

Also, I was informed that hunters don't "like to kill." They enjoy the outdoors, the camaraderie and the various skills involved. (One of these skills, the "cleankill," is prized precisely because it minimizes suffering.) Like vegetable gardeners, they enjoy providing food [for] themselves and their families with their own hands. Like those who fish, they enjoy a process of food acquisition that involves an animal's death, but not because it does. Again, this may seem a small point (especially to the prey), but I feel it is meaningful from the standpoint of the hunter's humanity.   8

In addition, I've come to see a certain integrity in hunters as meat-eaters who "do their own dirty work." Packaged cold-cuts and fast-food burgers mask the fact of lives bled out on the killing floor. Hunters never forget this, for they accept personal responsibility for it.   9

Furthermore, were I an animal that had to die to feed a human, I'd rather it happen one-on-one, at the hands of that person in the woods that were my home, than amidst the impersonal mass-production machinery of a meat factory. Either way is death, but one way has more dignity, less fear and less suffering.   10

There are bad hunters who trespass, shoot domestic animals, hunt intoxicated or disregard that cardinal rule of hunting's unwritten code of ethics: wounded prey must not be allowed to suffer. Last Thanksgiving morning in Chestnut Ridge Park, I found a fresh trail fo deer tracks in the snow, heavily splashed with blood. It was horrible.   11

One of my hunter co-workers was also upset when I told him about it, and had this story. He himself was able to hunt only one day last season and sighted a small, wounded doe. As a student on a tight budget with a family, he hunts for food and   12 would have preferred to ignore the doe's plight and meet his license limit with a large buck. Instead, he devoted a long, difficult day to trailing her until he was close enough to end her suffering. This was a act of mercy and even self-sacrifice, not the action of a heartless person insensitive to animals. It was reverence for life. He claims many hunters would do and have done the same.

And I realized that compassion has many faces, some of the truest the most [13] unexpected.

—*The Buffalo News*

DIRECTIONS   Skim each of the following selections. Then summarize each article in the space provided. For help writing summaries, see Chapter 16, p. 346.

Exercise 5

Selection 1: "Are There Perfect Answers About Greenness?"

_____

_____

_____

_____

_____

_____

_____

_____

Selection 2: "Sleep: The Great Restorer"

_____

_____

_____

_____

_____

_____

_____

_____

Tip *Staff morale* means "the attitude of employees toward their work environment." High morale refers to positive (good) impressions of the place; low morale refers to negative impressions. (Don't confuse *morale* with *moral*.)

1. Are There Perfect Answers About Greenness?

A growing list of U.S. firms have decided—for public relations, staff morale, and other reasons—to be socially responsible about the environment. This is called going "green." For example, Lever Brothers, a manufacturer of household products, has led the pack in recycling plastic bottles. DuPont has campaigned for chemical companies to take voluntary environmental initiatives. Monsanto, a chemical giant, took the lead in reducing air pollution long before passage of the Clean Air Act of 1990. Downy Fabric Softener can now be purchased in a "refill" pack.

Also, small firms in many businesses—bakers, painters, dry cleaners, and printing companies—have taken steps to comply with the law. Kinko's, a copying and business service firm, recycles paper and toner. Hannaford Brothers supermarkets, located in New England, offer shoppers canvas bags rather than plastic or paper bags. There is a lot of interest in and action toward being a responsible business and in achieving a "green," livable environment. However, there is also some debate about what is best.

In November 1990 McDonald's Corporation said it would phase out its use of polystyrene foam containers in favor of paper. McDonald's decision was based on evidence suggesting that the chemicals used in producing polystyrene were harmful to the environment. Now studies and researchers have suggested that the foam containers may be better for the environment than paper ones because the loss of trees used to produce paper is environmentally destructive. To settle similar debates, researchers have used a life-cycle analysis procedure to tote up every environmental risk associated with making, using, and disposing of products. In an unpublished study it sponsored, McDonald's claims that paper has lower environmental costs in most, if not all, respects. Therefore McDonald's will stick with paper.

The environmentally correct decision regarding greenness is equally unclear in the diaper industry. In a study sponsored by Procter & Gamble, the manufacturer of Luvs and Pampers disposable diapers, it was found that cloth diapers consume more than three times as much energy, cradle to grave, as disposables do. But a study sponsored by the National Association of Diaper Services found the opposite.

The diaper duel illustrates the toughest issue in life-cycle analysis; how to compare different kinds of environmental harm. Cloth diapers use about 60 percent more water and [create a] greater volume of water pollution than disposables do. But disposables generate more than seven times as much trash, hence filling landfills, and they take more energy to produce. Biodegradable disposables, the hoped-for compromise, only biodegrade in the sunlight, not when buried in a landfill.

Can all products be separated into good and bad categories? The public would like simple answers: foam or paper? disposables or cloth? It doesn't appear, however, that life-cycle analysis or any present analytical methodology is going to provide simple answers. Costs, green benefits, research to support and oppose, common sense, and leadership are all factors that society, the government, and individuals will have to weigh in making decisions about ecological issues.

—Kinnear, Bernhardt, and Krentler, *Principles of Marketing,* p. 61

2. Sleep: the Great Restorer

Sleep serves at least two biological purposes in the body: *conservation* of energy so that we are rested and ready to perform during high-performance daylight hours, and *restoration* so that neurotransmitters that have been depleted during waking hours can be replenished. This process clears the brain of daily minutiae as a means of preparing for a new day. Getting enough sleep to feel ready to meet daily challenges is a key factor in maintaining optimal physical and psychosocial health.

All of us can identify with that tired, listless feeling caused by sleep deprivation during periods of high stress. Either we can't find enough hours in the day for sleep, or once we get into bed, we can't fall asleep or stay asleep. **Insomnia**—difficulty in falling asleep quickly, frequent arousals during sleep, or early morning awakening—is a common complaint among 20 to 40 percent of Americans. Insomnia is more common among women than among men, and its prevalence is correlated with age and low socioeconomic status.

Some people have difficulty getting a good night's rest due to other sleep disorders. **Sleep apnea,** a condition in which a person may experience hundreds of episodes of breathing stoppage during a normal night's sleep, is increasingly common. Typically caused by upper respiratory tract problems in which weak muscle tone allows part of the airway to collapse, sleep apnea results in poor air exchange. This in turn causes a rise in blood pressure and low oxygen supply in the blood. Sleep apnea may do more than just disrupt sleeping cycles; in some cases, it can actually pose a serious health risk.

How much sleep each of us needs to feel refreshed depends on many factors. There is a genetically based need for sleep, different for each species. Sleep duration is also controlled by *circadian rhythms*, which are linked to the hormone *melatonin*. People may also control sleep patterns by staying up late, drinking coffee, getting lots of physical exercise, eating a heavy meal, or using alarm clocks. The most important period of sleep, known as the time of *rapid eye movement, or REM, sleep*, is essential to feeling rested and refreshed by sleep. This is the period of deepest sleep, during which we dream. If we miss this period of sleep, then we are left feeling groggy and sleep deprived.

Though many people turn to over-the-counter sleeping pills, barbiturates, or tranquilizers to get some sleep, the following methods for conquering sleeplessness are less harmful.

- *If your sleeplessness arises from worry or grief, try to correct what's bothering you.* If you can't correct it yourself, confide in a friend, join a support group, or find a qualified counselor to help you.
- *Don't drink alcohol or smoke before bedtime.* Alcohol can disrupt sleep patterns and make insomnia worse. Nicotine also makes you wakeful.
- *Avoid eating a heavy meal in the evening, particularly at bedtime.* Don't drink large amounts of fluid before retiring, either.
- *Eliminate or reduce consumption of caffeinated beverages except in the morning or early afternoon.*
- *Try a mid-afternoon nap, when circadian rhythms make you especially sleepy.* But avoid taking multiple catnaps—a practice that will keep you awake at night when you should be sleeping.
- *Spend an hour or more relaxing before retiring.* Read, listen to music, watch TV, or take a warm bath.
- *If you're unable to fall asleep, get up and do something rather than lie there.* Don't bring work to bed. If you wake up in the middle of the night and can't fall asleep again, try reading for a short time. Counting sheep or reconstructing a happy event or narrative in your mind may lull you to sleep.
- *Avoid reproaching yourself.* Don't make your sleeplessness a cause for additional worry. Insomnia is not a crime. Not everyone needs eight hours of sleep. You can feel well—and be quite healthy—on less. Don't worry that you have to make up lost sleep. One good night's sleep will reinvigorate you.

—Donatelle, *Access to Health*, pp. 40–41 ●

Visual Thinking
ANALYZING IMAGES

When skimming, how much attention should you pay to this image?

Scanning Techniques

Scanning is a method of selective reading that is used when you are searching for a particular fact or the answer to a question. Scanning can best be described as a looking rather than a reading process. As you look for the information you need, you ignore everything else. When you finish scanning a page, the only thing you should know is whether it contained the information you were looking for. You should *not* be able to recall topics, main ideas, or details presented on the page. You already use the technique of scanning daily: you regularly scan telephone books, television listings, and indexes. The purpose of this section is to help you develop a rapid, efficient approach for scanning.

Use the following step-by-step procedure to become more skilled in rapidly locating specific information:

1. **State in your mind the specific information you are looking for.** Phrase it in question form if possible.
2. **Try to anticipate how the answer will appear and what clues you might use to help you locate the answer.** If you are scanning to find the distance between two cities, you might expect either digits or numbers written out as words. Also, a unit of measurement, probably *miles* or *kilometers*, will appear after the number.
3. **Determine the organization of material.** It is your most important clue to where to begin looking for information. Especially when you are looking up information contained in charts and tables, the organization of the information is crucial to rapid scanning.
4. **Use headings and any other aids that will help you identify which sections might contain the information you are looking for.**
5. **Selectively read and skip through likely sections of the passage, keeping in mind the specific question you formed and your expectations of how the answer might appear.** Move your eyes down the page in a systematic way. There are various eye movement patterns, such as the "arrow pattern" (straight down the middle of the page) and the "Z pattern" (zig-zagging down the page). It is best to use a pattern that seems comfortable and easy for you.
6. **When you reach the fact you are looking for, the word or phrase will stand out, and you will notice it immediately.**
7. **When you have found the needed information, carefully read the sentences in which it appears in order to confirm that you have located the correct information.**

Exercise 6

DIRECTIONS   Scan each passage to locate and underline the answer to the question stated at the beginning of each.

1. *Question:* Why was an Irish militia supposedly formed?

Passage

Revolution in America also brought drastic changes to Ireland. Before 1775, that unhappy island, under English rule, had endured centuries of religious persecution, economic exploitation, and political domination. During the war, however, Henry Gratton (1746–1820) and Henry Flood (1732–91), two leaders of the Irish Protestant gentry, exploited English weakness to obtain concessions. An

Irish militia was formed, supposedly to protect the coasts against American or French attacks. With thousands of armed Irishmen behind them, the two leaders resorted successfully to American methods. In February 1782, a convention in Dublin, representing 80,000 militiamen, demanded legislative independence, which the English Parliament subsequently granted. An Irish legislature could now make its own laws, subject to veto only by the English king. Ireland thus acquired a status denied the American colonies in 1774.

—Wallbank et al., *Civilization Past and Present*, p. 533

2. *Question:* What three factors contributed to slavery?

Passage

Contrary to popular assumption, slavery was not usually based on racism, but on one of three other factors. The first was debt. In some cultures, an individual who could not pay a debt could be enslaved by the creditor. The second was crime. Instead of being killed, a murderer or thief might be enslaved by the family of the victim as compensation for their loss. The third was war and conquest. When one group of people conquered another, they often enslaved some of the vanquished. Historian Gerda Lerner notes that the first people enslaved through warfare were women. When premodern men raided a village or camp, they killed the men, raped the women, and then brought the women back as slaves. The women were valued for sexual purposes, for reproduction, and for their labor.

—Henslin, *Sociology: A Down-to-Earth Approach*, p. 246

3. *Question:* Who are secondary relatives?

Passage

Generally, relations with kin outside the parent-child unit play a significant role in American family life. But the strength of those ties and the functions they serve are extremely diverse. They vary according to the kind of relationship—parent, grandparent, cousin, uncle—as well as with social class, ethnic group, occupation, and region of the country. Indeed, in rural areas of the United States today, many families are still focused on extended kin—not just grandparents, but "secondary relatives" like aunts, uncles, cousins, and others. Table 5.1 illustrates the contrasts between this extended kin version of family values, and the kind of familism centered around nuclear or primary family relationships—husbands and wives, parents and children.

—Skolnick, *The Intimate Environment: Exploring Marriage and the Family*, p. 107

4. *Question:* What is a spiff?

Passage

Manufacturers often sponsor *contests* with prizes like free merchandise, trips, and plaques to dealers who reach certain specified sales levels. Additionally, they may get free *merchandise allowances* or even *money bonuses* for reaching sales performance goals. Once in a while, there is a sweepstakes, where "lucky" dealers can win substantial prizes. For example, Fisher-Price Toys had great success with a sweepstakes that gave cooperating dealers a chance to win a trip to Puerto Rico. These types of programs may also be directed at in-store sales personnel for their individual sales performances. A direct payment by a manufacturer to a channel member salesperson is called a *spiff*. This is very common at the consumer level for consumer durables and cosmetics, and at the wholesale level for beer and records. Another version of a spiff is when retailers pay their salespeople to push certain items. Clearly, this practice makes it possible for consumers to be deceived by a salesperson attempting to earn *push money*. As a result, these types of payments are controversial.

—Kinnear, Bernhardt, and Krentler, *Principles of Marketing,* p. 495

5. *Question:* What were the objectives of the New Deal?

Passage

In the 1932 elections, Franklin D. Roosevelt, only the third Democrat to be elected to the presidency since 1860, overwhelmed Hoover by assembling a coalition of labor, intellectuals, minorities, and farmers. The country had reached a crisis point by the time he was to be inaugurated in 1933, and quick action had to be taken in the face of bank closings. Under his leadership, the New Deal, a sweeping, pragmatic, often hit-or-miss program, was developed to cope with the emergency. The New Deal's three objectives were relief, recovery, and reform. Millions of dollars flowed from the federal treasury to feed the hungry, create jobs for the unemployed through public works, and provide for the sick and elderly through such reforms as the Social Security Act. In addition, Roosevelt's administration substantially reformed the banking and stock systems, greatly increased the rights of labor unions, invested in massive public power and conservation projects, and supported families who either needed homes or were in danger of losing the homes they inhabited.

—Wallbank et al., *Civilization Past and Present,* p. 781

USING COLLEGE TEXTBOOKS
Varying Your Reading Rate

To make the most of your valuable study time, vary your reading rate according to the difficulty of the textbook you are reading. Textbooks with big text, many headings, boldfaced words, and lots of graphics and visual elements allow you to read fast. Those with dense, small text, few headings, a lot of new vocabulary, and a lack of graphic elements require a slower reading rate. The two samples on pages 443–44 demonstrate these differences.

Use the following suggestions to vary your reading rate while reading textbooks.

- **Preview the chapter.** As part of your preview, assess its difficulty by looking for textual features such as those shown in the samples on the following pages.
- **Assess the content.** Determine whether the topics covered in the chapter are familiar and accessible or difficult and unfamiliar. Adjust your speed accordingly.
- **Evaluate your understanding as you read.** Test yourself as you read using the SQ3R method (p. 378). If you find yourself unable to remember what you just read, make immediate adjustments.
- **Vary your rate within a chapter.** As you encounter ideas you have determined to be important, slow down. When you encounter examples of ideas with which you are unfamiliar, speed up a little.

12.9 | A Brief History of Plastics

The search for a lightweight, nonbreakable, moldable material began with the invention of vulcanized rubber. This material is derived from natural rubber, which is a semisolid, elastic, natural polymer. The fundamental chemical unit of natural rubber is *polyisoprene*, which plants produce from *isoprene molecules*. In the 1700s, natural rubber was noted for its ability to rub off pencil marks, which is the origin of the term *rubber*. Natural rubber has few other uses, however, because it turns gooey at warm temperatures and brittle at cold temperatures.

In 1839, an American inventor, Charles Goodyear, discovered *rubber vulcanization,* a process in which natural rubber and sulfur are heated together. The product, vulcanized rubber, is harder than natural rubber and retains its elastic properties over a wide range of temperatures. This is the result of *disulfide cross-linking* between polymer chains. To help quench our ever-growing thirst for vulcanized rubber, the polymer of rubber (polyisoprene) is now also produced from petroleum.

Charles Goodyear was the classic eccentric inventor. He lived most of his life in poverty, obsessed with transforming rubber into a useful material. Goodyear was a man of ill health who died in debt, yet he remained stubbornly optimistic. The present-day Goodyear Corporation was founded not by Goodyear but by others who sought to pay tribute to his name 15 years after he died.

In 1845, as vulcanized rubber was becoming popular, the Swiss chemistry professor Christian Schönbein wiped up a spilled mixture of nitric and sulfuric acids with a cotton rag that he then hung up to dry. Within a few minutes, the rag burst into flames and then vanished, leaving only a tiny bit of ash. Schönbein had discovered nitrocellulose, in which most of the hydroxyl groups in cellulose are bonded to nitrate groups. Schönbein's attempts to market nitrocellulose as a smokeless gunpowder (*guncotton*) were unsuccessful, mainly because of a number of lethal explosions at plants producing the material.

Researchers in France discovered that solvents such as diethyl ether and alcohol transformed nitrocellulose to a gel that could be molded into various shapes. This workable nitrocellulose material was dubbed *collodion*, and its first application was as a medical dressing for cuts.

In 1870, John Hyatt, a young inventor from Albany, New York, discovered that collodion's moldable properties were vastly improved by using camphor as a solvent. This camphor-based nitrocellulose material was named *celluloid*, and it became the plastic of choice for the manufacture to many household items, such as combs and hair fasteners. In addition, thin transparent films of celluloid made excellent supports for photosensitive compounds, a boon to the photography industry and a first step in the development of motion pictures.

—adapted from Suchocki, *Conceptual Chemistry*, pp. 385–387

difficult vocabulary
no vocabulary defined in margins

no graphics or visual element

long section with no subheads

Small text new terminology

long sentences

Introduction to the Circulatory System

Circulation is the continuous one-way movement of blood throughout the body. All of the systems and organs depend on the circulatory system. Arteries carry blood with **oxygen** and nutrients to each cell, and veins carry away the cell's **waste products**. If the circulation is not **adequate**, cells die. When the cells die tissues begin to die, and the organs stop working properly. This may cause an entire system to stop functioning.

Kinds of Blood Vessels

- *Arteries* carry blood from the lower chambers of the heart (ventricles) to all parts of the body. Arteries carry **oxygenated** blood, with the exception of the pulmonary artery. The *pulmonary artery* carries **unoxygenated** blood.
- *Arteriols* are small arteries that connect arteries with capillaries.
- *Capillaries* have very thin walls that allow nutrients, oxygen, and *carbon dioxide* to move in and out of the blood. (Figure 13.17)
- *Venules* are small veins that connect veins with capillaries.

oxygen
(OX uh jin)
Element in the atmosphere that is essential for maintaining life in most organisms.

waste products
(WAYST praw dukts)
Elements that are unfit for the body's use and are eliminated from the body.

adequate
(AD uh kwit) Enough, sufficient.

oxygenated
(OX uh jin ate ed)
Containing oxygen.

unoxygenated
(UN ox uh jin ate ed)
Lacking oxygen.

carbon dioxide
(car buhn die OX eyed)
A gas, heavier than air; a waste product from the t body.

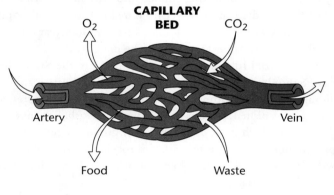

—Badasch, *Health Science Fundamentals*, pp. 349–350

vocabulary define in margin

short sentences

large sentences

bullet points

graphic

FURTHER PRACTICE WITH TEXTBOOK READING

Part A: Sample Textbook Chapter

Write an assessment of the sample textbook chapter's difficulty level. Where might you be able to speed up your reading rate? Where might you need to slow it down? Why?

Part B: Your College Textbook

Choose a textbook that you are using in one of your other courses. Select a chapter and assess its difficulty level. Where will you need to slow your reading rate? Where can you increase your reading rate? Why?

SELF-TEST SUMMARY

Goal 1 What techniques can you use to improve your overall reading rate?	You can improve your reading rate by eliminating roadblocks, previewing, eliminating regression, reading in meaning clusters, pacing, and rereading for speed.
Goal 2 What factors influence reading flexibility?	The type of material being read, the way the writer's ideas are expressed, and your purpose for reading all influence the rate and method of reading you use. Many types of material do not require a thorough, beginning-to-end, careful reading. There are also many situations in which reading everything is not necessary; reading some parts is more appropriate.

APPLYING YOUR SKILLS

DISCUSSING THE CHAPTER

1. Why is it important to become proficient with skimming and scanning techniques? How might you use these techniques in various professions and hobbies?
2. Why do college students tend to skip the previewing stage? Why is this stage so important in understanding various types of material?
3. Where and when do you read most effectively? Under what conditions are you best able to concentrate on technical material?

ANALYZING A STUDY SITUATION

Carla has been assigned a research paper for her business marketing class. In the paper, Carla is supposed to select a popular product, such as Pepsi or Reebok sneakers, survey its marketing history, analyze and critique its current marketing strategies, and make recommendations for widening the product's market.

Carla began with a specialized encyclopedia that provides company histories, and then checked reference books that give data on consumer spending habits as well as market share reports for products. She looked in the online catalog for books and then browsed the shelf near the one book she located in the catalog. Next she consulted the database Business Source Premier for journal articles. Finally she asked the librarian if there were any other sources she should consult.

1. Identify the reading strategies Carla might use for each source.
   - Specialized encyclopedia: _____
   - Reference books: _____
   - Online catalog: _____
   - Browsing the shelf: _____
   - Business Source Premier: _____
2. Evaluate Carla's approach to research for this assignment.

WORKING ON COLLABORATIVE PROJECTS

DIRECTIONS   Your instructor will assign one of the readings in Part Five or distribute an article of his or her choice. Choose a partner to work with. One student should read the article completely; the other should skim it. Then quiz each other and draw conclusions about the relative efficiency of skimming compared with that of reading. Also, list situations in which skimming would and would not be an appropriate strategy.

PEARSON
myreadinglab

For support in meeting this chapter's goals, go to **MyReadingLab** and select **Reading Rate**.

Quick **QUIZ**

DIRECTIONS   Write the letter of the choice that best completes each statement in the space provided.

CHECKING YOUR RECALL

_____ 1. All of the following statements about read- ing are true *except*

   a. the speed at which you read is measured in words per minute (wpm).

   b. you should be able to read at several speeds.

   c. good readers often skip words.

   d. you should read every paragraph the same way.

_____ 2. Your reading rate can be improved by all of the following techniques *except*

   a. previewing.

   b. rereading.

   c. pacing.

   d. regressing.

_____ 3. Of the following sentences, the one that is divided into meaning clusters is

   a. The professor / of psychology / waited patiently / to submit / his grades / to the registrar.

   b. The professor / of psychology / waited / patiently / to / submit / his / grades / to / the registrar.

   c. The / professor of / psychology waited / patiently to / submit his / grades to / the registrar.

   d. The professor of / psychology waited / patiently to submit / his / grades to / the registrar.

_____ 4. Reading flexibility refers to your ability to

   a. comprehend and recall what you read.

   b. adjust your rate to suit the material you are reading.

   c. predict points the author will make.

   d. adjust your comprehension to suit your rate.

_____ 5. Reading selectively is most appropriate for material that

   a. does not require a high level of comprehension.

   b. is unfamiliar.

   c. provides little or no background information.

   d. does not include any examples.

APPLYING YOUR SKILLS

_____ 6. Your reading rate would typically be fastest for material such as

   a. poetry.

   b. argumentative writing.

   c. textbooks.

   d. novels.

_____ 7. The primary objective of skimming is to

   a. locate a particular fact within a passage.

   b. get an overall picture of the material.

   c. find examples that support the material.

   d. make sure you understand the idea explained in a passage.

_____ 8. Jamil is writing a history paper and needs to find the date on which the United States entered World War I. The most appropriate reading technique for him to use in this situation is

   a. preview skimming.

   b. skim-reading.

   c. review skimming.

   d. scanning.

_____ 9. Woody has just finished review skimming a chapter in his physical therapy text. This information indicates that he

   a. plans to read the entire chapter later.

   b. is previewing as a way of getting ready to read.

   c. does not plan to give the chapter any more coverage.

   d. has already read the chapter and is going back over it.

_____ 10. Francine adjusts her reading rate based on the purpose of her reading assignments. In general, her reading rate should be slowest when her purpose for reading is to

   a. analyze or evaluate the material.

   b. be entertained.

   c. obtain an overview of the material.

   d. locate a specific fact.

Thematic Readings

Copyright © 2013 by Pearson Education, Inc.

THEME A Body Adornment

Sociology/Cultural Anthropology

Body adornment, the practice of decorating the human body, is present in almost all cultures. If you have any earrings, piercings, tattoos, or even hair color, you've adorned your body. Clothing and hairstyles are also considered forms of adornment. Body adornment is studied in the social sciences and is analyzed to understand why people do it, how the culture reacts, and what impact it has on behavior, social status, and relationships. It is also studied in the health sciences to examine how it affects the body and a person's mental health.

In this thematic section you will read about how body adornment is used as a form of communication ("Communication Through Body Adornment," page 449). You will also learn why people decorate their bodies ("Tribal Identity Through Body Art," page 452) and how Marines use a form of body adornment to memorialize fallen comrades ("Tattoos Honor Marines Killed in Iraq and Help Survivors," page 457).

A-1   Textbook Excerpt: Communication Through Body Adornment

Barbara Miller

1 Human communication, in one way or another, inevitably involves the body in sending and receiving messages. Beyond the mechanics of speaking, hearing, gesturing, and seeing, the body itself can function as a "text" that conveys messages. The full range of *body language* includes eye movements, posture, walking style, the way of standing and sitting, cultural *inscriptions* on the body such as tattoos and hairstyles, and accessories such as dress, shoes, and jewelry. Body language follows patterns and rules just as verbal language does. Like verbal language, the rules and meanings are learned, often unconsciously. Without learning the rules and meanings, one will commit communication errors, which are sometimes funny and sometimes serious.

2 Different cultures emphasize different body language channels more than others. Some are more touch oriented than others, and some use facial expressions more. Eye contact is valued during Euro-American conversations, but in many Asian contexts, direct eye contact is considered rude or perhaps a sexual invitation.

3 Modification of and marks on the body, clothing, and hairstyles convey messages about age, gender, sexual interest or availability, profession, wealth, and emotions. Color of clothing can send messages about a person's identity, class, gender, and more. In the United States, gender differentiation begins in the hospital nursery with the color coding of blue for boys and pink for girls. In some parts of the Middle East, public dress is black for women and white for men.

The *furisode* kimono is distinguished by its fine silk material, long sleeves, elaborate colors and designs. A girl's twentieth birthday gift is typically a furisode, marking her transition to young adulthood. Only unmarried women wear furisode, so wearing one is a statement of marital availability. Fluttering the long, wide sleeves at a man is a way to express love for him.

■ *Do sleeve styles and lengths in women's clothing convey special messages in your cultural world?*
(Source: © Around the World in a Viewfinder/Alamy Images)

kimono
traditional Japanese garment worn by both women and men

linguistic
related to language

4   Covering or not covering various parts of the body with clothing is another culturally coded matter. Consider the different meaning of veiling/head covering in Egypt and Kuwait. Kuwaiti women's head covering distinguishes them as relatively wealthy, leisured, and honorable, in contrast to the immigrant women workers from Asia who do not cover their heads. In contrast, the head covering in Egypt is done mainly by women from the lower and middle economic levels. For them, it is a way to accommodate conservative Islamic values while preserving their right to work outside the home. In Egypt, the head covering says, "I am a good Muslim and a good wife/daughter." In Kuwait, the headscarf says, "I am a wealthy Kuwaiti citizen."

5   In Japan, the **kimono** provides an elaborate coding system for gender and lifecycle stage. The higher one's status, the shorter the sleeve of one's kimono. Men's kimono sleeve comes in one length: short. Unmarried women's sleeve length is nearly to the ground, whereas a married woman's sleeve is nearly as short as that of a man's.

6   Lanita Jacobs-Huey's research on African American women's hair culture reveals the links among women's hair, their talk about hair, and identity. She also learned about the complex **linguistic** terminology that Black hair-stylists use to refer to various hair styling procedures. Stylists use specialized language and language correction to affirm their identities as hair-care specialists. In hair-care seminars, cosmetology schools, client–stylist negotiations, and even Bible study meetings, Black cosmetologists distinguish themselves from "hairdressers" and unlicensed "kitchen beauticians" by asserting their status as "hair doctors" and divinely "gifted" stylists.

REVIEWING THE READING

DIRECTIONS   Write the letter of the choice that best completes each statement in the space provided.

Checking Your Comprehension

_____ 1. The main purpose of this selection is to

    a. explain how clothing protects our bodies.
    b. discuss the patterns and rules of verbal language.
    c. describe how body adornment is used by people to communicate.
    d. discuss differences between American and Middle Eastern culture.

_____ 2. This selection answers all of the following questions _except:_

    a. What elements make up the full range of body language?
    b. How does body adornment reflect cultural differences?
    c. What messages are conveyed by clothing choices?
    d. How is the use of body adornment influenced by the media?

_____ 3. According to the selection, a woman who is wearing a head covering in Kuwait is saying

    a. "I am unmarried and available."
    b. "I am a good Muslim."
    c. "I am a wealthy Kuwaiti citizen."
    d. "I work outside the home."

_____ 4. In Japan, a person's high status is indicated by

    a. the color black.
    b. a kimono with short sleeves.
    c. a kimono with extremely long sleeves.
    d. the use of eye contact.

_____ 5. Research on African American women's hair culture indicates that black hairstylists affirm their identities and status through

    a. specialized language.
    b. body adornment.
    c. cultural inscriptions.
    d. gender differentiation.

Checking Your Vocabulary

_____ 6. Another word for _conveys_ (paragraph 1) is

    a. writes.
    b. prevents.
    c. conceals.
    d. communicates.

_____ 7. *Modification* (paragraph 3) means

    a. change or alteration.
    b. improvement or expansion.
    c. repetition.
    d. interpretation.

_____ 8. To *accommodate* (paragraph 4) is to

    a. dispute.
    b. overcome.
    c. perform.
    d. allow for.

_____ 9. Something that is *elaborate* (paragraph 5) is

    a. false.
    b. short.
    c. complex.
    d. optional.

_____ 10. Another word for *affirm* (paragraph 6) is

    a. alter.
    b. assert.
    c. challenge.
    d. damage.

Understanding Your Textbook

_____ 11. The title of this selection uses the term *body adornment,* which refers to all of the following *except*

    a. tattoos and marks on the body.
    b. clothing and shoes.
    c. posture and walking style.
    d. hairstyles.

_____ 12. By studying the photo and caption on page 450, you can tell that the young woman pictured is

    a. not yet twenty years old.
    b. celebrating her wedding.
    c. from a low or middle economic level.
    d. single and available for marriage.

A-2   Tribal Identity Through Body Art

Debbie Jefkin

1 Members of the Longia Saora tribe, in Orissa, Eastern India, stretch their ear lobes by placing increasingly larger balsa wood earplugs into their pierced ears. After several months, the earlobe is so elastic that it nearly reaches the shoulders.

scarify
make cuts or scratches in
the skin

2   Why do people adorn, tattoo, **scarify** or pierce their bodies? This question had never occurred to me until I traveled throughout tribal Africa and Asia. Of all the ways that a culture distinguishes itself—through architecture, religion, ceremonies—ritual decoration is the most fascinating of all. At first glance, each tribe or ethnic group is captivating for its own unique appearance. But, for all their differences, many of their reasons for adorning, tattooing, or piercing their bodies are the same: to convey beauty, wealth, status, bravery or even to appease the spirits.

The Beauty of Accessorizing

3   The remote parts of Orissa, Eastern India provide a perfect environment for the preservation of several tribal groups. The women of Bonda tribe (who live not too far from the Longia Saora tribe) are known for their colorful costumes. They artfully cover themselves with hundreds of strands of yellow, orange and white beads, which cascade elegantly like a brilliant bib. The crowning accessories include a beaded skullcap over a shaven head, silver necklace and earrings, and a brass nose ring.

4   The men of the elusive Dani tribe of Irian Jaya are immediately distinguished by their dress, or lack thereof. They wear only a privacy gourd for modesty. The Dani are well-attuned to the resources of their land, which provides them with superb accessories, such as white lime, flowers, fur, shells, feathers and curved bone nosepieces.

Courtship and Marriage

5   Hamer women of Ethiopia beautify their bodies with elaborate decorations and scars. They apply a concoction of red ochre and animal grease to their hair and style it according to their marital status. If a woman is married, she wears two iron torque necklaces, called *essentes*, or three if she is her husband's first wife. An engaged woman wears a leather band around her neck, signifying that her fiancé has completed the *bullah*, or "jumping of the bulls," a rite that testifies to his manhood and his right to marry. A young girl of marriageable age wears a metal visor called a *balle* to indicate her status. This symbol of eligibility simplifies things at the weekly market, which is a common meeting place for young men and women. A Hamer man notches his ear on the occasion of his first marriage, and the edges of his ears are pierced once for each wife he has.

6   In the Wodaabes of West Africa, the most dramatic beauty custom is the *gerewol* courting ritual. Young men adorn themselves with extravagant costumes and makeup, carefully applied to highlight their cherished elements of beauty: sinewy bodies, thin noses and lips, and white eyeballs and teeth. Once festooned in full *gerewol* **regalia**, the men hold hands, form a circle or line and start to chant and sway. The young girls choose the most handsome men, and many of these pairings result in marriage.

regalia
especially fine or
decorative clothing

Wealth and Status

7   Wealth is measured differently from one tribe to another, but one thing is consistent: if they've got it, they flaunt it.

8   Cowry shells are a measure of wealth in the Dani tribe, although these highlanders may not have seen the sea! The tribe's chiefs and most affluent members wear a breastplate made up of the shells to display wealth. The value of a shell is determined by its size, shape, color, ribbing and luster. The most valuable are the smaller shells with the convex back removed. Top-grade shells are given names and accompanied by a detailed history of every transaction in which they were involved. The shells take years to travel from the coastal region to the highlands, passing through many hands en route.

9   PaDaung women of Thailand are known for the practice of stretching their necks. The number and value of the rings confers status on the wearer's family. Girls are first fitted with the rings at the age of five or six, on a day prescribed by the **horoscopic** findings of the village **shaman**. A new ring is added to the stack each year until marriage. There are several theories about the origin of this practice. Some say that it rendered the women incapable of farming or heavy labor, thereby protecting them against kidnapping by invading tribes and slave traders. Others believe it prevented tiger bites. Yet another explanation is that it is purely an expression of feminine beauty.

horoscopic
based on a horoscope, using the positions of the planets to make predictions

shaman
spiritual leader

Intimidation and Bravery

10   Dani men are notorious for battles over pigs, women and land-rights. The warriors set forth for battle naked, but covered with a mixture of ashes and pig grease. This is meant to intimidate their adversaries by appearing so fierce that they paralyze the enemy with fear.

11   The Bume of Ethiopia are warriors who fight over grazing land, and their body scarification is closely related to their warfare. They are earned after a hunt or kill, and given in a complex ritual. These prestigious marks are a record of personal achievement.

12   Across the Omo River from the Bume, Hamer men wear their hair in a multi-colored, painted clay bun. It is a symbol of bravery and courage.

Appeasing the Spirits

13   Akha women of Thailand wear an elaborate silver headdress that might weigh as much as ten pounds, yet they wear it all the time: to festivals, to labor in the fields, even to bed. The point of these ornate adornments? Quite simply, as strict **animists** who practice spirit worship, they believe it would offend the spirits if they did not wear their finery.

14   The most distinguishing feature of Orissa's Dongariya Kondh women is the geometric tattoos on their hands. As animists, they believe that when they die and turn into spirits, these markings will help them recognize each other in the spirit world.

animists
those who believe that all natural objects have spirits or souls

Living in the Remnants of Time

15 Beyond the significant and bold symbolism of body-art, jewelry, clothing and hairstyles, there is another, more timeless reason for why tribes create a visual uniformity that so obviously sets them apart: They hold onto a fierce determination to maintain their cultural identity. This visual uniformity helps keep them together and also keeps everyone else out. The more rituals a tribe binds into its culture, the less likely that members of the group will **assimilate** into the surrounding society.

16 Some of these tribal groups have recently experienced their first contact with the outside world, while others have survived years of exploitation, repression or modernization. It is my hope that they will not be "civilized" into extinction.

17 By remaining true to tribal identity, they maintain a perpetual memorial to their ancestors. These rituals honor the past, nurture the future, and preserve extraordinary people living in the remnants of time.

assimilate
become similar to one's environment

REVIEWING THE READING

DIRECTIONS Write the letter of the choice that best completes each statement in the space provided.

Checking Your Comprehension

_____ 1. The author wrote this selection in order to

   a. explain how tribes preserve their customs.
   b. describe how religion influences tribal art.
   c. explore why people adorn their bodies.
   d. compare differing ideas of beauty.

_____ 2. The supporting details in this selection consist primarily of

   a. descriptions and examples.
   b. facts and statistics.
   c. cause–effect relationships.
   d. comparisons and analogies.

_____ 3. All of the following characteristics are associated with the Dani tribe of Irian Jaya *except*

   a. the men wear no clothes except for a privacy gourd for modesty.
   b. tribal chiefs show their wealth by wearing breastplates made of seashells.
   c. the women have geometric tattoos on their hands to help them recognize each other in the spirit world.
   d. warriors go into battle covered with a mixture of ashes and pig grease.

_____ 4. In the Hamer tribe of Ethiopia, a girl of marriageable age indicates her status by wearing

    a. a multi-colored, painted clay bun.
    b. two iron torque necklaces called *essentes*.
    c. a beaded skullcap over a shaven head.
    d. a metal visor called a *balle*.

_____ 5. The main idea of paragraph 15 is that body art helps tribes

    a. intimidate their enemies.
    b. maintain their cultural identity.
    c. establish contact with the outside world.
    d. become part of the surrounding society.

Checking Your Vocabulary

_____ 6. Another word for *appease* (paragraph 2) is

    a. reject.
    b. soothe.
    c. punish.
    d. challenge.

_____ 7. To be *elusive* (paragraph 4) is to be

    a. hard to find.
    b. physically strong.
    c. part of a small group.
    d. unable to communicate.

_____ 8. A *concoction* (paragraph 5) is a

    a. story.
    b. mixture.
    c. ceremony.
    d. poison.

_____ 9. Another word for *festooned* (paragraph 6) is

    a. removed.
    b. announced.
    c. decorated.
    d. startled.

_____ 10. Another word for *adversaries* (paragraph 10) is

    a. companions.
    b. families.
    c. rulers.
    d. enemies.

A-3 Tattoos Honor Marines Killed in Iraq and Help the Survivors

Michael M. Phillips

1 RAMADI, Iraq—Not long before the invasion of Iraq, when death still seemed far over the horizon, Jason Lemieux joked that he would tattoo Ruben Valdez's name on his arm if his buddy were killed in action. A few months after Lance Cpl. Valdez died in a gunfight on the Syrian border, Sgt. Lemieux remembered the conversation and decided the joke was a promise. When the sergeant made it home, he walked into a tattoo parlor and had the artist dye a rifle-helmet-and-boots memorial into his upper arm. Beneath is written "Never Forget," for Lance Cpl. Valdez and three other Marines who died that day in April 2004.

2 Somehow, the needle's prick relieved the sorrow of loss and the guilt of survival. "When I was feeling the pain of the tattoo, it was actually making it OK that those guys got killed and I didn't," recalls Sgt. Lemieux, now in Ramadi, a nest of the **insurgency**, on his third combat tour with Third Battalion, Seventh Marine Regiment. For many Marines in Iraq, memorial tattoos are becoming a way to give ink-and-skin permanence to friends taken young. "It's like death—it's forever," says Cpl. Joseph Giardino, a 23-year-old Chicagoan whose back reads "Some Gave All" in tattoo blue. The message had referred to two friends who lost their lives during his last tour of duty. Now it is also for two Marines killed here on his current tour, one by a hidden bomb and the other by a sniper.

3 "Fallen But Not Forgotten" marks the upper arm of Cpl. Francisco Villegas, 30, a three-tour veteran from Las Vegas. The words refer to the 17 Marines killed during Third Battalion's second tour of Iraq. Just three days after he stepped off the plane at the tour's end, Cpl. Villegas went to Paradise Tattoo in Twentynine Palms, Calif. "It's kind of like the respect and loyalty thing," he says, sitting in his **flak jacket** and helmet at a base here. "You find some way to remember your brothers."

4 Lance Cpl. Kelly Miller's tattoo commemorates the day his squad leader, Cpl. Jason Dunham, smothered a live grenade to save him and another Marine. "Remember the Fallen," it says, just above where **shrapnel** tore through his right triceps. "USMC 4-14-04." Another Marine from the **platoon** had the tattoo artist make a copy of Cpl. Dunham's own tattoo, an ace of spades superimposed with a skull gnawing an eight-ball. Marines have long been partial to tattoos of all sorts. But Sgt. Lemieux, a 22-year-old from Tupper Lake, N.Y., says his memorial tattoo—"Never Forget"—is a sort of warrior's warning label, to let civilians know what he has been through without having to explain. "It's for my guys," he says. "But it's also never forget the cost of war, to get people to understand what they're asking for when they support war." The sergeant hopes that if he goes home in a box, his buddies will take their grief to the tattoo parlor: "It would feel good to know that they cared that much."

insurgency
rebellion within a group

flak jacket
a jacket designed to protect the body from bullets or shrapnel

shrapnel
bomb, mine, or shell fragments

platoon
a military unit

Humvee
a military vehicle that combines the features of a jeep with those of a truck

5   Similar sentiments bound Mike Torres, Curt Stiver, Jesse White and Jeremy Dillon—who called themselves "wicked . . . super-friends" and gave each other their own gladiator salute before patrols. For strength, a fist in the air; for honor, a fist over the heart; for wicked strength, a fist with devil horns. Lance Cpl. Torres's nickname was Tex Man, being from El Paso, Texas, but the other three thought of him as their guardian angel because he kept them going through frightening times.

6   On July 5, 2004, Lance Cpl. Torres was riding in the open bed of a lightly armored **Humvee** when it was hit by an insurgent rocket. The day comes back to Cpl. White in brilliantly focused snapshots: A Navy corpsman tending to wounded Marines. A motionless leg with a black ammunition pouch, the kind only Lance Cpl. Torres had. Someone saying Lance Cpl. Torres was OK. Someone else saying he was one of three dead. Yelling, "What am I going to tell Stiver and Dillon?" Later, the three escorted Lance Cpl. Torres's casket to the airfield and gave him a gladiator salute as the plane took off. Months after, they went together to the Skin Factory in Las Vegas to make sure their friend would always be with them—and to show their tattoos to his mom. "It was natural," says Lance Cpl. Stiver, now 21.

7   Lance Cpl. Dillon, a 20-year-old from Maine, went with a variation on the helmet-rifle-boots memorial: a rifle with an attached grenade launcher, like Lance Cpl. Torres's, a cowboy hat, cowboy boots and, instead of the usual dog tags, a rosary. Lance Cpl. Stiver, a machine gunner from Oshkosh, Wis., had so many tattoos that he had lost count, so he chose some of the last available real estate on his body, his chest, for a portrait of Lance Cpl. Torres in a cowboy hat and sunglasses. The artist worked from a photo taken during infantry school. Cpl. White has already selected the tattoos he'll get if his remaining super-friends are killed before the battalion heads home in a couple of months. For Lance Cpl. Dillon, whose nickname is Rooster, he has in mind a tough-looking bird. For Lance Cpl. Stiver, it's a skull with devil horns, inspired by a favorite rock group. To remember Lance Cpl. Torres, Cpl. White, a 21-year-old from Bloomington, Ind., chose a tattoo of a stylized Sacred Heart for his upper arm, with the caption, "Tex Man 1983–2004." "There's not a day goes by when we don't think of Mike," says Cpl. White. "If ever a day did go by, all we have to do is take our shirts off."

REVIEWING THE READING

DIRECTIONS   Write the letter of the choice that best completes each statement in the space provided.

Checking Your Comprehension

_____   1. The main purpose of this selection is to describe

a. a typical Marine's tour of duty in Iraq.
b. different ways that soldiers cope with the stress of war.
c. friendships and relationships formed through military service.
d. Marines who have gotten tattoos to memorialize their friends.

_____ 2. According to the selection, getting tattoos has helped these Marines

    a. deal with their grief and the guilt of survival.
    b. honor their fallen comrades.
    c. remind others of the cost of war.
    d. do all of the above.

_____ 3. The supporting details in this selection consist primarily of

    a. research evidence about tattoos.
    b. facts and statistics about the Iraq war.
    c. descriptions from the soldiers themselves.
    d. the author's personal experiences.

_____ 4. The tattoo that Sgt. Jason Lemieux got in honor of Lance Cpl. Ruben Valdez included the words

    a. "Some Gave All."
    b. "Never Forget."
    c. "Remember the Fallen."
    d. "Fallen But Not Forgotten."

_____ 5. As part of the gladiator salute described in the selection, a fist over the heart signified

    a. strength.
    b. honor.
    c. loyalty.
    d. victory.

Checking Your Vocabulary

_____ 6. Another word for _commemorates_ (paragraph 4) is

    a. remembers.
    b. removes.
    c. ignores.
    d. imposes.

_____ 7. To be _partial_ (paragraph 4) to something is to

    a. change it.
    b. give it away.
    c. dislike it.
    d. prefer it.

_____ 8. A _gladiator_ (paragraph 5) is someone who

    a. celebrates.
    b. stands.
    c. fights.
    d. competes.

_____ 9. *Brilliantly* (paragraph 6) means

    a. vividly.
    b. loudly.
    c. quickly.
    d. strangely.

_____ 10. Something that is *stylized* (paragraph 7) is

    a. repeated.
    b. artistically designed.
    c. mistaken.
    d. commonplace.

MAKING CONNECTIONS

1. Define the phrase *body adornment*. Does the phrase have the same meaning for each author? Give examples to support your answer.
2. Each author offers reasons why people adorn their bodies. Make a list of the reasons given; then consider any similarities and differences among them.
3. What types of body adornment and "inscriptions" do humans use? Make a list of the types discussed in each reading. Are there types of adornment not discussed by any of the authors?
4. Compare the tone used in each of the readings. Which is most serious? Which is most academic?
5. How does the author's choice of supporting details affect your response to each reading? Which reading did you find most compelling? Explain why. ●

WHAT DO YOU THINK?

DIRECTIONS　On a separate sheet of paper, write about any four of these five choices.

1. Do you have a tattoo? If so, tell what it is and why you got it. If not, explain why you haven't gotten one and whether you ever will.
2. What kinds of body ornaments were common in the culture you grew up in?
3. Do you think it's a good idea for veterans to have a tattoo for a life-long reminder of comrades they lost in battle? Explain why or why not.
4. What do you think your clothes communicate to others? Do you ever wear clothes that are different from your usual attire because you want to make a different impression?
5. Have you ever gotten a gift of clothing or jewelry and said to yourself, "I can't wear this. It's not me"? What was the item? What message did it communicate that you couldn't identify with? ●

THEME B Controversies in Science: Genetics

Biology/Chemistry

Sometimes it is easy to think that science is all about learning facts, processes, and principles. These are often technical and theoretical; however, their application to our daily lives is interesting, practical, and often controversial. Scientific controversies include global warming, the Big Bang theory, the causes of certain diseases, and the reason for the extinction of the dinosaurs.

This section focuses on controversies raised by the study of genetics. The reading "You're Eating Genetically Modified Food," page 461, describes how the food we eat is affected by biotechnology. "The Genetic Crystal Ball," page 464, examines issues raised by the possible use of genetic information to control disease and to create desirable traits and behavior in humans. Genetics as it contributes to regenerative medicine (the regrowth of body parts and organs) is discussed in "Medicine's Cutting Edge: Re-Growing Organs," page 467.

B-1   You're Eating Genetically Modified Food

James Freeman

1   There's no escape. You are consuming mass quantities of genetically modified food. The milk on your Cheerios this morning came from a genetically modified cow, and the Cheerios themselves featured genetically modified whole grain goodness. At lunch you'll enjoy french fries from genetically modified potatoes and perhaps a bucket of genetically modified fried chicken. If you don't have any meetings this afternoon, maybe you'll wash it all down with the finest genetically modified hops, grains, and barley, brewed to perfection—or at least to completion if you're drinking Schaefer.

2   Everything you eat is the result of genetic modification. When a rancher in Wyoming selected his stud bull to mate with a certain cow to produce the calf that ultimately produced the milk on your breakfast table, he was manipulating genes. Sounds delicious, doesn't it? Sorry, but you get the point.

3   Long before you were ever born, farmers were **splicing** genes and manipulating seeds to create more robust plants. Genetic modification used to be called "breeding," and people have been doing it for centuries. Thomas Jefferson did it at Monticello, as he experimented in his gardens with literally hundreds of varieties of fruits and vegetables. (Hmm, Thomas Jefferson and genes. . . . This column is going to disappoint a lot of people doing Web searches.)

4   Anyway, to return to the topic at hand, breeding isn't a scary word, so people who oppose technology call it "genetic modification." They want to cast **biotechnology**, which is just a more precise and effective breeding tool, as some kind of threat to our lives, instead of the blessing that it is.

splicing
combining or inserting through genetic engineering

biotechnology
the use of biological substances or techniques to engineer or manufacture a product or substance

5 Have you ever seen corn in its natural state without genetic modification? It's disgusting. We're talking about that nasty, gnarled, multi-colored garbage used as ornamentation in Thanksgiving displays. The fear mongers should eat that the next time they want to criticize technology. In fact, the fear mongers are waging a very successful campaign against biotechnology, especially in Europe where they've lobbied to limit the availability of "genetically modified" foods. Even in the United States, where we generally embrace technology and its possibilities, the fear is spreading—not because of some horrible event related to the food supply, but because of more aggressive **spinning** of the media. In fact, you've been enjoying foods enhanced by biotechnology for most of the last decade. And the news is all good—lower prices and more abundant food.

6 As for the future, the potential to eliminate human suffering is enormous. Right now, according to the World Health Organization, more than a million kids die every year because they lack vitamin A in their diets. Millions more become blind. WHO estimates that more than a billion people suffer from anemia, caused by iron deficiency. What if we could develop rice or corn plants with all of the essential vitamins for children? Personally, I'd rather have an entire day's nutrition bio-engineered into a Twinkie or a pan pizza, but I recognize the benefits of more-nutritious crops. Reasonable people can disagree on the best applications for this technology.

7 Still, the critics want to talk about the dangers of genetically modified crops. The Environmental Protection Agency wants to regulate the use of certain bio-engineered corn seeds because they include a resistance to pests. Specifically, the seeds are bred to include a toxin called BT that kills little creatures called corn borers, so farmers don't need to spray pesticides. Turns out, according to the EPA, that the toxin in the corn can kill monarch butterflies, too. The butterflies don't eat corn, but the EPA is afraid that the corn pollen will blow over and land on a milkweed and stick to it and then confused monarch caterpillars will inadvertently eat the pollen. Not exactly the end of the world, but it sounds bad—until you consider the alternatives. According to Professor Nina Fedoroff, "A wide-spectrum pesticide sprayed from a plane is going to kill a lot more insects than will be killed by an in-plant toxin."

8 Of course, the anti-tech crowd will say that they don't like pesticides either. They promote organic farming—meaning we use more land to produce our food and we clear more wilderness. We also pay more for food, since we're not using the efficiencies that come from technology. Maybe that's not a problem for you or me, but it's bad news for those millions of malnourished kids around the world.

9 Says Fedoroff, "I think that most inhabitants of contemporary urban societies don't have a clue about how tough it is to grow enough food for the human population in competition with bacteria, fungi, insects, and animals and in the face of droughts, floods, and other climatic variations." That may be true, but I do think that most Americans understand the positive impact of technology. And that's why they'll ultimately reject the scare campaign against biotechnology.

spinning
presenting information in a particular way

REVIEWING THE READING

DIRECTIONS Write the letter of the choice that best completes each statement in the space provided.

Checking Your Comprehension

_____ 1. The main purpose of this selection is to

    a. describe new ways to genetically modify food.
    b. argue for the continued use of biotechnology.
    c. discuss alternatives to genetically modifying food.
    d. call for a ban on biotechnology and genetically modified food.

_____ 2. The thesis of this selection is that biotechnology is

    a. unnatural and unhealthy.
    b. harmful to the environment.
    c. a blessing rather than a threat.
    d. an essential part of organic farming.

_____ 3. According to the author, genetic modification is associated with

    a. lower prices.
    b. more abundant food.
    c. the potential to eliminate human suffering.
    d. all of the above.

_____ 4. The primary focus of paragraph 5 is on the

    a. differences between natural and genetically modified corn.
    b. campaign against biotechnology.
    c. food supply in Europe and the United States.
    d. widespread fear of technology.

_____ 5. The Environmental Protection Agency wants to regulate bio-engineered corn seeds because of their potential effect on

    a. milkweed plants.
    b. corn borers.
    c. monarch butterflies.
    d. corn-fed cattle.

Checking Your Vocabulary

_____ 6. Another word for _modified_ (paragraph 1) is

    a. limited.
    b. changed.
    c. repaired.
    d. secured.

_____ 7. *Robust* (paragraph 3) means

    a. broken.
    b. expensive.
    c. strong.
    d. simple.

_____ 8. Something that is a *toxin* (paragraph 7) is

    a. artificial.
    b. harmless.
    c. beneficial.
    d. poisonous.

_____ 9. To do something *inadvertently* (paragraph 7) is to do it

    a. forcefully.
    b. without meaning to.
    c. with assistance.
    d. on purpose.

_____ 10. Someone who is *malnourished* (paragraph 8) suffers from

    a. poor nutrition.
    b. a lack of shelter.
    c. a work injury.
    d. food poisoning.

B-2   Textbook Excerpt: The Genetic Crystal Ball: Do We Really Want to Look?

John J. Macionis

1 The liquid in the laboratory test tube seems ordinary enough, like a syrupy form of water. But this liquid is one of the greatest medical breakthroughs of all time; it may even hold the key to life itself. The liquid is deoxyribonucleic acid, or DNA, the spiraling molecule found in cells of the human body that contains the blueprint for making each one of us human as well as different from every other person.

2 The human body is composed of some 100 million cells, most of which contain a nucleus of twenty-three pairs of chromosomes (one of each pair comes from each parent). Each chromosome is packed with DNA, in segments called genes. Genes guide the production of protein, the building block of the human body.

3 If genetics sounds complicated (and it is), the social implications of genetic knowledge are even more complex. Scientists discovered the structure of the DNA molecule in 1952, and in recent years they have made great gains in "mapping" the human genome. Charting the genetic landscape may lead to understanding how each bit of DNA shapes our being.

4   But do we really want to turn the key to unlock the secrets of life itself? And what do we do with this knowledge once we have it? Research has already identified genetic abnormalities that cause sickle-cell anemia, muscular dystrophy, Huntington's disease, cystic fibrosis, some forms of cancer, and other crippling and deadly afflictions. Genetic screening—gazing into a person's genetic "crystal ball"—could let people know their medical destiny and allow doctors to manipulate segments of DNA to prevent diseases before they appear.

5   But many people urge caution in such research, warning that genetic information can easily be abused. At its worst, genetic mapping opens the door to Nazi-like efforts to breed a "super-race." In 1994, the People's Republic of China began to use genetic information to regulate marriage and childbirth with the purpose of avoiding "new births of inferior quality."

6   It seems inevitable that some parents will want to use genetic testing to evaluate the health (or even the eye color) of their future children. What if they want to abort a fetus because it falls short of their standards? Should parents be allowed to use genetic manipulation to create "designer children"?

7   Then there is the issue of "genetic privacy." Can a prospective spouse request a genetic evaluation of her fiancé before agreeing to marry? Can a life insurance company demand genetic testing before issuing a policy? Can an employer screen job applicants to weed out those whose future illnesses might drain the company's health care funds? Clearly, what is scientifically possible is not always morally desirable. Society is already struggling with questions about the proper use of our expanding knowledge of human genetics. Such ethical dilemmas will multiply as genetic research moves forward in the years to come.

REVIEWING THE READING

DIRECTIONS   Write the letter of the choice that best completes each statement in the space provided.

Checking Your Comprehension

_____   1. The main purpose of this selection is to

       a. criticize the use of genetic engineering.
       b. explore the potential effects of genetic research.
       c. promote the use of genetic screening.
       d. propose stricter regulation of genetic research.

_____   2. The thesis of this selection is that advances in genetic research

       a. have resulted in the misuse of genetic information.
       b. will improve our understanding of how DNA works.
       c. have led to an increasing number of ethical dilemmas.
       d. should be used only for the study and treatment of disease.

_____ 3. Of the following diseases, the only one that is not mentioned in the selection as being identified by genetic research is

    a. muscular dystrophy.
    b. sick-cell anemia.
    c. diabetes.
    d. cystic fibrosis.

_____ 4. The author points to China's use of genetic information as an example of

    a. progress made in mapping the human genome.
    b. the protection of personal genetic information.
    c. the importance of genetic research.
    d. the abuse of genetic information.

_____ 5. The issue of genetic privacy is illustrated by all of the following situations except

    a. employers ruling out job applicants with potential illnesses.
    b. parents using genetic information to create "designer children."
    c. prospective spouses asking for a genetic evaluation before marriage.
    d. life insurers requiring genetic testing before issuing a policy.

Checking Your Vocabulary

_____ 6. Another word for _blueprint_ (paragraph 1) is

    a. barrier.
    b. design.
    c. improvement.
    d. lesson.

_____ 7. _Manipulate_ (paragraph 4) means

    a. prevent.
    b. replace.
    c. change.
    d. remove.

_____ 8. To be _inevitable_ (paragraph 6) is to be

    a. unavoidable.
    b. impractical.
    c. doubtful.
    d. insufficient.

_____ 9. Another word for *evaluate* (paragraph 6) is

    a. alter.

    b. reveal.

    c. copy.

    d. assess.

_____ 10. *Prospective* (paragraph 7) means

    a. difficult.

    b. likely.

    c. regular.

    d. careful.

B-3 Medicine's Cutting Edge: Re-Growing Organs

The Future Is Here: Regenerative Powder, Ink Jet Heart Cells And Custom-Made Body Parts

Wyatt Andrews

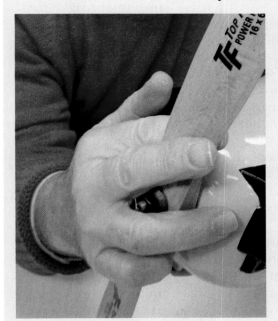

Lee Spievack sliced off a half-inch of this finger—but with the help of doctors and a special medical powder, he grew it back.

Imagine re-growing a severed fingertip, or creating an organ in the lab that can be transplanted into a patient without risk of rejection. It sounds like science fiction, but it's not. It's the burgeoning field of regenerative medicine, in which scientists are learning to harness the body's own power to regenerate itself, with astonishing results.

1   Three years ago, Lee Spievack sliced off the tip of his finger in the propeller of a hobby shop airplane. What happened next, **Andrews** reports, propelled him into the future of medicine.

2   Spievack's brother, Alan, a medical research scientist, sent him a special powder and told him to sprinkle it on the wound. "I powdered it on until it was covered," Spievack recalled. To his astonishment, every bit of his fingertip grew back.

3   "Your finger grew back," Andrews asked Spievack, "flesh, blood vessels and nail?" "Four weeks," he answered. Andrews spoke to Dr. Steven Badylak of the University of Pittsburgh's McGowan Institute of Regenerative Medicine and asked if that powder was the reason behind Spievack's new finger tip. Yes, it is," Badylak explained. "We took this and turned it into a powdered form."

4   That powder is a substance made from pig bladders called extracellular matrix. It is a mix of protein and connective tissue surgeons often use to repair tendons and it holds some of the secrets behind the emerging new science of regenerative medicine. "It tells the body, start that process of tissue regrowth," said Badylak.

5　Badlayk is one of the many scientists who now believe every tissue in the body has cells which are capable of regeneration. All scientists have to do is find enough of those cells and "direct" them to grow. "Somehow the matrix summons the cells and tell them what to do," Badylak explained. "It helps instruct them in terms of where they need to go, how they need to differentiate—should I become a blood vessel, a nerve, a muscle cell or whatever." If this helped Spievack's finger regrow, Badylak says, at least in theory, you should be able to grow a whole limb.

Advances That Go Beyond Theory

6　In his lab at Wake Forest University, a lab he calls a medical factory, Dr. Anthony Atala is growing body parts. Atala and his team have built, from the cell level up, 18 different types of tissue so far, including muscle tissue, whole organs and the pulsing heart valve of a sheep. "And is it growing?" Andrews asked. "Absolutely," Atala said, showing him, "All this white material is new tissue." "When people ask me 'what do you do,' we grow tissues and organs," he said. "We are making body parts that we can implant right back into patients."

7　Dr. Atala, one of the pioneers of regeneration, believes every type of tissue already has cells ready to regenerate if only researchers can prod them into action. Sometimes that prodding can look like science fiction. Emerging from an everyday ink jet printer is the heart of a mouse. Mouse heart cells go into the ink cartridge and are then sprayed down in a heart shaped pattern layer by layer. Dr. Atala believes it's a matter of time before someone grows a human heart. "The cells have all the genetic information necessary to make new tissue," Atala explained. "That's what they are programmed to do. So your heart cells are programmed to make more heart tissue, your bladder cells are programmed to make more bladder cells."

8　Atala's work with human bladder cells has pushed regenerative medicine to a transformational breakthrough. In this clinical trial at Thomas Jefferson Hospital in Philadelphia, Dr. Patrick Shenot is performing a bladder transplant with an organ built with this patient's own cells. In a process developed by Dr. Atala, the patient's cells were grown in a lab, and then **seeded** a biodegradable bladder-shaped scaffold. Eight weeks later, with the scaffold now infused with millions of regrown cells, it is transplanted into the patient. When the scaffold dissolves, Dr. Shenot says what's left will be a new, functioning organ. "The cells will differentiate into the two major cells in the bladder wall, the muscle cells and the lining cells," he explained. "It's very much the future, but it's today. We are doing this today."

Repairing the Wounded

9　Today, one of the biggest believers in regeneration is the United States military, which is especially interested in the matrix that regrew Lee

> ### Quote
>
> It's very much the future, but it's today. We are doing this today.
>
> Dr. Patrick Shenot

Spievack's finger. The Army, working in conjunction with the University of Pittsburgh, is about to use that matrix on the amputated fingers of soldiers home from the war.

10   Dr. Steven Wolf, at the Army Institute of Surgical Research, says the military has invested millions of dollars in regenerative research, hoping to re-grow limbs, lost muscle, even burned skin. "And it's hard to ignore this guy's missing half his skin, this guy's missing his leg," Wolf said. "You start asking the question, is there somebody out there with the technology that can do this for us?" "You mean regrow the tissue?" Andrews asked. "The answer," Wolf said, "is maybe."

11   At the burn unit at the Brooke Army Medical center, the very idea of regeneration brings a glimmer of hope. Army Staff Sgt. Robert Henline was the only survivor of an **IED** attack on his Humvee north of Baghdad. "It's a great idea," Henline said, talking with Andrews about the military's investment into the new technology. "If they can come up with something that's less painful and can heal it with natural growth, without all this scarring, it's definitely something to check into."

IED
improvised explosive device, makeshift bomb

Regeneration Race Goes Global

12 Several different technologies for harnessing regeneration are now in clinical trials around the world. One machine, being tested in Germany, sprays a burn patient's own cells onto a burn, signaling the skin to re-grow. Badylak is about to implant matrix material—shaped like an esophagus—into patients with throat cancer. "We fully expect that this material will cause the body to re-form normal esophageal tissue," Badylak said.

13   And in a clinical trial at the University of Pittsburgh Medical Center, patient Mary Beth Babo is getting her own adult stem cells injected into her heart, in hopes of growing new arteries. Her surgeon is Dr. Joon Lee. "It's what we consider the Holy Grail of our field for coronary heart disease," Lee said. The Holy Grail, because if stem cells can re-grow arteries, there's less need for surgery. "It's a big difference from open heart surgery to this," said Babo. "If people don't have to go through that, this would be the way to go . . . if it works."

The Business of Regeneration

14 Corporate America, meanwhile, already believes regeneration will work. Investment capital has been pouring in to commercialize and mass produce custom-made body parts. The Tengion Company has bought the license, built the factory, and is already making those bladders developed at Wake Forest that we told you about earlier. "We're actually building a very real business around a very real and compelling patient need," said Dr. Steven Nichtberger, Tengion's CEO.

15   Tengion believes regeneration will soon revolutionize transplant medicine. Transplant patients, instead of waiting years for a donated

organ, will ship cells off to a lab and wait a few weeks to have their own re-grown. "I look at the patients who are on the waitlist for transplant," said Nichtberger. "I look at the opportunity we have to build bladders, to build vessels, to build kidneys. In regenerative medicine, I think it is similar to the semi-conductor industry of the 1980s, you don't know where it's going to go, but you know it's big."

REVIEWING THE READING

DIRECTIONS   Write the letter of the choice that best completes each statement in the space provided.

Checking Your Comprehension

_____ 1. The main purpose of this selection is to

  a. describe the emerging science of regenerative medicine.
  b. present the pros and cons of regenerative medicine.
  c. argue for increased federal support of regenerative research.
  d. criticize the military's investment in regenerative technology.

_____ 2. The thesis of this selection is that the field of regenerative medicine

  a. is more like science fiction than reality.
  b. offers many promising uses for patients.
  c. is unlikely to advance beyond the lab.
  d. has little support in the corporate world.

_____ 3. The substance that allowed Lee Spievack to grow back his fingertip consisted of

  a. tissue grown in a Wake Forest lab.
  b. regenerated cells from an ink jet printer.
  c. powder made from pig bladders.
  d. stem cells developed on a scaffold.

_____ 4. The doctor who is performing a bladder transplant with an organ built from the patient's own cells is

  a. Mary Beth Babo.
  b. Patrick Shenot.
  c. Joon Lee.
  d. Steven Nichtberger.

_____ 5. In the selection, regenerative medicine is mentioned as a possible treatment for all of the following _except_

  a. burns.
  b. war injuries.
  c. diabetes.
  d. heart disease.

Checking Your Vocabulary

_____ 6. If something is *propelled* (paragraph 1) it is

a. kept away.
b. set aside.
c. moved forward.
d. not seen.

_____ 7. Another word for *prod* (paragraph 7) is

a. join.
b. push.
c. prevent.
d. copy.

_____ 8. *Transformational* (paragraph 8) refers to a change that is

a. dramatic.
b. minor.
c. expected.
d. insignificant.

_____ 9. Another word for *scaffold* (paragraph 8) is

a. scene.
b. arena.
c. scheme.
d. structure.

_____ 10. Something that is *compelling* (paragraph 14) is

a. convincing.
b. restrictive.
c. unnecessary.
d. worthless.

MAKING CONNECTIONS

1. For one of the issues discussed in this section, identify what information you would need to understand the issue more fully. If you were to write a paper or a speech on this issue, where would you look for additional information?
2. In your opinion, which of the issues addressed in this section is most compelling? Which issue is most relevant to your life?
3. What makes these topics controversial? What other topics could have been included as part of "Controversies in Science"?
4. Compare the tone used in each of the readings. Which is most convincing? Which is most academic? Which is most (and least) objective?
5. Consider the different types of supporting details each author used. Which details were most convincing and why? ●

WHAT DO YOU THINK?

DIRECTIONS On a separate sheet of paper, write about any four of these five choices.

1. What did you learn that was most surprising to you? What did you want to know more about after reading the selections? Did any of the selections change your opinion about an issue?

2. In what ways do you think your life will be affected by the issues discussed in these selections? Which issue do you feel most optimistic about and which causes you the most concern?

3. Imagine 25 years in the future. What predictions can you make about each of the issues described in this section?

4. If you were a scientist, in which of the fields described in this section would you be most interested in working? Which field do you believe has the most potential for improving life on Earth in the twenty-first century?

5. In the selection about genetically engineered food, the author calls it a blessing rather than a threat. Can you think of something that is considered a threat by some people and a blessing by others? ●

THEME C Technology and the Internet

Mass Media

The Internet has changed the world in many ways, offering many opportunities and many new threats and problems. Information access and instant communication are obvious benefits; identity theft and violation of privacy are threats associated with increased use of technology through the Internet.

This thematic section will examine several effects of the Internet. "Blogs and Democratization," page 473, explores how blogs create a new form of communication, expanding information access beyond that offered by the traditional media. In "Getting Found Out, Web 2.0 Style," page 479, you will learn some of the drawbacks of communication across the Internet. The reading "Impact of the Internet on Thinking," page 483, offers pro and con viewpoints on the controversy of whether Internet usage is detrimental to today's students.

C-1   Textbook Excerpt: Blogs and Democratization

John Vivian

Study Preview

Blogs hold promise for democratizing mass communication with affordable and technologically easy access. Critics note, however, that there is a polluting element. Blogging has no codes of conduct that require readers to be on guard against irresponsible postings. There are no gatekeepers.

1 As a mass communication tool, the Internet has outpaced older media in democratizing mass communication. This has become an era in which the price of entry to media ownership precludes most mortals. But the Internet, although young as a mass medium, is already democratizing mass communication. The rules are new. The most powerful member of the U.S. Senate, Trent Lott, never figured that his career would be sidelined under pressure created by a pip-squeak citizen in the **hinterlands**. It happened.

hinterlands
the remote parts of a country

People Power

2 Joshua Marshall, creator of his own Web site, talkingpointsmemo. com, picked up on a speech by Lott that, depending on your view, was either racist or racially insensitive. Lott uttered his comment at the 100th birthday party of Senator Strom Thurmond, once a strong segregationist. Mainstream news media missed the possible implications of Lott's comments. Not Joshua Marshall. In his blog on talkingpointsmemo.com, he hammered away at Lott day after day. Other bloggers, also outraged, joined in. Three days later the story hit NBC. Four days later Lott apologized. Two weeks later his Senate colleagues voted him out as majority leader.

Blog Fame Ana Marie Cox was born to blog. Every day at 7 A.M. she wrote 12 items, a self-set quota, on whatever struck her fancy. Though from Nebraska, Cox had transplanted herself to Washington and focused on Capitol gossip. The blog became a must-read in Washington power circles. Cox's satire was funny to some, irritating to others. At Wonkette world headquarters (Cox's spare bedroom), she got "hate mail," as she called it, from both liberals and conservatives. As she saw it, she must be doing something right. She sold the blog in 2007.

3   As a blogger who made a difference, Joshua Marshall is hardly alone. Best known is Matt Drudge, whose revelations propelled the Bill Clinton–Monica Lewinsky dalliances in the Oval Office into a national scandal. Another blogger, college student Russ Kirk, at his computer in Arizona, looked for information on government refusals to release photographs of caskets of fallen U.S. soldiers in Iraq and Afghanistan, which he regarded as documents to which the public, himself included, had legal access. Kirk filed a request for the documents under the Freedom of Information Act. Then on his Web site thememoryhole.org, he posted the photographs of the flag-draped coffins and also of the astronauts who had died in the Columbia disaster. The photos became front-page news. At one point Kirk's blog was receiving 4 million hits a day—almost twice the circulation of *USA Today.*

Accuracy, Truth

4   Both the beauty and the bane of blogs is their free-for-all nature. On the upside, the Web gives ordinary citizens access to mass audiences. It can be a loud and effective megaphone that is outside traditional news media, which have resulted from institutionalized practices and traditions. Joshua Marshall's work on Trent Lott is an example of outside-the-box news reporting.

5   The easy access that bloggers have to mass audiences is also a problem. Most bloggers are amateurs at news, and their lack of experience with journalistic traditions has a downside. It was bloggers, for example, who kept alive a story that presidential candidate John Kerry and an office intern had carried on an affair. So persistent were the bloggers that neither the mainstream news media nor Kerry could ignore it, although Kerry and the intern denied the allegations and there was

Glenn Reynolds
Blogger whose Instapundit.com has attracted a large audience

Glenn Reynolds

Never had **Glenn Reynolds** thought of himself as a media mogul. Although a young man of strong views, he saw his future as a college professor, not a media star. As a side line lark in 2001, he set up a Web site, Instapundit.com, and tapped out libertarian opinions for anybody who might be interested. At first nobody was.

Then, a month later, came the September 11 terrorism. People by the thousands turned to the Internet, found Reynolds' impassioned commentaries from Knoxville, Tennessee, and made Instapundit a daily routine. *Wired* magazine has declared Reynolds' site the world's most popular blog—a shortened word for "Web log" or diary.

Blogmeister. He never aspired to a major media career, but his blog site Instapundit attracts more hits a day than the average U.S. newspaper's circulation.

At 120,000 visits a day, Reynolds has a larger audience than the average U.S. daily newspaper and more than most cable television pundits. He's prolific, writing 20 to 30 opinion items a day, some fairly long, mostly political. He's also gotten the attention of the traditional media. *Fox News* has posted his stuff on its site. MSNBC gave him a separate blog on its site.

Reynolds' blog is not alone in its success. Thousands exist, created by individuals who have something to say. Blogs fulfill a promise of the Internet to give people of ordinary means a printing press to reach the world, enriching the dialogue in a free society to an extent once possible only to media moguls and those relatively few whom they chose to print and air.

The Internet is transforming the structure of mass communication.

What Do You Think?

- How are blogs democratizing mass communication?
- What does this democratization mean for existing mass media industries?
- What does this democratization mean for society as a whole?

no evidence that there was anything to it. Kevin Drum, of calpundit. com, calls himself "unedited and unplugged." Although Drum never touched the Kerry intern story and is respected by his followers, his point that bloggers are "unedited and unplugged" is both the good news and the bad news about the democratizing impact of the Internet.

New Gatekeeping

imprimatur
endorsement or mark
of approval

6 So-called mainstream media are introducing an element of old-fashioned, journalisitically valued gatekeeping into blogging. The New York *Times,* for example, picks up news generated by bloggers when it meets the paper's standards for what's worth reporting. The **imprimatur** of being cited in the *Times,* which involves fact-checking and news judgment, lends credibility to a blogger. When mainstream media are silent on blog content, their silence speaks volumes.

7   Increasingly common are mainstream-media summaries of blog content as a barometer of what's on the minds of participants in this emerging forum. Several times daily, CNN, as an example, reports what's new from the blogs.

8   Newsrooms everywhere keep an eye on YouTube and other self-post sites. Oddities worth reporting such as man-bites-dog items are picked up every day. YouTube attained a special status in the 2008 presidential elections when people were invited to upload questions for candidates. Questions were put to the candidates in CNN-hosted debates. Real issues by real people on video was undeniable as a new kind of vehicle for voters to assess candidates. The videos cut through carefully manipulated campaign tactics that had come to mark U.S. elections—staged photo-ops, town-hall meetings with only pre-screened participants, and politically **calibrated** 30-second spots. Not all YouTube-posted questions made the debates, though. As a gatekeeper, CNN used journalistic standards to winnow the chaff.

calibrated
carefully planned for a
specific effect or use

Learning Check

- Has blogging added a common person's voice to public dialogue on important issues?
- How is blogging being integrated into mainstream-media news reporting?

REVIEWING THE READING

DIRECTIONS   Write the letter of the choice that best completes each statement in the space provided.

Checking Your Comprehension

_____ 1. The main purpose of this selection is to describe

      a. different modes of communication on the Internet.
      b. advertising and marketing on the Internet.
      c. the effects of the widespread use of blogs.
      d. the latest technology for wireless networks.

_____ 2. The thesis of this selection is that

   a. the government should do more to enforce journalistic standards on the Internet.
   b. the type of information typically found on blogs is unreliable and misleading.
   c. mainstream media must start adapting its standards to compete with the Internet.
   d. blogs offer easy access to mass audiences but they lack codes of conduct or standards of quality.

_____ 3. The blog that led to the downfall of Senator Trent Lott is called

   a. talkingpointsmemo.com.
   b. thememoryhole.org.
   c. instapundit.com.
   d. calpundit.com.

_____ 4. The main idea of paragraph 6 is that bloggers

   a. rely on mainstream media for fact-checking.
   b. gain credibility when they are cited by mainstream media.
   c. influence the quality of mainstream news reporting.
   d. have high standards for what is considered newsworthy.

_____ 5. In this selection, the term _democratization_ refers to how the Internet has made mass communication

   a. politically oriented.
   b. accessible to many.
   c. more modern.
   d. free from censorship.

Checking Your Vocabulary

_____ 6. _Precludes_ (paragraph 1) means

   a. comes after.
   b. rules out.
   c. copies.
   d. adds to.

_____ 7. _Dalliances_ (paragraph 3) means

   a. business dealings.
   b. lies.
   c. fiascos.
   d. romantic entanglements.

_____ 8. Another word for *bane* (paragraph 4) is

    a. beauty.
    b. curse.
    c. benefit.
    d. argument.

_____ 9. *Allegations* (paragraph 5) are

    a. claims or assertions.
    b. illegal statements.
    c. conversations.
    d. demands.

_____ 10. A *barometer* (paragraph 7) is

    a. a summary.
    b. an introduction.
    c. a measuring device.
    d. an important announcement.

Understanding Your Textbook

_____ 11. The boxed feature about Glenn Reynolds deepens our understanding of

    a. what it takes to become famous by writing a blog.
    b. how blogging allows for the democratization of the news media.
    c. the amount of time it takes to write a blog each day.
    d. how easy it is to spread inaccurate stories with a blog.

_____ 12. The "Study Preview" alerts you that the selection will discuss the impact of irresponsible postings on blogs. This discussion can be found under the heading

    a. "People Power."
    b. "Accuracy, Truth."
    c. "Media People."
    d. "New Gatekeeping."

_____ 13. The sidebar called "Blog Fame" is intended to provide

    a. a brief history of one person's blog as an example.
    b. detailed instructions for how to go about writing a blog.
    c. an example of what makes a blog unsuccessful.
    d. proof that most blogs consist of hoaxes and similarly unreliable information.

C-2 Getting Found Out, Web 2.0 Style

Sarah Lacy

1 The other night I was watching a clip from *Ferris Bueller's Day Off*, the iconic teen movie of my generation. It's the scene where Ferris and Cameron are at the Cubs game and TV cameras pan Ferris catching a foul ball. Mr. Rooney, the obsessive high school principal who devotes his day to catching Ferris ditching, looks away from the TV just at that second. Ferris narrowly escapes.

2 It was then I realized just how dated this movie has become. A kid cutting school these days has a whole range of ways, beyond the chance pan of a TV camera, to get caught. Thanks to social media, there's an online trail of everything we do, with "friends" and "followers" as the audiences of the reality show starring each of us.

3 Imagine Ferris cutting class today. First, Mr. Rooney probably would have **TiVo'd** the game and had the chance to replay every hit caught by a fan. Ferris would have to resist the urge to change his Facebook status to "Ditching school today. Who's in?" He couldn't blog about his day afterwards. Nor could he post pictures on Yahoo's Flickr. And the hardest for any Web 2.0 devotee: He couldn't **Twitter** about any of it—not even convincing that snooty maître d' he was the sausage king of Chicago. (Although he could Yelp about those valets who racked up the miles in Cameron's dad's Ferrari.)

You Can't Hide Anything

4 The comparison underscores one of the downsides of Web 2.0: getting busted. I'm not talking about the dramatic, life-changing exposés, where a man gets caught cheating on his wife or an applicant doesn't get an interview because of incriminating college-party photos. No, I'm referring to the impact on the seemingly little white lies woven so tightly into our social fabric we don't even think about them anymore—until we get found out, that is.

5 Everywhere I go I hear of people getting busted because of what they disclose online. Valleywag editor Owen Thomas got additional inklings of an imminent Facebook-Microsoft deal when Facebook head of PR Brandee Barker had friended Adam Sohn, Microsoft's head of global sales and marketing PR, through her social network. Days later, Microsoft announced its $240 million investment in the social network. "Yeah, that was stupid," Barker confesses with a blush.

6 Of course most of us aren't **cyberstalked** by Valleywag. More common is a story like Shea Sylvia, a travel and entertainment writer for b5Media. She went out drinking with a friend, and both Twittered about it. She'd forgotten that her boss followed both of them. "Needless to say, he was not impressed with my 'I'm sick' when I called in the next day," Sylvia writes in an e-mail. "Not only did he not buy my excuse, he made me come in and work longer-than-usual hours." Sylvia would never again drink-and-Twitter on a work night.

7 Or there's the story of one Web 2.0 mover and shaker, who asked to remain nameless. He is a notorious people pleaser, so when he's

TiVo'd
recorded a TV program using a digital video recording device

Twitter
a free social networking and blogging service

cyberstalked
used the Internet to gather information about someone

invited somewhere he doesn't want to go, he instinctively makes up an alibi, à la "I'd love to, but my mother-in-law is in town and we're having a tree-planting day in the park." You know the excuse: just sane enough it could be true, but wacky enough he couldn't be making it up. But, because he works in Silicon Valley's Web scene, where everyone is using every new social media tool, he now has to keep track of all these excuses and what days they were on, so he doesn't Twitter or blog about whatever he really did that day instead. And of course, he has to make sure no one he's hanging out with Twitters, blogs, or posts a Facebook photo. If he really wants to be convincing, he has to Twitter missives such as "Just planted a tree!" to keep the ruse alive. That's a lot of work for a little white lie.

Communicating with a Mass Audience

8 But besides being an annoyance, the snowballing prevalence of these busted moments actually underscores the disruptiveness of sites like Facebook, Twitter, and the new social network aggregation tool FriendFeed.

9   These are distinctly different ways of communicating from everything we've seen to now, including e-mail, instant messaging, and even mobile messaging. Consider sending and receiving messages via Research In Motion's BlackBerry. It's still largely one-to-one communication, where you design a message with a specific person or group in mind. Ditto for IMs. But send a status update or a Tweet, and it's available to anyone you ever gave permission to see your information—and in some cases, anyone with a Web browser.

10   As this phenomenon spreads from early-adopter techies to mass audiences, it'll test some of the basic premises behind Web 2.0. Ning co-founder Marc Andreessen espouses the idea that people really want to hear from other people. Facebook founder Mark Zuckerberg believes people want tools that help them make sense of the world around them. Really? Maybe we've constructed social barriers in the offline world for a reason. Maybe we don't want to let everyone in.

11   Just as these new technologies get mainstream, there's likely to be a backlash. Remember the outcry when Facebook initiated the News Feed and Beacon tools, both aimed at disseminating information about what people are doing?

Making Sure Your Stories Jibe

12 The controversy reminds me of the *Seinfeld* episode where George freaks out about his worlds colliding when his fiancée starts hanging out with his friends. In the Web 2.0 Age, worlds collide all the time, at hyperspeed. Done right, these tools help us keep in touch in an amazingly efficient way. I log into Facebook every morning and scan the list of birthdays and take five minutes to make Wall posts. Voilà. I'm a more considerate friend than I am offline. One 140-character Twitter note can tell my 3,000-plus followers I just wrote a new blog post. I called my parents last week; now that they're accustomed to "communicating" with me via Twitter, e-mail, and my blog, they were stunned

to hear my voice. Yet because they knew the basics, we had a deeper, richer conversation. I even wrote my mother a blog post for Mother's Day, instead of sending a card. A former student found it and left a sweet post saying my mom was one of the best teachers she'd had. Beats a sappy Hallmark card!

13   For me, the convenience trumps the fear of the bust. I've accepted it: My worlds have collided, and there's no going back. When I'm late on a column, I know better than to make up excuses that will only be contradicted by Twitter feeds. My parents and in-laws read my Twitter stream, so I don't write anything I wouldn't want them to see. Valleywag scours the Web for photos of me, so I make sure nothing I don't want to see on the gossip blog is posted. If I don't want to go to a party, I don't make up a lame excuse. I just say: "Sorry, I'm really tired and a night at home with TiVo sounds better." It's made me more honest, and probably given everyone in my life a truer idea of who I really am.

14   Of course, it hasn't come without my own embarrassing "Busted!" moments. Fortunately, a column is still one-to-many communication, and I don't have to tell you about them. You'll have to follow me on Twitter for that.

REVIEWING THE READING

DIRECTIONS   Write the letter of the choice that best completes each statement in the space provided.

Checking Your Comprehension

_____ 1. The main purpose of this selection is to

    a. persuade Web users to sign up for social networking services.
    b. discuss the relationship between popular culture and technology.
    c. describe online communication options such as Facebook, Flickr, and Twitter.
    d. explain why communicating online with a mass audience can lead to problems.

_____ 2. The thesis of this selection is that social media tools have a downside, which is that they

    a. cause us to miss out on direct human contact.
    b. expose us to cyberstalkers and other online nuisances.
    c. create an online record of our activities for anyone to see.
    d. encourage us to be dishonest about ourselves and our activities.

_____ 3. The author supports her thesis primarily with

    a. facts and statistics.
    b. personal experience and examples.
    c. research evidence.
    d. comparisons and analogies.

_____ 4. The main idea of paragraph 7 is that

    a. most people using social networking sites prefer to remain anonymous.

    b. most people disclose too many details about their personal lives online.

    c. people working in Silicon Valley tend to try out every new social media tool.

    d. creating consistent stories to cover dishonesty is complicated by social networks.

_____ 5. According to the author, using social networking sites has made her more

    a. honest.

    b. suspicious.

    c. fearful.

    d. creative.

Checking Your Vocabulary

_____ 6. Something that is _iconic_ (paragraph 1) is

    a. sarcastic.

    b. characteristic.

    c. confusing.

    d. comical.

_____ 7. _Imminent_ (paragraph 5) means

    a. about to happen.

    b. well known.

    c. widespread.

    d. unlikely.

_____ 8. Another word for _ruse_ (paragraph 7) is

    a. accident.

    b. delay.

    c. deception.

    d. request.

_____ 9. _Espouses_ (paragraph 10) means

    a. seeks.

    b. promotes.

    c. records.

    d. denies.

_____ 10. Another word for _disseminating_ (paragraph 11) is

    a. lying.

    b. changing.

    c. spreading.

    d. leaving.

C-3   Impact of the Internet on Thinking

Is the Web Changing the Way We Think?

Alan Greenblatt

Pro

Cathleen A. Norris, Elliot Soloway

1 The Internet is just a roadway. But with mobile devices in the palms of their hands, all children, rich or poor, can hop onto that roadway to find answers to their own questions. Lest you missed it, let us repeat: A mobile device connected to the worldwide highway enables all children, regardless of economic situation, to explore their ideas, collaborate with friends and establish new contacts. For a youth living below the poverty line in Detroit, an Internet-connected smartphone is arguably the most empowering opportunity in that child's life.

2 Of course, we adults must provide instruction and guidance to help children make the best use of this truly unique opportunity. Although the temptations to squander the opportunity are but a finger-tap away, we are seeing that with proper adult support children can and do make effective use of their Internet-connected smartphones. As a young African-American girl commented to a CNN interviewer in describing her fifth-grade lesson on the Revolutionary War, "Now I can do something interesting with my phone, not just text."

3 The Internet naysayers say the Web encourages shallowness in thinking. But, in the context of the level of engagement that an Internet-connected smartphone affords and engenders, the naysayers' comments are mere quibbles. Paper, pencils, textbooks, blackboards—the stuff of America's classrooms—simply do not engage today's "mobile generation." For better or worse, this generation needs the interactivity and feedback provided by Internet-connected mobile devices.

4 In classrooms from Singapore to the U.K. to Toms River, N.J., where students use such devices as essential tools for learning for 40 to 70 percent of the school day—plus time on the school bus or in the bleachers at their brother's soccer match—understanding is improving, and so are test scores. "All 150 students in the project did every lick of homework—on time," says Mike Citta, principal of Hooper Avenue Elementary School in Toms River.

5 There is no magic in these devices; test scores improve because the students are spending more time on task because they are more engaged in their studies when using curriculum that is based on Internet-connected mobile devices.

6 There is no going back. Within five years every child in every grade in every school in America will be using mobile learning devices 24/7. And watch the test scores skyrocket!

Con

Elias Aboujaoude, M.D.

7 Much has been said about how digital media are changing the way we write. Not surprisingly, reading is also changing. Eye-tracking experiments suggest that online reading does not progress in a "logical" way but unfolds like a

giant-font letter "F" superimposed on the page. Users read in a horizontal movement across the upper part; move toward the bottom and read across in a second horizontal movement; then scan the left side in a quick vertical glance. Online reading seems just as foreign as online writing.

8 We scan and forage, rather than read, in part because of significant competition from other Web pages. Much of learning starts with a teacher imploring students to "pay attention." Yet many kids seem unable to focus for longer than it takes to write a status update.

9 Studies of students suggest a link between attention deficit/hyperactivity disorder (ADHD) and Internet use. For example, in a study involving 216 college students, 32 percent of Internet "addicts" had ADHD, compared to only 8 percent of normal users. While this does not prove causality, it suggests that our virtual lifestyle may be making us crave Ritalin, the drug used to control ADHD.

cognition
the process of thinking, understanding, learning, and remembering

10 Another cornerstone of **cognition** is memory: What good are reading, writing and attentiveness without retention? But more students are asking: Why bother to remember when all information is at our fingertips and when a Gmail account arrives with 7 gigabytes of storage? Memorizing has become a lost art as we have moved from cramming our brains to cramming our hard drives.

11 Where does this leave us? Because information is power, we feel empowered, but this is deceptive if we are gradually becoming less smart. The digital trend is moving us toward more superficiality. E-mail is a bastardization of language, and texting is a bastardization of e-mail. Blogging is a step down from intelligent debate, and micro-blogging, in the form of status updates like "Ach . . . fridge is empty," is a step down from blogging. Our ability to focus is compromised, which is one reason we love Twitter. But Twitter, in turn, further compromises our mental processing power, making us crave even speedier, less complex tools.

demagoguery
the practices of one who seeks power by appealing to popular desires and prejudices rather than reason

12 This cycle, and this dumbing-down, may prove counter-democratic. While the great equalizing effect of the Internet wipes out differences, instead of enhancing democracy, it may be moving us toward **demagoguery**. Demagogues' half-truths and propaganda require probing, dissection and debate, but one is too distracted. One just got tweeted.

REVIEWING THE READING

DIRECTIONS Write the letter of the choice that best completes each statement in the space provided.

Checking Your Comprehension

_____ 1. The main purpose of this selection is to

    a. describe ways in which the Internet has improved the way we think.

    b. present opposing positions about the effects of the Internet on students.

    c. compare how Internet-connected mobile devices are used around the world.

    d. criticize parents and teachers for not providing proper adult support to students.

_____ 2. Norris and Soloway argue that the Internet does all of the following *except*

    a. engage students.
    b. empower children.
    c. improve test scores.
    d. encourage shallow thinking.

_____ 3. The primary focus of paragraph 4 is on

    a. classrooms around the world.
    b. improvements in test scores.
    c. the use of Internet-connected devices by students.
    d. the principal of Hooper Avenue Elementary School.

_____ 4. The central thesis of paragraphs 7–12 is that the Internet

    a. has no effect on how we learn.
    b. is improving the way we learn.
    c. is negatively affecting how we learn.
    d. has become a vital tool for teachers.

_____ 5. Aboujaoude makes the claim that

    a. online reading progresses in a logical way.
    b. Internet use has been proven to cause ADHD.
    c. memorization has become increasingly important.
    d. we are gradually becoming less smart.

Checking Your Vocabulary

_____ 6. To *collaborate* (paragraph 1) is to

    a. take apart.
    b. compete against.
    c. work together.
    d. direct others.

_____ 7. Another word for *squander* (paragraph 2) is

    a. improve.
    b. waste.
    c. request.
    d. connect.

_____ 8. *Engenders* (paragraph 3) means

    a. avoids.
    b. returns.
    c. produces.
    d. injures.

_____ 9. Something that is *superimposed* (paragraph 7) is placed

    a. under.

    b. next to.

    c. away from.

    d. over or on top.

_____ 10. Another word for *forage* (paragraph 8) is

    a. search.

    b. form.

    c. replace.

    d. cover.

MAKING CONNECTIONS

1. Can you tell how each author feels about the use of the Internet for communication? For each reading, list the positive and negative elements associated with Internet communication.
2. Compare the tones of each of the readings. Which would you consider the most formal of the three selections? How does the topic of Internet communication lend itself to a more informal tone?
3. Which reading did you find most interesting? Which one was most relevant to you? Explain your answers.
4. The selections include several references to the online community. What value do you see in the "community-building" aspects of the Web? What negative aspects do you perceive? Consider how important online communities are in your own life.
5. Reread paragraph 10 in Reading C-2 ("Getting Found Out, Web 2.0 Style"). Do you agree that people really want to hear from other people, or do you think the social barriers in the offline world serve an important purpose? Discuss how the authors of each reading address these questions. ●

WHAT DO YOU THINK?

DIRECTIONS   On a separate sheet of paper, write about any four of these five choices.

1. Go online, and view one of the blogs mentioned in "Blogs and Democratization." Briefly summarize what you read, and tell if you thought it was interesting and believable.
2. Visit YouTube, watch a video, and then write a description and evaluation of it.
3. Are you interested in creating your own video or blog? What would it include?
4. How do you feel about social networking? Do you consider it fun, useful, a waste of time, or harmful?
5. Suppose you had a classmate who spent most of his or her time online with long-distance or virtual "friends" and rarely interacted with people whom he knew and could talk to in person. What would you say to encourage him or her to rejoin the real world? ●

This textbook chapter appears in *Think: Psychology,* a text widely used nationally in college introduction to psychology courses. Like most textbooks, it was written by a college professor. Because Abigail Baird is an expert in the field of psychology and an experienced teacher, she knows how students learn. She is careful to include a variety of learning aids to help her readers be successful in their psychology course.

This chapter is representative of most freshman level college textbooks and it features many of the same learning aids as many other textbooks do. For each textbook that you purchase, spend some time getting acquainted with its features and decide how to use them to help you study. (Hint: Check the book's preface; often, learning aids are described there.)

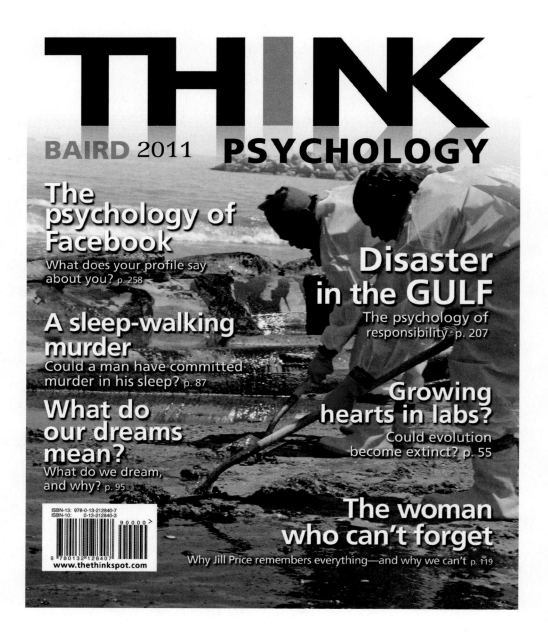

EMOTION AND MOTIVATION

Imagine

a world of 10 billion people, a growing number of man-made products, and not enough ways to reduce, reuse, or recycle everyday waste and garbage. Sound disgusting? Unhealthy? Without recycling and efforts to educate consumers about reducing waste and reusing materials, that world could exist in your lifetime.

Unfortunately, the prospect of an overpopulated, overburdened planet has not been enough to motivate the number of individuals and governments needed to make a significant enough change. Research has found that people will recycle if they think it is effective, if they are knowledgeable about and believe in the benefits of recycling, if they are concerned about the environment, if they feel social pressure to recycle, and if there are financial reasons that motivate them. People don't recycle for a variety of reasons: Some fail to see its benefits to society, while others find it inconvenient. There is a misconception that recycling requires a large commitment of time and energy—who has time to flatten aluminum cans or separate different types of plastics? Many people aren't aware that these steps are no longer required.

Companies such as RecycleBank try to increase recycling levels by motivating people with money. To do so, they give out recycling bins that have radio frequency chips on them that contain customers' account information. When a home's recycling is picked up, the truck weighs the amount recycled. The weight then gets converted to points that a customer can use to purchase items from RecycleBank's business partners.

Another way that people have been motivated to recycle is by seeing what they throw out. Waste-stream analysis, a method in which people sort and record information about the trash they produce, has been successful with groups such as high school students. Noticing how much reusable material gets thrown out can be a big motivator for recycling when coupled with the understanding of what each item is worth. Learning that a single glass bottle can save enough energy to run a laptop computer for a day can motivate a person to put the bottle in a recycling bin. Other motivations, such as offering fun activities as rewards, are especially great motivators for children.

Because governments need to meet both federal and state mandates for recycling, more ways to motivate people to recycle are quickly appearing. What ways can you think of to help keep the planet from becoming one giant landfill?

<<< *What motivates a person to recycle? As students become more aware of the fragile state of the environment, the push to "go green" is slowly sweeping colleges around the nation. As conservation becomes the norm, the social pressure to recycle and reuse increases, motivating many to join in. Whether we're aware of them or not, our emotions often provide the physical and mental drive behind our actions.*

CHAPTER **13**

Theories of Emotion

THE NATURE OF EMOTIONS

Laughing and crying are both expressions of emotions, but what do we mean when we talk about emotions themselves? Based on all the words we have for our emotions and all the artistic ways we express them, we know that emotions are complex. When we experience a subjective reaction to an object, event, person, or memory, we are experiencing **emotion**. Emotion includes an **affective component**, or the feelings associated with emotion. It also involves **mood**, a free-floating emotional feeling that does not relate directly to a stimulus.

Emotion includes three distinct but related parts: **physiological arousal**, **expressive behavior**, and **cognitive experience**. If your heart pounds in fear as you walk to the edge of a diving board or you feel choked up watching **Brokeback Mountain** or **Atonement**, you are experiencing physiological arousal. If you turn around and run back down the diving board ladder or cry during the film, you are exhibiting expressive behaviors. Your cognitive experience might include feeling embarrassed and deciding never to try diving off the high board again. On the other hand, you might feel moved and continue to rent sad movies.

THE UNIVERSALITY HYPOTHESIS

At some point in your life, you might have experienced emotions so painful that you wished you couldn't feel any emotions at all, but humans have evolved emotions in order to help us survive and reproduce. Fear might make us run away, anger might lead us to defend ourselves, and love might encourage us to bond with others. The facial expressions that indicate our emotions also help us communicate. In The Expression of the Emotions in Man and Animals, Charles Darwin's **universality hypothesis** supposes that facial expressions are understood across all cultures (1872/1965). For instance, a frown means sadness or disapproval in Japan, England, or Botswana, but gestures and other expressions of emotions can vary between cultures. But regardless of cultural norms, the expression of emotion seems fundamentally tied to the emotion itself.

THE JAMES-LANGE THEORY

Many psychologists have attempted to answer the question of whether the physiological experience, the expression, or the awareness of an emotion comes first and produces the other parts. At the end of the 19th century, American psychologist William James and Danish physiologist Carl Lange both simultaneously but independently arrived at the same theory of emotion. They believed that the physiological experience of emotion precedes our cognitive understanding of it. Instead of fear causing your heart to race or sadness causing tears to flow, the **James-Lange theory** proposes that the physiological experience of heart pounding or tears flowing causes you to feel afraid or sad (James, 1890/1950; Lange, 1887).

THE CANNON-BARD THEORY

Walter Cannon and Philip Bard, on the other hand, believed that physiological reactions did not precede emotions because sudden emotions don't allow for the delay in experiencing and then processing. According to the **Cannon-Bard theory**, the mental and physiological components of emotions happen simultaneously (Cannon, 1927).

When a 5.4 magnitude earthquake hit Los Angeles on July 30, 2008, Huntington Beach resident Danny Casler woke up from his sleep and ran out of the house in boxer shorts. According to the Cannon-Bard theory, Casler would have simultaneously felt fear and made the decision to run out of the house

SCHACHTER AND SINGER'S TWO-FACTOR THEORY

In the 1960s Stanley Schachter and Jerome Singer developed the **Schachter and Singer two-factor theory**, which says that the cognitive evaluation happens alongside our physiological arousal to create the emotion we experience (1962). Labels become important since

> Emotions involve physiological arousal, expressive behavior, and cognitive experience.

∨ ∨ ∨

Emotion is a subjective reaction to an object, event, person, or memory.

Affective component describes feelings associated with emotion.

Mood is a free-floating emotional feeling that does not relate directly to a stimulus.

Physiological arousal is a heightened bodily reaction to a stimulus.

Expressive behavior is an outward sign that a person is experiencing an emotion.

Cognitive experience is the brain's remembered response to experiencing an emotion.

Universality hypothesis supposes that facial expressions are understood across all cultures.

James-Lange theory proposes that the physiological experience of heart pounding or tears flowing causes a person to feel afraid or sad.

Cannon-Bard theory proposes that the mental and physiological components of emotions happen simultaneously.

physiological experiences can be very similar. **Schachter's cognition-plus-feedback theory** says that how we perceive an environment feeds back into the physiological arousal and influences what we feel. During a pilgrimage to a temple in India in August 2008, a broken railing led pilgrims to believe they were experiencing a landslide. As the landslide rumor spread through the crowd, an environment of panic was created, and the pilgrims rushed down the hill, killing 145 people in the stampede.

ZAJONC AND THE MERE EXPOSURE EFFECT

While cognition may be part of emotion, Robert Zajonc believed that some emotional reactions can bypass our conscious minds (1980, 1984). A flashed image of a smiling or angry face influenced people's emotions, although they had no conscious awareness of having seen the face (Duckworth et al., 2002; Murphy et al., 1995). Prior experience of a stimulus causes an **exposure effect**; the familiarity of the stimulus primes us to react a certain way (Zajonc, 1968). Some messages can go directly to the **amygdala**, a structure in the brain essential for unconscious emotional responses such as the fight-or-flight response, leaving our cortex to process the information afterward. More messages go to the cortex from the amygdala than the other way around.

COGNITIVE APPRAISAL THEORY

In contrast to Zajonc, Richard Lazarus believes that we have to think about our physiological

> *If you are taking an exam while sitting next to someone, you might think that you feel attracted to that person, when in fact you are simply terrified of failing the exam.*

responses in order to develop an emotion (1991, 1998). According to the **cognitive-appraisal theory**, if you notice a particular physiological response, you first have to decide what it means before you can feel an emotion. For instance, your heart could be pounding because you're nervous that you didn't prepare for an exam or because you're excited that the person you went on a date with last weekend just walked into the room. Having to decide what emotion a physiological response indicates could lead to **misattribution**. If you are taking an exam while sitting next to someone, you might think that you feel attracted to that person, when in fact you are simply terrified of failing the exam.

PLUTCHIK'S MODEL OF PRIMARY EMOTIONS

Robert Plutchik proposed understanding emotions by organizing them around a wheel (1980). He believed that the eight primary emotions were fear, surprise, sadness, disgust, anger, anticipation, joy, and acceptance.

Schachter and Singer two-factor theory states that cognitive evaluation happens alongside a person's physiological arousal to create the emotion he or she experiences.

Schachter's cognition-plus-feedback theory states that how a person perceives an environment feeds back into physiological arousal and influences what the person feels.

Exposure effect is caused by the prior experience of a stimulus, and primes us to react a certain way.

Amygdala is part of the limbic system; involved in fear detection and conditioning; it is essential for unconscious emotional responses such as the fight-or-flight response.

Cognitive-appraisal theory states that if a person notices a particular physiological response, that person has to decide what it means before he or she can feel an emotion.

Misattribution is assigning the incorrect meaning to an emotion because of a particular physiological response.

Thalamus is part of the brain located just above the brainstem that receives sensory information, processes it, and sends it to the cerebral cortex; helps to regulate the states of arousal, sleep and wakefulness, and consciousness.

Rapid subcortical pathway is a pathway between the thalamus and amygdala through which the amygdala receives projections from sensory organs.

Emotions on the opposite ends of the wheel contrasted with each other just as colors on a color wheel. Joy would be the opposite of sadness, and disgust the opposite of acceptance. The pie shape of each emotional sector indicated that emotions could vary in intensity, and emotions such as anger and anticipation could combine to produce aggression.

Emotion and the Body

BRAIN STRUCTURES
The Amygdala

The amygdala, a small structure in the brain that assesses the emotional significance of stimuli, receives projections from sensory organs via the **thalamus**, the brain's message-directing center, by way of the **rapid subcortical pathway**. The amygdala can analyze sensory data even before it reaches the cortex. If you hear a loud noise, the thalamus may direct that message directly to the amygdala so that you feel startled and jump. You might turn around and see that the

Plutchik's Emotion Wheel

Slower cortical pathway is a pathway that sends messages from the thalamus to the visual cortex and then back to the amygdala, allowing a person's perceptions to affect his or her emotions.

Visual cortex is a part of the brain that mediates the human sense of sight by encoding visual information.

Temporal lobe is a part of the brain involved in auditory processing.

Psychic blindness is the inability to interpret the significance of a sensory stimulus because of an inability to experience the correct emotional response.

Prefrontal cortex is the very front of the brain and part of the neocortex; responsible for the executive functions, such as mediating conflicting thoughts and making choices between right and wrong. It is essential for the cognitive experience of emotion.

Prefrontal lobotomy is a type of surgery in which the prefrontal area of the brain is disabled, causing people to feel less intense emotions but also leaving them unable to plan or manage their lives.

Autonomic nervous system (ANS) is the part of the peripheral nervous system that performs tasks that are not consciously controlled.

Sympathetic division is the part of the autonomic nervous system that tells the hypothalamus to release adrenaline to prepare the body for action.

Parasympathetic division is the part of the autonomic nervous system that brings the body back to its resting state after actions caused by intense emotions.

Nucleus accumbens is an area of the brain underneath the frontal cortex that is involved in experiencing pleasure.

loud noise came from the wind slamming a door shut, and you would relax. In that case, the slower **cortical pathway** would have sent messages from the thalamus to the **visual cortex** and then back to the amygdala, allowing your perceptions to affect your emotions. When researchers removed monkeys' amygdalae and parts of their **temporal lobes**, the monkeys developed **psychic blindness**—they saw and approached objects that ordinarily would frighten them (e.g., a rubber snake) but seemed to feel no fear or anger and became indifferent to the object's emotional significance (Kluver & Bucy, 1937).

>>> Communication between the amygdala, thalamus, and cortex allows us to attach emotional significance to what we experience.

The Prefrontal Cortex

At the anterior of the frontal lobes, the **prefrontal cortex** is essential for the cognitive experience of emotion. As a treatment for severe mental disorders, from 1949 to 1952, about 50,000 people in the United States, including John F. Kennedy's sister Rosemary and actress Frances Farmer, received **prefrontal lobotomies**. Disabling the prefrontal area of the brain left people feeling less intense emotions but also unable to plan or manage their lives. Because the prefrontal cortex receives input from the amygdala and the somatosensory cortex in the parietal lobes, emotion may be essential to the prefrontal cortex's ability to carry out the life functions it controls, such as planning, setting goals, and reasoning.

AUTONOMIC NERVOUS SYSTEM

In situations such as fight-or-flight crises, the **autonomic nervous system (ANS)** prepares our bodies for action and controls unconscious processes such as perspiration and respiration. The two divisions of the autonomic nervous system help us prepare for and recover from emotionally charged actions.

Sympathetic Division

Imagine that you suddenly realize the building you're in is on fire, or the man who was walking behind you is attacking you, or the bus you need to catch is driving off. Your emotions are high, and you need to act. To prepare for action, the **sympathetic division** of the ANS initiates what is often called the "fight-or-flight response." This system does its work primarily through spinal neurons and connections to peripheral sympathetic

ganglia. When the sympathetic nervous system is stimulated, it induces a cascade of adrenaline from the adrenal medulla. The binding of adrenaline to adrenergic receptors throughout the body results in the fight-or-flight response. The firing of sympathetic neurons, along with the release of adrenaline, causes dilated pupils, decreased salivation, increased perspiration and respiration, accelerated heart rate, and inhibited digestion. These changes allow the body to focus on what it needs to do to get out of the building, fight the attacker, or catch the bus.

In general, this state of arousal aids performance on well-known tasks but hinders new or complex ones. At the 2008 Olympics in Beijing, swimmer Michael Phelps won an unprecedented eight gold medals. Since swimming is a well-learned task for Phelps, the excitement of the Olympics may make him even more likely to succeed. However, if he suddenly changed his sport to table tennis, the arousal would likely not have the same benefit and could create anxiety that would hinder his performance.

The Parasympathetic Division

Once the crisis is over, the **parasympathetic division** takes over and brings the body back to its resting rate. As the adrenal glands stop releasing stress hormones, the heart rate and breathing slow down, perspiration decreases, the pupils contract, and digestion resumes.

COMPARING SPECIFIC EMOTIONS

Just as your heart might pound as a result of nervousness over an exam or an attractive person, arousal levels for many emotions are similar. Many emotions have physiological similarities. Being ecstatic about

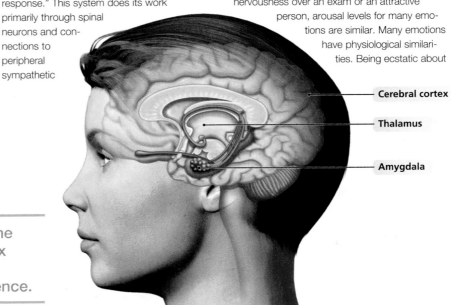

Cerebral cortex

Thalamus

Amygdala

winning the lottery produces the same heart rate increase as the fear you might feel while running away from a wild animal. So how can you tell if you're feeling ecstatic or afraid?

You might want to think of emotions as recipes: Each emotion is made up of different physiological ingredients that set it apart. Anger changes finger temperature more than joy or sadness. Anger, fear, or sadness, will increase your heart rate far more than happiness, surprise, or disgust. Fear moves different muscles in the face than joy, and the amygdala becomes much more active in someone looking at a fearful rather than an angry face.

Positive and negative emotions also engage different sides of the brain. Negativity, such as resentment or guilt, activates the right side of the prefrontal cortex more than the left. Depressed people often show less activity in the left side of the frontal cortex, which is associated with positive emotions. Research has shown that a major factor in drug addiction involves the way that certain drugs are able to directly tap into the reward system that allows us to feel pleasure functions in a very particular way. Special neurons at the base of the brain send dopamine along a dopaminergic pathway to an area underneath the frontal cortex called the **nucleus accumbens** (Nestler & Malenka, 2004). Electrical stimulation of the nucleus accumbens in depressed people releases dopamine and triggers smiling and laughing.

LIE DETECTION

On the game show **The Moment of Truth**, contestants must answer questions truthfully in order to win prize money. In this case, "truth" depends on what they answered during a polygraph test taken before appearing on the program. When someone lies, his or her body shows signs of arousal, which the polygraph test measures. Since many emotions

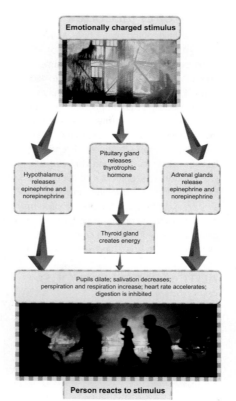

evoke physiological arousal, a person feeling nervous or afraid may appear to be lying. Conversely, spies famously tricked lie detectors because they knew how to control their physiological reactions or confuse results by showing arousal for baseline questions. Thermal imaging can also reveal the different patterns of facial blood flow that accompany a lie. However, many of these techniques may be no more reliable than the polygraph tests we have today.

Nonverbal Emotional Expression

FACIAL EXPRESSION AND EYE CONTACT

It's impressive how much we're able to communicate to each other without words: With just a "look," two people who know each other well can communicate when they want to leave a party or if they've hit on the same idea. Interestingly, not all expressions draw our attention equally. We seem to have radar for threats and will more easily pick out angry faces from a set of different facial expressions (Fox et al., 2000; Hansen & Hansen, 1988). Experiences also influence which emotions we see more easily. When shown a picture of a face that combined fear, sadness, and anger, physically abused children more frequently classified the expression as angry.

GENDER DIFFERENCES

Gender also informs how we read and express emotions. In general, women can detect and interpret nonverbal cues better than men (Hall, 1984, 1987). When asked to express happiness, sadness, and anger, women expressed happiness better than men, and men expressed anger better than women (Coats & Feldman, 1996). Psychologist Monica Moore found that while flirting, women also communicate better nonverbally and use 52 recorded flirting behaviors, such as hair flipping, head tilting, and smiling coyly, to invite men to approach.

CULTURE

Drawing from Darwin's universality of emotion theory, other researchers have shown that people throughout the world use the same facial expressions to show anger, fear, disgust, surprise, happiness, and sadness (Ekman & Friesen,

<<< A polygraph test measures vital signs such as blood pressure, heart rate, respiration, and perspiration in order to determine stress levels.

Facial feedback hypothesis states that a person who makes a certain facial expression will feel the corresponding emotion, as long as the person is not feeling some other competing emotion.

Action units are 46 unique movements involved in facial expressions that indicate emotion.

Intensification is an exaggeration of emotions.

Deintensification is a muting of emotions.

Masking refers to showing one emotion while feeling another.

Neutralizing refers to showing no emotion, even though the person is actually feeling one.

Morphology is the form or shape of something.

Mood-congruent processing is the selective perception of stimuli congruent with the emotional state of the person experiencing the stimuli.

Emotion regulation is the use of cognitive strategies to control and influence a person's own emotional responses.

1975; Ekman et al., 1987; Ekman, 1994). Blind children who have never seen facial expressions will express emotions with the same expressions as sighted people, a fact that argues for the innate biological basis of emotional expression. Although facial expressions seem to be universal, physical gestures and degree of emotional expression vary among cultures. Norwegians who saw President George Bush's 2005 inauguration interpreted his University of Texas "Hook 'em Horns" salute as the sign of the devil.

THE FACIAL FEEDBACK HYPOTHESIS AND FACIAL EXPRESSIONS

Darwin wrote in **The Expression of the Emotions in Man and Animals** that "free expression by outward signs of an emotion intensifies it" (1872). The **facial feedback hypothesis** says that a person who makes a certain facial expression will feel the corresponding emotion, as long as the person is not feeling some other competing emotion. When people were

>>> In 2009, Michelle Obama shocked British viewers when she greeted Queen Elizabeth with a friendly embrace. How might different cultures interpret this gesture?

asked to frown while watching sad films, they felt even sadder than they did while watching the films without frowning (Larsen et al., 1992). People who held pencils in their teeth, effectively forcing them to smile, while looking at cartoons reported that the cartoons were more amusing and enjoyable (Strack et al., 1988). Ekman and Friesen extensively studied the facial muscles involved in emotional expressions and found that the muscles make 46 unique movements, or **action units**. For instance, the zygomatic major on the cheek and orbicularis oculi around the eye move when we smile. These findings suggest that expressing emotions seems to intensify, not diminish, how we feel them.

DECEPTIVE EXPRESSION
Hiding Emotions

Although forcing yourself to smile might make you feel happy, true expressions actually differ from false ones. If you are pleased to see someone but act overjoyed, you're showing **intensification**, exaggerating your emotions. In public, someone feeling intense grief might find it necessary to use **deintensification**, to mute some of their emotions in order to be sociable. Showing one emotion while feeling another is **masking**; the runners-up at beauty pageants smile broadly while feeling miserable about losing the contest. Poker players routinely maintain the "poker face," **neutralizing** whatever they feel, so their opponents have no clues about their hands.

Detecting Emotions

Regardless of how much people hide their emotions, we can detect them if we know the signs of true and false emotions. False expressions involve different muscle groups than real ones, and studying their **morphology**, or shape, can tell us if the expressions are real. Sincere emotions have more symmetry than insincere ones, so both sides of the face show the same expression equally. Real expressions last about half a second; false ones can have a longer or shorter duration. Temporal patterning also differs in false and real emotions; sincere expressions come and go smoothly, but insincere ones start and end abruptly.

> **Cognition, or thought, can influence what we feel or believe we feel. Arousal from one event can spill over into the emotions we experience about other events.**

Experienced Emotion

COGNITION AND EMOTION

Cognition, or thought, can influence what we feel or believe we feel. Arousal from one event can spill over into the emotions we experience about other events. For example, if someone insults you just after you've completed a long run, you might react more angrily than usual because your body is aroused from physical exercise. Misattribution sometimes leads people to attribute their arousal to the wrong stimulus. When given an injection of epinephrine, a stimulating hormone, subjects attributed their arousal to an attraction to someone in the room (Schachter & Singer, 1962). Sometimes our emotions can influence what we choose to perceive through **mood-congruent processing**. Depressed patients noticed stimuli related to sadness more than to other emotions (Elliott et al., 2002; Erickson et al., 2005). In general, people will selectively perceive stimuli congruent with their emotional state (Ito, 2000).

Sometimes emotions do not reach our cognitive pathways or even have a cognitive element at all. People tend to prefer an image they have seen before, even if they didn't know they saw it (Elliott & Dolan, 1998). Since the message about the stimulus goes directly from the thalamic nuclei to the amygdala without reaching the cortex, the stimulus can elicit an emotional response without the element of cognition.

When we engage in **emotion regulation**, we use cognitive strategies to control and influence our own emotional responses. For example, if you see your boyfriend or girlfriend animatedly talking to another person, you could stop yourself from feeling jealous or worried by reappraising the situation and deciding that talking does not necessarily indicate romantic involvement. Thoughts can also help us make better decisions. You might have perused college Web sites to decide where to apply and imagined yourself as a student at each school.

If so, you engaged in **affective forecasting**, imagining how you would feel about something that might happen in the future.

VALENCE AND AROUSAL

All emotions have a **valence**, a positive or negative value along a continuum, and also vary in degree of arousal. An unpleasant feeling, fear has a negative valence. As a strong emotion, its high arousal makes you act quickly in a frightening situation. Because people don't enjoy feeling bored, boredom would have a negative valence but a low arousal, as a low-energy emotion. By contrast, elation has a positive valence and a high arousal; an elated person feels happy and excited. Sadness has a negative valence and low arousal, sadness feels unpleasant but does not feel particularly stimulating.

FEAR

Fear may not be a comfortable feeling, but it is an adaptive alarm system that prepares us for a fight-or-flight response when faced with danger. Children learn fear by watching others and by experiencing fear-inducing situations. But some fears, such as a fear of snakes and spiders, seem to be biologically hardwired into us. In a classic experiment of conditioning (that would never be conducted today), researchers Watson and Rayner taught an infant named Albert to transfer and generalize his fears (1920). Initially, the child showed fear of loud noises. The researchers synchronized loud noises with the presence of a rat, and the child gradually learned to feel frightened of the rat (as well as of all furry white things—for more on the "Little Albert" study, see Chapter 7). Likewise, children learn to fear heights by repeatedly falling or almost falling (Campos et al., 1992).

Physiologically, fear seems to be controlled largely by the amygdala, which receives input from the anterior cingulated cortex and sends projections to the brain areas involved in fear. People with damage to the amygdala showed more trust of scary-looking faces (Adolphs et al., 1998). Of course, some fears can be extreme. Phobias leave people so terrified of specific objects or situations that sufferers cannot function properly.

ANGER

Facial expressions of anger may be universal, but elements of anger expression can be culturally specific. To preserve group harmony, individuals from cultures that emphasize interdependence tend to express anger less often (Markus & Kitayama, 1991). Tahitians are particularly polite, and Japanese express anger less often than Westerners. In the West, the **catharsis theory**, the idea that expressing emotions to prevent them from building up and exploding, is generally accepted. Many forms of therapy encourage expressions of anger to release pent-up feelings, but studies have shown that "venting" does not decrease rage and actually makes people angrier (Bushman et al., 1999). Venting may give temporary relief, but distracting yourself or redirecting feelings are more effective coping mechanisms.

> **''**Children learn fear by watching others and by experiencing fear-inducing situations. But some fears, such as a fear of snakes and spiders, seem to be biologically hardwired into us.**"**

HAPPINESS

What's so great about happiness anyway? According to the **feel-good, do-good phenomenon**, when people are already happy, they are more likely to be helpful. Psychologists use **subjective well-being**—a person's self-perceived satisfaction with life—along with objective measures, such as income and health, to evaluate quality of life. Martin Seligman, one of the founders of a field known as positive psychology, believes that psychology should also study highly functioning, not just maladaptive, people. Positive psychology tries to determine the inner strengths, virtues, resources, and character traits that enable people to be happy. Studies have found that negative feelings caused by unpleasant daily events tend to last for a short period of time and often result in more positive feelings the next day (Affleck et al., 1994; Bolger et al., 1989; Stone & Neale, 1984). Similarly, an extremely positive event makes people feel only temporarily happier, and they soon return to their normal state (Brickman et al., 1978).

As the saying goes, money can't buy happiness. Those who value and pursue money often feel less happy than those who value love and friendship (Kasser, 2002; Perkins, 1991). People in affluent countries don't seem to be any happier than those in poor countries (Diener & Biswas-Diener, 2002; Eckersley, 2000). We tend to judge our present state by our previous ones, so because of the **adaptation-level phenomenon**, an elevated mood, more money, or greater prestige becomes the new norm (Campbell, 1975), and we start to want even more.

Affective forecasting refers to a person's imagining how he or she would feel about something that might happen in the future.

Valence is a positive or negative value along a continuum.

Catharsis theory states that a person should express emotions to prevent those emotions from building up and exploding.

Feel-good, do-good phenomenon refers to the idea that if a person is already happy, he or she is more likely to be helpful.

Subjective well-being is a person's self-perceived satisfaction with life.

Adaptation-level phenomenon is a phenomenon in which the things a person is currently experiencing become the norm for that person, causing the person to continually want more.

Relative deprivation relates to a person's comparison of himself or herself to others; when the person compares himself or herself to someone of higher social standing, he or she feels worse, and when the person compares himself or herself to someone of lower social standing, he or she feels better.

Our happiness also depends on how happy we perceive others to be. While not everyone rejoices in other people's miseries, most of us do judge our **relative deprivation** by comparing ourselves to others. When we compare ourselves to those of higher social standing, we feel worse; when we compare ourselves to those of lower social standing, we feel better. Similarly, soldiers in the WWII Army Air Corps felt more frustrated about their own prospects when they saw others being promoted quickly (Merton & Kitt, 1950).

So what does make people happy? Although the predictors for happiness vary somewhat by culture, they include optimism, close relationships, faith, meaningful work, good sleeping and eating patterns, and, in individualistic countries, high self-esteem. Age, gender, education levels, parenthood, and physical attractiveness are not reliable predictors of happiness (Diener et al., 2003).

Perspectives on Motivation, Drives, and Incentives

MOTIVATION

Early in 2008, the world found out that Jérôme Kerviel, a 31-year-old trader with the French bank Société Générale, had committed the largest banking fraud in history and racked up a $7.5 billion debt. Speculations about his motives

Motivation is a need or desire that energizes and directs behavior.

Dispositional forces are internal factors involved in motivation.

Situational forces are external factors involved in motivation.

Motivation states are internal conditions that make a person tend toward certain goals.

Drives are internal conditions that make a person tend toward certain goals; this is caused by a departure from optimal states.

Conscious motivation is a motivation that remains in a person's awareness.

Subconscious motivation is a motivation that is not in a person's awareness but can be easily accessed.

Unconscious motivation is a motivation that operates without a person's awareness.

Approach motivation is a motivation involved with striving to achieve a positive result.

Avoidance motivation is a motivation involved with striving to avoid a negative result.

Instincts are unlearned complex behaviors with a fixed pattern throughout a species.

Hedonic principle states that people want to experience pleasure and avoid pain.

Drive-reduction theory states that a person reacts when a physiological need creates an aroused state that drives him or her to reduce the need.

Homeostasis describes a steady and balanced inner state.

Regulatory drives seek to preserve homeostasis.

Nonregulatory drives initiate activities not required to preserve homeostasis.

Social learning theory emphasizes the role of cognition in motivation and the importance of expectations in shaping behavior.

Central-state theory explains drives by understanding them as corresponding to neural activity.

Central drive system is a set of neurons that create a drive.

Incentive is a positive or negative stimulus in the environment.

ranged from the recent death of his father and a bad break-up to his introverted personality and his overwhelming ambition. Why do we do the things we do? **Motivation** is the need or desire that energizes and directs behavior. It is made up of internal factors—**dispositional forces**—and external factors—**situational forces**—that drive us to do specific things in a particular situation.

Our **motivation states** and **drives** are internal conditions that make us tend toward certain goals, which may change over time. **Conscious motivations** remain in our awareness, but we can also be motivated by **subconscious motiva-**tions, which are not in our awareness but can be easily accessed, and **unconscious motivations**, which operate without our awareness. Studying to get a good grade on an exam—a positive result—is an example of **approach motivation**. **Avoidance motivation** would involve pulling an all-nighter so you don't fail. When we act to satisfy a requirement by eating a healthy meal, we fulfill a physical need and our drive for food. By eating ice cream after the meal, we satisfy a want, something not considered a requirement.

THEORIES OF MOTIVATION

As Darwin's theories of evolution became popular, so did labeling human instincts. William James believed that **instincts**—unlearned complex behaviors with a fixed pattern throughout a species—are purposeful in humans and other animals (1890). Sigmund Freud, who believed in the **hedonic principle**—that people want to experience pleasure and avoid pain—described the force of psychic energy initiated by drives as the root of life instincts (including sexuality).

According to Clark Hull's **drive-reduction theory**, we act when a physiological need creates an aroused state that drives us to reduce the need. If we feel tired, we take the action of going to bed to restore **homeostasis**—a steady and balanced inner state. Reducing the tension reinforces the behavior (Hull, 1943, 1952). Departures from optimal states create drives. **Regulatory drives**, such as hunger and thirst, preserve homeostasis. **Nonregulatory drives**, such as sex or social drives, initiate other activities. A drive to preserve safety motivates feelings of fear, anger, and even the need for sleep. Sexual drives and drives to protect offspring motivate sexual and family relationships. Social drives make people want to cooperate, and educative drives inspire curiosity and play, as well as the pursuit of art and literature.

Julian Rotter developed the **social learning theory** that emphasizes the role of cognition in motivation and the importance of expectations in shaping behavior (1954). Rogue trader Jérôme Kerviel may have engaged in risky trades with the expectation of making a lot of money because people do things based on the expectation of obtaining a goal and the importance of that goal to them. If individuals find that behaving in a specific way does not get them what they want, they might change their behavior. Kerviel's irrationality made him continue to trade despite his losses, instead of changing his behavior.

Central-state theory explains drives by understanding them as corresponding to neural activity. Different drives have different **central drive systems**—sets of neurons that create the drive. For example, hunger and sex have different but overlapping drive systems. Italian researchers have found a relationship between chocolate consumption and sexual desire, and women with low libido seem to become more interested in sex after eating chocolate.

Located in the base of the brain, the hypothalamus connects to the brainstem and the forebrain and plays a significant role in regulating many central drive systems. The hypothalamus is directly connected to nerves carrying input from internal organs and carrying autonomic motor output back to internal organs. The hypothalamus also connects to and works with the pituitary gland to control hormone release.

∧ ∧ ∧ ∧ **Why might offering chocolate to a loved one on Valentine's Day make sense physiologically?**

INCENTIVES

You may buy a soda because you feel thirsty, but you might also buy it because you watched a commercial touting its refreshing qualities. In addition to drives, **incentives**—positive or negative stimuli in the environment—motivate us to act. A strong drive can increase an incentive's value. If you are thirsty, you feel more influenced by the appearance of a refreshing drink.

Achieving a reward or a goal also reinforces incentives. An **intrinsic reward**, such as a desire to help others or learn new skills, creates its own joy just in performing the action. An **extrinsic reward**, such as studying to get a good grade, means we are motivated to perform an action that produces a separate, tangible reward. Triathlete Julie Ertel remembers to "have fun" in her sport and says that athletes get so caught up in winning (extrinsic reward), that they miss out on having fun (intrinsic reward).

Wanting and Liking

Both winning and enjoying a sport give an athlete a feeling of liking—a subjective feeling of pleasure derived from a reward. Wanting to win a medal at the Olympics gives athletes the desire to work hard for the reward. Reinforcement is the effect of the reward on learning and explains why athletes continue the pursuit of their sports.

Animals with reward neurons that are missing or damaged will lose all motivation and die unless artificially fed. The medial forebrain bundle, the brain's reward pathway, winds from the midbrain through the hypothalamus into the nucleus accumbens, the synaptic terminal for medial forebrain neurons. Because

> "Once an individual had met biological and safety needs, he or she would seek a feeling of belongingness—the need to feel loved and avoid alienation.

this pathway controls reward, animals will work long and hard to stimulate it. Rats with electrodes attached to the nucleus accumbens pressed a lever thousands of times to stimulate the brain reward areas (Wise, 1978).

The liking system involves pleasure and does not depend on dopamine. For instance, neuroscientists have found sweet tastes activate the liking system regardless of the level of dopamine. When rats received dopamine-reducing drugs, they still engaged in liking behaviors and only sought out rewards that were directly available. Endorphins, morphine-like substances released by the medial forebrain bundle, inhibit pain and may be involved in the immediate pleasure of rewards, such as the runner's high.

By contrast, the wanting system depends heavily on dopamine. Rats trained to press a lever for a reward have a short burst of dopamine activity in the nucleus accumbens just before but not after pressing the lever (Phillips et al., 2003). Dopamine also plays a role in learning. When rats are exposed to light just before they receive food, their dopamine activity starts occurring in response to the light. When they expect food, the rats start feeling an anticipation of reward, a feeling well-known to those with addictions.

Like a bad romantic relationship, an addiction creates "wanting" without much "liking." Addictions basically hijack the brain's reward

system. Cocaine, amphetamines, and narcotics imitate the effects of dopamine and endorphins in the nucleus accumbens. They also stimulate mechanisms that control reward-based learning that activate every time the drug is used, reinforcing the behavior. Gambling and games of chance also activate the nucleus accumbens and the reward pathway. Like the rats in the experiment, the simple anticipation of payoff causes dopaminergic activity and overrides dopamine conserving mechanisms. Kerviel's anticipation of huge profits from trades might also have fueled his behavior.

OPTIMAL AROUSAL

Olympic athletes need an optimal arousal that gives them enough motivation but not so much that they feel anxious and unable to perform. Sixteen-year-old gymnast Shawn Johnson feels anxiety at every competition, but performs with confidence by putting her feelings into the poetry she writes. At 41, Dara Torres has qualified for her fifth Olympics and says that she enjoys swimming and competing more than ever. The Yerkes-Dodson law states in general that performance peaks with a moderate level of arousal (Yerkes & Dodson, 1908). Described graphically, the Yerkes-Dodson law resembles an inverted U: Performance levels increase as arousal increases, but only up to a certain point (the peak of the inverted U). After that, performance levels decrease as arousal increases. Easier tasks have higher optimal levels of arousal, and more difficult tasks have lower optimal levels of arousal. Tasks requiring persistence also generally require more arousal than intellectual ones. Optimal arousal to compete in a sport would be higher than to play chess.

MASLOW'S HIERARCHY OF NEEDS

Abraham Maslow described motivation through a hierarchy of needs in which more basic levels had to be fulfilled before higher levels (1970). Physiological needs, such as hunger and thirst, appeared at the bottom of the hierarchy as the most basic level. Safety, a feeling of being in a secure and safe environment, came next on the hierarchy. Once an individual had met biological and safety needs, he or she would seek a feeling of belongingness—the need to feel loved and avoid alienation. Then come esteem needs, feelings of worthiness and achievement. At the very top of the hierarchy, Maslow placed self-actualization, a complete feeling of self-acceptance and an awareness of fulfilling one's unique potential (1971). (For more information about the hierarchy of needs, see Chapter 16.)

Intrinsic reward is a task that is pleasurable in and of itself.

Extrinsic reward is a reward that is achieved through the completion of a task.

Liking is a subjective feeling of pleasure derived from a reward.

Wanting is a desire to achieve a particular goal in order to receive a reward.

Reinforcement describes an act that causes a response to be more likely to recur.

Reward neurons are neurons involved with experiencing the positive emotions associated with receiving a reward.

Medial forebrain bundle is the brain's reward pathway.

Liking system is a system involved with experiencing pleasure; it does not depend on dopamine.

Endorphins are morphine-like chemicals that inhibit pain signals and are released by the medial forebrain bundle.

Wanting system is a system involved with achieving a goal to receive pleasure; depends heavily on dopamine.

Optimal arousal is an arousal state in which a person has enough motivation but not so much that he or she feels anxious and unable to perform.

Yerkes-Dodson law states in general that performance peaks with a moderate level of arousal.

Hierarchy of needs is a pyramidal structure that shows the five needs that must be satisfied for a person to achieve self-actualization.

Physiological needs are needs that affect a person's physiology, such as hunger and thirst.

Safety is a feeling of being in a secure and safe environment.

Belongingness is a need to feel loved and avoid alienation.

Esteem need is a need to feel achievement and self-worth.

Self-actualization is a complete feeling of self-acceptance and an awareness of fulfilling one's unique potential.

How might gambling addiction resemble drug addiction?

Glucose is blood sugar.

Insulin is a hormone that reduces the level of glucose in the blood.

Orexin is a hormone that brings on feelings of hunger.

Anorexogenic refers to signals that stop an animal from eating.

Arcuate nucleus is a part of the hypothalamus that contains both appetite-stimulating and appetite-suppressing neurons.

Gustatory sense is the sense of taste.

Preservation and protection theory explains sleep as a mechanism evolved to preserve energy and provide protection during the night.

Body restoration theory explains sleep as a time for necessary rest and recuperation.

Hunger

THE PHYSIOLOGY OF HUNGER

If you've ever skipped breakfast before an early morning class, you've probably experienced the embarrassment of your stomach growling loud enough to alert everyone in the room of your hunger. A. L. Washburn swallowed a balloon to monitor stomach contractions and discovered that feelings of hunger did indeed correspond to stomach contractions (Cannon & Washburn, 1912). But removing the stomach in rats and humans did not eliminate hunger, leading to new theories about its source.

Hunger, Body Chemistry, and the Brain

The levels of **glucose**—blood sugar—help determine hunger and satiety. When glucose levels drop, we feel hungry. If glucose levels rise, the hormone **insulin** reduces them by telling the body to convert glucose to fat. As the body monitors these chemical levels, it sends messages to the brain about whether to eat or not.

Research has shown the role the hypothalamus plays in regulating hunger along a dual center model. The lateral hypothalamus secretes the hormone **orexin**, which brings on feelings of hunger, an orexogenic response. When the lateral hypothalamus was electrically stimulated, rats that already felt full started eating. When the area was damaged or removed, even starving rats had no desire to eat (Sakurai et al., 1998). The ventromedial hypothalamus suppresses hunger and sends out **anorexogenic** signals that stop an animal from eating. The hypothalamus's **arcuate nucleus** contains both appetite-stimulating and appetite-suppressing neurons.

Not all hunger originates in internal body states. Many people seem to have room for dessert even when they already feel full after a meal. In this case, the **gustatory sense**—taste—mediates hunger. Satiety, a feeling of satisfaction, also involves sensory stimuli in the environment. The dessert looks appetizing, so we feel like eating it. Animals that eat a certain food until they feel satisfied will eat again if introduced to a novel food or taste. The sweet taste of dessert presents a new taste compared to the savory one of the meal.

> **Many people seem to have room for dessert even when they already feel full after a meal. In this case, the gustatory sense—taste—mediates hunger.**

Sexual Motivation

SYNCHRONY

Most mammals' sexual drives synchronize with their hormonal levels and chemical signals. The female cyclic production of estrogen and progesterone is the menstrual cycle in humans and the estrous cycle in other animals. In female rats, the ventromedial area of the hypothalamus corresponds to the preoptic area in males. For female mammals, estrogen peaks at ovulation, when the female becomes sexually receptive. Testosterone levels in male mammals remain more constant but still influence sexual behavior.

The human female's sex drive synchronizes less with her hormonal levels than in most other mammals. The female sex drive increases somewhat during ovulation but has more to do with testosterone levels than estrogen levels (Harvey, 1987; Meston & Frohlich, 2000; Meuwissen & Over, 1992; Reichman, 1998). Testosterone therapy, such as the testosterone patch, increases sex drive in women who feel a reduced desire for sex due to removal of the ovaries or adrenal glands. In males, testosterone also controls sex drive.

CASTRATION

In 17th- and 18th-century Europe, prepubescent boys who were castrated to preserve their high singing voices did not develop adult male sex characteristics or sexual desire. The 1994 film **Farinelli** depicts the life of the most famous

> **Sleep seems to be necessary to consolidate memories of the things we learn during the day and to promote learning.**

18th-century castrato, Carlo Broschi, thought to be one of the greatest opera singers of all time. In 2006, researchers exhumed Broschi's body to study castration's effects on the human body. While the study has not been fully completed, particularities in the bones do indicate castration. Castrated adult males also lose their desire for sex as their testosterone levels decline. Male sexual offenders given Depo-Provera to reduce testosterone to prepubescent levels also report less interest in sex. Some studies show a decrease in repeat offenses, but others indicate that the treatment does not reduce the rapist's desire to express aggression through sex (Criminal Justice Special Report, 1988). Implanting a testosterone crystal in the preoptic area of the hypothalamus restores sex drive in castrated animals (Everitt & Stacey 1987).

Sleep Motivation

WHY DO WE SLEEP?

The **preservation and protection theory** explains sleep as a mechanism evolved to preserve energy and provide protection during the night, when danger from predators was low and opportunities to get food were few. Sleep patterns do not depend on an animal's physical exertion levels but on how the animal finds food and protects itself. If predators hunt an animal during the day, the animal would be more likely to be nocturnal and out of harm's way during the daylight hours. Similarly, visually reliant species, such as human beings, tend to be diurnal to take advantage of sunlight for daily activities.

The **body restoration theory** explains sleep as a time for necessary rest and recuperation. During sleep, the metabolic rate goes down, muscles relax, and the body secretes growth hormones to promote tissue repair. Rats deprived of sleep experience tissue breakdown and eventually die (Rechtschaffen & Bergman, 1965). Sleep-deprived humans also experience declines in health and functioning.

Sleep seems to be necessary to consolidate memories of the things we learn during the day and to promote learning (Guzman-Marin et al., 2005; Leproult et al., 1997). Memory storage requires **long-term potentiation (LTP)**, two neurons firing together to extend the communication at the synapse, the junction where neurons meet. Rats that had been kept awake showed less long-term potentiation than those that had been allowed to sleep (Vyazovskiy et al., 2008).

The **activation-synthesis theory** understands sleep as a side effect of the visual and motor area neurons firing during **REM sleep**, the stage of sleep characterized by rapid eye movements. Dreams occur because neurons in different parts of the brain fire randomly, and the cortex synthesizes them into some kind of coherent story, but activation theory does not attribute any purpose to dreams or argue against any psychoanalytic theories.

INDIVIDUAL VARIATION

Although most people require about eight hours of sleep, some people need to sleep nine or ten hours to feel alert and rested. Former British Prime Minister Margaret Thatcher claimed that she only slept four hours a night, but sleep researcher Ian Hindmarch says that many photos showed Thatcher asleep during the day. Florence Nightingale and Napoleon also reportedly slept only a few hours a night. **Nonsomniacs** are those rare people who require much less than eight hours of sleep (sometimes only one hour a night). **Insomniacs** need as much sleep as most people but, for various reasons, are unable to get it.

Belongingness

When high school students try to be part of a clique or adults join professional groups, they are responding to a human need to belong. In the **Nichomachean Ethics**, Aristotle called humans the "social animal." Belonging does not simply make life more fulfilling; social bonds may have evolved to boost our ancestors' survival rates. Attachments between parents and children keep children close and protected. The word **wretched** comes from the Middle English word **wrecche**, meaning to be without kin nearby. Early humans probably fought, hunted, and foraged together to give themselves protection against predators and enemies.

Wanting to belong seems to be a cross-cultural need. A Zulu saying goes, "Umuntu ngumntu ngabantu," meaning "a person is a person through other persons." We act to increase our social acceptance because self-esteem tends to waver based on how

valued and accepted we feel. Our need to maintain relationships means that we stay in close contact with our friends and relatives. Bill and Hillary Clinton's marital problems played out very publicly, but the former President and the current Secretary of State remain together.

Being excluded hurts, and groups use social ostracism as a means of control. An online study showed that even the mildest forms of ostracism can control behavior powerfully (Williams et al., 2000). Participants playing a virtual game felt upset as other (computer-generated) participants began excluding them. In a second study, the ostracized participants complied more readily on tasks. Rejection literally hurts; social pain causes increased activity in the **anterior cingulate cortex**, an area involved in physical pain (Eisenberger & Lieberman, 2004). University students told during an experiment that they would be excluded from a group started showing more self-defeating and destructive behaviors (Twenge et al., 2001, Twenge et al., 2002). Conversely, social safety nets and a sense of belonging can improve and preserve health.

Motivation at Work

JOB SATISFACTION

If you've worked at a job you hated, you know how important job satisfaction can be to overall happiness. Those who think of work as a job, something they do to pay the bills, report the lowest job satisfaction. People who see work as a long-term career feel more satisfied. Individuals who see work as a "calling," something intrinsically important, feel the most satisfied (Wrzesniewski et al., 1997). Mihaly Csikszentmihalyi defined the feeling of being fully and comfortably engaged in work as "flow" (1990, 1999). We experience flow when tasks absorb us completely and demand enough from us, not too much or too little. A musician playing onstage, a chef busily

> **Long-term potentiation (LTP)** is the process in which neural connections are strengthened through the repetition of neurotransmitters traveling across the same synapses.
>
> **Activation-synthesis theory** is a theory that explains sleep as a side effect of the visual and motor area neurons firing during REM sleep. It states that dreams are the result of the brain's attempt to make sense of the random neural activity that occurs while a person sleeps.
>
> **REM sleep** is a recurring stage of sleep during which vivid dreams usually occur.
>
> **Nonsomniacs** are people who require much less than eight hours of sleep each day.
>
> **Insomniacs** are people who need as much sleep as most people but are unable to get it.
>
> **Anterior cingulate cortex** is an area of the brain that serves as an executive control system that helps control a person's behavior; it is involved in the perception of physical pain.
>
> **Equity theory** states that workers decide how satisfied they feel with their jobs by comparing themselves to others.
>
> **Expectancy theory** defines job satisfaction as a worker's sense of achieving a certain outcome based on expectancy, instrumentality, and valence.

preparing a dish, or a scientist engaged in research may all experience flow.

EQUITY THEORY AND EXPECTANCY THEORY

According to **equity theory**, workers decide how satisfied they feel with their jobs by comparing themselves to others. If they notice that they do a certain amount of work and get a specific reward while others do less work and get the same reward, they may feel unfairly treated. They may ask for a raise, work less, or leave their positions.

Expectancy theory defines job satisfaction as a worker's sense of achieving a certain outcome based on expectancy, instrumentality, and valence (Harder, 1991; Porter & Lawler, 1968; Vroom, 1964). For example, American International Group has offered new CEO Robert Willumstad an $8 million bonus. His expectancy would have to do with his ability to lead the company successfully. Instrumentality would involve the bonus he expects to receive for achieving the result, and valence would be defined by the value of the reward, the actual size of the bonus.

Popular series like Twilight speak to a need to belong.

13 · Review

Summary

WHAT ARE THE COMPONENTS OF EMOTION AND MOTIVATION?

• Emotions are made up of three distinct but related parts: physiological arousal, expressive behavior, and cognitive experience.

• We are motivated by both dispositional forces (internal states and drives) and situational forces (external stimuli).

WHAT ARE THE DOMINANT THEORIES OF EMOTION AND MOTIVATION?

• Theories of emotion are the James-Lange theory (physiological response precedes cognition), Cannon-Bard theory (physiology and cognition are simultaneous), Schachter-Singer two-factor theory (perception along with physiological response produces emotion), cognitive-appraisal theory (cognitive evaluation follows physiological response to produce emotion), and Plutchik's emotion wheel (eight primary emotions combine to form more complex emotions).

• Theories of motivation are drive-reduction theory (actions are motivated by a drive to reduce physiological need), social-learning theory (actions are motivated by the expectation of achieving goals), and central state theory (drives are created by neural systems).

HOW DO WE EXPLAIN THE EMOTIONS OF FEAR, ANGER, AND HAPPINESS?

• Fear protects us by initiating a flight-and-fight response. Controlled mostly by the amygdala, it is partially learned and partially innate.

• Anger is a universal emotion, but its expression is culturally specific.

• Happiness tends to be temporary, makes people helpful, depends on our sense of success relative to others, and does not depend on money.

HOW DO WE UNDERSTAND HUNGER, SLEEP, SEXUALITY, BELONGING, AND WORK?

• Hunger depends on stomach contractions, glucose levels, hypothalamic secretions of orexin, and the gustatory sense.

• Sleep protects us from predators and restores our minds and bodies.

• The levels of testosterone, estrogen, and other hormones in our bodies influence our sex drives.

• A feeling of belonging maximizes survival, and its absence resembles physical pain.

• People find intrinsically rewarding work to be most satisfying.

Test Your Understanding

1. Beth takes an inhaler for her asthma. One of the side effects of the medicine is that it makes her heart beat quickly. When this happens, Beth often feels anxious, even though there is nothing for her to feel anxious about. Beth's reaction to her inhaler is predicted by:

   a. the James-Lange theory.

   b. the Cannon-Bard theory.

   c. the mere exposure effect.

   d. the two-factor theory.

2. Lauren was surprised to hear that her best friend is moving, and also feels sad about it. According to Plutchik's emotion wheel, it is likely that Lauren is experiencing:

   a. awe.

   b. love.

   c. contempt.

   d. disappointment.

3. James punches a hole in the wall when he finds out he doesn't get the job he wants. The emotional component he is displaying is:

   a. cognitive experience.

   b. expressive behavior.

   c. physiological arousal.

   d. mood.

4. Melissa cries at her friend's wedding. Even though she just ended a relationship and has been crying for several days, she assumes she must be crying now because she loves weddings and is happy. Melissa may be demonstrating:

   a. the exposure effect.

   b. misattribution.

   c. psychic blindness.

   d. a negative mood.

5. Zach is camping and hears rustling in the woods near his tent. He begins to sweat and breathe more quickly. What is happening?

   a. He is developing psychic blindness.

   b. The sympathetic division of his nervous system is preparing him for flight or fight.

   c. His prefrontal cortex is malfunctioning.

   d. The parasympathetic division of his nervous system is highly activated.

6. Ashley's brother jumps out in front of her, yelling "Boo," and she screams before she realizes who it is. Ashley's scream is likely the result of:

   a. rapid subcortical pathway activity.

   b. cortical pathway activity.

c. psychic blindness.

d. parasympathetic activity.

7. When a person experiences an emotionally charged stimulus, epinephrine (adrenaline) is released by:

a. the prefrontal cortex.

b. the parasympathetic nervous system.

c. the pituitary gland.

d. the adrenal glands.

8. While their accuracy is controversial, polygraph machines are often used to determine if a person is lying. They work by detecting:

a. changes in brain waves.

b. physiological changes like heart rate and perspiration.

c. changes in body temperature.

d. changes in facial expression.

9. Janelle tries to make an effort to smile at parties so other people will think she is having a good time. As it turns out, Janelle usually has more fun at parties when she remembers to smile. This is likely an example of:

a. action units.

b. deintensification.

c. affective forecasting.

d. the facial feedback hypothesis.

10. Nancy's husband recently suffered a stroke and is in the hospital. Nancy is scared for him. When she goes to her daughter's house, she smiles and acts happy so that her daughter will not worry. What is Nancy doing?

a. neutralizing her emotions

b. deintensifying her emotions

c. masking her emotions

d. intensifying her emotions

11. Harold is clinically depressed. He watches a romantic comedy with his friends and cries during a scene in which the main characters break up. At the end of the movie, even though the main characters get married, Harold says it was a sad movie. Harold is demonstrating:

a. mood deintensification.

b. temporal patterning.

c. mood-congruent processing.

d. affective forecasting.

12. Max has been feeling depressed that he is unemployed and can't find work. He volunteers at a soup kitchen for the day feeding homeless families and feels better when he goes home. Which of the following might explain why Max felt better?

a. He re-evaluated his relative deprivation.

b. He engaged in affective forecasting.

c. He experienced the feel-good, do-good phenomenon.

d. He experienced the adaptation-level phenomenon.

13. Which of the following is a nonregulatory drive?

a. hunger

b. sex

c. thirst

d. all of the above

14. Which of the following does NOT demonstrate the hedonic principle?

a. an angry toddler hitting his head against the wall

b. a person trying to avoid hard work

c. a child refusing to eat foods he or she does not like

d. a person eating a large slice of pie

15. Which of the following LEAST demonstrates the concept of reinforcement?

a. teaching a dog to sit by giving it dog treats when it obeys

b. continuing to donate blood because it makes you feel good about yourself

c. giving your child money for receiving a good grade

d. yelling at a child for misbehaving

16. Which of the following is most likely to yield an intrinsic reward?

a. investing in the stock market

b. doing cartwheels

c. studying for a test

d. practicing for an ice-skating competition

17. A male with a low sex drive most likely has:

a. high estrogen levels.

b. low testosterone levels.

c. aggressive behavior issues.

d. high testosterone levels.

18. According to Maslow's hierarchy of needs, which of the following would a person make his first priority?

a. having a job

b. finding food

c. buying a house

d. being in a romantic relationship

19. Which of the following people are most likely to be tired during the day?

a. nonsomniacs

b. insomniacs

c. people given Depo-Provera shots

d. people with low testosterone

20. Which of the following most indicates an experience of "flow"?

a. the workday seeming to pass quickly

b. the workday seeming to drag on

c. keeping an eye on the clock to see how soon class gets out

d. looking around to see what everyone else is doing

Remember to check www.thethinkspot.com **for additional information, downloadable flashcards, and other helpful resources.**

UNDERSTANDING YOUR TEXTBOOK

DIRECTIONS   Write the letter of the choice that best completes each statement in the space provided.

_____ 1. The list of questions at the top of page 490 indicates that all of the following topics will be addressed in this chapter *except*

a. the components of emotion and motivation.
b. dominant theories of emotion and motivation.
c. strategies for managing interpersonal conflict.
d. explanations of the emotions of fear, anger, and happiness.

_____ 2. The purpose of the photo on pages 489–90 is to illustrate

a. why people should recycle.
b. what motivates people to recycle.
c. who is most likely to recycle.
d. what it means to "go green."

_____ 3. In this chapter, a list of key terms and definitions can be found

a. on the introductory page.
b. in the chapter summary.
c. in a box on nearly every page of the chapter.
d. in a glossary at the end of the chapter.

_____ 4. The aspect of emotion illustrated by the photo of a woman crying on page 491 is called

a. expressive behavior.
b. physiological arousal.
c. cognitive experience.
d. mood.

_____ 5. According to Plutchik's Emotion Wheel on page 492, feelings of joy and anticipation are associated with

a. submission.
b. remorse.
c. disappointment.
d. optimism.

_____ 6. The diagram of a brain on page 493 corresponds to information under the subheading

a. "Autonomic Nervous System."
b. "Brain Structures."
c. "Cognitive Appraisal Theory."
d. "Comparing Specific Emotions."

_____ 7. The photo of a man and woman on page 494 corresponds to a discussion of

a. facial feedback.
b. gender differences.
c. lie detection.
d. culture.

_____ 8. According to the process diagram on page 494, an emotionally charged stimulus triggers the release of thyrotrophic hormone by the

a. hypothalamus.
b. pituitary gland.
c. adrenal glands.
d. thyroid gland.

_____ 9. The concept of belongingness is illustrated by the photo of

a. a heart-shaped box of candy.
b. Michelle Obama and Queen Elizabeth.
c. slot machines in a casino.
d. a group of actors from the cast of *Twilight*.

_____ 10. The primary purpose of the "Test Your Understanding" feature on pages 501–02 is to allow readers to

a. measure their comprehension of important topics in the chapter.
b. create a summary of the theories and concepts in the chapter.
c. evaluate the accuracy and credibility of the material.
d. preview topics that will be covered in the next chapter.

CREDITS

PHOTO CREDITS

p. 8: iStockphoto.com/monkeybusinessimages; **p. 15:** Tor Eigeland/Alamy; **p. 27:** AP Images/The Syracuse Newspapers, Gary Watts; **p. 38:** Blend Images/SuperStock; **p. 46:** © HBO/Courtesy: Everett Collection; **p. 50:** Andrey Yurlov/Shutterstock.com; **p. 55:** Tetra Images/SuperStock; **p. 73:** Corbis Super RF/Alamy; **p. 99:** Radius/SuperStock; p. 106, top to bottom: Oredia/Alamy; David Young-Woolf/PhotoEdit Inc.; **p. 107,** left to right: Orange Line Media/ Shutterstock.com (2); Lasse Kristensen/ Shutterstock.com; wavebreakmedia/Shutterstock.com; Yuri Arcurs/ Shutterstock.com; **p. 108:** Lo-Random/ Shutterstock.com; **p. 156:** iStockphoto.com/deanmillar; **p. 171:** Masterpics/Alamy; **p. 198:** AP Images/Ed Bailey; **p. 216:** Stanislav Komogorov/Dreamstime.com; **p. 231:** Marc A. Hermann/Pool/Reuters; **p. 245:** NHPA/SuperStock; **p. 260:** © Tom Thaves; **p. 261:** Courtesy Merriam-Webster; **p. 288:** © Tom Thaves; p. 289, top to bottom: AP Images/Tina Fineberg; Gunter Marx/Alamy; **p. 290:** Courtesy Exploratorium.com; **p. 295:** United States Environmental Protection Agency. Photo: Jupiter Images/Thinkstock; p. 298, top to bottom: Jim Borgman/King Features Syndicate; Siu Chiu/Reuters; p. 299, top to bottom: 28/BrandX/Corbis; Paul Maguire/Shutterstock.com; **p. 306:** Mira/Alamy; **p. 318:** Prisma/SuperStock; **p. 320:** Radius/SuperStock; **p. 328:** DocCheck Medical Service GmbH/Alamy; **p. 333:** Justin Kase zninez/Alamy; **p. 364,** clockwise from top left: Kevin Radford/Purestock/SuperStock; Image Source/SuperStock; Tetra Images/SuperStock; p. 367, left to right: Fancy Collection/SuperStock; Ken Seet/Corbis; **p. 368:** Corbis Bridge/Alamy; **p. 374:** RelaxFoto.de/iStockphoto; **p. 391:** thumb/iStockphoto; **p. 420:** Martin Heitner/Purestock/SuperStock; **p. 439:** Jupiter Images/Thinkstock; **p. 450:** Robert Harding Picture Library Ltd./Alamy; **p. 467:** AP Photo/Al Behrman; **p. 474:** Courtesy Wonkette; **p. 475:** Christian Lange; **pp. 489–490:** Yellow Dog Productions/Getty Images; **p. 491:** Erik Dreyer/Getty Images; p. 494, top to bottom: Jurgen Vogt/Getty Images; Muntz/Getty Images; **p. 495:** Alpha/Landov; **p. 497:** Dorling Kindersley; **p. 498:** Dorling Kindersley; **p. 500:** Michael Buckner/Getty Images; Students studying icon: michaeljung/Shutterstock.com; Abstract color ring icon: Excellent Backgrounds HERE/Shutterstock.com.

TEXT CREDITS

p. 22: Belk, Colleen and Virginia Borden Maier, *Biology: Science for Life with Physiology*, 3rd ed., © 2010. Printed and electronically reproduced by permission of Pearson Education, Inc., Upper Saddle River, New Jersey.

p. 23: Baird, Abigail A., *THINK Psychology*, 2nd ed. © 2011. Printed and electronically reproduced by permission of Pearson Education, Inc., Upper Saddle River, New Jersey.

p. 44: Gronbeck, Bruce E., et al., *Principles of Speech Communication*, 11th brief ed. New York: HarperCollins College Publishers, 1992, pp. 217–218.

p. 46: Kunz, Jennifer, *THINK Marriages and Families*, 1st ed., p. 53, © 2011. Printed and electronically reproduced by permission of Pearson Education, Inc., Upper Saddle River, New Jersey.

p. 50: Katz, Jane, *Swimming for Total Fitness: A Progressive Aerobic Program*. Garden City, NY: Dolphin Books/Doubleday, 1981, p. 99.

p. 66: Frings, Gini Stephens, *Fashion: From Concept to Consumer*, 9th ed. Upper Saddle River, NJ: Pearson Prentice Hall, 2008.

p. 66: Thill, John V. and Courtland L. Bovée, *Excellence in Business*, 9th ed. Upper Saddle River, NJ: Pearson Prentice Hall, 2010, p. 355.

p. 66: Withgott, Jay and Scott Brennan, *Environment: The Science Behind the Stories*, 4th ed. San Francisco: Pearson Benjamin Cummings, 2011, p. 343.

p. 87: Thompson, Janice and Melinda Manore, *Nutrition for Life*, 2nd ed. San Francisco: Pearson Benjamin Cummings, 2010, pp. 148–150.

p. 101: Carl, John D., *THINK Sociology*, 1st ed., p. 143, © 2010. Printed and electronically reproduced by permission of Pearson Education, Inc., Upper Saddle River, New Jersey.

p. 106: Schiffman, Leon and Leslie Kanuk, *Consumer Behavior*, 10th ed., p. 364. © 2010. Printed and electronically reproduced by permission of Pearson Education, Inc., Upper Saddle River, New Jersey.

p. 106: Donatelle, Rebecca J., *Health: The Basics*, Green Edition, 9th ed., p. 132, © 2011. Printed and electronically reproduced by permission of Pearson Education, Inc., Upper Saddle River, New Jersey.

p. 107: Carl, John D., *THINK Sociology*, 1st ed., p. 197, © 2010. Line art printed and electronically reproduced by permission of Pearson Education, Inc., Upper Saddle River, New Jersey.

p. 114: Bovée, Courtland and John V. Thill, *Business Communication Today*, 9th ed., pp. 187–188, © 2008. Printed and electronically reproduced by permission of Pearson Education, Inc., Upper Saddle River, New Jersey.

p. 117: Zinn, Maxine Baca and D. Stanley Eitzen, *Diversity in Families*, 4th ed. New York: HarperCollins College Publishers, 1996, p. 205.

p. 118: Hewitt, Paul G., John A. Suchocki, and Leslie A. Hewitt, *Conceptual Physical Science Explorations*, 2nd ed., p. 138, © 2010. Text and figure printed and electronically reproduced by permission of Pearson Education, Inc., Upper Saddle River, New Jersey.

p. 123: Blake, Joan Salge, *Nutrition and You*, 2nd ed., p. 67. © 2012. Text and figure printed and electronically reproduced by permission of Pearson Education, Inc., Upper Saddle River, New Jersey.

p. 127: Kunz, Jennifer, *THINK Marriages and Families*, 1st ed., p. 5, © 2011. Printed and electronically reproduced by permission of Pearson Education, Inc., Upper Saddle River, New Jersey.

p. 127: Harris, C. Leon, *Concepts in Zoology*, 2nd ed. New York: HarperCollins College Publishers, 1996, p. 573. Reprinted by permission of the author.

p. 131: Wilson, R. Jackson, et al., *The Pursuit of Liberty: A History of the American People*, 3rd ed., Vol. 2. New York: HarperCollins College Publishers, 1996, p. 422.

p: 131: Kinnear, Thomas C., Kenneth L. Bernhardt, and Kathleen A. Krentler, *Principles of Marketing*, 4th ed., p. 637. © 1995. Printed and electronically reproduced by permission of Pearson Education, Inc., Upper Saddle River, New Jersey.

p. 131: Harris, C. Leon, *Concepts in Zoology*, 2nd ed. New York: HarperCollins College Publishers, 1996, p. 130. Reprinted by permission of the author.

p. 132: Schiffman, Leon and Leslie Kanuk, *Consumer Behavior*, 10th ed., p. 246. © 2010. Printed and electronically reproduced by permission of Pearson Education, Inc., Upper Saddle River, New Jersey.

p. 139: Loyd, Jason B. and James D. Richardson, *Fundamentals of Fire and Emergency Services*. Upper Saddle River, NJ: Pearson Prentice Hall, 2010, p. 12.

p. 140: Hicks, David and Margaret A. Gwynne, *Cultural Anthropology*, 2nd ed. New York: HarperCollins College Publishers, 1996, p. 270. Reprinted by permission of the authors.

p. 140: Ross, David A., *Introduction to Oceanography*. New York: HarperCollins College Publishers, 1995, p. 48.

p. 140: Ebert, Ronald J. and Ricky W. Griffin, *Business Essentials*, 8th ed. Upper Saddle River, NJ: Pearson Prentice Hall, 2011, pp. 30–31.

p. 141: Belk, Colleen and Virginia Borden, *Biology: Science for Life*, 2nd ed. San Francisco: Pearson Benjamin Cummings, 2006, pp. 392–393.

p. 141: Donatelle, Rebecca J., *Health: The Basics*, Green Edition, 9th ed., p. 109, © 2011. Printed and electronically reproduced by permission of Pearson Education, Inc., Upper Saddle River, New Jersey.

p. 141: Kinnear, Thomas C., Kenneth L. Bernhardt, and Kathleen A. Krentler, *Principles of Marketing*, 4th ed., pp. 79–81. © 1995. Printed and electronically reproduced by permission of Pearson Education, Inc., Upper Saddle River, New Jersey.

p. 141: Capron, H. L., *Computers: Tools for an Information Age*, Brief Edition. New York: Addison Wesley Longman Publishing Company, 1998, p. 82.

p. 142: Folkerts, Jean, et al., *The Media in Your Life: An Introduction to Mass Communication*, 4th ed. Boston, MA: Allyn and Bacon/Merrill Education, 2008, p. 257.

p. 142: Lutgens, Frederick K., Edward J. Tarbuck, and Dennis Tasa, *Essentials of Geology*, 10th ed. Upper Saddle River, NJ: Pearson Prentice Hall, 2009, p. 13.

p. 142: Gerow, Josh R., *Essentials of Psychology: Concepts and Applications*, 2nd ed. New York: HarperCollins College Publishers, 1996, p. 138.

p. 142: Edwards III, George C., Martin P. Wattenberg, and Robert L. Lineberry, *Government in America: People, Politics, and Policy*, 12th Edition, p. 16, © 2006. Printed and electronically reproduced by permission of Pearson Education, Inc., Upper Saddle River, New Jersey.

p. 143: Gronbeck, Bruce E., et al., *Principles of Speech Communication*, 12th brief ed. New York: HarperCollins College Publishers, 1995, p. 302.

p. 143: Thio, Alex, *Sociology*, 4th ed. New York: HarperCollins College Publishers, 1996, p. 181.

p. 143: Agee, Warren K., Phillip H. Ault, and Edwin Emery, *Introduction to Mass Communications*, 12th ed. New York: Longman, 1997, p. 225.

p. 143: Marieb, Elaine N., *Essentials of Human Anatomy and Physiology*, 5th ed. Menlo Park, CA: Benjamin/Cummings, 1997, p. 119.

p. 145: Gerow, Josh R., *Essentials of Psychology: Concepts and Applications*, 2nd ed. New York: HarperCollins College Publishers, 1996, p. 289.

p. 146: Audesirk, Teresa, Gerald Audesirk, and Bruce E. Byers, *Biology: Life on Earth*, 9th ed. San Francisco: Pearson Benjamin Cummings, 2011, p. 337.

p. 146: Thill, John V. and Courtland L. Bovée, *Excellence in Business Communication*, 9th ed. Upper Saddle River, NJ: Pearson Prentice Hall, 2011, p. xxxvi.

p. 146: Blake, Joan Salge, *Nutrition & You*. San Francisco: Pearson Benjamin Cummings, 2008, p. 513.

p. 146: Bovée, Courtland and John V. Thill, *Business Communication Today*, 9th ed., p. 54, © 2008. Printed and electronically reproduced by permission of Pearson Education, Inc., Upper Saddle River, New Jersey.

p. 146: Hewitt, Paul G., *Conceptual Physics*, 8th ed. Reading, MA: Addison Wesley Longman, 1998, p. 279.

p. 147: Miller, Roger Leroy, *Economics Today*, 8th ed. New York: HarperCollins College Publishers, 1994, p. 213.

p. 147: Weaver II, Richard, *Understanding Interpersonal Communication*, 7th ed. New York: HarperCollins College Publishers, 1996, p. 220.

p. 147: Frings, Gini Stephens, *Fashion: From Concept to Consumer*, 9th ed. Upper Saddle River, NJ: Pearson Prentice Hall, 2008, p. 80.

p. 147: Wallace, Robert A., *Biology: The World of Life*, 7th ed. Menlo Park, CA: Benjamin/Cummings, 1997, p. 167.

p. 148: DeVito, Joseph A., *Essentials of Human Communication*, 6th ed. Boston, MA: Allyn and Bacon, 2008, pp. 109–110.

p. 150: Blake, Joan Salge, *Nutrition & You*. San Francisco: Pearson Benjamin Cummings, 2008, p. 52.

p. 151: Miller, Roger Leroy, *Economics Today*, 8th ed. New York: HarperCollins College Publishers, 1994, p. 84.

p. 151: Wilcox, Dennis L. and Glen T. Cameron, *Public Relations: Strategies and Tactics*, 9th ed. Boston: MA: Pearson Allyn & Bacon, 2010, p. 145.

p. 151: Koch, Arthur, *Speaking with a Purpose*, 7th ed. Boston, MA: Pearson Allyn and Bacon, 2007, p. 110.

p. 152: Johnston, Mike, *The Pharmacy Technician: Foundations and Practices*. Upper Saddle River, NJ: Pearson Prentice Hall, 2009, p. 13.

504

p. 152: Withgott, Jay and Scott Brennan, *Environment: The Science Behind the Stories*, 4th ed. San Francisco: Pearson Benjamin Cummings, 2011, p. 59.
p. 152: DeVito, Joseph A., *Essentials of Human Communication*, 6th ed. Boston, MA: Allyn and Bacon, 2008, p. 278.
p. 153: Edwards III, George C., Martin P. Wattenberg, and Robert L. Lineberry, *Government in America: People, Politics, and Policy*, 12th Edition, p. 653, © 2006. Printed and electronically reproduced by permission of Pearson Education, Inc., Upper Saddle River, New Jersey.
p. 153: Ebert, Ronald J. and Ricky W. Griffin, *Business Essentials*, 8th ed. Upper Saddle River, NJ: Pearson Prentice Hall, 2011, pp. 211–212.
p. 153: Henslin, James M., *Essentials of Sociology: A Down-to-Earth Approach*, 7th ed. Boston, MA: Pearson Allyn & Bacon, 2007. p. 402.
p. 154: Gronbeck, Bruce E., et al., *Principles of Speech Communication*, 12th brief ed. New York: HarperCollins College Publishers, 1995, pp. 32–33.
p. 155: Blake, Joan Salge, *Nutrition & You*. San Francisco: Pearson Benjamin Cummings, 2008, p. 258.
p. 155: Donatelle, Rebecca J., *Health: The Basics*, Green Edition, 9th ed., p. 105, © 2011. Printed and electronically reproduced by permission of Pearson Education, Inc., Upper Saddle River, New Jersey.
p. 156: Donatelle, Rebecca J., *Health: The Basics*, Green Edition, 9th ed., p. 105, © 2011. Line graph printed and electronically reproduced by permission of Pearson Education, Inc., Upper Saddle River, New Jersey.
p. 156: Thill, John V. and Courtland L. Bovée, *Excellence in Business Communication*, 9th ed. Upper Saddle River, NJ: Pearson Prentice Hall, 2011, p. 73.
p. 156: Withgott, Jay and Scott Brennan, *Environment: The Science Behind the Stories*, 4th ed. San Francisco: Pearson Benjamin Cummings, 2011, p. 267.
p. 157: Krogh, David, *A Brief Guide to Biology*. Upper Saddle River, NJ: Pearson Prentice Hall, 2007, p. 148.
p. 157: Newcombe, Nora, *Child Development: Change Over Time*, 8th ed. New York: HarperCollins College Publishers, 1996, p. 354.
p. 157: Coleman, James William and Donald R. Cressey, *Social Problems*, 6th ed. New York: HarperCollins College Publisher, 1996, p. 130.
p. 157: Goldman, Thomas F. and Henry R. Cheeseman, *The Paralegal Profession*, 3rd ed. Upper Saddle River, NJ: Pearson Prentice Hall, 2011, p. 222.
p. 157: DeVito, Joseph A., *Messages: Building Interpersonal Communication Skills*, 3rd ed. New York: HarperCollins College Publishers, 1996, p. 153.
p. 158: Belk, Colleen and Virginia Borden, *Biology: Science for Life*, 2nd ed. San Francisco: Pearson Benjamin Cummings, 2006, p. 46.
p. 159: Folkerts, Jean, et al., *The Media in Your Life: An Introduction to Mass Communication*, p. 204.
p. 159: Suchocki, John, *Conceptual Chemistry*, 4th ed., p. ix, © 2011. Printed and electronically reproduced by permission of Pearson Education, Inc., Upper Saddle River, New Jersey.
p. 160: Audesirk, Teresa, Gerald Audesirk, and Bruce E. Byers, *Biology: Life on Earth*, 9th ed. San Francisco: Pearson Benjamin Cummings, 2011, p. 301.
p. 167: Mix, Michael C., Paul Farber, and Keith I. King, Biology: *The Network of Life*.
p. 168: Carl, John D., *THINK Sociology*, 1st ed., p. 31, © 2010. Printed and electronically reproduced by permission of Pearson Education, Inc., Upper Saddle River, New Jersey.
p. 168: Kunz, Jennifer, *THINK Marriages and Families*, 1st ed., p. 134, © 2011. Printed and electronically reproduced by permission of Pearson Education, Inc., Upper Saddle River, New Jersey.
p. 168: Preble, Duane, Sarah Preble, and Patrick Frank, *Artforms: An Introduction to the Visual Arts*, 6th ed. New York: Longman, 1999, p. 60.
p. 169: Audesirk, Teresa, Gerald Audesirk, and Bruce E. Byers, *Biology: Life on Earth*, 9th ed. San Francisco: Pearson Benjamin Cummings, 2011, p. 106.
p. 169: Wood, Samuel E., Ellen Green Wood, and Denise Boyd, *Mastering the World of Psychology*, 2nd ed. Boston, MA: Pearson Allyn and Bacon, 2005, p. 210.
p. 170: Preble, Duane, Sarah Preble, and Patrick Frank, *Artforms: An Introduction to the Visual Arts*, 6th ed. New York: Longman, 1999, pp. 98–99.
p. 170: Donatelle, Rebecca J., *Health: The Basics*, Green Edition, 9th ed., p. 186, © 2011. Printed and electronically reproduced by permission of Pearson Education, Inc., Upper Saddle River, New Jersey.
p. 170: Edwards III, George C., Martin P. Wattenberg, and Robert L. Lineberry, *Government in America: People, Politics, and Policy*, 12th Edition, p. 156, © 2006. Printed and electronically reproduced by permission of Pearson Education, Inc., Upper Saddle River, New Jersey.
p. 171: Frank, Patrick, *Artforms: An Introduction to the Visual Arts*, 9th ed. Upper Saddle River, NJ: Pearson Prentice Hall. 2009. p. 112.
p. 171: Carnes, Mark C. and John A. Garraty, *The American Nation: A History of the United States*, 12th ed. New York: Pearson Longman, 2006, p. 826.
p. 171: Solomon, Michael R., Greg W. Marshall, and Elnora W. Stuart, *Marketing: Real People, Real Choices*, 4th ed. Upper Saddle River, NJ: Pearson Prentice Hall, 2006, p. 202.
p. 171: Kinnear, Thomas C., Kenneth L. Bernhardt, and Kathleen A. Krentler, *Principles of Marketing*, 4th ed., p. 180. © 1995. Printed and electronically reproduced by permission of Pearson Education, Inc., Upper Saddle River, New Jersey.
p. 172: Lutgens, Frederick K., Edward J. Tarbuck, and Dennis Tasa, *Essentials of Geology*, 10th ed. Upper Saddle River, NJ: Pearson Prentice Hall, 2009, p. 261.
p. 172: Miller, Roger Leroy, *Economics Today*, 8th ed. New York: HarperCollins College Publishers, 1994, p. 147.
p. 172: Solomon, Michael R., Mary Anne Poatsy, and Kendall Martin, *Better Business*, 1st ed. Upper Saddle River, NJ: Pearson Prentice Hall, 2010, p. 8.
p. 175: Lutgens, Frederick K., Edward J. Tarbuck, and Dennis Tasa, *Essentials of Geology*, 10th ed. Upper Saddle River, NJ: Pearson Prentice Hall, 2009, p. 426.
p. 176: DeVito, Joseph A., *Essentials of Human Communication*, 6th ed. Boston, MA: Allyn and Bacon, 2008, pp. 131–133.
p. 178: Brands, H. W., et al., *American Stories: A History of the United States*, Vol. 1. New York: Pearson Longman, 2009, pp. 175–177.
p. 181: Krogh, David, *A Brief Guide to Biology*. Upper Saddle River, NJ: Pearson Prentice Hall, 2007, p. 406.
p. 183: Tortora, Gerard J., *Introduction to the Human Body: The Essentials of Anatomy and Physiology*, 2nd ed. New York: HarperCollins College Publishers, 1991, p. 56.
p. 184: Gitman, Lawrence J., *Principles of Managerial Finance*, 12th ed. Upper Saddle River: NJ, Pearson Prentice Hall, 2009, pp. 766–767.
p. 185: DeVito, Joseph A., *The Essentials of Public Speaking*, 3rd ed. Boston, MA: Pearson Allyn and Bacon, 2009, p. 8.
p. 187: Ferl, Robert J., Robert A. Wallace, and Gerald P. Sanders, *Biology: The Realm of Life*, 3rd ed. New York: HarperCollins College Publishers, 1996, pp. 252–253.
p. 187: Thompson, Janice and Melinda Manore, *Nutrition for Life*, 1st ed. San Francisco: Pearson Benjamin Cummings, 2007, p. 355.
p. 188: Fujishin, Randy, *The Natural Speaker*, 6th ed. Boston, MA: Pearson Allyn and Bacon, 2009, p. 21.
p. 188: Goldman, Thomas F. and Henry R. Cheeseman, *The Paralegal Profession*, 3rd ed. Upper Saddle River, NJ: Pearson Prentice Hall, 2011, p. 561.
p. 188: Carl, John D., *THINK Sociology*, 1st ed. © 2010. Printed and electronically reproduced by permission of Pearson Education, Inc., Upper Saddle River, New Jersey.
p. 189: Hicks, David and Margaret A. Gwynne, *Cultural Anthropology*, 2nd ed. New York: HarperCollins College Publishers, 1996, p. 304. Reprinted by permission of the authors.
p. 189: Henslin, James M., *Essentials of Sociology: A Down-to-Earth Approach*, 7th ed. Boston, MA: Pearson Allyn & Bacon, 2007, p. 226.
p. 189: Edwards III, George C., Martin P. Wattenberg, and Robert L. Lineberry, *Government in America: People, Politics, and Policy*, 12th Edition, p. 398, © 2006. Printed and electronically reproduced by permission of Pearson Education, Inc., Upper Saddle River, New Jersey.
p. 190: Blake, Joan Salge, *Nutrition & You*. San Francisco: Pearson Benjamin Cummings, 2008, p. 318.
p. 190: Thompson, Janice and Melinda Manore, *Nutrition for Life*, 1st ed. San Francisco: Pearson Benjamin Cummings, 2007, p. 205.
p. 191: Donatelle, Rebecca J., *Health: The Basics*, Green Edition, 9th ed., p. 158, © 2011. Printed and electronically reproduced by permission of Pearson Education, Inc., Upper Saddle River, New Jersey.
p. 191: Carl, John D., *THINK Sociology*, 1st ed., p. 83, © 2010. Printed and electronically reproduced by permission of Pearson Education, Inc., Upper Saddle River, New Jersey.
p. 191: Audesirk, Teresa, Gerald Audesirk, and Bruce E. Byers, *Biology: Life on Earth*, 9th ed. San Francisco: Pearson Benjamin Cummings, 2011, p. 317.
p. 191: Schiffman, Leon and Leslie Kanuk, *Consumer Behavior*, 10th ed., p. xi. © 2010. Printed and electronically reproduced by permission of Pearson Education, Inc., Upper Saddle River, New Jersey.
p. 191: Poatsy, Mary Anne and Kendall Martin, *Better Business*. Upper Saddle River, NJ: Pearson Prentice Hall, 2010, p. v.
p. 192: DeVito, Joseph A., *Interpersonal Messages: Communication and Relationship Skills*, 2nd ed. Boston, MA: Pearson Allyn & Bacon, 2011, p. v.
p. 196: Thio, Alex, *Sociology*, 5th ed. New York: Longman, 1998, pp. 376–377.
p. 196: Thio, Alex, *Sociology*, 5th ed. New York: Longman, 1998, p. 377.
From *The King's Drum and Other African Stories* by Harold Courlander, copyright © 1962, 1990 by Harold Courlander. Reprinted by permission of The Emma Courlander Trust.
p. 199: Zimbardo, Philip G. and Richard J. Gerrig, *Psychology and Life*, p. 501.
p. 203: Uba, Laura and Karen Huang. *Psychology*. New York: Longman, 1999, p. 323.
p. 203: Greenberg, Edward S. and Benjamin L. Page, *The Struggle for Democracy*, Brief Version, 1st ed. HarperCollins College Publishers, 1996, p. 186.
p. 205: Humorous quote attributed to Jay Leno, American Comedian and TV Talk Show Host.
p. 205: Vivian, John, *The Media of Mass Communication*, 9th ed., p. 136, © 2009. Printed and electronically reproduced by permission of Pearson Education, Inc., Upper Saddle River, New Jersey.
p. 205: Belk, Colleen and Virginia Borden, *Biology: Science for Life*, 2nd ed. San Francisco: Pearson Benjamin Cummings, 2006, p. 41.
p. 206: From Rebecca Terrell, "Are the Polar Ice Caps Melting?" *The New American*, vol. 26, issue 4 (February 15, 2010), p. 23. Copyright 2010 by New American [WI]. Reproduced with permission of New American [WI] in the format Textbook via Copyright Clearance Center.
p. 207: Oliveria, D.F., "Burning Will Go: That's Not All Good," *Spokesman Review*, July 24, 2002.
p. 207: Cook, Roy A., Laura J. Yale, and Joseph J. Marqua, *Tourism: The Business of Travel*, 2nd ed. Upper Saddle River, NJ: Prentice Hall, 2002, p. 245.
p. 207: "Not Always With Us," *The Economist*, September 15, 2005.
p. 207: Waltrip, Darrell, "Calling Dr. Phil: NASCAR Needs Black and White Penalties," FOXSports.com, September 2005.
p. 208: Bolte, Bill, "Jerry's Got to Be Kidding," *In These Times*, September 16, 1992. This article is reprinted with permission from *In These Times* magazine, © 1992.
p. 209: Mander, Jerry, from *In the Absence of the Sacred: The Failure of Technology and the Rise of the Indian Nations*. San Francisco: Sierra Club Books, 1991.
p. 209: Swardson, Roger, "Greetings from the Electronic Plantation," *City Pages*, October 21, 1992.
p. 210: Durst, Will, from "We Don't Know Squat" as appeared in *Utne Reader*, March/April 1995, originally from *The Nose*. Reprinted by permission of Will Durst.
p. 210: Otto, Whitney, *How to Make an American Quilt*. New York: Villard Books, 1991, p. 183.
p. 215: "Misstep on Video Violence," *USA Today*, June 6, 2005, p. 12A. Reprinted with permission.
p. 217: Reyes, Silvester, "Is a border fence the answer to the illegal immigration problem?" *CQ Researcher*, September 19, 2008. Copyright © 2008 CQ Press, a division of SAGE Publications, Inc. Reprinted by permission of CQ Press.
p. 218: Withgott, Jay and Scott Brennan, *Environment: The Science Behind the Stories*, 4th ed. San Francisco: Pearson Benjamin Cummings, 2011, p. 222.
p. 218: DeVito, Joseph A., *Human Communication: The Basic Course*, 12th ed. Boston, MA: Pearson Allyn & Bacon, 2012, p. 240.
p. 227: Bennett, Jeffrey, Seth Shostak, and Bruce Jakosky, *Life in the Universe*. San Francisco: Addison Wesley, 2003, p. 2.
p. 227: Kennedy, X. J. and Dana Gioia, *Literature: An Introduction to Fiction, Poetry, and Drama*, 3rd ed. New York: Longman, 2003, p. 454.

p. 227: Margolis, Mac, "A Plot of Their Own," *Newsweek*, January 21, 2002.

p. 235: Thompson, William E. and Joseph V. Hickey, *Society in Focus: An Introduction to Sociology*, 7th ed. Boston, MA: Pearson Allyn & Bacon, 2011, p. 167.

p. 235: Belk, Colleen and Virginia Borden Maier, *Biology: Science for Life with Physiology*, 3rd ed., p. 399, © 2010. Printed and electronically reproduced by permission of Pearson Education, Inc., Upper Saddle River, New Jersey.

p. 235: Donatelle, Rebecca J., *Health: The Basics*, Green Edition, 9th ed., p. 12, © 2011. Printed and electronically reproduced by permission of Pearson Education, Inc., Upper Saddle River, New Jersey.

p. 245: Wade, Carole and Carol Tavris, *Psychology*, 6th ed. Upper Saddle River, NJ: Prentice Hall, 2000, p. 337.

p. 245: Harris, C. Leon, *Concepts in Zoology*, 2nd ed. New York: HarperCollins College Publishers, 1996, pp. 408–409. Reprinted by permission of the author.

p. 246: Thio, Alex, *Sociology*, 5th ed. New York: Longman, 1998, p. 235.

p. 253: Solomon, Michael R., Mary Anne Poatsy, and Kendall Martin, *Better Business*, 1st ed. Upper Saddle River, NJ: Pearson Prentice Hall, 2010, p. 323.

p. 253: Bennion, Marion and Barbara Scheule, *Introductory Foods*, 13th ed. Upper Saddle River, NJ: Pearson, 2010, p. 179.

p. 253: Thompson, Janice and Melinda Manore, *Nutrition: An Applied Approach*, 2nd ed. San Francisco: Pearson Benjamin Cummings, 2009, p. 130.

p. 262: Copyright © 2009 by Houghton Mifflin Harcourt Publishing Company. Reproduced by permission from *The American Heritage Dictionary of the English Language, Fourth Edition*.

p. 268: Loyd, Jason B. and James D. Richardson, *Fundamentals of Fire and Emergency Services*. Upper Saddle River, NJ: Pearson Prentice Hall, 2010, p. 93.

p. 269: Kunz, Jennifer, *THINK Marriages and Families*, 1st ed., p. 291, © 2011. Printed and electronically reproduced by permission of Pearson Education, Inc., Upper Saddle River, New Jersey.

p. 274: Brennan, Scott and Jay Withgott, *Environment: The Science Behind the Stories*, 1st Edition, p. 461, © 2005. Printed and electronically reproduced by permission of Pearson Education, Inc., Upper Saddle River, New Jersey.

p. 277: Mix, Michael C., Paul Farber, and Keith I. King, *Biology: The Network of Life*, 1st Edition, p. 165. © 1992. Printed and electronically reproduced by permission of Pearson Education, Inc., Upper Saddle River, New Jersey.

p. 278: Kaufman, Donald G. and Cecilia M. Franz, *Biosphere 2000: Protecting Our Global Environment*, 1st Edition, p. 143, © 1993. Printed and electronically reproduced by permission of Pearson Education, Inc., Upper Saddle River, New Jersey.

p. 279: Belk, Colleen and Virginia Borden Maier, *Biology: Science for Life with Physiology*, 3rd ed., p. 364, © 2010. Printed and electronically reproduced by permission of Pearson Education, Inc., Upper Saddle River, New Jersey.

p. 279: Skolnick, Arlene S., *The Intimate Environment: Exploring Marriage and the Family*, 5th ed., p. 443. Copyright © 1992 by Arlene S. Skolnick. Reprinted by permission of Pearson Education, Inc.

p. 280: Edwards III, George C., Martin P. Wattenberg, and Robert L. Lineberry, *Government in America: People, Politics, and Policy*, 12th Edition, p. 180, © 2006. Printed and electronically reproduced by permission of Pearson Education, Inc., Upper Saddle River, New Jersey.

p. 281: Edwards III, George C., Martin P. Wattenberg, and Robert L. Lineberry, *Government in America: People, Politics, and Policy*, 9th Edition, p. 474, © 2000. Printed and electronically reproduced by permission of Pearson Education, Inc., Upper Saddle River, New Jersey.

p. 282: Hitt, Michael A., Stewart Black, and Lyman W. Porter, *Management*, 1st Edition, p. 241, © 2005. Printed and electronically reproduced by permission of Pearson Education, Inc., Upper Saddle River, New Jersey.

p. 283: Solomon, Michael R., *Consumer Behavior: Buying, Having, and Being*, 6th Edition, p. 293, © 2004. Printed and electronically reproduced by permission of Pearson Education, Inc., Upper Saddle River, New Jersey.

p. 284: Donatelle, Rebecca J., *Health: The Basics*, 4th Edition, p. 386, © 2001. Printed and electronically reproduced by permission of Pearson Education, Inc., Upper Saddle River, New Jersey.

p. 285: Edwards III, George C., Martin P. Wattenberg, and Robert L. Lineberry, *Government in America: People, Politics, and Policy*, 7th Edition, p. 47, © 1996. Printed and electronically reproduced by permission of Pearson Education, Inc., Upper Saddle River, New Jersey.

p. 287: Appelbaum, Richard P. and William J. Chambliss, *Sociology: Introduction*, 1st Edition, p. 427, © 1995. Printed and electronically reproduced by permission of Pearson Education, Inc., Upper Saddle River, New Jersey.

p. 297: Curry, Tim, Robert Jiobu, and Kent Schwirian, *Sociology for the Twenty-First Century*, 2nd ed. Upper Saddle River, NJ: Prentice Hall, 1999, p. 207.

p. 299: Kunz, Jennifer, *THINK Marriages and Families*, 1st ed., p. 241, © 2011. Printed and electronically reproduced by permission of Pearson Education, Inc., Upper Saddle River, New Jersey.

p. 299: Copyright © 2006 Polling Report, Inc., and polling/sponsoring organizations. PollingReport.com. From John D. Carl, *THINK Sociology*. Pearson Prentice Hall, 2010, p. 273.

p. 314: Edwards III, George, C., Martin P. Wattenberg, and Robert L. Lineberry, *Government in America: People, Politics, and Policy*, 15th ed. New York: Pearson Longman, 2011, p. 223.

p. 314: Thompson, William E. and Joseph V. Hickey, *Society in Focus: An Introduction to Sociology*, 7th ed. Boston, MA: Pearson Allyn & Bacon, 2011, p. 325.

p. 314: Gilbert, James N., *Criminal Investigation*, 8th ed. Upper Saddle River, NJ: Pearson Prentice Hall, 2010, p. 454.

p. 324: Thio, Alex, *Sociology*, 4th ed. New York: HarperCollins College Publishers, 1996, p. 100.

p. 324: DeVito, Joseph A., *The Interpersonal Communication Book*, 9th ed. New York: Longman, 2001, p. 191.

p. 325: Wallbank, T. Walter, et al., *Civilization Past and Present*, 8th ed. New York: HarperCollins College Publishers, 1996, pp. 1012–1013.

p. 326: DeVito, Joseph A., *Essentials of Human Communication*, 6th ed. Boston, MA: Allyn and Bacon, 2008, p. 125.

p. 327: Campbell, Bernard G. and James D. Loy, *Humankind Emerging*, 7th ed. New York: HarperCollins College Publishers, 1996, pp. 22–23.

p. 328: Thio, Alex, *Sociology: A Brief Introduction*, 7th ed., p. 105. © 2009. Printed and electronically reproduced by permission of Pearson Education, Inc., Upper Saddle River, New Jersey.

p. 328: Marieb, Elaine N., *Essentials of Human Anatomy & Physiology*, 9th ed. San Francisco: Pearson Benjamin Cummings 2009, p. 58.

p. 329: McCarty, Marilu Hurt, *Dollars and Sense: An Introduction to Economics*, 8th ed. Reading, MA: Addison-Wesley, 1997, pp. 213–214.

p. 332: Vivian, John, *The Media of Mass Communication*, 9th ed., pp. 336–338, © 2009. Printed and electronically reproduced by permission of Pearson Education, Inc., Upper Saddle River, New Jersey.

p. 333: Solomon, Michael R., *Consumer Behavior: Buying, Having, and Being*, 8th ed. Upper Saddle River:, NJ: Pearson Prentice Hall, 2009, pp. 465–466.

p. 335: Levens, Michael, *Marketing: Defined, Explained, Applied*. Upper Saddle River, NJ: Pearson Prentice Hall, 2010, p. 180.

p. 335: Badasch, Shirley A. and Doreen S. Chesebro, *Health Science Fundamentals*, 1st ed., p. 356, © 2009. Printed and electronically reproduced by permission of Pearson Education, Inc., Upper Saddle River, New Jersey.

p. 335: Thompson, Janice and Melinda Manore, *Nutrition for Life*, 2nd ed. San Francisco: Pearson Benjamin Cummings, 2010, p. 39.

p. 336: Frings, Gini Stephens, *Fashion: From Concept to Consumer*, 9th ed. Upper Saddle River, NJ: Pearson Prentice Hall, 2008, p. 158.

p. 336: Belk, Colleen and Virginia Borden Maier, *Biology: Science for Life with Physiology*, 3rd ed., p. 78, © 2010. Printed and electronically reproduced by permission of Pearson Education, Inc., Upper Saddle River, New Jersey.

p. 336: Kennedy, X. J. and Dana Gioia, *Literature: An Introduction to Fiction, Poetry, Drama, and Writing*, 11th ed. New York: Pearson Longman, 2010, p. 258.

p. 340: Devito, Joseph A., *The Interpersonal Communication Book*, 8th ed. New York: Longman, 1998, p. 266.

p. 344: Donatelle, Rebecca J., *Health: The Basics*, 4th ed. Boston, MA: Allyn and Bacon, 2001, p. 346.

p. 344: Solomon, Michael R. and Elnora W. Stuart, *Marketing: Real People, Real Choices*, 2nd ed., p. 135, © 2000. Printed and electronically reproduced by permission of Pearson Education, Inc., Upper Saddle River, New Jersey.

p. 347: Thompson, Janice and Melinda Manore, *Nutrition for Life*, 1st ed. San Francisco: Pearson Benjamin Cummings, 2007, p. 59.

p. 348: Thompson, Janice and Melinda Manore, *Nutrition for Life*, 1st ed. San Francisco: Pearson Benjamin Cummings, 2007, pp. 42–43.

p. 349: Donatelle, Rebecca J., *Health: The Basics*, Green Edition, 9th ed., p. 333, © 2011. Printed and electronically reproduced by permission of Pearson Education, Inc., Upper Saddle River, New Jersey.

p. 350: Donatelle, Rebecca J., *Health: The Basics*, 4th ed. Boston, MA: Allyn and Bacon, 2001, p. 282.

p. 350: Christopherson, Robert W., *Geosystems: An Introduction to Physical Geography*, 4th ed. Upper Saddle River, NJ: Prentice Hall, 2000, p. 470.

p. 351: Barlow, Hugh D., *Criminal Justice in America*. Upper Saddle River, NJ: Prentice Hall, 2000, p. 439.

p. 351: Solomon, Michael R. and Elnora W. Stuart, *Marketing: Real People, Real Choices*, 2nd ed., p. 418, © 2000. Printed and electronically reproduced by permission of Pearson Education, Inc., Upper Saddle River, New Jersey.

p. 351: Donatelle, Rebecca J., *Health: The Basics*, 4th ed. Boston, MA: Allyn and Bacon, 2001, p. 338.

p. 352: Macionis, John J., *Society: The Basics*, 5th ed. Upper Saddle River, NJ: Prentice Hall, 2000, p. 77.

p. 352: Solomon, Michael R. and Elnora W. Stuart, *Marketing: Real People, Real Choices*, 2nd ed., p. 427, © 2000. Printed and electronically reproduced by permission of Pearson Education, Inc., Upper Saddle River, New Jersey.

p. 358: Berman, Louis and J. C. Evans, *Exploring the Cosmos*, 5th ed. Boston: Little Brown, 1986, p. 145.

p. 360: Solomon, Michael R., Mary Anne Poatsy, and Kendall Martin, *Better Business*, 1st ed. Upper Saddle River, NJ: Pearson Prentice Hall, 2010, p. 56.

p. 360: Donatelle, Rebecca J., *Health: The Basics*, Green Edition, 9th ed., p. 218, © 2011. Printed and electronically reproduced by permission of Pearson Education, Inc., Upper Saddle River, New Jersey.

p. 360: Thompson, William E. and Joseph V. Hickey, *Society in Focus: An Introduction to Sociology*, 7th ed. Boston, MA: Pearson Allyn & Bacon, 2011, p. 481.

p. 372: Wade, Carole and Carol Tavris, *Psychology*, 4th ed. New York: HarperCollins College Publishers, 1996, pp. 124–125.

p. 372: Wallace, Robert A., *Biology: The World of Life*, 5th ed. Glenview, IL: Scott, Foresman, 1987, p. 443.

p. 372: Ross, David A., *Introduction to Oceanography*. New York: HarperCollins College Publishers, 1995, p. 239.

p. 383: Goldman, Thomas F. and Henry R. Cheeseman, *The Paralegal Profession*, 3rd ed. Upper Saddle River, NJ: Pearson Prentice Hall, 2011, p. 393.

p. 384: Divine, Robert A., et al., *America: Past and Present*, Combined Volume, 9th ed. New York: Pearson Longman, 2011, p. xv.

p. 384: Belk, Colleen and Virginia Borden Maier, *Biology: Science for Life with Physiology*, 3rd ed., pp. 30–31, © 2010. Printed and electronically reproduced by permission of Pearson Education, Inc., Upper Saddle River, New Jersey.

p. 400: Krogh, David, *Biology: A Guide to the Natural World*, 4th ed. San Francisco: Pearson Benjamin Cummings, 2009, p. 334.

p. 400: Suchocki, John, *Conceptual Chemistry*, 4th ed., p. 145, © 2011. Printed and electronically reproduced by permission of Pearson Education, Inc., Upper Saddle River, New Jersey.

p. 401: Withgott, Jay and Scott Brennan, *Environment: The Science Behind the Stories*, 4th ed. San Francisco: Pearson Benjamin Cummings, 2011, p. 688.

p. 401: Kunz, Jennifer, *THINK Marriages and Families*, 1st ed., p. 21, © 2011. Printed and electronically reproduced by permission of Pearson Education, Inc., Upper Saddle River, New Jersey.

p. 422: Carl, John D., *THINK Sociology*, 1st ed., p. vii, © 2010. Printed and electronically reproduced by permission of Pearson Education, Inc., Upper Saddle River, New Jersey.

p. 430: Kinnear, Thomas C., Kenneth L. Bernhardt, and Kathleen A. Krentler, *Principles of Marketing*, 4th ed., p. 654. © 1995. Printed and electronically reproduced by permission of Pearson Education, Inc., Upper Saddle River, New Jersey.

p. 435: Denesha, Timothy, "From a Vegetarian: Looking at Hunting from Both Sides Now," *Buffalo News*, November 24, 1996. Reprinted by permission of the author.

p. 437: Kinnear, Thomas C., Kenneth L. Bernhardt, and Kathleen A. Krentler, *Principles of Marketing*, 4th ed., p. 61. © 1995. Printed and electronically reproduced by permission of Pearson Education, Inc., Upper Saddle River, New Jersey.

p. 438: Donatelle, Rebecca J. and Lorraine G. Davis, *Access to Health*, 7th ed., pp. 40–41, © 2002. Printed and electronically reproduced by permission of Pearson Education, Inc., Upper Saddle River, New Jersey.

p. 440: Wallbank, T. Walter, et al., *Civilization Past and Present*, 6th ed., Vol. 2. Glenview, IL: Scott, Foresman, 1987, p. 533.

p. 441: Henslin, James M., *Sociology: A Down-to-Earth Approach*, 6th ed. Boston, MA: Allyn & Bacon, 2003, p. 246.

p. 441: Skolnick, Arlene S., *The Intimate Environment: Exploring Marriage and the Family*, 6th ed. New York: HarperCollins College Publishers, 1996, p. 107.

p. 441: Kinnear, Thomas C., Kenneth L. Bernhardt, and Kathleen A. Krentler, *Principles of Marketing*, 4th ed., p. 495. © 1995. Printed and electronically reproduced by permission of Pearson Education, Inc., Upper Saddle River, New Jersey.

p. 442: Wallbank, T. Walter, et al., *Civilization Past and Present*, 6th ed., Vol. 2. Glenview, IL: Scott, Foresman, 1987, p. 781.

p. 443: Suchocki, John, *Conceptual Chemistry*, 4th ed., pp. 385–387, © 2011. Printed and electronically reproduced by permission of Pearson Education, Inc., Upper Saddle River, New Jersey.

p. 444: Badasch, Shirley A. and Doreen S. Chesebro, *Health Science Fundamentals*, 1st ed., pp. 349–350 including Figure 13.17, © 2009. Printed and electronically reproduced by permission of Pearson Education, Inc., Upper Saddle River, New Jersey.

p. 449: Miller, Barbara D., *Anthropology*, 2nd ed., pp. 484–485, © 2008. Printed and electronically reproduced by permission of Pearson Education, Inc., Upper Saddle River, New Jersey.

p. 452: Jefkin-Elnekave, Debbie, "Tribal Identity Through Body Art," *Skipping Stones*, Vol. 16, Issue 1 (January/February 2004), pp. 34–35. Used with permission.

p. 457: Phillips, Michael M., "Tattoos Honor Marines Killed in Iraq and Help the Survivors." Reprinted by permission of *The Wall Street Journal*, Copyright © 2006 Dow Jones & Company, Inc. All Rights Reserved Worldwide. License number 2703211275720.

p. 461: Freeman, James, "You're Eating Genetically Modified Food," *USA Today*, April 10, 2000. Reprinted with permission.

p. 464: Macionis, John J., *Sociology*, 13th ed., p. 516, © 2010. Printed and electronically reproduced by permission of Pearson Education, Inc., Upper Saddle River, New Jersey.

p. 467: Andrews, Wyatt, "Medicine's Cutting Edge: Re-Growing Organs," CBSNews.com, March 23, 2008. CBS News Archives. Reprinted with permission.

p. 473: Vivian, John, *The Media of Mass Communication*, 9th ed., pp. 246–250, © 2009. Printed and electronically reproduced by permission of Pearson Education, Inc., Upper Saddle River, New Jersey.

p. 479: Lacy, Sarah, "Getting Found Out, Web 2.0 Style," *Business Week*, June 17, 2008. Used with permission of Bloomberg L.P. Copyright © 2008. All rights reserved.

p. 483: Norris, Cathleen A. and Elliot Soloway (Pro), and Elias Aboujaoude, M.D. (Con), "Impact of the Internet on Thinking," *CQ Researcher*, September 24, 2010. Copyright © 2010 CQ Press, a division of SAGE Publications, Inc. Reprinted by permission of CQ Press.

p. 489: Baird, Abigail A., *THINK Psychology*, 2nd ed., pp. 193–205, © 2011. Printed and electronically reproduced by permission of Pearson Education, Inc., Upper Saddle River, New Jersey.